Cognitive Psychology

Applying the Science of the Mind

Second Edition

Gregory Robinson-Riegler
University of St. Thomas

Bridget Robinson-Riegler
Augsburg College

Boston ■ *New York* ■ *San Francisco*
Mexico City ■ *Montreal* ■ *Toronto* ■ *London* ■ *Madrid* ■ *Munich* ■ *Paris*
Hong Kong ■ *Singapore* ■ *Tokyo* ■ *Cape Town* ■ *Sydney*

Acquisitions Editor: Stephen Frail
Series Editorial Assistant: Mary K. Tucker
Marketing Manager: Karen Natale
Production Supervisor: Liz Napolitano
Editorial Production Service: Elm Street Publishing Services, Inc.
Composition Buyer: Linda Cox
Manufacturing Buyer: JoAnne Sweeney
Electronic Composition: Elm Street Publishing Services, Inc.
Interior Design: Elm Street Publishing Services, Inc.
Photo Researcher: Sarah Evertson
Cover Designer: Joel Gendron

For related titles and support materials, visit our online catalog at www.ablongman.com.

Between the time website information is gathered and then published, it is not unusual for some sites to have closed. Also, the transcription of URLs can result in typographical errors. The publisher would appreciate a notification where these errors occur so that they may be corrected in subsequent editions.

Library of Congress Cataloging-in-Publication Data
Robinson-Riegler, Gregory.
    Cognitive psychology : applying the science of the mind / Gregory Robinson-Riegler, Bridget Robinson-Riegler. – 2nd ed.
        p.   cm.
    Includes bibliographical references and indexes.
    ISBN-13: 978-0-205-53139-4
    ISBN-10: 0-205-53139-3
        1. Cognitive psychology—Textbooks. I. Robinson-Riegler, Bridget. II. Title.

BF201.R63 2008
153—dc22

                                                                2007017864

Printed in the United States of America

10 9 8 7 6 5 4 3 2 1 RRD-VA 11 10 09 08 07

Credits appear on page 564, which constitutes an extension of the copyright page.

In memory of Bridget's dad, Dr. Frederick C. Robinson.

Contents

C h a p t e r   8

Remembering the Personal Past   289

C h a p t e r   9

Knowledge Representation and Retrieval   331

Chapter 10

Chapter 11

Preface

To the Instructor

When we first sat down to write the first edition of *Cognitive Psychology,* we asked ourselves, "Does the world really need another cognitive psychology textbook?" We thought maybe it did, and judging from the reception the first edition enjoyed, many instructors agreed with us. Between us, we've taught introductory cognition three or four dozen times, using seven different textbooks. The fact that we've used so many different texts is a testament to two things: Cognitive textbooks are at the same time satisfying and a bit wanting. All of the books we've used have their strengths: rigorous discussion of important empirical and theoretical principles, currency, good real-world examples and applications, good organization and pedagogy, engaging and student-friendly writing. The problem is, the texts have tended to be strong in two or three of these areas, and not as strong in the other three or two. We're shooting for five out of five.

Style. We listened to the complaints, comments, and suggestions of nearly a thousand students, who often found the texts to be a little dry and boring. They didn't seem as captivated by the field as we felt they should have been. We did our best to grab them (figuratively) in class, but we always sensed that something was missing. The books with the breezier writing styles seemed to lack depth of discussion. The books that went into depth seemed to be a little on the obtuse side. We've tried to write a text that strikes a balance—one that really grabs students and intrigues (even entertains) them, while still capturing the theoretical and empirical elegance and rigor that characterize cognitive psychology research.

Research Methods. Speaking of empirical elegance and rigor, we think that to gain a full appreciation of research in cognition, students need to have a firm foundation in research methods, particularly the experimental method. To this end, we've dedicated a chapter to the methods used in cognition research. While this may seem a bit unconventional, we feel that it's more than warranted. We are constantly faced with students who feel a little overmatched by the subject matter of cognition research because they don't have a firm hold on how experiments are conducted. To remedy this, Chapter 2 presents an overview of experiments and descriptive data analysis; importantly, we present these concepts *within the context of cognition research.* So even if students have had a methods course, they haven't had it the way we're presenting it. And if you feel that your students are well beyond the need for such an overview, you can simply skip the chapter, with no loss in organizational flow.

Organizational Structure. In organizing the chapters of the text, we attempted to follow the flow of a piece of information that enters the cognitive system. The information is perceived, attended to and placed in working memory, identified, and committed to memory. Later, the information serves as the basis for the higher-level processes of language, problem solving, and decision making. Admittedly, this is a serial approach, but we think it provides a nice intuitive description of cognition that will enhance understanding.

Although our text does feature a fairly standard approach to explaining the flow of cognition, there are a couple of notable exceptions. One is that attention and working memory are discussed in the same chapter. It always struck us (and our students) that when we're discussing the control processes of attention and the control processes used in short-term/working memory, we're talking about many of the same things. The two seem (in many ways) to be flip sides of the same coin. This view is certainly not new—indeed, much of the research on working memory span has emphasized attentional control as a key *component of* working memory. We therefore thought it highly appropriate to discuss these processes together. Another distinctive feature of our layout is that pattern recognition is presented *after* the discussion of attention and working memory. We placed it there because conscious recognition of a stimulus occurs only as the stimulus is processed by working memory. In other words, pattern recognition can be viewed as the first task of attention/working memory.

We've also tried to provide some organizational structure by referring to several important research themes in each chapter, including neuroscience, consciousness, individual differences, development, and culture. These research themes capture some of the most interesting and dynamic questions that currently define the field. We hope that the inclusion of these themes will enhance students' sense of these overarching issues.

Finally, we've strengthened the organizational flow of the text by making the interrelation of cognitive processes very apparent. The separate discussion of perception, attention, memory, etc., is completely a descriptive convention; when it comes to everyday thinking, these processes are inseparable. We've tried to give students a sense of this by pointing out, whenever possible, the relationship among the cognitive processes currently being discussed, those already covered, and/or those to come.

Everyday Relevance.   Cognition is constant; thinking is what we do. Despite the obvious relevance of thinking to our everyday lives, we sensed that our students didn't appreciate this relevance as fully as they should. To enhance this appreciation, we make liberal use of everyday examples in class, and give students thought-journaling assignments and experiments to do outside of class. The students really enjoy these and often are surprised at how interesting this stuff can be (needless to say, we're never surprised). We've adopted this tack in our book, sprinkling the discussion with numerous examples and sprinkling each chapter with exercises—titled "Stop and Think!"—to entice students to do just what the title says. These exercises can serve as homework assignments, as discussion generators for the classroom, or both.

Cool Experiments.   We also were never completely satisfied with the research presented in cognition texts. There are classic findings that merit extensive discussion, to be sure. But there are also some really intriguing empirical investigations, perhaps a little more off the beaten track, that merit mention and analysis. These investigations might be distinctive in their setting or in their empirical question (such as out-of-body experiences in touch caused by visual stimuli), but they still address fundamental questions of cognition. We've tried to include a good number of studies like this because they're likely to pique student interest and still convey the critical points.

Thanks for taking a look at our book. We hope your students enjoy reading it as much as we enjoyed putting it together (although we hope it won't take them as long!). We'd love to get your feedback and suggestions. If you spot errors or misrepresentations, know of an interesting study that may merit discussion, or otherwise want to comment on the text, please feel free to e-mail us at glriegler@stthomas.edu and Robinson@augsburg.edu.

Changes for the Second Edition

The second edition of the text features a number of changes, both in content and in pedagogy, that we believe strengthen the text. These changes are based on the comments of people who used the first edition, reviewers, and our own experiences with the text.

Content.   The major change to the content is an extensive updating, with much more discussion of and reference to studies that have been conducted in the past five years. In line with the continuing explosion of cognitive neuroscience in recent years, we have included more studies relating cognition to brain function. We have also made a more concerted attempt to tie our discussion into the research themes of consciousness, culture, individual differences, and development. In addition to these general content changes, some chapters have been reworked considerably, most notably those on perceptual processing, attention and working memory, and language.

Chapter-by-Chapter Changes.   All chapters have been significantly updated. Following is a list of some of the new topics covered in each chapter:

Chapter 1: Embodied cognition
Chapter 2: Expanded discussion of event-related potentials
Chapter 3: Embodied perception and action; change blindness; illusion of conscious will
Chapter 4: PRP paradigm in research on attention; ironic effects of thought suppression; updated discussion of working memory and expanded coverage of working memory as executive attention
Chapter 5: Expanded coverage of face recognition, folk biology, and biological essentialism
Chapter 6: Remembering action
Chapter 7: Expanded discussion of emotion and eyewitness memory, pictures and stories, and memory distortions
Chapter 8: Flashbulb memories for September 11
Chapter 9: Metacognitive account of tip-of-the-tongue experience
Chapter 10: Streamlined (one-chapter coverage)
Chapter 11: Expanded coverage of creativity
Chapter 12: Dread risk and September 11; discussion of decision-making heuristics as adaptive tools; discussion of the recognition heuristic

Pedagogy

Chapter Openers.   The chapter-opening device is now a series of short bullet points that highlight some thought-provoking phenomena and questions relevant to the chapter. These will get students thinking about the topic, and will allow them to see some of the topic's everyday applications.

Running Threads.   Our first edition included three running threads (consciousness, neuroscience, and individual differences). In each chapter, we highlighted three separate studies, one for each of these threads. However, because these discussions were long and "offset" to some extent, the intended implication—that these are constantly recurring themes in cognition research—may have been obscured a bit. So we've revised our style of highlighting these threads and have added a couple more. The threads are now consciousness, neuroscience, individual differences, culture, and development. Before, coverage of culture and development was relegated to the "individual differences" category. Given the extensive investigation of culture and development in current cognitive research, we thought it more appropriate to separate them and try to mention them more often than a "box" feature allows. Whenever discussion of one of the five themes comes up in a given chapter, the reader will be alerted with an appropriate icon.

Experimental Design.   We feel it's critical that students understand basic experimental design because it's so fundamentally important in cognitive psychology research. This is the basis for our inclusion of an entire chapter on research methods in cognitive psychology. In this edition, we reinforce this coverage by referring back to basic experimental design concepts in a sample study in each chapter. For this sample study, we highlight the independent variables and the resulting conditions.

Streamlined Coverage.   We shortened the text by a chapter. It seems nearly impossible to manage a textbook when it starts to ramble on into the teens of chapters. Our coverage of language has been streamlined into a single chapter; while this cut down on the number of specific topics we could cover in depth, we think that a one-chapter treatment is more manageable for the student and the instructor, and our streamlined chapter still manages to cover many of the high points of language.

To the Student:

The book you're about to read concerns something with which you're intimately familiar, yet probably haven't stopped to think about. It's something you engage in every single day but rarely notice unless something goes wrong. You couldn't live day to day without it, but you seldom stop to truly appreciate it. Is it TV? No. Coffee? No. Sleep? Nope. It's ***thinking.*** Ironically, although the mind is in constant use, most people take it for granted, noticing it only when it misfires. Consider the following examples of annoying little disturbances in thought:

- Why did I just put the cereal in the refrigerator and the milk in the cabinet?
- Why did I just get a D on an exam when I thought I knew everything "cold"?
- Why do I always find that answers to exam questions are right on "the tip of my tongue," but I can't quite spit them out?
- Why is it that I can stare at the same problem for hours and make little or no progress?
- Why do I find it so difficult to listen to a professor lecture and take notes (not to mention stay awake) at the same time?

Your average Joe/Jane understands relatively little about how thinking works, and how to improve it. But take heart! Thousands of scientists who call themselves cognitive psychologists have performed countless investigations on the thinking processes that we engage in every day, shedding tremendous light on the mechanics of thought. After reading this book, you will not be the average Joe/Jane.

What Is Cognitive Psychology?

Cognitive psychology is the subdiscipline of psychology that employs the scientific method to answer fundamental questions about how the mind works. By using controlled research (mostly experiments), cognitive psychologists attempt to explain the thinking processes that we use every day. A cognitive psychologist would have an analytic view of the problems described above and would view them technically, through the lens of a scientist. The following are how a cognitive psychologist might rework each of the questions posed above:

- What are the cognitive factors that underlie action slips? How do they relate to automatic processing?
- Why do people sometimes fail to monitor their own level of comprehension? What are the components of successful *metacognition*?
- What factors play a role in *retrieval blocks,* and how can retrieval blocks be successfully resolved?
- What leads a person to exhibit *mental set,* and how is it related to convergent thinking? What are some strategies that people can employ to overcome mental set?
- How do people successfully *divide their attention* between multiple sources of stimulation, given the limited nature of attention?

Why Study Cognition?

The study of cognition has tremendous ramifications for an overall understanding of how you "tick" on a day-to-day basis; it is in some ways the most applied (and applicable) of psychology's subdisciplines. As noted above, cognitive psychologists attempt to understand the processes that people use every day: perception, attention, memory, language, and reasoning. What could be more important as a subject of science? It's important from the standpoint of gaining a basic understanding of how people think and behave, which is the focus of psychology. And it's important for improving our lot in everyday life—who hasn't been frustrated by the (sometimes more than) occasional "brain lapse," and other difficulties in attention, memory, and the like?

Let's broaden the issue a bit. A full understanding of cognition is critical to an understanding of other subdisciplines in the field of psychology. This makes sense—psychology is typically defined as the scientific study of thinking and behavior, and questions of thinking are at the core of every other subdiscipline of psychology. Consider the following questions from other areas of psychology:

- *Clinical psychology:* Do depressed people remember events from their lives differently than nondepressed people?
- *Neuropsychology:* What's happening in different areas of the brain's cortex as people engage in cognitive processes like memory and problem solving?
- *Developmental psychology:* How do cognitive processes like memory and problem solving change as a person ages?
- *Personality:* Do a person's personality characteristics play a role in the types of decisions they make?
- *Social psychology:* What factors influence our ability to remember an individual?

These questions are wide ranging, but they have two common threads. First, they are fundamental psychological questions, and second, they all involve cognition. Unlocking and understanding the mechanisms that are involved in cognition is fundamental to psychological explanation.

Cognitive psychology can be a bit of a challenge to master, for a number of reasons. First, the subject matter of cognitive psychology (mental processes) can be difficult to grasp—you can't really see or touch them, and most often, they take place quickly and outside of conscious awareness. As a result, the discussion of mental processes often takes place on a rather abstract level, and discussions of findings from research on cognition are full of jargon that can be difficult to decipher. Second, cognitive psychology's roots are firmly in experimental methodology. So to understand cognitive psychology, you need to understand experimental methodology. Third, cognitive psychology is a sprawling field; no one has provided the one unifying theory of cognition, or even the theory of a simpler subprocess like memory. Findings and theories tend to conflict with one another, due to the relative youth of the field (experimental cognitive psychology has been around only about 50 years). As a result, students often don't gain a good sense of "the big picture." This text offers a number of features designed to help you organize, integrate, and apply the cognition research material you'll be reading about.

First, the overall structure of the book parallels the progression of thinking. Take a simple cognitive process—looking at an animal at a zoo, and realizing it's a duck-billed platypus. This involves (1) perceiving the animal, (2) paying attention to the animal, (3) retrieving the matching label for the animal from your store of concepts in memory, and (4) saying "duck-billed platypus." Then you may remember the summer when you had a duck-billed platypus for a pet, and, when it got too big, having to decide what to do with it. In line with this intuitive progression through the cognitive system, our text (after an initial foray into the history of cognitive psychology) proceeds from perception (initial perception of the animal), to attention and working memory (paying attention to the animal), to pattern recognition and concept representation (retrieving the label "duck-billed platypus" from memory). From there it's on to higher-level mental processes, including autobiographical memory, language, problem solving, and decision making (relating the story of the summer when you had a duck-billed platypus for a pet, and when it got too big, having to decide what to do with it).

A second feature of the text that will help you integrate the material is our inclusion of a number of recurring empirical threads in each chapter. These "threads" are topics that cut across all areas of cognition and serve as unifying themes for current research:

- *Neuroscience:* Perhaps the most active and exciting frontier of cognition research is the research in *cognitive neuroscience,* which attempts to relate cognitive processes to process and structure in the brain. What is occurring in the brain as we sense, pay attention, remember, and decide?

- *Consciousness:* Consciousness (which may be defined simply as one's awareness) is a mysterious concept that some say defies explanation, having confounded philosophers, cognitive psychologists, and physiologists over the years. Research in cognition has much to offer on the mystery of consciousness. To what extent do our everyday cognitive processes involve conscious awareness? How can we be influenced by things of which we are unaware?

- *Individual differences:* For the most part, research in cognition has focused on finding the *general* principles of how people think. *In general,* how do we pay attention? *In general,* how do we remember? *In general,* how do we solve problems? This tends to gloss over the fact that there are important differences in the ways that individuals think. We'll be discussing some of these differences within the context of our discussions of specific cognitive processes.

- *Development:* One of the most bustling areas of cognitive research relates to the notion of individual differences, more specifically, differences in age. Thinking changes throughout the life span. Throughout our discussions of cognition, we'll discuss how researchers are investigating thinking in subjects of all ages, from infancy to old age.

- *Culture:* It's probably not a big surprise to you that not everyone thinks exactly the same way; furthermore, many of these differences are observed when comparing people who have different cultural backgrounds. Throughout the text, we'll be highlighting investigations of similarities and differences in thinking among people of different cultures.

A third feature of the text that should help you gain a richer appreciation of cognitive psychology research is an entire chapter (Chapter 2) on research methods as they are applied to the study of thought. In that chapter, we explore the basics of experimental methodology within the context of cognitive psychology research. A chapter on research methods is a bit unusual for this type of textbook, but we think it's critical to your understanding and appreciation of the field. In addition, we revisit the important components of an experiment in a sample study in each of the subsequent chapters.

A fourth device that will assist you in integrating and applying the material is chapter-opening points that highlight thought-provoking questions or applications that will get you thinking about the material to be covered in the chapter.

In addition to the features that will assist you in organizing, integrating, and applying cognitive psychology research, our text provides several tools that we hope will help you understand and remember the material. These features include:

- **Stop and Review!:** To help you assess whether you've learned the important material in what you've just read, each major section of a chapter concludes with a short quiz. Following the quiz, a brief summary of the main points from the section (including the points covered in the preceding quiz) are presented.
- **Stop and Think!:** One of the best ways to understand and remember material is to become actively engaged with it. To help you accomplish this, each chapter features a number of exercises entitled "Stop and Think!" These exercises involve a number of hands-on and "mind-on" activities that will help you to more closely consider the material being discussed. The exercises include demonstrations of cognitive processes and principles through "mini-experiments," questions about how you might design a study to investigate some cognitive process, opinion questions about controversial issues in the field, and questions that require you to examine your own cognitive processing on a day-to-day basis and to evaluate it in the context of the topic being discussed.

As noted earlier, the newness, complexity, and breadth of cognitive psychology make it a challenging topic. However, these characteristics also make cognitive psychology an exciting and dynamic topic of study. Its newness means that there are many more exciting areas to explore and an endless array of questions waiting to be answered. Its complexity makes learning about it a great exercise in critical thinking. In reading this text, we hope that you gain a firm understanding of how seemingly vague questions about mental processes can be translated into experiments that provide concrete, empirical answers. The breadth of cognitive psychology makes it one of the most interesting and applicable of psychology's subdisciplines. Topics included in the text range from visual perception to eyewitness memory to language comprehension to problem solving, with many fascinating stops in between. Our sincere hope is that you enjoy learning about cognitive psychology as much as we enjoy talking about and teaching it. Turn the page, and start thinking about thinking!

Acknowledgements

We'd like to thank the following reviewers for their careful consideration and insightful suggestions:

Second Edition:
Paul F. Cunningham, Rivier College; Darryl Dietrich, The College of St. Scholastica; Kara Federmeier, University of Illinois-Champaign; Bennet L. Schwartz, Florida International University; and Yeatman, Stonehill College.

First Edition:
Martin Bink, University of North Texas; Tom Busy, Indiana University; Darryl Dietrich, College of St. Scholastica; Jocelyn R. Folk, Kent State University; Gary B. Forbach, Washburn University; Gary Ford, Stephen F. Austin State University; Nancy R. Gee, SUNY–Fredonia; Barry Gholson, University of Memphis; Janet M. Gibson, Grinnell College; Anita Hartmann, University of Alaska, Fairbanks; Jo Hector, University of Arizona; Andrew M. Herbert, University of North Texas; Douglas A. Hershey, Oklahoma State University; Lisa Isenberg, University of Wisconsin–River Falls; Paul W. Jeffries, SUNY–Stonybrook; Stephen Kitzis, Fort Hays State University; William Langston, Middle Tennessee State University; Andrew Lotto, Washington State University; Keith Millis, Northern Illinois University; Hal Pashler, University of California, San Diego; Danielle Polage, Pepperdine University; Christian Schunn, University of Pittsburgh; James Speer, Stephen F. Austin State University; Claudia J. Stanny, University of West Florida; Rick Stevens, University of Louisiana at Monroe; Evangeline Wheeler, Towson University; Stephen G. Yanchar, Brigham Young University; and Michael Young, Southern Illinois University.

1

An Introduction
to Cognition

What is thinking, exactly? How can there be a scientific discipline focusing on a process that is so complex, varied, and unobservable?

What are the roots of cognitive psychology? The study of mind sounds like it might involve philosophy—how does cognitive psychology differ? What were the important historical developments in study of mind?

Can thinking be broken down into sub-processes? What are the different types of thinking in which you engage throughout the course of a day, and what sorts of questions might be asked about these processes?

The mind seems to be a sort of "thinking machine;" technological devices like computers, cell phones, and Blackberries seem to have "minds of their own." Might those "minds" work in a way similar to ours?

What Is Cognition?

Psychology is generally defined as the scientific study of mental processes and behavior. **Cognitive psychology** could be defined by eliminating the last two words of that definition—the scientific study of mental processes. Behavior is examined by cognitive psychologists, but primarily as an avenue into the underlying mental processes, in the same way that physicists infer the force of gravity from the behavior of objects in the world.

And the study of *mental processes* covers a lot of ground. These processes include attention, remembering, producing and understanding language, solving problems, and making decisions. It is hard to imagine that we take such vital processes for granted. Thinking is something that is constantly happening, yet we rarely stop to . . . well . . . think about it. However, for the past five decades, cognitive psychologists have done exactly that, using the methods of science to answer questions about the mind. With the experimental method as their primary tool, these researchers approach the mind as a type of machine, attempting to elucidate its inner workings. Given that thinking is at the heart of everything we do on a day-to-day basis, it's difficult to imagine a more important field of study.

The Omnipresence of Cognitive Processes

One of our goals in this text is to help you appreciate and understand the importance of the cognitive processes in which you are constantly engaged. As an exercise in thinking about thinking, consider the mental processes that you go through on the first day of class.

Perception.   Imagine the visual and auditory information processing that occurs on the first day of class. Based on a quick glance of the room, you immediately separate the tables from the chairs and make out the back row, your area of choice. Scanning the room, you spot a couple of old friends from last semester. You take your seat and listen to the professor outline the thrilling experience you're about to have in their course. This scenario involves perception—the set of front-end processes through which you organize and interpret incoming information.

Attention.   Should you drift off in one of your classes, you may hear your professor bellow, "Pay attention!" Attention is the set of processes through which you focus on incoming information. Your ability to attend is flexible—you can divert your attention to that juicy gossip being discussed behind you. But it's also limited—if you shift your attention, you're not likely to remember much of what the professor has said.

Working Memory.   It's not enough to simply "zero in" on what the professor is saying at any given moment in time. In order to fully process and understand the facts and figures being discussed in class, you've got to perform a sort of mental juggling act. As the material is being presented, you've got to repeat it to yourself and/or jot it down in your notes. The online processor that makes this possible is working memory.

Identifying and Classifying Objects.   Two of the most important, yet most taken for granted, sets of cognitive processes in which we engage are the acts of identifying and classifying. Without thinking, you distinguish the professor from the students, you pull out your notebook rather than your planner to take notes, and you (without looking)

Sitting through the first day of class evokes a host of cognitive processes.

reach into your backpack to turn off that infernal cell phone. How do these acts of identification occur so seamlessly?

Long-Term Memory.   Let's go back to your juggling act. It's not over when the class winds to a close. When the class is finished, you must catch the balls you're juggling and put them in your pocket until the next juggling act. In cognitive psychology lingo, you have to store for later use the information that you're taking in. Taking notes helps serve this purpose—that is, if you engage in the note-taking process seriously and think about concepts as you are writing them down. Through conscientious note taking, you start to commit information to long-term memory. In our discussion of memory, we'll examine some of the processes involved in remembering, both when you're studying information and when you're trying to retrieve it.

Memory Distortion.   Memory's not perfect; far from it. It serves us well most of the time, but there are systematic ways in which it fails us. We're sure you've had the exasperating experience—especially on tests—of completely blanking on or misremembering information that you thought you knew. We'll discuss some of the processes involved in forgetting and memory distortion.

Autobiographical Memory.   Chances are good that the first day of classes will be one of the better-remembered days of your entire school year. You can probably think of some reasons for this: you meet new professors, hear about new classes, get reacquainted with old friends, and make new ones. Research on how we remember our personal past has exploded, and the study of autobiographical memory has become one of the more dynamic and interesting topics within the field of cognitive psychology.

Knowledge Representation.   It is truly stunning how much you know. Think about it: you no doubt recognized and understood just about every word that every professor said in class. These words and concepts are just some of the pieces of knowledge that you possess. Cognitive psychologists would term these *mental representations.* Just as a jpg file of your family pet is a *representation* of your pet, mental representations are representations of your stored knowledge, and you access them when necessary. How is general knowledge like this stored and retrieved? Computers read many different formats, including text files and the aforementioned jpg. Do our minds also represent things in different formats?

Language.   Your seamless processing of all the information from your first day is a testament to your skill in yet another important set of cognitive processes—those involved in the use of language. As the professor speaks, your implicit knowledge of and practice with sentence structure allows you to follow along just fine. What would happen if the professor came into class and said, "Class, and textbook turn your get page out OK to 28"? How about, "Pretty textbooks fly to the bookstore"? No doubt you'd be calling campus security. Your implicit knowledge of syntax (word arrangement rules) and semantics (rules for expressing meaning) allows you to comprehend instantly what makes sense and what doesn't. Your knowledge of language also allows you to ask questions that professors just love to hear, like, "Do we have to know this?" or "Will this be on the test?"

Problem Solving.   After you've been to all of your classes, you've got another juggling act to perform. Somehow, you're going to have to fit studying for 15 to 20 tests, writing for 15 to 20 papers, and attending class for about 150 one-hour periods all into the space of 14 or so weeks. And you've got to do it well. This is a fairly hefty example of problem solving. Problem solving involves operating within constraints (such as time) and reaching a goal from a starting state that is nowhere near that goal.

Decision Making.   You're going to have to make many decisions throughout the semester. "How much time should I devote to studying for each of my classes?" "If I miss class once in a while, am I going to pay for it in my final grade?" (Do you really need an answer to that one?) The process through which you arrive at decisions involves a complex interplay among other cognitive processes such as attention, memory, and knowledge retrieval.

THINKING ABOUT THOUGHT PROCESSES

Look at the list of cognitive processes that begins on page 2. You engage in all of these in some manner every day. Come up with an example of each of these from your daily life.

An Interdisciplinary Perspective

Not only is cognitive psychology central to everything we do in our day-to-day lives, it is also central to psychology's quest to understand how people think and act. As noted above in the definition of psychology, cognition comprises half of the subject matter! Because cognition is so fundamental to understanding how humans "tick," it is crucial to psychology's other subdisciplines. Social psychologists investigate the mental processes involved in thinking about others. Clinical psychologists investigate the role that mental processes play in psychopathology. Developmental psychologists are interested in the ways that cognitive processes change throughout the life span. Neuropsychologists are interested in the association between mental processing and brain activity. Industrial/organizational psychologists are interested in how cognitive processes such as remembering and decision making play out in the workplace. Understanding the fundamental mechanisms of human cognition provides critical insights into the other subdisciplines that define psychology.

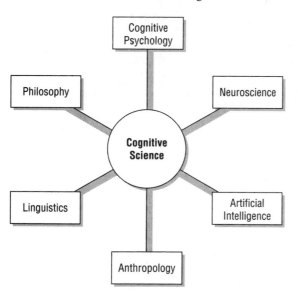

The study of cognition also lends insights beyond psychology. Cognitive psychology is a key player within the interdisciplinary field of study termed "cognitive science." **Cognitive science,** simply defined, is an interdisciplinary effort to understand the mind. It includes a number of (seemingly disparate) disciplines, five of them plus cognitive psychology lying at its "core" (Gardner, 1985). Philosophy, the first discipline to systematically examine the mind, helps to formulate and examine the fundamental questions that define the field. Neuroscience attempts to specify the relationship between mind and brain. Artificial intelligence addresses issues of mind by modeling human thought processes with computer hardware and software. The field of linguistics investigates the structure of language and the specifics of language use and what they tell us about the mind. Anthropology explores the mind through quite a different lens—the lens of culture. How do our physical and cultural surroundings impact our thinking? Since each of these disciplinary approaches is reflected to some degree in the work of cognitive psychologists, you'll be getting a taste of most of these disciplines in this text.

STOP *and* REVIEW!

1. Define cognitive psychology.
2. Identify the major topics covered by cognitive psychologists.
3. True or false? Cognitive science is a specific field within cognitive psychology.
4. Identify the disciplines that comprise "cognitive science."

➤ Cognitive psychology can be defined as the scientific study of mental processes.

➤ Cognitive psychologists study a wide range of abilities—perception, sensory memory, attention, working memory, pattern recognition, concept representation, long-term memory, knowledge representation, language, problem solving, and decision making.

➤ Cognitive psychology lies at the core of an interdisciplinary approach termed *cognitive science.*

➤ Cognitive science attempts to bring together research from the fields of philosophy, neuroscience, artificial intelligence, linguistics, and anthropology in an effort to understand the mind.

Psychology B. C. (*Before Cognitive Psychology*)

As pioneering cognitive psychologist Hermann Ebbinghaus observed, psychology has a long past but a short history. Thinking has long been a topic of interest—no doubt since we, as humans, started thinking. It shouldn't be a surprise that philosophy is generally considered to be the primary disciplinary "parent" of psychology, particularly cognitive psychology. Ancient philosophers such as Aristotle were interested in the mechanics of mind. He (and others) sought to establish **laws of association** to explain why the activation of some concepts seems to automatically lead to the activation of others. Consider a word association task: What is the first word that pops to mind when we say "black"? How about "chair"? We'd be willing to bet that you thought of the concepts "white" and "table." Aristotle assumed, as do modern-day cognitive psychologists, that mental processes are lawful and predictable.

Although philosophers have long been interested in the mind, the subject was not thoroughly examined with the scientific method of controlled observation until the 1800s. At that point a second disciplinary "parent" of psychology, physiology, had begun to establish itself as a legitimate area of scientific inquiry. Physiologists looked at the body as a sort of machine and employed scientific methods to determine its inner workings. How do nerve impulses travel? How does information from the outside world enter into our sensory systems? How is this information interpreted? These latter two questions bring physiology right to the doorstep of psychology because they are questions of human experience and thinking. Once physiologists started applying their methods to these types of questions, a complete science of mind was inevitable.

STOP *and* THINK!

COMPARING COGNITIVE PSYCHOLOGY TO ITS FORERUNNERS

Philosophy and physiology are generally recognized as the parent disciplines of psychology.

- Do you consider cognitive psychology to be more like philosophy or more like physiology?
- Why do you think so?
- What are some of their similarities and differences?

Psychophysics

The scientific study of mind can be traced back to a number of origins, none more important than the work of early psychophysicists. **Psychophysics** refers to the study of the relationship between the physical properties of a stimulus and the properties taken on when the stimulus is filtered through subjective experience. For instance, suppose we see two lights in succession. The first light is double the luminance of the second light. Does the first light *seem* twice as *bright*? Note that while luminance is a physical measure of light intensity, *seem* is a subjective term and *brightness* is a psychological dimension, not a physical one.

Mapping out these sorts of relationships between the physical and the psychological was a primary concern of early psychophysicists such as Gustav Fechner (1801–1878). One of Fechner's major contributions was his quantification of the relationship between incoming stimuli and corresponding perceptions. Fechner demonstrated that there is

Surrounding context plays an important role in determining what stimuli are perceivable.

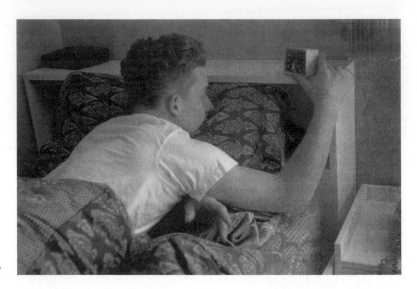

Giant clock?

not a one-to-one relationship between changes in the physical intensity of a stimulus and changes in its *psychological* (or perceived) intensity. Think about it. If someone snaps their fingers at a rock concert, no one would notice. If somebody snaps their fingers in a quiet room, you notice it easily. Clearly, there is some process of translation occurring between the presentation of the physical stimulus and the actual experience of that stimulus.

Hermann von Helmholtz (1821–1894) influenced the newly developing science of mind primarily through his work on visual perception, which Helmholtz argued involved a process of **unconscious inference.** An inference is a conclusion that we arrive at through some type of evidence. According to Helmholtz, our visual systems are constantly making inferences about the external world based on the information gathered as well as on the "evidence" of previous experience. Consider what happens when you pick up your alarm clock in the morning and hold it close enough to read it (leaving aside the revulsion you feel that it's 7:30 and you have to get up for an 8:00 class). The image picked up by the retina in the back of your eye gets larger as you move the clock close to your face. Do you recoil in horror at the sight of a giant clock? Perhaps, if you had a particularly rough evening immediately before; but we're betting you don't. Based on life experiences, you make an unconscious inference that alarm clocks (and other objects) do not spontaneously increase in size. Therefore, you know that the clock is closer, not larger. Three important principles are highlighted by Helmholtz's concept of unconscious inferences. First, the perceiver plays an interpretive role in what is perceived; perception is not just a passive process of registering incoming physical energy. Second, perceptual and cognitive processes are influenced by previous experience. Third, perceptual and cognitive processes often occur outside of conscious awareness (as implied in the term *unconscious inference*).

COGNITIVE PROCESSES—CONSCIOUS OR UNCONSCIOUS?

In proposing the concept of unconscious inference, Helmholtz helped make it clear that many cognitive processes occur outside conscious awareness. Look again at the list of cognitive processes that begins on page 2. Rate each process on the following continuum and explain your rating.

$$1 \longleftarrow 2 \longrightarrow 3 \longrightarrow 4 \longrightarrow 5$$

mostly unconscious   mostly conscious

It's not difficult to see why the work of early psychophysicists provided an important step toward a science of cognition. Psychophysicists were among the first to apply the scientific method to bridge the physical and the mental. Both psychophysicists and cognitive psychologists are interested in how stimulation and information in the outside world are linked with internal processes, representations, and conscious experience.

While psychophysicists tend to focus on the early stages of how we process information, cognitive psychologists focus on *all* stages of information processing. Let's turn our attention back to that blasted alarm clock that shatters your nighttime reverie. Psychophysicists might be interested in how bright the LED read-out on the clock needs to be for you to read it, or on how loud the alarm has to be for you to hear it, or on whether you think the light is as bright as the alarm is loud—in other words, your psychological interpretation of physical experiences. A cognitive psychologist, on the other hand, would be interested in these processes and more: How do you focus your attention on the clock? How do you recognize and understand the sound coming from it? What are the processes that may lead you to decide to sleep in?

Structuralism: The Contents of Mental Experience

Although psychophysics may have helped lay the foundation, modern experimental psychology is generally traced back to 1879, when Wilhelm Wundt (1832–1920) established the first psychological laboratory at the University of Leipzig in Germany. Wundt believed that a science of psychology should be concerned with how people consciously experience the world. Given that psychology was a fledgling scientific enterprise, some thought it wise to model psychology after a well-established science—chemistry. Simple chemical elements combine to form more complex compounds. The structuralists, as they would later be dubbed, wondered whether this approach could be applied to conscious experience. Perhaps the complexities of how we experience everyday events could be broken down into distinct and basic elements of consciousness. According to the structuralists, these elements could likely be classified into three broad categories: sensations (the basic sensory dimensions that we encode from a stimulus), feelings (emotions aroused by a stimulus), and images (purely mental impressions that seem sensory in nature).

Consider an example: Wundt and his colleagues might characterize looking at a sunrise as a complex experience made up of simpler ones. These would include simple sensations (e.g., warmth on the skin), simple images (e.g., hearing bird calls), and simple feelings (e.g., contentment). Wundt attempted to identify these simple components of complex experiences through the use of **introspection,** a procedure that requires subjects to provide a rigorous, unbiased report of every element of the conscious experience that accompanies the presentation of some stimulus (e.g., the presentation of a tone). It was hoped that applying this method of thorough, objective, journalistic analysis to a wide range of everyday experiences would yield the elemental sensations, images, and feelings that combine to produce everyday consciousness. One of Wundt's students, Edward Titchener (1867–1927), popularized this approach in the United States, terming it **structuralism.** While this early approach to the study of psychology may seem simplistic at best, you must remember the context in which it emerged. Psychology was new and trying to establish itself as a scientific discipline, so it made sense to emulate the approach used by another science.

Functionalism: The Functions of Mental Experience

At about the same time that structuralists were attempting to distill consciousness into its basic elements, a decidedly different approach was evolving. William James (1842–1910) and others were highly critical of the structuralist approach (see Kimble, 1985), contending that their atomistic approach to consciousness was wrong-headed. James invoked the well-known phrase *stream of consciousness* to capture the continuous, ever-changing nature of our experience. Analyzing it at any discrete point in time (as the structuralists did with introspection) violates its very nature. A related point is that the mere act of scrutinizing and analyzing one's conscious experience changes the experience. You're no longer studying consciousness.

Rather than using introspection to provide moment-to-moment snapshots of what was currently in mind, James thought psychology should devote itself to figuring out the *functions* of the mind—what it does in everyday life (hence the name given to this approach—**functionalism**). While a structuralist would attempt to determine the basic images, feelings, and sensations that comprise the conscious experience of being angry, a functionalist would study the emotion of anger by trying to determine the purpose or function of being angry. Given its emphasis on mental processing rather than on mental structure, functionalism ultimately had a more profound influence on cognitive psychology than did structuralism. Indeed, the table of contents of James's famous text *Principles of Psychology* reads like a "what's what" of the study of cognition, including chapters on attention, remembering, emotions, and thinking.

Behaviorism: The Rejection of Mental Experience

While the structuralists and functionalists were debating the proper focus of a scientific study of consciousness, a storm was brewing. The study of the mind and conscious experience was entering what might be termed a sort of "dark age." Psychologist John B. Watson (1878–1958), intensely dissatisfied with psychology's lack of progress, suggested a shift that he believed would make the fledgling enterprise of psychology truly scientific. Watson's radical notion was the banishment of consciousness from scientific study. Why would he propose such a radical move? The hallmarks of scientific study are observation, measurement, and repeatability. The study of consciousness lends itself to none of these. It cannot be reliably observed or measured, and the results of an

Stimulus ⟶ Response

introspective analysis cannot be reliably reproduced. But behavior can be observed, measured, and repeated; hence, it should serve as the focus of scientific psychology. Watson's approach, termed **behaviorism,** discarded both the subject matter and the approach of the structuralists and functionalists, instead emphasizing the study of observable responses and their relation to observable stimuli. Given its emphasis on observable stimuli and responses, it makes sense that behaviorism is sometimes referred to as **S-R psychology.** According to behaviorists, psychology should dedicate itself to discovering these S-R connections. Between stimulus and response is a "black box" that houses consciousness. Investigation of the contents of the black box is a futile enterprise, according to the behaviorists, because the contents do not lend themselves to scientific investigation.

The behaviorists were not denying that we experience consciousness; for example, they wouldn't have a problem with acknowledging that people have a conscious experience of hunger. They simply rejected the idea that this conscious experience could be meaningfully studied, owing to its inherently subjective nature. They also gave consciousness no causal role in producing behavior; we don't eat because we *feel hungry.* Eating is an observable response that occurs in the presence of some verifiable stimulus, such as low insulin levels or a plate of fresh-out-of-the-oven cookies. The complete rejection of consciousness from scientific study was a radical move, but it struck a resounding chord. In the United States, the behaviorist approach dominated experimental psychology for the first half of the 20th century.

STOP *and* **THINK!**

THINKING ABOUT BEHAVIORISM

The behaviorists believed that all behavior and action could be understood purely in terms of observable stimuli and responses. Consider each of the following everyday activities:

hanging out with a friend
getting lunch
feeling nervous over an upcoming test
screaming for your team at a football game
going out to see the latest gross-out comedy film
working a crossword puzzle
telling a joke
going for a half-hour jog

For each activity, apply an S-R analysis by answering the following questions:

What would fit into the S box?
What would fit into the R box?
What would fit into the "black box" (that behaviorists would want to ignore)?

- Did you have any difficulties explaining these behaviors solely in terms of the S's and R's?
- If so, what were the difficulties?
- Which of the activities are most difficult to account for with an S-R view? (In other words, which activities involve a great deal of activity in the black box?)
- Does the S-R view of these activities offer any advantages?

Laying the Foundation for Cognitive Psychology

The rejection of consciousness as a topic for scientific study was not without good intent. The behaviorists wanted to establish psychology as a rigorous experimental science alongside other disciplines more readily acknowledged as "scientific," such as biology and chemistry. Their sincere belief was that the study of mind was never going to get us there. But scientists throughout the short history of psychology have demonstrated time and time again that rigorous observation and measurement of mental processes is possible. In fact, even before the behaviorists "threw down the gauntlet" to scientists interested in human behavior, Hermann Ebbinghaus was quietly conducting a strikingly methodical and precise series of experiments on remembering.

Ebbinghaus: Pioneering Experiments on Memory.   In the late 1800s, Ebbinghaus embarked on an investigation of his own memory—an investigation that demonstrated convincingly that complex mental processes could be submitted to experimental test. Ebbinghaus was a truly dedicated researcher; he served as his only subject, tirelessly testing and retesting his own memory under rigorously controlled conditions of presentation and testing. He did this by memorizing list after list of nonsense syllables—letter strings that do not form words (e.g., DBJ). For a given list, he would record the number of study trials it took to learn the list to perfection. Then, after varying periods of time, he would attempt to relearn the list to perfection again. As you might imagine, it took him fewer trials to relearn lists that he had memorized previously. Ebbinghaus coined the term **savings** to refer to this reduction in the number of trials it took to relearn a list. His previous experience in perfectly learning the material *saved* him some trials the second time he tried to learn it. Think about it: if you've already learned to do something well and then take some time off, you're not going to have to start from scratch when you attempt to redo or relearn the task.

Using the method of savings, Ebbinghaus revealed a number of fundamental principles of memory. He found that recall was more difficult as list length increased, a harbinger of later research that would investigate the limited nature of working memory. He found that his retention increased with the frequency of repetitions (if you study more, you'll remember more). And he captured the pattern of forgetting over time in what has been termed the **forgetting curve,** which relates the amount recalled to the time that has elapsed since study. Forgetting occurs rapidly early in the retention interval, then slows down considerably. This pattern has been replicated in countless investigations of memory, but as you'll read later, the precise function that relates what we remember and forget to the passage of time depends on myriad variables.

Ebbinghaus's research was significant for a number of reasons. First, it demonstrated that precise and well-controlled experimental methods could be applied to study complex mental processes, setting the stage for the experimental approach to cognition that was to follow. Second, it provided a well-conceived research paradigm for the study of memory that inspired a legion of later researchers. Finally, as noted above, it established a number of core principles of memory function that are still being replicated and extended in laboratory research today.

Bartlett's Memory Research.   Sir Frederick Bartlett objected to the use of tightly controlled laboratory procedures for revealing memory function. He believed that if psychological research was to be generalizable, it should be as naturalistic as possible. Following this principle, his procedure involved the presentation of materials that were meaningful rather than nonsensical. In assessing subjects' memory for stories and folk tales, Bartlett (1932) discovered a fair amount of reconstruction. Some details were left out of the story; other details were inserted. Based on his results, Bartlett characterized memory as a reconstructive process rather than a reproductive one. This reconstruction was guided by what Bartlett termed *schemata,* generalized knowledge structures about events and situations that are constructed based on past experience.

Note that in contrast to the behaviorist explanations of the day, Bartlett was postulating that mental structures (schemata) exerted a causal influence over behavior. Bartlett's work was distinctive and important in a couple of ways. First, it provided an alternative to the mechanistic, S-R view of remembering as a group of simple verbal associations. Second, it showed incredible prescience, foreshadowing some major concerns that have taken center stage in present-day cognitive psychology—the reconstructive nature of memory. A social anthropologist at heart, Bartlett was interested in remembering as a dynamic, social process that helps us make sense of our daily lives. His classic book was titled *Remembering: A Study in Experimental and *Social* Psychology* (emphasis added). Cognitive psychology's current emphasis on the study of cognition within natural contexts owes much to Bartlett's early investigations.

It's interesting to note the strong contrast between the methods used by Ebbinghaus and those used by Bartlett to study remembering. Ebbinghaus's method involved the precisely controlled presentation and remembering of lists of nonsense syllables, while Bartlett's method (though somewhat controlled) left more to chance, as subjects were exposed to stories and asked to remember them. The tension between precise control and realism in procedures and materials will be discussed in Chapter 2.

◆ **STOP *and* THINK!** ━━━━━━━━━━━

TWO APPROACHES TO THE STUDY OF COGNITION

Look at the list of cognitive processes that begins on page 2 (again!). For each process, give a brief description of how you would study it

- in the laboratory
- in the real world

━━━━━━━━━━━━━━━━━━━━━

Gestalt Psychology.   The Gestalt perspective in psychology, developed in Germany and very active in the first half of the last century, emphasized the role that organizational processes play in perception and problem solving. Roughly translated, the German word *gestalt* means something like *configuration.* Psychologists who adopted the **Gestalt approach** were interested in the organizational principles that guide mental processing. So a Gestalt psychologist would be interested in investigating the way that you organize visual stimuli in your environment—do you see the items in Figure 1.1 as rows or columns of X's? The Gestaltists believed that the answer to this question revealed something fundamental about visual perception.

The spirit of the Gestalt approach is captured well by their oft-cited credo "The whole is different than the sum of its parts." One cannot capture the

Figure 1.1 Three rows or five columns?

essence of conscious experience by analyzing it into its elements, as the structuralists attempted to do. Experience is more than just a summary of elementary sensations, images, and feelings. When combined in a particular way, these elements of experience form a particular gestalt, or whole. And one cannot understand human experience and behavior by eliminating all talk of conscious experience, as the behaviorists attempted to do. Current cognitive psychology embodies the spirit of the Gestalt view by placing the mind center stage and viewing it as an active processor of information. In addition, the Gestalt approach still has a strong influence on how we view particular cognitive processes, most notably, perception and problem solving, as we'll see in Chapters 3 and 12.

STOP *and* **REVIEW!**

1. True or false? Philosophy provided the content of cognitive psychology, while physiology provided the method used by cognitive psychology.
2. True or false? Functionalism ultimately had a greater influence on psychology than did structuralism.
3. The behaviorist approach in psychology
    a. was theoretically aligned with Gestalt psychology
    b. followed the assumptions and methods established by structuralists and functionalists
    c. emphasized the study of observable phenomena
    d. focused on the role of mind in behavior
4. What are the basic ideas of Ebbinghaus, Bartlett, and the Gestalt approach to psychology?

➤ The scientific study of thinking has its roots in philosophy, which provided the basic questions that empirical research in cognition attempts to answer. The science of physiology provided a basic method for the investigation of perceptual processes. Modern attempts to understand the mind can be traced to the psychophysicists, who studied the relationship between physical stimulation and psychological experience.

➤ Psychology was established in 1879, when the structuralists began to formally investigate the elements of conscious experience. Their primary method was introspection, an intensive analysis of the contents (images, feelings, and sensations) of one's own consciousness. The functionalists were concerned with specifying the functions of consciousness rather than its structure, and ultimately had a much larger impact on the field.

➤ Behaviorists favored the elimination of consciousness as a topic of study, given its subjective nature. Behaviorists believed a science of psychology should focus on observables like behavior. Behaviorism is sometimes referred to as S-R psychology because of its emphasis on the analysis of observable stimuli and responses and their relation to one another.

➤ Ebbinghaus demonstrated that rigorous experimental work on cognition was possible. His research on memory for nonsense syllables established a number of key principles of memory that are still recognized today. Bartlett investigated memory for more realistic materials and, based on his results, argued that memory involves processes of reconstruction. Gestalt psychologists were interested in the organizational tendencies of the mind and had a significant influence on views of perception and problem solving.

The Emergence of Cognitive Psychology

Although behaviorism had struck a chord, to many it rang hollow in its failing to capture the richness and diversity of human behavior and creativity. The challenges to behaviorism came from outside and from within and were both empirical and theoretical. From within the behavioristic camp, some studies of animal behavior were producing results that were problematic for S-R accounts, results revealing that rats could rightfully be described as "thinking" under some circumstances. The momentum from these research challenges began to build in the 1930s, posing a threat to the behaviorist stronghold on scientific psychology. In addition, psychologists were growing increasingly frustrated with the narrowness of explanations offered within the behaviorist paradigm, arguing that such explanations captured virtually nothing of what human beings do on a day-to-day basis, such as our use of language. Another major influence on the emergence of cognitive psychology was the development of new technologies like calculators, computers, and communication systems. These developments revolutionized how humans viewed machines and their capabilities. This, in turn, revolutionized the way humans viewed *themselves* and *their* capabilities.

S-R Explanations: *Seriously wRong?*

Failure to Account for Data.　As we've seen, behaviorists viewed reference to mental states or mental representations as useless, preferring to focus only on behavior, and using only the concepts of stimuli, responses, and the associations between them. Consider the following example: Suppose we have a rat that we place in a T-maze; the rat has to learn to run down the straightaway and choose the side with food in it. Over a series of trials, what do you suppose happens? As you might suspect, the rat starts to make the correct turn to obtain the food. Rats may not be the brightest of animals, but they can learn that simple association. A behaviorist would explain the rat's learning of the maze with three simple concepts: stimuli, responses, and reinforcement. Associations are formed between stimuli and responses, with reinforcement as the "glue" that holds

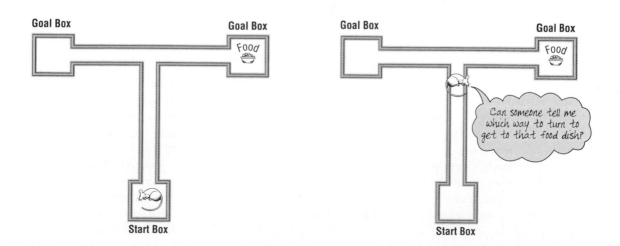

the associations together. When placed in a particular *stimulus* situation (the feel and smell of a maze), the rat engages in a particular *response* (running forward in the maze). If it receives reinforcement at the end of the maze, this bonds the stimulus and the response together—an S-R association. The next time the rat is confronted with the feel and smell of the maze (the S), the response of running (the R) will be triggered. Each time the rat is placed in the maze, this association plays itself out again and becomes stronger with each reinforcement. The rat runs faster. Over time, it zips down the alley and without hesitation makes the correct turn, without asking for directions.

The behaviorist account of the learning process is simple and elegant and does not rely on reference to unobservable mental processes, like the rat *expecting* or *knowing* that the food is on the right. The rat doesn't "know" anything; it is simply executing a chain of S-R associations that have been built up over a series of trials. But the trouble is that there are too many scenarios in which this simple account doesn't apply. Let's briefly review a few of these findings.

Learning without Responding.

According to the behaviorists, responding is absolutely essential for learning. It's the R in the S-R association link. Demonstrating that learning occurs in the absence of R would be difficult, if not impossible, to explain. A study by McNamara, Long, and Wike (1956) investigated whether learning would occur in this type of situation. Rats were tested in a T-maze, as described above. Some of the rats ran the maze themselves, eventually learning that they had to turn right to get to the food. Other rats were pushed by the experimenters down the alleyway in small carts. At the end of the runway, the experimenters turned the cart to the right and let the rat out to eat the food.

Which group of rats will know where the food is? "Isn't it obvious?" you must be thinking. They both will. They both saw the maze and saw that food was on the right. So now they *expect* the food to be on the right. But this is exactly the type of mentalistic explanation that behaviorists rejected. Behaviorists would say only the group of rats that ran on their own would learn the correct response. Why? Because R is required for learning. The results, however, failed to support the behaviorist prediction. When allowed to run on their own, the rats that had previously gotten a ride to the food showed a preference for the right side, just like the rats that had run there on their own from the beginning. Clearly, the hitchhiking rats learned—and without responding.

Learning without Reinforcement.

Recall that, according to the behaviorist view, reinforcement is necessary for learning to occur; as described above, it's the "glue" that holds the S and the R together. If there is no reinforcement, stimulus and response will not be bonded, and there will be no learning. Tolman and Honzik (1930) tested this in a classic study. Over the course of two weeks, they placed three different groups of rats in a complex maze like the one in Figure 1.2 and had them explore it. One group of rats was reinforced every time they reached the goal box, starting on day 1. A second group was never reinforced. A third group was not reinforced during the first 10 days but began

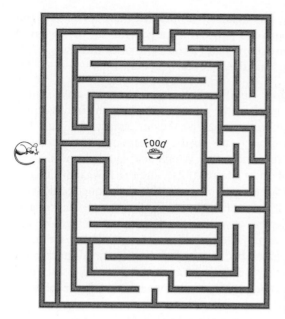

Figure 1.2 A complex garden-style maze used in some early studies of simple learning.

receiving a reinforcement in the goal box on the 11th day.

Consider the prediction of the S-R view. The rats in group 1 should show a steady decrease in error rate. The reinforcement in the goal box strengthens the response (R) of running when placed in the stimulus (S) of the maze. Group 2 rats should show no decrease in error rate; they were never reinforced, so S and R were never bonded. Group 3 should look exactly like group 2 until day 11, when the rats see food in the goal box. Then, starting on day 12, group 3 rats should show the same gradual decrease in error rate shown in group 1, as the goal box reinforcement starts to strengthen the S-R connection.

The findings were surprising, at least to those operating from an S-R perspective. The rats in groups 1 and 2 behaved exactly as predicted, showing a gradual decrease in error rate and no decrease in error rate, respectively. But the results from group 3 proved problematic for the behaviorists. As you can see in Figure 1.3, starting on day 12, these rats were as error free as rats in group 1. Clearly, they had been learning the maze all along, even without reinforcement. Tolman termed this phenomenon **latent learning.** This finding is difficult to handle from a behaviorist standpoint: How could learning occur if the stimulus and response were never associated? Once again, a cognitive explanation seems like a more

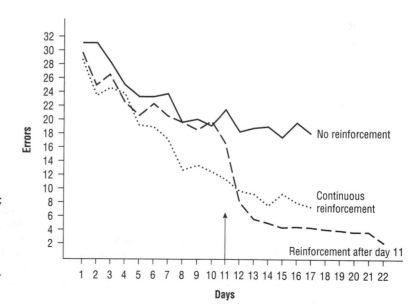

Figure 1.3 Latent learning; results from Tolman and Honzik's (1930) study.

From Tolman, E. C., & Honzik, C. H. (1930). Introduction and removal of reward, and maze performance in rats. *University of California Publications in Psychology, 4,* 257–275.

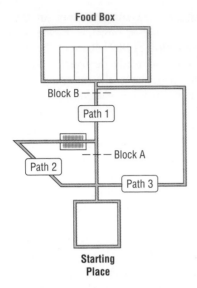

Figure 1.4 Maze used to study latent learning. On different trials, blocks were placed at various places in the maze.

From Tolman, E. C. (1948). Cognitive maps in rats and men. *Psychological Review, 55*, 189–208.

reasonable one. The rats wandered around the maze for 11 days and picked up what Tolman (1948) termed a general "lay of the land." They were well aware of the maze layout, and once there was a reason to demonstrate what they had learned, they did.

Cognitive Maps. In 1948, Tolman conducted a classic study that would put another fly in the behaviorists' ointment. In this experiment, rats were faced with a maze like the one pictured in Figure 1.4. There are three possible routes to the destination—three possible *responses:* path 1, path 2, and path 3. Which one would you pick, if you were hungry? The shortest one, of course, and this is what S-R theory would predict. In behaviorist terms, path 1 has the strongest S-R association because the reinforcement is obtained the most quickly, and the less time that elapses between responding and reinforcement, the stronger the association. Following this logic, path 2 has the next-strongest S-R association because food can be obtained quicker via this path relative to path 3. Path 3 has the weakest S-R association because taking this path would take the longest to get to the food.

The cognitive view of rat behavior in this situation is quite different. Recall Tolman's proposal that rats acquired a "lay of the land" as they explored the maze. Another way of putting this is that the rats formed a **mental map** of the maze layout and consulted it to determine which path would get them to the food most quickly. Note that this explanation is exactly the type of view that the behaviorists railed against because it appeals to the notion of mental representations (i.e., mental maps) and their influence on behavior. Behaviorists believed that behavior could be explained without any appeal to such factors.

In his study, Tolman allowed rats to freely explore the maze over a series of trials. True to S-R predictions, the rats preferred path 1, choosing it most. Then the investigators teased the rats by placing a block at point A. When rats ran into this block, they were forced to retreat to the choice point and go a different way. The S-R approach would predict that at this point, the rats should behave according to the next-strongest S-R association and take path 2. The cognitive approach would also make this prediction, because when placed in this situation, the rats would consult their mental map and realize that path 2 was shorter.

The key condition was when a block was placed at point B. What is a rat to do? The behaviorist and cognitive predictions diverge in this case. According to the behaviorist view, the rats will take path 1, because path 1 has the strongest S-R association. When blocked, they will go back to the choice point and take path 2, which has the next-strongest S-R association. Finally, when blocked again, they should return to the choice point and choose

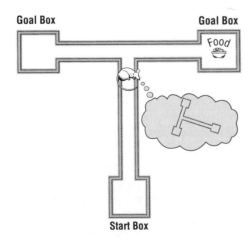

path 3. The cognitive view gives the rats a little more credit. According to this view, the rats have a general mental map for the entire maze arrangement, so when the rats see the block at point B, they'll realize that path 2 is also blocked. Therefore, they won't even bother with it. They'll run back to the choice point and take path 3. This is exactly what Tolman found. On the first trial with the block at point B, the rats chose path 3 over 90% of the time.

Because behaviorists claim that both reinforcement and responding are necessary for learning, they were bedeviled by the discovery of learning without responding and latent learning, as well as by the seeming reality of mental maps. Theorists such as Clark Hull (1943) attempted to repair the damage done to behaviorist theory by postulating additional mechanisms and processes, but these changes (postulating unseen mechanisms) brought S-R theory perilously close to cognitive theory. Change was afoot: the failure of S-R theory was helping to set the stage for the new science of mind.

Lashley Lashes Out.   As the middle of the 20th century approached, the theoretical tide was shifting away from behavioristic explanations of action. In 1948, a group of scientists convened at the Hixon Symposium in what was to be a seminal event for the emergence of a scientific study of mind. As described by Gardner (1985), this conference featured a number of papers that championed a new approach to studying mind and

Skilled performance: Amenable to an S-R analysis?

brain and cast severe doubt on behaviorism's rigidity. One of the most devastating blows was dealt by Karl Lashley, who argued that any science of human behavior must be able to explain forms both simple (rats running in a T-maze) and complex (a human playing the piano). Complex behaviors, Lashley argued, could not possibly play out via a series of S-R connections, as the behaviorists claimed. Consider Jerry Lee Lewis playing "Whole Lotta Shakin' Goin' On," a breathlessly fast song. According to the behaviorists, the performance of this song can be explained through S-R connections. Jerry Lee's finger movements are the *responses* that are connected to the *stimuli* (the piano and the keys) by some type of *reinforcement* (be it audience applause, the sound of the music, or something else). The problem is, the sequence of movements involved in such a performance play out with such speed that there is no conceivable way that a chain of S-R connections could be the explanation. Complex behaviors like this need to be planned out and organized in advance, according to Lashley. Any complete science of behavior should have to address the question of internal mental plans for action. It was becoming more and more apparent that the banishment of mental representations from scientific explanations of behavior was threatening to lead psychology to a dead end.

Chomsky's Challenge. Challenges to standard behaviorist explanations came not only from inside the domain of animal learning research, but also from disciplines outside of psychology, such as linguistics. Remember that behaviorism offered a general explanation of all behavior, animal and human. Indeed, renowned behaviorist B. F. Skinner termed language *verbal behavior* and applied an S-R analysis to the acquisition of language, arguing that even complex abilities like language could be captured in purely S-R terms. Skinner viewed language as the acquisition of a set of responses, explainable through the principles of reinforcement. Linguist Noam Chomsky (1959) wrote a scathing review of Skinner's analysis in what Leahey (1992) calls "perhaps the single most influential psychological paper published since Watson's behaviorist manifesto of 1913." In his review, Chomsky completely rejected the S-R view of language, characterizing it as more vague and unscientific than the very cognitive explanations that Skinner himself criticized (Lachman, Lachman, & Butterfield, 1979).

Behaviorists explained language, as they did all human behavior, in terms of stimulus, response, and reinforcement. When little two-year-old Jimmy drinks his favorite drink, looks up at Mommy, and happily says, "Chocolate!", his mother says enthusiastically, "That's *right*, Jimmy!" Skinner applied a simple S-R account to such scenarios. The stimulus is the beverage Jimmy is drinking, the response is "Chocolate!", and the reinforcement is Mommy's smile and exclamation that solidifies the bond between the stimulus and the response. In Skinnerian terms, the *response* "Chocolate" comes under control of the *stimulus* of a glass of chocolate milk. This mechanism is typically labeled "stimulus control."

Chomsky challenged this conceptualization, pointing out gaping holes in Skinner's account. He argued that the concept of stimulus control has no meaning in language. Consider an example. If we hand you a glass filled with a brown-colored bubbling liquid (the stimulus), you could respond by saying, "Coke?" or "cold" or "tasty." No matter what you said, a behaviorist would say that your response was elicited by some stimulus property; but there would be no way of predicting *which* stimulus property. Skinner would just say that whatever response you gave was elicited by a stimulus property. Chomsky pointed out that this explanation is no explanation at all. The term *stimulus* might mean something when a rat runs in a maze, but it loses virtually all meaning when applied to the subtleties and complexities of language.

Consider the following sentence: *After the storm, the sun came out, and the leprechaun started searching for the gold.* We just created this sentence. We've never heard it before. We've never been reinforced for saying it or writing it. It seems kind of silly to say that the *response* of typing it came about because of the *stimulus* of the laptop computer. The behaviorists really have no satisfactory explanation for how this sentence was created. They also have no explanation for the wonder of sentence comprehension—the process by which you understood the sentence and probably inferred that the leprechaun would first need to find a rainbow or his search would be unsuccessful. The term *reinforcement* doesn't hold up very well either. It's not really apparent what the reinforcement is for speaking. What's reinforcing about people talking to themselves as they read or a child talking to one of her dolls? Skinner's explanation was *automatic self-reinforcement;* but once again, if such a slippery concept is allowed as an explanation of language, then we really have no explanation at all. Chomsky argued that Skinner's account of language learning was nothing more than a fuzzy, metaphorical description of language learning that happened to sound vaguely scientific.

Chomsky's critique of Skinner was so devastating that it was met by silence from the behaviorists for over a decade (Lachman, Lachman, & Butterfield, 1979); they simply didn't have an answer for it. The basic premise of Chomsky's account was that the productivity and novelty observed in language use can be explained only by appealing to mental representations—"rules in the head" that allow a person to produce and comprehend language. As you'll see throughout the text, the concept of mental representation is central to the study of cognition, and Chomsky deserves much of the credit for legitimizing it.

The movement toward a new science of mind now had undeniable momentum. Conceptually, behaviorism was failing as a satisfactory explanation of behavior. The issues discussed in the preceding sections were all converging on a single, very important point that lies at the heart of cognitive psychology—any satisfactory account of behavior must make reference to mental processes and mental representations. The time was right for a new approach to the study of mind to emerge. Behaviorism, the dominant explanatory paradigm, was failing. Around the same time that behaviorism was faltering, emerging technologies, such as communication systems and computers, provided useful models for describing the process of thinking and investigating its components.

Technological Influences

Communications Engineering. Communication devices such as televisions, radios, and cell phones are all examples of information transmission systems. In 1948, Bell Telephone mathematician Claude Shannon developed a general theory of how such systems work. According to Shannon, any communications system has several key components, including an information source, a transmitter, a channel through which a message is transmitted, and a receiver. An effective communications system will transmit information with as much fidelity as possible, minimizing distortion and the effects of outside interference, or "noise." These issues are obviously of interest to engineers working with communications systems. But this description of a communications system is also a fairly good model of how humans process information. Consider yourself as you listen to your professor's riveting lecture on the history of cognitive psychology. The professor is the information source, and the lecture is the transmitter. You listen to the message via your auditory channel, and after reception, the message is interpreted. The noise in the system could be the students behind you whispering or someone's cell phone ringing. Shannon's concept of a communications system provided a fruitful metaphor for considering how human thought processes might work and suggested ways they might be analyzed and investigated.

Computer Science. A second technological advance that had a dramatic impact on the newly developing science of mind was the development of the computer. It became apparent that machines could be programmed to perform some of the intelligent functions thought to be the exclusive province of humans. Simply put, computers could, in a sense, "think." It wasn't long before the analogy was more actively pursued. Could the way computers "think" be similar to the way humans think? After all, like communications systems, the computer provides a good descriptive model of how the mind might work. Computers handle information in three basic stages: input, some type of processing,

The computer has been a rich metaphor for conceptualizing mental processing.

and output. Humans can be thought of in exactly the same way. We take in information through our sensory systems, process it in some way, and respond to it in some way. A promising direction for a science of mind might be to specify the mechanisms whereby humans process data and how the data are stored, retrieved, and used. As you'll see, cognitive psychology research has these basic aims.

STOP *and* THINK!

CONSIDERING COGNITION'S HISTORICAL INFLUENCES

Look over the developments that led to the decline of behaviorism and the ascendance of cognitive psychology, and think about their relative importance. Provide a ranking of the following developments, from most important to least important, and explain your ranking.

Lashley's argument   learning-without-reinforcement study
Chomsky's argument   learning-without-responding study
cognitive map study   advances in communications engineering

STOP *and* REVIEW!

1. True or false? Research has shown that learning can occur without responding.
2. Explain Chomsky's objection to the behaviorist account of language learning.
3. True or false? Lashley argued that many behaviors are carried out too slowly for an S-R explanation to be correct.
4. Describe the ways in which technology was instrumental in the development of cognitive psychology.

➤ According to behaviorism, learning requires both a response and a reinforcement. Contrary to this view, research indicated that rats were capable of learning in the absence of reinforcement and in the absence of a response, suggesting that behavior is guided by mental representations like maps and expectations.

➤ Chomsky sharply criticized Skinner's simplistic S-R view of learning language, citing the tremendous novelty and generativity of language.

➤ Lashley pointed out the inadequacy of the behaviorist approach in explaining rapid behavioral sequences, like those involved in playing the piano.

➤ The development of new technologies such as computers and communication systems provided new models of how the mind might work and helped inspire the new science of cognition.

Psychology A. D. (After the *Decline* of Behaviorism)

By the mid-1950s, cognitive psychology was well on its way to establishing itself as a legitimate paradigm within psychology. The failure of the S-R approach, coupled with the promise and excitement generated by new theoretical approaches and new technologies, fueled what some have termed the *cognitive revolution*. One of cognitive psychology's pioneers, George Miller (cited in Gardner, 1985), fixed the birthdate of cognitive psychology as September 11, 1956. On this date, psychologists interested in the study of mind gathered at the Massachusetts Institute of Technology for the Symposium on Information Theory. As outlined by Gardner (1985), this conference featured a number of seminal papers that employed the new approach to mind. Chomsky presented his newly developed theory of language; computer scientists Allen Newell and Herbert Simon presented a paper detailing their "Logic Theory Machine"—a complete theorem proof carried out by a computing machine; and George Miller presented his now-classic view of short-term memory as a limited information-processing mechanism that could hold approximately 7 ± 2 items. Clearly, times had changed.

Behaviorism Reconsidered

But before we kick the last bit of dirt onto the behaviorists' grave, we should emphasize the immeasurable positive influence they had on the study of mind. As you'll see, the methodologies employed by modern-day cognitive psychologists are truly impressive in their objectivity and precision, almost to a fault. Whereas introspection was an "easy mark" in terms of criticism, the same cannot be said of today's investigations of mind, which are rigorously controlled and feature careful measurement and observation. Behaviorists threw down the gauntlet of challenge to investigators of mind, and the challenge was answered.

And, as it turns out, behaviorism never really went away after all. In a recent essay entitled "What Happened to Behaviorism," Roediger (2004) gives his answer: not much. Behaviorism is still alive and well, and is well represented in much of the research and theorizing in current cognitive psychology. For example, all psychologists (including cognitive psychologists) must ultimately measure behavior to reach any type of conclusion. And, as Roediger points out, "The scientist's hope is to discover fundamentally interesting principles from simple, elegant experimental analyses," and when cognitive psychologists engage in this process of discovery, they use behavioral measures to arrive at the "fundamentally interesting principles." So the behaviorist approach continues to hold some sway, although different from in its heyday.

Information Processing: A Computer Metaphor for Cognition

As cognitive psychology evolved, the **information-processing model** emerged as the preeminent paradigm in cognitive psychology. This paradigm uses the computer as a model for human cognition and has dominated theory and research in cognitive psychology for its first five decades.

Lachman, Lachman, and Butterfield (1979) identified some of the major assumptions of the information-processing approach. The first assumption is that humans are *symbol manipulators* who encode, store, retrieve, and manipulate symbolic data stored in memory. Flowing from this is the idea of *representation;* the data of the human information-processing system consist of representations that correspond to information from the environment (e.g., objects and events) and processes (e.g., remembering and problem solving). Another assumption is that human thought is best characterized as a *system* of interrelated capacities and processes that all affect each other. The components cannot be fully understood in isolation from one another. This view also assumes that humans are active and creative information scanners and seekers; we don't just passively react to the environment. This idea contrasts powerfully with the behaviorist approach, which considers humans to be passive responders waiting for the environment to elicit responses. According to the information-processing approach, thinking is a step-by-step process in which the products of a given stage serve as the input for the next stage, and so on. Each of these processes takes time and can be examined separately, to some extent. For example, we can attempt to isolate processes such as encoding, processing, and retrieval and estimate their duration. This assumption paved the way for using reaction time to measure mental processing, something we will discuss in Chapter 2.

STOP and THINK!

CONSTRUCT YOUR OWN INFORMATION-PROCESSING DIAGRAMS

As discussed in the chapter, you're constantly engaged in cognitive processing. According to the information-processing approach to cognition, thinking is a step-by-step process that can be broken down into a number of simpler subcomponents. For each everyday task listed below, construct a simple flowchart that represents the information processing involved. See if you can take each subcomponent and divide it into smaller components, trying to get to the very basic elements of cognition. Here's an example to get you started:

Component tasks of doing a crossword puzzle:

- **read clues** ⇨ **figure out words that fit clues** ⇨ **write word in puzzle**
- **read clues**
  component tasks: perceive letters ⇨ recognize words ⇨ figure out what words mean together
- **figure out words that fit clues**
  component tasks: search for word that fits ⇨ retrieve word from memory
- **write word in puzzle**
  component tasks: perceive blank spaces ⇨ write each letter in blank space

Each of these component tasks can be subdivided into further components, which in turn can be further subdivided, and so on.

Try to break down the following processes in the same way:

taking notes in class
looking up and dialing the number of a pizza joint
ordering something at a restaurant
getting dressed for the day

Connectionism: A Brain Metaphor for Cognition

One might say that the information-processing approach would characterize the brain as the "hardware" of the human computer system and the numerous cognitive processes as the "software"; engaging in different mental operations is analogous to running different software packages. This analogy has proved to be a fairly appropriate characterization, as thousands of studies have helped to specify the "software" that is cognitive processing. However, some feel that the human-computer analogy has been taken to (perhaps beyond) the limits of its usefulness. Do humans really process information in a way similar to computers? It turns out there are some major differences between the two. The most important difference is that computers typically have some type of central processing unit that does things one at a time; that is, computers tend to operate in a serial (step-by-step) fashion. This is not how the human brain works. Investigations of the brain's basic function

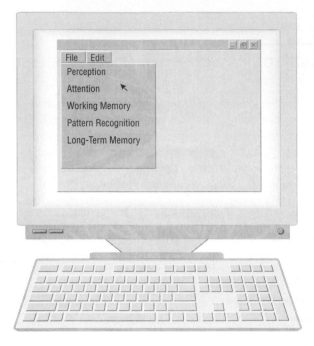

File   Edit

Perception

Attention

Working Memory

Pattern Recognition

Long-Term Memory

Perceptual Processing

Attentive Processing

Recognition

LTM Activation

Problem Solving

Decision Making

have failed to reveal any central processor and have made it apparent that much of the brain's functioning occurs in parallel, not serially.

Instead of a very rapid and serially operating computer, the mind seems better characterized as a set of slower computers that operate in parallel, all working on relatively specific tasks (Martindale, 1991). Computers can do things that humans find difficult (e.g., error-free calculation), and humans can do things that computers find difficult (e.g., recognizing variations in a familiar pattern). Unlike a computer, we can quickly recognize **A**, *A*, A, **A**, A, A, *A* as all representing the same thing; consequently, it's clear that information is processed differently in each system. The inadequacies of the information-processing metaphor have led most psychologists to abandon it as a model for the way cognitive processes work. As you'll see throughout the text, however, this metaphor is employed as a descriptive device. Though significant differences exist in how humans and computers process information, certain similarities do remain.

In a continuing search for a good model, many cognitive psychologists have turned to structural aspects of the brain for answers to the riddle of cognition. A different model of cognitive processes has evolved and threatened to replace information processing as the dominant paradigm for exploring and explaining cognition. This approach, termed **connectionism,** uses the brain (rather than the computer) as a basis for modeling cognitive processes. Connectionist models (e.g., McClelland & Rumelhart, 1981; Rumelhart & McClelland, 1986) describe cognitive processing in terms of connections between simple units, which correspond to the basic unit of the brain, the neuron. The billions of neurons in the human brain form complex neural networks, which serve as the basis for knowledge representation and cognitive processing. This model attempts to account for cognition solely in terms of the underlying "hardware" (in the computer terms used earlier) without the need to postulate extra "software" that "runs" on the hardware. In addition, psychologists (and scientists) prefer simpler theories to more complex ones, all things being equal. (The simplicity of a theory is termed *parsimony*.) Explaining cognition solely in terms of existing brain structure and function has a theoretically appealing simplicity—and it also makes a great deal of intuitive sense. It's not difficult to understand why these models generate a great deal of interest and enthusiasm.

Let's consider some of the key assumptions of the connectionist approach. The cognitive system (which corresponds to the brain) is made up of billions of interconnected nodes (corresponding to the billions of interconnected neurons in the brain) that come together to form complex networks. Nodes within a network can be activated, and the pattern of activation among these nodes corresponds to conscious experience. Connectionism is also referred to as **parallel distributed processing,** which hints at how connectionists think mental processing takes place. Let's unpack this term and look at some basic assumptions underlying this approach. First, the approach proposes that the networks underlying cognitive processing operate largely *in parallel;* information processors throughout the brain work simultaneously on some specific component of a cognitive task. Second, the processing involved in a given task (e.g., retrieving a memory) does not occur in only one specific location. Rather, the networks involved in cognitive processing are *distributed* throughout the brain. This idea of parallel processing contrasts strongly with the idea of cognition as a serial (step-by-step) process, as proposed in the information-processing approach.

If cognition is characterized as the parallel activity of a complex series of networks distributed throughout the brain, you might be asking yourself, "How are these networks formed?" The basic building block of these networks is a connection between two individual nodes. Once again, the dynamics of interconnection between nodes is modeled on the way neurons interact. The effect of one neuron on another may be excitatory, inhibitory, or nonexistent. So, within a neural network, nodes may have an excitatory connection (activation of one node makes activation of another node more likely), an inhibitory connection (activation of one node makes activation of another node less likely), or no connection (activation of one node has no effect on another node). These connections are built up, solidified, and modified as we experience the world day to day, just as our memories, general knowledge, and skills are built up, solidified, and modified. Connectionist models postulate some type of learning rule to model this process. One intuitively sensible rule often employed is that connections between nodes are strengthened if they are activated at the same time.

Consider this simple example: Imagine that you meet Greg (one of your authors) at a party. It probably won't be more than about 15 minutes before he makes some reference to either *The Simpsons* ("Homer Simpson is the greatest comic creation in TV

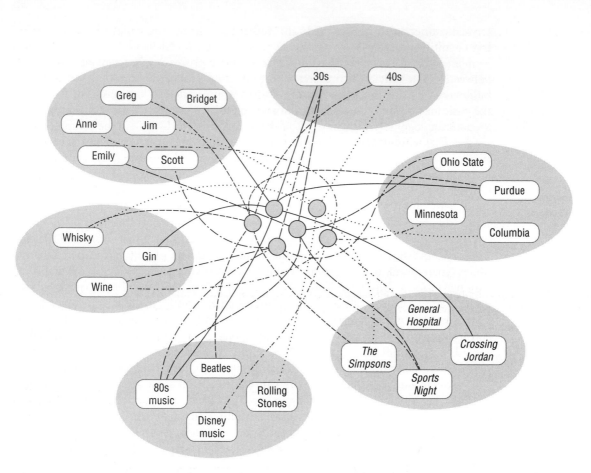

Adapted from Rumelhart, D. E., & McClelland, J. L. (1986). *Parallel distributed processing: Explorations in the microstructure of cognition.* Cambridge, MA: MIT Press. Reprinted by permission.

history") or the Beatles ("The Beatles are bigger than cognitive psychology"). From this encounter, you will have the beginnings of a connectionist network that corresponds to your memory of Greg—essentially, it *is* your memory of him. The nodes distributed throughout your neural network correspond to the bits of information you have about Greg and are connected one to another. There are excitatory connections between Greg's name, *The Simpsons*, the Beatles, and whatever other information you might pick up. Every time you meet Greg and he bores you with yet another piece of trivia about the Beatles, that particular connection gets stronger. When you are asked about him, all of the nodes in your network that are Greg are activated in parallel as you bring him to mind. From this simpleminded example, you can imagine how your brain might encode the thousands of memories and bits of information that you know and encounter.

Connectionist models have advanced far beyond simple accounts of how knowledge is represented. In recent years, cognitive scientists have developed connectionist models of everything from face recognition to problem solving to how we form attitudes about other people. These models are used to generate predictions, which are assessed with regard to existing and future experimental results. When predictions are correct, models are extended and elaborated; when incorrect, they undergo revision. Although connectionist modeling may hold an important key to truly understanding cognitive processes, most current research in cognitive psychology focuses on straightforward empirical investigations of cognitive processes and does not involve modeling, so our discussion of it will be limited.

Alternative Approaches to Cognitive Psychology

Modern-day cognitive psychology was profoundly influenced by the renowned French philosopher Descartes. One of Descartes' many claims to fame was his dualistic view of human beings. **Dualism** refers to the belief that mind and body are separable entities. This distinction is implicit in the definition of cognitive psychology that we gave earlier—the scientific study of mental processes. In other words, cognitive psychology is the study of "mind."

Two "frustrations" have resulted from the Cartesian roots of cognitive psychology. One is dualism itself—most cognitive psychologists would probably consider themselves *materialists* rather than dualists. **Materialism** is the view that mind and body are one and the same—they are both "material." In fact, mind doesn't really exist at all, except as a label for the processes of the brain. And once neuroscience has delineated the functions of the human brain, there will be nothing else to explain with regard to mind, soul, or consciousness since these are all just manifestations of brain activity. In fact, some believe that cognitive psychology itself may be rendered irrelevant. Happily for us cognitive psychologists, that day isn't here yet; neuroscientists are far from delineating the functions of the human brain, and cognitive psychologists work to help define the terrain of the field; so we still have jobs.

Embodied Cognition and the Question of Meaning.   The other "frustration" that dualism has created is an embedded assumption about mind, an assumption also embedded in the information-processing approach just described. The information-processing approach assumes a sort of "idealized" thinking mechanism, and as a result, tends to study cognition in idealized settings. In fact, researchers have strived to remove any "impure" influence from the picture in order to figure out how the "thinking machine" works; consider Ebbinghaus's use of nonsense syllables as an example of this approach. But studying cognition in these isolated and pure settings isn't really studying cognition, is it? Think about the thinking you engage in every day—how much of it takes place while you are sitting a precise distance from a computer screen with your index finger poised to press down a key as quickly as possible? We're willing to bet . . . um . . . none.

This approach to studying cognition might be considered "disembodied." It's almost as if the researchers conducting these studies conceive of the mind as a machine that's been plopped into our skull—and the task is to take the machine out and learn how it works. A recent trend in cognition research and theory is attempting to counter this with an approach appropriately termed **embodied cognition.** Embodied cognition applies to a constellation of ideas about how we think and interact with the world. It makes the important point that thinking is dynamic and situated—it occurs in conjunction with action and within a broader context that guides and shapes it. It follows that cognition should be studied within the context of actions, situations, and differing task demands that mimic conditions of everyday life.

A similar disillusionment with current cognitive psychology is encapsulated in what cognitive developmental psychologist Jerome Bruner (1990, 1996) has termed the *problem of meaning.* According to Bruner, cognitive psychology has lost its way. The computer-based information-processing approach, with its antiseptic view of the thinking machine, has tended to remove cognitive processes from any type of meaningful setting. In so doing, cognitive psychology has largely ignored the processes whereby we use our everyday experiences to make some type of broader sense of the world. It may sound a bit touchy-feely, but the point is well taken. As an example, think again about memory. Memories are our personal histories; they're critical to our identity, and to our place in the world. Practically, they serve as a critical basis for many important cognitive processes, such as reminiscing, telling stories, or making important life decisions. How much does the retention of a list of nonsense syllables really tell us about these more meaningful uses of memory? Not much, according to Bruner's view. What is needed is a much broader and richer evaluation of memory (and other cognitive processes) in *meaningful* situations, complete with the concomitant, albeit "messy," influences of personality and emotion that cognitive psychology has traditionally taken great pains to avoid.

The Ecological Approach.   A similar concept invoked to describe cognitive psychology's lack of grounding in the "real world" refers to the idea of **ecological validity** (discussed earlier in the context of Ebbinghaus and Bartlett). In response to what some see as the rather restrictive approach to studying cognition in the laboratory, the last couple of decades have been characterized by an ever-growing number of studies that investigate cognition in more real-world settings. This growing trend will be reflected in many of the studies discussed in this text. Another outgrowth of the move toward more ecologically valid cognition research is a greater appreciation for the role that culture plays in cognition. It seems more than a bit presumptuous to assume that everyone around the world remembers, speaks, solves problems, and makes decisions in the same way. Therefore, current research is dealing more and more with the relationship between culture and cognition.

STOP *and* **REVIEW!**

1. When did cognitive psychology develop as a field?
2. True or false? The information-processing model has been the dominant paradigm for explaining cognition since the 1950s.
3. The connectionist approach uses _____ as a model for how cognitive processing takes place.
   a. communication systems
   b. a library
   c. an interstate highway system
   d. the brain
4. True or false? Since the late 1970s, the trend in cognitive research is to emphasize ecological validity.

➤ Some call the emergence of cognitive psychology the "cognitive revolution." Some place the birthdate of cognitive psychology at September 11, 1956, when psychologists interested in the study of mind gathered at the Massachusetts Institute of Technology for the Symposium on Information Theory.

➤ The information-processing approach compares mental processing to the serial operation of a computer. Humans, like computers, encode and store information for later retrieval and use. This model has proved to be an extremely useful framework for investigating cognitive processes and has been the dominant approach to describing and investigating cognition since the 1950s.

➤ The connectionist approach uses the neural networks of the brain, rather than the computer, as a model for how thinking takes place. According to this approach (also termed *parallel distributed processing*), the interactive and parallel activity of neural networks distributed throughout the brain forms the basis for mental representations and processes.

➤ Since the late 1970s, the trend in cognitive research has been to feature investigations of cognition in ecologically valid contexts. In this spirit, more researchers are investigating cultural and individual differences in basic cognitive processes.

Research Themes

Throughout the text, we'll be touching on a number of running research themes that reflect fundamental trends in the experimental investigation of cognitive processes. When we discuss research studies related to each theme, the icon associated with each one will appear in the margin. Below is a brief description of each theme.

◁ Research Theme: Neuroscience

Neuroscience. As discussed earlier in the chapter, the investigation of brain substrates for cognition is perhaps the most exciting frontier of modern-day cognition research. Research on this frontier will be a prominent theme in subsequent chapters.

● Research Theme: Consciousness

Consciousness. Many of the most intriguing findings to emerge from cognitive psychology in the past couple of decades relate to interactions between cognitive processes and our awareness of those processes. To what extent do our thought processes occur outside of our awareness?

⬡ Research Theme: Development

Development. We aren't born ready to remember, reason, or speak. These abilities emerge over time. Throughout the text, we'll be discussing research on developmental highlights of cognition.

◆ Research Theme: Individual Differences

Individual Differences. Not everyone thinks alike—consistent differences in thinking have been found among all sorts of subject groups: men versus women, depressed versus nondepressed, gifted versus nongifted. Throughout the text, we'll be taking a look at some of the ways cognition varies among individuals.

■ Research Theme: Culture

Culture. Does everyone in the world have the same basic cognitive machinery, or are there different habits of mind in different parts of the world? How might culture have shaped the manner in which individuals think?

G L O S S A R Y

behaviorism: an early approach that eschewed the study of consciousness in favor of a scientific analysis of overt behavior (p. 11)

cognitive psychology: the scientific study of mental processes (p. 1)

cognitive science: an interdisciplinary effort to understand the mind; includes the disciplines of cognitive psychology, philosophy, neuroscience, artificial intelligence, linguistics, and anthropology (p. 5)

connectionism (also **parallel distributed processing**): a model that uses a brain-based metaphor to describe cognitive processes in terms of complex and interconnected networks of individual processing units that operate in parallel (p. 27)

dualism: the belief (often associated with the philosopher Descartes) that mind and body are separable entities; mind is separate from brain (p. 29)

ecological validity: the degree to which results from a research investigation can be generalized to everyday situations (p. 30)

embodied cognition: a constellation of ideas emphasizing the belief that thinking is dynamic and occurs in conjunction with action and within a broader context that guides and shapes it (p. 30)

forgetting curve: a function relating memory to time passage. A good deal of forgetting occurs soon after study, then slows down over time (p. 12)

functionalism: an early approach to the study of consciousness that emphasized the discovery of the basic uses of consciousness and how it helps us adapt in daily life (p. 10)

Gestalt approach: an early approach to the study of consciousness that emphasized the inherent organizing tendencies of the mind (p. 13)

information-processing model: a descriptive approach that likens the functioning of the mind to the operation of a computer (p. 24)

introspection: a rigorous and systematic self-report of the basic elements of an experience (p. 10)

latent learning: learning that occurs in the absence of any reinforcement (p. 17)

laws of association: principles that underlie the act of relating two ideas or concepts (p. 6)

materialism: the view that mind and body are one and the same; mind is completely accounted for by brain (p. 29)

mental map: a mental representation of a spatial layout (p. 18)

psychophysics: the study of the relationship between the physical properties of a stimulus and the properties taken on when the stimulus is filtered through subjective experience (p. 7)

savings: a measure of memory developed by Ebbinghaus that refers to the reduction in learning trials needed to learn some set of information due to previous learning trials (p. 12)

S-R psychology: another term for the behaviorist approach; emphasizes the observation of relationships between observable stimuli and responses (p. 11)

structuralism: an early approach to the study of consciousness that emphasized breaking it down in terms of its most elemental components (p. 10)

unconscious inference: an implicit assumption made by our perceptual systems about some characteristic of an incoming stimulus (p. 8)

2

Research Methods
in Cognition

How in the world does a researcher ever get a handle on something as mysterious and immaterial as thought? Can it be measured or manipulated in any sort of meaningful way?

Are simple research methods like surveys and observations of any use in the investigation of thinking, given that thinking is private and difficult to reflect on?

Are people sensitive enough about how they think to provide useful information? Is it even possible to "experiment" with mind? If so, how?

How does the study of thinking interface with the study of the brain? Is thinking the same as brain activity? If we understand brain activity, might that be all we need to understand thinking?

In this chapter, we review the nuts and bolts of psychology research as it applies to cognitive psychology. As we discussed in the previous chapter, cognitive psychology is the scientific study of mental processes. Consequently, cognitive researchers face a unique challenge: reaching firm conclusions about a subject matter that is, for the most part, completely unobservable. As you learned in Chapter 1, the behaviorists didn't think this was possible and deemed the "scientific study of mental processes" a contradiction in terms. They believed that it was impossible to study in a scientific way something so hidden and subjective. And because the initial attempts to establish a science of consciousness were based heavily on introspection, the behaviorists' objections were largely on the mark. Try as they might, early pioneers of psychology could not completely remove the subjectivity and guesswork from their study of cognitive processes.

Much has changed from the late 1800s to the turn of the 21st century. The scientific study of consciousness was rejected and then reestablished as a legitimate field of scientific study, and technological and theoretical developments opened up a new world of possibilities for a controlled and methodical approach to the study of thinking. Today, research on cognitive processes is thriving. And the recently established field of cognitive neuroscience has added a new dimension to this research as it seeks to delineate the connections between mind and brain. In this chapter, we'll introduce you to some of the basic issues confronted by researchers in cognition and cognitive neuroscience.

All scientific research seeks to describe, predict, explain, and modify some set of phenomena. Research in cognition is no different; it is designed to describe, predict, explain, and modify the processes that make up thinking. "Modifying thinking" doesn't indicate sinister cognitive psychologists attempting mind control. This phrase basically implies efforts to improve cognitive skills like memory. Accomplishing the goals of description, prediction, explanation, and modification in the domain of thinking is a challenging task because the processes are wholly unobservable. You can't see what or how someone is thinking. So the existence of various internal representations (like mental images) and processes (like memorization or rehearsal) must be *inferred,* based on something that *is* observable—namely, behavior. As you'll see, cognitive psychologists have come up with some very creative methods for uncovering the processes of thought and making them observable.

Descriptive Research

Descriptive research techniques, as the name suggests, allow us to describe some set of phenomena. Descriptive methods include naturalistic observation, case studies, and self-reports. These methods can provide some interesting observations about behavior, but that's really all they provide. Descriptive research could indicate that factor A and factor B seem to go together but not *how* or *why* they go together. Typically, descriptive investigations serve as a sort of springboard for subsequent experimental research. Although their use in the study of cognition is limited, examples of each technique can be found.

Naturalistic Observation

Naturalistic observation involves the observation of behavior in its natural setting, uninfluenced by the researcher (hence the term *naturalistic*). As you might guess, this method is of relatively little use to cognitive psychologists. Mental processes are, by their very nature, unobservable. Simply watching people do something tells you little or nothing about what they are thinking. You could try to infer what they're thinking based on their behavior, but this would be (at best) an educated guess, and probably a very general one at that. This is not to say that research in cognition has not benefitted from observational techniques. Quite the contrary; in Chapter 12 you'll read about pioneering cognitive researcher Wolfgang Kohler, who based much initial conjecture about problem-solving processes on systematic observations of chimpanzees. His observational studies helped spur human research on insight (the sudden realization of a problem's solution).

STOP *and* **THINK!**

NATURALISTIC OBSERVATION OF COGNITION

Kohler (1925) used naturalistic observation to gain some insight into the way chimps solve problems. You can use the same approach with people:

- Identify a cognitive process.
- Observe people engaging in this type of mental activity. (Remember: the observation location must be public—the library, student union, local mall, etc.)
- Identify the inferences you are able to make about what people must be thinking based on what they are doing.
- List the limitations of the inferences you made.

Case Studies

Case studies involve an in-depth investigation of a single case or a small number of cases. Typically, this method is used to study unique conditions that could not be created in a laboratory. Case studies of cognition have played a prominent role in one area in particular—brain research. (You'll read about this topic throughout this book in the neuroscience research theme sections.) A good deal of basic information that relates brain systems to cognition and behavior is based on the study of individuals who have suffered some sort of brain damage. For instance, research on the brain mechanisms underlying memory has benefitted from work with amnesics, people who have lost much of their memory functioning due to brain trauma (discussed in Chapter 6). Although case studies add an important dimension to research on cognition, they are limited in one important way—**generalizability.** Because case studies are, by definition, based on a small number of unique cases, their results may not apply (be generalizable) to the majority of individuals. Basic cognitive functioning in those who have suffered brain damage may differ in important ways from basic functioning in normal individuals. Therefore, generalizing from one to the other can be tenuous. However, as you'll see at several points throughout the text, the usefulness of case studies in cognitive neuroscience is undeniable.

Self-Report

Another descriptive research technique involves individuals reporting on their own knowledge, attitudes, feelings, or opinions through some type of **self-report** questionnaire or interview. Within the realm of cognition, this might involve asking people what they know or how they think. And indeed, some cognitive research has done just that. Think back to introspection (discussed in Chapter 1), one of the earliest tools for assessing the contents of the mind. This technique basically amounts to asking people to report what is currently in their consciousness. Introspection is a close cousin of one method that is sometimes used to investigate problem solving—the collection of verbal protocols (discussed in Chapter 12). A verbal protocol is literally "thinking out loud." Subjects are given problems to solve and asked to provide descriptions of what they're thinking as they solve the problems. Some of the *Stop and Think!* exercises featured throughout this text involve self-report investigations of cognition and are designed to help you observe your own cognitive processes more analytically.

One benefit of observing your own thinking processes may be an improvement in metacognitive skills. **Metacognition** refers to people's understanding of their own cognitive processing and can be assessed using questionnaires or interviews. For example, a number of studies have investigated an interesting state called the "tip-of-the-tongue phenomenon," which occurs when you're sure you know some fact but just can't seem to bring it to mind—the answer is on the tip of your tongue (discussed in Chapter 9). Cohen and Faulkner (1986) asked subjects in their study to note any tip-of-the-tongue experiences they had over a period of two weeks. They found that the most common type of block (68% of the total) was for proper names of acquaintances or friends; the second (17%) was for names of famous people; and the third was for names of places (7%). Note that this study, while informative, is purely descriptive. It gives us some basic information about when tip-of-the-tongue blocks occur but doesn't really explain how or why they occur.

STOP *and* THINK! ━━━━━━━━━━━━━━━━━━━

USING THE INTERVIEW TECHNIQUE TO STUDY COGNITION

Interview four friends and ask them about

- the study strategies they use
- which ones they use most frequently
- which ones are most effective and least effective

Based on their responses

- What do you conclude about the prevalence and effectiveness of these study strategies?
- What are the limitations of these conclusions?

STOP *and* REVIEW!

1. Why does the scientific study of cognitive processes present such a difficult challenge?
2. True or false? Descriptive research methods don't allow for assessing how or why two variables relate to each other.
3. What is naturalistic observation?
4. Why is the use of case studies valuable, and why is it limited?
5. How might self-report techniques be used in cognitive psychology research?

➤ Research in cognition is designed to describe, predict, explain, and modify the processes that comprise thought. Accomplishing these goals is a challenging task because the processes are unobservable. The existence of internal representations and processes must be inferred based on behavior.

➤ Descriptive research techniques allow for simple descriptions of a phenomenon. They provide interesting observations about behavior but can't explain why or how something happens. Therefore, their use in cognitive research is limited.

➤ Naturalistic observation involves the unobtrusive observation of behavior in its natural setting. It is of little use for cognitive psychologists because mental processing is, for the most part, unobservable.

➤ Case studies involve an in-depth investigation of a single case or a small number of cases. This method is used to study unique conditions that could not be created in a laboratory, such as human brain trauma. Case studies, while valuable in cognitive research, are limited in generalizability.

➤ Self-report techniques involve individuals reporting on their own knowledge, attitudes, feelings, or opinions. In cognitive studies, this may involve asking people to describe their thinking process during different tasks.

Experimental Research

As stated above, descriptive methods are designed to do just that—describe. While these techniques have provided some useful information to cognitive psychologists, the information is limited. If cognitive psychologists want to provide *explanations* of cognitive processes rather than just educated guesses or *descriptions,* it's necessary for them to be more controlled and systematic when observing behaviors and inferring thought processes. To accomplish this, cognitive psychologists rely heavily on experiments.

Experimental research involves the systematic manipulation and measurement of variables and the observation of their effects on one another in controlled settings. The data yielded from experimental investigations go beyond simple descriptions of behavior and guesses about the underlying thought processes. A well-controlled experiment allows for causal statements to be made about the effects of variables on one another, a goal that even the most well-designed descriptive studies cannot reach.

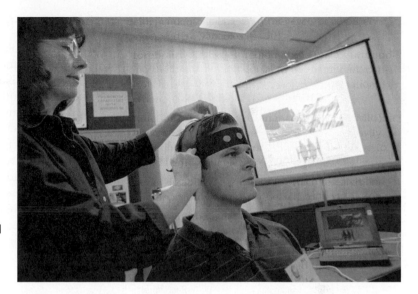

The computer has proved vital not only as a metaphor for cognition, but also as a research tool.

The Importance of the Computer

In Chapter 1, you learned that the computer was central to the development of some of the ideas that remain at the core of current cognitive psychology. In addition to its role as a model for how thinking might take place, the computer has also been vital to actually conducting cognition research. Much of the research you'll read about in later chapters was conducted using a desktop computer. Computers are used for two primary reasons: automation and precision. Conducting an experiment on a computer allows for precision in how stimuli are presented (e.g., presentation duration, time between stimuli, etc.) and how responses are recorded. This is not to say that all of cognitive research is conducted via computers; it is not. But certainly, the advantages offered by computer technology have had an enormous impact on how cognitive psychology research is conducted.

What Happens in an Experiment?

In an experiment, researchers manipulate factors they believe influence some mental process(es). Suppose we wanted to determine whether forming mental images is an effective technique for remembering information later. We could address this in a very simple experiment by having subjects study a list of words, one group using mental imagery and the other group using simple mental rehearsal (repeating the items as they are presented). In the lingo of experimentation, we would be *manipulating* study strategy. Such manipulated variables (e.g., study strategy) are termed **independent variables.** Then, to find out if we're correct that imagery is an effective study strategy, we need to *measure* memory for each group and compare performance. Such measures are termed **dependent variables.** One measure could be the total number of words recalled. If we're right about the effects of imagery, then the subjects who studied with imagery should recall more words than those who simply repeated the items silently.

The Advantages and Disadvantages of an Experiment

Experiments are the preferred method in cognitive psychology because of the explanatory power they offer. The results of a well-controlled experiment allow a researcher to state nearly definitively which of the manipulated variables had an effect on the measured variables and to describe the nature of these effects. In other words, experiments allow researchers to make statements about the "hows" and "whys" of mental processes, unlike descriptive studies, which limit researchers to simple conclusions about the "whats." Take the example of whether imagery helps memory: A descriptive study that addresses this question might involve interviewing individuals about their study strategies and whether they use imagery, or it might involve observing participants as they use mental imagery. This type of study might generate some interesting guesses about imagery and what it may do to help studying, but the conclusions remain guesses only. Really knowing the effect of a study strategy on memory requires a controlled series of experiments.

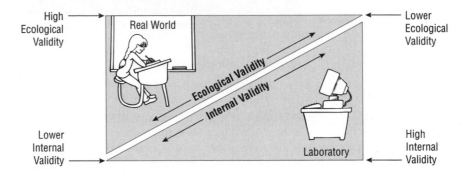

Do experiments have any disadvantages? One disadvantage is the artificial nature of the research. Well-designed experiments offer a great deal in the way of control and precision, which enhances their **internal validity.** However, they sometimes fall short in terms of naturalness, or how well they represent everyday life. In Chapter 1, we talked about this characteristic, termed **ecological validity.** Also in that chapter you read about the work of Ebbinghaus and Bartlett. We can look at the relationship between internal and ecological validity in the context of the research conducted by these pioneering cognitive psychologists. Ecological and internal validity typically have an inverse relationship; you trade off one to get more of the other. The addition of more realism to an experimental procedure often comes at the expense of experimental control. Bartlett's procedures and materials were not as tightly controlled as Ebbinghaus's, opening up the possibility that Bartlett's results may have been the product of uncontrolled variables. However, if you impose too much control, you may create a situation that doesn't really mirror real life, thereby limiting your findings. Some might claim that Ebbinghaus's research, while rigorously controlled, is of limited value because nonsense syllables do not resemble the types of material that we encode and remember on a daily basis.

A problem with experiments arises if subjects and/or experimenters have expectancies about what should or shouldn't happen in the experiment. These **expectancy effects** are typically controlled by keeping subjects blind to the purposes of the study and keeping researchers blind to the particular treatment or condition being received by the subjects. This is termed a **double-blind procedure.** Making researchers blind to the expected results of an experiment is quite difficult, given that they designed it, so experimenters need to take special care not to unintentionally influence the results of an experiment. Another way to control for expectancy effects is to minimize contact between experimenter and subjects through the use of a computer to present instructions and stimuli.

STOP *and* **REVIEW!**

1. True or false? Cognitive psychology relies most heavily on experimental research.
2. Why are computers used in cognitive psychology experiments?
3. True or false? A well-designed experiment allows for causal explanations.
4. Discuss the relationship between ecological and internal validity in experimental research.

➤ Experiments are the preferred method in cognitive psychology because of their explanatory power.

➤ Conducting an experiment on a computer allows for precision in how stimuli are presented and in how responses are collected. Using a computer also minimizes contact between experimenter and subjects, thus reducing expectancy effects.

➤ The results of a well-controlled experiment allow for causal statements to be made about the effects of one variable (the independent variable) on another variable (the dependent variable).

➤ Experiments offer control and precision (internal validity) but often at the expense of generalizability (ecological validity). Subject and/or experimenter expectancies can inadvertently influence research results. These unwanted effects can be controlled by keeping subjects blind to the purposes of the study and researchers blind to the condition being received by the subjects.

The Cognitive Psychology Experiment

How Can We See Thinking?: The Dependent Variable

Because cognitive processes are unobservable, researchers must come up with behaviors or measures of performance that reflect specific cognitive processes. In other words, the cognitive process in question—be it perception, attention, memory, decision making, or problem solving—must be given an operational definition. An **operational definition** involves defining a variable in terms of precise, measurable procedures that can be repeated by other researchers. Memory, a vague concept, might be defined in terms of how many words can be recalled from a previously studied list. Problem-solving ability might be

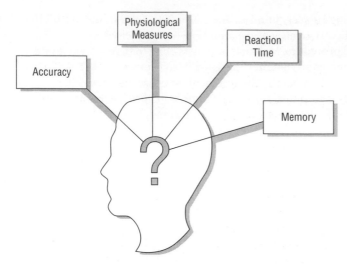

defined in terms of the time it takes for someone to solve a given problem. Following are some of the more common ways to operationalize mental processes.

Speed and Accuracy.   As you learned in Chapter 1, one of the fundamental assumptions of the information-processing approach is that cognitive processes involve a flow of information through a series of stages. Implicit in this characterization is the notion that cognitive processes take time, so a common measure of performance is **reaction time (RT).** The speed with which someone engages in a particular cognitive process can provide useful information about how that process is being carried out. For example, people are quicker to respond affirmatively to "Is a robin a bird?" than to "Is a penguin a bird?" This is a consistent difference, and as we'll see in Chapter 9, it lends insight into how categories are represented, and how we retrieve information about them.

Another common measure is the **accuracy** of responding. If subjects in a study are consistently less accurate in one condition relative to another condition, this may reveal important information about the thought processes involved. For example, when you try to attend to two different things, you make more errors than when your attention is focused on only one thing. As we'll see in Chapter 4, this gives us important information about the nature of attention. Often, speed and accuracy have a reciprocal relationship. That is, as responses get faster, the accuracy of those responses sometimes suffers, a relationship termed the **speed-accuracy trade-off.** Researchers need to keep this trade-off in mind when they interpret the results of any study using speed and accuracy as their dependent variables.

STOP *and* THINK!

A SPEED-ACCURACY TRADE-OFF

Get ready for a typing test. Go to a keyboard and type out this tried-and-true sentence (which includes every letter in the alphabet):

The quick brown fox jumps over the lazy dog.

Try typing this sentence five times under two different conditions:

1. Type it at a moderate pace five times, maybe a little slower than you normally do.
2. Type it as fast as you possibly can five times.

Count the number of errors you made in conditions 1 and 2.

- Did your results show a speed-accuracy trade-off?
- Why?

Do you note any problems with the "design" of this experiment?

- What are they?
- How could you fix them?

Other Characteristics of Responding.   Speed and accuracy serve as general and useful indicators in nearly all areas of cognitive research, but there are a myriad other dependent variables that researchers use to assess mental processing. For the most part, the particular dependent variable used depends on the cognitive process being studied. A researcher interested in reading might measure reading comprehension. A researcher interested in problem solving might look at the level of creativity in the solution to the problem. A researcher interested in decision making might assess the types of choices that are made in particular situations.

Physiological Measures.   Recent advances in neuroscientific technology have introduced a whole new class of dependent variables into the study of cognition. Researchers in cognitive neuroscience investigate not only the characteristics of mental processing, but also the corresponding brain activity as revealed by physiological measures like positron-emission tomography (PET), functional magnetic resonance imaging (fMRI), or event-related potentials (ERP). These dependent variables will continue to play a critical role as researchers bridge the gap between mind and brain. We'll talk more about these dependent variables later in this chapter.

What Variables Influence Cognition?: The Independent Variable

As you might imagine, cognitive processes can be influenced by a host of variables, which are called the *independent variables* in an experiment. An independent variable has at least two levels; the levels of the independent variable determine the **experimental conditions.** The simplest experiment involves one independent variable with two levels and therefore two conditions. For example, suppose we wanted to look at how the type of memory test affects the amount that people can remember. We can study a real-world analog—the tests you take in class. Which would you prefer—a test where we give you a term and ask for a definition, or a test where we give you a term along with four possible definitions and have you pick the correct one? Chances are you'd perform differently in each situation.

How would we test this idea in the laboratory? We would present you with a list of words and test your memory of the list in different ways. The independent variable in this simple experiment would be the type of test. This variable has two levels—recall (you are given a blank sheet of paper and asked to write down everything you remember) and recognition (you are given a list of words and asked to circle the ones you saw before). In experimentation, there is no real difference between the terms *level* and *condition*. When you're talking about the design of the experiment, you talk about *levels* of the independent variable. When you're actually testing subjects, you assign the *conditions* that correspond to these levels. What are the important independent variables in studies of cognition? Jenkins (1979) proposed a classification of independent variables that could be investigated in a memory experiment. However, this scheme is quite useful for classifying variables in all sorts of cognition experiments.

Subject Variables.   Not everyone thinks in the same way, so it should come as no surprise that many cognition studies focus on how thinking is affected by *who* is doing the thinking: man or woman, young or elderly, Asian or European. Studies using **subject variables** will be featured in the *Individual Differences* research theme that appears throughout the textbook. Subject variables are unique in that the experimenter does not assign subjects to a condition. For example, we can't tell Bob that he's in the female condition of our experiment. Subjects are "assigned" to different conditions by virtue of circumstances. A study by Channon and Baker (1996) investigated the subject variable of depression, assessing its influence on problem solving. The problem-solving task was to review electrical wiring diagrams and find errors. The investigators' primary interest was strategy differences that might exist between nondepressed and depressed subjects. The results showed that depressed subjects were no less accurate than nondepressed subjects but were slower and tended to carry out more redundant tests of the wiring.

Material Variables.   The way that people think also depends on *what* it is they're thinking about. Cognitive processes vary depending on whether people are processing individual words, stories, pictures, computer screens, pieces of general knowledge, or brain-teasing puzzles. So a great deal of cognitive research manipulates what might be termed **material variables.** Consider a study by Kemp (1988) concerning a person's ability to date events. For example, do you know what year the space shuttle *Challenger* exploded shortly after takeoff? It was 1986. Kemp investigated individuals' ability to date events and varied the material, comparing subjects' recall of recent events (like the *Challenger* disaster) to more remote events (like the year Abraham Lincoln was assassinated). Kemp's study revealed that people tend to underestimate the age of remote events (i.e., they think the Lincoln assassination occurred later than it did) and to overestimate the age of recent events (they think that the *Challenger* disaster occurred earlier than it did).

Experimental Context Variables.   Cognitive processing may be influenced by many aspects of the experimental context. For example, a researcher may manipulate the instructions given to subjects (e.g., having them use different study strategies), the situation in which an experimental task is performed (e.g., having subjects perform a task under time pressure or no time pressure), or the situation in which a particular material is encountered (e.g., having subjects identify the perpetrator of a crime they witnessed when a weapon was used and when a weapon was not used). A study by King (1991) provides a good (and relevant) example of the use of **experimental context variables.** In this study, the effect of listening strategy on lecture comprehension was investigated. Some students simply listened to the lecture, while other students used self-questioning during the lecture. The results demonstrated an effect of listening strategy. The group that engaged in self-questioning was superior in their comprehension of the lecture material to that of subjects who simply listened to the lecture.

Performance-Measure Variables.   These variables are a bit more subtle than the others. Basically, the dependent variable is used as an independent variable, because sometimes cognitive processing depends on exactly how you measure the particular cognitive process. Andersson and Roennberg (1996) provide an example of the use of **performance-measure variables.** These authors were interested in the process of collaborative memory in dyads. Put more simply, what happens when two people (a dyad) remember an event, and does this recall depend on the type of memory test? The researchers investigated these questions by comparing dyads' performance on two different types of tests: one that requires recall of a story presented earlier and one that involves answering general information questions. The results showed that the type of memory test made a difference. Recall of the story suffered when subjects recalled in pairs relative to when they recalled on their own. However, on the fact retrieval test there was no such difference. The way in which memory was queried proved to be an important factor.

STOP *and* THINK!

IDENTIFYING AND LABELING VARIABLES

For the following descriptions of actual studies, identify the independent variable(s) and dependent variable(s). For each of the independent variable(s), determine which of the four types of independent variable it is and specify the levels of the variable.

1. Bauer and Johnson-Laird (1993) were interested in whether diagrams could improve reasoning with different types of disjunctive logic problems (type A and B). They investigated people's ability to solve these types of problems, comparing conditions in which the problems were presented with a diagram to conditions in which the problems were presented verbally.

2. Holtgraves (1997) was interested in people's memory for the exact wording of remarks made in everyday situations. Subjects heard statements that were made by a high-status (e.g., a professor) or equal status (e.g., another student) person. Holtgraves compared recall and recognition memory for these statements.

3. Forsterlee and Horowitz (1997) were interested in the effects of taking notes on mock jurors' decisions in a complex trial. Subjects saw a complex trial on videotape, and either did or did not take notes. Performance was measured by looking at the amount of compensation awarded to the plaintiff.

4. Coleman and Shore (1991) were interested in how people who varied in their knowledge of physics would vary in problem solving. They compared experts (graduate students in physics), high achievers from a high school class, and average achievers from a high school class. Coleman and Shore looked at performance by classifying and counting the types of statements made by these subjects as they were solving the problems.

5. Schmidt (1994) was interested in the effects of humor on people's ability to remember sentences. In one experiment, he presented both humorous and nonhumorous sentences and tested recall of these sentences with either free recall or cued recall.

After the independent and dependent variables have been chosen and operationally defined, other issues must be addressed. Let's examine some of the major concerns we should have in designing a study comparing performance on tests of recall and recognition.

Confounding Variables

Confounding variables are factors that vary along with the independent variable, making the results difficult to interpret. For example, in the memory test experiment, we would want to make sure that everything is as equivalent as possible in the two conditions being examined—the subjects, the testing conditions, the words presented—everything. The only difference between the two conditions being compared should be the type of memory test that subjects get (i.e., the independent variable). If something else is different (say, we give milk and cookies to the subjects in the recall condition but not to the subjects in the recognition condition), then we won't know if it was the food or the type of memory test that caused the difference in results. A researcher must ensure that the conditions being compared are as equivalent as possible. Once we have anticipated possible confounding variables, we have another decision to make: Should we use different subjects in each of the conditions (i.e., a between-subjects design) or the same subjects in each condition (i.e., a within-subjects design)?

Assigning Subjects to Conditions

In practice, a wide variety of factors are likely to influence a given behavior. Therefore, many experiments in cognitive psychology will examine more than one of these factors. However, for the sake of simplicity, we will limit our discussion to a **single-factor experiment,** which examines the influence of a single **factor** on behavior. In other words, there is one independent variable in the experiment; the terms *factor* and *independent variable* are synonymous. Each independent variable in an experiment must have at least two levels. Again, for simplicity's sake, we will limit our discussion to independent variables with only two levels. Our memory test experiment is an example of a simple single-factor experiment. We are manipulating one independent variable (memory test) with two levels (recall and recognition) and investigating its effect on one dependent variable (the amount remembered).

Within-Subjects Designs.   In a **within-subjects design,** the same subjects take part in each condition of the experiment. Suppose we have 12 subjects in our memory test experiment. If we are using a within-subjects design, we would have each of the 12 subjects perform both the recall and the recognition tests. Testing the same subjects in all conditions offers a big advantage. Remember that the conditions of an experiment should be as similar as possible (with the exception of the independent variable). When we use a within-subjects design, the subjects in the conditions are *identical,* which eliminates one possible difference between the conditions. However, this design suffers from some disadvantages—namely, **practice effects** and **carryover effects.** When subjects take part in more than one condition, there is a strong likelihood that participation in one condition will affect performance in the other condition, either by giving the subjects practice on the task (practice effect) or by giving them a strategy that influences performance in the other conditions (carryover effect). Let's look at our memory test experiment. Suppose we test a subject in recall first, then in recognition. It's quite likely that the initial act of attempting to recall all of the words is going to influence how the subject does on the recognition test. This influence could be characterized as a general practice effect: taking one memory test helps you on a second one. This influence could also be characterized as a strategy carryover effect: taking the first memory test may change the way you approach the second one. In either case, we are not really getting a pure comparison of these two conditions.

Between-Subjects Designs.   In a **between-subjects design,** different subjects are assigned to each condition of the experiment. So if we recruit 12 subjects to be in our memory test experiment, we would assign six of them to each of the two memory test conditions. One major advantage of a between-subjects design is that there is no danger of performance in one condition influencing performance in another condition, because each condition involves different subjects. A between-subjects design is preferable when there is a strong likelihood of carryover from one condition to another. Carryover is very likely in the memory test experiment. If subjects attempt to recall words, then there will probably be a contaminating effect of this recall on a later test of recognition. Therefore, it's preferable to use a between-subjects design in such cases.

Between or Within?   If possible, researchers prefer to use within-subjects designs, because fewer subjects are required. Also, within-subjects designs have more statistical power than do between-subjects designs. That is, an effect is more likely to be revealed using a within-subjects design. A statistical test determines if the independent variable was responsible for the difference found between the conditions. Reducing other differences between the groups makes the difference due to the independent variable more likely to be detected (i.e., gives the test more statistical power). As we just noted, in a within-subjects design, the subjects in the conditions are identical, thus eliminating a major source of variation between conditions. While within-subjects designs are typically the design of choice, the chance of practice or carryover effects occurring from one condition to another makes the choice of a between-subjects design preferable in many cases.

Let's review the four types of independent variables in the context of the between-subjects versus the within-subjects choice. *Subject variables,* by definition, involve a between-subjects comparison, because the comparison of interest involves different groups of subjects. Recall that Channon and Baker (1996) compared depressed and non-depressed subjects on their problem-solving abilities. *Experimental context variables* are often manipulated in between-subjects designs. This was the choice made in the King (1991) study that investigated the effect of listening strategy on lecture comprehension. Because different subjects were used in the each of the strategy conditions, the experimenter did not need to worry about a strategy in one condition carrying over to another condition. When experimenters vary *materials,* they commonly do so using a within-subjects manipulation; the same subjects experience each type of material. As you read earlier, Kemp (1988) was interested in comparing people's ability to date historical and recent events and presented each subject with both types of events. It is unlikely that there would be any influence of one type of event on the other, so the choice of a within-subjects design was appropriate. Studies that manipulate *performance-measure variables* do so either within or between subjects, depending on the particular issue being investigated. A between-subjects manipulation is often used when the two measures are likely to influence each other, obscuring their comparison (like recall and recognition of the same information). However, when the two measures are unlikely to influence each other, a within-subjects design is chosen. As you may remember, this was the choice of Andersson and Roennberg (1996), who used a within-subjects design to compare dyadic memory performance in different retrieval situations. Recalling facts from a story you just read is unlikely to influence the way in which you recall general information facts. Therefore, the added power of a within-subjects design was the obvious choice.

The decision about whether to manipulate a given variable within or between subjects is dependent on the particular experimental question being investigated and must be made with caution and a clear understanding of previous research. In fact, choosing a within-subjects or a between-subjects design can determine whether you get an effect or not. For example, forming bizarre images of a concept helps you remember it, but only when subjects see both bizarre images and common images. Bizarre images are remembered better when they contrast with more common images in the same context (e.g., Cox & Wollen, 1981; McDaniel & Einstein, 1986). On the other hand, if you give one group of subjects a bunch of bizarre images and the other group a bunch of common images (i.e., if you manipulate bizarre imagery between subjects), you get no effect. There is nothing for the bizarre images to clash with in this design, so they aren't very well remembered. Clearly, the decision to manipulate a particular variable between or within subjects is a critical one. Researchers must consider the variables being manipulated and their impact on one another.

STOP and THINK!

MANIPULATING VARIABLES—BETWEEN OR WITHIN?

Below are some independent variables that might be of interest to a cognitive psychologist. For each, identify the levels of the independent variable and identify whether to assign subjects to the conditions in a between-subjects or a within-subjects manner. Be sure to justify your choices.

1. the effects of the type of word people are trying to remember—positive (i.e., *wedding*) or negative (i.e., *funeral*)
2. the effects of the way in which a problem is presented on people's ability to solve a problem
3. the effects of modality (whether something is presented visually or auditorily) on memory for words
4. the effects of gender on the ability to form mental images
5. the effects of listening to Mozart or Britney Spears on people's reaction time and accuracy in a cognitive task
6. the effects of TV commercials on people's memory for the commercial itself and on brand preference

1. Identify and define the four types of independent variables.
2. True or false? The terms *independent variable* and *factor* mean the same thing.
3. What is RT and the speed-accuracy trade-off?
4. True or false? All things being equal, researchers prefer to use within-subjects designs rather than between-subjects designs.

➤ The dependent variable in an experiment must be given an operational definition, which involves defining a variable in terms of precise and replicable measurable procedures. Independent variables have at least two levels that determine the experimental conditions. There are four types of independent variables. Subject variables involve groups of subjects who differ on some critical factor. Material variables involve varying the nature of the material being processed. Experimental context variables involve varying the nature of the instructions given to subjects. Performance-measure variables involve varying the response measures given to subjects.

➤ A factor is another name for an independent variable. A single-factor experiment has one independent variable. Researchers attempt to make experimental conditions as similar as possible, except for the manipulation of the independent variable. Confounding variables can obscure the interpretation of experimental results because they inadvertently vary along with the independent variable.

➤ Reaction time (RT) is the time taken to respond to a stimulus. A speed-accuracy trade-off refers to the tendency for decreases in response time to be associated with increases in error.

➤ In a within-subjects design, the same subjects participate in each condition. Possible problems are practice effects (performance changes as a result of continuous participation in the study) and carryover effects (specific effects of processing in one condition affect processing in another condition). In a between-subjects design, different subjects are assigned to each condition. Generally, within-subjects designs are preferable because they require fewer subjects and are more likely to reveal an effect.

The Factorial Design

As we noted earlier, a wide variety of factors can influence a given behavior or cognitive process. Because of this, cognitive psychologists often conduct studies that investigate more than one factor. Let's go back to our memory test experiment. Suppose that we are interested not only in how the type of test affects memory, but also if there is any difference in how well we remember high-frequency words like *house* and low-frequency words like *aardvark*. We could accomplish this by conducting another experiment in

		Memory Test	
		recall	recognition
Word Frequency	high	high/recall	high/recognition
	low	low/recall	low/recognition

Figure 2.1 In a factorial design, each level of one independent variable is crossed with each level of the other independent variables.

which we compare words that are encountered frequently in the English language (high-frequency words) to those that are encountered less frequently (low-frequency words). By conducting these two independent studies, we could determine how memory is affected by the type of memory test employed and word frequency.

However, it is possible that these variables may have a different effect on memory performance when they are examined together, relative to when they are examined in isolation. For example, the effect of word frequency might vary based on whether the memory test is free recall or recognition. In other words, the effects of one variable may *depend on* the other variable. Manipulating both independent variables in the same study allows us to look at the joint effects of these variables, as well as the effect of each variable in isolation. This is called a **factorial design**—a design that completely crosses each level of one independent variable with each level of the other independent variables. In order to conduct our experiment, we would completely cross each level of the memory test variable (recognition and recall) with each level of the word frequency variable (low and high word frequency) to produce four conditions: high-frequency words/recognition test, high-frequency words/recall test, low-frequency words/recognition test, low-frequency words/recall test (see Figure 2.1).

A factorial design may employ any number of independent variables, each having any number of levels. To keep our discussion clear, we'll consider the simplest case: a factorial design with two independent variables, each with two levels (e.g., the memory test/word frequency experiment). For each of these independent variables, the researcher has the choice of manipulating it between subjects (using different subjects for each level of the independent variable) or within subjects (using the same subjects for each level of the independent variable). In a **between-subjects factorial,** both variables are manipulated between subjects. Subjects are assigned to one of the four conditions. In a **within-subjects factorial,** both variables are manipulated within subjects. Each subject experiences all four of the conditions.

The best design for our study would probably be a hybrid between the two just mentioned: a mixed-factorial design. In a **mixed-factorial design,** some variables are manipulated between subjects and other variables are manipulated within subjects. For the present study, all subjects would see a list that includes both high- and low-frequency words (a within-subjects manipulation of word frequency). The independent variable of word frequency is a *materials* variable, which is commonly manipulated within subjects. The independent variable of memory test is a *performance-measure* variable and should probably be manipulated between subjects in this situation. If we were to use a within-subjects design and test recognition followed by recall (or vice versa), the second test would be affected by the first because it's a second attempt to remember the same words. So, half of the subjects would be tested with recall, and the other half would be tested with recognition. Mixed-factorial designs like this are extremely common in cognition research. Once the data from a factorial design have been collected, a researcher needs to summarize, analyze, and present the results. This involves a number of statistical procedures that are beyond the scope of this text, but we'll briefly review some of the highlights.

Analyzing and Presenting Results

Researchers submit data to a number of statistical procedures in order to determine whether their hypotheses have been supported. **Descriptive statistics** are used to provide a thumbnail sketch of the data. The major class of descriptive statistics we will discuss is called *central tendency*. Measures of **central tendency** (the *mean* is the most commonly used) give an idea of the typical score for a given condition. Common practice is to present means in the form of data graphs or data tables. However, descriptive statistics do not provide a complete picture of the data. For example, in our memory test experiment we may find that recall percentages for the two conditions are 40% and 50%. It may seem as though these are different levels of performance, but differences such as these can arise purely through chance, and this possibility needs to be assessed. This involves the use of **inferential statistics,** which goes further than simply summarizing the data. Inferential tests allow a researcher to determine how likely it is that a difference between conditions occurred due to chance. And if it is unlikely that the difference occurred by chance, the *inference* is that it must have occurred due to the differences in the levels of the independent variable. In other words, the differences between conditions are "real" and the effect is said to have achieved **statistical significance.**

Main Effects.   Let's say that we carried out our memory test/word frequency experiment. As described above, the experiment is a mixed-factorial design with four conditions, which are yielded by crossing a two-level independent variable (memory test) with another two-level independent variable (word frequency). This design allows us to assess if either of the independent variables influences performance and whether the variables interact. Given the proposed design, two **main effects** would be assessed, one for each of the independent variables. We can assess the effect of memory test on memory performance by examining recall and recognition scores regardless of the type of word. We can also assess the effect of word frequency on memory performance by examining memory for high- and low-frequency words regardless of memory test.

These data can be presented in the form of a table like the one in Figure 2.2a, which presents the main effect data for our hypothetical memory experiment. The overall means for the levels of each independent variable are presented at the bottom (for type of memory test) and far right (for word frequency). A statistical comparison of the means for the memory test variable reveals a statistically significant main effect: overall, recognition leads to better memory than recall. Now, shifting to the side of the table, we can assess whether there is a main effect of word frequency. We see that there is not a statistically significant difference between these two conditions; high- and low-frequency words are remembered equally well. The same data can be captured in the form of a graph, as displayed in Figure 2.2b. Take a look at the pair of bar graphs for the memory

		Memory Test		
		recall	recognition	
Word Frequency	high			52
	low			57
		37	72	

(a)

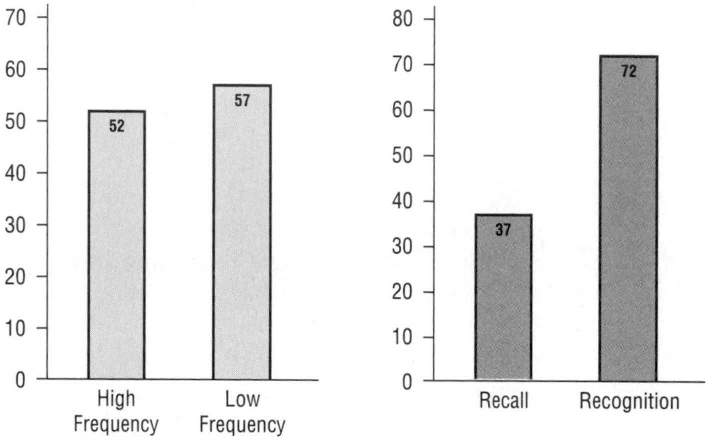

Figure 2.2 Main effects are assessed by looking at the overall means for each of the conditions, often displayed in the margins of the table. The table (a) shows the main effect data from the hypothetical memory experiment. The graphs (b) show the main effect data for the hypothetical memory experiment.

(b)

data. In the graph on the right, the bar representing recognition is higher than the bar representing recall. In the graph on the left, the bars representing memory for high-frequency words and low-frequency words are nearly identical in height, indicating equivalent performance.

Interactions.   If we want to know whether these two independent variables influence each other, we need to look at the means for *each* of the four conditions created by the factorial design. Take a look at Figure 2.3a, which shows the means for all four conditions in our hypothetical memory experiment. Looking at these means reveals that the previously stated conclusions based on the main effects do not ring completely true. This is because the data indicate a statistically significant interaction between the two variables. When examined in isolation, the independent variable of word frequency seems to have no influence on remembering; but when we look at the means for all four conditions, this overall effect is quite misleading. The ability to remember high- and low-frequency words depends critically on how memory is tested. High-frequency

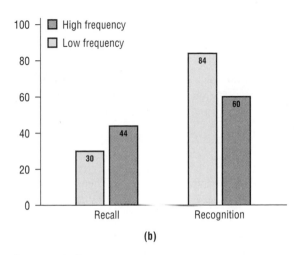

		Memory Test	
		recall	recognition
Word Frequency	high	44	60
	low	30	84

(a)

(b)

Figure 2.3 Hypothetical data showing an interaction between word frequency and type of memory test, presented as a table and a bar graph.

words are remembered better in recall, while low-frequency words are remembered better in recognition. In other words, there is an **interaction** between the effects of memory test and word frequency.

An interaction might be described as a "difference of differences." In Figure 2.3a, it's apparent that this is exactly what we have. In recall, there is a 14% advantage for high-frequency words; in recognition, the difference is reversed, with a 24% advantage for low-frequency words. So the high-frequency/low-frequency difference is different for the two memory tests. The same interaction can be viewed from another angle. Compare memory for recognition and recall. Recognition is superior to recall overall, but the superiority is much more evident in the case of low-frequency words. Once again, we see a difference between differences; the difference between recognition and recall is 54% for low-frequency words but only 16% for high-frequency words. So viewed either way, the effects of word frequency and memory test *depend on* each other. This interaction also emerges from the bar graph in Figure 2.3b, which includes all four conditions. Compare the pattern observed in each half of this graph. In the recall panel, the bar representing highfrequency words is higher than the bar representing memory for low-frequency words. The converse can be seen in the recognition panel, demonstrating the interactive effect of word frequency and memory test.

STOP *and* **THINK!**

SPOTTING MAIN EFFECTS AND INTERACTIONS

On the next page are some hypothetical experimental designs and results. Look at the patterns and determine whether the results indicate main effects and/or interactions. Given that the data have not been submitted to inferential statistics, the assumption about statistical significance is given with each experimental example.

Dependent measure: Comprehension rating for a baseball story presented in different formats. Rating is on a scale from 1 to 10. Following are scores averaged across subjects. (Assume that a difference of 2 is statistically significant.)

		Presentation Format		
		Video	Written Story	
Baseball	High	6	6	6
Expertise	Low	4	2	3
		5	4	

Dependent measure: Reaction time (in seconds) for solving word puzzles and math puzzles that are either simple or complex. (Assume that a difference of 8 is statistically significant.)

		Difficulty Level of Problem		
		Simple	Complex	
Puzzle	Word	4.9	13.1	9.0
Type	Math	6.6	23.8	15.2
		5.8	18.5	

Dependent measure: Percentage accuracy in detecting odd and even digits presented visually or auditorily. (Assume that a difference of 10 is statistically significant.)

	Odd Numbers	Even Numbers	
Distracted	55	56	55.5
Full Attention	93	92	92.5
	74	74	

Dependent measure: Knowledge of material (% correct on either a fill-in-the-blank test or an essay test) from a textbook chapter for different study strategies (memorization of terms and outlining). (Assume that a difference of 10 is statistically significant.)

		Test Type		
		Fill-in-the-Blanks	Essay	
Study	Memorize	60	42	51
Strategy	Outline	50	66	58
		55	54	

A Sample Experiment

Let's put all of the pieces together and dissect a classic experiment by Chase and Simon (1973). These authors were interested in the cognitive processes involved in playing chess and how these processes might depend on a player's skill level. One process they were interested in was memory—more specifically, memory for chess pieces laid out on a board. As you might guess, they postulated that people at different skill levels would differ in their memory for chess positions.

Variables and Design.   Let's restate the research question: How does level of expertise influence memory for chess pieces placed on a board in various configurations? Chase and Simon compared master chess players to beginning chess players. The players were exposed to chessboard configurations that were either typical of a game situation or randomly rearranged versions of these typical configurations. Subjects looked at a given board arrangement for five seconds. Then the board was covered and they were asked to reconstruct what they had seen by placing pieces on an empty chessboard.

The dependent variable in this experiment was performance on the chessboard reconstruction task, measured in terms of how many pieces could be placed on the board in the correct position. Can you guess the independent variables? There are two. One is level of subject expertise, which is a *subject variable* with two levels (master and beginner). By definition, subject variables involve *between-subjects* comparisons. One person cannot simultaneously be an expert and a beginner. The other independent variable is chessboard configuration, a *materials* variable with two levels (game configuration and random configuration). This variable was manipulated *within subjects*—all subjects saw both types of board configurations. So this investigation was a *mixed-factorial* that featured four conditions. This design allowed Chase and Simon to examine the *interactive* effect of expertise and board configuration. It wouldn't be surprising to find that masters remember chess positions better than beginning players, but would this advantage depend on type of board configuration?

		Expertise Level		
		experts	novices	
Chessboard Configuration	random arrangements	3	4	3.5
	game arrangements	16	4	10
		9.5	4	

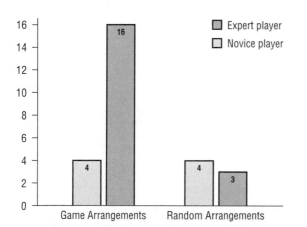

Figure 2.4 Data from Chase and Simon's (1973) experiment, presented as a table and as a bar graph. Main effects of expertise level and chessboard configuration are apparent, as is an interaction between the two variables.

From Chase, W. G., & Simon, H. A. (1973). Perception in chess. *Cognitive Psychology, 4,* 55–81. Copyright 1973 by Elsevier Science (USA). Reprinted by permission.

Results and Conclusions.   Chase and Simon analyzed the number of pieces correctly placed by the subjects as a function of expertise level and chessboard configuration. The results are pictured in Figure 2.4. First, let's examine the main effects of the two independent variables. There was a significant main effect of expertise; overall, masters were better at remembering the piece positions than novices. There was also a significant main effect of board configuration; configurations that represented actual game positions were much better remembered than random board configurations.

But once again, the main effects don't tell the whole story. The results reveal a significant interaction between expertise and board configuration: the pattern of results differs starkly between the two conditions. When it comes to actual game positions, masters are markedly better than novices. But there is *no difference* between masters and novices in remembering chess pieces randomly strewn about the board; in this condition, expertise offers no memory advantage. Chase and Simon explained this result by suggesting that when viewing the chessboards, experts categorized the pieces on the board into groupings that were familiar from their own experience. This categorization allowed for easier encoding and retrieval of the information. However, since the categorization was based on actual game experience, it was possible only for board configurations from actual games. So expertise led to benefits in memory performance, but only for game configurations. Once again, the simultaneous investigation of more than one variable allowed for more elaborate conclusions than could have been gathered from investigating the variables in isolation.

STOP *and* THINK!

IDENTIFYING THE VARIABLES THAT AFFECT THINKING

You no doubt realize that what you think and do on any given day is affected by a host of variables. For example, Greg's memory for a joke from *The Simpsons* can be affected by (1) the fact that he's a big fan, (2) what time of day it is, (3) whether he's just seen the episode that has that particular joke, (4) whether a friend is helping him remember it . . . you get the idea. Pick a cognitive ability that you use on a daily basis and come up with five variables that affect it (based on your intuition).

For two of the variables that you identify, create a factorial design to determine the effect of the variables on that cognitive ability. Then follow these steps:

1. Identify and operationalize your independent variables (with the levels).
2. Operationalize your dependent variable.
3. Identify and state how you would attempt to control for any confounding variables.
4. Identify and justify whether the design should be within subjects, between subjects, or mixed.

STOP *and* REVIEW!

1. True or false? Factorial design experiments involve more than one independent variable.
2. Identify and define the three types of factorial designs.
3. Briefly describe the purpose of descriptive and inferential statistics.
4. An interaction can only be assessed if
   a. a researcher uses more than one dependent variable
   b. a researcher uses only between-subjects variables
   c. a researcher uses only within-subjects variables
   d. a researcher manipulates more than one independent variable

➤ A factorial design involves the manipulation of more than one independent variable, completely crossing each level of one independent variable with each level of the others. Factorial designs allow researchers to determine how different variables affect one another.

➤ In a between-subjects factorial, all independent variables are manipulated between subjects. In a within-subjects factorial, all independent variables are manipulated within subjects. A mixed factorial involves the joint manipulation of at least one between-subjects variable and one within-subjects variable. Mixed-factorial designs are extremely common in cognition research.

➤ Descriptive statistics are used to summarize the data. Measures of central tendency (most commonly, the *mean*) give an idea of the typical score for a given condition. Inferential statistics are used to determine how likely it is that a difference between conditions occurred due to chance. If this likelihood is low, the effect is said to be statistically significant.

➤ A main effect refers to the overall effect of an independent variable on the dependent variable. An interaction occurs when the effect of an independent variable depends on the level of the other independent variable(s).

Cognitive Neuroscience: Investigating Mind and Brain

There is little doubt that the most rapidly expanding research frontier within psychology is **cognitive neuroscience,** which involves relating cognitive processes to their neural substrates—in other words, what the brain is doing when the mind is thinking. Gazzaniga, Ivry, and Mangun (2002) describe cognitive neuroscience as a coalescence of biology and psychology. According to these authors, cognitive neuroscience began to emerge in the 1970s out of necessity. At that time, neuroscientists began to move beyond the simple method of destroying brain tissue and relating the destruction to behavioral function and to use increasingly sophisticated methods to address more complex questions, such as how visual cells process and combine information to produce percepts. As neuroscientists advanced beyond simple approaches, so did psychologists. Recall that by the 1960s, psychologists were developing theories and models of cognition and action that were based on mental representations (whose basis, ultimately, is the brain). Given that the interests of many neuroscientists were getting more cognitive and that the interest of many cognitive psychologists was turning toward brain representation, a union of the two approaches was inevitable.

An Overview of the Nervous System

Throughout the text, we'll be discussing cognitive neuroscience research. Before we do, it would be helpful to review some basics about the nervous system. We'll start at the most basic level with a discussion of the basic nerve cell, the neuron. We'll then proceed to the brain, highlighting its structure and discussing some of the important questions posed by cognitive neuroscientists as well as their tools of investigation.

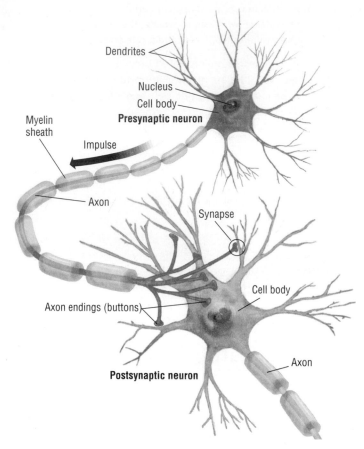

Figure 2.5   A neuron and its major structures.

The Neuron. The nervous system is the body's system for processing information, and the **neuron,** or nerve cell, is its basic unit. It is estimated that there are about 100 billion neurons throughout the nervous system. Many of these are located in the brain's cerebral cortex, the seat of complex thought. A simple neuron is pictured in Figure 2.5. This is a general representation; there are many different types of neurons, with different sizes, shapes, and functions. Given that there are billions of them, you might imagine that they're interconnected in incredibly complex networks. Indeed, this aspect of brain structure forms the basis for the connectionist approach to cognition, discussed in Chapter 1.

Neurons are electrochemical information processors. Within a neuron, communication is basically an electrical process whereby a signal travels from the dendrites to the cell body down the length of the axon. This process is called an **action potential,** and it occurs in an all-or-none fashion if the stimulation of the neuron reaches some critical value, or threshold. At this point, the communication process becomes chemical; the action potential causes the release of neurotransmitters into the tiny gap between neurons, the synapse. The neurotransmitters released into the synapse interact with dendrites of many receiving neurons, leading to their excitation or inhibition. This system of excitatory and inhibitory connections between these basic units of the nervous system underlies all thinking and behavior. Indeed, many believe it *is* thinking (e.g., LeDoux, 2002), although this assertion generates some philosophical argument.

Hebb (1949) suggested a basic principle of neuronal functioning. According to Hebb, "When an axon of cell A is near enough to excite a cell B, and repeatedly takes part in firing it, some growth process or metabolic change takes place in one or both cells such that A's efficiency as one of the cells firing B is increased" (p. 62). In other words, the association between neurons can become stronger with experience; neural networks can learn. Hebb's suggestion has been supported by research and has served as a partial basis for the connectionist approach to mental processes, which attempts to explain thinking in terms of the strengthening and weakening (i.e., the changes) in association among simple units. These simple units and their interconnections correspond to the brain's neurons and neural networks. Researchers have attempted to simulate thinking tasks like problem solving or object recognition with computer models that have an architecture similar to that of the brain, in hopes that these models might provide some insight into how the microstructure and activity of the brain subserve cognitive processes.

Research in cognitive neuroscience has not progressed to the point of explaining cognition in terms of how individual neurons and neural networks actually work in their seemingly infinite complexity and variety. But researchers have come a long way in modeling how cognition *might* work, given the properties of neurons (e.g., Pinker, 1994b). So while we can't map out the exact grouping and activity of neurons that underlie the cognitive processes that occur as we're deciding what to watch on TV tonight, we are fairly certain where in the brain the relevant activity takes place and how some of the component processes may play themselves out in a system modeled on the neural networks of the brain. So some of the pieces of the puzzle about how the brain works are in place, and cognitive neuroscientists continue to look for the remaining ones.

The Brain.   The brain serves as the primary focus of cognitive neuroscience because the brain is the center of information processing. Cognitive neuroscientists investigate a number of questions about brain structure and its relation to cognitive processing. A great deal of research has investigated exactly what brain areas are active during different mental processes. Based on this general information, researchers can pinpoint more specifically the brain substrates of cognition.

Neuroscientists commonly divide the brain into three major areas. The **hindbrain** is located at the base of the brain, just above the spinal cord, and its primary function is to monitor, maintain, and control basic life functions such as breathing and heartbeat. Just above the hindbrain, a relatively small area termed the **midbrain** contains areas that are involved in some sensory reflexes and help to regulate brain arousal. The remainder of the brain, the forebrain, is the area of primary interest for cognitive neuroscientists. The **forebrain** comprises most of the brain and consists mainly of the **cerebral cortex,** the familiar wrinkled outer shell of the brain, which is actually a sheet of billions of neurons. The cerebral cortex is the primary neural substrate for what might be termed *higher cognitive functions*—remembering, planning, deciding, communicating—essentially, all the stuff that you'll be reading about in this text. Beneath the cortex lies an array of important subcortical structures that are involved in basic processes such as the regulation of memory and emotion.

The Cerebral Cortex.   The cerebral cortex consists of two nonsymmetrical hemispheres that are made up of layered sheets of neurons that form tremendously complex interconnections and networks. Each hemisphere can be subdivided into four major areas, or *lobes* (see Figure 2.6a). Some areas within each of the lobes are specialized for particular functions. The frontal lobe is the anterior portion (i.e., the "front part") of your cortex, located immediately behind your forehead and running back to about the middle of the top of your head. The posterior area (i.e., the "back part") of the frontal lobe, the motor cortex,

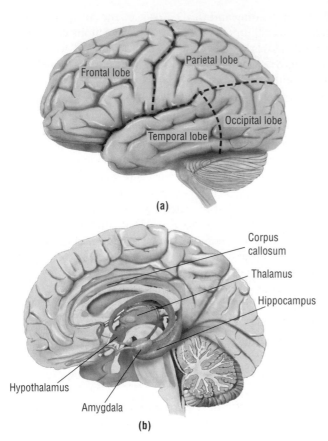

(a)

(b)

Figure 2.6 (a) The major divisions and anatomical regions of the brain. (b) The cerebral cortex and major subcortical structures.

plays an important role in carrying out voluntary movements. Areas in the anterior portion of the frontal lobe (commonly called the *prefrontal cortex*) are important in higher aspects of motor control, such as planning and executing complex behaviors. The frontal lobe also includes Broca's area, an important region that's related to the physical production of speech. Behind the frontal lobe lies the parietal lobe, centered more or less under the crown of your skull. In the anterior portion of the parietal lobe resides the somatosensory cortex, which controls the experience of bodily sensations such as touch, temperature, and pain. In terms of cognitive processes, the parietal lobe houses areas important in regulating (among other things) the processes of attention and working memory. Beneath the parietal lobe in the posterior portion of the cortex is the occipital lobe, which contains the primary visual cortex, the area of the brain primarily responsible for vision and the ability to recognize visual patterns. (So you really do have "eyes" in the back of your head!) Finally, the temporal lobe is appropriately located behind the ears. It contains the auditory cortex, the brain's primary sensory area for audition. It also includes Wernicke's area, which is involved in speech comprehension. Many areas of the cortex are not specifically devoted to motor or sensory function and have been dubbed "association areas." Association areas of the cortex are believed to integrate the processing of other brain areas, serving as the basis for higher mental processes that require integration, such as language processing, problem solving, and decision making.

The cerebral cortex is made up of two hemispheres, the right and the left. The hemispheres appear more or less symmetrical in their appearance, but as we'll see, each features some interesting processing differences. In general, the operation of the hemispheres is lateralized—that is, the left hemisphere receives information from and controls the right side of the body, while the right hemisphere receives information from and controls the left side of the body. The two hemispheres communicate primarily by means of the corpus callosum, a nerve bundle located in the center of the brain above the limbic system.

Beneath the cerebral cortex lies a complex system of structures that play an important role in a variety of cognitive processes (see Figure 2.6b). Most of the structures are grouped together and termed the *limbic system*. The **limbic system** is integral to learning and remembering new information as well as the processing of emotion. Important structures in the limbic system include the hippocampus, which is vital for encoding new information into memory. The amygdala plays a key role in regulating emotions and in forming emotional memories. The thalamus serves primarily as a relay point that routes incoming sensory information to the appropriate area of the brain (directing visual information to the visual cortex and so on) and also seems to play a role in attention. Below the thalamus lies the hypothalamus ("hypo" means "under" in Latin), which controls the endocrine system (the body's system of hormones) and plays an important role in emotion as well as the maintenance of important and basic survival processes, such as temperature regulation and food intake. Together, the thalamus and hypothalamus are termed the *diencephalon*. The basal ganglia play a critical role in controlling movement and are important for motor-based memories, such as the procedures involved in riding a bike.

Although brain areas and brain structures are to a considerable extent specialized for certain types of functions, it is important not to lose sight of the brain as an integrated system. No function (particularly cognitive functions like remembering) takes place in a single brain structure or area. While some subcomponents of cognitive processes may be localized in one area, complex cognition involves an intricate interplay between brain areas and brain structures that are distributed throughout the brain.

The Tools of Cognitive Neuroscience

Cognitive neuroscientists rely on a number of investigative techniques to discover the neural underpinnings of cognition. Before the development of sophisticated technologies, much of the information we know about the brain, and what happens where, was discovered through investigations of people who had suffered brain damage. In the last 25 years, there has been an explosion in the development of brain investigation techniques. Some of these techniques involve the assessment of the electrophysiological activity occurring in the brain during cognitive processes, while others involve "taking a picture" of the brain activity that accompanies mental processing.

Brain Trauma.   Much of the early knowledge about what brain areas are involved in various cognitive functions came from studies of patients who had suffered some sort of trauma to the brain through injury or disease. A prominent example relevant to cognitive psychology is the work of Paul Broca, a neuroscience pioneer in the mid-1850s. Broca had a famous patient who was dubbed "Tan" because this syllable was all he could say. In spite of this inability to speak normally, Tan's ability to understand was relatively unimpaired. Broca discovered that this patient had damage to the left frontal lobe. Later, in the 1870s, Carl Wernicke had a patient who could speak, but what he said was gibberish. Furthermore, he was unable to understand written or spoken language. Wernicke discovered that this patient had damage to the left temporal lobe. Based on these and other patients with language impairment, researchers were able to more clearly delineate the role of left-hemisphere areas in language processing.

The most severe limitation of using cases such as these to study cognitive processes is that they allow absolutely no control. A researcher can't map out the human brain by systematically damaging different areas and observing the associated deficits. (How would you like to volunteer for that study?) Studies of brain trauma cases also suffer the limitations in generalizability that we discussed in Chapter 1 in conjunction with case studies. There may be critical differences in the functioning of a normal and a damaged brain. And finally (and this is true of most brain investigation techniques), the evidence yielded is purely descriptive. It provides a relatively simple sketch of the relationship between brain areas and cognitive function.

Single and Double Dissociations.   So what modes of assessment do cognitive neuroscientists use in studying individuals with brain damage? Often they will compare performance on two tasks that differ in the use of one proposed mental operation. Let's consider an example from Coltheart (2001). Suppose we find a person who has brain damage in area X and exhibits deficits in comprehending written language (i.e., reading) but has no deficits in comprehending spoken language. This would be an example of a **single dissociation**—performance deficits in one task but no performance deficits in another task. Based on these data, it's tempting to conclude that area X is responsible for written comprehension but not for spoken comprehension. Perhaps spoken comprehension depends on some other area, Y. Do you see a problem with this conclusion? Maybe area X is responsible for *both* written and spoken comprehension, but the damage is not severe enough to reveal the deficits in spoken comprehension. (We use this example for discussion purposes only; whether this is a reasonable argument will depend on the nature of the differences between spoken and written comprehension.)

So what can researchers do? They could examine patients with different areas of brain damage—X *and* Y. Suppose we found a patient with damage to area X who shows deficits in reading but not in understanding spoken language *and* a patient with damage to area Y who has deficits in understanding spoken language but not in reading. This pattern is termed a **double dissociation** and serves as stronger evidence for the claim stated above—that area X is responsible for written comprehension and area Y is responsible for spoken language comprehension. Although double dissociations are quite informative, they still do not conclusively show that written and spoken comprehension are based on *completely* different brain processes and structures. However, the double dissociation in this case certainly suggests that written comprehension and spoken comprehension are partially independent and controlled by areas X and Y, respectively.

The value of double dissociations extends well beyond cognitive neuroscience. Double dissociations have also been used to argue that the performance on two different experimental conditions or tasks relies on different mental processes, or different cognitive systems. Let's consider the memory test/word frequency experiment we discussed to explain the basic principles of a factorial design. As you'll recall, high-frequency words were better recalled than low-frequency words. However, low-frequency words were better recognized than high-frequency words. This double dissociation indicates that recall and recognition are influenced, at least to some extent, by different factors. Throughout this text, you'll encounter numerous examples of dissociations that indicate the operation of distinct brain systems, or distinct sets of cognitive processes.

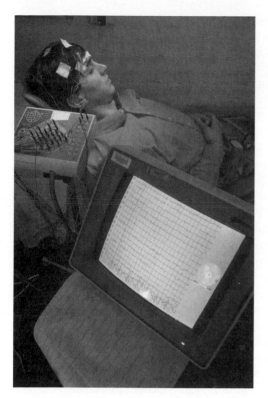

The EEG allows a researcher to record summed action potentials from different brain sites.

The Electroencephalograph. Remember the way neurons work—they are electrochemical information processors. Because the activity of neurons is electrical in part, some research techniques involve recording the electrical activity of the brain and relating it to cognitive functioning. The **electroencephalograph (EEG)** uses electrodes placed on the scalp to pick up the electrical current being conducted through the skull by the activity of neurons underneath, essentially providing a global recording of the action potentials occurring in the brain. Although researchers have used this method to localize the brain processes underlying cognition, the results have been somewhat disappointing. The electroencephalograph simply records a combination of the activity of millions of neurons at the brain's surface, making it difficult to pinpoint specific areas underlying cognitive processes. Also, because the neural impulses are traveling over the brain and through the skull and scalp, some distortion in the recorded signal is inevitable, further confounding attempts to localize where the important brain processing is occurring. Some have likened this use of the EEG to trying to diagnose a computer malfunction by holding up a voltmeter in front of it. As we'll see, neuroscientists have developed much better techniques for mapping out brain function.

Event-Related Potentials. Although electroencephalography leaves something to be desired in terms of brain-mapping precision, it does have one advantage over some other techniques. It has fairly good temporal resolution, or precision, in specifying the time course of events. Researchers can observe EEG tracings over time and look for *changes* in the brain's electrical activity at certain critical points, like when something surprising occurs. These changes are termed **event-related potentials (ERP)** because they represent the action *potentials* that occur in *relation* to some *event.* These potentials allow researchers to plot out *when* (in addition to *where*) important brain activity is occurring.

Event-related potentials have become increasingly popular in recent years because of their unique ability to pinpoint highlights of cognitive processing in real time—something the brain-imaging techniques that we'll be talking about cannot do. Let's take a closer look at the makeup of an event-related potential and review some of the terminology; a sample is provided in Figure 2.7. The x-axis represents time in milliseconds, and the y-axis represents the magnitude/direction of the brain's electrical response, typically measured in millivolts. The plot defined by these axes represents the brain's response to a stimulus over time. As you can see, shortly after stimulus presentation, the ERP response begins. The response curve has several features to note. First is the *amplitude*

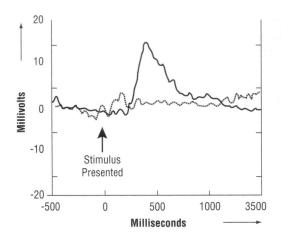

Figure 2.7 An event-related potential (ERP).

of response, indicated by the distance of the response from a control condition that serves as a baseline. Second is whether the change in amplitude occurs in a positive or a negative direction (i.e., deflection above or below the baseline condition). Third is the point in time at which the peak level of response occurs relative to stimulus presentation. Also keep in mind that ERPs are being collected from a myriad of points along the surface of the scalp, so a given ERP may represent activity from a particular location on the scalp (and, correspondingly, the brain).

As noted earlier, ERP responses always involve a comparison between at least two conditions. Let's make this more concrete with an example. A researcher might compare the brain's responses to "Jocelyn put the cookies into the *oven*" and the responses to "Jocelyn put the cookies into the *shoe*" in order to find out the brain's response to a semantic anomaly. It turns out that the pattern generated in response to the aforementioned kooky cookie sentence would be a pronounced negative deflection in the wave 400 ms after stimulus presentation, relative to the normal (i.e., baseline) cookie sentence. This more pronounced deflection is termed an **N400 response** (Kutas & Hillyard, 1980); this response (often shortened to N4) tends to be larger over parietal and temporal regions of the right hemisphere (Atchley & Kwasny, 2003).

The N400 response is just one of a number of typical responses that researchers look for when analyzing the time course and location of various cognitive processes. Another informative pattern is the **P300 response** (Sutton, Tueting, Zubin, & John, 1965), a pronounced positive deflection in the brain's response 300 ms after stimulus presentation, relative to a baseline condition. Actually, this response (often shortened to P3) is probably the most analyzed component of the ERP response (Key, Dove, & Maguire, 2005). It occurs in response to an unexpected stimulus—sometimes termed an "oddball." For example, if someone had been observing a series of bird pictures, an oddball picture of a panda bear inserted in the middle would result in a P300 response. Although sources of the P300 are unclear, one seems to be the medial (i.e., toward the middle) temporal regions of the brain.

The P300 and N400 components are only two of many that researchers attempt to extract from the EEG in order to plot out the time course and locations of cognitive processing. All components are affected by a host of independent variables like stimulus probability, presentation time, modality of presentation (visual vs. auditory), and more. Indeed, observing the variation in ERP components as a function of these independent variables is critical in mapping out brain function. You'll be encountering more of these component-variable interactions in subsequent chapters, within the context of specific cognitive processes and paradigms, such as face recognition, autobiographical remembering, and problem solving.

Functional Imaging Techniques: PET and fMRI Scans.   The greatest strides in cognitive neuroscience have been made by using functional imaging techniques. These imaging techniques have proved much more successful than EEGs in precisely localizing the brain areas associated with various cognitive processes. Unlike EEGs, imaging techniques do not involve the direct measurement of neural activity. Rather, changes in blood flow are used as indices of where brain activity is occurring during various cognitive processes, essentially providing a map of brain activity.

Imaging techniques involve a comparison between an active and a (relatively) inactive brain. In a test scan, researchers present some type of task that is thought to reflect a given cognitive process. For example, to investigate how we access words from our mental dictionary, researchers might have subjects generate synonyms for words as they are presented. Brain activity would be monitored as subjects engage in this task, and the results would yield an *image* of what the brain is doing. But this image isn't enough to indicate the brain centers important for performing the task. These brain centers might be active anyway, because the brain is never simply "turned off." Therefore, researchers must also get an image of the brain activity that occurs when the brain is at rest or is involved in some simpler task. This image is termed a *baseline,* or *control scan.* By comparing the *difference* in the two images, researchers can extract the areas of the brain that seem to be consistently associated with the task in question. Let's take a closer look at the two major brain-imaging techniques: positron-emission tomography (PET) and functional magnetic resonance imaging (fMRI).

A PET scanning machine.

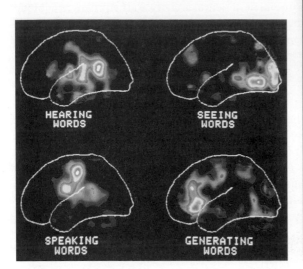 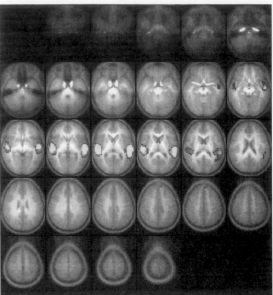

Both PET scans and fMRI images allow researchers to note active and less active areas of the brain.

A **positron-emission tomography scan (PET scan)** uses radioactive substances ingested (in harmless amounts!) by a willing subject to trace brain activity. The technique is based on one feature of brain metabolism: active areas of the brain are associated with increased blood flow, and a decaying radioactive substance can gauge where this blood flow is occurring. Detectors pick up this blood flow and convert it into a visual image—essentially a map of the brain in which "hot" colors, like red and yellow, indicate increased activity and "cool" colors, like blue and green, indicate less active brain areas.

Functional magnetic resonance imaging (fMRI) is similar to a PET scan in that it reflects brain activity through changes in blood flow. But fMRI picks up this activity with magnetic detectors that are sensitive to hemoglobin levels in the blood. Basically, a magnetic scanner picks up differences in hemoglobin that is oxygenated (carrying oxygen) or nonoxygenated (no longer carrying oxygen). The larger the difference, the more neuronal activity is occurring in that area (Gazzaniga, Ivry, & Mangun, 2002). This activity is displayed in much the same way as in PET scanning—as a multicolored map of more and less active brain areas.

fMRI offers a number of advantages over PET scanning. First, it's noninvasive. In other words, no foreign agent has to be introduced into the body, like the radioactive substance used in PET scan studies. Functional magnetic resonance imaging is also cheaper. Equipment that's already present in many hospitals and clinics can be modified to conduct fMRI, whereas PET scanning equipment is relatively exotic. A third advantage of fMRI is a little more subtle, and relates to how the brain scans are collected over time. Because a PET scan uses a radioactive substance to trace brain activity, some time must elapse between test and control scans to allow the substance to dissipate; the next scan needs to start with a "clean slate." Therefore, over a given period of time, only a limited number of scans can be taken, and these scans are combined into an average image.

In fMRI research, there is no decaying radioactive tracer to worry about, so test and control scans can be interspersed with much greater frequency. In other words, researchers can collect many more control scans and many more test scans in a given period of time. Why is this important? Common sense probably tells you that the more subjects in an experiment, the higher the likelihood is that the results of the experiment will be valid and representative. The same principle applies here; the more scans that are obtained, the more likely it is that a researcher is getting a valid and representative idea of brain activity.

Imaging techniques such as PET and fMRI have led to crucial insights about where the neural substrates for cognitive activity may lie. These techniques do have a number of limitations, however. One major limitation is their relative inability to provide a time-based analysis of cognition. Most basic cognitive processes occur on the order of fractions of a second, and the temporal (time) resolution of imaging techniques is not nearly this precise, so what we get is only a global picture of brain functioning.

Hemispheric Asymmetries.   The fact that the brain is divided into two separate hemispheres is a happy coincidence for brain researchers, because the asymmetries in the processing of the hemispheres have revealed some interesting features of brain processing. The main distinction between the brain's hemispheres relates to verbal ability. In most people, the left hemisphere is specialized for verbal processing, while the right hemisphere is relatively nonverbal. One major source of evidence for this asymmetry has been research on **split-brain patients,** people who have had their corpus callosum severed to alleviate the severity of epileptic seizures. While successful in alleviating seizures, cutting the main source of communication between the right and left hemispheres does lead to some oddities in processing that have illuminated some of the differences in hemispheric functions. These oddities are revealed only in a special laboratory setup. Were you to meet a split-brain person on the street, you likely wouldn't notice anything.

Split-brain research takes advantage of the wiring of the visual system, which is structured so that if you were to stare straight ahead, information right of center would go predominantly to the left hemisphere, while information left of center would go predominantly to the right hemisphere. When a split-brain patient is presented with a stimulus (e.g., a word) left of center fixation, it goes to the right hemisphere, but cannot get to the left due to the severed corpus callosum. If the patient is asked to read aloud the word, they will have a great deal of difficulty because the right hemisphere is relatively poor in its verbal ability. But interestingly, if asked to take their left hand and reach behind a screen to pick up the item that the word names, they are able to do so because the right hemisphere directs the left hand. The right hemisphere "knows" the word it saw, but it is limited because it cannot demonstrate this knowledge verbally. However, if a word is presented right of center fixation, it goes to the left hemisphere, and the patient will have no trouble reading it aloud because the left hemisphere is specialized for verbal processing.

Differences in left and right brain function can also be seen in people with intact brains. This research has revealed that the left hemisphere is specialized for language processing, while the right hemisphere is specialized for spatial tasks like assembling the pieces of a puzzle or orienting oneself within the environment. And there are some other asymmetries in processing, some of which you'll learn about in subsequent chapters. But one should be careful not to overgeneralize—the two hemispheres of the brain form an elegantly integrated system that features close interactions between right and left.

A Critical Look at Brain Investigation.   There can be no denying that breathtaking strides have been made in delineating the neural substrates of cognition. At the same time, there can be no denying that we know very little about how any specific daily cognition—getting a book out to study and reading the first page, for example—is realized at the level of a specific neural network. On a microlevel, we know a good deal about the general mechanics of how neurons fire action potentials; on a macrolevel, brain-imaging techniques have provided a good deal of information about the brain areas that are active during certain cognitive processes. However, a gaping chasm continues to exist between these two levels of analysis, and work continues to build a critical bridge between them.

Wacky Brain Claims.   As just stated, although neuroscience hurtles ahead, we are at least several orders of magnitude away from anything approaching a complete understanding of how the brain subserves cognition. Indeed, that full understanding may never come. But alas, there are always hucksters eager to make a buck by watering down what is known about brain and mind, and serving it up as oversimplified tripe. Let's briefly examine two examples. First is the claim that we use only 10% of our brains. Given that the brain is the center for cognitive processing, it's no surprise that you hear claims about "unleashing your brain power" or "tapping into the unused portion of your brain." There is no evidence whatsoever for this ridiculous assertion (except maybe the fact that people make the assertion), yet it persists like the weeds in our backyard. Radford (1999) notes that this idea may have originated from the functions of the different cortical areas and the prevalence of association areas. Some have misinterpreted the lack of specialization of the association areas as a lack of important function that, if used, could enhance our "brain power." It's almost as if the association areas are perceived as just lying there, doing nothing. Nothing could be further from the truth! There are no unused areas in the brain. Areas that are not specialized for particular functions are critical for combining and integrating information from other brain areas.

A second wacky brain claim is based in empirical fact. As you read earlier, scads of research evidence support the notion that the left and right hemispheres of the brain are specialized for different sorts of functions. No one would deny this. But in the decades that have ensued since this discovery and subsequent investigations, pop psychology schlockmeisters have taken the distinction to unfounded extremes. Rather than subtle differences between the hemispheres in their responses to certain types of stimuli, you hear about the logical, linear, mathematical, and verbal left hemisphere and the creative, freethinking, spatial, and nonverbal right hemisphere. An associated claim is that the abilities of the right hemisphere go largely untapped relative to those of the left (which may relate to the 10% myth), and that the right hemisphere needs selective exercise.

This overdichotomization of hemispheric specialization represents a series of gross oversimplifications. First, the differences between the hemispheres on these various tasks is

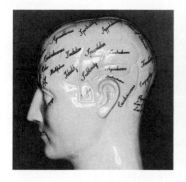

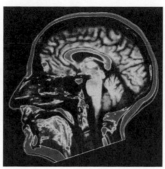

The new phrenology?

a matter of degree. Neither hemisphere lies there completely inactive during *any* cognitive task. Second, tasks and abilities are much more intricate and complex than implied by these wacky claims. *Nothing* we do can be pigeon-holed as purely a left-hemisphere or a right-hemisphere task. Take reading a novel, for example. . . . Verbal task, right? Well, in some ways, yes. We're reading, following a linear plot, ana-lyzing the logic of the characters' actions, and so on. But at the same time, we're no doubt engaged in some serious right-hemisphere activity as well, as we form mental images of the events in the novel, create our own alternate plotlines, and attempt to follow the stream-of-consciousness writing of an author like William Faulkner. The point is, nothing is simple. Everything we do requires a complex interplay of processing between the hemispheres and can't be neatly classified as "right-brained" or "left-brained."

Neuroimaging: The New Phrenology?

The extreme brain claims discussed above are "straw men" and rather easy to dismiss. However, the more sophisticated analy-ses of brain function provided by researchers who do functional imaging studies are not such an easy mark. Nonetheless, there are more nuanced criticisms that can be offered. A serious limitation to studies that associate cognitive processes with active brain areas is that they provide only *descriptive* information about the location of the brain activity that accompanies a given set of cognitive processes.

Some think this concern is grave enough to question the entire enterprise of map-ping the brain with functional imaging, referring to it as "the new phrenology" (e.g., Uttal, 2003). You may recall phrenology from your introductory psychology course; it's the (now totally discredited) attempt to link brain functions to bumps on the skull, pop-ular in the 19th century. Although functional imaging has certainly not been discredited (indeed, it has been enthusiastically embraced), the criticism would seem to be well taken. The concern is that simply pointing to brain areas and saying, for example, "These three areas are quite active when people make a decision" doesn't really say much about the underlying processes.

In spite of these reservations, researchers continue to plot brain function with functional imaging techniques. Although the comparison to phrenology seems on the mark in some ways, it is a bit extreme. After all, we have excellent reasons to attribute (or at least to relate) cognitive processes to the operation of the brain's neural net-works. The same cannot be said of attempts to relate cognitive processes to skull bumps. But the comparison to phrenology serves as an important caveat and guide to researchers: general information about *where* cognitive processes seem to be taking place is only one piece of the puzzle that, when complete, will describe exactly *how* they take place.

STOP and REVIEW!

1. What is the basic unit of processing? What are the major divisions in the brain?
2. True or false? The four lobes of the brain are referred to as left, right, parietal, and temporal.
3. Describe the difference between a single dissociation and a double dissociation.
4. What do brain-imaging techniques such as PET scanning allow researchers to do? What is a major limitation of imaging techniques?

➤ The basic unit of processing in the brain is the neuron. The brain provides the physiological machinery used in thinking and can be subdivided into the hindbrain, midbrain, and forebrain.

➤ The majority of higher-level processing that underlies cognition occurs in the forebrain, particularly in the cerebral cortex, which is typically divided into four lobes: frontal, parietal, occipital, and temporal. Beneath the cortex are subcortical structures involved in memory and emotion. The left and right hemispheres of the brain are specialized in their processing capacities. The most prominent example is a left-hemisphere specialization for language.

➤ Investigation of thinking in patients with brain trauma can provide evidence regarding the locus of cognitive processes. Single dissociations occur when some change influences the operation of one particular process but leaves another unaffected. Double dissociations occur when two measures of performance are affected in an opposite fashion by different experimental variables.

➤ The EEG involves recording brain potentials (through the scalp) from different sites in the cerebral cortex. Event-related potentials can reveal the time course of brain activity in response to stimuli. Brain-imaging techniques (e.g., PET scanning and fMRI) allow researchers to pinpoint brain regions active in conjunction with various cognitive tasks, but they are limited to simple descriptions of the localization of brain activity.

GLOSSARY

accuracy: the percentage of trials on which a subject is correct (p. 42)

action potential: an all-or-none reaction of a neuron that occurs when stimulation reaches some critical threshold value (p. 58)

between-subjects design: an experimental design in which different subjects receive each level of the independent variable (p. 47)

between-subjects factorial: a factorial design in which different subjects are assigned to each of the experimental groups created by the factorial design (p. 50)

carryover effects: occur when processing or strategy effects from one condition influence processing in a subsequent condition (p. 46)

case studies: intensive investigations of a single case or a small number of cases (p. 36)

central tendency: a descriptive measure that gives an indication of a typical score (p. 51)

cerebral cortex: the outer shell of the brain that comprises the majority of the forebrain and is made up of billions of neurons (p. 59)

cognitive neuroscience: an interdisciplinary field of study, combining neuroscience and cognitive psychology, that attempts to relate cognitive processing to its neural substrates (p. 57)

confounding variables: the factors that vary in conjunction with the independent variable (p. 46)

dependent variables: the variables measured in an experiment that are influenced by changes in the independent variables (p. 39)

descriptive statistics: the numbers that provide an overview of basic characteristics about some set of data, such as central tendency (p. 51)

double-blind procedure: a technique for preventing expectancy effects by keeping both the subjects and the experimenter naive as to the purposes and particular treatments of the study (p. 41)

double dissociation: occurs when two measures of performance are affected in an opposite fashion by different experimental variables (p. 62)

ecological validity: the degree to which the experimental methodology simulates the real world (p. 40)

electroencephalograph (EEG): a brain investigation technique that involves recording summed action potentials (through the scalp) from different areas of the brain (p. 63)

event-related potentials (ERP): changes in the brain's electrical activity at critical points that are measured to show the temporal relationship between stimulus presentation and brain response (a technique used in conjunction with the EEG) (p. 63)

expectancy effects: the influence of subject or experimenter beliefs on the results of a study (p. 40)

experimental conditions: the groups being compared in an experiment; the circumstances formed by the manipulation of the independent variable (p. 43)

experimental context variables: varying the nature of the instructions given to subjects or the situations in which subjects are tested (p. 44)

experimental research: the systematic manipulation and measurement of variables in a controlled setting, designed to allow for causal explanations (p. 38)

factor: a synonym for the independent variable in an experiment (p. 46)

factorial design: an experimental design that involves completely crossing the levels of one

independent variable with the levels of all other independent variables (p. 50)

forebrain: the largest region of the brain, surrounding the midbrain and dorsal to the hindbrain; controls higher-level processes involved in sensation, emotion, and thought (p. 59)

functional magnetic resonance imaging (fMRI): a brain-imaging technique that traces brain activity through the use of magnetic detectors sensitive to blood hemoglobin levels (p. 66)

generalizability: the extent to which research findings apply outside of the research context (p. 36)

hindbrain: the brain region that lies under the base of the skull and controls basic life functions (p. 59)

independent variables: the variables manipulated in an experiment that are assumed to cause changes in the dependent variables (p. 39)

inferential statistics: statistical tests that provide an indication of the probability that the results obtained were due to chance (p. 51)

interaction: occurs when the particular influence of one independent variable depends on the level of another independent variable (p. 53)

internal validity: the degree to which extraneous variables are controlled (p. 40)

limbic system: system of structures in the lower forebrain that is important in learning, memory, and basic emotion (p. 60)

main effects: the overall effects of an independent variable on the dependent variable (p. 51)

material variables: varying the nature of the material being processed by subjects (p. 44)

metacognition: one's awareness of one's own cognitive processing tendencies and abilities (p. 37)

midbrain: a small brain region dorsal to the hindbrain that controls some sensory reactions and relates to overall brain arousal (p. 59)

mixed-factorial design: a factorial design that involves the joint manipulation of at least one between-subjects factor and at least one within-subjects factor (p. 50)

N400 response: a pronounced negative deflection in the brain's response to a stimulus relative to a baseline condition that occurs approximately 400 ms after the onset of the stimulus (p. 64)

naturalistic observation: watching and recording a behavior of interest in its natural setting (p. 35)

neuron: a nerve cell; the basic building block of the nervous system (p. 58)

operational definition: defining a variable in terms of precise, measurable procedures that can be repeated by other researchers (p. 41)

P300 response: a pronounced positive deflection in the brain's response to a stimulus relative to a baseline condition that occurs approximately 300 ms after the onset of the stimulus (p. 64)

performance-measure variables: varying the nature of the response measures given to subjects (p. 45)

positron-emission tomography scan (PET scan): a brain-imaging technique that traces brain activity by observing the distribution of an ingested radioactive substance (p. 66)

practice effects: the general improvement in participant performance that occurs over the course of participation in an experiment (p. 46)

reaction time (RT): the time taken to respond to a stimulus, usually measured in milliseconds (p. 42)

self-report: the use of interviews or questionnaires to gather subject data (p. 37)

single dissociation: occurs when some change influences the operation of one particular process but leaves another unaffected (p. 62)

single-factor experiment: an experiment in which the effects of only one independent variable are assessed (p. 46)

speed-accuracy trade-off: the tendency for (all other things being equal) faster responding to be associated with higher error rates (p. 42)

split-brain patients: people whose corpus callosum has been severed, usually as a treatment for severe epilepsy (p. 67)

statistical significance: a term used to describe results that are unlikely to have arisen through simple chance variation (p. 51)

subject variables: varying the nature of research subjects (e.g., female or male, young or old, etc.) (p. 44)

within-subjects design: an experimental design in which the same subjects receive each level of the independent variable (p. 46)

within-subjects factorial: a factorial design in which the same subjects partake in each of the conditions created by the factorial design (p. 50)

3

Basics of Perception and Awareness

Look up from what you're doing right now, and reflect on what's happening as you view the scene. As soon as you set your sights on it—instantly—it's neatly organized, everything is sorted and separated. How does this "perceptual packaging" occur?

How might people differ in their perceptual reports? No doubt you've experienced sights or sounds that others around you haven't. Have you ever heard a "bump in the night" that someone else swears didn't happen? What could give rise to such different perceptions?

You hear the claims and the warnings—subliminal messages are all around us, in magazine ads, in music, and who knows where else? Can we really be influenced by things that we can't even perceive?

How is it that you can be completely engrossed in something like a conversation or a movie, yet somehow you happen to hear your name? How much processing occurs when we aren't paying attention to something?

Basic Issues in Perception

Perception is truly a masterful achievement. Consider vision. A two-dimensional array of light appears on the retina, which houses the visual receptors. Instead of a random array of color dots, we instantaneously experience a rich, coherent, veridical, three-dimensional perception of an object, person, or event (i.e., a **percept**). Perhaps the most astonishing fact is that this all occurs instantaneously, mostly outside of conscious awareness. You're aware only of the product, not the process. Perception is indeed an incredible achievement, not to mention a brilliantly engineered one. Attempts at computer vision and speech recognition—basically, getting computers to "see" and "hear"—have met with extremely limited success. No machine can yet match the speed and flexibility of human perceptual systems.

Sensation and Perception

Given that cognition is often characterized in terms of information processing, it makes sense to say that cognition begins as soon as "information" enters the cognitive system. A series of processes is responsible for the transformation from "two-dimensional array of light," "air vibration," and "pressure" to the percepts of "cat," "car horn," and "kiss." Because the resulting percept forms the basis of all subsequent cognition and action, a complete understanding of cognitive processes requires an understanding of the basic processes that lead to these percepts.

Psychologists usually distinguish between *sensation* and *perception*. Although the distinction is somewhat artificial, there are a number of bases for making it. The most relevant basis for our purposes is a distinction between the physiological and the psychological. The term *sensation* is sometimes loosely associated with the physiological processes that underlie information intake. Within the examples mentioned above, this would include the processes whereby eye, ear, and skin receptors take the initial stimuli (the light, vibration, and pressure, respectively), and register them in the chemical language of the nervous system. From there, it's on to the neurons and then to the brain, where the processes typically labeled "perception" transform this electrochemical message into a rich percept. This latter set of processes, termed *perception,* refers to the psychological processes involved in the immediate organization and interpretation of sensations.

We sense and perceive through a myriad of channels that include the ubiquitous five major senses of vision, audition, touch, taste, and smell. Information taken in through any of these channels can and does initiate information processing. However, there can be little doubt that thinking is dominated by things we see and hear. Vision and audition are the primary modes through which we take in information from the world. As a result, most of the research done by cognitive psychologists focuses on information from these two sense modalities.

Fans of the other senses shouldn't lose heart! In this chapter we will have some brief discussion of how the senses commingle and interact. Also, information processing initiated by the other senses will make brief appearances in subsequent chapters as we consider identification via touch (Chapter 5) and smell as a cue for autobiographical memories (Chapter 8).

Bottom-Up and Top-Down Processing

The processes of perception are the product of what are commonly termed *bottom-up* and *top-down processes*. **Bottom-up processing** basically refers to a flow of information that proceeds from the stimulus to the neural activity driven by this stimulus to its eventual identification. Bottom-up processing is sometimes termed **data-driven processing,** because it refers to the processes whereby the stimulus itself (i.e., the *data*) leads to the sensible percept. **Top-down processing** refers to the processes whereby we bring what we expect, what we know, and surrounding context to bear in determining what it is we're sensing and subsequently perceiving. Because it refers to the application of concepts to perception, top-down processing is sometimes dubbed **conceptually driven processing.**

Are Our Perceptions Constructions?   The distinction between bottom-up and top-down processes is related to another fundamental question that arises in perceptual research and theory. To what degree are our percepts *constructed* by interpretive processes or *directly experienced* (with little or no interpretation) from the external environment? This issue has been debated most thoroughly with regard to visual perception, although the basic arguments apply to any modality. The **constructive view** of visual perception emphasizes the role of active construction and interpretation in arriving at a three-dimensional percept of the world. This view has its psychological roots in the work of Helmholtz, whom you read about in Chapter 1. Recall that Helmholtz advanced the notion of *unconscious inference* in perception. His basic idea was that we *infer* or construct a percept based on the sensory information we're receiving and on our previous knowledge and experience. This view emphasizes the role of top-down factors in perception. Perception, in this view, is a process of problem solving. Take golf, which often (always, for Greg) involves the difficult perceptual task of locating where one's drive off the tee ended up. Finding a golf ball amounts to detecting a round, light-colored speck in a field of green. There is no doubt that Greg's ability to locate the ball depends on expectations—he watched it as it flew away from him, he knows that he doesn't typically hit it far (a pathetic 150 yards at best), and he knows he usually hits it straight. This cluster of knowledge, which cognitive psychologists term a **schema,** "tunes" his perception of the ball as he searches for it.

According to an alternative view proposed by theorist J. J. Gibson (1950, 1966, 1987), perception is not a matter of construction or interpretation. What we perceive about our visual environment is picked up directly, hence the name: the **direct view** of perception. This view is closely aligned with the concept of bottom-up processing because it emphasizes the actual data being analyzed by visual mechanisms. Let's go back to our golf example. According to the direct view of perception, when Greg searches for his golf ball and scans the surrounding grass (which is usually very deep), two important pieces of data guide his search. One is *optical flow*—as you move through a given environment (say, a particular fairway on a golf course), the image on your retina changes; as you move toward some object or destination, that image expands, and the rate of expansion offers information about how fast you're moving and how close you are to objects. *Texture gradients* also serve as unambiguous sources of information. As you move closer to an object in the environment (say, the golf ball and surrounding grass), the apparent density of the object changes; this change in density provides information about depth that needs no interpretation.

You may be wondering how Gibson's view corresponds to the distinction between sensation and perception, but perhaps you can hazard a guess. Sensation involves the initial registration of information through sensory receptors, and perception involves processes of construction and interpretation. Since the direct view of perception eschews the importance of these sorts of interpretive processes, Gibson would probably minimize the distinction between sensation and perception and fuse them more closely in terms of what they accomplish.

The constructive and direct views aren't necessarily oppositional. It's almost certainly the case that both "modes" of perception are at work as we take in visual information. Rochat (1999) points out that the two approaches are explanations of different aspects of visual perception. He likens the direct approach to *perceiving* and the constructive approach to *pondering*. The direct approach, in emphasizing the richness of the visual environment, is really more of an explanation of how we move through and act on our environment from moment to moment. The constructive approach is an account of what might be considered the subsequent steps in visual experience, including the roles that expectations, memory, imagination, and problem solving play in how we interpret the world. As such, the constructive approach tends to focus more on cognitive factors like knowledge and expectation rather than on the specific aspects of the visual stimulus.

STOP *and* REVIEW!

1. Sensation is to perception as:
   a. physiological is to psychological
   b. vision is to the other senses
   c. responding is to information intake
   d. organization is to interpretation
2. Describe the basic difference between bottom-up processing and top-down processing.
3. True or false? According to the direct view of perception, top-down processing is more important to perception than is bottom-up processing.

➤ Sensation generally refers to the physiological processes that underlie information intake, while perception generally refers to the psychological processes involved in the immediate organization and interpretation of those sensations.

➤ Some perceptual processes are primarily bottom-up, or data-driven, featuring a flow of information that proceeds from the stimulus to subsequent neural activity to stimulus identification. These processes are complemented by top-down, conceptually driven processes through which we bring our expectation, our knowledge, and the surrounding context to bear in identification.

➤ The constructive view of visual perception emphasizes the role of top-down, active interpretation in perception. The direct view of visual perception emphasizes the bottom-up processing of information inherent in the stimulus itself, and minimizes the role of interpretation.

The Basic Tasks of Visual Perception

Palmer (2003) separates the processes of visual perception into two major subsets that correspond neatly to the progression of information processing that will structure the next few chapters. The first subset of processes involves the organization of an incoming stimulus array into discrete perceptual parts and elements; the second set of processes involves the identification and further processing of these elements and their categorization as people, golf balls, computers, books, etc. This chapter will deal primarily with the first set of processes—those whereby we impose some initial order on incoming information. Traditionally, these processes have been characterized as primarily pre-attentive, or "early," in the information-processing sequence. Toward the end of this chapter, we'll move into discussion of post-attentive processes (i.e., those that occur as soon as attention has been directed at a stimulus), and how attentional focus impacts perceptual processing. In the following two chapters, we'll discuss the second set of processes proposed by Palmer (2003), those that are responsible for identification and further processing of perceptual inputs. Chapter 4 ("Attending to and Manipulating Information") will focus on the control and manipulation of attention, and Chapter 5 ("Identification and Classification") will focus on the identification and classification of incoming information.

Perceptual Organizational Processes

Palmer (2003) proposes that when confronted with a stimulus array, the first major task of the visual system—the pre-attentive tasks mentioned above—is to impose structure on it. In other words, we must figure out which parts of the image go together and which do not. Following is a discussion of some of the factors that the visual system uses to accomplish this first step.

Grouping and Region Segmentation. A vital aspect of visual organization is **grouping,** our ability to sort things in our environment so that the percept is a neat, orderly package rather than a jumbled mess of randomly arranged stimulus patterns. The importance of this process was noted by Wertheimer (1923/1938) and other Gestalt psychologists, who were briefly introduced in Chapter 1. The Gestalt psychologists were interested in the processes underlying perceptual and mental organization. Perhaps most notable were their proposed **principles of visual organization.** These principles account for most of the "order" that we see in our visual environment. The Gestalt psychologists believed that these principles were the cornerstone of perception.

Several of the Gestalt grouping principles are depicted in Figure 3.1. **Proximity** refers to the tendency for objects that are near one another (i.e., *proximal*) to be grouped. The elements of Figure 3.1a look like

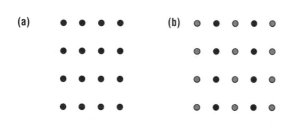

Figure 3.1 The Gestalt grouping principles that guide perceptual organization.

rows rather than columns because the row elements are closer to one another than are the column elements. The principle of **similarity** dictates that items be grouped to the degree that they are similar to one another. The elements of Figure 3.1b seem to be columns rather than rows because the columns have like elements. The principle of **good continuation** refers to our tendency to perceive lines as flowing naturally, in a single direction. For example, the letter X seems to be two lines that cross rather than two connected 45° angles. According to the principle of **closure,** we tend to complete the incomplete, perceptually connecting contours that are almost, but not quite, connected. Finally, **common fate** refers to our tendency to group elements together if they are moving in the same direction or at the same speed. Palmer and his colleagues have relatively recently added a couple of other organizational cues to these "classics." One is **common region**—elements that seem to belong to a common designated area, or region, will be grouped. Another is **synchrony,** which refers to our tendency to group elements that occur at the same time. It's important to note that these principles of organization are all interrelated and that one may dominate another, given the particular nature of the visual stimulus. For example, in Figure 3.1c, the principle of common region dominates the principle of similarity.

STOP *and* THINK!

GROUPING

Right now, stop reading, look up, and make a list of all of the Gestalt grouping cues that are assisting you in organizing your visual environment. If you're near a window, walk to it and see if any other grouping cues seem apparent.

Figure 3.2 Can you find the object?

As noted by Palmer (2002), it's tempting to think of these organizational tendencies as vague generalizations that don't really apply to our perception of objects in the real world. Nothing could be further from the truth. Can you find the camouflaged object in Figure 3.2? The difficulty you're having results from the breakdown of grouping cues. If these cues were not available in your everyday visual experience, you'd be missing objects you reach for, failing to recognize friends' faces, and walking into walls. By the way, the picture is a Dalmatian sniffing something on the ground.

Grouping: Bottom-Up or Top-Down? A good deal of discussion has centered on the issue of how grouping happens. Is grouping more of a bottom-up or a

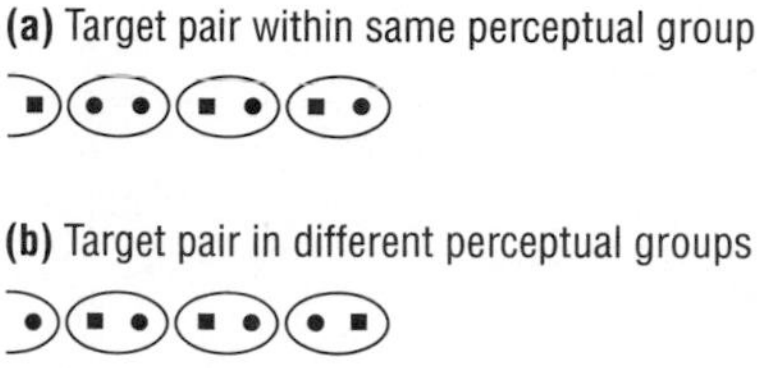

(a) Target pair within same perceptual group

(b) Target pair in different perceptual groups

Figure 3.3 Sample stimuli used by Beck and Palmer (2002) in their study of strategic effects in perceptual grouping.

top-down process? Grouping has traditionally been considered a bottom-up process, based solely on analysis of the data that comprise a visual scene (e.g., Marr, 1982; Neisser, 1967). Top-down processes—analyses based on previous knowledge, expectation, and strategy—were thought to play little or no role. Recent results have challenged this view.

Beck and Palmer (2002) designed a study to find out whether strategic effects occur in perceptual grouping, using a *repetition discrimination task*. In this task, subjects receive a series of displays like the ones in Figure 3.3. For each display the subjects are to indicate as quickly as possible whether the repeated elements are indicated as circles or squares. Reaction time for this judgment is the dependent variable. A critical independent variable is the status of these repeated elements. On some trials the repeated elements are indicated as part of the same perceptual group by means of a particular cue we've just discussed (e.g., common region). On other trials, the repeated elements are from different groups (i.e., not part of the same region). The typical finding is that observers are 200–300 ms faster in identifying repeated elements when those elements are in the same region (i.e., perceptual group). In other words, subjects indicate "circle" when presented with the display in Figure 3.3a significantly faster than when presented with the display in Figure 3.3b. That is, there's a same-perceptual-group advantage.

In their variation of this procedure, Beck and Palmer (2002) added one more critical independent variable to assess possible strategic effects in grouping. They varied the percentage of trials in which the repeated element appeared in the same perceptual group. The repeated element appeared in the same group on 25%, 50%, or 75% of the trials (and, of course, in a different group on the other 75%, 50%, or 25% of the trials). Why this manipulation? Basically, the researchers wanted to manipulate subject expectations. What effect do you think this manipulation would have on the subjects and on the same-perceptual-group advantage? Well, if perceptual grouping primarily involves bottom-up processing, the manipulation shouldn't have any impact at all. Grouping will occur and will have its effect of producing a same-perceptual-group advantage in spite of subject expectation or effort. However, if perceptual grouping involves top-down processing, then one might expect that when most of the trials feature repeated elements in different groups, subjects will look for this and engage in some type of strategy to "defeat" the natural grouping and pick out the pair. That is, if they're expecting repeated elements to be in different groups, they'll be able to reduce the same-perceptual-group advantage.

The results are presented in Figure 3.4. As you can see, there was a sizable effect of the probability manipulation. In the baseline condition in which there are an equal number of same-group and different-group trials, the typical same-group advantage occurs. Subjects have an easier time finding the repeated elements if these elements are in the same perceptual group. But look at the condition in which same-group trials occurred only 25% of the time. In that condition, the same-group advantage was all but wiped out. Basically, subjects were able to alter their strategies and overcome the natural grouping offered by the stimulus display, indicating a role for top-down processing in perceptual grouping.

A simple thought experiment also shows that top-down, knowledge-based factors impact perceptual grouping. Look again at Figure 3.2 (p. 78). After learning what this

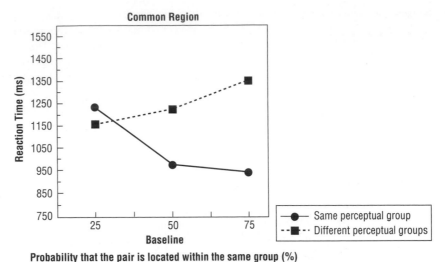

Figure 3.4 Results of Beck and Palmer's (2002) study of strategic effects in perceptual grouping.

From Beck, D.M & Palmer, S.E. (2002). Top-down influences on perceptual grouping. *Journal of Experimental Psychology, 28*(5), 1071–1084. Reprinted with permission from the American Psychological Association and the author.

figure represents, can you look at it and prevent yourself from seeing the Dalmatian? You almost certainly cannot. As noted by Wertheimer (1923), once you've experienced a particular perceptual grouping, especially an ambiguous stimulus, it's nearly impossible not to see it that way every time you look at it. This is another indication of top-down, experience-based influence on perceptual grouping (see also Kimchi & Hadad, 2002).

Figure-Ground.   Another fundamental principle of organization, termed **figure-ground,** refers to our tendency to segregate visual scenes into a background and a figure that appears to be superimposed against that background. Several cues allow us to parse figure from ground. Regions identified as figure tend to be smaller and have more symmetrical features than regions designated as background. In addition, a region is more likely to be seen as figure to the degree that it is meaningful (a person is more meaningful than a wall) and is surrounded by other elements of the visual array (Palmer, 2003). Vecera, Vogel, and Woodman (2002) add another feature to the mix. Elements in the lower region of the visual field are more likely to be seen as figure relative to elements in the upper region of the visual field. According to Vecera et al., this tendency develops with visual experience; in most natural scenes, regions below the horizon line are closer and comprise the figure. Experience tunes our visual systems to parse the scene in this way, which is yet another indication of top-down processing.

STOP and THINK! ━━━━━━━━━━━━━━━━━━

FIGURING OUT FIGURE-GROUND

Put this book aside and look up, taking note of the scene in front of you, wherever you may happen to be. Jot down all the elements of the scene. Then take your list of elements and classify each of them as (a) figure or (b) ground. Once you have your list, see if you notice any general differences in the sorts of things that comprise figure and ground. Do the things that seem like "figure" reflect the characteristics discussed in the text and summarized below?

- Smaller
- More symmetrical
- More meaningful
- Lower region of visual scene

Global Precedence.   When we hear a symphony or look at a painting, it seems that (phenomenologically, at least) we tend to blend the elements into an integrated whole rather than isolate separate elements. The Gestalt credo that "the whole is different from the sum of its parts" does a nice job of capturing this phenomenological experience. The Gestaltists viewed perception (and thinking in general) as a process of apprehending whole configurations or relationships—and this apprehension is more than just the sum of a group of independent sensations and thoughts. Basically, the Gestalt view is that apprehending wholes or configurations is a primitive. It's the natural tendency of our perceptual system and, as such, is done fairly easily and automatically. In other words, the "forest" is apparent before the "trees" are.

A classic study by Navon (1977) provides some ammunition for this perspective. Navon was interested in how people process visual displays. More specifically, would this processing be dominated by the specific and individual features within the pattern (i.e., local features), or would it be dominated by the overall pattern (i.e., global features)? Navon (1977) addressed this question rather cleverly, by composing stimuli that could be perceived in one of two ways, depending on whether subjects were influenced more by global or local features. He pitted these two modes of processing against one another by using stimuli like those pictured in Figure 3.5 to see which would dominate. When viewed globally, the figure is an H; however, the local features are made up of a different letter (S). When you glance at this figure, what do you notice first?

Navon (1977, experiment 3) investigated this question with a fairly straightforward procedure. Subjects viewed letters like the one in Figure 3.5 under different instructional conditions. In the *global-directed* condition, the task was to indicate whether the global figure was H or S; in the *local-directed* condition, the task was to indicate whether the component letters were H's or S's. The big letters presented to subjects were of three types: (1) the global and local features were consistent (a big H made of little H's); (2) the global and local features conflicted (a big H made of little S's); (3) the global and local features were neutral with respect to one another (a big H made of little rectangles). If global processing takes precedence, then conflicting letters should pose a problem only in the local-directed condition, because in this condition, one can't help but see the big letter. Also in this condition, where the large letter conflicts with the one subjects have to identify, responses should be slower and more prone to error.

```
S        S
S        S
S        S
SSSSSSS
S        S
S        S
S        S
```

Figure 3.5 Sample stimulus from Navon's (1977) study of global precedence.

From Navon, D. (1977). Forest before trees: The precedence of global features in visual perception. *Cognitive Psychology, 9,* 353–383. Copyright 1977 by Elsevier Science (USA). Reprinted with permission.

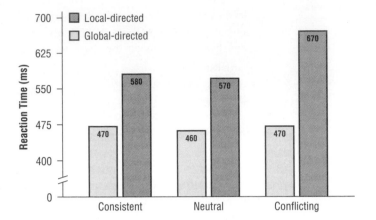

Figure 3.6 Results from Navon's (1977) study.

From Navon, D. (1977). Forest before trees: The precedence of global features in visual perception. *Cognitive Psychology, 9,* 353–383. Copyright 1977 by Elsevier Science (USA). Reprinted by permission.

The results are shown in Figure 3.6. The first thing you see in the graph is that the reaction time (RT) for the big letters (global-directed) was much less than that for the small ones (local-directed). This demonstrates that perceptually, it's easier to "grab" what's represented by the big letter. This could be due simply to the size of the stimulus—it's easier to identify something that's bigger. This explanation would suffice, were it not for the striking interaction that's apparent in the graph. Interference from the conflicting letter had markedly different effects on global-directed and local-directed conditions. When subjects were directed to notice the global aspects of the presented stimulus (identify the large letter), it didn't matter whether the local (small component) letters were consistent, conflicting, or neutral. The global (large) letter was easily apprehended. Such was not the case for the local (small) letters; whether the global letter was consistent or conflicting made a huge difference. If the large letter conflicted, subjects' RT was slowed by 100 milliseconds (relative to the neutral condition), a sizable inhibition effect. This implies that even when instructed to look for the local letters, subjects couldn't help but encode the global one. The finding of **global precedence** has proved to be quite general (see Kimchi, 1992, for a review). A series of studies by Cassia, Simion, Milani, and Umilta (2002) showed that the global over local advantage exists even from birth!

Some research (e.g., Evans, Shedden, Hevenor, & Hahn, 2000) indicates that differences in the processing of global and local features of a stimulus correspond to asymmetries of processing in the brain's right and left hemispheres. Specifically, this evidence places the locus of global processing in the right hemisphere, and the locus of local processing in the left hemisphere. Roalf, Lowery, and Turetsky (2006) extended this brain research to the domain of sex differences. Relevant to the present question are findings of structural differences between male and female brains that indicate stronger lateralization of function in male brains (Kolb & Whishaw, 1996). **Lateralization** is the degree to which particular cognitive processes are localized in one hemisphere or the other. So, men are more likely to have particular cognitive processes localized in one hemisphere, whereas the same cognitive processes in women are more diffusely spread between the hemispheres. This would lead

Research Theme: Individual Differences

to the prediction that the processing of global and local stimulus features would be more balanced between the hemispheres in women, relative to men.

Two other sex differences in hemispheric processing are relevant to the present discussion. First, women tend to excel on tasks that involve the left hemisphere (e.g., Halpern, 2000; Herlitz, Nilsson, & Backman, 1997). Combining this finding with evidence that indicates left-hemisphere dominance in processing local features of a stimulus leads to the prediction that women should be especially good at analyzing local features relative to global ones. A complementary finding is that men show strongly lateralized right-hemisphere processing. Given that the processing of global stimulus features seems to be localized in the right hemisphere, one might expect men to be more proficient in processing global features than in processing local features.

Roalf, Lowery, and Turetsky (2006) used the Navon global/local task to test these hypothesized sex differences. In addition, they wanted to explore possible sex differences in the time course of global/local processing. To do this, they measured event-related potentials. As you may recall from Chapter 2, ERPs are brain responses to presented stimuli that can be viewed in real time, allowing researchers to both localize and plot the time course of processing. In their study, Roalf et al. presented stimuli like those used in Navon's study, and had subjects respond as quickly as possible whenever they saw an H (either globally or locally). While performing this task, event-related potentials were recorded.

The reaction time data presented in Figure 3.7 reveal a number of interesting patterns. First, women responded faster to the local feature (the H's in the figure) than to the global feature (the figure of an H), which is consistent with the findings that women tend to excel in left-hemisphere tasks (e.g., Halpern, 1997) and that the left hemisphere seems more efficient in its processing of local features (e.g., Kimchi, 1992). A converse difference—faster processing of global features, relative to local ones—was expected for men. However, although the reaction time difference was in the predicted direction, the difference was not significant; this was an unexpected finding.

Another unexpected finding is apparent in the reaction time data; the authors failed to find the basic global precedence effect! In fact, local features were associated with a small, yet consistent, reaction time advantage. The authors noted several features of their study that may have enhanced the processing of local features and led to this surprising failure to replicate. First, the size ratio of global to local letters was different from that in previous studies, and may have tipped the scales in favor of local processing. In addition, the global processing bias is strongest with periperhal stimulus presentation, and is reduced in size when stimuli are presented centrally, as they were in this study. A final factor was the fact that a relatively small number of local elements were used to make the global stimulus, thus enhancing the salience of the local stimulus.

	Men	Women
Global Targets	643	702
Local Targets	650	663

Figure 3.7 Reaction time findings from the Roalf, Lowery, and Turetsky (2006) study of sex differences in the global precedence effect.

From Roalf, D., Lowery, N., & Turetsky, B. (2006). Behavioral and physiological findings of gender differences in global-local visual processing. *Brain and Cognition, 60*(1), 32–42. Reprinted with permission from Elsevier.

Failure to replicate the effect aside, the brain's relative response to global and local elements, as revealed through event-related potentials, did show some interesting differences in response to global and local elements. As expected, women

Research Theme: Neuroscience ▶

showed a stronger P300 response to local features than to global features. In contrast, male responses were similar across conditions. Because P300 responses occur upon presentation of important or salient stimuli (Johnson, 1984), this difference between male and female responses suggests that women attach more salience to local features than to global features. In fact, further analysis of other ERP components revealed that the processing bias toward local features in women was present a scant 100 ms after stimulus presentation! This indicates extremely quick discernment of the local features of a stimulus. In sum, the results from both the RT and physiological measures indicate consistent sex differences in the processing of local and global stimuli.

STOP and REVIEW!

1. Which of these is not one of the Gestalt principles of visual organization?
   a. similarity
   b. proximity
   c. common fate
   d. lateralization
2. True or false? Perceptual grouping is unaffected by top-down factors.
3. Describe the global precedence effect.

➤ A first basic task of visual perception is to organize the incoming information into sensible groups and regions. This is accomplished in part with the help of Gestalt principles of visual organization, which include similarity, proximity, common fate, synchrony, common region, and closure.

➤ Although early research generally characterized grouping as mostly a bottom-up process, recent evidence indicates that it can be influenced by top-down factors such as strategy. Another fundamental grouping principle is figure-ground, which refers to our tendency to segregate visual scenes into a background and a figure superimposed upon it.

➤ The global precedence effect refers to the finding that global elements of a visual scene tend to dominate local elements; all other things being equal, people tend to see "forest" before they see "trees." Some evidence suggests that women have a left-hemisphere/local feature processing bias, relative to men.

Multisensory Interaction and Integration

Devoting separate discussions to perception, attention, memory, and the like is largely a matter of descriptive convenience. Parsing the processes into separate chapters might lead one to lose sight of the interrelation among cognitive processes. The same is true (albeit on a smaller scale) for perceptual processes. For example, what we see affects what we hear; what we hear impacts our sense of touch.

Synesthesia

An intriguing example of interactions between sensory systems is involved in the phenomenon known as synesthesia. **Synesthesia** refers to experiences in which input from one sensory system produces an experience not only in that modality but in another as well. For example, synesthetes, as they're termed, might experience a particular musical chord as green. These cases, termed *strong synesthesia* by Martino and Marks (2001), are very rare (occurring in fewer than 1 out of every 2,000 individuals); interestingly, female synesthetes outnumber males about 6 to 1 (Baron-Cohen, Burt, Smith-Laittan, & Harrison, 1996). This disproportionate distribution combined with the fact that synesthesia runs in families (Barron-Cohen et al., 1996) indicates that the phenomenon may have a genetic basis.

Synesthesia is generally thought to be unidirectional in nature (e.g., Mills, Boteler, & Oliver, 1999). For example, some synesthetes associate colors with digits, with the digits serving as inducers. So a synesthete may see the number 9, and have an experience of orange. However, the converse experience does not occur; the experience of orange does not lead to an experience of 9. However, some recent evidence indicates that there is some bidirectionality in the association between colors and digits in synesthetes (e.g., Knoch, Gianotti, Mohr, & Brugger, 2005).

Synesthetic experiences are not as exotic or uncommon as it may seem. Most people have cross-modal experiences in which stimuli from one sensory modality are experienced in terms of another. Martino and Marks (2001) term these garden-variety synesthetic experiences *weak synesthesia*. For example, people commonly blend touch and vision in distinguishing between "warm" and "cool" colors. Weak synesthesia is also evident in controlled laboratory settings. For example, in a study by Martino and Marks (2001), tones were presented and subjects were to rapidly classify them as high or low. Tones were accompanied either by a black or a white square. Results indicate a cross-modal interaction (weak synesthesia); high-pitched tones were more quickly classified when presented along with white squares than when presented with black squares. The opposite pattern held for low-pitched tones. This pattern is termed a *congruence effect*.

What leads to synesthetic correspondences, and do similar mechanisms underlie the strong and weak varieties? It's too early to tell. Some believe that these effects derive from the way we process sensory data at lower levels; others believe these effects derive from the way we think about the sensory dimensions. One explanation of the first type appeals to the notion of "sensory leakage" (Harrison & Baron-Cohen, 1997), in that information from one sensory modality is miscoded and/or misprocessed by another modality. In strong synesthesia, this could be due to some abnormality in the development of neural connections. A similar account can be applied to weak synesthesia. For example, the congruence between high-pitched tones and the color white could occur due to low-level sensory processes. For example, transduction processes that convert stimulus energy into neural activity may transduce high-pitched tones and the color white in a similar manner, causing the two to be perceptually associated.

Conversely, Martino and Marks (1999) propose that synesthetic effects arise from higher-level mechanisms. More specifically, they propose that the associations between sensory modalities that give rise to synesthetic effects are the product of knowledge. Synesthetic effects derive from the way we think about and linguistically code our sensory experiences. According to Martino and Marks (1999), as we experience and describe our perceptions, we build up an abstract network of concepts that applies to these experiences. With further experience, some of these concepts become strongly associated (e.g., white and high pitched, black and low pitched) such that one can automatically activate the other. So the experience of light blue activates a related concept (at least within this network)—coolness.

STOP and THINK!

A SENSE OF SYNESTHESIA

As you've read, a weak form of synesthesia occurs when we form a semantic, or meaning-based, connection between two concepts based in different senses. As we experience and describe our perceptions, we build up an abstract network of concepts that applies to these experiences.

Think about this idea, and see if you can come up with any examples of this "linguistic" synesthesia. We'll start you with a sample: Some music might be described as "bright," mixing the visual and auditory senses. Musical notes are sometimes termed "sharp," mixing the tactile and auditory senses. Colors are sometimes described as "warm" or "cool." Can you come up with any other "sense mixing" in everyday language? For the examples you generate, come up with reasons they might be connected.

Comparing the Senses

As mentioned at the outset of the chapter, vision tends to dominate research on sensation and perception, no doubt because it is the dominant sensory modality for information intake. The visual sense's domination over the other modalities has been demonstrated empirically in a variety of research paradigms, a sampling of which we now discuss.

Vision and Audition.   A great deal of information processing involves the joint intake of visual and auditory stimuli, so it's not surprising that there are some powerful interactions between the two. You'll see that in each, vision tends to dominate audition. Two examples of such interaction involve the process of sound localization. In a movie theater, the sound appears to be coming from the appropriate sources on the screen—the actors, the ringing phones, and so on. But in reality, the sound is coming from speakers positioned around the theater. Ventriloquism relies on the same effect; the voice seems to be coming from the dummy, not from the ventriloquist. The so-called **ventriloquist effect** (Bertelson, 1999) occurs when a visual cue that is presented simultaneously with an auditory stimulus biases the localization of that auditory stimulus toward the location of the visual cue.

Another example of visual dominance in audition comes from a study by Saldana and Rosenblum (1993). They presented one group of subjects visually with a video of a cello being either plucked or bowed in conjunction with a corresponding auditory stimulus—a tape recording of a cello being plucked or bowed. Other subjects were presented with only the auditory stimulus. Subjects in the visual-plus-auditory condition tended to "hear" what they saw rather than what was presented auditorially. In other words, if the subjects in both conditions heard a cello pluck, those in the auditory-only condition indicated that they heard the pluck. However, those subjects who heard the pluck and saw a cello bow indicated that they heard a bow, not a pluck.

MacDonald and McGurk (1978) investigated the role of visual information in speech perception. In their study, subjects were presented with speech sounds (e.g., /bə/); simultaneously, they were presented with a (silent) visual display of a speaker pronouncing a different speech sound (e.g., /gə/). That is, the auditory and visual information was in conflict. What "wins" in this case? Interestingly, a sort of "average" of the two speech sounds (/də/) is the resulting perception. This phenomenon has been dubbed the **McGurk effect.** Some neurological evidence provides further support for the importance of visual information in speech perception. Calvert, Bullmore, Brammer, and Campbell (1997) performed functional magnetic resonance imaging (fMRI) on individuals who were watching a speaker's lips in the absence of any auditory stimulation. Intriguingly, simply watching these speech-related lip movements led to the activation of the auditory cortex of the brain. This activation didn't occur for just any type of facial movement, however. The auditory cortex was activated only when facial movements were linguistic in nature. This neurological evidence converges with laboratory evidence indicating an important role for visual cues in speech.

Vision and Chemical Senses.   It takes only a moment's reflection to realize that there's probably an association between the look of a plate of food and how good it smells/tastes (aside from the obvious fact that spoiled food doesn't look good). Morrot, Brochet, and Dubourdieu (2001) showed evidence of just such an interaction within the

Cherry? Clove? Cocoa?

context of smelling wine. They presented a white wine that had been artificially colored to look like red wine, and gave the concoction to a panel of 54 wine experts. They then performed an analysis of the words the experts used to describe the smell of the wine. They found what might be termed a "smell illusion." The wine experts described the white wine with words typically associated with red wine (e.g., *cherry, clove, cocoa*). Basically, visual information led the experts to discount the olfactory information they were receiving.

Vision and Touch.   Vision and touch allow us to gather richly elaborate information about objects in the world. But what happens when these two senses are placed in conflict? Evidence indicates that vision exerts undue influence, just as it does in the cases of conflict between vision and audition.

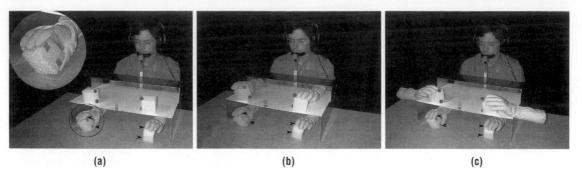

(a)   (b)   (c)

Figure 3.8 Interaction between vision and touch; setup for the Pavani, Spence, and Driver (2000) phantom hand study.

From Pavani, F., Spence, C., & Driver, J. (2000). Visual capture of touch: Out-of-body experiences with rubber gloves. *Psychological Science, 11,* 353–359. Copyright 2000 by Blackwell, Inc. Reprinted by permission.

Pavani, Spence, and Driver (2000) devised a unique test of the possible dominance of vision in touch. They placed subjects in the setup pictured in Figure 3.8a. In this experiment, subjects wore rubber gloves, and their hands were placed out of sight. Each subject held a small sponge cube with the thumb and forefinger of each hand. The cubes were equipped with tiny vibrators that could vibrate either the thumb or the forefinger position. Directly above the handheld sponge cubes were two visible sponge cubes. These sponge cubes were equipped with an LED at the top and bottom that would light up simultaneously when the respective handheld cube below was vibrated. The relationship between which LED was activated (top or bottom) and which position received the vibration (forefinger/top or thumb/bottom) was random on any given trial; sometimes they matched, and sometimes they mismatched. But activation of the lights and vibration always occurred at the same time. The subjects were to identify the source of the vibration, and reaction time for this judgment was recorded. A question of interest is the possible facilitatory or inhibitory effect of the light. Would the location of the light on the cube (top or bottom) being viewed affect the reaction time to identify the source of the vibration (top or bottom)?

Here's where the fun starts: On half of the trials, dummy hands in rubber gloves were placed on the visible cubes (the ones with the LEDs). Subjects' hands (situated below, and out of sight) were in identical rubber gloves, and the fake hands were positioned so that they looked like they could have been subjects' hands (see Figure 3.8b). Imagine what subjects would experience in this condition. They'd be looking at "hands" that are holding cubes; the LEDs on these cubes would light up at the same time they'd feel a vibration directly underneath. *Now* what happens when the visual cue and tactile stimulation match or mismatch?

The results are presented in Figure 3.9a. Subjects' speed in identifying the source of the vibration is plotted as a function of whether the viewed light matched or mismatched the position of the vibration and whether or not there were dummy hands holding the cubes. As you can see, the reaction time to identify the source of the vibration was slower

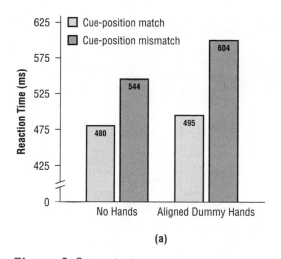
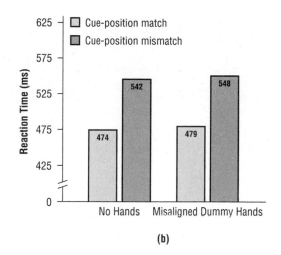

Figure 3.9 Results from the Pavani, Spence, and Driver (2000) study.

From Pavani, F., Spence, C., & Driver, J. (2000). Visual capture of touch: Out-of-body experiences with rubber gloves. *Psychological Science, 11,* 353–359. Copyright 2000 by Blackwell, Inc. Reprinted by permission.

when the light mismatched the vibration position than when it matched. More important, however, is that the dummy hands significantly accentuated this interfering effect! In the dummy hand condition, subjects were even slower (reaction time was greater) at identifying the source of the vibration when the light mismatched the vibration position. Seeing the light at a given position on the dummy hand gave rise to an illusory sensation of feeling that vibration was occurring in the corresponding position below.

Perhaps, you might think, subjects were confused because they were seeing another set of hands. In a second experiment, Pavani and colleagues (2000) replicated the same procedure but with misaligned dummy hands that were clearly fake (see Figure 3.8c). The results, shown in Figure 3.9b, make it clear that the dummy hands had no effect under these conditions. Therefore, the results of the first experiment show that subjects experienced the dummy hands as their own (to some extent). The results of this and a number of other studies underscore the fact that tactile sensations are the result of a complex blend of tactile, kinesthetic, and visual information.

Audition and Touch.   Another interesting study of a cross-modal interaction involving touch was conducted by Hötting and Röder (2004). These researchers

Research Theme: Individual Differences

were interested in the degree to which life experience shapes multisensory integration and function. They compared blind and sighted individuals in a task that involved both the tactile and the auditory modalities. Subjects were presented with a series of one to four tactile stimuli to the right index finger; simultaneously, they heard a series of one to four irrelevant tones. Their task was simply to judge the number of times their index finger had been touched. If multisensory integration occurs, one would expect the report of the number of tactile stimulations reported to be influenced by the number of irrelevant tones. You may be thinking, "Why did they compare sighted and blind individuals?" The

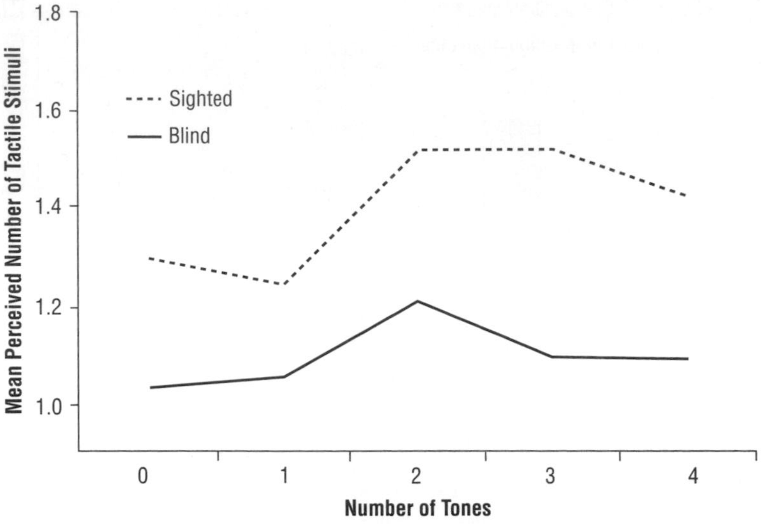

Figure 3.10 Results from the Hötting and Röder (2004) study of sensory interaction between touch and audition.

From Hötting, K., & Röder, B. (2004). Hearing cheats touch, but less in congenitally blind than in sighted individuals. *Psychological Science, 15*(1), 60–64. Copyright 2004 by Blackwell, Inc. Reprinted with permission.

researchers' thinking was that blind and sighted individuals differ not only in their unimodal (single-sense) experiences, but also in their multisensory integration. Because blind individuals are bound to have profoundly different perceptual experiences and combinations of perceptual experiences than those of sighted individuals, one might expect their processes of multisensory integration to differ.

Let's consider the design of the study. The independent variables included a subject variable (congenitally blind vs. sighted) and one critical experimental context variable (number of distractor tones presented). The dependent variable was the subjects' report of the number of tactile stimulations. The results from this study are presented in Figure 3.10. For simplicity's sake, these results are limited to the trials in which a single tactile stimulus was presented. As in the Pavani, Spence, and Driver (2000) study, the sense of touch was fooled. The more tones that subjects heard along with a single tactile stimulus, the more likely subjects were to experience more than one tactile stimulation. In addition, you'll notice an interaction between the number of tones presented and the type of subject. The disruptve effect of the tones on tactile perception was more pronounced in sighted individuals, relative to those who were congenitally blind. This supports the notion that processes of multisensory integration develop differently in the blind and the sighted. One plausible alternative account that Hötting and Röder offered was the fact that all blind subjects were experienced Braille readers. Due to this tactile expertise, they had more confidence in their tactile judgments, and were less susceptible to auditory interference. So while it's apparent that multisensory integration changes as a function of visual deprivation, it remains an open question whether the changes are due to enhanced skill in the intact modalities or to some fundamental difference in the way the senses interact.

Perception and Action

So far, we've been talking about perception in pretty passive contexts—sitting around with electrodes attached to your scalp, sitting around having your fingers stimulated, sitting around smelling wine . . . provocative research to say the least. But truth be told, much of your perception occurs not while you're sitting around, but *while you are moving.* Not only that, sometimes the objects you're perceiving are moving as well. Viewing perception in terms of one's dynamic interaction with their everyday environment is sometimes termed **embodied perception.** This notion resonates strongly with Gibson's view of direct perception, described at the outset of the chapter. According to this approach, perception is not a matter of constructing, interpreting, and building models of the environment based on previous knowledge. Instead, according to this view, perception is dynamic, immediate, and requires no previous knowledge to "construct" some sort of representation.

Proffitt (2006), in a recent review of work on embodied perception, makes the provocative statement that "A principal function of perception" is to defend people from having to think" (p. 119). According to this view, perception doesn't involve "thinking" as much as it involves "reacting." And this "reaction" is influenced by a variety of nonvisual factors such as bodily state, emotional state, and a person's goals. Proffitt's view of perception is expressly evolutionary—he claims that visual perception aids survival by making people aware of both the opportunities and the costs of action.

Some fascinating research on perception of distance and slant supports these claims. Proffitt and his colleagues have shown that perception of these two factors is quite mutable in some unexpected ways. For example, Proffitt, Bhalla, Gossweiler, and Midgett (1995) looked at the effects of fatigue on judgments of slant. They recruited subjects who were regular runners and asked them to have their most demanding run of the week coincide with the experiment. Upon arriving at the experiment site, the runners stood at the foot of a hill and were asked to make three estimates of its slant. For the verbal estimate, they simply looked at the hill and estimated how steep it was, in degrees. For the visual estimation, they took a handheld pie chart and adjusted a "piece of the pie" to reflect their estimate of the hill's slant (see Figure 3.11). For the haptic estimation, they stood at the foot of the hill and placed a hand on a movable palmboard (see Figure 3.12). They then adjusted the palmboard (without looking at their hand) to reflect their judgment of the hill's slant. After making these estimates, the subjects took their demanding run and arrived at a second hill where the same estimates were made.

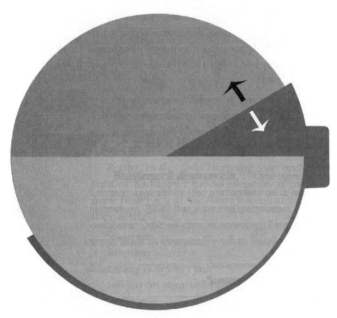

Figure 3.11 Device used for visual estimation in the Proffitt, Bhalla, Gossweiler, and Midgett (1995) study of embodied perception. Subjects estimated the slant of a hill by adjusting a small segment of the pie chart device to match the degree of slant.

From Proffitt, D.R. (2006). Embodied perception and the economy of action. *Perspectives on Psychological Science, 1*(2), 110–122. Published by Blackwell, Inc. Reprinted with permission of the author.

Figure 3.13 presents the results for the estimations of two different 5° hills. The independent variables are the time

Figure 3.12 Device used for haptic estimation in the Proffitt, Bhalla, Gossweiler, and Midgett (1995) study of embodied perception. Subjects estimated the slant of a hill by placing a hand on the movable palmboard and adjusting it (without looking at their hand) to reflect their judgment of the hill's slant.

From Proffitt, D.R. (2006). Embodied perception and the economy of action. *Perspectives on Psychological Science, 1*(2), 110–122. Published by Blackwell, Inc. Reprinted with permission of the author.

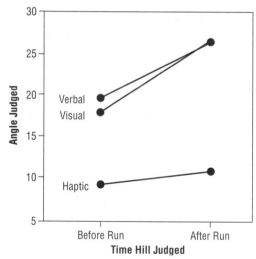

Figure 3.13 Results from the Proffitt, Bhalla, Gossweiler, and Midgett (1995) study on the effects of fatigue on slant estimation.

From Proffitt, D.R. (2006). Embodied perception and the economy of action. *Perspectives on Psychological Science, 1*(2), 110–122. Published by Blackwell, Inc. Reprinted with permission of the author.

the slant of the hill was estimated (before or after a run; you might also label this independent variable "fatigue") and type of estimation (verbal, visual, or haptic). The dependent variable is slant estimation. The results are striking. The visual and verbal estimates of slant weren't great to begin with, and the effects of fatigue were powerful. Estimates of slant for the (post-fatigue) second hill were nearly 10° greater than the estimates for the (pre-fatigue) first hill, in spite of the fact that the slant of the hills was the same! And it's not just that we're poor estimators of slant to begin with; the haptic judgments are pretty good, and unaffected by fatigue. These findings indicate that visual perception—in this case, the perception of geographic slant—is modulated by what Proffitt (2006) terms "energetic considerations," in order to promote "efficient energy expenditure." In other words, if you feel dead-tired (an energetic consideration), you probably need to rest. The illusory perception of a 5° hill as a 25° hill is more likely to prompt you to rest, which in this case, would aid the goal of "efficient energy expenditure."

It's important to note that Proffitt's view of perception is expressly evolutionary. As you probably know, the basic notion behind the evolutionary approach is that we evolve in ways that maximize our chances of survival. A key principle in survival is that energy consumption has to exceed energy expenditure. So how does this tie in with perception? Well, as Proffitt points out, perception aids in the process whereby we "economize our actions." If the energy we need to expend to accomplish something exceeds the amount of energy we have, then the action isn't worth doing. Our perceptual processes have evolved to aid in making these decisions.

STOP *and* **THINK!**

EMBODIED PERCEPTION

According to Proffitt's (2006) view of embodied perception, perceptual processes are critical in helping us assess how much energy we're going to need to expend in order to accomplish something. This aids us in deciding whether or not to engage in the action. The study you read about shows that fatigue can make hills look steeper than they really are. Might fatigue make backpacks seem heavier than they really are?

For this demonstration, you're going to annoy your friends by having them make perceptual estimates under different conditions of fatigue. Get a backpack, fill it with several books, and find out the weight of it. Then ask your friends to make estimates of its weight by just looking at it (keep the backpack open so they can see what is inside). Do this in the following conditions (you'll need to test different people in each one):

a. early in the morning
b. midday
c. late in the evening

These different conditions are meant as a manipulation of fatigue. You should also have your "subjects" rate their level of fatigue on a 1 to 10 scale after they make their weight estimate. In which conditions should the estimates of weight be the heaviest? Did your results match the prediction? Why or why not?

The previous discussion makes it apparent that our perception of the world around us isn't some static process of our sensory receptors obtaining information and subsequently calculating their respective inputs. Rather, it's a dynamic process that involves an exquisite orchestration and integration of input from all of the sensory systems, a process that occurs within the rich context of our previous experiences as well as our motives and goals.

STOP and REVIEW!

1. Distinguish between strong and weak synesthesia.
2. True or false? Vision tends to dominate all senses with the exception of audition.
3. Which of these is NOT true of the embodied perception view?
   a. It fits well with Gibson's view of direct perception.
   b. It characterizes perception as dynamic and not constructed.
   c. It characterizes perception as an evolved survival mechanism.
   d. It proposes that previous knowledge guides perception.

➤ Strong synesthesia refers to experiences in which input from one sensory system produces an experience not only in that modality but in another as well. A weaker form of synesthesia involves cross-modal associations between concepts that are based in different modalities, like dark and low-pitched tones.

➤ Vision tends to dominate the other senses. Dominance of audition is shown by the *McGurk effect*, which occurs when a visual stimulus distorts the identification of an auditory (speech) stimulus, and the *ventriloquist effect*, which occurs when a visual cue that is presented simultaneously with an auditory stimulus biases the localization of that auditory stimulus toward the location of the visual cue.

➤ Embodied perception (similar to Gibson's notion of direct perception) describes the view that perception is dynamic, immediate, and requires no previous knowledge to "construct" some sort of representation. This evolutionary view proposes that perception aids in the process whereby we "economize our actions."

Consciousness

Have you ever had the experience of driving somewhere via a familiar route and, upon arriving at your destination, having no memory whatsoever of the drive? It's a common, yet striking, phenomenon. It's frankly amazing that in spite of being engaged in the highly complex set of activities that comprise driving, you aren't particularly aware of what you're doing. Have you ever been operating in this mode, and then a squirrel darts out in front of your car? All of a sudden, you're in full-thinking mode! The squirrel (as squirrels so often do) prompted a profound change in your **consciousness** (our awareness of internal and external events). Your "autopilot" process of driving became a much more conscious one.

Within the study of cognition, no general topic has stimulated more interest than the notion of consciousness, and how consciousness relates to cognitive processes. Our consciousness of the world around us is at the very root of how we experience daily life, and many believe it is at the very root of who we are. It's an elusive concept, and has proved exceedingly difficult to define or pin down. The proliferation of terms thrown around to describe things outside of conscious awareness attests to this—we hear about things being nonconscious, subconscious, preconscious, and unconscious—and there is relatively little agreement about exactly what *non-, sub-, pre-,* and *un-* refer to, much less exactly what *conscious* means. The quest to account for the phenomenon of consciousness is currently one of the hottest topics within the interdisciplinary field of cognitive science, which spans the disciplines of (most notably) psychology, biology, and philosophy. In 2005, this quest—finding the biological basis for consciousness—was designated by the prestigious journal *Science* as one of the top 25 unanswered questions facing scientists.

Varieties of Consciousness

Block (1995) offers a helpful framework that distinguishes between four different senses of consciousness (which Block contends is a "mongrel concept" that refers to a number of different phenomena). *Monitoring* consciousness refers to one's ability to reflect on their own thinking processes; this concept was briefly mentioned in Chapter 2 as *metacognition. Self*-consciousness refers to one's general knowledge about themselves. For example, Bridget knows she's from Indiana, knows she loves to teach, and knows she loves to read mystery novels. **Access consciousness** is used when you're manipulating representations, and manipulation of representations has the potential to influence your reasoning, communication, or behavior. For example, the processes that underlie your ability to drive a car would be considered access consciousness. Whenever we process information, we're demonstrating access consciousness. But this doesn't mean that we're aware of the fact that we're processing information. This sense of subjective awareness of what our mind is currently doing is termed **phenomenal consciousness.**

STOP *and* THINK!

PHENOMENAL CONSCIOUSNESS OF CONSCIOUSNESS

Think about phenomenal consciousness; reflect on what you're thinking right now and how you think and respond throughout the day (examples would be reading, driving, etc.).

- Which sets of cognitive processes seem open enough to conscious awareness that you might be able to describe correctly how they work? That is, there seems to be some convergence of access and phenomenal consciousness.
- Which processes seem completely closed to phenomenal consciousness, and therefore are comprised almost completely of access consciousness processes?

Let's return to our driving example. When you're cruising along, not a care in the world, you are deeply involved in access consciousness. All of your mental processes are whirring and clicking, with predictable results: you stop at the red, go at the green, and make all the necessary turns. The fact that you barely notice it and don't remember it later indicates that you had little phenomenal consciousness of the act of driving—it's almost as if you had no subjective experience of driving at all. But the picture changes drastically when the squirrel makes its appearance. When that happens, you are jolted into phenomenal consciousness as you stop and pay attention to what you were thinking, doing, and feeling. The vast majority of the research you'll read about in the rest of the text deals with the processes of access consciousness. Cognitive psychology research is all about the nature of the representations that allow us to reason and communicate, and how those representations are accessed and manipulated. And, as implied by our driving example, many of these processes operate outside of our phenomenal consciousness—that is, our subjective experience.

The fact that cognitive processes lie largely outside of our phenomenal consciousness creates a bit of a pickle for researchers. It renders subjective experience highly suspect; I can't just ask you how you read, remember, or perceive things, because these processes in large part are not open to introspection. Indeed, this is a major reason the structuralist approach to cognition discussed in Chapter 1 was doomed to fail.

Let's examine this point a little more closely within the context of perception. As you might imagine, access consciousness and phenomenal consciousness are associated with quite different dependent variables. If I want to assess your phenomenal consciousness, I simply ask you what you're perceiving, thinking, or feeling, and take careful notes on your responses. But, as noted above, verbal report isn't a complete or unbiased reflection of cognitive processing. Perception also involves a willingness to report an event. Think about bumps you may have heard in the night. Did you really perceive them, or were they a product of your imagination? The important point here is that, in addition to a discrimination process based on sensitivity, perception involves a *decision* regarding whether a stimulus was perceived. This important insight forms part of the basis for **signal detection theory,** an approach to psychophysics that characterizes perceptual experiences as the joint product of **sensitivity** and **response bias.** Of two people, one may succeed and the other fail to perceive some stimulus (e.g., a sound) because one observer is more sensitive than the other, or because one observer is more willing to report that they perceived the stimulus. Due to response bias and other possible biases on the part of the subject, not many studies rely on phenomenal consciousness to assess cognitive processing. A final strike against the reliance on phenomenal consciousness as a tool for assessing cognitive processing is that most of the cognitive processes of interest take place rapidly. Therefore, more subtle measures like reaction time and accuracy are needed to reveal their intricacies.

Dissociations of Access and Phenomenal Consciousness.   As you've probably gathered from the discussion up to this point, one of the most interesting topics of investigation in perception is cases in which access consciousness and phenomenal consciousness diverge. Another way of stating this is that different types of consciousness dissociate from one another. They behave in different ways and are influenced by different variables.

Authorship Processing.   Stop reading right now, and raise your hand. Go ahead, do it! Now, how would you describe the sequence of events that led you to raise your hand? Sounds like a stupid question, right? You're probably thinking, "I read a command

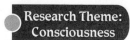
Research Theme: Consciousness

to raise my hand, processed those instructions, and decided to raise my hand." So your belief is that you had *authorship* of that action. Consciousness led to will, and will caused you to raise

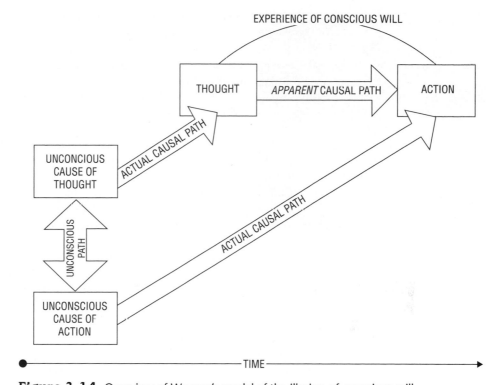

Figure 3.14 Overview of Wegner's model of the illusion of conscious will.

Adapted from Wegner, D.M. & Wheatley, T. (1999). Apparent mental causation: Sources of the experience of will. *American Psychologist, 54*(7), 480–492.

your hand. While that may be your subjective experience of what happened (i.e., your phenomenal consciousness), this is what Wegner (Wegner, 2003; Wegner & Sparrow, 2004) and his colleagues term the **illusion of conscious will**—the "mind's best trick."

It's quite a challenging notion, that our conscious experience of will is illusory; it's a notion that fits uncomfortably well with the idea that free will itself is an illusion. Now that's a metaphysical quagmire into which we dare not tread. We'll settle for explaining Wegner's major assumptions. A simple overview of the conscious will illusion is presented in Figure 3.14. Note that subjectively (phenomenal consciousness), the apparent causal path is from our conscious will to an action. However, both the feeling of conscious will and the action itself are caused by separate, unconscious processes. Another way of thinking about it is in terms of correlation not equaling causation—even though our feeling of will is highly correlated with our actions, that association does not necessarily indicate a causal relationship.

This illusion is a product of **authorship processing,** the set of processes that leads us to attribute events to the entities that are thought to have caused them. Why would we even question this feeling? Aren't we pretty good at figuring out whether we (or someone else) authored an action? Not according to Wegner, who points out many instances of mistakes in authorship processing. One such example is the infamous Ouija

Who's in control?

board, a game in which users place their fingers on a device termed a *planchet,* and (supposedly) spirits guide their movements to spell out messages from beyond. This certainly seems to be a situation in which our attribution of authorship is mistaken.

What are the preconditions for a subjective experience of conscious will that might be mistaken? Wegner and Sparrow (2004) mention several, including direct bodily feedback, feedback from visual perception, and action-relevant thought. For example, at the start of this section, we asked you to raise your hand. You no doubt had the subjective experience that you consciously willed your arm up. This experience (illusory, in Wegner's view) was encouraged by the facts that (a) you felt your arm raise, (b) you saw your arm raise, and (c) this was in close coincidence with the thought that "the authors want me to raise my arm."

A more detailed account of the theory, along with critiques from other researchers and theorists, can be found in Wegner (2004). But a closer look at one of the studies supporting this view is warranted. Wegner, Sparrow, and Winerman (2004) were interested in the conditions that might lead one to have an illusory experience of control over the movements of others. To investigate the question, they used a unique setup in which they recruited pairs of subjects and put them in the situation pictured in Figure 3.15. As you can see, the setup was rather odd. The person in back was the one moving their own arms, but the situation was arranged so that it appeared to the person in front (passive observer) that it was their own arms that were

(a)

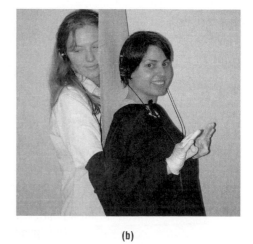

(b)

Figure 3.15 A passive observer subject from the study by Wegner, Sparrow, and Winerman (2004).

From Wegner, D. M, Sparrow, B., Winerman, L. (2004). Vicarious agency: experiencing control over the movements of others. *Journal of Personality and Social Psychology, 86*(6), 838–848. Reprinted with permission from the American Psychological Association and the author.

moving. The person in front is the subject of interest. Wegner et al. wanted to find out whether that person might experience an illusion of conscious will over the movements of another—in this case, the person behind them. The person in back was given commands to raise their arm, wave their hand while the person in front stood passively (arms down and covered by a smock), and watched the odd scenario in a mirror that they were facing.

Now, here's the critical manipulation: In one condition, the passive observer was hearing the instructions through headphones as they were given; in another condition, the passive observer heard nothing. Recall Wegner et al.'s idea that the experience of conscious will is having a relevant thought in close conjunction with an action. Therefore, if the passive observer was listening to the commands being given to the person in back, this would increase the feeling that they were somehow controlling or willing the action that occurred. Obviously this feeling would be in striking error, as the passive observer did nothing. Wegner et al. assessed the observer's experience with a simple rating scale in which subjects rated the degree to which they felt they were consciously willing the arm movement that they were viewing in the mirror. Consistent with the authors' suspicions, passive observers who heard the instructions as they were given gave higher ratings of conscious will and control than did those who had not heard the instructions. So basically, people had a strong experience of phenomenal consciousness. But they had absolutely no access consciousness of the action, because they weren't doing anything!

What vs. Where: Blindsight.   Now let's consider a converse dissociation—a case in which a person has no subjective experience of something but their behavior is affected by it.

Research Theme: Neuroscience ▶

In other words, there is access consciousness in the absence of phenomenal consciousness. This is what happens in the surprising phenomenon termed **blindsight**, detailed in a case study by Weiskrantz (1986). His patient, D. B., was blind to the entire left side of his visual field as the result of surgery to remove enlarged blood vessels in his right visual cortex. The wiring of the visual system is such that information presented to the left of center goes to the right part of each eye, and ends up being processed in the right visual cortex. The opposite is true for visual information presented to the right of center. So the right hemisphere receives information from the left visual field, and the left hemisphere receives information from the right. Consistent with this, D. B. reported no awareness of objects or events on his left. However, there were some intriguing suggestions that he had some knowledge of them. For example, he could accurately reach for a person's outstretched hand in order to shake it. He attributed this type of success to lucky guessing, swearing up and down that he didn't see it—that is, he was visually unaware. In Block's terms, he was demonstrating access consciousness in the absence of phenomenal consciousness.

To investigate D. B.'s deficits and abilities more systematically, Weiskrantz (1986) placed him in controlled visual settings and presented a variety of stimuli to his left and right visual fields. Whenever stimuli were presented to the left visual field, D. B. reported seeing nothing (self-reported blindness). Weiskrantz then employed a *forced-choice procedure* to find out what if anything D. B. knew about the stimulus he claimed not to see. In a forced-choice procedure, subjects are given two alternative answers and are *forced* to choose the correct one—"I don't know" is not an acceptable answer. After presenting visual stimuli, Weiskrantz asked D. B. to make a forced choice about some aspect of the stimulus, such as where it occurred, or in the case of stimulus lines, the orientation of the lines. His performance under these conditions was quite surprising—his accuracy was well above chance. In spite of his lack of visual awareness (i.e., no phenomenal consciousness), he was able to process some information about the stimuli (i.e., there was access consciousness). Weiskrantz termed the phenomenon *blindsight* to underscore the seeming contradiction between the capacity to classify presented stimuli in some respect while being unaware that it has been presented.

Subsequent research on blindsight (along with other research on the visual system) has indicated that there are two distinct neurological systems underlying vision that are dissociated in the case of blindsight. One of these systems, based primarily in the visual cortex, is responsible for identifying, recognizing, and becoming aware of visual stimuli. This is often termed a *what system*. The other system, which functions at an earlier point in visual processing (i.e., a subcortical system), is concerned with detection and localization (i.e., a *where system*). So basically, the patient D. B. had an intact "where" system but a deficient "what" system. Analogous "what versus where" systems seem to exist in audition (e.g., Rauschecker & Tian, 2000) and touch (e.g., Reed, Klatzky, & Halgren, 2005).

Subliminal Perception

An issue that has been the subject of hot debate both in the public arena and in cognition laboratories is the relative influence of stimuli of which we are unaware. You saw that such stimuli can have an influence in cases of blindsight. In the lay literature, the effects of **subliminal perception** can allegedly be seen in many different guises. Many proponents (e.g., Key, 1973) claim that ice cubes in vodka ads, heavy metal rock songs, and the frames of movies contain insidious subliminal messages that exert an influence on our behavior. One of the most famous examples of supposed subliminal influence (the example most students relate when they claim that subliminal influence is for real) was reported in 1957 by advertising expert James Vicary, who (self-) reportedly embedded the messages "eat popcorn" and "drink Coke" in a movie, resulting in a rush of movie watchers to the concession stands to buy refreshments. Almost everyone has heard some version of this story. However, almost no one knows that Vicary later admitted that it was a hoax—a story he cooked up to generate some publicity for a struggling advertising firm (see Weir, 1984). But based on stories like this and other anecdotal evidence, people tend to believe in the reality of subliminal influence.

Cognitive research has revealed extremely subtle (though consistent) effects of subliminally presented stimuli, but not the large-scale effects claimed by Vicary and others. One reason for the gulf between popular opinion and research results is a lack of precision in definition. When your local newscaster or your Aunt Edna says something about subliminal perception, the term *subliminal* could simply mean "not attended." This is unfortunate, since the difference between "not attended" and "not perceived" proves to be critical when assessing whether a stimulus is likely to affect processing. As you'll see in Chapter 4, it's clear that unattended stimuli can exert an influence on behavior. In Chapter 6, you'll see that information we don't remember can also influence our behavior. But subliminal literally means "below threshold"—that is, it cannot be perceived. So the sound of people murmuring behind you in class is not subliminal; it's simply not attended to (hopefully!). The real question of subliminal perception is whether stimuli that aren't even judged as being present at all can influence behavior. As you'll see, there are even subtler definitional shadings to the notion of subliminal.

Contrary to popular belief, there's no reason to believe that subliminal messages in music influence behavior; they may not even exist at all!

The Empirical Evidence. Marcel (1983) conducted a series of studies to investigate the possibility of subliminal perception. The procedure involved a task in which subjects

Research Theme: Consciousness

were presented with a color patch on a screen and were asked to name the color as quickly as possible. The presentation of the color patch was preceded by a word that either was neutral (table-orange patch) or matched the color patch (orange-orange patch). Comparison of these two conditions should indicate what is termed **priming**—reaction time should be faster when the color patch is preceded by a matching word, relative to when it is preceded by a neutral word.

So what makes this procedure a test of subliminal perception? The catch was that the word presented before the color patch (called a *prime*) was (on some trials) presented subliminally—that is, subjects could not see it. To ensure that the prime could not be seen, Marcel ran a pretest for each subject in which color words were presented extremely quickly. He basically wanted to find the point at which the subjects achieved approximately chance performance in saying that they had detected a word. He then used these individualized exposure times to present the primes subliminally. He also tested subjects in a **supraliminal** (above the threshold of conscious awareness, or clearly visible) prime condition, in which prime words were clearly visible.

Would a prime presented at a level at which subjects had reported not seeing anything at all produce an effect on responding? Marcel's results showed that it did. If the prime word matched the color of the patch, it facilitated (speeded) responding, relative to a condition in which the prime word was neutral. The prime words influenced the speed of color naming even if the primes were presented at a level in which subjects reported not being aware of them. It's important to note that these effects were much greater when primes were presented supraliminally rather than subliminally.

Subjective and Objective Thresholds.

A great deal of consternation about the study of subliminal perception has centered on exactly how to define *subliminal*. Marcel (1983) defined it in terms of what subjects *said* they perceived. *Subliminal* was defined as the conditions under which subjects guessed about half the time that there was a prime presented. You might say that Marcel defined the threshold *subjectively*—solely in terms of the subjects' phenomenal consciousness. Others (e.g., Cheesman & Merikle, 1984) have emphasized the importance of what is termed an objective threshold—that is, the level at which *performance on some task* (not subjects' self-report) indicates that the prime was not perceived.

They point out that in the Marcel procedure, in which awareness was defined subjectively, subjects may have perceived the prime but were conservative in saying that they had. So even though they said they were unaware, they may have been aware. This relates to two concepts of psychophysics discussed earlier: When subjects reported that they hadn't perceived the subliminal prime, it may have been a matter of *sensitivity* (they truly did not detect it), or a matter of *response bias* (they were conservative in their reporting). A third possibility is that they truly were not aware of the stimulus (i.e., they had no phenomenal consciousness), but some low-level processing occurred outside of their conscious awareness (i.e., they were engaged in access consciousness). In this case, their report of "I don't see it" was only partially true.

Cheesman and Merikle (1984) were concerned about this third possibility and attempted to replicate Marcel's study while adding a twist of their own. They used the same task—a primed color identification task—but they were more stringent about the way they determined that a prime was presented *subliminally*. Recall that Marcel defined subliminal as the level at which subjects said about half the time that a word had occurred. Cheesman and Merikle defined it differently—in a pretest, they presented prime words for different durations. After each presentation, subjects were asked (as they were in the Marcel study) if they had seen anything. In cases where they failed to detect a word, they were then presented with four color names and forced to choose which they had seen. Note that if their guessing performance matched their self-report, they shouldn't have been able to guess the color more than 25% of the time. But even under conditions in which subjects reported seeing nothing, they guessed the color they had seen at a level much higher than chance. This demonstrates that some information about the stimulus must had been processed (which is evidence of access consciousness); otherwise, guessing would have been at chance levels.

Cheesman and Merikle (1984) tested the effects of prime words presented under the conditions identified in the pretest. In the objective threshold condition, primes were presented under conditions that had led to chance levels of performance in the forced-choice pretest (25%). The authors believed that this was the condition that truly involved subliminal presentation, because at this level of exposure, subjects couldn't guess what color had occurred with any level of proficiency. Thus, this condition used what was termed an **objective threshold.** In a second condition, they presented primes under conditions that had led to 55% accurate guessing in the pretest (percentage used by Marcel). This latter condition used what Cheesman and Merikle termed a **subjective threshold**—subjects

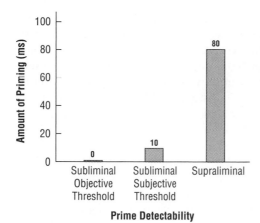

Figure 3.16 Results from the Cheesman and Merikle (1984) priming study. The bars indicate priming scores, which reflect the difference between reaction times on trials that included a prime and trials that did not include a prime.

From Cheesman, J., & Merikle, P. M. (1984). Priming with and without awareness. *Perception & Psychophysics, 36,* 387–395. Reprinted with permission of the Psychonomic Society, Inc.

reported that they couldn't see the prime words, yet their guessing performance indicated otherwise.

The results of this study are presented in Figure 13.16, which shows the amount of priming observed in reaction times as a function of prime condition—supraliminal, subliminal as defined objectively, and subliminal as defined subjectively. As you can see, primes presented below an objective threshold failed to influence performance (i.e., reaction time did not differ from a neutral prime). But primes that were presented below a subjective threshold did produce a statistically significant (albeit small) degree of priming, replicating Marcel's results; priming occurred even though subjects reported not being aware of the prime. Cheesman and Merikle concluded that the reality of subliminal perception depends on how one defines the threshold of awareness below which the stimuli presented are deemed *subliminal*. Defined subjectively, subliminal perception exists; objectively, subliminal perception does not exist. It's important to note that even when subliminal influences are found, they tend to be small effects, on the order of 1/20th of a second.

Subliminal Self-Help? Do the subtle effects reported in laboratory studies of subliminal influence translate into any real effects? One common application of what might be termed *subliminal perception technology* involves presenting subliminal messages on tapes. Such tapes claim to offer assistance with everything from weight loss to alleviating depression to curing acne (see Druckman & Bjork, 1991, for a more complete list). Is there any evidence that such tapes work? Usually, their advertisers cite the evidence of testimonials from satisfied customers. But even if these testimonials are real, they aren't very compelling evidence. Satisfied customers represent a biased sample; people who listen to self-help tapes are certainly motivated to make the change targeted by the tape. Any observed behavioral change may simply be the result of these motivational factors.

STOP *and* **THINK!**

SUBHELPFUL SUBLIMINAL PROGRAMS

Search the Internet and magazines for advertisements and descriptions of subliminal self-help programs (or other subliminal claims). Take note of what they claim and how the subliminal message is delivered.

To separate the possible effects of subliminal self-help messages from motivational effects, one needs to conduct a double-blind study of the effects. Greenwald,

Spangenberg, Pratkanis, and Eskenazi (1991) conducted a double-blind study on the effectiveness of subliminal message tapes. They used commercially manufactured tapes that had subliminal messages embedded within classical music, popular music, or nature sounds. In a clever procedure, they gave subjects one of two tapes with an embedded subliminal message; the message was designed to improve either self-esteem or memory. However, the label on each tape was randomly assigned. A tape labeled "memory improvement" was actually a self-esteem tape for some subjects, and a tape labeled "self-esteem improvement" was actually a memory improvement tape for some subjects. Subjects were given pretests that included measures of memory and self-esteem and were then instructed to listen to their tapes every day for one month. They then returned for a series of posttests, including retests of memory and self-esteem. Subjects were also asked to rate whether they believed their self-esteem and memory had improved.

The results were clear: the posttest measures of self-esteem and memory showed none of the expected improvement over the pretest measures in any of the conditions. The only consistent effect that emerged was a subject-expectancy effect. When asked about their perceived improvement, subjects were generally of the opinion that they had improved in whatever quality (memory or self-esteem) was on the tape label (even if the tape had been labeled incorrectly). For example, subjects who saw a "self-esteem improvement" label on their tape thought that they had made improvements in their self-esteem, regardless of what was actually on the tape.

Subliminal Perception and Top-Down Processing.   Subliminal messaging is also challenged by another line of research, one that indicates that messages embedded in various media (e.g., print ads and rock music) are actually creations of the lookers' or listeners' imaginations. Vokey and Read (1988) demonstrated this in an informative series of studies. In one of their studies, they investigated the phenomenon of backmasking—the alleged presence and influence of messages on record albums (which were all the rage before CDs) that are supposedly discernible if the records are played backward. According to some, these backmasked messages embedded in rock albums are capable of eliciting negative effects in listeners. In an especially tragic case, the heavy metal band Judas Priest was sued by the parents of two teenagers who jointly attempted suicide. Sadly, one of the boys succeeded; the other died from drug complications a few years later (Moore, 1996). The plaintiffs alleged that subliminal messages in the music played a role in prompting this tragedy. After hearing expert testimony on both sides, the judge ruled in favor of the defendants. (See Moore, 1996, for an excellent discussion of this case, as well as an informative discussion of lay and legal belief about the effectiveness of subliminal messaging.)

Vokey and Read demonstrated that you can hear just about anything in a garbled message, as long as you have an expectation that you're going to hear something. In one of their studies, they made backward recordings of Lewis Carroll's *Jabberwocky* ("Twas Brillig and the Slithy Toves . . .") and the 23rd Psalm ("The Lord is my shepherd . . ."). The experimenters did some (in their words) "creative listening" to these backward tapes and detected a few sequences that could be heard as something meaningful. Among these were "Saw a girl with a weasel in her mouth" and "I saw Satan." Now, mind you, these messages weren't really there; the garbled noise that was there could be construed into these messages by the creative listener. The experimenters found six such passages for each of the two recordings. They then gave subjects a simple task: they were to listen to the backward recordings to see if they could hear the messages designated by the experimenter. Each subject was given only the six messages for one of the passages; for the other passage, they listened without any prior prompting about what they might hear. As Vokey and Read suspected, subjects were very good at hearing the backmasked messages, but only the ones that they were told to expect. The six messages in the control passage, extracted by the experimenters but not mentioned to the subjects, were never heard by the control group. So in essence, the subjects created the backmasked messages because they expected to hear them; when they didn't expect them, they didn't hear them. Clearly, top-down processing is at work here: the data are garbled, but expectations and knowledge impose order on this garbled data.

To sum up: the only solid evidence for subliminal influence consists of smallish reaction time effects on laboratory tasks. The empirical evidence for successful application of subliminal messaging in real-world situations is extremely weak, almost nonexistent.

STOP *and* **REVIEW!**

1. Phenomenal consciousness is to access consciousness as:
   a. aware is to unaware
   b. sensation is to perception
   c. subjective experience is to manipulation
   d. mind is to brain
2. True or false? Blindsight is an example of access consciousness in the absence of phenomenal consciousness.
3. How does the presence of a subliminal priming effect relate to how the threshold of awareness is defined?

➤ Phenomenal consciousness refers to subjective awareness of what our mind is currently doing; access consciousness refers to the manipulation of representations in the service of thinking. Dissociations between these types of consciousness (i.e., one is present in the absence of the other) are commonplace.

➤ People often experience illusions of authorship, believing that they consciously willed an action when in reality, they did not. Blindsight is associated with a specific type of visual impairment, and occurs when an individual reports not seeing a stimulus (absence of phenomenal conscious) that had been presented. In spite of this, they often guess correctly about the location of the stimulus (presence of access consciousness).

➤ One example of a dissociation is the effect of subliminal primes. Primes presented below a subjectively defined threshold of conscious awareness have the capacity to speed reaction times to target stimuli. However, if the threshold of awareness is defined objectively, subliminal primes have no effect. The long-term effects of subliminal stimuli are limited.

Perceptual Processing and Attention

We've seen that stimuli that lie below our threshold of awareness have minimal impact. They may have a short-run influence on reaction times to computerized stimuli but little or no long-term impact. A subliminally presented message to buy Coke probably won't make you go out and buy Coke the next day. Information doesn't really have a long-term impact unless it is brought into the focus of our attention. As defined earlier, attention refers to the processes used to monitor and focus on incoming information. Recall the distinction between pre-attentive and post-attentive processing; much of what we've talked about thus far would be considered pre-attentive, or at least "early" in the stages of attentional processing. In this section as well as in the next chapter, we'll take a look at some of the particulars of post-attentive (or simply, attentive) processing—how it's allocated, and how it goes awry.

Visual Attention

One essential characteristic of our attention is that it's limited. Because you simply can't process all of the information in the environment at once, there needs to be some type of mechanism(s) for directing attention. So what makes you pay attention to a certain object as you look at a scene? This is actually (at least) two different questions. The first involves what you monitor or focus on during processing. The second involves what "grabs," or captures, your attention.

Spatial and Object-Based Attention.   When you drive, how do you pay attention? If you think about it, you probably realize that there are at least two possible modes. First, you pay attention to what's in front of you, almost as if you're shining a sort of attentional "spotlight" on the scene. Things in the middle of the scene get the most attentional "light," and this light dims a bit as you move into the periphery. Now suppose you notice a rather erratic driver, their car weaving in and out of its lane—another inconsiderate driver on their cell phone, perhaps? Don't get me started. Anyway, you're likely to begin paying attention to *that car in particular* (in addition to the more diffuse attention already discussed). This example highlights the difference between the two basic types of attention.

The first type of attention, paying attention to the region of space in front of you, can be termed **spatial attention.** According to this view of attention, you direct your attention to a spatial location within a scene. This mode of attention has been likened to a spotlight (e.g., Posner, 1980) or to the zoom lens of a camera (Eriksen & Yeh, 1985). The second type of attention, paying attention to particular objects of importance or salience, has been termed **object-based attention** (e.g., Cave & Bichot, 1999). In the driving example, you are likely going to be following the swerving car with your visual attention even as the car weaves in and out of the "spotlight." A good deal of research now indicates that we can operate in either of these attentional modes, although the nature of their interaction remains unclear and is being actively investigated (e.g., Lamy & Tsal, 2000; Soto & Blanco, 2004).

Attentional Capture and Inattentional Blindness.   So when we are focusing our attention on a visual scene, what objects grab the spotlight? This issue, termed **attentional capture,** refers to occasions in which a person's attention is involuntarily drawn by some stimulus. And as you'll see, some of the most provocative findings from the study of visual attention are startling demonstrations of failures in attentional capture. You couldn't miss a gorilla walking into a room . . . or could you?

Studies of what grabs or fails to grab someone's attention have been conducted within two quite different research paradigms, recently distinguished by Most, Scholl, Clifford, and Simons (2005) as *implicit* and *explicit* attentional capture. Both lines of research attempt to specify what stimulus changes lead to (or don't lead to) shifts in attention. Studies that investigate attentional capture in the implicit sense look at whether changes in visual displays lead to changes in subtle measures of subject performance like eye movements or response time. For example, in the attention-cuing research paradigm, subjects are presented with a visual display in which they must find some target stimulus. The target is preceded by a cue that indicates where the stimulus will likely appear. When the cue is valid, reaction times to the target are fast; when it's invalid, reaction times to the target are slow (e.g., Colegate, Hoffman, & Eriksen, 1973; Posner, 1980). Hence, differences in reaction times are used to indicate attentional shifts. Whether or not subjects are consciously aware of their attentional shifts isn't at all clear. Here we again see the divergence of access and phenomenal consciousness. Changes in access consciousness (i.e., shifts in attention) aren't necessarily noticed phenomenologically.

Most et al. (2005) argue that studies measuring implicit effects of attentional shifts are of limited practical relevance. They provide the following example: Suppose you're driving down the street, fiddling with the radio as a child runs out in front of you. An implicit reflection of the attentional shift might be that you slow down in turning the radio knob. This change in attention is almost certainly occurring outside of conscious awareness. However, this level of attentional shifting isn't going to help the child. The most critical measure of an attentional shift in this case is that you *notice* the child running in front of you—an instance of *explicit* attentional capture. Studies that investigate attentional capture in the explicit sense are expressly designed to figure out which stimulus changes do and do not capture conscious awareness and have yielded some startling results.

Consider the strange phenomenon of **inattentional blindness** (e.g., Mack & Rock, 1998), which refers to a failure to notice obvious changes or events in our visual environment. Basically, you can be staring right at something and not see it. This phenomenon and a related one, failures in **change detection** (Rensink, 2002; Simons & Levin, 1997), have been demonstrated in many studies using a variety of research paradigms. For example, Simons and Chabris (1999) showed observers an experimenter-created video of two teams of three players each passing a basketball around. The players moved, threw bounce passes, waved their arms, and generally kept moving around while passing to one another. One team was dressed in black T-shirts, the other in white. The task of the subjects was to watch the "game" and keep track of some activity—for example, the number of bounce passes thrown by the black-shirted team. The twist was that right in the middle of the game, an extremely bizarre event occurred: A person in a gorilla suit strolled into the scene in plain view, beat its chest a few times, and strolled off

Research Theme: Consciousness

Figure 3.17 Still photos from film shown to subjects in the Simon and Chabris (1999) study. (Photos provided by Daniel Simons.)

Simons, D. J., & Chabris, C. F. (1999). Gorillas in our midst: Sustained inattentional blindness for dynamic events. *Perception, 28,* 1059–1074.

(see Figure 3.17). The major empirical questions of interest were: Would subjects fail to notice the unusual event, and what variables might affect the probability of their noticing? Simons and Chabris (1999) manipulated task difficulty by having some subjects count the total number of passes by the attended team (easy condition) while having others keep separate counts of bounce and aerial passes by the attended team (difficult condition). They also manipulated whether the attended team was perceptually similar to the critical event (the gorilla) by having some subjects count passes for the black-shirted team (similar condition) and others count passes for the white-shirted team (different condition).

After the observation session, subjects reported their counts, and then they were asked whether they had noticed anything unusual during the game. Figure 3.18 displays the percentage of people who reported the unusual event. You'd no doubt expect 100% across the board. But astoundingly, a significant proportion of subjects completely missed the gorilla! A demanding visual task essentially compromised their ability to notice other things that had occurred *in the same visual space.* As you can see, the probability of noticing was dependent on two variables. First, subjects were less likely to notice the unusual event if their visual task was hard rather than easy. Second, subjects were less likely to notice the unusual event if the features of the attended task mismatched those of the unusual event. The gorilla suit was black; subjects were more likely to notice it if they had been counting the passes of the black-shirted team rather than those of the white-shirted team.

Striking failures to pick up on rather obvious changes in visual scenes have also been investigated using a change detection paradigm in which subjects are presented with two versions of a scene that alternate with one another rapidly (termed a **flicker paradigm**). One feature changes between the two versions, essentially disappearing and reappearing. Although the difference is obvious when the scenes are viewed side by side, viewing them in rapid alternation makes it surprisingly difficult to detect the change.

	Easy Attentional Task	Difficult Attentional Task
High Similarity	83	58
Low Similarity	42	50

Figure 3.18 Results from the Simon and Chabris (1999) study. Numbers refer to the percentage of subjects who noticed the gorilla, as a function of attentional task difficulty and T-shirt similarity to the gorilla.

From Simons, D. J. & Chabris, C. F. (1999). Gorillas in our midst: Sustained inattentional blindness for dynamic events. *Percerption, 28,* 1059–1074. Pion Limited, London. Reprinted with permission of Pion Limited and the author.

STOP *and* **THINK!** ━━━━━━━━━━━━━━━━

A couple great change blindness demonstrations are available on the Web. One of them is at Daniel Simons's Web site, which features footage from his famous gorilla study (among others). Several different short videos show the passing game interrupted by the gorilla. http://viscog.beckman.uiuc.edu/djs_lab/demos.html

Another set of demonstrations is available at Ronald Rensink's Web site; these feature the flicker paradigm in which two pictures rapidly alternate. The twist is that something changes between the two frames, and it's exceptionally hard to see what it is when the frames alternate rapidly. http://www.psych.ubc.ca/~viscoglab/demos.htm

Show either or both of these to some of your friends, and see if they can catch the changes/unusual events. You may even want to make it a little more interesting by varying the instructions you give them. For example, when having them view the gorilla video, vary whether you tell them to count the passes of the white-shirted team or the black-shirted team, or whether you make them sort out aerial passes and bounce passes.

━━━

A cross-cultural study by Nisbett and Masuda (2003) yielded some interesting results that suggest fundamental differences between Eastern (e.g., Japan, Korea, China) and Western (e.g., United States and Europe) cultures in scene perception. They based their hypothesis about perceptual differences on well-established differences between Eastern and Western views of the world. Generally, Eastern cultures tend to view the world holistically in terms of change, interrelatedness, and an emphasis on context. Western cultures have converse inclinations, with the tendencies to de-emphasize change and context and to emphasize the importance of objects rather than backgrounds. The investigators believed that these deeply rooted differences might be associated with a **perceptual set**, or a tendency to attend to and visually analyze scenes in a particular way. More specifically, they hypothesized that Eastern observers (in this case, Japanese) would be better at detecting changes in scenes when those changes involved background context than when the changes involved central objects. They made the converse set of prediction for Western observers. Their results fit the hypothesis neatly, as you can see in Figure 3.19. Japanese subjects found it easier to detect changes that occurred in the background rather than those that occurred in focal objects, whereas U.S. subjects found it easier to detect changes that occurred in the focal objects rather than those that occurred in the background.

Research Theme: Culture

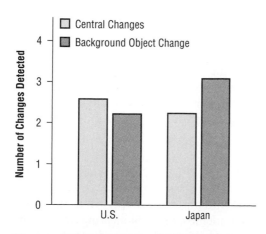

Figure 3.19 Results from Nisbett and Masuda's (2003) study of cultural differences in change detection.

From Nisbett, R. E., & Masuda, T. (2003). Culture and point of view. *Proceedings of the National Academy of Sciences, 100,* 11163–11170. Reprinted with permission of the author.

The phenomena of inattentional and change blindness highlight a couple of important general concepts in visual attention. For example, Rensink (2002) emphasizes the importance of *coherence*—the notion that visual attention is necessary to hold the elements of a visual scene together (Treisman & Gormican, 1988). Visual attention is like "perceptual glue," and when it is absent, features become transient and difficult to perceive—in a word, "unglued." In the Simons and Chabris (1999) gorilla-noticing study, subjects were so focused on counting the basketball passes—in other words, on keeping that scene glued together—that they had precious little attention left to notice the gorilla; to stretch the metaphor to its limit, the gorilla didn't "stick."

Another important issue proposed by Most, Scholl, Clifford, and Simons (2005) is what they term an **attentional set,** which refers basically to one's strategy or mind-set when watching a visual scene. Again, consider the subjects in the Simon and Chabris (1999) study. They watched a scene in which individuals moved around and continually passed basketballs to one other, and were instructed to count the number of passes for a given team. This gave them the attentional set "OK, I have to watch this game and pay particular attention to bounce passes from people wearing the black T-shirts"—a set that basically "tuned their attention to a certain frequency," if you will. Note that they were more likely to notice the surprising event when the features of that event matched the "frequency" (black gorilla suit, black T-shirts).

The phenomena of inattentional blindness and change blindness underscore the importance of visual attention in providing a coherent view of the world around us. Simply looking is not enough. As you'll see in the next chapter, there are very good empirical reasons to be worried about driving while on your cell phone, in terms of trying to juggle the tasks of driving and talking on the cell phone. The phenomenon of inattentional blindness also provides a grave caution to those who try to stretch their visual attention too far. As the Simons and Chabris (1999) study shows, you can be looking at the exact region where something critical is happening and flat out miss it—particularly when your attention is drained, like it is when you're chatting it up on your cell phone. Indeed, Strayer, Drews, and Johnston (2003) found that the degree of inattentional blindness experienced while driving increases with concurrent cell phone use. As eloquently summarized by Most et al. (2005), an understanding of the factors that lead one to notice an unexpected event ". . . carries with it important applications to everyday life, where the difference between comedy, tragedy, and fortune often rides on whether one sees the unexpected."

Auditory Attention

Many of the phenomena of perception and attention just discussed within the visual domain have an auditory analog. In fact, much if not most of the pioneering work on the limited nature of attention and the fate of unattended stimuli was conducted using the auditory sense. Much of the pioneering work, done in the middle of the 20th century, was inspired by the applied problems of the day. British psychologists Donald Broadbent (1958) and Colin Cherry (1953) were interested in the difficulties pilots encountered in World War II. These pilots faced complex control panels with a bewildering combination of visual and auditory displays. Monitoring these displays and responding appropriately

A formidable problem of selective and divided attention.

presented an incredible challenge—a situation of sensory overload! Therefore, early theories of attention attempted to explain how our cognitive systems operate under conditions of sensory overload. This sensory overload is sometimes conceived of as a "bottleneck"—a passageway that gets jammed if too much information tries to get through. Some type of selective mechanism would seem to be a necessity.

Recall the "spotlight" conception of selectively attending in vision—we shine our spotlight on certain locations that we need to "illuminate." The analogous mechanism for auditory attention is a "gateway"—a sort of passive filtering mechanism that allows only some of the information through the bottleneck and into conscious awareness. The studies that test this sort of mechanism utilize selective attention tasks in which some information must be processed and responded to and some must be ignored. The questions that emerge from this scenario parallel those from studies of visual attention: What are we aware of when we are focusing our auditory attention on one aspect of an auditory scene? Are we "deaf" to some aspects of the auditory scene, just like we're blind to some aspects of a visual scene? Do certain auditory stimuli get privileged access through the gateway of auditory attention, just as certain visual stimuli manage to grab the spotlight?

Attention as a Gateway.   Before we venture into the theories that view attention as a gateway, let's take a look at one of the classic auditory attention tasks. Cherry (1953) had subjects engage in **dichotic listening**—specially rigged headphones presented a different message to each ear. But simply having a person listen to two messages doesn't allow the researcher a window into their attentional processes. To control attention,

Cherry had subjects perform **speech shadowing** (repeating speech, word for word) for one of the messages. Speech shadowing forced subjects to selectively attend to one message (the *attended message*) while ignoring the other (the *unattended message*).

One of the most intriguing questions that emerges from this situation is whether subjects notice or process the ignored elements of the auditory scene (i.e., the unattended message). It turns out that subjects were fairly successful in their attempts to shadow the attended message, but they seemed to know very little about the content of the unattended message. They *were* aware that a message was being played and tended to notice some of its physical characteristics such as changes in pitch (e.g., whether the speaker was male or female). But as for what was actually said, they were aware of practically nothing. This basic pattern—minimal processing of information presented in an unattended channel—was a common finding in early studies of selective attention (e.g., Moray, 1959).

Early Selection Theories.   The basic findings of studies like those conducted by Cherry led to the development of a theory typically referred to as **early selection theory,** which is depicted in the top panel of Figure 3.20. First, the initial processing of auditory

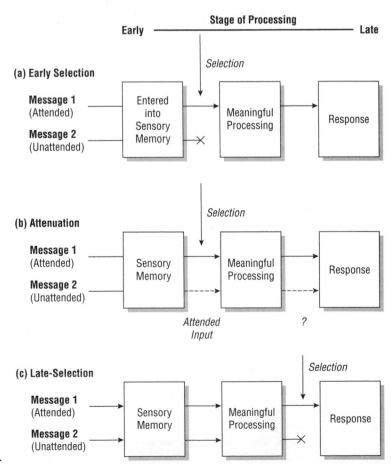

Figure 3.20 Attentional processing according to (a) early selection theory, (b) attenuation theory, and (c) late-selection theory.

information encodes each source of information in terms of its physical characteristics. At this point, the information sources are *filtered* based on this information, with only one source selected for further processing. This approach is termed *early selection* because the *selection* process whereby we designate information for further processing occurs *early* in processing, as the information is first registered by the senses. The process of early selection was evident in Cherry's study—the only things that subjects seemed to notice about the message in the unattended channel were its physical characteristics— exactly what would be expected if all messages were processed only to an early stage of analysis. After the selection of the attended message, the other messages were essentially discarded. However, further investigation of auditory selective attention made it clear that more is going on than meets the ear. Just as your visual attention can be grabbed by an erratic driver whom you hadn't previously noticed, your auditory attention can be grabbed by a similarly salient stimulus.

Consider the **cocktail-party phenomenon.** You've no doubt been at a party where there were many conversations occurring all at once, yet you had little or no trouble focusing on only one. This is an everyday example of selective attention. According to early selection theories, the unattended conversations are like static—you're not really processing them. Yet (and this is where the problem lies) if someone in another conversation says your name, you are very likely to notice. Based on a strict interpretation of early selection theories, this shouldn't happen; the analysis of unattended information stops *early*, at the point of noticing only sensory characteristics. Therefore, you shouldn't be able to recognize your name (or anything else), because doing so requires analysis at the level of meaning (i.e., analysis at a *later* stage of processing).

Now, this demonstration doesn't necessarily give psychologists cause to toss out the theory—after all, it is just a demonstration. But the results of a classic (not to mention ingenious) study by Treisman (1960) give empirical support to this phenomenon. Treisman employed dichotic listening in her study, but with an interesting twist: Subjects heard a different message in each ear and were required to shadow one of them. Occasionally, *the meaning of the shadowed message switched ears,* as depicted in Figure 3.21. The question is whether this switch in meaning grabs the listener's attention so that they will say, "Psychology is a really interesting major for students . . ." (the meaningful response) or "Psychology is a really interesting walk on the beach . . ." (the correct response). As you might have anticipated, the meaningful message grabbed subjects' attention, leading to shadowing mistakes.

Right Ear

Psychology is a really interesting / walk on the beach.

Left Ear

On our vacation we went for a / major for students.

"an interesting— uh—major for students"

Figure 3.21 The procedure employed in the Treisman (1960) selective attention study.

Adapted from Treismam, A. (1960). Contextual cues in selective listening. *Quarterly Journal of Experimental Psychology, 12,* 242–248.

The intriguing results from Treisman's (1960) classic study demonstrate clearly that we process a good deal more of the auditory scene than we might be aware

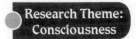

Research Theme: Consciousness

of, and that, when appropriate, an auditory stimulus can grab our attention. But what if a stimulus doesn't grab our conscious attention—do we still register it on some level? Corteen and Wood (1972) conducted a two-phase study to find out. In the first phase, subjects were asked to listen to a series of words. Each list contained three city names (e.g., Minneapolis, Lafayette, Cincinnati) that were each followed by a slight electric shock. The shock produced an autonomic nervous system response called a *galvanic skin response (GSR)*—slight sweating in the fingertips. In the second phase, subjects performed a dichotic listening and shadowing task. The unattended message was a list of words that consisted of 12 critical words—6 words presented in phase 1 (3 shock-associated city words plus 3 nouns not associated with shock) and 6 words not presented in phase 1 (3 new city words and 3 new nouns). When the dichotic listening/shadowing task was complete, some of the subjects reported that they had heard words in the unattended ear but were unaware that some of these words were city names. To put it in earlier terms, subjects had no phenomenal consciousness of identifying these words.

But recall the commonplace dissociations between phenomenal consciousness and access consciousness that we discussed in the context of visual perception, and apply them to this case of auditory attention. Did subjects show evidence of access consciousness? Indeed they did; during the dichotic listening task, the 3 shock-associated city words from phase 1 produced a higher galvanic skin response relative to that produced by the 3 non-shock-associated nouns from phase 1 (37.7% vs. 12.3%). As noted earlier, these words were not consciously identified (or at least they weren't remembered shortly after their presentation). But they must have been meaningfully identified because they produced a GSR. In addition, the 3 new city words not presented in phase 1 produced a more intense GSR than the 3 new nouns not presented in phase 1 (22.8% vs. 8.7%). The fact that the heightened GSR generalized to control items from the same semantic category (i.e., city names) is further evidence that the city names presented in the unattended channel in phase 1 were indeed recognized at some level, a la the subliminal primes that exerted a slight but statistically significant priming effect with visual stimuli.

Attenuation Theory. To account for the apparent fact that even unattended events in the auditory scene are processed somewhat, and may even overtly grab our attention, Treisman (1960) proposed the **attenuation theory,** which is essentially a slight modification of early selection theories. This theory is depicted in the middle panel of Figure 3.20 (p. 112). According to this model, unattended information is not completely blocked from further analysis. Rather, it is *attenuated* or "turned down," if you will. So the early filtering of messages is partial, not complete. Unattended information does make it through the filter, but weakly. So how does this weak trickle of information grab our attention?

Treisman proposed that some words in our "mental dictionary" are permanently more available than others (e.g., one's name) because of personal importance. Similarly, other words are temporarily more available due to present circumstances (e.g., the context of the sentence in Treisman's ear-switching study or the words that might indicate the arrival of a shock in the Corteen and Wood study). Therefore, even the small trickle of information that makes it through the attenuating filter might be enough to trigger recognition and grab our attention. To put it in terms of a basic issue in perception that was discussed at the beginning of the chapter, some stimuli require less information from bottom-up processing to trigger recognition because of the facilitatory effect of top-down processing (e.g., personal importance or current circumstances).

Late-Selection Theories.   Of course, Treisman's attenuation theory is only one of many ways researchers might account for how unattended information grabs our attention; another is a **late-selection theory** (e.g., Deutsch & Deutsch, 1963). This theory is depicted in the bottom panel of Figure 3.20 (p. 112). According to late-selection theories, *all* incoming information is identified or recognized at a level outside of phenomenal consciousness. *After* the information is identified, only the selected piece of information emerges into phenomenal consciousness.

The late-selection approach easily accounts for how unattended elements of an auditory scene grab our attention. For example, the cocktail-party phenomenon is no surprise—because unattended stimuli are identified, one's name certainly would be, leading to an attention switch. The experimental demonstrations of Treisman (1960) and Corteen and Wood (1972) are also explained quite easily. All incoming information (the unattended passage in the Treisman study and the word list in the Corteen and Wood study) is identified. This identification leads to an attention switch (as in the Treisman study) or to an emotional reaction (as in the Corteen and Wood study).

You might find it difficult to differentiate between attenuation and late-selection because both theories seem to make similar predictions and allow for the identification of unattended information. Driver (2001) provides a useful way to distinguish the two approaches. Attenuation theory proposes that identification of unattended information is the *exception rather than the rule*. Whether or not information is identified depends on the context or the exact nature of the information. Conversely, late-selection theories argue that the identification of meaning is the *rule rather than the exception*. The identification of meaning is obligatory; all information (attended and unattended) is identified. So which is correct? Driver (2001) indicates that neurological studies of attention are more consistent with an attenuation-type account. While the attenuation theory proposed by Treisman may be a bit simplistic, it is clear that attention is influenced by the type of top-down processing (e.g., context, current task demands, goals of the attender, etc.) proposed by the attenuation theory.

Our discussion of visual and auditory attention seems to imply that how we focus our attention is passive. Nothing could be further from the truth. Rather, the *way in which* we pay attention can be strategically varied according to the situational demands. This may remind you of the Most, Scholl, Clifford, and Simons (2005) notion of attentional set within the context of visual attention. Recall that in vision, you can basically decide what you're going to look at and attend to visually; what you notice and don't notice depends on this set. Similarly, in auditory attention you can make the same decision, choosing to listen to your professor instead of the inconsiderate students chatting behind you. How we choose to pay attention is largely a matter of strategy and situational demands. In the next chapter, we will explore the processes involved in what is sometimes termed "executive attention."

STOP *and* REVIEW!

1. Object-based attention is to spatial attention as:
   a. region is to element
   b. thing is to place
   c. salient is to noticeable
   d. visual is to auditory
2. True or false? We're more likely to notice a bizarre event or a change in a scene if the event/change looks different from the elements of the scene to which we're attending.
3. Describe how dichotic listening and speech shadowing are used to study auditory attention.
4. Can early selection theories of attention explain the identification of meaningful information? Why or why not?

➤ Visual attention can be spatial or object-based. Spatial attention refers to our tendency to focus on a region in space. Object-based attention refers to our tendency to isolate and attend to specific elements of the visual scene. Attentional capture occurs when one's attention is involuntarily drawn to some salient stimulus.

➤ Inattentional blindness and change blindness refer to instances in which we fail to notice obvious changes or events in our visual environment. These failures are more likely to occur when we're distracted by a visually demanding task and when the change event is different from the attended events.

➤ Auditory attention is studied with dichotic listening (having people listen to two distinct messages) and speech shadowing (requiring that they repeat one of the messages). These techniques show that attention is limited; people seem able to attend to only one stimulus at a time. In spite of these limits, unattended information does sometimes receive meaningful analysis.

➤ Early selection theories propose that the processes whereby we designate information for further processing occur as the information is first registered by the senses. This view fails to account for cases in which the meaning of unattended information grabs our attention. A variation, attenuation theory, accounts for these cases by proposing that early filtering of messages is partial, so especially salient stimuli can be noticed.

➤ Late selection theories propose that all incoming stimuli are processed for meaning.

GLOSSARY

access consciousness: processes whereby we manipulate representations in the service of reasoning, communication, or behavior (p. 95)

attentional capture: occasions in which a person's attention is involuntarily drawn to some stimulus (p. 107)

attentional set: the strategy or mind-set you have as you attend to a visual scene (p. 110)

attenuation theory: a theory positing an attenuation mechanism that minimizes, but does not eliminate, analysis of unattended information; salient or context-relevant information can be recognized (p. 114)

authorship processing: the set of processes that leads us to attribute events to the entities that are thought to have caused them (p. 97)

blindsight: a neurological disorder characterized by a lack of visual awareness but the preserved ability to report on some aspects of a stimulus (p. 99)

bottom-up (data-driven) processing: the identification of a stimulus through the assembly of its component features (p. 74)

change detection: the ability to notice variations in the perceptual environment (p. 107)

closure: a tendency to perceptually complete incomplete objects (p. 78)

cocktail-party phenomenon: a tendency to notice highly relevant stimuli presented in an unattended channel (p. 113)

common fate: a tendency to group elements together if they are moving in the same direction or at the same speed (p. 78)

common region: a tendency to group together elements that seem to belong to a common designated area or region (p. 78)

consciousness: awareness of internal and external events (p. 94)

constructive view (of perception): emphasizes the role of active construction and interpretation in arriving at a 3-D percept of the world (p. 75)

dichotic listening: simultaneous listening to two different messages, one in each ear (p. 111)

direct view (of perception): emphasizes the direct pickup of information from the environment and de-emphasizes the role of constructive processes in producing a percept (p. 75)

early selection theory: a theory positing a sensory processing filter for incoming messages; limitations in attention occur immediately after sensory processing (p. 112)

embodied perception: a view of perception that emphasizes dynamic interaction with the everyday environment (p. 91)

figure-ground: a tendency to segregate visual scenes into a background and a figure that appears to be superimposed against it (p. 80)

flicker paradigm: procedure used to study change detection in which two slightly different versions of a scene alternate with one another rapidly (p. 108)

global precedence: a tendency to encode the overall features of a scene before apprehending scene details (p. 82)

good continuation: a tendency to perceive lines as flowing naturally, in a single direction (p. 78)

grouping: processes whereby we organize incoming sensations (p. 77)

illusion of conscious will: the often-erroneous belief that our efforts and actions are controlled through conscious force of thought (p. 97)

inattentional blindness: a failure to notice obvious changes or events in our visual environment (p. 107)

lateralization: the degree to which particular cognitive processes are localized in a particular brain hemisphere (p. 82)

late-selection theory: a theory of attention positing that selection occurs after all incoming stimuli have been identified; limitations in attention are at the stage of response (p. 115)

McGurk effect: a speech perception effect in which visual information conflicts with auditory signals, changing the perceived speech sound (p. 87)

object-based attention: focusing on objects of particular importance or salience (p. 106)

objective threshold: the level of stimulus energy below which participants report not seeing a stimulus; forced-choice procedures also indicate a lack of awareness (p. 102)

percept: the coherent representation of an object, person, or event that results from the processes of sensation and perception (p. 73)

perceptual set: a tendency to visually analyze scenes in a particular way (p. 109)

phenomenal consciousness: subjective awareness of what our minds are currently doing (p. 95)

priming: a change in reaction time produced by the prior presentation of a related stimulus (p. 101)

principles of visual organization: the principles followed by our perceptual system to organize incoming sensations in a sensible and simple manner (p. 77)

proximity: a tendency for objects that are near one another (i.e., *proximal*) to be grouped (p. 77)

response bias: a subject's willingness to report the presence of some stimulus (p. 96)

schema: a cluster of knowledge about some object or event (p. 75)

sensitivity: one's perceptual acuity; the ability to detect the presence or absence of a stimulus or a change in a stimulus (p. 96)

signal detection theory: an approach to psychophysics that characterizes perceptual experiences as the joint product of sensitivity and response bias (p. 96)

similarity: a tendency for objects that are similar to one another to be grouped together (p. 78)

spatial attention: focusing on a particular region in space (p. 106)

speech shadowing: repeating a message word for word (p. 112)

subjective threshold: the level of stimulus energy below which subjects report not seeing a stimulus; forced-choice procedures indicate some minimal awareness (p. 102)

subliminal perception: the purported tendency to be influenced by stimuli presented below the level of awareness (p. 100)

supraliminal: above the threshold of conscious awareness (p. 101)

synchrony: a perceptual tendency to group elements that occur at the same time (p. 78)

synesthesia: experiences in which input from one sensory system produces an experience not only in that modality but in another as well (p. 85)

top-down (conceptually driven) processing: the identification of a stimulus with the help of context, previous knowledge, and/or expectations (p. 75)

ventriloquist effect: occurs when a visual cue that is presented simultaneously with an auditory stimulus biases the localization of that auditory stimulus toward the location of the visual cue (p. 86)

4

Attending to and Manipulating Information

Is it really that risky to talk on a cell phone and drive at the same time? It seems easy enough, and it seems that a lot of people do it with no problem. Do hands-free devices help?

Have you ever put the milk in the cabinet and the cereal in the refrigerator? Walked into a room, and then forgot what you went there for? Responded to someone who says, "How's it going?" with a brilliant response of, "Not much!" Are you losing your mind?

You're golfing, playing tennis, or (fill in your favorite skill here) and have a pesky habit of making the same mistake over and over. And when you really try to tell yourself not to make the mistake, and pay extra close attention . . . you're even *more* likely to make the mistake! What's going on?

Why do certain tasks—walking and talking, for example—seem to go together so seamlessly, whereas other tasks—taking notes and listening to a professor lecture—seem to be so difficult to do at the same time?

Selection and Division: The Strategic Nature of Attention

As was evident from our initial discussion in the previous chapter of cognitive processes, we're constantly being bombarded by information moving in and out of our conscious awareness. As I write this, I can hear the air conditioner humming; water from the sprinkler is hitting the windows because it isn't set quite right; a baseball game is on TV; and my laptop computer is threatening to fall and become a floortop computer.

Obviously, there is a nearly constant need to monitor the events that are occurring in our external environment, not to mention the "events" in our internal environment (i.e., thoughts). As you learned in Chapter 3, cognitive psychologists term this monitoring process **attention.** You'll learn in this chapter that attention is strategic and actively manipulated as we attempt to examine, consider, manage, and respond to events appropriately. The processes that allow us to perform these dynamic cognitive operations on the information that is held in consciousness comprise what is referred to as **working memory.** This chapter will feature a closer look at these strategic and active processes of cognitive control.

Control of Selective Attention

The last chapter concluded with a discussion of visual and auditory attention. One of the major themes of the final section was the idea that attention is limited—we can't possibly process everything we see and hear. So there has to be some sort of regulatory mechanism whereby we allow information to enter the information-processing system. Now, you may have missed a subtle yet key word from the previous sentence—*allow*. Stating that we *allow* information to pass through implies that we have some choice about it, and indeed we do. In other words, attention is strategic.

Multimode Theory of Attention.   A series of investigations by Johnston and Heinz (1978) provides evidence for a **multimode theory** of attention. According to Johnston and Heinz, attention is flexible in that people can shift from early modes of attention (processing only the physical characteristics of incoming stimuli) to late modes (processing the meaning of incoming stimuli). Given that we have voluntary control over how we deal with incoming information, we are capable of determining the basis on which we select information for further processing (an early or late processing mode). However, attending in each of these modes has an associated set of costs. As selection proceeds to a later point in the information-processing system, attending takes more mental effort. To test their multimode theory of attention, Johnston and Heinz developed a clever attention task. Subjects were given two tasks—speech shadowing lists of words and light detection. During the speech shadowing task, subjects had to watch for a light signal and press a key as quickly as possible when they saw it.

Recall Johnston and Heinz's basic idea—attention can operate in different modes that have corresponding costs. They varied the mode of attention (early vs. late) by manipulating the nature of the shadowing task. In a control condition, the speech shadowing task was easy; only one list was presented, so subjects simply had to repeat it. In the other two conditions, the shadowing task required *selecting* between two lists. In one of these conditions, the presented lists were different physically; one was read by a female voice, the other by a male voice. Subjects had to shadow one. Repeating one of these lists required only a simple discrimination of the lists' physical characteristics; in other words, only early selection was required. In a more challenging condition, the two lists had similar physical characteristics (i.e., they were read by speakers of the same gender), so easy selection based on physical characteristics wasn't possible. For these two lists, only the meaning differed. Therefore, the shadowing task required late selection.

The difference in attentional capacity required by the various shadowing tasks was assessed by examining how the light detection task was affected. According to the multi-mode theory, early and late selection are both possible, but late selection costs more in terms of capacity. The condition in which the messages were physically similar and differed only in meaning (semantically different) required late selection; in order to selectively listen, subjects had to pay attention to *what* was being said. This is expensive in terms of attentional capacity. Therefore, there would be little capacity left to detect the light. The condition in which the lists differed physically required only early selection; in order to selectively listen, subjects had only to note the lists' gross physical characteristics. This is cheap in terms of attentional capacity, leaving more to perform the light detection task.

(a) Late-Selection Condition

(b) Early Selection Condition

The results, presented in Figure 4.1, support these predictions. The figure plots RT cost, which is calculated by subtracting simple reaction time (light detection task only) from reaction time to detect the light in each of the other three conditions. The first was the control condition (one-list shadowing) described earlier. The other two conditions required that subjects discriminate between two lists and shadow one. As you can see, the listening task exacted a cost on RT in each condition. More importantly, the "price" was different, depending on the degree of selection required. The one-list control condition exacted only a slight cost on RT. But the requirement to listen to two lists and select one for shadowing was much more challenging and more costly in terms of attention. Consistent with Johnston and Heinz's analysis, the cost was greater in the late-selection condition, where subjects had to discriminate between two lists on the basis of meaning. These findings supported Johnston and Heinz's view that both early and late selection are possible, but late selection requires a greater amount of mental effort or capacity.

Dividing Attention

The results of Johnston and Heinz (1978) make it apparent that we have a choice of operating in an early selection mode, a late-selection mode, or somewhere in between. They also underscore the idea that attention is strategic. The strategic nature of attention is made even more obvious when one considers the processes of divided attention. Whereas selective attention involves choosing one input to process at the expense of others, **divided attention** involves the processing of multiple inputs.

Figure 4.1 Results from Johnston and Heinz (1978, experiment 4).

From Johnston, W. A., & Heinz, S. P. (1978). Flexibility and capacity demands of attention. *Journal of Experimental Psychology: General, 107,* 420–435. Copyright 1978 by the American Psychological Association. Reprinted by permission.

Assessing Divided Attention. The ability to divide attention and the factors that affect this ability

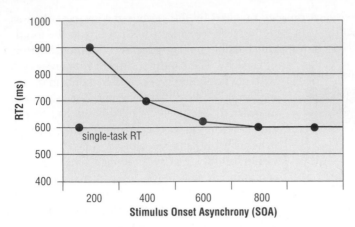

Figure 4.2 The psychological refractory period. Reaction time to a second stimulus (RT2) is elevated the more closely in time it occurs after a first stimulus.

have been investigated within a variety of dual-task paradigms in which subjects are faced with having to juggle two tasks at once. Characteristics of task performance and the factors that influence performance are examined to determine the nature of attentional processing and the attentional system.

The PRP Paradigm.   One very simple, yet classic, method for investigating dual-task interference is termed the *psychological refractory period (PRP) paradigm* (Telford, 1931; see Pashler, 1994, for a review); it's sort of a "double reaction time" task in which two different signals are presented in rapid succession, and each of the signals requires a separate fast response. Either task on its own would be trivially simple, but when they're paired, responding becomes quite challenging. The major independent variable of interest in this paradigm is **stimulus onset asynchrony (SOA),** the time that lapses between the presentation of the two stimuli. The major dependent variable of interest is reaction time to the second stimulus (RT2). The typical finding can be seen in Figure 4.2, which plots RT2 as a function of stimulus onset asynchrony. As you can see, reaction time to the second stimulus relative to performing that task alone (single-task RT) is greatly elevated when the second stimulus is presented immediately after the first stimulus. As this interval (the SOA) increases, RT2 becomes faster, finally mirroring single-task reaction times at long SOAs. This improvement in RT as a function of time is taken as evidence of a **psychological refractory period,** a period of time during which the response to a second stimulus will be significantly slowed because of the processing still occurring on the earlier stimulus.

Complex Task Sharing.   The PRP paradigm is an exceedingly simple way to look at the interference that occurs when people are required to do two things at once. What about more complex tasks like the ones you engage in every day—walking, talking, eating, reading, taking notes? Another way to look at divided attention is to require someone to concurrently perform two different complex tasks like these, and observe deficits in the task(s) relative to when each is performed alone. Recently, a growing number of researchers has looked at complex task sharing within a growingly commonplace setting: behind the steering wheel, cell phone in hand. Given the ever-growing ubiquity of those infernal little instruments, there's been quite a spate of research on the consequences for our everyday attention (e.g., Beede & Kass, 2006; Lesch & Hancock, 2004; Raukaskas, Gugerty, & Ward, 2004; Strayer & Johnston, 2001; Treffner & Barrett, 2004). In fact, an entire edition of the applied journal *Human Factors* was devoted to the problem of driver distraction. So turn off your cell phone and read up!

For a sample empirical investigation of this phenomenon, let's look at a study by Beede and Kass (2006). Whereas previous studies had generally focused on only a couple of dependent variables to measure driving performance, these investigators assessed the effects of engaging in a cell phone conversation on a wide variety of driving measures. Because earlier research had already established the detrimental effects of hand held devices on driving (e.g., Briem & Hedman, 1995; Strayer & Johnston, 2001), Beede and Kass had subjects use a hands-free version to focus on the question of how general attentional interference (rather than motor requirements) might relate to driving deficits. They had subjects perform a simulated driving task in a set up that was complete with a steering wheel, brake pedal, gas pedal, and turn signals. They measured performance on a variety of measures that included traffic violations (i.e., running a stop sign), driving maintenance (i.e., variations in speed and lane position), attention lapses (occasions in which the subject did something absentmindedly; categories were predefined by the experimenter and included stopping at a green light), and reaction time to driving events (e.g., starting after a red light turned green). Subjects were tested in both no-phone (single-task) and hands-free phone (dual-task) conditions.

Beede and Kass's (2006) findings are presented in Table 4.1, and the news isn't good. Engaging in cell phone conversations had a significant negative impact on just about every measure of driving performance. Cell phone conversations were associated with more traffic violations and attentional lapses, and also slower reaction times to critical events relative to trials without a cell phone conversation. Clearly, driving while talking on a cell phone isn't safe, and using a hands-free version doesn't make it any safer.

Accounts of Dual-Task Interference.   So what's going on? It may be obvious that trying to do two things at once is more difficult than focusing on just one. But what are the underlying mechanisms that may lead to the deficits? In this section, we lay out a couple of theories that are often proffered to account for findings of dual-task interference.

Bottleneck Approach.   One type of model proposed to account for dual-task interference appeals to the metaphor of a bottleneck (e.g., Pashler, 1992; see Lien, Ruthruff, & Johnston, 2006, for a recent overview). You've no doubt been in bottlenecked traffic, where only one lane of cars is moving. Everyone has to stop, get into the queue, and wait their turn. This is essentially what bottleneck theories of attention propose. Recall the classic

Table 4.1 Summary of Results from Beede and Kass (2006)

	Without Phone	With Phone
Attention Lapses	1.56	2.17
Total Violations	3.81	5.33
Stop Sign Delay (sec)	6.83	7.41
Traffic Light Delay (sec)	1.37	1.79

From Beede, K. E., & Kass, S. J. (2006). Engrossed in conversation: The impact of cell phones on simulated driving performance. *Accident Analysis & Prevention, 38*, 415–421. Adapted with permission from Elsevier and the author.

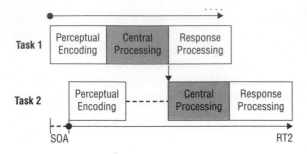

Figure 4.3 Bottleneck model of attention. Central processing of task 2 must wait until the central processing for task 1 has been completed.

Lien, M., Ruthruff, E., & Johnston, J. C. (2006). Attentional limitations in doing two tasks at once: the search for exceptions. *Current Directions in Psychological Science, 15*, 89–93. Published by Blackwell, Inc. Reprinted with permission from Blackwell, Inc., and the author.

finding from the PRP paradigm—that reaction time to a second stimulus increases as SOA decreases. It makes sense—if a first stimulus is already being processed, any other stimulus that occurs in that time is going to have to wait its turn, due to the bottleneck in processing; only one thing can be dealt with at a time. This will delay responding to the second stimulus—and will delay responding longer—the more closely in time it occurs to the first stimulus.

A diagram of this type of model is presented in Figure 4.3. The two sets of bars represent two different tasks (T1 and T2). For each of the tasks, the subject must engage in three sets of processes: perceptual encoding (the initial intake of the stimulus), central processing (the stages of classification and judgment), and response processing (the processes that lead to the required behavior). Time is moving from left to right—note that this is a serial (i.e., step-by-step) depiction of stimulus processing. In this particular depiction, there is a bottleneck in central processing. In the diagram, the first stimulus has been presented, has progressed through perceptual encoding, and is currently undergoing central processing. When the second stimulus is presented, its processing proceeds through perceptual encoding, but because of the bottleneck in central processing, it needs to wait until those processes finish with the first stimulus. So basically, processing of the second stimulus gets temporarily postponed, lengthening overall RT. And of course, the postponement will be longer, the closer in time T2 is to T1.

Although this type of model applies most readily to the simple PRP paradigm, it isn't hard to imagine how such bottlenecks and "waiting in line" would play themselves out in a more complex scenario like driving and talking on a cell phone. Both of these complex tasks have simpler subtasks in common; for example, you need to process numbers to think about and dial a cell phone number and also to check your speed and how many miles it is to the next destination. You need to interpret words to have the cell phone conversation and also to read and interpret highway signs. It's not hard to imagine how the specific processes that ultimately comprise driving and conversing would be cued up behind one another, waiting, which would lead to slow and error-prone performance.

Capacity Approach. Another way of capturing what is going on in situations that require the division of attention between two tasks is by appealing to the notion of limited mental resources, or capacity that is shared (e.g., Kahneman, 1973; Navon & Gopher, 1979). Two tasks can be performed simultaneously by sharing the common "pool" of resources, as long as they don't empty the pool; performance on either task, both tasks, or neither task could suffer. The major difference between this view and the bottleneck view is that the capacity view proposes no information-processing bottleneck that "holds up" processing in terms of time. According to the capacity view, processing of multiple tasks can be simultaneous; each doesn't have to wait in line for the others.

STOP *and* THINK!

THE PRICE OF ATTENDING

Imagine that all of the attention you could possibly focus on some everyday task has a value of $100. That is, the most mentally challenging task in the world costs $100. Based on this idea, "price" each of the following tasks.

watching TV
listening to music
taking notes in class
talking on your cell phone
walking
driving in an unfamiliar location
driving a familiar route
listening to a professor lecture
eating

Based on your "pricing system,"

- Which pairs of tasks would not send you "over budget"?
- Which combinations would send you "over budget"?
- What makes tasks easy or difficult to combine?

One issue that has been bandied about within the context of capacity theories is whether the capacity is unitary or not. In other words, do we have one general type of resource from which we draw to perform tasks, or do we have multiple specific resources? And if there are multiple types of resources, what differentiates them? Consider your ability to balance two tasks at once—you have no doubt noticed that this ability depends on the nature of the two tasks. For example, you probably find it relatively easy to talk and drive at the same time. However, you would find it much more difficult to drive and read at the same time (although we have seen people reading their papers while driving!). Performing two visual monitoring tasks seems more difficult than performing one primarily visual task along with one primarily auditory task. No doubt a great deal of the ease or difficulty relates to the physical operations required by each of the tasks, but some researchers (e.g., Navon & Gopher, 1979; Wickens, 1984) have proposed that it also relates to a likely difference in the type of mental capacity required.

What differentiates these types, or pools, of capacity? Wickens (1984) suggests that pools are differentiated according to a number of factors, such as whether the input modality is visual or auditory, and whether the response required is vocal or manual. According to this view, tasks interfere to the degree that they tap into the same pool of resources. For example, an auditory and visual task or tasks requiring a vocal and a manual response will interfere less with each other than will two visual tasks or two tasks requiring a manual response. This may get you thinking about driving and cell phone usage—driving relies primarily on the visual modality, while talking on a cell phone relies primarily on the auditory modality. Therefore, you might figure that, given the previous analysis, the two should not interfere with one another. But even if two tasks are in different modalities, there is a central limit to the total amount of capacity that can be devoted to them together, with predictable results when that amount is exceeded. As you saw in the Beede and Kass (2006) study, almost every measure of driving performance suffered when combined with the second task of talking on the cell phone, even though the tasks were in separate modalities.

In spite of the general success of the notion of capacity as a descriptor of task sharing, the concept has some pretty harsh critics (e.g., Logan, 1997). Whether we have one

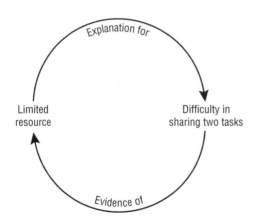

general type of resource from which we draw to perform tasks or multiple specific resources begs a more fundamental question—what exactly *is* a mental resource? The term is just a vague concept that's used as an explanation of attention, but it doesn't really explain anything; it simply redescribes it. In addition, the definition of resources is circular. That is, the notion of limited resources is used to explain why sharing two tasks is difficult; but the fact that two tasks are difficult to share is used as the reason there are limited resources! Using a concept to explain some phenomenon, and then using the phenomenon as evidence of the original concept is shoddy theorizing. There needs to be some concrete measure or definition of a *resource* that is independent of increases in the difficulty of a task; however, a satisfactory one has not yet emerged. Given the difficulty in pinning down the concept, some (e.g., Logan, 1997) have urged restraint in use of the term.

So which model provides a better account of divided-attention data? It's hard to say. When one gets down to the nitty-gritty of the models, they are actually more difficult to tell apart than it would seem. In a very broad sense, the approaches are similar in that they each propose some sort of basic limit on how much mental activity we can engage in. Some even propose that the bottleneck notion is subsumed by the capacity approach (e.g., Navon & Miller, 2002). After all, a serial bottleneck mechanism is an example of a mental resource, and indeed may be a part of a more complex system. As is so often the case when theories conflict, it is quite likely the case that the division of attention features both the "queueing" of the bottleneck approach and the "sharing" of the capacity approach.

Individual Differences in Divided Attention.   As you might imagine, it's difficult to reach more than broad generalizations about divided-attention performance because tasks, people, and situations vary so wildly. In this section, we'll examine two factors that have been shown to influence attention: age and culture.

Aging. As the baby boom generation (of which your authors are at the tail end) gets older and grayer, there seems to be more and more concern about the relationship between
aging and cognitive function. Research on the relationship between aging, cognition, and brain has accelerated in the past couple of decades, and we are finding out a great deal about how cognition changes with age. Until recently, it's been pretty much accepted that the ability to do two things at once deteriorates with age—that is, elderly adults show more dual-task interference (e.g., Hartley, 1992; Kramer & Larish, 1996) relative to younger adults. But some more recent results cast considerable doubt on such a blanket conclusion. As it turns out, age deficits in divided attention are highly task- and situation-dependent. One critical factor in whether age differences in dual-task interference are found is the degree to which skills are routine or well practiced. Deficits in dual-task performance are less likely to be seen with routine or extremely well-practiced activities than they are with novel tasks (Jennings & Jacoby, 1993; see Riby, Perfect, & Stollery, 2004, for a review).

This conclusion fits well with the results of a study by Strayer and Drews (2004) that investigated dual-task interference between driving and conversing on (hands-free) cell phones in both younger and older adults. You may be rushing to the thought that older folks aren't very good drivers, and that the results of the study probably confirmed this speculation. Guess again. In their study, Strayer and Drews employed a procedure similar to the one discussed earlier in the Beede and Kass (2006) study. Subjects drove in a simulator while engaged in a cell phone conversation with a research assistant. The results were consistent with our earlier discussion: there was a detrimental effect of cell phone use on driving performance. Notably, however, this effect was identical in younger and older adults. So the impact of dual-tasking doesn't seem to be any more drastic for older adults than it is for younger adults, at least in the task situation investigated by Strayer and Drews. The lack of an interaction fits with the notion that when it comes to highly practiced tasks like driving, age-related differences in dual-task performance are minimal to nonexistent. There certainly is dual-task interference between driving and other tasks, but that interference is no worse for older folks relative to youngsters.

Culture. In a recent investigation of cross-cultural differences in patterns of divided attention, Correa-Chávez, Rogoff, and Arauz (2005) were interested in how different *modes* of attention might be employed by children from European American and indigenous North and Central American cultural backgrounds. More specifically, they were interested in comparing what they termed *simultaneous* and *focused* styles of managing attention. A *focused* attentional style is characterized by concentration on one activity at a time. A *simultaneous* attention style is seen when, as stated by Correa-Chávez et al., ". . . people attend keenly and actively in a broad manner that focuses skillfully on several events at once" (p. 664). The concept of an attentional management style is similar to the notion of an attentional set, which we discussed in Chapter 3. Attentional set refers to how a person tends to focus in a given situation.

The researchers hypothesized that differences in ethnic and cultural backgrounds, in addition to differences in formal education, lead to divergent patterns of paying attention. Specifically, children in indigenous North and Central American families and communities are expected to learn by participating in family and social activities, keenly and closely observing everything that is going on—kind of a "hands-on" approach to absorbing the customs, traditions, and history of the community (e.g., Rogoff et al., 2003). Through these sorts of interactions, children might be expected to develop a more simultaneous "try and absorb as many things as you can" attentional style. The authors are careful to point out that this *simultaneous attention* does not necessarily imply a lack of focus.

In contrast, children from European American families are less likely to participate in the activities of the adult community, and are more likely to have highly structured and formal educational experiences focused exclusively on them (the individual children). The type of attention that emerges from these experiences is a more focused "try and learn these individual facts" attentional style. Children with this type of style are more likely to pay attention to one thing at a time. They may be able to attend to different things over time, but to only one thing at any one time. Hence, they engage primarily in focused attention and alternate this focus among tasks. From this point on, we will label this style *alternating attention*.

The procedure used by Correa-Chávez et al. involved groups of children (7–8 years of age) learning the paper-folding art of origami. The children were instructed by a first-grade teacher who was blind to the researchers' hypotheses. The interaction between the teacher and the children (tested in groups of three) took a total of about 15 minutes and involved a few minutes of getting acquainted and playing with some already-made figures. The rest of the period involved the teacher showing the children how to make the figures. The teacher was instructed to interact with the students informally, as an "auntie" rather than as a teacher; children were free to attend or not attend, to fold figures on their own, or to help their classmates. These interactions were videotaped and later coded in terms of the type of attention the children engaged in as they struggled with the most difficult phase of the instructions, learning how to fold an origami frog.

Two critical types of attention were operationally defined and subsequently coded from the videotaped interactions. *Simultaneous attentional style* was defined as instances in which children managed to attend to at least two events effectively, without stopping one in favor of another. *Alternating attentional style* was marked by instances in which children were attending to multiple events in a serial fashion such that they were interrupting one event in order to switch to another. So in contrast to simultaneous attention, alternating attention involves attending to only one stimulus at a time. Table 4.2 displays

Table 4.2 Results from Correa-Chávez, Rogoff, and Arauz (2005) Study of Cultural Differences in Divided Attention

Form of Attention Management	North and Central American	European American
Simultaneous	48.3	27.1
Alternating	37.7	53.3

Correa-Chávez, M., Rogoff, B., & Arauz, R. M (2005). Cultural patterns in attending to two events at once. *Child Development, 76,* 664–678. Copyright 2005 Blackwell, Inc. Reprinted with permission from Blackwell, Inc.

the percentage of 10-second periods in which the children engaged in these two types of attention. As you can see, the predicted dissociation was observed. Children from indigenous North and Central American family backgrounds spent more of their time engaged in simultaneous attention relative to alternating attention, while children from European American backgrounds showed the opposite pattern.

STOP *and* **REVIEW!**

1. True or False? According to the multimode theory of attention, early selection seems to demand less attentional capacity than late selection.
2. Research on using cell phones while driving
   a. provides evidence of a psychological refractory period.
   b. indicates that the use of hands-free devices eliminates interference.
   c. indicates that if driving is highly automatized, then cell phones do not interfere.
   d. indicates that any type of cell phone use has a negative impact on concurrent driving.
3. Distinguish between bottleneck and capacity theories of divided attention.
4. Should you be more worried about an older adult driving and talking on a cell phone than you would be about a younger adult doing the same thing? Explain.

➤ According to multimode theory, attenders can choose to attend in either early or late-selection "modes," but this choice has consequences in terms of the capacity that is needed; late selection requires more attentional capacity than early selection.

➤ Divided attention is investigated by looking at dual-task interference. In one paradigm, subjects are given two concurrent tasks, and reaction time to perform the second task is assessed, typically showing a psychological refractory period, slower reaction time on the second task the closer in time it occurs relative to the first task. Research on the combination of more complex tasks reveals that the use of cell phones (including hands-free devices) has detrimental effects on driving.

➤ Bottleneck theories of divided attention propose that when one stimulus is already being processed, any other stimulus that occurs in that time is going to have to wait in line to be processed. In contrast, capacity theories of divided attention propose that we have mental resources that are shared among tasks. When the attention demanded exceeds capacity, task performance will suffer.

➤ Some research indicates that older adults do not suffer any more dual-task interference than younger adults, as long as the tasks being combined are well practiced (i.e., driving). Research also indicates cross-cultural differences in the way children distribute their attention.

Automaticity

You have probably noticed that many of the daily activities in which you engage seem to involve little or no attention. Tasks such as these are said to involve *automatic processing*. This **automaticity** typically develops as the result of extensive practice. After years of repeatedly engaging in a set of processes, these processes occur with relatively little effort.

Characteristics of Automatic Processes

In a recent review of research and theory, Moors and De Houwer (2006; also see Posner & Snyder, 1975) summarize the characteristics generally thought to differentiate between automatic processes and nonautomatic (i.e., controlled) processes. One of the most salient distinctions between automatic and controlled processes is the degree to which actions are subjected to conscious *control*. Control involves the ability or propensity to monitor, alter, change, or stop doing something. This control is lessened to the degree that a task is automatic. A related difference is the degree to which there is a conscious *intention* present. When activities are automatic, you aren't really consciously intending to engage in them; they're more autonomous, seeming to occur on their own, without any central control. A third characteristic of automatic processes is their *attentional efficiency*. Activities involving automatic processes take place with a minimum of attentional capacity, which leaves more capacity for the performance of other tasks.

Let's highlight these characteristics in the context of a particularly salient example: driving. When you drive, particularly in a low-traffic situation (i.e., on a non-busy highway), you may have the phenomenal experience of "zoning out." You aren't attentively monitoring the environment, so altering or changing what you're doing—say, if something falls off of a truck in front of you—would be difficult. Also, the activities involved in driving do seem to be relatively autonomous. You don't consciously form a goal like "Now I have to accelerate"; you just do it, almost as if the behavior comes out of you. Finally, when you're driving in this situation, you have little problem doing something else at the same time, like talking (except on a cell phone, as discussed earlier!), because driving in a low-traffic situation doesn't take much in the way of capacity.

Another example of automatic processing is the development of simple math skills (e.g., Ashcraft, 1992). We'll use this example in order to compare two major accounts of what's happening as a task becomes automatic. Greg (your first author) was quite into mental arithmetic while in college—no, not as a hobby. He was a mail clerk, and one of a mail clerk's many exciting tasks is the tabulation of mail charges for bundles of mail. When Greg was a mail clerk, a piece of pre-sort mail cost 17¢ to mail (yes, he's that old). His first few months on the job, he would painstakingly multiply 17 by any and all numbers rather laboriously in his head, or sometimes on paper. But after two years of clerking, he was extremely fast at multiplying any number by 17 (a feat that now serves no useful purpose, other than to win the occasional bet at a party).

Accounts of Automaticity

One account of the transition from controlled processing to automatic processing might be termed a sort of *increased speed approach* (e.g., Schneider & Shiffrin, 1977). According to this view, as the performance of a task undergoes the transition from controlled to automatic, the component processes used to carry out the task become faster and faster. There are no fundamental differences in the mental procedures (also termed *algorithms*) used to carry out the task. They just get increasingly faster with repetition. So Greg's ability to rapidly multiply numbers after extended practice occurred because each of the component processes of multiplication (i.e., multiply the 1's, carry over 10's, multiply

10's) got faster. In addition, this view proposes a gradual transition from serial (step-by-step) processing to parallel (all-at-once) processing. In the case of mental arithmetic, this might mean that the three stages of multiplication mentioned parenthetically above might eventually progress to the point where they could be done in a somewhat overlapping (i.e., parallel) fashion.

Logan (1988) has a different interpretation of what is going on as a task becomes automatic. According to his approach, termed the *instance-based view,* there is a fundamental change in the way tasks are performed as people get more and more practice. Performance of a task in the early stages tends to be conscious and deliberate, involving effortful memory search and information manipulation. Each encounter with the task leads to the formation of a new memory trace, so after a great deal of practice, there are countless *instances* of having performed the task stored in memory. After sufficient practice, performance of the task switches from the deliberate algorithmic mode to the quick and simple retrieval of an instance from memory. So after a great deal of practice, instead of having to rely on repeating a mental computation, a person performs the task by quickly retrieving relevant information from memory.

Turning again to Greg's party trick, according to Logan's view, after years of practice, the way Greg was accomplishing the task had changed fundamentally. Instead of carrying out the actual multiplication each time he was holding 23 envelopes ($3.91!!), he was instantly and directly retrieving an instance from his hundreds of memories of having multiplied 17 by 23. This transition from computation to memory retrieval is what is happening as a task becomes automatic.

A recent study by Tronsky (2005) demonstrates this transition quite nicely and, as luck would have it, in an empirical setting that mirrors Greg's real-world experience.

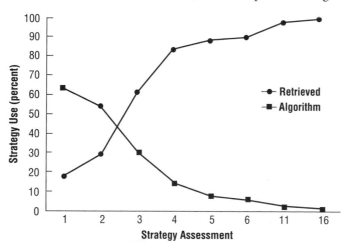

Tronksy was interested in investigating how automaticity develops in complex multiplication. To find out, he assessed subject skill and strategy in computing products of single-digit/multiple-digit (e.g., 9×17) multiplication problems. Over the course of several phases, subjects solved 60 different multiplication problems more than 120 times each! In addition to the multiple phases of multiplication, Tronsky also required the subjects to provide regular assessments of the strategies they were using to calculate the products. Needless to say, accuracy of calculation wasn't of much interest in the study. For their purposes, the most interesting findings were those from the strategy assessment, which are presented in Figure 4.4. As you can see, reported strategies from early phases of the experiment were

Figure 4.4 Results of Tronsky (2005), showing changes in strategy use for multiplication problems over time.

Tronsky, L. N. (2005). Strategy use, the development of automaticity, and working memory involvement in complex multiplication. *Memory & Cognition, 33,* 927–940. Published by Blackwell, Inc. Reprinted with permission from Blackwell, Inc., and the author.

formulaic or algorithmic. Subjects followed the sometimes arduous rules of multiplication. However, over time, their strategies had changed completely. By the end of the experiment, they were relying almost exclusively on memory to retrieve the products of the multiplication problems. Rather than getting faster and faster at carrying out the same computations, it seems that (consistent with Logan's 1988 view), subjects were changing how they performed the task, moving from the relatively slow and laborious application of an algorithm to the quick and efficient retrieval of an answer from memory.

Costs of Automaticity

Although the nature of automaticity is still debated, there is little doubt about the practical implications of automatic processing. Automaticity seems to be largely a good thing; after all, we perform tasks more quickly and efficiently and are better able to share attention between tasks. But there is a downside to automaticity. Automatic processes can be quite difficult to abort or modify, due in part to the fact that they involve relatively little in the way of conscious monitoring. Therefore, it's often the case that people make absentminded mistakes when they are engaged in automatic processing. These mistakes can range from the amusing to the downright dangerous. Norman (1981) coined a term for these all-too-common bouts of absentmindedness—**action slips.**

Action Slips.   We've all done it—put the cereal in the refrigerator; gone to a room to fetch something only to return with the wrong object; called someone on the phone and forgotten who it was we were calling. Norman (1988) would label each of these an action slip. Action slips tend to occur in the absence of attention (hence the term *absentmindedness*). Recall that one characteristic of automatic processes is that they are performed with relatively little conscious control or monitoring. Given this, it's not surprising that many action slips occur in the context of automatic processing; quite literally, when we do things automatically, *we aren't thinking*.

Norman (1988) proposes that highly learned action sequences (like driving a car) are controlled by organized memory structures termed *schemas*—an organized body of knowledge (or set of movements) that guides motor activities. Each schema is assumed to cover only a limited range of knowledge. Therefore, a given action sequence must be made up of a number of hierarchically organized schemas. The highest-level schema is called the *parent schema* and consists of a series of *child schemas* that are initiated by the parent schema at the appropriate time. A sample parent schema might be driving to school in the morning, which is made up of many child schemas, such as walking to the car, starting the car, and parking. Norman contends that once an action becomes highly skilled, only higher-level (parent) schemas need be activated to set a behavior chain in motion; once set in motion, it basically "runs" fairly mindlessly.

Action slips can occur at any time during this schema activation. Table 4.3 lists the various types of action slips. Let's take a look at each one. Some action slips can occur when schemas are triggered inappropriately. One type of slip, termed a *capture error,* occurs when some sequence being performed is similar to one that is very familiar and well practiced. The schemas controlling the well practiced action sequence may become activated and take over. For example, if you were a hockey player for your college team,

Table 4.3 Types of Action Slips

Capture error	A well-practiced, but unintended, action takes over when it shares initial sequence elements with a more unfamiliar action.
Data-driven error	External events cause the (inappropriate) activation of a schema and force some type of unwanted behavior.
Associative activation error	The intention to do or say something activates a strongly related but inappropriate schema.
Loss-of-activation error	The error lies in forgetting an intention to do something or remembering the intention but forgetting what to do.
Description error	The desired action is carried out but with the wrong object.

Adapted from Norman, D. A. (1981). Categorization of action slips. *Psychological Review, 88,* 1–15. Copyright 1981 by the American Psychological Association.

you would be very familiar with the way you stop while on ice skates. When on roller skates, you might try to stop in the same manner, because the ice-skate-stopping action is more familiar than the roller-skate-stopping action. Consequently, you might find yourself on the ground rather than on your skates!

A *data-driven error* occurs when external events cause the (inappropriate) activation of a schema and force some type of unwanted behavior. Have you ever been typing an e-mail, when a word from the music you are listening to appears on your screen? If so, you've experienced a data-driven error. An *associative activation error* occurs when your intention to do or say something activates a strongly related but inappropriate schema. For example, you might respond to a friend's question, "What's up?" with "Great!" This happens because what might be termed a *greeting schema* activates a number of *reply schemas* that are closely associated, and the wrong one wins.

Given that the associative activation error, the capture error, and the data-driven error all occur because an inappropriate schema is activated, you may find it difficult to differentiate between them. To distinguish them, think about the familiarity level and the nature of the intruding action sequence. If the intruding action sequence is more familiar than the intended action sequence, then a capture error has occurred. If the intruding action sequence is not more familiar but simply related to the intended action sequence, then an associative activation error has occurred. If the intruding action sequence is initiated by some aspect of the environment, regardless of whether it was more familiar or less familiar, then a data-driven error has occurred.

Activation of inappropriate schemas isn't the only route to an action slip. Some slips involve a failure to completely activate or maintain the activation of a schema. One of the most frustrating types of slips is the *loss-of-activation error,* which basically involves going to do something and forgetting what it was you wanted to do. This occurs when an activated schema loses activation because of decay or interference (two mechanisms for forgetting we'll discuss later in the chapter). Some slips can occur because an intention to do something is formed, but not correctly or completely. In other words, an incomplete description of what to do is formed, leading to what Norman terms a *description error.* This occurs when you carry out the action you wanted to but on the wrong object. For example, in a rush to put things away in the kitchen, you may find yourself putting cereal in the refrigerator and milk in the cupboard. The actions are appropriate, but they're performed on the wrong objects.

According to Norman (1981), all of these action slips occur because their prevention and/or detection requires feedback from the information-processing system about ongoing processing. Because such conscious monitoring is at a relatively low level when actions are automatic, slips are more likely to occur. Slips are prevalent in other situations that involve lowered conscious monitoring of behavior, such as when you're tired, stressed, or doing too many things at once.

STOP *and* THINK! ————————

ABSENTMINDEDNESS

Start a diary of all the absentminded mistakes you make over the next couple of weeks. Classify each error according to the scheme discussed in the text. Write them down in detail, including what happened, what should have happened, and what was going on externally (i.e., in the environment around you) and internally (your own thoughts, how you felt).

- When do these slips seem to occur?
- Relate their occurrence to the characteristics of automatic processing.

Ironic Processes of Control.   As you've seen, action slips are situations in which a behavior seems to come out of nowhere due to lowered attention and a lack of conscious monitoring. It might also interest you to know that sometimes, behaviors can come out of nowhere due to *heightened* attention and the presence of *too much* conscious monitoring! Basically, paying *too much* attention leads to what Wegner (1994) terms "ironic" effects. In other words, the processes involved in guarding against some type of mistaken action actually *encourage* the mistaken action to occur! Wegner, Ansfield, and Pilloff (1998) summarize it well: "Our bodies mock us as we double dribble, slice into the rough, miss our first serve, and otherwise work our way out of the record books and into blooper videos" (p. 196).

Wegner and his colleagues (Wegner, 1994, 2003; Wegner, Ansfield, & Pilloff, 1998) propose a two-factor theory of cognitive control to account for situations in which we make the very mistakes that we're trying to avoid making. According to this account, two different control processes come together in the service of action. The first process is termed an *intentional operating process,* and it is responsible for activating thoughts relevant to the goal at hand (e.g., hitting a golf ball off a tee). The second process is termed the *ironic monitoring process,* and it is responsible for keeping track of thoughts that might foil the goal at hand (e.g., a desire to see where your drive went makes you lift your head up too soon). The purpose of the ironic processes is to prevent the thoughts being monitored from surfacing. According to Wegner's (1994) analysis, the intentional operating process is conscious and effortful, while the ironic monitoring process is not conscious, does not demand effort, and is usually less influential. Its work is more "behind the scenes."

The two systems usually combine happily to produce the desired outcome. The intentional operating process fills the mind with goal-achieving thoughts and feelings while the ironic monitoring process concurrently tracks goal-thwarting thoughts or emotions. If the ironic monitoring process finds evidence of these, the intentional operating process initiates an act of control to keep the thoughts and emotions at bay. Here's where the irony starts to rear its ugly head: Because the ironic monitoring process is tracking unwanted thoughts and feelings, these thoughts and feelings are in an activated state. This is fine when the intentional operating process has sufficient capacity (say, when you're engaging in a task that's highly practiced, and you have nothing else on your mind). But if mental capacity is drained in some way (you're engaged in a task that takes a good deal of effort, or you're distracted or nervous), the intentional operating process is compromised in its ability to keep these now highly activated thoughts and feelings at bay, so they spill over into consciousness and impact behavior.

Wegner, Ansfield, and Pilloff (1998) tested this account in the context of what can be an exquisitely difficult motor skill to execute—putting a golf ball. If you've ever partaken in the grand game of golf, you know that you spend almost as much time considering how things could go wrong as you do considering how things could go right. This is certainly true of putting. And, according to the ironic process of control theory, this is OK—monitoring for unwanted thoughts is an important part of mental and physical control. But problems will arise in cases of increased mental load. Wegner et al. had all subjects make a baseline putt (they putted to a spot that was highlighted on the floor). Then, for their next (experimental) putt, they were given an extra instruction—they were told to be particularly careful not to overshoot the spot. For this second putt, half of the subjects were told to keep in mind a six-digit number that they would have to report after the putt. The other half was given no extra task.

According to the ironic process theory, the group given the mental load task should have been especially likely to overshoot. Can you figure out why? The intentional operating process would be activating all the thoughts and sensations that lead to a good putt, while the ironic monitoring process would be trying to find all of the thoughts and sensations related to overshooting. If such thoughts and sensations were found, the intentional operating process would deal with it, making the proper adjustment. But in this study, subjects were distracted by the requirement to keep a six-digit number in mind. Hence, the intentional process would be compromised in its ability to adjust—and so wouldn't be able to. Wegner et al.'s results (1998) fit neatly with this analysis. Figure 4.5 plots the difference (in centimeters) between the experimental ("don't overshoot") and baseline putts. A positive value on this measure indicates overshooting; a negative value indicates undershooting. Right in line with the predictions, overshooting proved to be a problem for subjects who were given a mental load; they overshot the putt by an average of over 20 cm! Subjects not given a mental load actually undershot the target by an average of 11 cm, which makes sense. Because there was no extra mental load, the intentional operating process could make the proper

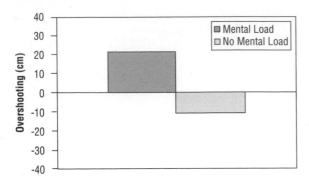

Figure 4.5 Results from Wegner, Ansfield, and Pilloff (1998).

From Wegner, D. M., Ansfield, M., & Pilloff, D. (1998). The putt and the pendulum: Ironic effects of the mental control of action. *Psychological Science, 9,* 196–199. Published by the American Psychological Association. Reprinted with permission of the author.

adjustments to avoid overshooting. So the lesson here may be that to avoid these ironic effects, you have to try not to think about the mistakes you tend to make. Unfortunately, that sets up a sort of double-irony situation (not to mention a syntactic disaster).

The ironic effects of control seem evident in situations far more serious than your occasional trip out to the Pirate's Cove Mini-Golf. Clinical psychologists have found the paradigm particularly applicable to disorders that feature the inability to control anxiety-producing thoughts, such as insomnia (Harvey, 2005), post-traumatic stress disorder (e.g., Shipherd & Beck, 2005), depression (Wenzlaff & Luxton, 2003), and obsessive-compulsive disorder (Smári, 2001).

1. Describe the major characteristics of an automatic process, and discuss two different views of what's happening as a task becomes automatic.
2. George was making pumpkin bread for his wife. He usually makes her banana bread, but today he decided to make pumpkin bread. When it came time to put in the pumpkin, he found himself peeling bananas. What type of action slip is this?
   a. associative activation error
   b. capture error
   c. data-driven error
   d. loss-of-activation error
3. True or false? If one is mentally overloaded, they are less apt to be a victim of ironic thought processes.

➤ Automaticity characterizes tasks that have received extensive practice and, as a result, seem to operate without intention, outside of conscious awareness, and with a minimum demand on attention. One view of their development is that there is a dramatic increase in the speed of processing. An alternative account is that, with practice, processing shifts from algorithm to memory retrieval.

➤ Action slips refer to absentminded actions that can occur during the course of automatic processing due to a lack of conscious monitoring. A capture error occurs when a well-practiced action sequence takes over an intended one. Other types of errors include loss-of-activation errors, data-driven errors, and associative activation errors.

➤ Processes of mental control can have ironic effects, in that they actually contribute to the mistakes in behavior that they are guarding against. These ironic effects seem more prevalent in cognitively demanding situations.

Processing in Immediate Memory

At several points in our discussion of attention, we said that once information has passed through the limited-capacity gateway of attention, it receives further processing. What is the nature of this further processing? These processes are referred to collectively as short-term memory, or working memory. The distinction between a temporarily activated, conscious form of memory and a nonactive, nonconscious store of knowledge that can be brought into an active state when necessary is not a new one. William James (1890) himself proposed such a distinction, labeling the former "primary memory" and the latter "secondary memory."

The Information-Processing Approach to Memory

Waugh and Norman (1965) and Atkinson and Shiffrin (1968) formalized and popularized this distinction, making it a centerpiece of their information-processing view of memory. The Atkinson-Shiffrin view has been so influential that it is often termed the *modal model* of how memory works. The **modal model** (also called the *information-processing model*) is summarized in Figure 4.6. As you can see, the model is clearly in the tradition of information-processing models, postulating a series of chronologically arranged stages through which incoming information passes. Although current researchers are unsure about this stagelike progression, not to mention the idea of three distinct memory stores, the model provides an extremely useful way to describe what phenomenologically seem to be different types of memory processing.

Three Memory Systems. Atkinson and Shiffrin (1968) propose three different types of memory storage: sensory memory, short-term memory, and long-term memory. As originally conceptualized, **sensory memory** serves as an initial storage system and refers to an extremely brief representation of a just-presented stimulus. Although some type of sensory memory is thought to exist for all major senses, it's easiest to imagine in the context of vision; Atkinson and Shiffrin label this quickly fleeting form of storage "iconic memory." The notion of an icon is evident when viewing a scene during a lightning flash. Although the flash lasts only about 50 ms, the scene illuminated by the flash seems to be visible for much longer. In the laboratory, this phenomenon is demonstrated by presenting a stimulus array very briefly to subjects and having them report as many letters as possible. Evidence from laboratory studies indicated that when presented with a stimulus array, the entire array remained available for about 1/4 of a second (just as the scene illuminated by a lightning flash remains available). Basically, for that brief period, subjects could "read off" any part of the array, given that they had an "icon" to look at. However, the icon was found to fade almost instantly.

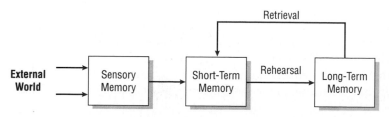

Figure 4.6 The modal model: An information-processing view of memory.

The notion of a rapidly decaying iconic memory store has become a bit outmoded in the eyes of many researchers (e.g., Massaro & Loftus, 1996; Nairne, 2002b). Rather than viewing iconic memory as a passive buffer or "box" that holds information for a brief time, iconic memory is usually conceived of as a phenomenon of **visual persistence** that results from the way the visual system processes stimuli over the course of time. Put another way, the *decaying icon* is simply a by-product of the way our neural systems process visual information. For example, when a visual stimulus is presented, the presentation begins a neural response that lasts for a few hundred milliseconds. If the stimulus is removed immediately after presentation (as it is in many studies of iconic memory), the neural response will continue to its natural end; this continuation is experienced as the fading icon.

The centerpiece of the theory has proved to be the other two memory stores and the postulated distinction between them. **Long-term memory (LTM)** can be conceptualized as a vast repository that houses all of the experiences, knowledge, and skills that we have accumulated throughout our lifetimes. (Keep in mind that this simple spatial metaphor is only a convenient description of LTM and fails to capture anything about LTM storage on a physiological level.) We'll address issues of LTM in much more depth in Chapters 6 through 9.

Short-Term Memory

So what lies between the transient sensory buffer and the long-term storage of everything we know? **Short-term memory (STM)** is the set of processes that we use to hold and rehearse information that occupies our current awareness. This *temporary* form of memory can be conceptualized as a sort of mental workbench in which we rehearse or recycle information. You'll notice that in Figure 4.6 (p. 137), there are arrows running from STM to LTM and vice versa. This signifies that rehearsal in STM is thought to result in LTM storage. And when information in LTM is appropriate for dealing with present circumstances, it is *brought back into STM*.

Since the inception of the modal model in 1968, research on short-term memory has exploded, and many investigators' conceptualization of it has gone well beyond the original idea of STM as a holding and recycling buffer. Short-term memory is often investigated in the context of other more complex cognitive processes, such as reading and problem solving. There is no doubt that these abilities are critically dependent on the elaborate processing of information that currently resides in consciousness, not just on temporarily holding a set of items in mind. In discussing this expanded conceptualization of short-term memory, researchers often use the term *working memory (WM)*, a concept we'll examine in more detail later in the chapter. It is important to note that the term *working memory* is now the modal terminology used by cognitive researchers (and will be used throughout this book). However, from a historical perspective, investigations into this area began with what was traditionally termed STM. Therefore, we'll start our discussion in the same manner, by examining the basic characteristics of STM.

Limited Duration and Capacity. When keeping track of your instructor's riveting lectures, you've no doubt experienced one of the defining characteristics of STM—the fact that it has a limited duration. The information seems gone pretty quickly after it is presented. Information is active in STM only temporarily; in order to maintain information in STM, it needs to be rehearsed. In Chapter 6, you'll read more about the basic rehearsal of information and its effect on long-term retention.

The limited duration of STM has been most often demonstrated with the **Brown-Peterson task** (Brown, 1958; Peterson & Peterson, 1959). In this task, people receive a brief presentation of a consonant trigram (e.g., JDL) immediately followed by the presentation of a three-digit number. Subjects must count backward by threes from that number. The purpose of the counting task is to prevent the subjects from rehearsing the material. The amount of time they're required to count defines the **retention interval.** The amount of time that lapses between encoding and retrieval is a common independent variable in memory experiments. Peterson and Peterson's results are presented in Figure 4.7. As you can see, forgetting was quite extreme and quite quick; within about 20 seconds, the probability of recalling the trigram was only 0.10 (or 10%).

Duration isn't the only limit on STM processing. As you're well aware from frenzied attempts to write down what your professor is saying, there are severe limits in what STM can handle at one time. A loose analogy can be drawn between STM and storage on some type of media like CDs, which can hold only a finite amount of information, depending on their capacity. Analogously, the amount of information we can hold in STM is also limited (we'll return later to this analogy).

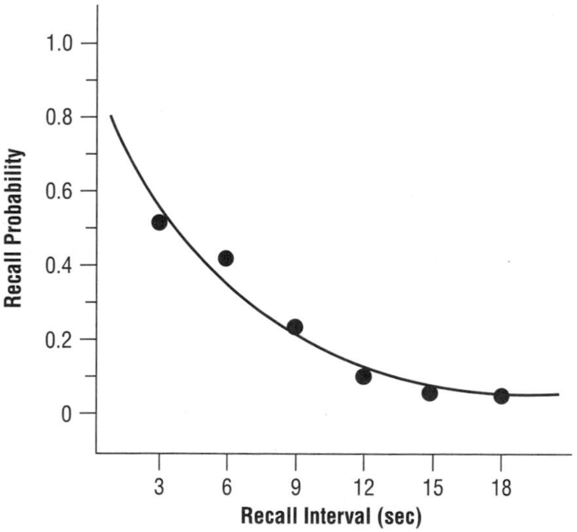

Limitations in STM capacity were noted by George Miller, one of the leading figures in the cognitive revolution of the 1950s. In a classic paper, Miller (1956) notes the prominence of what he coined the **magical number,** 7 ± 2. He was referring to a strikingly consistent limitation in the number of items we can hold in STM. Miller noted that this number is applicable across a wide array of different stimulus types, from letters to numbers to words to musical notes. So "magical" is this number that it was the basis for our seven-digit phone numbers. Based on the early work investigating STM capacity, seven digits were chosen as the most reasonable load an individual could remember that would still allow for various phone number combinations.

The limited capacity of STM is most often assessed through **memory span,** the longest string of information (e.g., numbers, letters) that a person can immediately recall. A legion of research findings from studies of STM memory

Figure 4.7 Short-term memory fades with time.

From Peterson, L., & Peterson, M. J. (1959). Short-term retention of individual verbal items. *Journal of Experimental Psychology, 58,* 193–198.

span confirm what Miller originally proposed: that we have a fundamental limit in our ability to keep track of incoming information (e.g., Baddeley, 1993; Shiffrin & Nosofsky, 1994). Nairne (1996) likens the limited capacity of STM to the capacity of a juggler. Just as a juggler can keep only so many balls in the air at a time, our STM can keep only so much information "in the air" at a time. Miller puts the limit at 7 ± 2 items. Now the question is, what exactly constitutes an item?

Chunking in STM.   It turns out that our STM is considerably more powerful than the magic number would imply. Although there is no doubt that there is a limit to memory span, we can functionally increase the limits by recoding information, combining it into larger and larger "chunks." Through this process, called **chunking** or **recoding,** you translate incoming information into a more manageable form. The capacity limits of STM never get beyond the magic number, but with efficient use of recoding strategies, we can functionally increase the capacity. In the juggling analogy to STM, we can think of this as being able to juggle seven large balls or seven small balls, but seven is all that can be juggled. And according to Cowan (2001), it's not even really seven. He contends that Miller's "magic number" was mainly meant to be a rough estimate, almost as a rhetorical device to describe the capacity limit of short-term memory (which, by the way, does fit with the folksy manner in which Miller lays out his argument). Cowan's thorough review of STM literature post-Miller suggests that the limit is actually about four chunks of information, with a chunk defined as ". . . a collection of concepts that have strong associations to one another and much weaker connections to other chunks currently in use" (p. 89).

However one conceives of this limit, our ability to chunk or recode information is affected by a number of variables. First, because STM has a relatively brief duration, the rate of presentation can be a limiting factor in chunking. For instance, when someone tells you a phone number too quickly, with no pauses, these *characteristics of presentation* have a significant effect on your recoding. Recoding is also profoundly affected by *knowledge base.* When you're taking notes based on a professor's lecture, you are recoding the information. This ability is enhanced the more you know about the topic; previous knowledge aids your reorganization of the information. (That's why it helps to read the material from the textbook before you come to class!)

Effects of Word Length.   Because the information in STM seems to be lost relatively quickly, it shouldn't be surprising that the longer an item takes to pronounce, the fewer such items you can hold in STM. Since Miller's (1956) original formulation of the magic number, research has demonstrated that this number may not be as "magic" as was first thought. Short-term memory span seems to be limited not necessarily by the number of items being encoded but by the time it takes to encode a given set of items. Consider again the CD analogy: the amount of information that will fit on a disc is not only determined by the capacity allowed by the disc, but also by how fast you talk. (The faster you talk, the more information you can get on the disc.) Similarly, retaining 7 ± 2 long items (e.g., *hippopotamus*) in STM proves to be much more difficult than retaining 7 ± 2 short items (e.g., *cat*). This **word-length effect** is a consistent finding in studies of STM (e.g., Baddeley, Thompson, & Buchanan, 1975; Schweickert, McDaniel, & Riegler, 1993) and serves as another illustration of the time-based nature of STM.

STOP *and* THINK!

WORD LENGTH AND STM CAPACITY

Find two friends to serve as cognitive guinea pigs. For each subject, pick one condition, and test their short-term memory of each list by reading each item at a rate of about one second per item and having them recall after each list.

Condition 1	Condition 2
1. ham	**1.** mystery
dog	vanilla
gem	bicycle
skill	pyramid
heart	condiment
bag	television
ring	automobile
2. cat	**2.** gigantic
beef	anatomy
stone	octopus
tin	factory
job	ladybug
fruit	metallic
blue	cabinet
3. shoe	**3.** tornado
bow	animal
book	martini
jaw	surgery
song	radio
can	cantaloupe
jug	barbaric

- Did the subject in each condition demonstrate the same or different results?
- Did the results fit Miller's "magic number"?
- If not, what factor(s) may have led to the discrepancy?
- Why?

Coding in STM. How is information typically coded in STM? When you're listening to something, whether it's a phone number or an important fact from class discussion, how do you keep track of it in consciousness? Your answer is almost certainly that you repeat it to yourself. A great deal of research indicates that *auditory coding* is the dominant mode of processing in STM. That is, we "hear" information as it is being rehearsed via a sort of "inner voice." One piece of experimental evidence supporting this idea is the **phonological similarity effect,** the finding that lists of similar-sounding items are more difficult to keep track of in STM than are lists of different-sounding items. This basic effect has been replicated many times (e.g., Baddeley, 1966; Conrad, 1964; Schiano & Watkins, 1981). It even occurs when material is presented visually, strongly implying that visually presented information is quickly converted into an auditory form. The word-length effect, described earlier, is also cited as evidence for auditory coding in STM: the longer it takes to say an item, the fewer such items can be held. We tend to maintain information in STM by repeating it, so it makes sense that when it takes a long time to say information, it's going to place more of a strain on STM.

STOP *and* THINK!

PHONOLOGICAL SIMILARITY AND STM

Same instructions as last time. Find two friends to serve as cognitive guinea pigs. For each subject, pick one of the list conditions (1 or 2) and test memory of each list by reading each item at a rate of about one second per item and having the subject recall the items.

List 1a: f, z, k, w, r, p, m
List 1b: e, g, z, b, t, p, v
List 2a: cat, chair, joy, hat, book, run, tree
List 2b: cake, lake, bake, sake, take, make, rake

• Did you notice any differences in subjects' ability to recall the two lists?
• If so, what factor(s) seem to relate to this difference?

But is audition the only modality in which information can be coded in STM? Simple introspection tells us that STM processing is not limited to some type of auditory rehearsal. The processing of material in your conscious awareness also allows for visual coding. The use of a visual code is easy to demonstrate. Look up from this book (yes, we know that's hard to do), close your eyes, and think about the steps involved in getting to your first class in the morning. It's a good bet that you aren't verbally saying, "Walk out door, turn right, turn left, enter elevator, go outside." It's more likely that you're visualizing the path you take; this is a simple example of visual coding in STM.

A study by Brandimonte and Gerbino (1993) provides an interesting demonstration of auditory and visual coding in STM. Their experiment made use of reversible figures (pictures with two possible interpretations that alternate as you're viewing them). One question that emerges from the investigation of these figures is whether mental images (i.e., visual codings) of these reversible figures can be ambiguous—that is, interpreted in two different ways. For example, if you briefly view a reversible figure and then simply hold it in memory, does it reverse just as it does when you're actually looking at it? If the answer is yes, this provides strong evidence for the presence of a visual coding mechanism in STM.

Brandimonte and Gerbino (1993) reasoned that image reversal in STM probably is possible, but only under certain conditions. Consider what might happen if you were presented very briefly with the reversible picture depicted in Figure 4.8. Chances are, if your inner voice says "duck," the image being held in STM will look like a duck. (Or conversely,

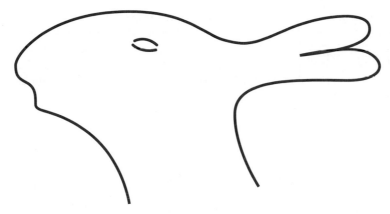

Figure 4.8 Rabbit or duck?

From Brandimonte, M. A., & Gerbino, W. (1993). Mental image reversal and verbal recording: When ducks become rabbits. *Memory and Cognition, 21,* 23–33. Reprinted by permission of the Psychonomic Society, Inc.

if your inner voice says "rabbit" the image being held in STM will look like a rabbit.) But (and this is the important point) if the image is quickly labeled as either a duck or a rabbit, seeing the other version will be much less likely. In other words, the auditory code that enjoys such prominence in STM leads to a particular interpretation of the figure and blocks the other interpretation. But if the auditory processing of STM is somehow prevented, both interpretations might remain equally viable and allow for a spontaneous figure reversal.

To test this idea, Brandimonte and Gerbino trained subjects using a couple of reversible figures so that they would be familiar with the general idea and experience the image reversals that can occur. After this training phase, subjects were presented with a new reversible figure (the duck/rabbit figure); the presentation duration was brief (two seconds) to prevent subjects from experiencing the reversal while actually viewing it. But this brief presentation was sufficient for an auditory coding of the stimulus. During this brief presentation, half of the subjects remained silent; the other half was required to say, "La, la, la" (which helps prevent auditory rehearsal). After the image was taken away, subjects were asked what they had seen. Next, subjects were told to hold the figure in mind and attempt to reverse it in order to reveal the second possible interpretation. The investigators wanted to see if image reversals would depend on whether or not subjects were able to use an auditory code during the initial encoding.

An interesting aspect of this study is that Brandimonte and Gerbino investigated both children and adults. Citing other experimental evidence that young children tend to rely

Research Theme: Development

on a visual code in STM tasks, they argued that young children's ability to imagine the reversals would not differ in the silent and "la, la, la" conditions. That is, since young children don't rely on auditory coding, it should not matter whether they are allowed to rehearse or not. But because older children and adults tend to code information in an auditory form, they should be affected by the prevention of auditory rehearsal and therefore imagine more reversals in the "la, la, la" condition.

The results from the study are presented in Figure 4.9. Consistent with the researchers' analysis, reversals of the mental image were much more likely to occur when auditory rehearsal was prevented; for example, preventing subjects from silently saying, "Rabbit" when they first saw the item made it more likely that they would be able to see a "duck" when they imagined it later. Clearly, we have the ability to encode information in a visual format in STM. Interestingly, the effect did depend on age. As predicted by the investigators, young children experience just as many image reversals when auditory rehearsal is prevented as when it isn't, suggesting that auditory coding isn't that important in their

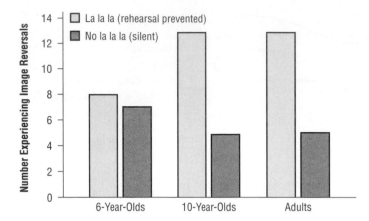

Figure 4.9 Results from the Brandimonte and Gerbino (1993) study.

From Brandimonte, M. A., & Gerbino, W. (1993). Mental image reversal and verbal recoding: When ducks become rabbits. *Memory and Cognition, 21,* 23–33. Reprinted by permission of the Psychonomic Society, Inc.

initial encoding. The Brandimonte and Gerbino study is just one of many that support the existence of visual coding in STM. In other words, our STM seems to feature both an "inner voice" and an "inner eye."

Forgetting in STM. As stated before, one of the most palpable characteristics of STM is the fact that information is lost fairly quickly. Two mechanisms have received a great deal of attention as the primary culprits in this loss of information: decay and interference. Let's examine each of these in more detail.

Decay.   The loss of information from STM due to the passage of time is referred to as **decay.** The initial evidence for this rather simple view consists of findings from early studies that employed the Brown-Peterson technique. Forgetting in this task seemed to occur even with minimal interference. It was assumed that counting backward did not interfere with the maintenance of information in STM because the corresponding stimuli (letters and numbers) are so dissimilar. Therefore, any forgetting that occurred was attributable to decay.

The decay view of forgetting may be seen as a little insufficient. As everyone knows, time passes, and we forget. As noted by Nairne (1996) in a critique of the decay account of forgetting, the fact that iron rusts over time does not mean that the rust was caused by time's passage. It's caused by something that happens over the time interval—namely, oxidation. In the same way, many researchers believe that a better account of STM forgetting must involve the specification of the events that happen during the retention interval. The most likely candidate is interference.

Interference.   According to the notion of **interference,** information is lost from STM because information currently being processed is negatively influenced by the presentation of other information. In a broad sense, interference can occur in one of two basic patterns. When earlier information interferes with the ability to retain information that comes later, it's termed **proactive interference.** The complementary case, in which later information interferes with the ability to retain information that occurred earlier, is termed **retroactive interference.** These two can be distinguished by considering the temporal relationship between the to-be-remembered information and the interfering information. Figure 4.10 should help you distinguish between the two.

So what causes forgetting in STM—a simple process of erosion, or the confusion that arises when we encode additional information? There still exists a fair amount of disagreement on this score, although most researchers probably look to interference as the more likely culprit. There are a number of findings that cast serious doubt on simple

Here's a scheme that should help you discriminate between retroactive and proactive interference. Imagine that you've spent your weekend studying for two tests—psychology and sociology. You studied psychology on Saturday and sociology on Sunday.

Which information was learned first? Write it down:

> *psychology*

Which information was learned second? Write it down to the right of the item that was learned first; it was learned after the first item:

> psychology   *sociology*

Which of the two pieces of information is trying to be remembered? Let's say you're taking your psychology exam. Underline that item and draw an arrow from the nonunderlined item (i.e., the item that is not being remembered) to the underlined item (i.e., the item that is being remembered).

If the arrow is pointing in the backward direction (pointing backward in time from what was learned second to what was learned first), the type of interference is *retroactive* (*retro* means "backward"). Sociology information is retroactively interfering with your ability to remember information for your psychology exam.

Now let's imagine you are in your sociology exam.

If the arrow is pointing in the forward direction, the type of interference is *proactive* (*pro* means "forward"). Psychology information is proactively interfering with your ability to remember information for your sociology exam.

Figure 4.10 Scheme/mnemonic for distinguishing retroactive and proactive interference.

From Robinson-Riegler, M. B., Robinson-Riegler, G., & Kohn, A. J. (1999). *Instructor's resource guide* for J. Kalat, *Introduction to psychology* (5th ed.). Belmont, CA: Wadsworth. Copyright 1999. Reprinted by permission of Wadsworth, a division of Thomson Learning.

decay theory. For example, Keppel and Underwood (1962) used the Brown-Peterson task to assess forgetting and found that there was virtually no forgetting on the first of a set of Brown-Peterson trials. Not only that, it didn't matter how long the delay interval was; even with long delays, there was almost no forgetting on the initial trial. There seemed to be little or no effect of longer retention intervals until trials started to accumulate. Put another way, there seemed to be little or no effect of delay until there was significant potential for interference (proactive, in this case) to occur. Hence, interference is implicated as the more important cause of forgetting.

STOP *and* **THINK!**

INTERFERENCE AND FORGETTING IN STM

Go back to the results you gathered from the *Stop and Think!* on the word-length effect (pg. 141). Better yet, rerun the experiment, this time with a different set of questions in mind.

- Should the number of words recalled change from group 1 to group 3, regardless of condition?
- If so, how should it change? Why?
- What did your results show? (Think about it in terms of interference.)

Trial 1	*Recall*	Trial 2	*Recall*	Trial 3	*Recall*	Trial 4	*Recall*
daisy		tulip		orchid		plum	
rose		sunflower		carnation		peach	
daffodil		hyacinth		marigold		banana	

Figure 4.11 A rendition of the Wickens et al. (1976) procedure for demonstrating release from proactive interference.

Adapted from Wickens, D. D., Dalezman, R. E., & Eggemeier, F. T. (1976). Multiple encoding of word attributes in memory. *Memory and Cognition, 4,* 307–310.

An experiment by Wickens, Dalezman, and Eggemeier (1976) provides another classic demonstration of proactive interference, and adds a twist to the coding picture in short-term memory. In this study, Wickens et al. employed the Brown-Peterson task but used categorized lists instead of letters. On a given trial, subjects would read three flowers—daisy, rose, daffodil—and then be required to count backward. After this distractor period, they were asked to recall the professions.

Wickens et al. presented three of these Brown-Peterson trials in a row, each time using three more items from the same category (see Figure 4.11). As you can see in Figure 4.12, the subjects in this study were profoundly affected by this proactive interference; recall fell by 60% from the first to the third trials. But the most intriguing finding from this study emerged on a fourth Brown-Peterson trial. Recall that subjects had received three successive lists from the same category. On the fourth trial, they were presented with three items but this time from a different category—fruits. (A control group received fruits on all four trials.) The last data point in the figure shows the surprising result: recall bounced back up. This bounce-back effect is termed **release from proactive interference.** Interestingly, the greater the difference between the original lists and the final list, the greater the release. As it turns out, the Wickens study is a classic, not only for its demonstration of proactive interference and release from proactive interference, but also for its revealing another dimension of STM: STM is also (at least somewhat) sensitive to meaning.

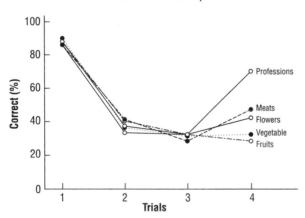

Figure 4.12 Trial-by-trial recall in the Wickens et al. (1976) study.

From Wickens, D. D., Dalezman, R. E., & Eggemeier, F. T. (1976). Multiple encoding of word attributes in memory. *Memory and Cognition, 4,* 307–310. Reprinted by permission of the Psychonomic Society, Inc.

STOP *and* **REVIEW!**

1. Which of the memory stores originally proposed in the modal model is no longer considered to be a form of memory?

2. The duration of STM
   a. is about two minutes.
   b. is less than one second.
   c. is about 20 seconds.
   d. depends upon the length of the word.

3. Consider the following two lists of letters:
   B P C Z D T
   J F R Q N W
   Which would be easier to keep track of in STM, and why?

4. Describe the two types of forgetting in STM. Which is most cognitive researchers' preferred account of forgetting?

➤ The modal model is an information-processing view of memory that proposes three memory systems: sensory memory, originally thought to hold a rapidly fading trace of presented formation (but now viewed as a form of sensory persistence and not really memory); long-term memory, our vast storehouse of knowledge about the world and our lives; and short-term memory, which allows for the processing of information in consciousness.

➤ STM refers to the processes that are used for temporarily holding, rehearsing, and responding to information currently in consciousness. STM is limited in duration, lasting less than 20 seconds without rehearsal. STM capacity is limited (7 ±2 items), but can be functionally increased by chunking incoming information.

➤ Information in STM is processed predominantly in auditory (sound-based) form as indicated by the phonological similarity effect (similar-sounding items are more difficult to keep track of in STM than are different-sounding items). Visual coding is also possible in STM.

➤ Information loss from STM is thought to result from decay (the simple passage of time) or interference (inhibition from other sources of information)—proactive interference (earlier information interferes with the ability to retain information that comes later) and retroactive interference (later information interferes with the ability to retain information that occurred earlier). Researchers prefer interference as an account of STM forgetting.

A Modular Approach to STM: Working Memory

Three decades of research on STM have liberated it from its conceptualization as a simple information recycler, as conceived of in the early days of information-processing theory. Based on years of research demonstrating the richness and variety of STM processing,

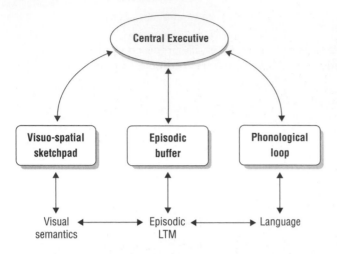

Figure 4.13 Baddeley's model of working memory.

Reprinted by permission from Macmillan Publishers LTD: NATURE REVIEWS NEUROSCIENCE. Baddeley, A. (2003). Working memory: Looking back and looking forward. *Nature Reviews Neuroscience, 4,* 829–839.

investigators have proposed increasingly elaborate models of STM function, the most popular of which is a model termed *working memory (WM)* (Baddeley, 1986, 2000b; Hitch & Baddeley, 1976). The model has captured researchers' fancy to such a degree that working memory is how many psychologists refer to the collective set of processes we've been discussing. According to this model, working memory is actually a number of closely interacting subsystems that combine to subserve a host of higher-level mental processes, including language comprehension, problem solving, and reasoning. Figure 4.13 provides an overview of Baddeley's model. Two of the subsystems incorporate notions of auditory (articulatory loop) and visual (visuo-spatial sketchpad) coding in STM. A recently added subsystem (episodic buffer) is a "go-between" that allows for integration among the articulatory loop and the visuo-spatial sketchpad and long-term memory. The final component (central executive) serves as the "boss" of STM, supervising the operation of the other subsystems and carrying out important duties of its own.

The Articulatory Loop

Intuition, along with the results of many investigations (discussed earlier in this chapter) of STM, tells us that information can be temporarily held in some type of active form and that the dominant mode for holding the information is based on some type of auditory code (the "inner voice" discussed earlier). According to the working memory model, this is accomplished by the **articulatory loop.** This component is actually made up of two subcomponents: a *phonological store* that holds information temporarily and an articulatory process, called the *subvocal rehearsal mechanism,* that allows for the rehearsal of information. According to this model, the effects we discussed earlier (the effects of word length and phonological similarity) result from the mechanics of the articulatory loop. The word-length effect derives from the fact that information in the phonological store is extremely limited in duration. Our difficulty remembering similar-sounding items results from the subvocal rehearsal mechanism.

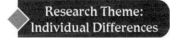

The name "sub*vocal* rehearsal mechanism" and research indicating the dominance of auditory coding in STM (the "inner voice") may make you think that the WM system is based solely on audition. But what about deaf individuals? They lack normal auditory sensory capabilities, but it seems unlikely that they have no rehearsal mechanism. Therefore, the mechanism must be more general in nature, allowing for internal rehearsal in whatever mode the rehearser is accustomed to using.

All uses of language—including American Sign Language—involve the articulatory loop.

The name of the working memory (WM) subsystem that contains the subvocal rehearsal mechanism provides a hint—it's called the *articulatory loop*. Articulation requires the coordination of various motor movements to produce the basic units of the communication system, whether those units are sounds (in the case of speech, which we'll discuss further in Chapter 10) or hand movements, for users of American Sign Language (ASL). The prominence of auditory coding discussed earlier occurs because the subjects in these studies used speech to communicate. So while it is functionally accurate to say that the dominant mode is auditory (most people use speech to communicate), this fact may lead one to have an oversimplified view of WM. Audition is prominent not because the basic mechanisms of WM rely on the auditory modality but because WM relies on articulatory processes, which happen to be auditory in hearing adults. With this revised viewpoint, let's reconsider some of the findings we discussed earlier.

For users of speech, researchers find a phonological similarity effect: similar-sounding words are more difficult to keep track of than different-sounding words. But the critical factor is not that the words sound similar, but that similar motor movements are required to articulate the words. Given that the important dimension is the particular mode of articulation rather than the sound itself, we should expect to obtain an analogous finding for users of ASL in their articulatory mode—namely, signing. In other words, deaf signers of ASL should show a sign-based similarity effect. Similar-looking signs should be more difficult to keep track of than different-looking signs, because similar-looking signs share similar motor movements. This has been found by several

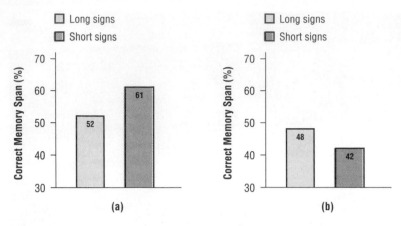

Figure 4.14 Results from the Wilson and Emmorey (1998) study.

From Wilson, M., & Emmorey, K. (1998). A "word-length effect" for sign-language: Further evidence for the role of language in structuring working memory. *Memory and Cognition, 26,* 584–590. Reprinted by permission of the Psychonomic Society, Inc.

investigators (e.g., Beluggi, Klima, & Siple, 1974; Hanson, 1982; Wilson & Emmorey, 1997); signs that share the same hand movements are more difficult for deaf signers to retain in WM than are signs that vary in hand movements.

Second, one would expect to find a word-length effect; long signs should be just as difficult for deaf signers to keep straight as long words are for hearing speakers. To test this idea, Wilson and Emmorey (1998) presented deaf users of ASL with signs that varied in terms of the movement features. Long signs featured movements that were large and circular, covered distance, or featured a change in direction; short signs involved short movements, with no change of direction. Importantly, the long and short signs were matched for other features, such as the hand shapes used. The signs were filmed and presented to subjects via videotape. At the end of each sign sequence, a probe sign was presented that signaled subjects to recall the list. The results are presented in Figure 4.14a. As you can see, the researchers did indeed find a word-length effect for sign language. Signs involving more distance, changes in direction, or large circular motions were more difficult to remember.

Effects of Articulatory Suppression. Given that articulation is the critical factor in the operation of the articulatory loop, what would happen if we prevent a person from articulating the information they are attempting to rehearse? Remember the "la, la, la" distractor discussed in the rabbit/duck study? Well, it has a name—**articulatory suppression task.** The task is designed to prevent a person from using articulation mechanisms to rehearse information by tying up their "inner voice" with another silly task (saying, "La, la, la, . . .). As you might expect, this makes the retention of information in WM much more difficult, decreasing memory span (Murray, 1968).

Articulatory suppression also influences the effects of phonological similarity and word length. Recall that even visually presented stimuli (e.g., printed words or nameable pictures) seem to be quickly translated into an auditory form (Posner & Keele, 1968) and therefore are subject to the negative effects of phonological similarity. However, something interesting happens when you introduce articulatory suppression during the encoding of visually presented items: there is no negative effect of phonological similarity (e.g., Coltheart, 1993; Murray, 1968). It makes sense if you think about it. Seeing a picture of a tiger, or the printed word *tiger,* will lead you to silently rehearse "tiger" using the subvocal rehearsal mechanism—unless I prevent you from doing so through articulatory suppression. In that case, the item cannot be coded in terms of the articulatory mode of your communication system—sound—so the way the words sound doesn't influence performance. Therefore, it doesn't matter whether the items sound alike or not; you can't use articulation mechanisms anyway.

Articulatory suppression has similar effects on the word-length effect. An articulatory suppression task prevents rehearsal with the subvocal rehearsal mechanism. Therefore, it makes no difference whether the incoming information is long or short; it can't be rehearsed through articulatory mechanisms anyway. Indeed, articulatory suppression tends to eliminate the effects of word length on recall from WM (e.g., Baddeley, Lewis, & Vallar, 1984).

In investigations of the word-length effect in users of ASL, subjects were presented with hand signs that were either long or short. Would articulatory suppression make this effect go away, as it does with hearing subjects? And what would articulatory suppression be for deaf subjects? Wilson and Emmorey (1998) looked at the effects of suppression in a second condition of their study. To do this, half of the subjects had to engage in a suppression task. These subjects were required to touch their middle fingers to their respective thumbs (the ASL 8 hand shape) while at the same time having their hands circle one another, with contact at the end of each circle (this is the sign for "world"). Just as saying "La, la, la" prevents a hearing person from using the "inner voice" to vocally rehearse, making hand motions should prevent a nonhearing person from using what might be termed the "inner hands" to manually rehearse. As you can see in Figure 4.14b, this is exactly what Wilson and Emmorey found: suppression not only disrupted WM performance overall, it also eliminated the effects of sign length. And interestingly, an earlier study by Wilson and Emmorey (1997) produced the corresponding finding: articulatory suppression eliminated the sign-based similarity effect. So whether you're dealing with the spoken word or ASL hand movements, it's pretty clear that there is an articulation mechanism that immediately codes incoming information in terms of one's customary language and developmental experience (Wilson & Emmorey, 1998) and that this articulation mechanism can be blocked.

Research Theme: Individual Differences

The Visuo-Spatial Sketchpad

Based on findings that indicate visual coding in STM, Baddeley (1986) proposes a corresponding subsystem within WM, termed the **visuo-spatial sketchpad.** This component of WM is responsible for the storage and manipulation of visual and spatial information and seems to operate (in large part) independently of the other subsystem (the articulatory loop). In other words, visual/spatial encoding and articulatory coding do not interfere with one another.

This lack of interference was demonstrated in a study by Brooks (1967). Brooks manipulated the task mode (visual or verbal) and the response mode (visual or verbal). His results showed that while subjects had a great deal of difficulty when the task mode and the response mode were in the same modality—both visual (i.e., both engaging the visuo-spatial sketchpad) or both verbal (i.e., both engaging the articulatory loop)—they had little difficulty if the task mode and response mode were different. It seems that the visuo-spatial sketchpad and articulatory loop can operate together with little loss in performance efficiency.

Some evidence indicates a further division of duties within the visuo-spatial sketchpad. Della Sala, Gray, Baddeley, Allamano, and Wilson (1999) propose separable

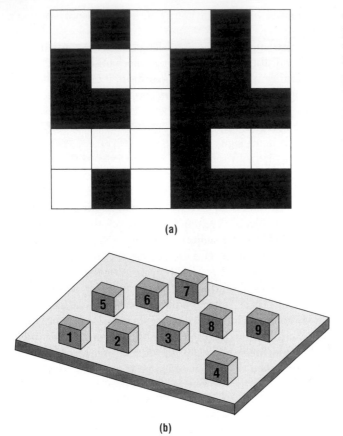

(a)

(b)

Figure 4.15 Tasks used by Della Sala et al. (1999) to assess processing of the visuo-spatial sketchpad. The figure in (a) depicts the visual processing task; the figure in (b) depicts the spatial processing task.

Reprinted from Della Sala, S., Gray, C., Baddeley, A., Allamano, N., Wilson, L. (1999). Pattern span: A tool for unwelding visuo-spatial memory. *Neuropsychologia. 37*, 1189–1199. Copyright 1999 Elsevier. Reprinted with permission from Elsevier.

components corresponding to *spatial* processing and *visual* processing. To see the difference, take a look at the tasks used by Della Sala et al. to assess each subcomponent. Figure 4.15a presents the visual processing task (the VPT); Figure 4.15b presents the spatial processing task (SPT). For the VPT, subjects are presented with a visual matrix—a checkerboard pattern with randomly alternating black and white squares. After a three-second presentation, subjects must replicate the pattern by filling in squares in a blank matrix. The SPT is called the *Corsi blocks test*. The subject watches the experimenter using a stick to tap out a pattern on the wood blocks. Once the pattern has been tapped out, the subject has to replicate it. Like the VPT, this SPT is visual, but it ups the ante by adding the requirement of remembering a positional sequence. Whereas the VPT requires only memory for the appearance of a matrix, the SPT requires that subjects mentally reason about distance, direction, and order.

Della Sala et al. (1999) tested the notion of separate visual and spatial processes by using an interference paradigm. On noninterference trials, subjects were presented with a visual or a spatial pattern and were tested on the pattern after an unfilled 10-second interval. On interference trials, the 10-second interval was filled with an interference task. On half of these interference trials, the subjects had to view irrelevant pictures before reconstructing the visual matrix. This task was thought primarily to involve visual processing, and was expected to interfere primarily with the VPT. On the other half of the interference trials, subjects had to reach under a screen and haptically (i.e., by touch) follow a sequence of pegs. This task was thought primarily to involve spatial processing, and was expected to interfere primarily with the SPT.

The results from the study are presented in Figure 4.16. As you can see, a double dissociation occurred. Recall from Chapter 2 that a double dissociation occurs when two levels of an independent variable have opposite effects on two different cognitive tasks. This is precisely what happened in the Della Sala et al. (1999) study. Performance on the VPT was disrupted much more by the picture-viewing interference task than it was by the peg-following task. The converse was true of the SPT, which was disrupted much more by

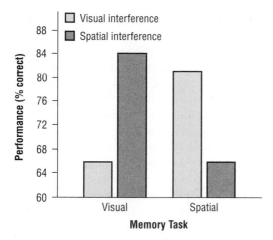

Figure 4.16 Results from Della Sala et al. (1999).

Reprinted from Della Sala, S., Gray, C., Baddeley, A., Allamano, N., Wilson, L. (1999). Pattern span: A tool for unwelding visuo-spatial memory. *Neuropsychologia. 37,* 1189–1199. Copyright 1999 Elsevier. Reprinted with permission from Elsevier.

the peg-following interference task than by the picture-viewing interference task. As you may also remember from Chapter 2, a double dissociation is generally considered to be evidence that two tasks rely on different underlying mechanisms. So, based on the dissociation they obtained, Della Sala et al. concluded that there are separable visual and spatial components that make up the visuo-spatial sketchpad.

The Episodic Buffer

Baddeley (2000a) added another piece to complete the puzzle of working memory. He terms this fourth component the **episodic buffer.** He proposed this component in an attempt to account for some of the failings of the three-component model. One such failing is the sensitivity of immediate memory to meaning. You saw this phenomenon earlier in our discussion of release from proactive interference. Other meaning-based effects have been found as well. For example, memory span is affected by meaning-based factors such as how easy it is to form an image of a word (Hulme, Roodenrys, Brown, & Mercer, 1995). This shows that processing in working memory is influenced by representations in long-term memory. The episodic buffer provides a mechanism to allow for this influence. According to Baddeley (2006), this new component holds information that has been processed through articulation (the articulatory loop) and visualization (the visuo-spatial sketchpad), as well as relevant information from long-term memory, and from them forms a coherent scene or episode that is held in conscious awareness.

Central Executive

The linchpin component of Baddeley's WM system is a central controller, termed the **central executive.** Recall our earlier statement that the attentional system could be conceptualized in two ways: as a gateway or as a pool of resources that is allocated to the tasks of consciousness. Baddeley's central executive might be conceived of as the "gatekeeper" or "capacity allocator" for the attentional system. When a particular task demands extensive involvement of either the articulatory loop or the visuo-spatial sketchpad, the central executive deploys the necessary resources. The central executive is also thought to be responsible for the higher-level thought processes involved in reasoning and language comprehension. Because the capacity of the attentional system is limited, the central executive has only so much to give; if a task is too demanding, the central executive's resources will be drained, and complex thinking will suffer. If you think the foregoing description of the central executive sounds a bit vague, many researchers—Baddeley (2006) included—would agree! Until very recently, the central executive remained the least well-specified component of the working memory system. But a number of recent studies have clarified the possible roles of the central executive.

Executive Attention.   Recall our discussion at the outset of this chapter when we emphasized the importance of attention for cognitive processing, as well as attention's strategic nature. The multimode theory proposed that we can choose to attend selectively in either early or late-selection mode. Later you saw that capacity theories of attention emphasize the strategic nature of divided attention. To some extent, we can parcel out our attention to ongoing events as we see fit. Well, recent investigations of working memory have revealed that the central executive system is the set of mechanisms that allows us to control our attention in these ways. According to the work of Engle and his colleagues (Engle, 2002; Engle & Kane, 2004; Kane, Poole, Tuholski, & Engle, 2006), these functions of working memory can be conceived of as **executive attention.**

The importance of working memory in the control of attention and in subserving more complex processing (like reasoning, language comprehension, and problem solving) has become especially evident in recent years. Researchers have developed measures of **working memory span** and attempted to relate performance on these measures to other aspects of cognitive processing. Recall that *short-term memory span* (typically referred to as memory span) is a simple measure of how many items can be held in immediate memory. Working memory span provides a more dynamic and valid characterization of immediate memory's capacity. Consider one of several tasks used to measure WM span, a task termed *operation span*. This, along with a more standard memory span task, are depicted in Figure 4.17. Note that while the memory span task involves the simple rote repetition of a list of words after their presentation, the operation span task requires a good deal more. Subjects are to read the problems aloud and solve them. After each of the three problems in a trial has been presented, subjects are to recall the words that accompanied each problem. The operation span task is essentially a divided-attention situation; subjects must process and answer the simple math problems while at the same time keep track of the words. As Engle (2002) notes in his review, a person's working memory span is a strikingly good predictor of a broad range of more complex abilities, including spoken and written language comprehension, writing, note taking, vocabulary learning, and even bridge playing!

Why might working memory span be such a good indicator of other more complex abilities? According to Engle and his colleagues, it's because the tasks involved in WM span are a microcosm of what is required during complex cognitive processing. We must process multiple streams of information, keeping some of it active and easily retrievable even in the face of interference from other material that may be more relevant at the time. Consider the operation span task; subjects need to somehow keep the words fresh and active, yet manage to keep them at bay in order to perform those annoying little calculations. You have to do this in class if you have professors like us, who put notes up on a projector and lecture at the same time. You somehow have to get down what's in the notes while also tracking what the professor is saying.

Engle (2002; see also Engle & Kane, 2004) discusses the importance of *inhibition*

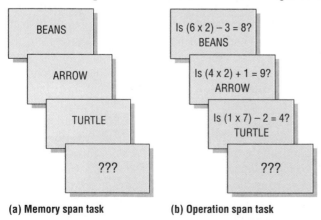

(a) **Memory span task**   (b) **Operation span task**

Figure 4.17 Comparison of (a) memory span task and (b) operation span task.

in the control of attention. It's easy to acknowledge the value of attending to important information and keeping it active in memory. What may not be as obvious is the role of inhibition in attention. We have to be able to screen out what isn't immediately important because of the interference it may produce. Kane and Engle tested this idea (2000) within a proactive interference paradigm. Recall that proactive interference refers to the detrimental effect that early information has on the subsequent recall of more recently presented information. Kane and Engle reasoned that if working memory involves the executive control of attention, then those who are particularly good at this control—that is, subjects with high working memory capacity—might be able to stave off the effects of proactive interference. This is exactly what Kane and Engle found—over trials, the recall of individuals who had higher working memory capacity showed less of a deterioration with the presentation of subsequent lists, relative to the recall of individuals with lower working memory capacity.

Working memory capacity has also been shown to interact with another classic effect—the *cocktail-party phenomenon*, discussed in Chapter 3. Recall that this refers to circumstances in which you catch your name even though it has been presented in an unattended channel. So in some ways, this might be considered a *failure* of selective attention—after all, you shouldn't be picking up on anything from an unattended channel, salient or not. Conway, Cowan, and Bunting (2001) compared high and low WM capacity subjects in a dichotic listening situation and found that those with higher WM capacity were less likely to notice their name in an unattended message; that is, they were less susceptible to the cocktail-party phenomenon. Engle (2002) sees this as one more piece of evidence that working memory is intimately involved in the control of attention, in the service of more complex cognitive activities like reasoning, problem solving, and language comprehension.

STOP *and* **THINK!** ━━━━━━━━━━━━━━━

WORKING WITH WORKING MEMORY

Return to the tasks from the *Stop and Think! The Price of Attending* and reconsider them in light of Baddeley's model of working memory. For each of the tasks (relisted below), determine how each of the three subcomponents of working memory might be involved, and how they actually are.

watching TV
listening to music
taking notes in class
talking on your cell phone
walking
driving in an unfamiliar location
driving a familiar route
listening to a professor lecture
eating

As you did earlier, consider these questions:

- Which pairs of tasks would be easy to share?
- Which pairs would be difficult to share?
- Why are certain combinations more or less manageable, given Baddeley's view?

Working Memory and the Brain

Given the variety of processes thought to comprise working memory, it shouldn't surprise you to learn that neuroscience research has made a good deal of progress in delineating the neural substrates of the various processes involved in working memory. Overviews of this work are provided in Jonides and Smith (1997), Baddeley (2003), and Jonides, Lacey, and Nee (2005). A brain diagram summarizing some of the brain-mapping research work on the processes underlying working memory is presented in Figure 4.18. As you can see, the different subprocesses of working memory seem to be based in distinct portions of the brain. It's interesting (but perhaps not surprising) to note that the areas responsible for the "inner ear" and the "inner eye" are quite similar to those that underlie your "outer ear" and your "outer eye," as it were.

> **Research Theme: Neuroscience**

Areas important in the articulatory processes of working memory are similar to the ones we use in speech perception. Generally, these processes tend to be localized in the left hemisphere. Recall that the articulatory processes of working memory are thought to be comprised of two subprocesses, subvocal rehearsal and phonological storage. Brain mapping of working memory supports this distinction. Areas in the posterior parietal cortex seem to be important in phonological storage, while motor areas in the frontal lobe are important in subvocal rehearsal. These frontal areas are near Broca's area, which plays an important role in speech production.

Those areas important in the visuo-spatial sketchpad are very similar to those involved in visual perception, and seem to be localized primarily in the right hemisphere. Jonides and Smith (1997) note that these areas have a similar storage-rehearsal parallel to articulatory processes; that is, different regions seem to be involved in the storage and rehearsal of visual/spatial information. These (right hemisphere) areas seem to be rough analogs of the areas that underlie articulatory processes in the left hemisphere, namely, posterior parietal regions and the premotor areas of the frontal lobes. In addition to these areas, some evidence indicates the involvement of areas in the occipital lobe, which, as you'll see in Chapter 9, are involved in mental imagery.

So, what of the executive processes, those that seem to be instrumental in manipulating the contents of working memory in the service of higher-level cognition? You may have heard in your introductory psychology class that the frontal lobe of the brain's cortex is responsible for "higher-level"

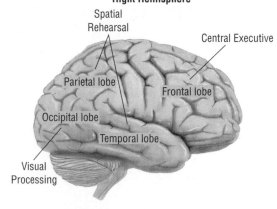

Figure 4.18 Brain areas involved in working memory.

thought processes like thinking, planning, and deciding. Given the importance of working memory in these complex processes, it probably comes as no surprise that the executive functions of working memory have been found to be localized primarily within the frontal lobe, more specifically, the dorsolateral (toward the top and side) of the prefrontal area (the "back" area of the frontal cortex) (Jonides & Smith, 1997).

In summarizing the available evidence regarding brain substrates of working memory processing, Jonides, Lacey, and Nee (2005) propose that the immediate processing of incoming information is accomplished via the same mechanisms that were engaged in the perception of that information. This stored information will be either lost over time or passed onward to higher-level processes if the information is rehearsed. Then the information will be processed by mechanisms in the parietal and temporal regions.

The Working Memory Model Reconsidered

Baddeley's model has served as an extremely useful heuristic for organizing and explaining much of what researchers have found about the duration, capacity limitations, and coding mechanisms in STM. It certainly does a better job of describing STM than the relatively simple mechanisms proposed in the original modal model. The original model characterized immediate memory as a static holding place for information. The working memory model represents immediate memory as a dynamic set of processes used not only for storage, but also for active manipulation and consideration. And over the last 30 years or so, a great deal of evidence has accumulated indicating that working memory is indeed an extremely important mechanism that serves as a sort of foundation for more complex abilities like reasoning and language comprehension.

However, despite its dominance, Baddeley's approach is not without its problems. Neath (2000) summarizes a number of them. One criticism is that the label "working memory" is somewhat misleading. As you just read, what working memory is (supposedly) all about is the executive control of attention; this is the centerpiece of the theory. So, working memory isn't really about memory; it's about attention. The term "working attention" might therefore be more apt (Kintsch, 1998). A second problem relates to the notion that working memory is for the temporary storage of information that is needed for higher-level cognitive tasks. The problem is that the amount of information we need for bridge playing, math, reading comprehension, and the like exceeds the capacity limitations most researchers espouse for immediate memory.

A related problem is the mechanism proposed to account for the forgetting that occurs in immediate memory. Baddeley's model is a "rehearsal and decay" model that emphasizes the importance of activation in maintaining information in the face of decay. But, as noted earlier, Nairne (1996, 2002b) points out that decay is not an explanation for memory loss. It's simply a restatement of the phenomenon: information is lost. As Neath (2000) points out, Baddeley's model fails to specify exactly what is lost and doesn't specify the mechanisms whereby it is lost. A final problem with the model is that it focuses on sensory (i.e., visual and auditory) processing of incoming information, but is mute on the concept of meaning. As you saw in the discussion of release from proactive interference, immediate memory is sensitive to the meaning of encoded information. Obviously, then, immediate contact with long-term memory occurs in working memory, something that earlier versions of Baddeley's model failed to account for. As you saw, an episodic buffer was added to provide for a mechanism of contact between working memory and long-term memory, but the mechanism is vaguely specified, and given its recent foray into theory, the jury is still out on how well the episodic buffer accounts for the interaction among the memory systems.

STOP *and* **REVIEW!**

1. Give a basic definition of working memory.
2. What is the function of (a) the articulatory loop and (b) the visuo-spatial sketchpad?
3. Which of the following components allows for the integration of information in working memory with representations in long-term memory?
   a. visuo-spatial sketchpad
   b. subvocal rehearsal mechanism
   c. episodic buffer
   d. articulatory loop
4. What is executive attention?

➤ Working memory, the most common conceptualization of STM memory processing, is comprised of a number of closely interacting subsystems that combine to subserve a host of higher-level mental processes, including language comprehension, problem solving, and reasoning.

➤ The articulatory loop allows one to hold information temporarily and rehearse it. The word-length and phonological similarity effects derive from the characteristics of the articulatory loop. The visuo-spatial sketchpad is responsible for the storage and manipulation of visual and spatial information in immediate memory.

➤ The central executive is responsible for higher-level thought processes and for allocating attention. If a task is too demanding, the central executive's resources will be drained, and complex thinking will suffer. An episodic buffer allows for the integration of working memory processes with information in long-term memory.

➤ Some conceptualize the central executive as executive attention responsible for controlling attention to subserve more complex processing. Measures of WM span provide strikingly good predictions of performance on a wide range of more complex thinking tasks.

GLOSSARY

action slips: absentminded actions that are often the result of automatic processing (p. 132)

articulatory loop: a subcomponent of working memory that allows for the mental rehearsal of incoming information (p. 148)

articulatory suppression task: a task designed to prevent the rehearsal of information in the subvocal rehearsal mechanism of the articulatory loop (p. 150)

attention: limited-capacity processes devoted to the monitoring of internal and external events (p. 120)

automaticity: the tendency for cognitive processes to occur nonintentionally, unconsciously, and with little effort after extensive practice (p. 129)

Brown-Peterson task: a sequence of letters is encoded, followed by a distraction task of counting backward, followed by recall of the letter sequence (p. 139)

central executive: a limited-capacity control mechanism for working memory that is responsible for the higher-level thought processes involved in planning, reasoning, and language comprehension (p. 153)

chunking (recoding): regrouping items in STM (p. 140)

decay: the loss of information from memory with the passage of time (p. 144)

divided attention: monitoring and responding to more than one source of information (p. 121)

episodic buffer: component of working memory that is responsible for integrating information processed by the articulatory loop and the visuo-spatial sketchpad, as well as relevant information from long-term memory (p. 153)

executive attention: function of working memory whereby we control the allocation of attention (p. 154)

interference: when information currently in memory is negatively influenced by the presentation of other information (p. 144)

long-term memory (LTM): the representations of experiences, knowledge, and skills that we have accumulated throughout our lifetimes (p. 138)

magical number: 7 ± 2, the number of items we can hold in STM (p. 139)

memory span: the capacity of STM; the longest string of information a person can immediately recall (p. 139)

modal model: the information-processing view of memory that postulates a series of chronologically arranged stages through which incoming information passes (sensory memory, STM, and LTM) (p. 137)

multimode theory: a theory of attention positing that we can engage in early or late selection depending on the situation; late selection requires more attentional resources than early selection (p. 120)

phonological similarity effect: the finding that lists of similar-sounding items are more difficult to keep

track of in STM than are lists of different-sounding items (p. 141)

proactive interference: occurs when earlier information interferes with the ability to retain information that comes later (p. 144)

psychological refractory period: a period of time during which the response to a second stimulus will be significantly slowed because of the processing still occurring on a stimulus presented earlier (p. 122)

release from proactive interference: the release from the cumulative effects of proactive interference when there is a change in the nature of the stimuli being encoded (p. 146)

retention interval: the amount of time between encoding and retrieval (p. 139)

retroactive interference: occurs when later information interferes with the ability to retain information that came earlier (p. 144)

sensory memory: proposed by the modal model of memory; an extremely brief representation of a just-presented stimulus (p. 137)

short-term memory (STM): the set of processes that we use to hold and rehearse information that occupies our current awareness (p. 138)

stimulus onset asynchrony (SOA): the time that lapses between the presentation of two stimuli (p. 122)

visual persistence: the continuation of the neural response to a visually presented stimulus after its removal; experienced as a fading icon or image (p. 138)

visuo-spatial sketchpad: a subcomponent of working memory that allows for the processing of spatial information and manipulation of visual images (p. 151)

word-length effect: the finding that STM span is negatively related to the length of encoded items (p. 140)

working memory: the processes involved in examining, considering, manipulating, and responding to internal and external events (p. 120)

working memory span: a measure of the cognitive processing capacity that is available when a person does two tasks (e.g., memory and computation) concurrently (p. 154)

5

Identification and Classification

It seems pretty amazing that you can instantly recognize a chair as a chair, no matter if its upright, lying on its side, or in a picture that you're looking at upside down. Furthermore, you recognize all different kinds of chairs—rocking, folding, and high chairs. What processes might underlie this ability?

As many types of chairs as there may be in the world, there seem to be several orders of magnitude more faces. How in the world do we ever manage to distinguish between them? Are we specially equipped to deal with the recognition of faces?

Have you ever watched ESPN and wondered why you were watching poker, dance competitions, or hunting? Are these things really sports? Football, baseball, and basketball sure seem to fit the sports category. How do we fit certain things into certain categories?

Children seem to be faced with a monumental, nearly insurmountable task—learning which new things in the world belong in which categories. How do they go about sorting the world, learning that sharks and dolphins are in different categories, yet robins and flamingos are in the same category?

Identification and Classification: An Overview

In this chapter, we continue our "tour" through the early components of the information-processing system. Up to this point, we've talked about how we look or listen, pay attention, and hold information in our working memories for further processing. The first step in further processing involves *identifying* and *classifying* what it is you've latched onto through attentional processing. The process of identification is typically labeled **object recognition**—the processes whereby we match an incoming stimulus with stored representations for the purpose of identification.

The fact that we can look at a pattern of stimulation and say "bird," "football," "tree," or "chair" begs the question of how we know what birds, footballs, trees, and chairs are. That is, how do we represent these *concepts,* and how did we arrive at these representations? What is a tree, exactly? You've probably never thought too much about questions like this (unless you major in philosophy), but this chapter will introduce you to some of the answers that cognitive psychologists have proposed to these questions.

Identification: Recognizing from the Bottom Up and from the Top Down

In Chapter 3, we discussed the basic processes of visual perception through which an incoming stimulus is translated into a percept. In order to deal with these incoming stimuli, we need to identify them (*recognize* these objects). It turns out that a distinction we introduced in Chapter 3 is critical to an account of object recognition—namely, the notions of *bottom-up* and *top-down processing.* Bottom-up processes employ the information in the stimulus itself (what you might call "data") to aid in its identification. That is, we build and identify stimuli "from the bottom up." For example, you recognize a chair because of the data of brown cylindrical lines, four pointing to the ground and a couple pointed in the air, and two flat surfaces, one parallel to the ground and one perpendicular. It's not difficult to see that bottom-up processing is necessary for recognizing objects. It's obvious that we can't identify something without any data at all; there would be nothing to identify. While bottom-up processing may be necessary to account for object recognition, it isn't sufficient. A fundamental fact about object recognition is that both bottom-up and top-down processes play an important role.

The importance of top-down processes may not be as obvious, but they do play a vital role in our ability to recognize what we see. Quite often, incoming data are incomplete or obscured in some manner and are thus unidentifiable. In these cases, we must rely on expectations, knowledge, and/or surrounding context to supplement the data (i.e., top-down processing). Even if the aforementioned chair were partially obscured, chances are you'd be able to identify it, particularly if it were in a familiar context (e.g., a living room or furniture store). Our knowledge of chairs enhances identification. In other words, we identify what things are "from the top down."

STOP *and* **THINK!**

BOTTOM-UP AND TOP-DOWN PROCESSING YOUR ENVIRONMENT

Recognizing objects is a matter of both bottom-up processes (the processing of data) and top-down processes (bringing previous knowledge and context to bear on the data). Look at the objects within view and make note of (1) the data that comprise them—what are the component elements that allow you to know what the thing is? and (2) the contextual elements in the scene that may be aiding your recognition—what is it about the situation you're in that aids in your identification of the objects you see?

- Are there any objects for which you lack data yet can still identify the object?
- What aspects of the situation or your previous knowledge allow you to do that?

The number of objects we are able to recognize is nothing short of phenomenal. Look around you and identify all of the things you can. Chances are you were able to name at least 10 or so things in the space of 10 or so seconds. A computer recognition system can't touch this level of performance. Decades of work in artificial intelligence have not cracked the problem of getting computers to "see" in the rapid, flexible, and accurate manner that we can. In the first section of the chapter, we'll examine some of the mechanisms researchers propose to account for object recognition.

Concepts and Categories: The Database for Recognition

The fact that we are able to identify and classify everything around us raises a fundamental issue: What is the classification database, and how is it formed, organized, and accessed? In the latter half of the chapter, we'll explore some of the answers that have emerged to these basic questions. One aspect of categorization has significant implications for the processes of object and face recognition, so we'll discuss that aspect next.

Levels of Categorization.   Think about the objects we mentioned above that you would quickly and effortlessly recognize: bird, football, tree, and chair. Notice that we didn't write "animal," "sports equipment," "plant," or "piece of furniture." Those seem to be too general. Nor did we say "black-capped chickadee," "Rawlings Collegiate Size Composite Leather Football," "white dogwood," or "beanbag chair." These seem to be ridiculously specific (not to mention much more wordy and space consuming!). What we've just done is outline three fundamental **levels of categorization,** or gradations of specificity that can be used in describing everyday categories.

In a classic discussion, Rosch (1976) summarizes these levels of categorization. The superordinate level of categorization—animal—is the most general; the subordinate level of categorization—black-capped chickadee—is the most specific. The midpoint between these lies at what is termed the **basic level of categorization:** bird. In the same look at categorization, Rosch (1976) also discusses a number of features that characterize items at the basic level. The basic level seems to be the most general level of categorization in which (a) items share similar shapes, (b) the same movements and postures are used to interact with the items, and (c) the items lead to the formation of a single mental image. Rosch notes that this level of categorization is by far the most salient, and dominates our cognitive processing. Intuitively, this makes sense—superordinate terms like *animal* would seem to provide too little information to be of much use. Subordinate terms like *black-capped chickadee* often provide more information than is necessary. The basic level is "just right" in that it specifies what type of animal yet doesn't bore you with the details.

As you'll see, the differing levels of specificity of everyday categories and concepts have important ramifications for the task of object recognition. In more concrete terms, it seems that distinguishing between two quite different objects like chairs and birds (which differentiate at the basic level) might involve a different set of recognition processes than distinguishing between two quite similar objects like a black-capped chickadee and a tufted titmouse (which differentiate at the subordinate level). Another way of saying this is that the basic level turns out to be the **entry point for recognition.** The entry point refers to the default level of categorization that we use for familiar objects.

STOP *and* **REVIEW!**

1. Distinguish between the role of bottom-up and top-down processing in object recognition.
2. Which of the following levels of categorization is most often used when describing objects?

    a. superordinate level
    b. basic level
    c. subordinate level

➤ Object recognition refers to the processes whereby we match an incoming stimulus with stored representations for the purpose of identification. Bottom-up processing employs the information in the stimulus itself to aid in identification. Top-down processes rely on expectations, knowledge, and/or surrounding context to help identify an object.

➤ Categories are represented at varying levels of specificity. The most general is the super-ordinate level (e.g., tools); the most specific is the subordinate level (e.g., ball peen hammer). The intermediate, and most-often-used, level is the basic level (e.g., hammer).

Object Recognition

Consider the processes of recognition, as outlined by Tarr (2002). A messy array of light information strikes the retina, where early visual processes extract some basic information and impose some basic order on the chaos via the perceptual organizational processes we discussed in Chapter 3. These processes include the discernment of boundaries, edges, contours, and surfaces as well as more global organizational processes that lead us to discern the shapes and objects that will ultimately lead to recognition. The next step in recognition is a matching process whereby the now-analyzed visual pattern is compared with representations in memory. Evidence accumulates for the most likely candidates, and ultimately, we come to the conclusion that the object in the picture is indeed . . . a . . . bunny rabbit!

In theory, the process of recognition seems pretty straightforward, but keep in mind what it's up against. The view of an object that falls on the retina (the "stuff" of recognition) is woefully inconsistent. A given object is rarely, if ever, viewed in exactly the same way.

Can you identify this wascally object?

Objects can rotate, shift, change position; viewers can move and radically change their perspective on an object; the lighting on the object can change; parts of the object can be blocked out. There are also incredible variations in the object itself. Are you viewing it live, in a movie, in a photo, or in a pencil sketch? You can also recognize the bunny rabbit at the different levels of categorization—you could recognize it as an animal, a mammal, a rabbit, a jackrabbit, or Bugs Bunny. In spite of these challenges, you're nearly flawless in execution. Before discussing theoretical accounts of the process, let's talk about some of the "nuts and bolts"—empirical research on how recognition occurs.

Effects of Orientation and Perspective

It's obvious, for practical purposes at least, that the particular perspective from which we view objects doesn't really affect our ability to identify them. We know what they are in a split second. But are the processes of recognition really impervious to orientation and perspective when viewed with a more fine-grained analysis? This question—whether recognition is *viewpoint invariant*—is a critical one for evaluating the theories of recognition that we'll talk about a little later. It also turns out that the answer to the question is, well, . . . yes and no.

A classic study of perspective effects on recognition was done by Palmer, Rosch, and Chase (1981). These investigators collected ratings from subjects regarding how well each of several photos represented a particular object (e.g., how well the photos in Figure 5.1 represent a car). Then they gave a separate group of subjects an identification task in which they were to name as quickly as possible the objects pictured. Recognition turned out to be fastest for objects in a canonical perspective—that is, the perspective rated as the best representation of the object. For the lower-rated perspectives, recognition was slower. You might think that perhaps this RT pattern occurs because the canonical perspective is the most familiar one. Good intuition, but it turns out that similar effects are found for unfamiliar objects (e.g., Edelman & Bülthoff, 1992).

Since one's perspective of an object seems to affect object recognition, object rotation itself must, too, right? Well, no. . . . Answers in cognitive psychology are rarely so simple. Some pioneering work done by Biederman and his colleagues (Biederman & Cooper, 1991; Biederman & Gerhardstein, 1993) suggests that orientation might not matter all that much in object recognition. They used a technique commonly employed in all sorts of studies of cognition, a technique termed *priming*. As you read in Chapter 3, priming refers to a benefit gained from earlier exposure to a stimulus. After having thought about or identified an object once, you're "primed" to think of it or identify it more easily afterward. Biederman and Gerhardstein (1993) presented subjects with a series of objects like the

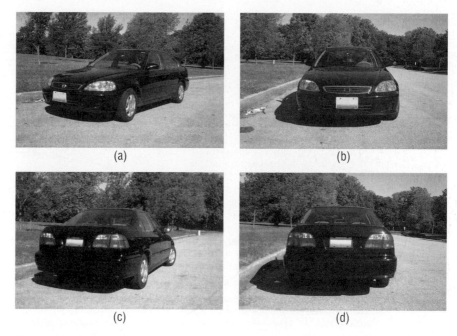

(a)   (b)

(c)   (d)

Figure 5.1 Based on the findings of the Palmer, Rosch, and Chase (1981) study, photo (a) would be the canonical perspective.

From Palmer, S., Rosch, E., & Chase, P. Canonical perspective and the perception of objects. In J. Long & A. Baddeley (Eds). *Attention & Performance IX* (pp.135–151). Erlbaum; Hillsdale, NJ: 1981. Adapted with permission from the author and from Lawrence Erlbaum Associates, Inc.

ones pictured in Figure 5.2a, and subjects were simply to name each one as quickly as possible (phase 1). In the second phase of the experiment, subjects were once again presented with a series of objects to name. Half of these objects were the same as those seen in phase 1, but presented at varying degrees of rotation. The other half of the objects were different exemplars (i.e., a different type of flashlight), also presented at varying degrees of rotation. Their measure of performance was priming—would the first presentation speed up the identification time in the second phase? And would priming depend at all on rotation?

Figure 5.2b shows phase 1 reaction time as a single point because degree of rotation was not varied in this phase. Phase 1 provided a baseline identification RT, which was needed for comparison with phase 2 reaction times. The graph also depicts phase 2 RT for the same exemplars and for different exemplars, plotted as a function of degree of rotation. As you can see, for both types of objects, reaction time was faster in phase 2 than in phase 1. Seeing a flashlight in phase 1 primed identification of all flashlights (whether the same exemplar or a different exemplar)—this is termed *semantic priming*. However, same exemplar reaction times were faster than different exemplar reaction times. Seeing the same exemplar produced more priming than seeing a different exemplar. But most important for the present discussion were the effects of rotation, which were negligible. This indicates that rotation doesn't really matter to object recognition.

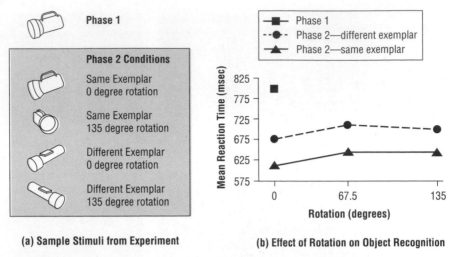

(a) Sample Stimuli from Experiment   **(b) Effect of Rotation on Object Recognition**

Figure 5.2 Sample stimuli from the Biederman and Gerhardstein (1993) study, and graph of the major results.

From Biederman, I., & Gerhardstein, P. C. (1993). Recognizing depth-rotated objects: Evidence and conditions for three-dimensional viewpoint invariance. *Journal of Experimental Psychology: Learning, Memory, and Cognition, 19,* 1162–1182. Copyright 1993 by the American Psychological Association. Reprinted by permission.

Effects of Context

Our discussion of recognition thus far is missing something; we've been talking about lab studies that investigate speed of recognition of isolated objects. But in everyday life you rarely see things in complete isolation. Instead, you view them within some sort of meaningful context. You see a bunny rabbit sitting in the grass underneath a tree; you see a pencil in the hand of someone sitting in a classroom taking notes. One classic demonstration of the beneficial effects of context on recognition was conducted by Palmer (1975). In his study, simple sketches of various everyday scenes were presented, and then sketches of single objects were presented briefly for identification. Palmer varied the relationship between the objects and the scenes: In some cases, the preceding scene (e.g., a kitchen) was consistent with the object to be identified (e.g., a loaf of bread), while in other cases it was inconsistent (e.g., a drum). In others it was inconsistent *and* misleading (e.g., a mailbox, which has features in common with a loaf of bread). Identification of objects was best when the objects followed a scene that was consistent and worst when the objects were misleading. In fact, in this condition, subjects were likely to name the scene-appropriate object (i.e., a loaf of bread and not a mailbox).

A more recent study by Davenport and Potter (2004) shows the interactive effect that objects and scenes have on identification of the other. While most previous investigations of scenes and object recognition had used line sketches, these investigators decided to use more naturalistic stimuli—photographs of familiar scenes. Their general procedure involved a brief (80 ms) presentation of a scene, followed by a mask. A *mask* is a briefly presented visual pattern that serves to "erase" the just-observed stimulus so that identification can't be based on a fleeting visual afterimage. They wanted to isolate the identification process to the presentation of the photograph itself. Following the mask,

Figure 5.3 Sample photos used by Davenport and Potter (2004). Photos in the top row are from the consistent condition, and photos in the bottom row are from the inconsistent condition.

From Davenport, J. L. & Potter, M. C. (2004). Scene Consistency in Object and Background Perception. *Psychological Science*, 15, 559–564. Reprinted with permission from the author and from Elsevier.

subjects had to identify either the object in the foreground (i.e., a football player) or the scene itself (the football field). If you look at a sample of the stimuli that the investigators used (see Figure 5.3), you'll notice that a couple of the pictures are a little odd. A football player is ready to receive a pass from someone at an altar, and a cardinal is dispensing a blessing at midfield. These mismatched photos allowed for an assessment of the relative effects of consistent and inconsistent context.

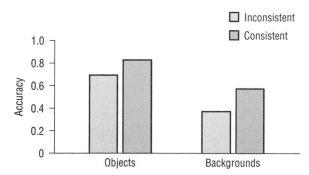

Figure 5.4 Results of Davenport and Potter (2004) study.

From Davenport, J. L. & Potter, M. C. (2004). Scene Consistency in Object and Background Perception. *Psychological Science*, 15, 559–564. Reprinted with permission from the author and from Elsevier.

Let's break down the experimental design of this study. Davenport and Potter (2004) were interested in two independent variables—whether subjects were to identify foreground objects or background scenes (a performance-measure variable), and whether the relationship between the objects and the scenes was consistent or inconsistent. So the design was a simple 2 × 2 factorial design. The results are presented in Figure 5.4, and show accuracy in naming as a function of the two variables. As you can see, subjects had an easier time identifying foreground objects than background scenes. This makes sense, as we're no doubt more used to identifying objects than their backgrounds, a finding that fits well with our discussion of basic figure-ground processing in Chapter 3. More importantly, there was a strong effect of consistency between object and background. Both objects and scenes were recognized more easily in cases in which the corresponding background and object were consistent.

Theories of Visual Object Recognition

Now that we've looked at some of the factors that influence recognition, let's consider some of the processes that might be involved. The last 20 years or so have witnessed a lively theoretical debate regarding the nature of recognition processes. As noted earlier, any theory of recognition needs to explain how various changes in an incoming stimulus can have little or no effect on our recognition processes. Two basic approaches have been proposed; let's introduce them briefly within the context of our proverbial bunny rabbit. **Parts-based approaches** propose that the incoming pattern of stimulation produced by the rabbit is parsed into its component parts (little sphere; bigger sphere; long, thin triangles); we then compare this set of components to information in memory, and recognize that this set of basic components in this particular combination equals a rabbit. **View-based approaches** propose a more holistic process whereby we take the whole image of the rabbit, in the orientation that we're viewing it, and compare it to corresponding representations in memory until we find a match. Let's look at these views in a little more detail.

Parts-Based (PB) Approaches.   According to the parts-based approach to visual recognition (e.g., Biederman, 1987; Marr & Nishihara, 1982), we compare the features of the object we've just encoded to a description of the object's structure, which is stored in memory. This description includes a list of the parts (features) of the object, as well as the relationship among them. Given the emphasis on features, it may not surprise you that some parts-based approaches are often given the label **feature analysis**. An important feature of PB approaches is that the representation stored in memory is *not* visually or spatially analogous to the object being recognized. Rather, we compare the features of the incoming visual stimulus to an abstract description of those features in memory.

Recognition based on parts offers an obvious advantage: the particular orientation or view of the object is not important. No matter the perspective, objects are broken down into component parts and compared to a set of features. So orientation or transformation of objects doesn't matter, as long as the component parts are still identifiable. Therefore, these approaches are also termed *viewpoint independent* because identification of the object does not depend on the particular view that we have of the object; identification depends only on the component features of the object itself.

Recognition-by-Components (RBC) Theory.   One influential parts-based theory has been proposed by Biederman and colleagues (e.g., Biederman, 1987; Biederman & Cooper, 1991; Biederman & Gerhardstein, 1993). Its name—**recognition-by-components**—makes the general approach pretty clear. Object recognition is a matter of separating, analyzing, and recombining the features of whatever we're looking at.

The features into which we parse objects are basic three-dimensional shapes that Biederman terms **geons** (derived from the phrase "geometrical ions"). A sample of these shapes is presented in Figure 5.5, along with a variety of ways in which they might combine

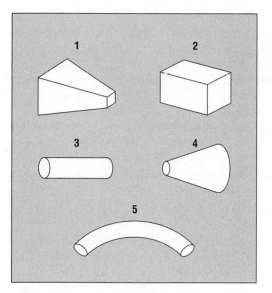
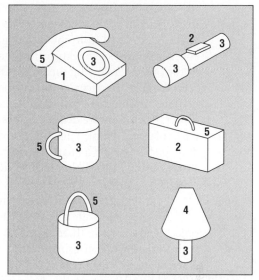

Figure 5.5 Some of the 36 geons proposed by Biederman (1987) and how they combine to form simple objects.

From Biederman, I. (1987). Human image understanding: Recent research and a theory. *Computer Vision, Graphics, and Image Processing, 32*, 29–73. Copyright 1987. Reprinted by permission of Elsevier Science.

to form everyday objects. According to Biederman's theory, there are a total of 36 geons that serve as *visual primitives*—simple shapes that can combine to form most other more complex shapes. Importantly, these geons are viewed the same way regardless of orientation; a cylinder almost always looks like a cylinder, no matter what visual perspective you happen to have on it.

 **STOP *and* THINK!**

SPOTTING GEONS

From where you're sitting, look around at all of the various objects you are able to easily identify.

- How many basic parts (i.e., geonlike parts) make up each object?
- How do the objects break down into component parts?

Also note whether anything in your field of view is difficult to identify.

- Why is it?
- Is the object at an odd angle?
- Is most of it blocked?
- Are geons unidentifiable?
- Are there any objects that seem indistinguishable?
- Does it seem like orientation would influence your ability to recognize any of these objects?

The RBC theory proposes a series of hierarchically arranged stages whereby information about component features is used to identify the object. First, information about edges is extracted from the retinal image. This edge-extraction process looks for differences in features like texture, luminance, and color and results in a simple line drawing of the object. Following this edge extraction, we encode the *nonaccidental features* of the retinal image. Nonaccidental features are those that are almost sure to be actual features of the stimulus rather than some accident of the perspective the observer has on the object. Put simply, we detect features of the stimulus and assume they don't vary with the particular viewpoint. This should sound familiar. Recall from Chapter 3 that Gestalt psychologists were particularly interested in how cognitive processes impose organization on incoming information. A basic theme underlying their principles of organization is *simplicity;* we tend to parse objects in the simplest way possible. The segmentation of objects, as proposed by RBC theory, is guided by this basic assumption (Biederman, 1987).

Concurrently with this search for regularities, the visual system is also parsing the object at areas where there appear to be boundaries between the parts of the object. Next, with the information gained to this point, the components of the figure (the geons) are determined, and this set of components is matched with object representations in memory. When a match is found, the object is identified. You may be wondering whether 36 geons is a sufficient number, given the incredible variety of objects we view on a daily basis. Biederman argues that it is; he estimates that humans are familiar with up to 30,000 visually discriminable objects (see Biederman, 1987, for more information on how this estimate was derived). This estimate is no match for the number of objects that could be formed by the 36 geons. Given only two geons—and considering differences in their size, where they join together, and their position relative to one another—over 50,000 shapes are possible. Add a third geon to the mix, and the estimate goes to over 150 million! Clearly, 36 geons provide enough representational power to account for the power of object recognition.

The RBC approach does a fairly good job of accounting for the general processes of object recognition as described earlier. As you saw, Biederman and Gerhardstein (1993) found that object rotation had minimal to no effect on object recognition. This fits with the RBC assumption that recognition of an object should be unaffected as long as the component parts (i.e., the geons) are identifiable. But what about the effects of perspective found by Palmer, Rosch, and Chase (1981)? Recall their finding that objects are best recognized in a canonical perspective. According to RBC theory, this result may occur because certain orientations—most notably the canonical perspective—allow more readily for geon recovery.

So, all is well for the recognition-by-components approach? Well, it turns out that sometimes orientation does have an impact on visual recognition, a finding that poses a problem for the parts-based approach. Consider a study conducted by Tarr and Pinker (1989), which used a priming procedure but a different sort of stimulus than did Biederman and Gerhardstein (1993): two-dimensional novel shapes like the ones in Figure 5.6. During a training phase, subjects memorized names for three such shapes, which were always presented in the same orientation. Once the three target shapes and their names had been memorized, Tarr and Pinker assessed their

Figure 5.6 Sample stimuli from the Tarr and Pinker (1989) study.

From Tarr, M. J., & Pinker, S. (1989). Mental rotation and orientation-dependence in shape recognition. *Cognitive Psychology, 21,* 233–282. Copyright 1989, Elsevier Science (USA). Reprinted by permission.

subjects' recognition during a test phase. During this phase, the targets were presented at varying degrees of rotation, and subjects were asked to identify them by pressing one of three keys. Target reaction times showed a significant effect of rotation; subjects responded quickly if the shapes were presented in the same orientation as in training, but responded successively slower as the degree of rotation from that original position increased, indicating that visual recognition might be tuned to specific views, or a particular perspective, on an object.

View-Based (VB) Approaches.   In contrast to a PB approach, a view-based (VB) approach to object recognition contends that objects are recognized holistically through a process of comparison with a stored analog. When a match is found, the object is recognized. In contrast to PB approaches, VB approaches are considered *viewpoint dependent,* because identification of an object depends critically on the particular perspective the viewer has. To identify the object, an image matching this particular view must be found, or the incoming stimulus image must be manipulated in some way (e.g., rotated) until a match is found with images represented in memory.

An Early Version of the View-Based Approach.   The first systematic attempt to account for recognition in the early history of cognitive psychology was proposed by Neisser (1967), who proposed an account of how we recognize simple line patterns like letters. He suggested that such pattern recognition was a process of *template matching.* According to this **template-matching theory,** our store of general knowledge includes a set of **templates,** or copies, of every pattern that we might encounter. You may have seen (or used) plastic stencils that allow you to trace perfect forms (provided you have a steady hand). You might picture templates this way—as perfect forms or replicas of a pattern. The basic notion behind template-matching theory is that when we encounter some pattern that needs to be identified, the mind quickly rifles through its set of templates, and then when a match is found, the pattern is given the label stored with the template (i.e., the pattern is recognized).

Template matching is a VB approach in that pattern recognition involves a comparison with a stored analog. Many simple computer-based recognition systems are based on this sort of process. For example, the somewhat odd-looking numbers at the bottom of your checks are rigidly structured such that they fit the templates that computers use for recognition. These recognition systems are "stupid" in that even the slightest change in the pattern will lead to a recognition failure. This strict version of the template-matching theory is too limited to even begin to account for the tremendous flexibility of human pattern recognition. We have no problem recognizing patterns that are distorted, upside down, backward, tilted, partially blocked, bent, twisted . . . you get the idea. Another problem is the lack of economy implied by the template approach. To recognize all of the patterns we are able to, we'd need countless templates. Also, we'd need different templates for different versions of patterns (tilted, upside down, partially blocked). This means we'd need to have an essentially infinite number of templates, something that just doesn't seem feasible. This seems especially true when one considers that not only would we need letter templates, but object templates as well, in all of their different versions.

Modern Versions of the View-Based Approach.   The strict version of the template-matching theory described above is really a sort of straw-man argument that's not very difficult to dismiss. But this general approach is not without its merit. The basic mechanism—matching our view of an object with a representation of that view stored in memory—is quite sensible. The problems arise from the rigidity implied in the original approach. Based on our overwhelming "hit" rate in correctly identifying objects in the world, it seems pretty apparent that misorientation and distortion don't seem to hurt visual recognition as much as the template-matching theory would imply. Biederman and Gerhardstein lent empirical support to this intuition in their research, as discussed earlier, revealing minimal effects of orientation on object recognition.

To deal with these sorts of issues, VB theorists (e.g., Tarr & Pinker, 1989) propose that through experience with objects in many different orientations and viewed from many different perspectives, we develop multiple representations, or *views,* of the objects. These *multiple views* serve as the templates for later recognition. The reason orientation tends not to affect our visual recognition under most circumstances is that everything we must recognize has received extensive exposure from different perspectives. For example, think of all the different perspectives from which you've viewed your car. Based on extensive exposure to these different perspectives, you've developed multiple views of your car that you use in recognizing it.

This **multiple-views approach** is consistent with some findings from studies of basic visual processing in monkeys (who have visual systems comparable to our own). Logothetis, Pauls, and Poggio (1995) taught monkeys to recognize novel three-dimensional objects from a variety of different perspectives, and like humans, the monkeys eventually became equally proficient at recognizing these objects, given any of the rotations. Especially compelling was the neural activity associated with recognition during a later testing phase; different sets of cells responded most strongly to certain objects, indicating that certain networks were devoted to certain objects. More important, a given set of cells responded most strongly when that object appeared in the same orientation as it had during training. The responses of these cells decreased systematically with increases in the rotation from that perspective. Consistent with the basic assumption of the multiple-views approach, these monkeys seemed to have what might be termed *physiological templates* that were devoted to recognizing a specific object in a specific orientation (Tarr, 2000).

Object Recognition: Parts or Views?   So we've seen conflicting evidence regarding whether object recognition is impacted by transformations of the stimulus. Both the view-based and the parts-based approaches to recognition have garnered some support. Hayward (2003) even declared the debate over, reviewing findings that lend support to the existence and operation of both sorts of mechanisms; both seem to be important in recognizing objects. For example, Foster and Gilson (2002) found that objects are recognized with a combination of information gathered from particular views as well as from an analysis of component parts.

The problem then becomes determining the situations in which each type of object-recognition mechanism tends to be important. It turns out that an early idea by Tarr and Bülthoff (1995) provides quite a nice explanation. These authors suggest that object recognition be conceived as a continuum. At one end are heavily viewpoint-independent

The processes used to distinguish between two subordinate-level category members (two types of birds) may be different from those used to distinguish between two basic-level category members (a bird and a hammer).

mechanisms like those proposed by the PB approaches. These mechanisms will be recruited when more gross categorical judgments are required, such as when we need to distinguish among two different basic-level category members, like a hammer and a sparrow. In this sort of judgment, orientation is not likely to matter much. At the other end of the continuum are heavily viewpoint-dependent mechanisms like those proposed by the VB approaches that are used for making subtle discriminations among subordinate-level category members like a finch and a sparrow. Here, orientation is likely to play a role, particularly if we're not experts in the particular domain (e.g., birds). We'll return to this discussion later in the context of face recognition.

Nonvisual Recognition

Although there would be little disagreement that vision is the most important and prominent mode for the recognition of objects, recognition also occurs in the other senses. The most important tasks of auditory recognition occur within the context of language use and will be discussed further in Chapter 10. Along with vision and audition, we do gain a good deal of information that aids in our identification from both the tactile and chemical senses.

Tactile Recognition.   Given our incredible proficiency at visual identification, we fail to notice how much information is available through touch (Gibson, 1966). We tend to think of vision as the primary mode for environmental exploration and information intake. However, **haptics** provide useful and distinct information that is often taken for granted. Klatzky, Lederman, and Reed (1987) suggest the following thought experiment: think of what you would likely see if you were looking at a cat. Chances are, this visual image includes a head, pointy ears, whiskers, four legs, and a tail, along with the respective sizes and layout of these features. If you were asked to think of how a cat feels to the touch, you'd likely come up with quite different attributes: furriness, warmth, and softness. There's a great deal of information about objects in the environment that you can't get just from looking.

So how do you gain this information? Klatzky, Lederman, and Metzger (1985) coined the term **exploratory procedures** (**EPs**) to describe the precise motor patterns performed by the hands in the exploration and identification of an object. They asked subjects to identify 100 common objects using nothing but their hands. It may seem surprising that subjects were able to identify each object in a matter of one to two seconds, with virtually no wrong identifications. Clearly, we can gather an incredible amount of information with what Klatzky and Lederman (1995) call a *haptic glance*.

Based on their observations of subjects' haptic exploration, Klatzky, Lederman, and Metzger (1985) identified six exploratory procedures (depicted in Figure 5.7): static contact, unsupported lifting, lateral motion, pressure, contour following, and enclosure.

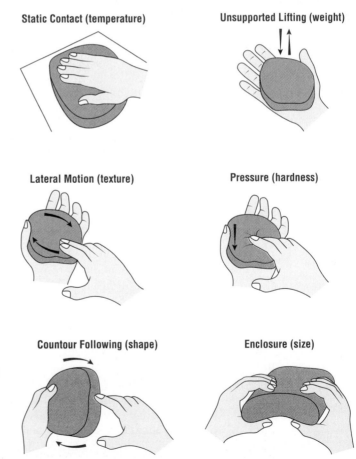

Static Contact (temperature)

Unsupported Lifting (weight)

Lateral Motion (texture)

Pressure (hardness)

Countour Following (shape)

Enclosure (size)

Figure 5.7 Exploratory procedures identified by Klatzky et al. (1985) and the information each procedure obtains about an object.

From Klatzky, R. L., Lederman, S. J., & Metzger, V. A. (1985). Identifying objects by touch: An "expert system." *Perception & Psychophysics, 37,* 299–302. Reprinted by permission of the Psychonomic Society, Inc.

Each of these EPs is directed specifically toward obtaining information about a specific characteristic of an object. Static contact is used to ascertain the temperature of an object; unsupported lifting helps ascertain information about weight; lateral motion is used to extract information about texture; pressure is used to extract information about hardness; contour following provides information about shape; and enclosure provides information about object size. Lederman and Klatzky (1990) found that haptic exploration proceeded in a quite orderly manner. The first EPs performed by subjects tended to be enclosure and unsupported lifting. In other words, subjects began their exploration by grasping and hoisting the object to determine its size and weight. Subsequently, the rest of the EPs described above were used in further exploration to determine such things as texture, shape, and hardness.

STOP *and* THINK!

EXPLORING EPS

Gather three objects that can be easily held and keep them out of view. Recruit some friends and have them attempt to identify each object through haptic exploration. You'll have to direct your "subjects" to close their eyes. Take careful note of their hand movements as they attempt to identify each object and identify the hand movements as static contact, unsupported lifting, lateral motion, pressure, contour following, or enclosure.

- Do they use hand movements not identified by Klatzky, Lederman, and Metzger? If so, explain what they are.
- Do the hand movements seem to take place in a particular order? If so, explain the order.
- Does this order correspond to that identified by Klatzky, Lederman, and Metzger? Explain.

Chemical Senses.   Not much research has been done on recognition of basic tastes and smells, probably because taste and smell identification often takes a back seat to visual recognition. After all, you typically see and identify your food before you eat it or smell it; and because taste is strongly related to and determined by our sense of smell, we'll focus on the latter. Smell can be a powerful cue that we use to identify objects, particularly foodstuff like peanuts. But smells can be a bit bedeviling, too; people sometimes have a tough time describing the perceptual characteristics of smell, a deficit demonstrated by what Lawless (1997) terms the **olfactory-verbal gap**—people tend to have difficulty describing and correctly identifying odors. In fact, studies show that subjects often label as few as 50% of presented odors correctly (e.g., Cain, 1977; Desor & Beauchamp, 1974). The picture changes considerably if odor identification is tested with a choice of labels. Under these conditions, odors are quite reliably named and, for reasons not yet completely understood, women are better at labeling smells than men. Another indicator of the olfactory-verbal gap is sometimes termed **tip-of-the-nose phenomenon** (Lawless & Engen, 1977), which refers to a frustrating inability to come up with the verbal label for an odor in spite of a strong feeling that one knows what the odor is. The *smeller* can describe the odor and name similar ones, but the label is stuck on the tip of the nose.

STOP *and* THINK!

WHAT'S THAT SMELL?

Gather up some basic household items (such as peanut butter, chocolate, baby powder, rubbing alcohol, garlic, onion, vanilla, deodorant, household cleaner, pencil shavings, crayons). For each smell you choose to present, come up with some alternatives you could give on a multiple-choice labeling test.

Recruit your friends. Place the smell substance in a small paper cup so that the "smellers" can't see the items as you present them. Have them take a good whiff of the item and then attempt to identify it. Try to test both men and women. First, have them describe the smell; then ask them to identify it. If they cannot, give them the multiple-choice options you created.

- Were there any signs of the olfactory-verbal gap?
- Were they able to readily identify the smells? Was the tip-of-the-nose phenomenon evident?
- Did providing choices aid in their identification of the smells?
- Did you find a difference between men and women in identification ability?

STOP *and* REVIEW!

1. True or false? Objects are more difficult to recognize if they're placed in an appropriate scene than if they're viewed in an inappropriate scene.
2. View-based approach is to parts-based approach as
   a. view dependent is to view independent.
   b. template matching is to multiple views.
   c. bottom-up processing is to top-down processing.
   d. valid is to invalid.
3. Describe how view-based mechanisms and parts-based mechanisms might both be involved in object recognition.
4. What are exploratory procedures and what information does each detect about an object?

➤ Object recognition is influenced by a number of variables including one's perspective on an object. Objects seem to be identified most easily when viewed from a canonical perspective, the perspective that serves as the best representation of the object. Context also aids in object recognition; objects are recognized more easily in an appropriate context than in an inappropriate context.

➤ According to parts-based approaches, object recognition is based on an analysis of object parts. These approaches are termed *viewpoint independent;* identification does not depend on perspective. View-based approaches contend that objects are recognized holistically through a process of comparison to a stored analog. These approaches are termed *viewpoint dependent* because they contend that identification does depend on perspective.

➤ Some contend that object recognition is likely to involve both parts-based (viewpoint-independent) and view-based (viewpoint-dependent) mechanisms, depending on the nature of the identification task. Recognition at the basic level may involve primarily parts-based mechanisms, while the finer discriminations required at the subordinate level involve primarily view-based mechanisms.

➤ The olfactory-verbal gap refers to the difficulty people have in identifying smells. Exploratory procedures are the hand movements we use for tactile identification. These procedures include contour following (shape), enclosure (size), lateral motion (texture), static contact (temperature), unsupported lifting (weight), and pressure (hardness).

Recognizing Faces

If there's one class of stimuli for which recognition is the most important, significant, and frequent, it's the recognition of faces. Without the ability to recognize familiar faces, we would be awash in a sea of strangers. Indeed, this is the disconcerting dilemma faced by those suffering from **prosopagnosia,** an inability to recognize familiar faces. Consider the experience of a prosopagnosic described by Farah (1992). She recounts the story of a prosopagnosic who was sitting in a country club wondering why another gentleman was staring so intently at him. He asked one of the servers to investigate and found that the man staring at him was his own reflection in a mirror!

Face Inversion

Let's take a closer look at face recognition and a particularly revealing finding—that turning a face upside down has a disproportionately disrupting effect on the recognition of faces relative to its effects on the recognition of objects (Yin, 1969). Look at the man in the photo on page 178. Do you recognize him? He is none other than the "Governator," Arnold Schwarzenegger. If you hesitated in recognizing him, it is because he is upside down.

The Thatcher Illusion.   The effects of face inversion have been studied quite extensively within what has come to be known as the Thatcher illusion (Thompson, 1980). Take a look at the left-hand panel of Figure 5.8. What you see is an upside down picture of Britney Spears. The right-hand panel shows the same picture . . . or does it? Flip the book over, and be horrified. When placed in the proper orientation you can see that the picture is actually a seriously distorted version of the "normal" picture. (In the original study, pictures of former British Prime Minister Margaret Thatcher were used.

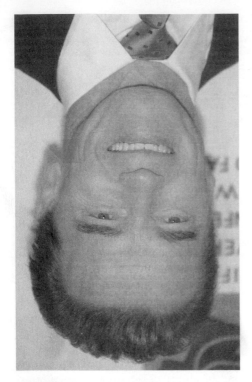

I'll be back. . . . Who am I?

Pity poor Margaret Thatcher, whose frightening upside-down visage has become a staple of psychology books.) Anyway, the point of the demonstration is that turning a face upside down—that is, inverting it—is severely disruptive to face recognition.

What makes the recognition of faces so different from that of other objects, and how does this lead to the inversion effect? Diamond and Carey (1986) propose that to recognize objects, we need *first-order relational information*—that is, information about the parts of an object and how those parts relate to one another. For face recognition, this would involve an analysis of the person's facial features and the relationship among those features. However, first-order relational information is not enough to recognize faces; simply noticing that two eyes are above the nose, which is above the mouth, may be enough for recognition that something is a face but doesn't allow for recognition of who the face is. To recognize faces, we need what Diamond and Carey term *second-order relational information*. Second-order relational information involves comparing the first-order analysis to facial features of a "typical," or "average," face. This typical face is built up through experience and serves as an implicit standard against which we compare the faces we see. Inverting a face disrupts the encoding of second-order relational information. Given that this information is most important for recognizing faces, inversion disproportionately harms face recognition.

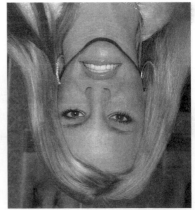

Figure 5.8 An example of the Thatcher illusion.

Diamond and Carey (1986) performed an interesting test of this idea. In addition to replicating the basic inversion effect with human faces, they also investigated recognition of dogs (no, not ugly people—actual dogs). The twist was that they compared dog experts with dog nonexperts. Their reasoning was as follows: Everyone is an expert at recognizing faces. Through countless *practice trials,* we've formed views of the "typical" face, and we encode the faces that we see relative to this example in terms of second-order relational properties. The same should be true of dog experts: they're so experienced with dogs that they should encode dogs in terms of second-order relational properties. This leads to an interesting prediction. Inversion should have adverse effects on the dog nonexperts' recognition of human faces but not of dogs. To a nonexpert, a dog is like an object, and inversion should not harm recognition. But inversion should have adverse effects on dog experts' recognition of both human faces and dogs. This is exactly what occurred. Inversion disrupted memory for earlier-presented faces for all subjects, but disrupted memory for earlier-presented dogs only in dog experts.

A Body-Inversion Effect. Some evidence (Reed, Stone, Bozova, & Tanaka, 2003; Reed, Stone, Grubb, & McGoldrick, 2006) indicates that upright faces might not be alone in their alleged "special" status. As noted by Reed, Stone, Bozova, and Tanaka (2003), the human body is special, too. Just like the face, bodies carry information about a person's identity, age, gender, intentions, and emotions. And, just like the face, they have strong configural properties that vary across individuals. The authors reasoned that if there is a parallel between faces and bodies, then an inversion effect might be expected to occur for the latter, as it does for the former.

Reed et al. (2003) employed a 2 × 2 factorial design to test their idea. Let's revisit that type of design within the context of their study. A 2 × 2 design features the manipulation of two different independent variables, with two levels (conditions) of each. In this study, those two factors were inversion (upright vs. inverted) and stimulus type (bodies vs. houses). Both of these variables were manipulated in a within-subjects fashion. That is, subjects had to make judgments for both bodies and houses, in both upright and inverted configurations. Subjects were presented one body (or house) for 250 ms, then after a short interval (1,000 ms) they were shown a second body (or house) and had to judge whether the second figure was the same as or different from the previously presented one. Figure 5.9 depicts a sample trial of the body stimuli.

Does inversion have the same effect on recognition of faces and dogs?

Same or different

Figure 5.9 Sample trial from body-inversion study of Reed, Stone, Bozova, and Tanaka (2003).

From Reed, C. L., Stone, V., Bozova, S., & Tanaka, J. (2003). The body inversion effect. *Psychological Science, 14,* 302–308. Published by the American Psychological Association. Reprinted with permission from the American Psychological Association and the author.

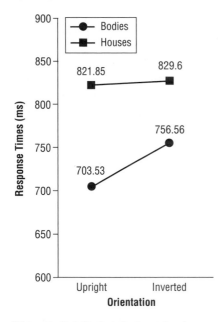

Figure 5.10 Results from body-inversion study of Reed, Stone, Bozova, and Tanaka (2003).

From Reed, C. L., Stone, V., Bozova, S., & Tanaka, J. (2003). The body inversion effect. *Psychological Science, 14,* 302–308. Published by the American Psychological Association. Reprinted with permission from the American Psychological Association and the author.

The results are presented in Figure 5.10. First, you can see main effects for both stimuli. Recall that a main effect refers to an overall effect of an independent variable. First, judgments about bodies were faster than judgments about houses. This makes some sense, as you probably have much more practice in looking at the human body than you do in looking at houses, unless you're a realtor (hey, there's another possible experiment!). Second, judgments about inverted stimuli were slower than judgments about upright ones; however, this main effect is qualified by a significant interaction. The effect of inversion really influenced only the judgments of bodies; there was virtually no effect on judgments of houses. This interaction is precisely what the authors had predicted.

Configural Processing

As you've read, face recognition seems to depend on second-order relational information, or the relationship among the features. Inverting a face disrupts these relationships profoundly, and thus disrupts face recognition. This underscores the fact that faces are encoded as whole configurations (like templates) that are best processed holistically. The upright face is a unique pattern, and when that pattern is disrupted (e.g., is turned upside down), so is recognition. This is true in spite of the fact that none of the individual parts has changed. This isn't the case with objects—rearranging the parts of objects doesn't really disrupt their recognition too much. This difference between face and object recognition was evident in a study by Tanaka and Farah (1993). These authors reasoned that to the degree that a given pattern (e.g., a face or some other object) is stored as a set of features, then those features ought to be useful cues in retrieving the remaining information about the object. However, if a pattern is stored as a whole configuration (as seems to be the case with faces), then presenting part of that whole will not be particularly helpful in recognition.

To test their hypotheses, Tanaka and Farah presented subjects with sketches of faces and sketches of houses, both decomposable in terms of distinct features. Each face and house was

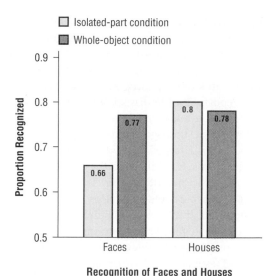

☐ Isolated-part condition
■ Whole-object condition

Recognition of Faces and Houses

Figure 5.11 Results from Tanaka and Farah (1993).

From Tanaka, J. W., & Farah, M. J. (1993). Parts and wholes in face recognition. *Quarterly Journal of Experimental Psychology, 46A,* 225–245. Copyright 1993. Reprinted with permission of Psychology Press, Ltd.

given a label, such as "Larry's house" or "Larry's face." On a later recognition test, subjects were asked about the faces and houses in either an isolated-part condition or a whole-object condition. In the isolated-part condition, they were given a choice of two object parts and had to pick which one of them had been part of an object presented earlier (e.g., "Which of these is Larry's nose?" or "Which of these is Larry's door?"). In the whole-object condition, they were given a choice of two whole objects and had to pick out the one they had seen earlier (e.g., "Which of these is Larry's face?" or "Which of these is Larry's house?").

The results are presented in Figure 5.11. As you can see, the type of question asked didn't matter for recognition of houses; subjects were just as good at recognizing parts of houses as they were at recognizing whole houses. But for faces, the type of question did matter. Subjects were not as good at recognizing face parts as they were at recognizing whole faces. This fits with the view that faces are encoded and retrieved as whole configurations and that disrupting this configuration harms recognition. Sound familiar? While face recognition is assumed to be different from the recognition of other objects, the previous finding hearkens back to one difference between view-based approaches and parts-based approaches to object recognition. To which one is face recognition more similar? Recall that view-based approaches assume holistic processing of objects whereas parts-based approaches assume an analysis and assembly of component features. The processes involved in face recognition seem to be more akin to those proposed by the view-based approaches. Keep this thought in mind as we move on to discuss the nature of face recognition in more depth.

So, *Is* Face Recognition Special?

As our discussion implies, one of the central questions addressed by researchers and theorists who study face recognition is whether the mechanisms used to recognize faces are "special"—specialized for face recognition, and used solely for face recognition. Is there a brain *module* devoted only to recognizing upright faces?

Face Recognition as a Specialized Module.   The notion that face recognition is a highly specialized ability (e.g., Kanwisher, 2006) would certainly seem to make evolutionary sense. It would be hard to come up with a more important thing to recognize and respond to than a human face. So it would make sense that there are highly specialized mechanisms devoted only to that task. The evidence seems pretty strong that face recognition is much different from the recognition of other types of stimuli like houses, birds, or hammers. Recall the concept of dissociations from Chapter 2—dissociations are often taken as one piece of converging evidence that two different abilities are based on different processes. The face-inversion effect is an example of such a dissociation, and indicates that face and object recognition are based on different mechanisms.

Research Theme: Neuroscience   A number of brain-related findings are also cited as evidence for the special status of face recognition. For example, Farah (1991, 1994) reports double dissociations among case studies of object and face recognition. In reviewing a number of cases of neurological patients, she reports that some patients show intact object recognition without face recognition, while others show the converse pattern. This is compelling evidence that the two types of recognition are based on different mechanisms. In addition to these case studies, brain-imaging studies consistently show that a specific area of the brain's visual cortex, labeled the **fusiform face area,** is highly activated when people view faces but not when they view other objects (Kanwisher, McDermott, & Chun, 1997). Finally, event-related potentials taken from the visual cortex show an early negative peak response to faces (an N170 response) that is not shown in response to other objects. Taken together, these findings offer compelling evidence for the existence of a specialized face-recognition module.

Face Recognition as Perceptual Expertise.   Not all agree that face recognition is a specialized module (e.g., Gauthier & Curby, 2005; Tanaka, 2001; Tarr & Cheng, 2003), instead citing the incredible efficiency and speed of face recognition as evidence of perceptual **expertise.** Expertise refers to the superior knowledge and skill that develops after extensive practice in some domain, and there's no doubt that all human beings (except perhaps infants) could be considered experts in the domain of face recognition. A simple way to test this notion would be to test experts in some domain other than human faces and determine the effects of inversion on their recognition processes. Astute readers might be thinking, "Hey . . . didn't I just read about a study like this?" If so, give yourself a doggie biscuit. This comparison was a feature of the Diamond and Carey (1986) classic study that compared dog experts and nonexperts. Recall that the recognition of dogs was disrupted by inversion, but only for dog experts. This finding indicates that human faces might not be so special after all.

Entry Points Revisited.   As an alternative to the existence of separate processing systems for the recognition of faces and objects, Tarr and Cheng (2003) propose a different type of taxonomy. According to their view, recognition of faces differs from that of other objects because of the typical *entry point* required for recognition. As you read earlier in the context of levels of categorization, the entry point refers to the default level of categorization that we assign to familiar objects. In our earlier discussion, we noted that another way of thinking about the basic-level categorization advantage is that the basic level serves as the most common entry point for recognition. But given the seemingly infinite variety of faces that we encounter in our lives, recognition at the basic level would not be enough. No one looks at their best friend and thinks, "Hey, there's a human"; they don't even recognize a face at the subordinate level: "Hey, there's a young Caucasian American." Instead, they recognize individuals: "Hey, there's Allison." So the entry point required for recognition of human faces is at the *individual* level, a more specific level than we've addressed thus far.

This still doesn't explain why the recognition of faces and objects might depend on different sorts of processes. Recall our discussion of recognition theories and the resolution of those theories proposed by Tarr and Bulthoff (1995). They propose that parts-based mechanisms are important for making gross discriminations (i.e., at the basic level), while more holistic view-based mechanisms are used for making fine discriminations (i.e., at the subordinate level). Tarr and Cheng (2003) apply this distinction to the recognition of objects and faces, proposing that objects can be discriminated and recognized based on their parts, while faces can be recognized only holistically, in terms of the particular configuration of their features. This distinction would also explain why rotation would harm face recognition disproportionately. As you saw earlier, parts-based recognition is unaffected by rotation, while view-based recognition is affected by it. So basically, Tarr and Cheng (2003) propose that expertise leads one to shift the default level of categorization and recognition from the basic level to the individual level. Faces aren't special; expertise is.

Some recent neurological evidence would seem to support this view. Gauthier, Skudlarski, Gore, and Anderson (2000) found that the fusiform face area, thought to be associated exclusively with the recognition of faces, is also active when bird experts recognize birds, and when car experts recognize cars. In addition, another piece of neurological evidence cited as support for a face-recognition module would seem to be on tenuous ground; the early peak ERP response seen exclusively for faces turns out not to be exclusive *to* faces (Tanaka & Curran, 2001).

Research Theme: Neuroscience ▶

The view that expertise is the operative factor in recognition gets further support from an ERP study of expert recognition conducted by Gauthier, Curran, Curby, and Collins (2003). Their procedure provided a direct test of whether face and object recognition engage precisely the same brain areas and cognitive processes. They looked at dual experts, people who were highly skilled at recognizing both faces (as everyone is) and, in this particular case, cars. The researchers' basic idea was simple yet elegant. They set up a situation in which the dual experts had to process faces and cars concurrently. Basically, they were using a logic similar to the dual-task paradigms discussed in Chapter 4. If two concurrent tasks interfere with one another, they are more than likely engaging similar mechanisms, overloading a central resource, or creating a perceptual bottleneck. The procedure was a little too complex to get into a detailed exposition here, but basically, subjects were presented with an alternating series of faces and cars and had to make judgments about each stimulus. The judgments required that subjects hold the previous *two* stimuli in mind; so, while they were making a judgment about a presented face, subjects also were holding in mind an image about a just-presented car (and vice versa).

The results of the study were consistent with the expertise hypothesis. There was a significant correlation between the level of car expertise of the subjects and how much interference they experienced in facial recognition. The more expertise they had, the more their judgments about cars interfered with their judgments about faces and vice versa. The researchers' interpretation is that both car and face recognition vie for the same holistic pattern-recognition processes, and interference is the result. In addition, Gauthier et al. (2003) also recorded ERPs in subjects as they engaged in the face-car interference task. These findings paralleled the reaction time findings. The N170 component—the face-selective neural response to faces, discussed earlier in the chapter—occurred in response to cars, but only for car experts. More importantly, the N170 response to faces was significantly lessened when faces had to be processed in the context of cars. This is another indication that face processing and car processing (in car experts) were tapping the same sets of processes. That is, face processing was not special.

Self-Recognition

Let's return to the plight of the man in the anecdote related by Farah (1992) who failed to recognize his own face. His visual recognition deficit is striking, reminding us of the degree to which we take this ability for granted. Our knowledge of our own face seems inseparable from our general knowledge of self—who we are, our likes and dislikes, our personal history. Whether face recognition involves a special mechanism or is simply a matter of perceptual expertise, there does seem to be evidence to suggest that recognition of one's own face may be particularly special. One indicator of this is that although nonhuman primates have shown face-recognition ability, they fail on tests of self-recognition even after extended training (Keenan, Wheeler, Gallup, & Pascual-Leone, 2000). Might our own face recognition rely on different brain areas than general face recognition?

Research Theme: Neuroscience

Both case study and brain-imaging evidence suggest that the area of the brain called the fusiform face area (located in the temporal lobes) is specialized for recognizing faces. Prosopagnosics (those with an inability to recognize faces) show selective damage to this area (e.g., Sergent & Signoret, 1992), and brain-imaging studies with normal individuals demonstrate increased activation in this area during face recognition (Kanwisher, McDermott, & Chun, 1997). Despite the paucity of research regarding the neural substrates of self-face recognition, Keenan and colleagues (Keenan, Freund, Hamilton, Ganis, & Pascual-Leone, 2000; Keenan, McCutcheon, Freund, Gallup, Sanders, & Pascual-Leone, 1999) found some intriguing evidence that self-recognition may involve the right pre-frontal area of the cortex. This evidence is especially intriguing in light of what others have found—that this same area is especially active during other tasks involving the self, such as recalling the events from one's own life story (Fink, Markowitsch, & Reinkemeier, 1996). (We'll talk more about recall of one's life story—autobiographical memory—in Chapter 8.)

Consider an investigation by Keenan, Freund, Hamilton, Ganis, and Pascual-Leone (2000). Their first study employed a simple recognition task. Subjects were presented with pictures of faces and as quickly as possible had to identify each face as their own face, the face of a coworker, or the face of a stranger. For half of the trials, they used their left hand to respond; for the other half, they used their right. Why the hand switch? This was actually a critical component of the study, given the contralateral organization of the brain's hemispheres: a left-hand response is controlled by the right hemisphere of the brain, and the converse is true for a right-hand response. If the right hemisphere is specialized for self-recognition, then one might expect to find a left-hand reaction time (RT) advantage. This is exactly what happened. RTs for recognizing one's own face were faster than those for recognizing the other two types of faces; more important, this advantage was seen only when subjects responded with their left hand! This result would be expected if the right hemisphere enjoys an advantage in processing one's own face relative to the faces of others.

Another study by Keenan et al (1999) bolsters this conclusion. In this study, subjects saw a series of rapidly presented faces—a sort of "face movie." The series of faces began with the person's own face and ended with the face of a famous person (e.g., Bill Clinton or Marilyn Monroe). In between was a sequence of morphed pictures that were combinations of the two (see Figure 5.12). Imagine yourself watching a gradual sequence of pictures in which you turn into Marilyn Monroe or Bill Clinton. (The researchers also

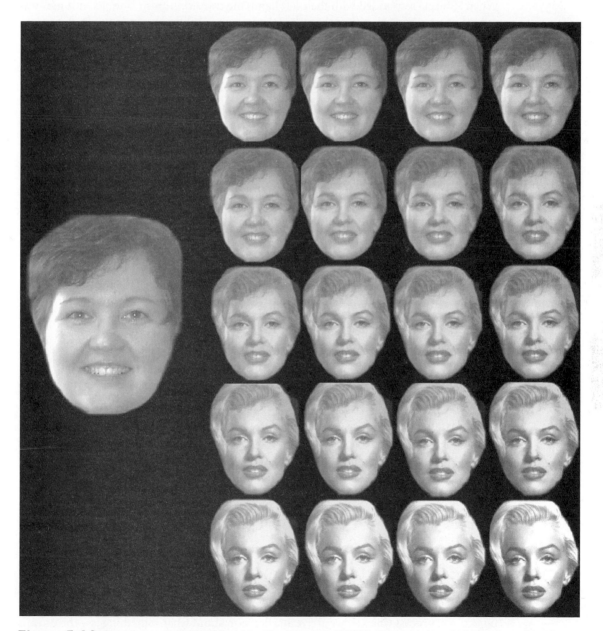

Figure 5.12   Facial morph like that used by Keenan et al. (1999). Over a series of pictures, a subject's face morphs into a famous face.

From Keenan, J. P., McCutcheon, B., Freund, S., Gallup, G. G., Sanders, G., & Pascual-Leone, A. (1999). Left-hand advantage in a self-face recognition task. *Neuropsychologia, 37,* 1421–1425. Copyright 1999. Reprinted by permission of Elsevier Science.

used the opposite sequence in which the famous face would gradually morph into the subject's face.) Subjects were told to watch the series and press a key when they felt that each picture had become more "not themselves" than "themselves" (or vice versa, in the reverse condition). Once again, they used either their right or left hand to press the key. When subjects responded with their left hand, the transition from "me" to "not me" was judged as occurring significantly earlier than when subjects responded with their right hand. This again seems to confirm that the right hemisphere (which controls the left hand) has an advantage in self-recognition.

STOP *and* **REVIEW!**

1. The Thatcher illusion shows that:
   a. turning a face upside down impacts recognition of the faces of celebrities, but not faces of noncelebrities.
   b. turning a face upside down impairs the ability to recognize it.
   c. people recognize the parts of a face, but can't recognize the whole face.
   d. faces can't be recognized as faces if they're presented upside down.
2. Briefly describe the claims of the "specialized module" and "perceptual expertise" accounts of how we recognize faces.
3. True or false? The right hemisphere seems especially proficient at recognizing one's own face.

➤ The Thatcher illusion demonstrates that inverting a face has a disproportionate effect on recognition, relative to its effect on objects. This suggests that faces are encoded and subsequently recognized holistically, while objects are encoded more in terms of separate elements. Inversion has much more of an effect on faces than it does on other objects due to the strong configural properties of faces.

➤ Some view faces as "special" stimuli, with a dedicated brain module or set of mechanisms devoted specifically to their recognition. Others characterize the proficiency of face recognition as expertise, citing evidence of face-like holistic processing within a person's domain of expertise.

➤ Evidence of the ability to recognize one's own face demonstrates a hemispheric asymmetry. The right hemisphere seems to be selectively involved in self-face recognition.

Concepts and Categories

We've seen that object recognition involves the identification and classification of some object. The process whereby we arrive at a decision about what something is—the process of object recognition—begs a basic question: What makes a thing what it is? In other words, what is it about a poodle, a Lhasa apso, and a Great Dane that would lead us to

Different, but the same. What allows us to classify each of these as members of the same category?

look at all of them and apply the same label—"dog"? And why would animals that seem similar enough to belong to the dog category (e.g., a Minnesota timber wolf—the animal, not the basketball player) be classified in a different category? In this section of the chapter, we'll discuss some fundamental work on concepts and categories. A **category** refers to a grouping of objects or ideas that have some common underlying feature or set of features. The term **concept** is typically used to refer to the more abstract notion of what that category represents in one's mind. To simplify matters, we'll follow a common convention and use the terms *category* and *concept* interchangeably.

Types of Categories ("Categories" as a Category)

There are a number of different schemes one might use to distinguish between category types (see Medin, Lynch, & Solomon, 2000 for an extensive consideration of this issue). Goldstein and Kersten (2003) suggest that different types of categories can be ordered in terms of how similar members of the category seem to be to one another. **Natural kinds** (also termed *natural categories*) are those that occur naturally in the world; they essentially define themselves. Members within these types of categories seem to share important characteristics or features. For example, all flowers are grouped into a single category by virtue of the naturally occurring attributes that they share. These naturally occurring concepts are labeled only after their discovery (Medin & Heit, 1994). **Artifacts** (also termed *artifact categories*) include objects or conventions designed or invented by humans to serve particular functions (e.g., tools, sports, furniture). Members of artifact categories don't seem to share the same sorts of basic features shared by members of a natural category. For example, soccer and cross-country (two members of the artifact category *sport*) don't quite hang together as well as rose and daisy (two members of the natural kind category *flower*).

Two other sorts of categories seem even more loosely associated than natural kinds and artifacts; however, there's no question that there is a concept underlying them. For example, **ad hoc categories** (Barsalou, 1983) are those formed in the service of some goal. The members of the category cohere only by virtue of their relation to the context at hand. For example, we doubt that *things to take on vacation* has the same presence in your knowledge representation as does the natural kind category *fruit*. Nonetheless, asking for *things to take on vacation* would lead to consistent responses across individuals within a particular cultural context, suggesting that we can form categories "on the fly," given a particular goal. These categories are labeled "ad hoc" because they're formed only for a purpose. In Goldstein and Kersten's (2003) similarity scheme, members of ad hoc categories would seem to be pretty low in terms of their similarity. It seems that, other than all belonging to the ad hoc category *things people take on vacation*, there's virtually nothing in common among suitcases, swimsuits, cameras, and books. Even less coherent is the *metaphorical concept*. An example of this type of concept is an emotional prison, which could describe an unrewarding job, a relationship that can't be ended for some reason, or a person who can't share some dark secret. The specific situations underlying these three category members may be radically different, yet there is a common underlying theme that unites them.

Folk Biology.   A review by Medin and Atran (2004) ascribes special status to natural kind categories or, more generally, to our knowledge of the biological world. This everyday knowledge or intuition about living things and how they work is termed **folk biology,** which invokes the image of "common folk" discussing their knowledge. In fact, these investigators propose that knowledge of biological systems constitutes a cognitive module that has evolved in the service of adaptation to the environment. Recall that you read a similar argument about face recognition earlier in the chapter. As noted by Medin and Atran, a biological-knowledge system would certainly make evolutionary sense given that survival of humans and their ancestors no doubt depended on the ability to learn and reason about animals, plants, and other natural phenom-

> Research Theme: Culture

ena. This evolutionary claim is consistent with the fact that across all cultures of the world, people seem to think about biological entities in the same way, in terms of hierarchies of (i.e., different levels of) categorization (Atran, 1990). Even the gradation of these hierarchical categories (say, into fruit, apple, and Honey Crisp apple) seems to be the same across cultures, indicating that the levels into which categories are divided reflect a natural reality, rather than a cultural convenience (Berlin, 1992; Malt, 1995).

Functions of Concepts

Just reading through the different sorts of concepts that we use in everyday thought and language ought to give you some feel for just how important concepts are. Indeed, as succinctly summarized by Solomon, Medin, and Lynch (1999), "Concepts are the building blocks of thought." Their functions go well beyond just providing us with labels convenient for grouping things. Medin and Rips (2005) review these various and sundry functions of concepts.

Concepts are extremely important in our everyday thinking—they serve as a sort of mental shorthand that allows for quick and efficient *understanding*. They also allow us to go beyond the present moment and make *predictions*. Suppose Greg tells you that his favorite TV show is a sitcom (a situation comedy); he probably doesn't need to add that the show is funny, that it lasts 30 minutes, that it's on at night between 7 p.m. and 9 p.m., or that he watches it on a little box that projects color images. "Sitcom" immediately evokes all of these ideas. Put another way, our knowledge of concepts allows us to infer knowledge not explicitly stated. In addition, if you don't like sitcoms, based on his use of the label "sitcom" you can predict that you won't like the show. Concepts can also support new *learning*. In the 1980s there was a pretty standard formula for a situation comedy—and this formula did not involve animation. That concept has changed, due largely to the success of Greg's favorite show, *The Simpsons*. People updated their concepts so thoroughly that now animated sitcoms like *South Park* and *Family Guy* have become all the rage.

Finally, concepts are important for communication. As you'll see in Chapter 10, people are wizards in their ability to combine concepts via language in order to get their idea across. For example Greg makes a distinction between "restaurant coffee" and "real coffee," and he's willing to bet that many if not most readers of this text know what he means.

Which place sells "real coffee"?

Restaurant coffee is weak—hot water flavored with a hint of coffee bean. Real coffee is the kind you get at a coffee shop—it packs more flavor and gives you more of a jolt. Clearly, concepts are subtle and complex entities.

Approaches to Concept Representation

A number of approaches have been proposed to explain how we represent and think about everyday concepts. Central to these accounts is the question of what makes category members *cohere,* or stick together. Approaches to concept representation can be classified into two broad categories (see how pervasive categorization is!): similarity-based approaches and essentialist approaches.

Similarity-Based Approaches.   **Similarity-based approaches** to concept representation assert that categorization is a matter of judging the similarity between the target object and some standard in long-term memory. That standard might be a clearly specified set of features or characteristics, an abstracted "best example" version of the category, or all of the other members of the category. We now examine each of these possibilities.

The Classical View.   The earliest and perhaps most straightforward account of how we use concepts is termed the **classical view.** According to the classical view, items are classified into particular categories if they have certain features or characteristics. These features are both necessary and sufficient for defining the concept. For example, the concept "triangle" is a closed, three-sided figure whose angles sum to 180°. Shapes that have these characteristics are triangles; shapes that don't are not. The classical view is considered similarity based, because categorization is based on whether the set of features that characterize a given entity is similar to the features that define the concept.

STOP *and* **THINK!**

DEFINING CONCEPTS WITH RULES

Consider the following concepts:

gemstone
sport
square
plant
grandmother
furniture
spice
game

For each of these concepts, try and come up with a list of features that define it—a set of features that, if possessed by some object or person, would make them a member of the category. After you've defined each concept, try and think of exceptions to the "rules" you just made.

- Which set of concepts had the most exceptions (i.e., "problem concepts")?
- Which concepts didn't have any?
- Can you refine your definitions of the "problem concepts" to accommodate more examples?
- What are they?

Although the classical view provides a ready description of how we might classify concepts that have clearly defined properties, closer inspection reveals some serious flaws. The most significant criticism gets at the very core of the approach: it's very difficult to specify many concepts in terms of features that are both necessary and sufficient. For example, take the concept "game," which can include Ring around the Rosie, Monopoly, football, and cribbage—what on earth are the common features that define them as games and make them members of that category? Which features are necessary and sufficient for something to be called a game?

Graded Structure and Fuzzy Boundaries.   Another serious problem with the classical view is that it can't explain a fundamental characteristic of categorization—the fact that our representations of categories have a **graded structure.** When we think of a category like "furniture," it's not the case that all furniture is created equal. The vast majority of respondents, when asked to name a member of the category "furniture," will say "table," "chair," or "couch." The classical view of concepts has no way to deal with this finding, termed the *typicality effect.* According to the classical view, if something has all of the features that define "furniture," then it's a piece of furniture; if it doesn't, then it's not. The view has no mechanism that explains why certain category members (e.g., tables) are

Sport, or not a sport?

more "furniturey" than others. An interesting side note: even members of ad hoc categories, like "things to take on vacation," vary in their typicality (typical: "swimsuit"; less typical: "deck of cards"). The graded nature of category representation is evident from many research studies, most notably the work of Eleanor Rosch and colleagues (e.g., Rosch & Mervis, 1975). When subjects are asked to rate which members of categories are typical, there is overwhelming agreement about which members are more and less typical.

A second problem with the classical view is the implication that categories are separated by absolute, clear-cut boundaries. If something has the necessary and sufficient features of a category, then it's a member; if not, it's not. If the categories of "game" and "sport" were well defined, it would be a trivial task to classify "bowling." But in reality, categories have what have been called **fuzzy boundaries;** one person's game is another person's sport. When we invite opinion from our students regarding whether bowling is a sport, we invariably get a split. Bowling is "kind of" a sport; like other sports, it requires well-coordinated motor movements, and it's shown on the sports channel. But still, it seems (at most) like "sort of" a sport. But the classical view doesn't allow for this "sort of" view of categories. Something is a sport or it isn't. This absolute view fails to capture many of the categories we think about every day.

The Prototype Approach.   The **prototype approach** to categorization provides a more flexible view. Rather than specifying necessary and sufficient features that each category member must have, the prototype approach contends that there are features of the category that members are likely to have. Instances of the category are evaluated and classified based on their resemblance to other members. Instances that have a high **family resemblance** (i.e., those that share many features with other category members) are classified as typical members of the category and serve as the standard to which other category members are compared (this standard is called the prototype). Those with a low family resemblance are seen as less typical members. For example, typical bird features might be the following: flies, chirps, has feathers, has a beak. The instance "robin," because it is characterized by all four of these features, is perceived as more typical than "penguin," which is characterized by only two. (Penguins are one of the aberrations of the bird category.) This is why the prototype approach is classified as similarity based: category membership is determined by an item's similarity to the prototype.

The prototype approach solves the problems encountered by the classical view. First, it avoids the rigidity of the classical view. One doesn't need to come up with the set of features that absolutely defines a category. The prototype approach contends that there are features that tend to be present. The second problem—the fact that some category members are perceived as more typical, or "better," members than others—certainly poses no difficulty. In fact, it's the very basis for the prototype approach. Finally, the fuzzy boundary issue isn't really a problem for the prototype approach. The fuzzy boundary between the categories of "game" and "sport" fits well with this view. "Bowling" is difficult to classify because it lies near the boundaries for each category (about equidistant from each category's prototype), and the category boundaries aren't really clear.

STOP *and* THINK!

AND THE NUMBER 1 FRUIT IS . . .

Recruit a few willing friends as subjects, and give them this concept task. Present the following category names and have the subjects generate the first four examples that come to mind.

fruits
games
weapons
beverages
things you'd save in a fire

Tally up the responses and consider the following questions:

- Did prototypes emerge from the categories? What were those prototypes?
- Did your "subjects" have any trouble with the "ad hoc" category? Did generation of members of this category take any longer than generation of the more "traditional" categories?
- Is the graded nature of category structure apparent from the responses?

How does a category member become a prototype? Prototypes are thought to be abstracted through repeated experience with category members. Through repeated encounters with birds, we arrive at a representation of a "bird" that includes the features we've seen the most often; smallish, flies, builds nests, has feathers, and so on. A particularly compelling demonstration of prototype formation is provided by Posner, Goldsmith, and Welton (1967). These investigators used an unusual sort of category—dot patterns—to investigate prototype formation. Figure 5.13 presents some sample patterns. Unbeknownst to the subjects, all of the dot patterns presented were statistically generated distortions of a prototype; the presented examples differed from the prototype by varying amounts. However, the prototype itself was never presented. During a test phase, subjects were presented with both old (previously presented) and new dot patterns and were to determine whether or not they had seen each pattern in the earlier phase.

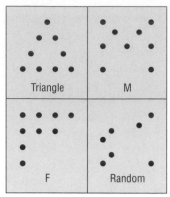

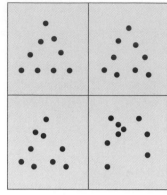

Figure 5.13 Stimuli used in the Posner et al. (1967) study of prototypes.

From Posner, M. I., Goldsmith, R., & Welton, K. E. (1967). Perceived distance and the classification of distorted patterns. *Journal of Experimental Psychology, 73,* 28–38. Copyright 1967 by the American Psychological Society. Reprinted by permission.

(a) Prototypical Pattern   **(b) Triangle Distortions**

The most compelling result came from test trials on which the prototype pattern was presented. Subjects tended to confidently confirm that they had seen the prototype pattern, even though they never had. They were considerably less likely to make this same mistake with other new patterns. Later in the session, after only the one test presentation, the prototype was recognized just as well as patterns that had been presented throughout the experiment, almost as if the prototype itself had been repeatedly presented. In a sense, it had, according to the prototype approach. Throughout the initial presentation trials, subjects were abstracting a prototype that represented the average of all the patterns they were observing.

Characteristics of Prototypes.   As previously mentioned, the term **prototype** refers not only to the theoretical approach to concept representation but also to the most representative member (or members) of a given category. These *anchoring,* or *standard,* category members are afforded advantages in processing.

Let's take a look at some of the processing advantages enjoyed by prototypes (reviewed by Rosch, 1975a). First, *speed of access* is quicker the more prototypical the category member. In reaction time studies, people are quicker to verify the category membership of prototypical category members like "hammer" relative to less prototypical members like "T-square." *Ease of access* to prototypes is also indicated by the fact that when asked to generate members of a category, the order in which people generate the items (e.g., Battig & Montague, 1969) corresponds closely to prototypicality ratings (Rosch, 1975a). In other words, the more prototypical the word, the earlier it is listed. *Rate of learning* also seems to be faster for prototypical category members. Rosch (1973) compared children's and adults' ability to verify category membership of prototypes and nonprototypes and found a much larger difference in children relative to adults. Children were much slower at verifying the category membership of nonprototypes relative to prototypes, implying that the prototypes had been more quickly learned.

Research Theme: Development

Prototypes are also more likely to be *primed* by presenting the category name. Rosch (1975a, b) found that presenting the name of a category (e.g., "weapon") speeds the recognition of a prototypical member (e.g., "knife"), but can inhibit the recognition of a nonprototypical member (e.g., "brick").

Prototypical category members also have some primacy in terms of how they're used linguistically—that is, when we communicate. Take the example of a *linguistic hedge* (Lakoff, 1972) in which we qualify what we're saying with phrases like "technically," "in essence," or "when you come right down to it." For example, we're more likely to say that "when it comes right down to it, a penguin is a bird," than we are to say "when it comes right down to it, a robin is a bird" (cf., Rosch, 1975a). The latter sounds preposterous, because "robin" and "bird" seem nearly synonymous.

Problems with the Prototype Approach.   There is no question about the descriptive value of the term *prototype*. As just discussed, the idea that certain category members serve as the basis to which other members are compared is not in doubt. But *prototype* as a theoretical explanation for how we represent concepts has fared less well than *prototype* as a descriptive term. One problem is that people's representations of categories and their characteristics seem to be much more complex than would be implied by the prototype approach. Categorical knowledge extends beyond the simple average representation suggested by the prototype approach. Evidence indicates that people are sensitive to the ways in which certain properties of category members do and do not go together. For example, people are sensitive to the fact that small birds tend to sing but large birds tend to squawk, not sing (Mervis & Rosch, 1981); furthermore, people use this type of information in classifying objects. It's not clear how an average representation could allow for this rather sophisticated representation of object properties and their intercorrelations.

The prototype approach also fails to capture another key feature of category representation—the fact that it's sensitive to context (Roth & Shoben, 1983). Research shows that what we view as a typical category member depends on how we think about the category. For example, if I ask you to name a musical instrument, you're quite likely to say "piano"; but if I ask you to name a "campfire musical instrument," you're likely to say "guitar" or "harmonica." If our representation of a category is centered on one (or two or three) typical member(s), it's not clear why context should matter at all. A similar problem arises when one considers the conjunction of two concepts (Hampton, 1993). Take the concept "pet fish," for example; most people would say "guppy" or "goldfish" if asked for an example, but neither is prototypical of either individual concept ("pet" or "fish").

The Exemplar Approach.   Partially in response to the problems encountered with the prototype approach, some researchers have proposed the **exemplar approach,** which suggests that we represent categories in terms of examples, or category exemplars. According to this view, there is no single representation of a category that gets abstracted over time. There are a number of different versions of the exemplar approach (e. g., Brooks, 1978; Hintzman, 1986; Nosofsky, 1984). The extreme version of the exemplar view proposes no abstraction or generalization process. Rather, our representation of a

Exemplars of the concept "guitar."

concept (i.e., "guitar") consists of every single encounter we've had with it. When we think about the concept, we retrieve one of these encounters (e.g., Brooks, 1987). Note that like the prototype approach, the exemplar approach is similarity based: objects and events are assessed in terms of their similarity to a standard. But in this case, the standard is a specific example of the category rather than a generalized representation. Also, the standard that is used (i.e., the particular example) will depend on circumstances. When asked if an eagle is a bird, the example retrieved will be some relatively large bird of prey (Ross & Spalding, 1994).

Like the prototype approach, the exemplar approach can deal readily with the difficulties of the classical view. The effect of typicality poses no problem for the exemplar approach. The reason we're most likely to think of "robin" when we encounter the concept "bird" is that the majority of our stored examples of birds are robins (or similar to robins). When we retrieve an instance, we're more likely to retrieve one that's been encoded frequently.

The exemplar approach can also deal quite readily with some of the problems encountered by the prototype approach. The biasing effect of context ("harmonica" as an example of "a campfire musical instrument") is no problem for the exemplar approach, which claims that a particular context can activate certain exemplars, essentially *priming* their retrieval. When we're in the middle of the Christmas season, for example, Christmas songs abound. So if asked in December to give an example of the category "song," "Jingle Bells" may well be the answer; in this case, temporal context serves to make this particular exemplar especially retrievable. The exemplar approach also has no problem with the finding that people are sensitive to correlations in the properties of category members (Malt & Smith, 1984). (Remember the previous example that little birds sing and big birds don't?) Since we store every single encounter with category members, all the information about the category's members is available. So although you may not be particularly aware that small birds tend to sing and big birds tend to squawk, you are able to arrive at this conclusion if asked. (Of course, who would ask but a cognitive researcher?)

But alas, it seems that every theory has its problems, and the exemplar approach is no exception. For one thing, it seems that in some circumstances people are truly using an abstracted representation—one that's constructed from repeated encounters. Think back to the dot-pattern classification study conducted by Posner and colleagues (1967). In that study, people were very likely to say they had seen the prototype they had never seen, so there was no corresponding exemplar. Obviously, the exemplar approach has no explanation for these results. How would one recognize an exemplar that was never encoded? Another problem with the more extreme versions of the exemplar approach is one of economy (Komatsu, 1992). It strains credulity to think that every single encounter with every single object is stored in memory. (This recalls the problem of economy faced by the template view of pattern recognition.) Even if only some exemplars are stored, what determines the ones that are? As is often the case in theoretical debates, it appears that both the prototype approach and the exemplar approach have some merit and that both may serve as accurate descriptions of concept representations. Malt (1989) demonstrated that under different circumstances, people may classify based on either exemplars or prototypes. It seems that the boundary between these two categories of theories is definitely fuzzy!

The Essentialist Approach.

Similarity-based approaches to categorization take what might be termed a bottom-up approach to categorization. These approaches emphasize the processing of the particular features possessed by members of the concept; a robin is a bird because it has the features of a bird, or is similar in features to some prototypical bird or to an exemplar. Alternatively, one might conceive of categorization in more of a top-down manner. It could be that categorization is not based on encoding the particular properties of entities in the external world and comparing these properties to those of stored exemplars or prototypes. Instead, categorization of external entities may be based on a person's general idea (or "theory") regarding the essence of the concept. And this essence isn't always obvious, or even related closely to physical appearance or obvious characteristics. Because of this notion—that categories have some underlying nature or essence—these accounts are sometimes labeled as **essentialist approaches** (Medin & Ortony, 1989). One critical implication of the notion of an essence is that categories are not represented or thought of solely in terms of their characteristics or features. And by extension, when we compare categories, or use them in reasoning, we aren't just doing some type of simple comparison and arriving at some judgment of similarity, as the classical, prototype, and exemplar approaches would propose. Categorization goes well beyond superficial comparison of perceptual similarity.

REPRESENTING CONCEPTS

Ask two friends to tell you what they think about when they hear each category name:

vegetable
vehicle
tool
four-footed animal
type of reading material

- Does it seem like a general prototype or a specific exemplar comes to mind?
- If it's a specific exemplar, why might this particular exemplar have been brought to mind? Was it seen recently? Was it appropriate to the context they're in?
- Was there any indication that they were using an essentialist approach? How so?

A study by Rips (1989) provides a compelling demonstration of the inadequacy of the similarity-based approaches, and of the validity of the essentialist approaches. He used an intriguing procedure in which he presented subjects with stories that involved made-up organisms—but although they were made up, subjects were likely to label them as a member of a familiar category, like a bird or insect (importantly, however, these labels were never presented to subjects). They compared two conditions (see Figure 5.14 for example stories from each condition). In the *accident* condition, the organism (e.g., a birdlike creature called a *sorp*) underwent a catastrophic accident that resulted in many of its external features being altered, such that it now looked like a member of a different category (e.g., an insect) but still behaved like a member of its original category (e.g., behaved like a bird). In the *essence* condition, the sorp underwent the same type of external change (e.g., looked like an insect rather than a bird). But now it behaved like its new category rather than its old category (e.g., behaved like an insect, not a bird), and was given a new name (e.g., a *doon*). So in one condition, there were *accidental* changes in the organism; in the other, there were *essential* changes in the organism.

After reading these stories, subjects were given (1) a categorization task in which they were to rate the degree to which the sorp (or doon) fit into the category of bird on a scale from 1 to 10; and (2) a similarity-rating task in which they were to rate the similarity between sorps and birds (or the similarity between doons and birds) on a scale from 1 to 10. If the basis for categorization *is* similarity, then a measure of categorization should behave the same way as a measure of similarity. It should be influenced by the same variables, and in the same way. If some manipulation leads an organism to seem like a better member of a certain category, that manipulation should also lead the organism to be rated as more similar to members of the category. In the present experiment, changes in the accident and essence conditions should influence judgments of similarity and judgments of categorization in the same manner. Given that the basis for categorization is similarity to a prototype or exemplar, any manipulation that increases similarity ratings for an item should also make that item seem like a better member of the category.

Accident Condition:

There was an animal called a sorp which, when it was fully grown, was like other sorps, having a diet which consisted of seeds and berries found on the ground or on plants. The sorp had two wings, two legs, and lived in a nest high in the branches of a tree. Its nest was composed of twigs and other fibrous plant material. This sorp was covered with bluish-gray feathers.

The sorp's nest happened to be not too far from a place where hazardous chemicals were buried. The chemicals contaminated the vegetation that the sorp ate, and as time went by it gradually began to change. The sorp shed its feathers and sprouted a new set of wings composed of a transparent membrane. The sorp abandoned its nest, developed a brittle iridescent outer shell, and grew two more pairs of legs. At the tip of each of the sorp's six legs an adhesive pad was formed so that it was able to hold onto smooth surfaces; for example, the sorp learned to take shelter during rainstorms by clinging upside down to the undersides of tree leaves. The sorp eventually sustained itself entirely on the nectar of flowers.

Eventually this sorp mated with a normal female sorp one spring. The female laid the fertilized eggs in her nest and incubated them for three weeks. After that time normal young sorps broke out of their shells.

During an early stage of the doon's life it is known as a sorp. A sorp's diet mainly consists of seeds and berries found on the ground or on plants. A sorp has two wings, two legs, and lives in a nest high in the branches of a tree. Its nest is composed of twigs and other fibrous plant material. A sorp is covered with bluish-gray feathers.

Essence Condition:

After a few months, the doon sheds its feathers, revealing that its wings are composed of a transparent membrane. The doon abandons its nest, develops a brittle, iridescent outer shell, and grows two more pairs of legs. At the tip of each of the doon's six legs an adhesive pad is formed so that it can hold onto smooth surfaces; for example, doons take shelter during rainstorms by clinging upside down to the undersides of tree leaves. A doon sustains itself entirely on the nectar of flowers.

Doons mate in the late summer. The female doon deposits the eggs among thick vegetation where they will remain in safety until they hatch.

Figure 5.14 Transformation stories used in the study by Rips (1989).

From Rips, L. J. (1989). Similarity, typicality, and categorization. In S. Vosniadu & A. Ortony (Eds.), *Similarity and analogical reasoning* (pp. 21–59). Cambridge, UK: Cambridge University Press. Reprinted by permission of Cambridge University Press.

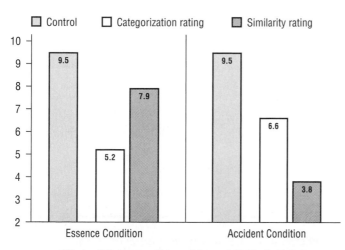

Effects of Changes on Categorizing and Similarity Ratings

Figure 5.15 Data from Rips (1989).

From Rips, L. J. (1989). Similarity, typicality, and categorization. In S. Vosniadu & A. Ortony (Eds.), *Similarity and analogical reasoning* (pp. 21–59). Cambridge, UK: Cambridge University Press. Reprinted by permission of Cambridge University Press.

The results were striking. Take a look at Figure 5.15. Presented are ratings of category membership in and similarity to birds, relative to a control group (who read only the description of the birdlike sorps). In the accident condition (in which the organism eventually looked like an insect but still behaved like a bird), the change lowered similarity ratings more than categorization ratings. So basically, in the case of an accidental change, subjects saw the new organism as much less similar to birds than it had been. However, in terms of its category, it still seemed basically like a bird. In the essence condition (in which the organism eventually looked and behaved like an insect), the change lowered categorization ratings more than similarity ratings. Basically, in the case of an essential change, subjects saw the new organism as still somewhat similar to birds. However, in terms of its category, it seemed less like a bird. The striking finding here is that similarity judgments and categorization judgments were influenced differently by the change manipulation.

This pattern should be getting more familiar to you now; it's yet another example of a dissociation. Different variables influenced the two different judgment tasks in varying ways. Recall that a dissociation is a fairly strong piece of evidence that two tasks are based on different underlying processes. So basically, Rips's (1989) finding suggests that similarity judgments and categorization judgments are based on different underlying processes! This finding poses serious challenges to the prototype and exemplar approaches, which basically say that judgments of category membership and judgments of similarity are one and the same. Clearly, they aren't. These findings led Rips (1989) and others to propose essentialist approaches of categories. According to these approaches, representation is a matter of what might be termed a *personal theory* about what a concept represents; that is, our views of categories are based on implicit theories about what makes a thing what it is—in other words, what is the essence of a bird?

STOP *and* THINK!

WHAT'S THE ESSENCE OF . . .?

Consider once again what makes a thing what it is and what makes a category cohere. Think about the following items and what makes each of them a member of their respective category. Also think of why the third item in each example isn't a member of its category although it might share some features with the other two.

- What makes a brick a weapon? What makes a chain a weapon? Why isn't a sponge a weapon? What is the essence of a weapon?
- What makes water a beverage? What makes tomato juice a beverage? Why isn't motor oil a beverage? What is the essence of a beverage?
- What makes a bus a vehicle? What makes a bicycle a vehicle? Why isn't an escalator a vehicle? What is the essence of a vehicle?
- What makes a piano a musical instrument? What makes cymbals a musical instrument? Why aren't two garbage can lids a musical instrument? What is the essence of a musical instrument?

In answering each set of questions, what should emerge is your own explanation-based view of the category—-the "essence" of the category. Try the same demonstration with your oh-so-patient friends.

Essentialist approaches do a better job of explaining the notion of *category coherence* than do the exemplar and prototype approaches. When asked to list examples of the category "weapons," how do disparate items such as guns, knives, missiles, candlesticks, and baseball bats all gain membership in this category? What is it about these objects that allows them to "hang together," or cohere, as members of the same concept? They certainly don't look similar, yet we have no trouble grouping them together. And conversely, what is it about two seemingly similar animals—a shark and a dolphin—that leads them to be placed in different categories (Ross & Spalding, 1994)? They look similar but we categorize them differently. According to an essentialist approach, a category is not the set of common features that objects share. So the fact that guns and knives don't look like each other and don't share an identifiable set of features doesn't matter; it's our idea about the essence of a weapon that must be similar. And our idea about the essence of a weapon is consistent with guns, knives, and baseball bats; consequently, they are placed in the same category. Also, the fact that dolphins and sharks share structural similarities doesn't matter. What matters is that our knowledge of dolphins and their essence (they're mammals) is not similar to our knowledge of sharks and their essence (they're fish). Based on these essential differences, these two do not cohere and are categorized differently.

Biological Essentialism.   Recall the notion proposed by Medin and Atran (2004) that biological classification is a universal and special cognitive ability. These researchers take their argument one step further and argue that the notion of a biological *essence* is also universal. That is, all cultures seem to share the notion that biological organisms have some type of underlying structure (i.e., essence) that dictates the organism's appearance, behavior, and interaction with other organisms in the environment (Atran, 1998; Sousa, Atran, & Medin, 2002). Medin and Atran give the example of a frog and a tadpole; these organisms are universally considered to be the same basic animal, despite some pretty big differences in how they look, behave, and live. Although these are perceptually salient differences, they're more superficial than essential.

Essentialism in Children.   Recent research indicates that even young children have an idea about the essence of categories. This more recent research challenges earlier thinking

Research Theme: Development

on how children form concepts, including that of the venerable pioneer of child development theory, Jean Piaget (e.g., Piaget, 1929). Piaget's view was that young children place things into categories according to their superficial similarity. Rather than classifying objects in terms of essence or causal power (i.e., what the object *does* or *is*), children focus on perceptual attributes (i.e., size, color, shape). Piaget's basic assumption does make some sense; an essence seems like a rather abstract concept, and it would seem that children

Same underlying essence?

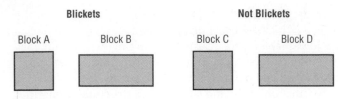

Figure 5.16 Stimulus blocks used in the Gopnik and Sobel (2000) study.

From Gopnik, A., & Sobel, D. M. (2000). Detecting blickets: How young children use information about novel causal powers in categorization and induction. *Child Development, 71*, 1205–1222. Reprinted by permission of the Society for Research in Child Development.

might take a while to intuit the essence of a category. But recent work has shown children to be fairly astute in this regard.

According to developmental theorist Susan Gelman (2003), children are not tied to obvious perceptual characteristics in their groupings of the objects they encounter in their young lives. They seem to understand nonobvious and fundamental properties. A rather whimsical example of this can be seen in a study by Gopnik and Sobel (2000). These researchers "invented" a machine termed a *blicket detector*. This machine would light up and play music when certain objects were placed on it. These objects were termed (of course) *blickets*. Although activation of the blicket detector was under the control of an unseen confederate, children didn't suspect this at all. They accepted the machine and its capabilities at face value.

To find out the basis for children's categorization, Gopnik and Sobel (2000) tested three- and four-year-old children on a category-inference task. The children were shown the blicket detector (they weren't told its name at this point) and the four blocks (A and C were square, B and D were rectangular) presented in Figure 5.16. The experimenter told the children that blocks A and B were blickets and blocks C and D were not blickets. Then block A was placed on the blicket detector, which went off. At this point, the experimenter simply exclaimed, "Look! See, this one set the machine off." Then the experimenter asked the children to indicate which of the other objects (blocks B, C, or D) would set the machine off.

As you can see, Gopnik and Sobel pitted perceptual characteristics against causal characteristics, placing them in conflict to find out which one was more salient to children as they made their classification decision. As just noted, the two blickets are different in shape: one is square and one is rectangular. The question of interest is this: On being informed that blocks A and B are blickets and then seeing block A set off the blicket machine, which property of block A would they apply to the experimenter's question? A focus on perceptual characteristics would lead the children to choose the perceptually similar object (block C); a focus on the concept that block A is a blicket would lead them to choose the other blicket (block B). The results demonstrated that the fact that something was called a "blicket" meant much more than perceptual similarity. On 73% of the trials, children chose the item that had the same label (block B) but had a conflicting shape. The perceptually similar item (block C) was chosen on 15% of the trials; and on 12% of the trials, children chose block D, which was neither causally nor perceptually similar.

These results demonstrate that even very young children have the ability to go beyond appearance and use information about causal power to classify objects. A blicket was conceived of not as an object with certain physical properties, but as a causal agent that influenced other entities in predictable ways. Placing items into categories is not a simple judgment of physical similarity; such information can be overridden by deeper conceptual relations, supporting the notion that children are sensitive to the nature, or essences of, the objects they encounter. In fact, this sensitivity seems to be present for children as young as one or two (e.g., Graham, Kilbreath, & Welder, 2004)!

Gelman and Wellman (1991) provided another clever test of the idea that children understand essences. They presented scenarios in which an animal is born to its biological parents but is switched at birth, and grows up in a new environment, with a new set of parents. In one scenario, children were presented with a story of a kangaroo switched at birth, such that it grew up with goats. They were then asked questions about characteristics and behaviors of the kangaroo. Would it hop like a kangaroo or climb like a goat? Would it have a pouch or not? Gelman and Wellman found that even preschool children understood that the kangaroo would have a pouch and would hop even though its parents couldn't hop, and couldn't teach it to hop. They seemed to understand that this is what kangaroos do; it is part of the essence of being a kangaroo.

STOP _and_ REVIEW!

1. True or false? The graded structure of categories cannot be accounted for by the classical view of categorization.
2. What are the prototype and exemplar approaches of categorization?
3. The essentialist approach of categorization
   a. seems to apply to children as well as to adults.
   b. states that categorization is based on similarity.
   c. would predict that similarity judgments and categorization judgments should be affected by the same variables.
   d. states that categorization is based on an item's outward appearance.

➤ Similarity-based approaches to categorization assume that categorization is a matter of judging the similarity between the target and a representation stored in long-term memory. According to the classical view, we compare targets to a set of features that defines the concept. The classical view is too rigid to account for the graded structure of categories and fuzzy boundaries between them.

➤ Another similarity-based view, prototype approach, assumes that we compare objects to a best example from the category. Although this approach accounts for graded structure and fuzzy boundaries, it does not account for the variability of categories in context. The exemplar approach proposes that we think of concepts in terms of specific examples, and accounts better for the sensitivity of concepts to contextual factors.

➤ Some research shows that categorization and similarity judgments dissociate under certain conditions, which casts doubt on the view that categorization is based on similarity. According to essentialist approaches, concepts are represented in terms of their essence, or basic underlying nature. There is good evidence that even young children base their categorization on underlying essences rather than on similarity.

G L O S S A R Y

ad hoc categories: categories formed "on the fly" in the service of a goal (p. 188)

artifacts (artifact categories): categories of objects designed or invented by humans to serve particular functions (p. 188)

basic level of categorization: level of categorization between superordinate and subordinate; represents the preferred level of specificity (p. 162)

category: a grouping of objects or ideas that have some common underlying feature or set of features (p. 188)

classical view: the view that items are classified into particular categories if they have certain features or characteristics (p. 190)

concept: the mental representation of a category (p. 188)

entry point for recognition: the default level of categorization that we use for familiar objects (p. 163)

essentialist approach: the view that categorization is based on a person's general idea or explanation of the essence of a particular concept (p. 197)

exemplar approach: a view of categorization that suggests that we represent categories in terms of examples, or exemplars; when we think about the concept, we retrieve one of these examples (p. 195)

expertise: superior knowledge and skill that develops after extensive practice in some domain (p. 182)

exploratory procedures (EPs): movements we use for tactile identification (p. 174)

family resemblance: the degree of overlap between members of a category (p. 192)

feature analysis: one version of the parts-based approach to object recognition; contends that we recognize objects via an analysis and recombination of their component parts (p. 168)

folk biology: the notion that knowledge of biological systems constitutes a cognitive module that has evolved in the service of adaptation to the environment (p. 189)

fusiform face area: area in the brain's visual cortex thought to be specialized for the recognition of faces (p. 182)

fuzzy boundaries: the notion that separation between some categories (e.g., "games" and "sports") is indistinct (p. 192)

geons: the basic three-dimensional shapes that form the basis for object recognition, according to the RBC approach (p. 168)

graded structure: the fact that category members differ in how well they represent the category (p. 191)

haptics: information gathered from hand position and hand movement (p. 173)

levels of categorization: the notion that categories can be described at varying levels of specificity and generality (p. 162)

multiple-views approach: proposes that object recognition is based primarily on a process whereby we match our view of an object with a representation of views stored in memory (p. 172)

natural kinds (natural categories): categories of objects that occur naturally in the world (p. 188)

object recognition: the processes whereby we match an incoming stimulus with stored representations for the purpose of identification (p. 161)

olfactory-verbal gap: people have difficulty describing and correctly identifying colors (p. 175)

parts-based (PB) approaches: propose that object recognition is based primarily on a process of parsing an object into its component parts (p. 168)

prosopagnosia: a neurological disorder characterized by an inability to recognize faces (p. 177)

prototype: the most representative member (or members) of a given category (p. 194)

prototype approach: a view of categorization proposing that we categorize by judging similarity between a target concept and a best example from the category (p. 192)

recognition-by-components (RBC): Biederman's view of object recognition; contends that recognition is a matter of separating an image into a structural description and using this description for identification (p. 168)

similarity-based approaches: the view that categorization is a matter of judging the similarity between the target object and some standard in long-term memory (p. 190)

template-matching theory: a view of pattern/object recognition whereby we compare incoming patterns to stored whole patterns in memory until we find a match (p. 171)

templates: the stored replicas of patterns that need to be identified (p. 171)

tip-of-the-nose phenomenon: a difficulty in labeling an odor in spite of a strong feeling that one knows its identity (p. 175)

view-based (VB) approaches: contend that we recognize objects by comparing incoming visual information to stored whole-object images representing the objects (p. 168)

6

Encoding and Retrieval Processes in Long-Term Memory

Have you ever had the experience of studying hour upon hour, yet when faced with some of the test material for which you've put in all this time, it might as well be in Greek—you draw an absolute blank. How can this be? You studied and you never miss class!

You've no doubt had the experience of visiting an "old haunt"—a place where you used to hang out, like your high school, a club, or a family vacation spot. Memories come flowing back spontaneously in situations like these. Why do these memories pop back up in those circumstances but not in others?

Have you ever had something running through your mind over and over—a song, maybe—but for the life of you, you can't figure out why? Is it a random thing, or did something happen earlier that prompted you to think of *that* particular song?

Have you ever experienced a profound sense of familiarity in some location or situation that you know you've never been in before (the often-experienced feeling of déjà vu)? The feeling of recollection is palpable, but you know it can't be an actual memory. What's going on?

It would be difficult to overestimate the importance of memory. It serves as the cornerstone of cognition, informing and assisting every process in our cognitive arsenal. As discussed in Chapter 4, working memory is critical for online processing of incoming information. Another vital component of memory is our long-term memory. In previous chapters (and subsequent ones) the importance of long-term memory is readily apparent. Long-term memory forms the database for object recognition (Chapter 5), language (Chapter 10), problem solving (Chapter 11), and decision making (Chapter 12). Memory is also important from a personal standpoint; it houses our autobiographies, the personal histories that give us our sense of identity and place in the world (Chapter 8). In this chapter, we're going to take you through the basic workings of long-term memory, including the processes by which you manage to store and retrieve the countless bits of information that form the core of thinking.

Fundamental Issues and Distinctions

Short-Term vs. Long-Term Memory

As discussed in Chapter 4, the modal model of memory (Atkinson & Shiffrin, 1968) proposes three memory stores (sensory memory, short-term memory, and long-term memory). The distinction between short-term memory (STM) and long-term memory (LTM) has proved to be controversial. What might be termed a *memory* systems *view* (e.g., Cowan, 1995; Pashler & Carrier, 1996) argues that there is good reason for making such a distinction. Alternatively, some theorists (e.g., Crowder, 1993; Nairne, 1992) espouse a *unitary view,* suggesting that short-term and long-term memory are manifestations of the same underlying memory system. While a complete discussion of these theoretical alternatives is beyond the scope of this text, let's briefly consider a phenomenon at the center of the debate—the **serial position effect.** This refers to the finding that items at the beginning of a list **(primacy effect)** and items presented at the end of the list **(recency effect)** are remembered better than items presented in the middle of the list. The existence of this phenomenon is not in question (the general prominence of information that comes first and last is a common pattern in many areas of cognition, as you'll see throughout this book), but the explanation for the recency effect has served as a sort of flash point for the STM/LTM debate.

Waugh and Norman (1965) were early proponents of the *memory* systems view. By their account, the recency effect occurs because the items currently being rehearsed (i.e., the items currently in STM) are easily retrieved. Essentially, they're "dumped out" immediately in response to a recall cue. This explanation runs into problems when one considers another finding: there are also recency effects in long-term memory (Bjork & Whitten, 1974). Long-term recency effects would seem to provide partial support for the unitary view that one memory is responsible for both effects. However, it is important to note that recency effects in immediate recall are indeed greater than those found in delayed recall. This indicates that there may be different bases for the two recency effects, which is consistent with the memory systems view. Currently, the debate continues. Cowan (1995) suggests that future research attempting to resolve the issue should focus on the neural mechanisms underlying short-term and long-term memory processing. Whatever the resolution of the STM/LTM debate turns out to be, there is certainly enough evidence to justify using the distinction as a descriptive device. We will adopt this convention in our subsequent discussion.

The STM/LTM distinction certainly fits well with our conscious experience of memory. Clearly, memory exists in both a limited, immediate, "thinking about it right now" form as well as a more vast "warehouse of information" form that is largely removed from conscious awareness. Let's review some of the characteristics that distinguish our temporary working memory from our more permanent long-term memory. Probably the most salient differences are the limitations (or lack thereof) of the respective systems. Working memory is quite limited, in both duration and capacity. Information can be held by working memory for only a limited period of time, and doing so requires mental rehearsal. Working memory also has severe capacity limits; one can do only so much in the "mental work space." There are ways to get around these limits, to be sure, but the limits are there. Contrast this with long-term memory, which is virtually limitless, in terms of both capacity and duration. Consider all of the important and inane information your friendly author Greg knows. He knows where he lives, how to drive a car, the lyrics to every Beatles song, what he did last night, and what he did on the Fourth of July in 1976. Information in long-term memory has the potential to last a lifetime. In addition, there is always room for more information—a testament to long-term memory's tremendous capacity.

Types of Long-Term Memory

Tulving (1972, 1983) suggests that there are two distinct types of **long-term memory (LTM)**: episodic memory and semantic memory. **Episodic memory** refers to one's memory for personally experienced events that include contextual elements like the time and place of the event's occurrence. **Semantic memory** refers to knowledge or information about the world that does not include contextual elements like the time or place the information was learned. Greg's memory of his first rock concert (the Doobie Brothers on their first of three farewell tours) is an episodic memory. He experienced it in a specific time and place (August 30, 1982, in Colorado). Greg's knowing that the Declaration of Independence was signed on July 4, 1776, is a semantic memory. It's just something that he knows. He wasn't at the signing, so he has no personal memories of it. Tulving (1983) outlines several other key differences between episodic and semantic memory (see Table 6.1). The retrieval of an episodic memory is typically associated with

Table 6.1 Contrasting Characteristics of Episodic and Semantic Memory

Characteristic	Memory System	
	Episodic	Semantic
Likelihood of forgetting	High	Low
Usefulness	Low	High
Recollective experience	Present	Not present
Sensory component	Present	Not present
Presence of emotion	Present	Not present

Based on information in Tulving, E. (1983). *Elements of episodic memory.* New York: Oxford University Press.

a recollective experience. Greg's memory of his first concert is accompanied by a strong feeling of recollection, almost as if he can place himself there. Semantic memories feature no such recollective experience. They involve the simple retrieval of an isolated fact. Episodic memories are more vulnerable to forgetting. Many of the details of Greg's first concert have faded over time. Semantic memories are relatively resistant to forgetting. Greg will never forget that particular fact about the American Revolution. Episodic memories often include an affective (emotional) component. Seeing his first rock concert was an exciting experience and is a positive memory. This contrasts sharply with semantic memories. Greg has no emotional connection to the historical fact of the signing of the Declaration of Independence.

As with the distinction between short-term and long-term memory, not all researchers agree that episodic and semantic memory represent two different memory systems; many believe the same memory system underlies both. They point out that there may be as many similarities as differences in the two. Still, as with the STM/LTM distinction, there does seem to be good intuitive and empirical evidence to use the distinction on a descriptive level, and most memory researchers accept the notion of separate memory systems as a given (e.g., Squire, 2004; Tulving, 2002). At the end of the chapter, after having discussed a wide range of memory phenomena, we will revisit this distinction in richer detail, including the possible neural substrates of these systems.

In this chapter, we will be dealing primarily with episodic memory, discussing the processes that are used to encode and retrieve events. Semantic memory, our general knowledge base, will be discussed further in Chapter 9. We should note that most of the research in this chapter is tightly controlled laboratory research, so the remembering done by subjects (on the face of it) might not always bear a close resemblance to the way you remember every day. Most of the characteristics of episodic memory proposed by Tulving (1983) are more descriptive of this everyday remembering (autobiographical memory), which we will discuss in Chapter 8. But in this chapter, we'll be discussing the basic laboratory work that serves as its foundation. This basic laboratory research still represents episodic memory—remembering a list of words that a cognitive researcher showed you is a personally experienced event that you will remember later.

STOP *and* THINK!

DISTINGUISHING EPISODIC AND SEMANTIC MEMORIES

Come up with examples of episodic memories (episodes from one's life) and semantic memory (general knowledge about the world). Then examine Table 6.1, which summarizes the key distinctions between these two types of memory. Assess the distinction between these types of memory by analyzing your examples.

- How well does each example fit each of the characteristics listed?
- Do episodic and semantic memories seem truly distinct?
- Why or why not?

A third memory system not proposed in Tulving's original formulation, but later added to the memory systems picture, is **procedural memory** (e.g., Squire, 1987). This system underlies (among other things) the execution of extremely well-learned skills like driving a car or riding a bike. As you'll see later in the chapter, the "recall" of skills based on procedural memory (i.e., the execution of skilled actions) can be easily dissociated from the recall of episodic and semantic memories. For example, the old saying "You never forget how to ride a bike" is more or less true, and this distinguishes procedural memory from semantic and particularly episodic memories. We'll talk more about these dissociations later in the chapter.

A Descriptive Framework: Encoding, Storage, and Retrieval

When memory researchers discuss the processes involved in memory, they often appeal to a disarmingly simple and useful description of memory proposed by Melton (1963), who suggested that the processes of remembering can be characterized in terms of three stages: encoding, storage, and retrieval. **Encoding** refers to the processes involved in the acquisition of material. Encoding processes are what you engage in when you're studying material for your next test. You study the material repetitively, generate notes based on what you read, relate it to other material you already know, and/or form a silly picture of it in your head, all in the hope of remembering it later. **Storage** of information involves the formation of some type of memory representation, or *memory trace*. If you've encoded some event (like a class lecture) successfully, there should be some remnant of the study experience. (And to do well on an exam, it had better be a pretty big remnant!)

But simply having this stored remnant of experience is no guarantee that you're going to remember it. Memory depends critically on the final process in this sequence— retrieval. **Retrieval** refers to your ability to get something out of memory once it has been encoded and stored. Think of all the times you've been frustrated while you're taking a test, thinking, "I *know* this, but I just can't think of the answer right now!" This is a retrieval failure, and, unfortunately, professors don't give partial credit for retrieval failures (although you never know—check your syllabus).

The distinction between encoding, storage, and retrieval provides a useful thumbnail sketch for discussing how memory works. In this chapter, the focus will be on the processes of encoding and retrieval and how these processes interact. What about storage, you ask? The term *storage* is used to refer to the state of information once it has been encoded; it doesn't really describe a process. *Encoding* is the term typically used to describe processes of study and retention and is really inseparable from the notion of storage. If something is processed effectively at encoding, then it will be stored. In this chapter, we'll examine exactly what comprises effective processing.

We're going to discuss encoding processes and retrieval processes separately, but discussing them in this way is mostly a matter of convenience. It turns out that remembering depends critically on the interaction between the two. You no doubt have some intuitive sense that this is the case. Do you study differently based on the type of test you're going to take? In other words, do you change how you encode based on how you'll have to retrieve? As you'll see, memory research has borne out that this intuitive strategy is based on solid empirical ground. The first major section of this chapter will deal with how various encoding factors influence memory. To enhance your understanding of these effects, you should be aware of an important retrieval distinction.

Remembering is a more complex concept than you might suspect. Memory researchers have drawn a critical distinction between explicit and implicit memory tests. **Explicit memory tests** (or *direct memory tests*) involve conscious recollection of some specific event from the past. The first few decades of cognitive psychology research focused on explicit tests, and the first several sections of this chapter will focus on how encoding processes influence remembering in these sorts of situations.

Sometimes, however, experiences and events have an influence on our behavior in the complete absence of conscious memory for that event. Tests that assess these implicit influences have been collectively termed **implicit memory tests** (or *indirect memory tests*). Consider a story from the French neuropsychologist Edouarde Claparede (1911/1951). Claparede had a patient who suffered from **amnesia,** or memory loss due to brain damage. One day, Claparede hid a pin in his hand and greeted his patient with a prickly handshake. The patient quickly forgot the incident. The next time the two met, the amnesic denied having met Claparede. But when Claparede held out his hand for the customary shake (this time without the pin!), the patient refused. When pressed for the reason, she insisted that she had the right to not shake hands. This is quite remarkable; the amnesic demonstrated that she both did and did not remember what had happened previously. In other words, the amnesic demonstrated a failure of explicit memory by failing to recall having met Claparede but showed successful implicit memory in refusing to shake hands with him. As you'll see, the distinction between explicit and implicit memory tests has proved to be essential for describing how various encoding factors affect remembering.

STOP *and* **REVIEW!**

1. The unitary view assumes
   a. that STM and LTM are distinct memory stores or processes.
   b. that STM and LTM are based on the same underlying memory system.
   c. that episodic and semantic memory are distinct memory stores or processes.
   d. that episodic and semantic memory are based on the same underlying memory system.
2. Identify and define the three subdivisions of long-term memory.
3. Name the three general stages of remembering and briefly describe each.

➤ The unitary view contends that one underlying memory mechanism is responsible for STM and LTM processing. The memory systems view contends that STM and LTM are distinct systems, with distinct underlying processes. Serial position effects (better memory for the initial and final items in a list) are sometimes offered as evidence for the distinction.

➤ Long-term memory is often subdivided into episodic memory (memory for personally experienced events that include context), semantic memory (context-free general knowledge about the world), and procedural memory (memory for how to perform skills). Explicit tests of memory (often termed *direct*) require the conscious recollection of a specific event, while implicit tests of memory (often termed *indirect*) do not.

➤ There are three basic stages involved in memory: Encoding refers to the processes whereby events are taken in; storage refers to the retention of these events over time; retrieval refers to the processes whereby information is recalled.

Encoding Processes in Explicit Long-Term Remembering

It's obvious that your ability to remember something depends on what you do as the information is coming in. Think about the steps you take when you really want to remember something. What do you do to increase your chances of remembering it? In this section, we'll talk about some of the fundamental encoding factors that influence LTM. Keep in mind that the research discussed in this section deals primarily with explicit memory tests—memory tests that require conscious recollection. The rules may be different for implicit memory tests, as you'll see later.

Attention and Repetition

As you learned in Chapter 4, attention is the mechanism whereby we bring information into the focus of conscious awareness. So it should come as no surprise that attention plays a critical role in long-term memory. Quite simply, you're more likely to recollect something to which you paid attention. Think about sitting in class, listening to your professor. You're not going to recollect much of anything from the lecture if you're tuning in to the juicy gossip behind you instead of to what the professor is saying. A simple-minded explanation might be that attention leads to a longer-lasting and more retrievable memory trace. The role of attention is considerably more complex than this simple statement would imply, but there is little doubt that focused attention is necessary for explicit and detailed recollection of some event.

Another factor that affects retention is **repetition.** Material that is presented more than once is easier to remember. This principle is so fundamental that Crowder (1976) notes, "If any generalization is basic to the field of learning it is that an experience that occurs twice is more likely to be remembered than a single experience" (p. 264). But the picture gets a bit more complex when we consider the issue of exactly how material is repeated.

The Spacing Effect.   One important distinction involves how repetitions occur over time. **Massed repetition** involves repeated presentations that occur closely together in time, while **distributed repetition** involves repeated presentations spread out over time. Which do you think works better? The advantage of distributed repetitions over massed repetitions has been termed the **spacing effect,** and this effect has been found in numerous empirical investigations (Glenberg, 1974; Melton, 1970). Why should repetitions spaced out over time be better than repetitions that are crammed together? Researchers have proposed two likely explanations, both of which have some empirical support (Greene, 1992). These accounts place the locus of the spacing effect at different stages of the remembering process. The *deficient-processing view* focuses on encoding, suggesting that massed repetitions lead to deficient processing of the second presentation—you simply don't pay much attention to the later presentations relative to the first (Hintzman, Block, & Summers, 1973). As a result, you have only one fully encoded memory representation rather than many. The *encoding variability view* is similar in that it contends that massed presentations amount to little more than one presentation, but it places the locus of the effect at retrieval. According to this view, under massed presentation conditions, there is little or no variation in how the repeated events are encoded into memory, so the corresponding memory representations will be similar and relatively indiscriminable.

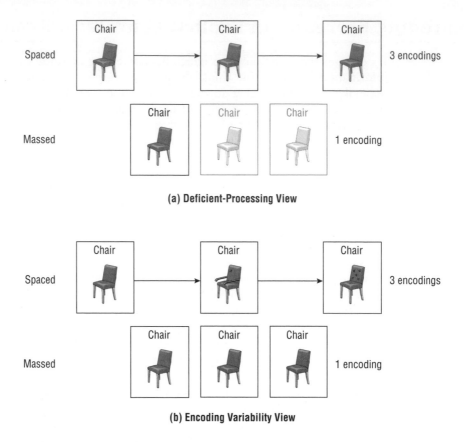

(a) Deficient-Processing View

(b) Encoding Variability View

This will make them more difficult to "find" in a memory search relative to when presentations have been distributed. When repetitions are distributed in time, each encoding will be relatively distinct from the others, so you're more likely to "stumble on" one of them during your memory search.

The spacing effect is what researchers term a *robust phenomenon*—it's been found in many studies, using a variety of experimental contexts and tasks including the classroom (Seabrook, Brown, & Solity, 2005), so it's definitely relevant to how you study. If you're like many students, you cram more often than you should. Cramming—trying to learn material with massed repetition within a short time span—is a relatively ineffective study technique if your goal in college is to learn what is being taught (a sensible goal, given that you're investing a not-so-small fortune in it!). Research on the spacing effect suggests that your study time would be better spent spread out over a longer period. That is, when presenting yourself with stimuli from your classes (i.e., studying your notes and your text), you should distribute your presentations. But if you have tuition money to burn and are interested only in learning information for the next test, then massed repetitions are the ticket. But get your tuition dollar's worth—you never know, you may need the information on a cumulative final, in a later class, or (gasp) in real life!

Rehearsal

It should come as no surprise to you that **rehearsal,** which is basically mental practice, improves memory. It's easy to confuse the concepts of repetition and rehearsal because they are closely related. Repetition refers to the fact that an item is experienced more than once, whereas rehearsal refers to how that item is thought about internally. Let's consider the processes involved in the mental practice of information and how these processes relate to remembering.

Maintenance and Elaborative Rehearsal.   To a large extent, memory follows the old axiom "Practice makes perfect." As discussed in Chapter 4, rehearsal is important for maintaining information in working memory and, according to some early models of memory (Atkinson & Shiffrin, 1968; Waugh & Norman, 1965), may be instrumental in encoding it permanently in LTM. But as was the case with the seemingly straightforward variable of repetition, simple rehearsal isn't as effective as you might think. An experiment by Craik and Watkins (1973) demonstrates how truly ineffective it can be. Subjects were presented with lists of words, and their task was to keep track of the words that began with a specific letter (e.g., *p*). At the end of each list, subjects were to report the last word that had begun with that letter. If you were a subject, you might be presented with *cherry, plow, tiger, desk, house.* After presentation of the list, your job would be to say "plow." How would you accomplish this fairly simple task? Probably by mentally repeating the word *plow* over and over until you got another *p* word or until you had to report the word *plow,* whichever came first. Consider this list: *tree, peach, carpet, table, igloo, garlic, bird, clock.* Your response would be *peach.* In this case, you would have to repeat the word *peach* approximately twice as many times as the word *plow.* At the end of the experiment, when asked to recall all of the words from each list, you might think that this increase in rehearsal would have made it more likely that you'd remember the rehearsed word. It didn't. Craik and Watkins varied the number of intervening items (and hence the amount of rehearsal) from 2 to 12 items, and found no difference in later recall.

The type of rehearsal employed in this situation is aptly termed **maintenance rehearsal,** because all you're doing is maintaining the item in consciousness, with little or no embellishment. Trying to memorize information from your class notes by simply repeating the information over and over is not a very effective technique. Certainly, repeating it once is better than not repeating it at all, but after one presentation there seems to be little additional memory benefit. So if you use maintenance rehearsal to study, one thorough exposure is as good as several. Based on your experience with college tests, you're probably thinking that one simple rehearsal would not be sufficient to pass most professors' tests.

But the story on maintenance rehearsal isn't quite so simple. Recall the earlier discussion about the importance of the interaction between the stages of encoding and retrieval. Whether or not you get any benefit from maintenance rehearsal depends on the retrieval task. Let's take a short detour and talk about the two most common explicit retrieval tasks, recall and recognition. Suppose you're a subject in a memory experiment and you're presented with 48 words, followed by a memory test. If you're tested with **recall,** you are given little or nothing to work with in terms of hints, and your task is to come up with as many of the 48 items as you can. In **recognition,** your task is a bit easier. You're presented with a large set of items that includes the items presented earlier and some other items. Your task is to distinguish the two. Usually, recognition proves to be easier than recall because in recognition you actually get to see the correct answers—you need only recognize them.

Now, back to the effects of maintenance rehearsal. While maintenance rehearsal is relatively ineffective in enhancing one's ability to recall information, it does lead to some improvement in the ability to recognize it. Successful recognition depends on the degree to which you've thoroughly processed an individual item, whereas recall depends more on making associations between the to-be-remembered items (Anderson & Bower, 1973; Gillund & Shiffrin, 1984). When you consider this, it's not difficult to see why maintenance rehearsal helps recognition but not recall. Repeating an individual item over and over will lead to more thorough processing of that individual item but will do little or nothing to build associations between items on a list (Nairne, 1983).

Let's consider the practical implications of these findings. In general, maintenance rehearsal is a relatively ineffective way to remember something. It helps in laboratory tests of recognition in which you have to answer the question, "Did you see this concept before?" But real-world memory situations are never this simple. Professors never ask, "Do you remember the term *rehearsal* from your reading?" If they did, everyone would get 100% on every test. You're more likely to be asked, "What's the difference between rehearsal and repetition?" Simply recognizing the word *rehearsal* isn't going to help you answer this question. So although maintenance rehearsal may be effective in certain laboratory settings, it is a relatively inefficient technique for committing information to memory (Greene, 1992). There are much better uses for your study time.

A better alternative to maintenance rehearsal is **elaborative rehearsal**. This involves thinking about the meaning of the information that is to be remembered, as well as making associations between that information and information already stored in memory.

An early study by Hyde and Jenkins (1969) demonstrates the effectiveness of this type of processing. Subjects encoded single words by making a simple judgment about each one. They were to rate the pleasantness of the word, estimate the number of letters in the word, or determine whether the word had an *e*. Hyde and Jenkins were interested in how well the words themselves would be remembered. The results were clear-cut. Memory was much better when subjects were required to judge the pleasantness of words relative to when they were noticing *e*'s or counting letters.

Consider the differences in these tasks. Judging the pleasantness of words requires that you think about what the word means and may even make you think about some associated information. For example, judging whether Jell-O is pleasant or unpleasant requires you to think about what Jell-O is and may even trigger a thought about the red-white-and-blue layered Jell-O salad you enjoy at family picnics on the Fourth of July. Counting the number of *e*'s in Jell-O would produce nothing like this. You would give the word cursory consideration but little quality thought.

One surprising aspect of this finding is that this advantage occurred in both incidental learning and intentional learning. Under **incidental learning** conditions, subjects are not told that memory will be tested. Instead, they are under the impression that the encoding task is the sole focus of the experiment. Under **intentional learning** conditions, subjects are explicitly told that they are participating in a memory experiment and that the encoded material will be tested later. Hyde and Jenkins found a memory advantage when subjects were just reading words and making simple judgments about them, as long as the judgments made subjects consider the meaning of the concept. It didn't even matter if subjects were trying to remember the words. They just ended up doing so, because they gave the words quality processing. Given these findings, memory research began to focus on the effects of different types of processing on memory.

STOP *and* THINK!

MASSING, DISTRIBUTING, MAINTAINING, AND ELABORATING

You've read about the benefits of repetition and rehearsal as well as their variations. Suppose you combined these two variables and came up with the following four encoding conditions:

1. massed repetitions/maintenance rehearsal
2. distributed repetitions/maintenance rehearsal
3. massed repetitions/elaborative rehearsal
4. distributed repetitions/elaborative rehearsal

Rank each of these four conditions in terms of the quality of memory you think they would produce. Explain your ordering. Test your predictions by getting four friends and reading them each one of the list versions below, along with the appropriate instruction. The numbering of the following instructions corresponds to the numbering of the conditions presented above: Did you find your predicted results?

1. *Instruction:* As each word is presented, repeat it over and over silently. (Use the list on the left.)
2. *Instruction:* As each word is presented, repeat it over and over silently. (Use the list on the right.)
3. *Instruction:* As each word is presented, think of an associate of the word. For example, if presented with the word *tiger,* you might think of *lion.* (Use the list on the left.)
4. *Instruction:* As each word is presented, think of an associate of the word. For example, if presented with the word *tiger,* you might think of *lion.* (Use the list on the right.)

List for 1 and 3	List for 2 and 4
earth	earth
earth	ambulance
spinach	cotton
spinach	square
ambulance	spinach
ambulance	earth
cotton	machine
cotton	nutmeg
machine	oxygen
machine	cotton
square	square
square	ambulance
nutmeg	spinach
nutmeg	oxygen
oxygen	machine
oxygen	nutmeg

Levels of Processing.   The notion that memory depends on how information is processed at encoding served as the foundation for Craik and Lockhart's (1972) land-mark **levels-of-processing theory**. This theory served as an alternative to the modal model of memory. Recall that the modal model focused primarily on structural aspects of memory, proposing the existence of separate storage systems along with principles regulating the transfer of information between them. How the incoming information was processed was not ignored by this model, but it was not central.

Craik and Lockhart made processing the focus of their approach, proposing that how incoming information is processed is the critical determinant of whether that infor-mation is remembered. According to their theory, analysis of incoming information pro-ceeds from a shallow and superficial analysis of structural features to a more deep and thorough analysis of meaning. The primary determinant of whether information is remembered is how far processing gets on this continuum. Information that is processed to a deep level will be better remembered than information processed only to a shallow level. Craik and Tulving (1975) proposed that maintenance rehearsal has relatively little impact on later memory, because processing never gets beyond the superficial level. They proposed *elaborative rehearsal* as a superior alternative. During elaborative rehearsal, the analysis of incoming information proceeds to a deeper, more meaningful level.

Let's apply this analysis to Hyde and Jenkins's (1969) study. According to the levels-of-processing approach, the different encoding tasks led subjects to process information to different levels. Simply noting *e*'s or estimating the number of letters in a word can be accomplished with only a superficial level of analysis. Deciding whether a word is pleasant, however, requires more; you need to proceed all the way from encoding the physical fea-tures of the word to thinking of the word's meaning and whether or not it is a pleasing concept. This more extensive level of analysis leads to a more enduring and retrievable memory trace.

As fresh and popular as the levels-of-processing approach was when it was intro-duced, its vagueness was troublesome to many. For example, the word *mouse* is remem-bered better when it's presented with the question, "Is this an animal?" relative to when it's presented with the question, "Does this word rhyme with *house?*" Why? Because the first condition leads to a deeper level of processing. But how do we know that the first question leads to deeper processing than the second? There seems to be no clear answer other than "Because you remember it better." Depth of processing is used as an explana-tion for memory performance, and then memory performance is used to define depth of processing. This circular definition is really no definition at all. (You may remember the notion of a circular definition from our discussion of capacity in Chapter 4.) In order to avoid this circularity, we need something else (besides memory performance) that indi-cates a deep level of processing.

Several such specifications have been offered. One is **elaboration** (Craik & Tulving, 1975), which basically refers to the degree to which information is specified, described, and/or related to other information in memory. The better elaborated a concept is at encoding, the more access routes you have to get to it at retrieval. A deep orienting task will probably lead you to think about associated information (like the information about Jell-O mentioned earlier). These associations can serve as routes to the information at retrieval. Conversely, a shallow orienting task does not lead to the production of such associates and hence produces a memory trace with relatively few (if any) retrieval routes. The more the retrieval routes, the better the memory will be.

Another independent definition of depth was **distinctiveness,** which refers to how well information is distinguished from other information. According to this analysis, encoding an item in terms of what it means distinguishes the item better from its neighbors in memory, relative to encoding an item in terms of how it sounds or looks. The more distinct an item, the easier it will be to find during retrieval. A classic demonstration of the effects of distinctiveness on memory, the **von Restorff phenomenon** (von Restorff, 1933) was studied extensively in the early days of cognitive psychology. Early investigations of the phenomenon involved presenting a list of items with one item that "stuck out like a sore thumb" (e.g., in a different color); the "isolated" item was often particularly well remembered (Wallace, 1965).

Depth of Processing or Transfer-Appropriate Processing?   In general, research inspired by the levels-of-processing paradigm has told us a great deal about the nature of encoding processes and how they relate to remembering. However, the levels-of-processing paradigm is a bit narrow in that it emphasizes encoding processes as the primary determinant of memory and fails to discuss retrieval at any length. Morris, Bransford, and Franks (1977) propose the notion of **transfer-appropriate processing** as an alternative. According to these researchers, no encoding task is inherently better than another in terms of leading to retrievable memory representations, as the levels-of-processing paradigm implies. According to the notion of transfer-appropriate processing, what qualifies as memorable processing at encoding is defined by what is required at retrieval. In other words, the information gained in the study phase is going to have to transfer to the retrieval situation, so the processing performed at encoding should be appropriate for how it's going to be retrieved. That is, processing should be transfer-appropriate.

Morris, Bransford, and Franks (1977) claimed that the memory that results from a surface encoding task might indeed be durable, but the typical memory test doesn't pick up on the information that was encoded (i.e., structural information about a word). According to this analysis, if the memory test *did* make use of this information, then shallow processing might actually lead to *better* performance than deep processing.

The researchers tested their hypothesis in a clever series of experiments. In one experiment, subjects encoded words either semantically (deep processing) by judging whether a word (e.g., *train*) fit in a sentence ("The _____ had a silver engine"), or phonologically (shallow processing) by judging whether a word (e.g., *eagle*) rhymed with a second word (e.g., *legal*). They tested memory with either a traditional recognition test (described earlier) or a *rhyme-recognition test.* In the rhyme-recognition test, subjects had to recognize words that rhymed with the words they'd encoded. For example, the word *regal* would appear on the recognition test, and subjects would have to indicate if this word rhymed with one of the studied words. According to the levels-of-processing approach, a more durable memory trace is created in the semantic condition, so subjects in this condition should remember more words, regardless of the test. According to transfer-appropriate processing, both encoding conditions create durable memory traces, but ones that contain different information. Semantically encoded words should

Table 6.2 Data from the Morris, Bransford, and Franks (1977) Study

	Rhyme Recognition	Standard Recognition
Semantic Encoding	0.33	0.84
Rhyme Encoding	0.49	0.63

From Morris, D. C., Bransford, J. D., & Franks, J. J. (1977). Levels of processing versus transfer-appropriate processing. *Journal of Verbal Learning and Behavior, 16,* 519–533. Copyright 1977, Elsevier Science (USA). Reprinted by permission.

be better remembered on the typical recognition test, which requires access to the concepts represented by the words. Conversely, phonologically encoded words should be better remembered on the rhyming recognition test, which requires access to phonological information—that is, the spoken label for the word.

The results, displayed in Table 6.2, support the transfer-appropriate processing analysis, demonstrating what might be termed a *reverse levels-of-processing effect*. On the rhyme-recognition test, words processed less deeply were remembered better. What mattered the most was not the depth of processing but whether the encoding process was appropriate for the memory test. The practical implications for your studying are clear: Be sure that the memory trace you create for the material on an upcoming test is *appropriate* to the type of test you'll receive. In other words, the way you study should depend on the way you'll be tested. The notion of transfer-appropriate processing was part of the shifting terrain of memory research, which was moving away from the simple analysis of encoding variables toward a focus on the *interaction* between encoding and retrieval. You'll read more about this later.

Organization. In our discussion of levels of processing, we noted that the degree to which we think about the meaning of an event is important for memory. Conversely (or perhaps we should say, "In a complementary manner"), memory also depends on the degree to which individual events are organized or structured. The term **organization** can refer either to the characteristics of the incoming information (i.e., whether this information is structured in some way) or to the strategic orientation of the encoder (i.e., whether a person attempts to organize the incoming information).

The degree to which incoming information is structured exerts powerful effects on memory, as demonstrated in a study by Bower, Clark, Lesgold, and Winzenz (1969). It's extremely unusual for subjects in a memory study to achieve perfect recall, but that is exactly what happened in this study. Bower and colleagues presented subjects with four different lists of items to be encoded. Each set of items belonged to a particular category. For example, a list of items could belong to the category "minerals," and the subcategories "metals" and "stones." The experiment featured a very simple design. Subjects in the organized condition saw the items organized into their respective taxonomic categories (e.g., "precious stones"), while subjects in the unorganized condition were presented with the items in a random arrangement. Memory was tested with *multitrial free recall*. Subjects attempted to learn the lists and then recall them; this learn-and-recall cycle was done three more times (four total cycles). The results were striking: subjects in the organized condition recalled over 90% of the items by the second trial and were perfect on the final two trials. In contrast, the unorganized group never got up to 70% recall, even after studying the same lists four times.

In addition to the organizational structure inherent in the to-be-remembered information, deliberately imposing structure on incoming information can also be a powerful determinant of effective encoding. Such organization might be considered a close companion to chunking in working memory (discussed in Chapter 4). Recall that chunking refers to recoding information into meaningful groupings of information, thereby lightening the load of what must be recycled in working memory. Imposing structure while encoding the information for later recall accomplishes the same thing. The organizational scheme employed facilitates the rehearsal and/or formation of associations between the bits of information as they are being encoded. It also serves as a structure that can be used for later retrieval as we retrace the associations formed at encoding.

We are such resourceful information processors that we will use organization to aid our memory even in the absence of an obvious list structure. Tulving (1962) was interested in the degree to which subjects would impose their own organizational schemes on incoming information, so he used lists of words that had no inherent structure; that is, the list items were unrelated to one another. As in the Bower and colleagues (1969) study, memory was tested with multitrial free recall. Over the course of the first two presentations, Tulving thought that subjects would form idiosyncratic categories. They would think of certain words together and use this subjective organization to impose structure on the unstructured list. And, in keeping with the finding that organization helps memory, he hypothesized that people who showed more of these idiosyncratic categories (i.e., people who employed subjective organization) would recall more on the third recall trial. The results supported his hypothesis. The patterns of recall for the first two trials revealed that subjects consistently grouped certain items together, and subjects who did this to a greater degree remembered more. So, even when the materials do not lend themselves to organization, we impose our own organization in order to help us recall the information.

Organization or Distinctiveness?: Material-Appropriate Processing.

You may be a little puzzled with the foregoing discussion. First we said that information that is distinctive or different from other information is especially well remembered. Then we championed the benefits of organizing incoming information, which places importance on seeing structure and relationships among the pieces of information that we need to remember. These two statements would seem to be at odds with one another; how can we make distinctions among items while at the same time draw relationships among them? The notion of **material-appropriate processing** (Hunt & Einstein, 1981; McDaniel & Einstein, 2005) provides an answer.

According to this framework, both ways of looking at information are critical for optimal memory performance. **Relational processing** describes the degree to which we process items in terms of their interrelationships and is aided to the degree that incoming information affords *organization*. **Individual-item processing** describes the degree to which we process items in terms of their *individual* characteristics and is aided by conditions that lead to distinctive processing. The key idea of the material-appropriate processing approach is that the type of processing that one should use in studying material for later retention depends on the nature of the material. If the material that one is trying to remember has a high degree of structure or is well organized, then the best type of processing would be individual-item (i.e., distinctive) processing. The converse is also true; if the material that one is trying to remember has little structure and is focused on specifics, then the best way to study it would be to use relational processing (i.e., organization). The processing strategy that one takes in approaching material they want to learn should be whatever strategy provides a complement to the information offered by that material. You may actually engage in material-appropriate processing without really knowing it. For example, if you outline the major points of a chapter and highlight important terms and their definitions, then you're engaging in both organizational and distinctive processing. The point of the material-appropriate processing framework is that you should be a little more deliberate in noticing what type of processing is afforded by the material you're studying, and use its complement.

Mnemonic Techniques.   Highlighting and outlining are examples of **mnemonic techniques,** devices employed to improve memory. These techniques range from the mundane (yet effective) techniques that we use every day such as elaborative rehearsal to the slightly bizarre procedures involved in structured mnemonic techniques. One example of a structured mnemonic is the **method of loci,** captured nicely with a rather gruesome story related by Yates (1968). In 477 B.C., the Greek poet Simonides was addressing the attendees of an indoor banquet when he was called outside by some messengers. While he was outside, the roof of the banquet structure collapsed, killing everyone inside and mangling their remains beyond recognition. However, Simonides was able to identify their bodies based on his memory of the banquet. Can you guess how? During the banquet, he had paid enough attention to everyone that he knew where they were all sitting. So he imagined the banquet table and mentally went around it, naming the person who had been sitting in a given position. In other words, he used the method of loci, or *location*.

This method involves memorizing a set of familiar locations (like landmarks on your college campus), taking a mental stroll through those locations, and placing a piece of information that must be remembered (such as items on a grocery list) at each location. When it comes time to remember the information, you simply take another mental stroll, and pick up each item. The technique sounds a little flaky, but it can be quite effective. Think about why, in terms of the factors that promote successful encoding and retrieval. The method of loci promotes both organizational processing (as we use the organizational structure of a set of points in a known location) and distinctive processing (as we imagine each item singly, sitting in its location). A good deal of research demonstrates the effectiveness of this technique (e.g., Cornoldi & DeBeni, 1991; Groninger, 1971; Moè & DeBeni, 2005).

The effectiveness of the method of loci highlights another factor that can have a pronounced influence on memory: visual encoding. As with organization, the use of visual encoding can be either an aspect of the information being encoded (pictorial stimuli) or an imagery-based encoding strategy (imagining something as you study it). Information that is encoded in pictorial form or with the use of imagery-based rehearsal processes tends to be well remembered. This basic finding has been demonstrated in a couple of different experimental contexts. First, a number of studies (e.g., Paivio & Csapo, 1969; Yuille & Paivio, 1969) have compared memory for concrete and easy-to-imagine concepts like "candle" with memory for abstract and difficult-to-imagine concepts like "truth." As you might expect, concrete concepts are more likely to be remembered than are more abstract ones. In a similar vein, Madigan (1983) demonstrated what has been coined the **picture-superiority effect.** In his experiment, subjects either read simple concepts (e.g., "tiger") or viewed simple line drawings of the same concepts (e.g., a picture of a tiger). Concepts were more likely to be remembered if they were presented as pictures rather than words.

Self-Reference.   As we've seen, research on levels of processing has demonstrated that words processed deeply (i.e., in terms of their meaning) are remembered well. Later research by Rogers, Kuiper, and Kirker (1977) revealed an encoding condition that seems deeper than deep. In this experiment, subjects encoded words (e.g., *happy*) with different types of encoding questions, as in the levels-of-processing studies, with one exception: the researchers added an encoding condition they termed "self-reference." Words in this condition (e.g., *generous*) were encoded with the question, "Does this term describe you?" The results demonstrated the standard levels-of-processing effect, with a twist: words that were self-referenced were remembered even better than those deeply processed. Over the last quarter-century, many studies have replicated and extended this basic **self-reference effect,** establishing it as a robust memory phenomenon (Symons & Johnson, 1997).

Why is relating information to yourself such an effective technique? In their review of studies on the self-reference effect, Symons and Johnson (1997) conclude that self-reference promotes good memory through elaboration and organization. Because the self is such an elaborate, well-developed, and well-practiced network of knowledge, it offers incredible potential for both elaborative and organizational processing. The implications for your own memory are clear: Chances are that you'll increase the likelihood of remembering something to the degree that you can relate it to yourself. Processing in this way encourages both organization and elaboration of the incoming information, and this, in turn, makes it more likely that you'll remember it.

STOP *and* **THINK!**

YOU'RE THE PROFESSOR!

Congratulations! You've just been designated "Professor for a Day." (Prepare for a pay cut!) Imagine that you have to teach a class of first year college students about what cognitive psychology is (some of the basic information from Chapter 1) and make sure that the information sticks. What techniques could you use to develop an effective and memorable presentation of the important concepts? (Give specific examples.)

Remembering Actions

All of the foregoing discussion of memory is deficient in a major way. Every study we've talked about has dealt only with one specific domain of memory. More specifically, we've discussed only **retrospective memory** for verbal materials, or memory for information that was presented to you in the past. Although this scenario does characterize many of the situations in which you have to remember, it by no means is the only important one. Let's look at two memory scenarios not directly addressed by the research discussed thus far.

Enactment Effect.   The issue of memory for action has enjoyed a surge of interest in recent years, another indication of the growing influence of a notion we discussed in Chapter 1—embodied cognition (Gibbs, 2006; Wilson, 2002). As you may recall, this refers to the notion that cognitive processes must be investigated within the context of the body's interaction with the environment. Research reveals that people are quite good at remembering actions. This memory advantage has been termed the **enactment effect.** People are better at remembering action phrases like "hammer the nail" if they enact the activity, relative to conditions in which they simply read verbal descriptions. Most accounts of this effect propose that enacting an event results in a richer, more retrievable memory representation. Enacting an event brings in a motor component, not to mention richer visual and auditory components (e.g., Engelkamp & Zimmer, 1985). Couched in terms of what you learned earlier in the chapter, you could view this as a more richly *elaborated* encoding rather than merely reading a phrase.

STOP *and* THINK! ──────────────────────

ENACTING ENACTMENT

The enactment effect is fairly easy to demonstrate. All you'll need to do is set up two basic conditions, and test a couple of people in each. In one condition, read the phrases below to the "subjects" and have them repeat the phrases out loud. In the other condition, read the phrases below to the subjects and have them do the activity described. Of course, this condition will require a bit of setup. And actually, the "control" condition (those who simply hear the phrases) should probably be in the presence of the items mentioned below as well, to control for the effects of simply seeing toothpicks, pencils, etc.!

After you've read the phrases or had the subjects enact the phrases, give them some type of distractor—talk to them about how great your cognitive psych class is—for a few minutes. Then, test recall of the phrases by having the subjects write them down.

Total Cost of Materials: 57¢
Demonstrating the Enactment Effect: Priceless

Break the toothpick.
Pick up the pencil.
Bend the paper clip.
Drink from the cup.
Flip the light switch.
Rip the paper.
Kick the chair.
Close the folder.
Stack the books.
Open the envelope.

It turns out that the mere *intention* to carry out an act leads to a similar memory advantage (Badets, Blandin, Bouquet, & Shea, 2006; Goschke & Kuhl, 1993). For example, Goschke and Kuhl (1993) asked subjects to learn two procedural scripts. Each script consisted of five specific activities that served one goal (e.g., clearing a messy desk). After learning each of the scripts, subjects were told that they would later have to perform one of them. This was done to activate an expectation or intention in the subjects for later performance of the task. In the next phase of the experiment, subjects were given single words and had to decide as quickly as possible whether each of the words had appeared in the earlier scripts. The interesting finding was that subjects were quicker to respond to words taken from the scripts that they thought they were going to have to act out. This indicates that simply forming an intention to do something by thinking about it leads to increased memory activation of that activity.

Prospective Memory.   Have you ever reminded yourself that you need to do something in the future, like go to a meeting or take some medication? You've probably found that you often fail to follow through on those intended actions. These situations involve remembering to carry out future activities and plans, termed **prospective memory.** Contrast this with retrospective memory, the focus of the chapter thus far. Retrospective memory involves the retrieval of events that occurred in the past.

You may notice a parallel between the enactment effect and prospective memory. While the enactment effect involves remembering an action, prospective memory involves remembering an *intention* to act and following through on it. In a prospective memory situation—in which the intention to act must be triggered and an action actually carried out—the intention to act can be triggered in one of two ways, according to Einstein and McDaniel (1990). Intentions to act can be triggered by some event; for example, when you see a friend, you have to remember to pay them back the $5 you borrowed for lunch yesterday. This is termed *event-based* prospective memory. Alternatively, intentions might be triggered by the mere passage of time; for example, you need to remember to turn off the sprinkler watering your lawn an hour from now. This is termed *time-based* prospective memory.

These triggering situations highlight a fundamental difference between retrospective memory and prospective memory. In retrospective memory (recognition and free recall), retrieval is triggered by some external instruction that initiates a search of memory, such as, "Tell me all of the words that appeared on the previous list." In prospective memory there is no instruction to initiate the memory search; retrieval needs to be self-initiated. Suppose you see the friend to whom you owe $5. When you see them, no one tells you to give them the money. The idea must spontaneously occur to you. And once you realize that you have to give them some money, you must remember how much. This "half" of prospective memory is similar to retrospective memory—the content of the intended action (e.g., the amount of $5) must be recalled. So the unique feature of prospective memory seems to be the requirement of "remembering to remember," which is sometimes termed **self-initiated retrieval.**

This concept turns out to be important in considering age-related differences in prospective memory. Craik (1986) proposed that many age-related deficits in memory occur in

Research Theme:
Development

tasks that involve self-initiated retrieval. Consider the self-initiated retrieval required by prospective memory. Because prospective memory has the distinctive feature of having to "remember to remember," a person must initiate the memory process. And the requirement to initiate is much more acute in time-based prospective memory situations, relative to event-based ones. Think about it—event-based situations include a salient cue (e.g., seeing the friend to whom you owe money) that something needs to be done, whereas time-based situations do not. Einstein and McDaniel (1990) suggested that the elderly may be more likely to show deficits in time-based prospective memory because it requires more self-initiation—you have to truly "remember to remember" without any external cues. This idea has been put to the experimental test by a number of investigators, and the results have generally supported the prediction (Henry, MacLeod, Phillips, & Crawford, 2004). Age-related deficits in prospective remembering are more pronounced on tasks that are time based, relative to those that are event based.

STOP *and* **REVIEW!**

1. True or false? Distributed repetition is more effective than massed repetition.
2. How does transfer-appropriate processing differ from levels-of-processing?
3. Mnemonic devices tend to emphasize
   a. individual-item processing over relational processing.
   b. relational processing over individual-item processing.
   c. both relational processing and individual-item processing.
   d. neither relational processing nor individual-item processing.
4. Describe prospective memory, and indicate what makes it different from retrospective memory.

➤ Attention brings information into conscious awareness, enhancing the likelihood that the information will be stored for the long term. Repetition of information is more effective if distributed over time, rather than massed. Maintenance rehearsal refers to simple mental repetition, while elaborative rehearsal involves making associations between the information to be remembered and other information. Elaborative rehearsal is more likely to result in long-term memory storage.

➤ The levels-of-processing approach emphasizes that how information is processed at encoding is the key determinant of memory. Processing involving the analysis of meaning (i.e., deep processing) is more likely to lead to long-term storage than processing that involves a more superficial analysis (i.e., shallow processing). In transfer-appropriate processing, retrieval is a critical factor, meaning that the effectiveness of a study technique will depend on how memory is tested.

➤ Material that is organized tends to be better remembered. Distinctive encodings (i.e., those that stand out from other events) are more likely to be remembered. According to the material-appropriate processing framework, relational processing (i.e., organization) and individual-item processing (i.e., distinctive encoding) combine to produce optimal retention. Mnemonic devices are memory-enhancement techniques that tend to combine these two types of processing.

➤ The enactment effect refers to the finding that people are better at remembering action phrases, relative to verbal descriptions. Prospective memory involves remembering to carry out future activities and plans, and differs from retrospective memory because of the unique requirement of self-initiated retrieval; a person must "remember to remember."

Retrieval Processes in Long-Term Memory

Successful encoding and storage of information is necessary but not sufficient to guarantee later memory recall. Remembering also involves the processes of retrieval, whereby we regain access to encoded information. Of course, as mentioned early in the chapter, retrieval is not isolated from encoding and storage. The effectiveness of retrieval depends on the effectiveness of those two processes as well as on whatever reminders (i.e., **retrieval cues**) are present. This section will focus on the effectiveness of various retrieval cues and will consider how various retrieval tasks and situations interact with the encoding variables discussed earlier.

Availability and Accessibility

It's interesting to note that the process of retrieval went relatively unnoticed in the early days of memory research as investigations focused on encoding and storage (Roediger & Guynn, 1996). Retrieval tasks were seen basically as a means to an end, namely, revealing the contents of storage. Failures to retrieve information were seen as failures of encoding (e.g., the material was not processed deeply enough) and/or storage (the material was lost due to disuse or interference). Retrieval itself was rarely varied and investigated systematically. However, early research by Endel Tulving (e.g., Tulving & Pearlstone, 1966) suggested that failure to remember information was not necessarily due to encoding or storage failure. Tulving thought it likely that a great deal of information was available in memory but was not accessible. You've experienced this distinction every time you've stared at a test question and the critical information fails to come to mind. The problem is not necessarily that the information isn't stored; the information may be there (i.e., it's available), but you can't get to it given the information (retrieval cues) in front of you (i.e., it's inaccessible). The problem is, this is still forgetting, and you're still going to lose points on the test. **Retrieval failure** is now widely recognized as a primary cause (perhaps *the* primary cause) of forgetting.

An investigation by Tulving and Pearlstone (1966) provides a simple illustration of the distinction between **availability** and **accessibility.** In this study, subjects encoded categorized lists that contained two target words from each of 24 categories. If you were a subject, you might be presented with "type of spice: garlic, parsley." Subjects were instructed to remember the target words for a memory test. Some subjects were tested with *free recall.* Under these conditions, subjects recalled substantially less than half of the items. Tulving and Pearlstone suspected that this failure of recall was not necessarily a complete failure of memory. It was conceivable that all 48 encoded items were available in memory but that a blank piece of paper and instructions to recall the words were not good enough cues to allow access to the information. In other words, memory failure in this situation was due largely to problems in accessibility, or retrieval failure. To test this notion, the researchers had other subjects take a *cued-recall test* in which information is presented to assist the retrieval process. Tulving and Pearlstone provided these subjects with the category names (i.e., type of spice) as retrieval cues. Incredibly, in this condition subjects recalled nearly three-quarters of the words. Clearly, they had successfully encoded and stored the information. The locus of the problem had indeed been at retrieval. The information was available, and the right retrieval cues made it accessible.

Encoding Specificity

It's clear that retrieval cues are critical to remembering. This begs another question: What types of cues are most effective? One clue comes from those spontaneous memories (mentioned at the beginning of the chapter) that flood back to you when you visit a familiar location. It turns out that memory retrieval is aided by a cue to the extent that the cue helps reconstruct the encoding situation. In other words, memory depends on the amount of overlap between what's happening at retrieval and what happened at encoding. This fundamental retrieval principle is termed *encoding specificity*.

Let's consider a classic investigation by Thomson and Tulving (1970) that demonstrated the **encoding specificity principle.** Subjects encoded weakly related word pairs, like *plant-bug*, in which the word *bug* was the word that had to be remembered (i.e., the target). After encoding a list of such pairs, a cued-recall test was given in which a cue was presented for each of the targets. Thomson and Tulving compared two retrieval conditions. In one condition, a strongly related word was presented to cue the target. For example, the subject would see *insect* as a cue for *bug*. In the other condition, the word from the original word pair was presented as a cue for *bug* (i.e., *plant*). Intuitively, which word do you think would be a better cue for *bug*? It seems as though *insect* would be; it's a synonym for the target. But as it turns out, it was a relatively ineffective cue for recall relative to *plant*. Consider why this was the case in light of the encoding specificity principle. The event that has to be retrieved is encountering the pair *plant-bug*. The best retrieval cue will be one that helps reactivate that specific encoding situation, and *plant* is much more effective for this purpose because it was *part* of the encoding situation. If I wanted you to simply say the word *bug, insect* might be a good cue, but if I want you to remember an episode in which you saw the words *plant* and *bug* together, then *plant* is much more effective. By the way, this was part of the basis for Tulving's distinction between a memory system that stores episodes, complete with context (episodic memory), and one that stores contextless pieces of knowledge (semantic memory).

You may have noticed a similarity between the encoding specificity principle and the transfer-appropriate processing principle discussed earlier. The two are quite similar in that they emphasize the overlap between encoding and retrieval as the key determinant of remembering. You might consider them to be opposite sides of the encoding-retrieval coin. The transfer-appropriate processing principle focuses on encoding and emphasizes that the encoding processes one uses should be appropriate for how memory is going to be tested. The encoding specificity principle focuses on retrieval and emphasizes that the best retrieval cues are those that tap into how something was encoded. For example, knowledge of the transfer-appropriate processing principle should influence the way you study for a test: you should study in a manner appropriate for the type of test you will be given. Conversely, knowledge of the encoding specificity principle should influence the type of retrieval cues that will be helpful for that test, given the way you studied.

STOP *and* THINK!

STUDY SKILLS COUNSELING

Suppose your friends are worried about how to effectively study for their finals. Use the encoding principles and the retrieval principles discussed to generate some study tips that may help. Be specific about what you think your friends should do.

- Would you emphasize encoding or retrieval more? Why?
- What specific factors would you emphasize as extremely important? Why?
- What factors do you consider less important? Why?

Extensions of Encoding Specificity: Context Dependency Effects.   Clearly, the nature of retrieval cues is a critical determinant of memory. You might be wondering how wide-ranging this principle is. Does it extend to the physical environment? Since you learn much of the information in your class in a particular room, should you be in the same room when you're tested? Does the principle extend to how you feel? If you've had a couple of drinks and then meet some new friends, are you more likely to remember their names at the next party after you've had a couple of drinks? Evidence indicates that the encoding specificity principle is quite general. Studies manipulating physical context (e.g., Smith, 1979), presence or absence of music (e.g., Balch, Bowman, & Mohler, 1992), odor (e.g., Schab, 1990), drug or alcohol intake (e.g., Petersen, 1977), and mood (e.g., Eich & Metcalfe, 1989) at encoding and retrieval have all revealed **context-dependency effects.** That is, given a particular encoding context, memory is better when retrieval reinstates that context.

The general structure of a context-dependency experiment is outlined in Table 6.3. These experiments generally involve four groups of subjects. Some subjects encode in context A and also take their memory test in context A. A second group of subjects encodes in context A but is switched to context B for their memory test. A third group encodes in context B and is switched to context A for their memory test. Finally, a fourth group encodes in context B and is tested in context B. The prediction from the encoding specificity principle is that for a given encoding condition, memory will be

Table 6.3 General Format of a Context-Dependency Study

	Retrieval Condition A	Retrieval Condition B
Encoding Condition A	AA—match	AB—mismatch
Encoding Condition B	BA—mismatch	BB—match

better if the same context is reinstated at retrieval. So condition AA should be better than condition AB, and condition BB should be better than condition BA. It is important to point out that these comparisons are the only ones relevant to the encoding specificity principle. While it may seem reasonable to infer that AA should be better than BA and that BB should be better than AB, this can't be predicted by the encoding specificity principle. The encoding specificity principle states that *for a given encoding condition,* memory is best when the retrieval condition matches the encoding condition. A comparison between AA and BA involves different encoding conditions, and therefore would not represent the proper conditions to test this principle. This comparison would provide a test of the other encoding-retrieval overlap principle that we discussed earlier—transfer-appropriate processing. The prediction based on this principle is that for a given retrieval condition, memory is best when the encoding condition matches the retrieval condition. A comparison of BB to AB and AA to BA involves the same retrieval conditions and therefore is a test of the transfer-appropriate processing principle and *not* the encoding specificity principle. Regardless of which principle is being tested, the overriding message is that memory is best when encoding and retrieval conditions match.

If the physical environment in which an event occurs is truly part of the memory representation for the event, then a switch of environments between encoding and retrieval might result in poorer memory due to an encoding-retrieval mismatch. Godden and Baddeley (1975) tested this idea in a unique situation by having deep-sea divers participate in an underwater memory experiment. Divers encoded words in one of two conditions: on a beach or under several feet of water. Later, recall was tested in the environment in which divers had encoded the information or in the other environment. As you can see in Table 6.4, the results revealed a context-dependency effect. If divers had

Table 6.4 Results of the Godden and Baddeley (1975) Study

		Retrieval Condition	
		Underwater	On Land
Encoding Condition	Underwater	32	22
	On Land	24	37

From Godden, D. R., & Baddeley, A. D. (1975). Context-dependent memory in two natural environments: On land and underwater. *British Journal of Psychology, 66,* 325–331. Copyright the British Journal of Psychology. Reprinted with the kind permission of the British Psychological Society.

been on the beach during encoding, they were better off on the beach at retrieval. If they had been underwater during encoding, they were better off underwater during retrieval. Consider why this was the case. The divers' memory did not just consist of the encoded words. It also included the physical environment in which the encoding had taken place. When this physical environment was presented as a cue at retrieval, memory was enhanced. This general finding has been found across a variety of experimental situations (Smith, 1988).

Miles and Hardman (1998) investigated whether context-dependent memory might extend to the internal context associated with aerobic exercise. These researchers manipulated the encoding context by having some of their subjects pedal an exercise bike vigorously enough to double their heart rate. The other half of the subjects simply learned the words while at rest (sitting on the bike but not pedaling). Physiological context was manipulated in the same way at retrieval. The results revealed a context-dependency effect. If subjects had been sweating it out during encoding, they were better off sweating it out during retrieval. If subjects had been taking a breather during encoding, they were better off taking a breather during retrieval. Miles and Hardman point out that the findings may have implications for athletes who need to retrieve information in the context of competition. If such retrieval is necessary, it would behoove athletes to encode the information under competition-like conditions, in order to enhance the encoding-retrieval match.

Effects of Test Type. A theme that should be increasingly obvious is that various memory phenomena depend on exactly how memory is tested. Therefore, it should come as no surprise that context-dependency effects vary with the type of memory test given. Research has shown that context-dependency effects are more likely to occur in free recall than in cued recall or recognition. For example, in the Godden and Baddeley (1975) underwater memory experiment, a context-dependency effect was not found when memory was tested with recognition. According to Eich (1980), the more direct the contact between the retrieval cue and the memory trace, the less likely it is that context will be needed to help retrieve the encoded episode. Cued recall and recognition both offer this direct contact and typically do not show context-dependency effects. Basically, you'll turn to context as a cue as a last resort, only when better cues are unavailable. Smith (1988) proposed a similar notion, terming it the *outshining hypothesis.* Basically, it claims that context can be a useful cue for memory, but only when you need it. In recall, there are no retrieval cues, so context reinstatement provides some aid to the retrieval process. But in recognition, the retrieval cues are extremely strong (you get to see the item itself), so context reinstatement is not critical. In other words, on recognition tests, test items themselves "outshine" context as a cue.

Practical Implications. What are the practical implications of this principle? Students often hear about these dependency effects and worry that perhaps they should eat, sleep, and (mostly) study in the room where they're going to be tested. The results are mixed on whether switching classrooms between study and test has any impact on performance. Metzger and colleagues (1979) found a negative effect of room switching, but other studies

Mismatch between encoding and retrieval.

(e.g., Saufley, Otaka, & Bravaresco, 1985) have found no effect. There are a few reasons you needn't worry about taking a test in a different location than where you studied. First, most of the studies demonstrating context dependency use lists of unrelated words as the material to be remembered, which is hopefully not what you're learning in class (see the dean if you are!). Second, context almost certainly gets outshined by other more useful retrieval cues. Smith (1988) suggests that processing information in a meaningful way produces retrieval cues that are likely to outshine context. In other words, if you know the material well, you won't need to rely on the physical context for retrieval help. Also, many tests provide a great deal of cues (e.g., multiple-choice stems) that would outshine context at retrieval.

Although the effects of context dependency may be slight or nonexistent in many classroom situations, a study by Grant, Bredahl, Clay, Ferrie, Groves, McDorman, and Dark (1998) suggests that the principle should not be dismissed altogether. If you're like many students, you study under conditions of distraction. The TV or stereo is on, your roommates are talking, or there's a buzz of activity at the library. But you're not tested in the presence of the TV, your stereo, your blabbing roommates, or the noisy library; you're tested in a completely silent room. Is there an effect of this mismatch of conditions (studying with background noise and activity and testing in silence)? To investigate this, Grant and colleagues followed the standard context dependency research design, manipulating the presence or absence of general background noise at both encoding and retrieval. They had subjects encode a two-page article on psychoimmunology and tested them with a fill-in-the-blank exam followed by multiple-choice questions. In this study, one of the independent variables was encoding environment. Two levels were tested: presence or absence of background noise. The other independent variable was retrieval condition, and its two levels were also the presence or absence of background noise. The dependent variable for the study was test performance.

The results, shown in Table 6.5, are intriguing; there was no main effect of background noise at encoding. Subjects who studied in the presence of background noise remembered just as much as subjects who studied in the absence of background noise, which seems to support many a student's claim that studying with background noise, such as music, does not hurt memory. However, this main effect is mediated by an

Table 6.5 Results from Grant et al. (1998)

a. Percentage correct on short-answer test

		Test Condition		
		Silent	Noisy	Row Mean
Study Condition	Silent	67	46	56.5
	Noisy	54	62	58.0
Column Mean		60.5	54.0	

b. Percentage correct on multiple-choice test

		Test Condition		
		Silent	Noisy	Row Mean
Study Condition	Silent	89	79	84
	Noisy	79	89	84
Column Mean		84	84	

From Grant, H. M., Bredahl, L. C., Clay, J., Ferrie, J., Groves, J. E., McDorman, T. A., & Dark, V. J. (1998). Context-dependent memory for meaningful material: Information for students. *Applied Cognitive Psychology, 12,* 617–623. Copyright 1998, John Wiley & Sons, Ltd. Reprinted by permission.

interaction: whether or not subjects studied in the presence or absence of noise at encoding, they were better off in the same environment at retrieval. Consider the ramifications for test performance. Because tests are given in quiet conditions, studying should occur under quiet conditions, maximizing the encoding-retrieval match.

STOP *and* THINK!

ENCODING SPECIFICITY AND FOND MEMORIES

Go somewhere you haven't been for a while—a place on campus, a restaurant, anyplace—and see if any memories spontaneously pop into mind. Use the encoding specificity principle to explain why this might have happened.

A Critique of the Encoding Specificity Principle.   Encoding specificity effects are so commonplace that the effects have been elevated to the level of a "principle," one of only a handful of cognitive psychology findings that could make that claim. However, Nairne (2002a) proposes that the basic tenet of encoding specificity—that successful memory depends on a match between retrieval and encoding circumstances—is a myth! According to Nairne, what determines successful memory performance is *cue distinctiveness*, or the effectiveness of a cue in singling out a specific memory representation. It just so happens that when encoding and retrieval overlap, you're more likely to have some cues that really are distinctive. But it is not the match between encoding and retrieval per se that leads to successful memory. So even circumstances in which there is almost no overlap between encoding and retrieval could produce good memory, if the minimal overlap is highly distinctive. So, according to Nairne (2002a), the relationship between the encoding-retrieval match and successful memory performance is correlational, not causal. Having a rich set of retrieval cues increases both (1) encoding and retrieval overlap and (2) the chances of having highly distinctive cues. It is the highly distinctive cues that determine performance, rather than encoding and retrieval overlap. Nairne does not quibble with the practical implications of the encoding specificity principle, only the explanation of why an encoding-retrieval match is beneficial.

Retrieval: An Effective Encoding Strategy?

Retrieval is necessary to demonstrate that information has been effectively encoded and stored in memory. However, retrieval itself can also be utilized to enhance your ability to retrieve information at a later point in time. In other words, while studying information that you need to remember, it is useful to periodically attempt to retrieve the information you are trying to encode. This **testing effect** has been found in tests of free recall (Hogan & Kintsch, 1971), cued recall (Allen, Mahler, & Estes, 1969; Carrier & Pashler, 1992), and recognition (Wenger, Thompson, & Bartling, 1980). However, these studies were conducted with structured lists of words, not exactly the stuff of classroom learning.

A recent study by Roediger and Karpicke (2006) investigated the testing effect in a context more generalizable to the classroom setting. In one part of the study, they presented prose passages about scientific topics (much like this textbook!). One independent variable was the encoding conditions used in the first phase of the experiment. Half of the subjects studied the passage for four separate five-minute periods (SSSS). The other half studied the passage for only one five-minute period and took a test in each of the subsequent three periods (STTT). The other independent variable was the *retention interval,* which refers to the amount of time between the first phase of the experiment and the final testing phase. Half of the subjects were tested five minutes after the completion of phase 1, while the other half were tested one week later. In the final test, subjects were told to try hard to recall the entire passage and write down as much of it as they could. The memory test was scored in terms of the number of basic ideas recalled from the passage.

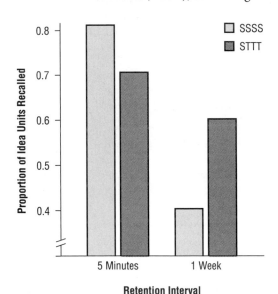

Figure 6.1 Results from Roediger and Karpicke's (2006) study of the effects of testing on retention.

From Roediger, H. L. & Karpicke, J. D. (2006). Test-enhanced learning: Taking memory tests improves long-term retention. *Psychological Science, 17*(3), 249–255. Blackwell Publishing. Reprinted with permission from the author.

The results are presented in Figure 6.1. The findings are rather striking. When the final test was given after a short delay (five minutes), studying the passage four times led to a clear advantage in memory. However, the advantage was a short-lived one. When tests were given a week later, the pattern of results was the opposite! The group who had experienced repeated testing remembered much more than the groups who had studied repeatedly. Put another way, the two encoding conditions seemed to lead to markedly different forgetting rates. Subjects who studied by testing themselves repeatedly forgot much less than those who had read repeatedly, almost as if the repeated testing was an inoculation against forgetting.

Roediger and Karpicke's (2006) results may remind you of the study we discussed earlier. Recall that Craik and Watkins (1973) found rote repetition of single words to be fairly ineffective for long-term retention. The present finding would seem to provide a prose analog, with obvious implications for your study habits—your study sessions shouldn't be all about reading the text repeatedly. Such maintenance rehearsal is woefully inefficient, and what you learn isn't likely to last. A much better use of your time would be a combination of elaborative rehearsal and repeatedly testing your knowledge of the material.

Encoding, Retrieval, and Hemispheric Asymmetry

As you read in Chapter 2, research on brain functioning has revealed asymmetries in the functioning of the right and left hemispheres, with each half of the brain specialized for different types of processing. Recent research has revealed that this asymmetry in processing extends to the two fundamental processes that we have just discussed: encoding and retrieval. Tulving and his colleagues (Habib, Nyberg, & Tulving, 2003) have proposed the HERA (hemispheric encoding/retrieval asymmetry) model.

> Research Theme:
> Neuroscience

The HERA model is based largely on the results of neuroimaging studies. As you know, neuroimaging techniques such as positron-emission tomography (PET) and functional magnetic resonance imaging (fMRI) allow researchers to observe which areas of the brain are more and less active during cognitive processing. Let's take a look at some of the evidence reviewed by Nyber, Cabeza, and Tulving (1996). One task that has been employed extensively in neuroimaging studies of cognition is a verb-generation task (e.g., Petersen, Fox, Posner, Mintun, & Raichle, 1988), in which subjects are presented with nouns, one at a time, and are required to generate an appropriate verb. For example, when presented with the word *joke*, the correct response would be "laugh" (unless it's a joke a professor tells in class, in which case you would say "groan"). This task involves *retrieval from semantic memory*. Knowing the verb that goes along with *joke* is a fact that you just know. It also involves *encoding into episodic memory*. Seeing words like *joke* and thinking of their associates while you're being PET scanned is an event that you'll remember later. Neuroimaging evidence from the verb-generation task shows greater activation in the left prefrontal area relative to the same area in the right hemisphere, indicating that the left is instrumental in retrieval of information from semantic memory and encoding episodic memories. It's also interesting to note that left-hemisphere activation is influenced by exactly *how* incoming information is processed. Kapur and colleagues (1994) found that processing items deeply at encoding led to greater left-hemisphere activation than processing items shallowly.

Let's contrast this with circumstances in which the right hemisphere is more active than the left hemisphere. Nyber, Cabeza, and Tulving (1996) reviewed evidence from neuroimaging studies of episodic retrieval. These studies investigated a wide range of retrieval situations (e.g., free recall, cued recall, recognition) and a wide range of material to be remembered (words, sentences, objects, locations, odors). These situations all involved *episodic retrieval*, because the task was to recollect a specific encoding episode—what happened at some point in the past. Imaging studies of episodic retrieval have produced pretty consistent results. Nearly all of the studies reviewed demonstrated that when recalling or recognizing the occurrence of some past event, there tends to be more intense activation in the prefrontal area of the right hemisphere than in the left.

STOP *and* **REVIEW!**

1. What does it mean to say that a memory is available but inaccessible?
2. The encoding specificity principle indicates that retrieval will be best when
   a. encoding conditions and retrieval conditions are different.
   b. encoding conditions and retrieval conditions are the same.
   c. multiple retrieval attempts are made.
   d. the person's mood at encoding matches their mood at retrieval.
3. True or false? If you test memory with recognition, you're more likely to find a context-dependency effect than if you test it with recall.
4. In studying for a Spanish test, would it be more beneficial to repeatedly read a Spanish word and its English translation or present yourself with the Spanish word and try to retrieve its English translation? Why?

➤ Information stored in LTM (i.e., it's available) may not be remembered because the retrieval cues are insufficient (i.e., it's not accessible). Retrieval failure is a common cause of forgetting.

➤ According to the encoding specificity principle, a retrieval cue will be effective to the degree that it overlaps with the information provided at encoding. A closely related finding is that memory tends to be better when the context present at retrieval matches the context that was present at encoding (context-dependency effect). This applies to both external (i.e., physical surroundings) and internal (i.e., mood, body state) context.

➤ These context-dependency effects depend on how memory is tested. According to the outshining hypothesis, context-dependency effects are more likely to be found on free recall tests (few retrieval cues) than in cued-recall or recognition tests (more retrieval cues) because the presence of other retrieval cues tends to outshine the context cue.

➤ Testing oneself on material is more beneficial for later retention than simply studying the material repeatedly. Hemispheric asymmetries seem to characterize the processing of information in memory. Retrieving information from semantic memory seems to be associated with left frontal lobe activity in the brain, while retrieving information from episodic memory is associated with right prefrontal activity.

Memory and Consciousness

In recent years, the question of how consciousness relates to memory has become a question of intense interest. This stands in stark contrast to 20 or 30 years ago, when the mystery of consciousness seemed too subjective to assess with the scientific method, and thus remained outside the realm of experimental psychology. The tide began to shift with research on implicit memory, which made it apparent that questions of consciousness could be addressed scientifically. Tulving's (1972, 1983) proposal of distinct memory systems also focused researchers' attention on questions of consciousness. As you'll recall, one of the major factors that distinguishes episodic from semantic memory is that episodic retrieval is accompanied by an experience of recollection, or a *reliving* of the past experience. In the past decade, investigators have developed methods to assess directly the relationship between consciousness and memory.

Remembering and Knowing

One of the more popular approaches for separating the conscious and nonconscious components of memory is to ask about one's state of awareness during the retrieval of a previous experience. This has been termed the **remember-know paradigm** (Gardiner, 1988). In this paradigm, subjects are asked to recognize events (typically words) that occurred in an earlier list. For items that are recognized, another judgment is made: Subjects are asked whether they *remember* seeing the word or just *know* that they saw it earlier. A *remember* judgment means that subjects can vividly recall the presentation of the word, basically reliving the experience. They can consciously recollect that the word was indeed presented (Rajaram, 1993). A *know* judgment means that although one knows that the word was part of the study list, they have no experience of recollection or reliving; the person just "knows" that the word appeared earlier. So if we "remember" that an event occurred, this reflects conscious and effortful retrieval. If we just "know" that an event occurred, this reflects nonconscious, automatic memory retrieval.

Research employing the remember-know paradigm has demonstrated a number of dissociations. Remember and know judgments are influenced by different variables. For example, both Gardiner (1988) and Rajaram (1993) found that a levels-of-processing manipulation had different effects on these two types of judgments. Rajaram (experiment 1) presented words (e.g., *cat*) to subjects and had them generate either a rhyme associate (*bat*) or a semantic associate (*dog*). Memory was tested with recognition. If a word was recognized, subjects also had to make a remember-know judgment. Based on what you've read about the levels-of-processing effect, you might correctly anticipate that subjects better remembered words for which a semantic associate was provided. So overall, there was a levels-of-processing effect. But when the conscious and nonconscious components of memory were teased apart, an interesting pattern emerged. The levels-of-processing effect was limited to remember judgments. In fact, as you can see in Table 6.6, the effect was reversed in know judgments.

Research employing the remember-know paradigm (see Gardiner & Richardson-Klavehn, 2000, for a review) has revealed that many of the encoding factors that improve performance in explicit memory tasks (i.e., recall and recognition) also influence

Research Theme: Consciousness

Table 6.6 Data from Rajaram (1993, experiment 1) Study

	Percent Correct Responses		
	Overall Recognition	Remember Judgments	Know Judgments
Shallow Processing	62	32	30
Deep Processing	86	66	20

From Rajaram, S. (1993). Remembering and knowing: Two means of access to the personal past. *Memory and Cognition, 21,* 89–102. Reprinted by permission of the Psychonomic Society, Inc.

remember judgments. These factors include attention (Gardiner & Parkin, 1990), picture presentation (Rajaram, 1993), and stimulus generation (Gardiner, 1988). These same encoding factors exert relatively little influence on *know* judgments. Some have used the concept of memory systems to account for the remember-know results (e.g., Gardiner & Parkin, 1990; Tulving, 1985), suggesting that remember judgments are based on the episodic memory system, while know judgments are based on the procedural system.

Implicit Memory

For the first part of the chapter, we talked about memory retrieval as a deliberate, conscious process. All of the retrieval situations we discussed involved people consciously thinking back to some previous experience (an encoded list or story) and remembering everything they could. These retrieval situations require conscious recollection of a previous episode for successful performance. Free recall, cued recall, and recognition all have one thing in common—an explicit instruction to mentally reinstate a previous experience and recollect what happened. Over the past 20 years, it's become apparent that this is only part of the retrieval story. Even if something isn't remembered explicitly, it may still have an impact on your attitudes, feelings, or behavior. In other words, you may "remember" something without really "remembering" it. Memory tests that reflect this type of remembering are termed *implicit memory tests* and do not require conscious recollection of a previous episode for successful performance. Memory is reflected implicitly—as an improvement or change in some task that occurs even if the subject remembers nothing about the original event. It is important to note that implicit memory (and explicit memory) are not *types* of memory but *tests* of memory; the effects we will be discussing center on the way in which memory is assessed (i.e., tested), not the type of memory that is encoded.

Everyday Examples of Implicit Memory Retrieval.   Here's an example of implicit memory from Greg's life. We were moving into our new house, carrying box after box into the house and up the stairs. Later that day, Greg found that a song was running through his head. He was whistling and humming it, and he had no idea why, much to his frustration (you know the feeling). The song was "Handle with Care" by the Traveling Wilburys (an old rock group you may not remember or even have heard of!). After thinking about it for a few hours, it finally came to him why he was whistling that song. Most of the boxes he had carried up the stairs earlier had "Handle with care" printed on the side, which in turn had led him to whistle that song. Although throughout the day he had no explicit memory of reading that phrase, his whistling of the tune was a reflection of implicit memory.

Schacter (1996) and Brown (2003, 2004) suggest that implicit memory may lie at the heart of **unconscious plagiarism.** In some instances, you come up with what you think is a brilliant idea—that is, until the friend you're describing it to informs you they had the same idea and discussed it with you three months ago. Your failure to recall that it was your friend's idea is a failure of explicit memory. Yet you do remember the encoding episode implicitly, as reflected by your generating the idea you encountered in your earlier conversation. Former Beatle George Harrison (who was one of the Traveling Wilburys, by the way) may have been an unwitting victim of implicit memory. The melody for Harrison's song "My Sweet Lord" sounded a little bit too much like "He's So Fine," an earlier hit by the Chiffons. Harrison acknowledged being aware of the song but denied copying it. The court found the similarity between the tunes too great to be an accident and ruled against Harrison. Interestingly, the actual ruling included language basically stating that in composing the song, Harrison must have been "subconsciously" primed by the earlier song (Schacter, 1996).

Schacter (1996) also suggests that implicit memory may lie at the heart of déjà vu experiences. Déjà vu occurs when we have the distinct impression or feeling that we've been in some place or had some experience before, when in reality we have not. These experiences are commonplace; in a review of the literature on déjà vu, Brown (2004) estimates that about two-thirds of individuals have had the experience at least once in their lifetimes, and most of these have had multiple experiences. He also notes that the experiences tend to be triggered by some physical context. This notion fits nicely with an analysis by Berrios (1995), who claims (in keeping with the encoding specificity principle) that some piece of a memory gets activated by a cue, but the entire memory is not retrieved. Instead, one is left with a feeling of familiarity that cannot be readily explained. Hence, déjà vu may be an expression of the encoding specificity principle in the form of an implicit memory.

Implicit Memory Tests.   Experiments that investigate implicit memory start out the same way as the studies we've been discussing: subjects study some type of information, most commonly a word list. Later, their memory is tested. Just like the battery of explicit memory tests (free recall, cued recall, and recognition), there are a number of implicit memory tests. In **word-fragment completion,** you're faced with a word in which some letters are there and some aren't, and your task is to come up with the appropriate word. (Think of the game show *Wh_ _l of F_rt_ne.*) In **word-stem completion,** the initial three letters of a word are presented, and your task is to complete the stem with the first word that comes to mind.

A subject in an implicit memory experiment encodes a list of words. Later, when given the implicit memory test, there is no mention of these previously encoded words. But presenting the word earlier primes the person to come up with it later, either by successfully completing the word fragment with a previously seen word or by blurting out a previously seen word, given a stem that could be completed by several possibilities. For example, if you saw the word *garlic* in a list an hour ago, when you see the word stem *gar_____,* you're quite likely to respond "garlic" (rather than "garbage," "gargoyle," "garden," or some other nonpresented word).

Table 6.7 A Word-Fragment Completion Study Example

Encoding	Retrieval
List A (studied):	
giraffe	g _ r _ f f _
paper	p_ p_ r
tongue	_ o n _ u _
chapel	c h _ _ e _
List B (unstudied):	
clock	_ l o _ k
bottle	b _ _ t l _
picture	p i _ _ u r _
staple	_ _ a p _ e

Implicit memory is typically measured in terms of **priming,** or the benefit in performance from previous exposure to a word. Let's get a little more specific with regard to the methodology used to assess priming in the typical implicit memory experiment (see Table 6.7). Subjects in an implicit memory experiment would encode a list of words (let's call it Word List A). Another list of words (List B) remains unstudied. Later, subjects attempt to complete word fragments (or word stems) for words from both lists. Another group of subjects gets precisely the opposite arrangement: they study List B but don't study List A. Later, they attempt to complete the same set of word fragments (or stems). This arrangement may seem overly elaborate, but it allows the researcher to compare completion rates for the same words under both studied and nonstudied conditions.

Now that you know how to methodologically implement an implicit memory test (e.g., word-fragment completion), let's return to the example in Table 6.7 and explain how priming is measured. Let's say you encode a list of 4 words and are tested later with 8 word fragments that include those 4 words and 4 other words that were not previously encoded. Let's say you successfully complete 3 of the 4 fragments with previously encoded words, or 75%. For the other 4 word fragments, you manage to complete only 1, or 25%. In this example, priming is 50%—there is a 50% benefit in performance from having seen the words earlier. And it's important to note that you may not be able to consciously recollect any of the words you saw; still, having seen them will help you complete a word fragment. So a memory benefit can occur from previous exposure to a word in the absence of conscious recollection of the word.

STOP and THINK! ———————

WHEEL OF FORTUNE!!

See if you can complete the following word fragments. Spend only about 5 to 10 seconds on each fragment. *Do not read below the fragments until you are done.*

1. c _ r t _ _ n   3. i _ _ li _ _ t   5. c a _ p _ _   7. e _ _od _n _   9. c _ v _ r _
2. ga _ _ i _   4. b _ _ e m _ n _   6. c _ n t _ x _   8. m _ _ or _   10. a _ s _ ss _ _

Take note of the fragments you successfully completed. Calculate the percentage you got correct for questions 2, 3, 6, 7, and 8. Do the same thing for the other five items (questions 1, 4, 5, 9, and 10). Questions 2, 3, 6, 7, and 8 were "studied," because you saw them earlier in the chapter. Questions 1, 4, 5, 9, and 10 were "nonstudied"—you didn't see them earlier.

- Did you show any priming?
- What is your explanation?

6. *context* 7. *encoding* 8. *memory* 9. *cavern* 10. *assassin*

1. *curtain* (or *cartoon*) 2. *garlic* 3. *implicit* 4. *basement* 5. *carpet*

Dissociations in Implicit and Explicit Tests of Memory.   Laboratory research on implicit memory began its rise to prominence in the 1960s, as researchers investigated memory functioning in amnesics (people with severely impaired memory function). For a while, it was believed that many amnesics lacked the ability to move things into long-term storage. This was based on the observation that amnesics demonstrated relatively normal short-term memory ability but suffered profound long-term memory deficits. So it seemed that short-term memory was intact but the mechanism whereby new information is transferred to long-term memory was nonfunctional (and, indeed, this dissociation was cited as evidence for a distinction between a short-term and a long-term memory store). But as it turned out, the story wasn't so simple. (Recall that STM/LTM memory distinction has suffered a similar fate.) In spite of their inability to consciously recollect previous events, the amnesics showed signs of long-term retention (as evidenced by the prickly handshake story discussed at the beginning of this chapter).

Let's consider an early investigation by Warrington and Weiskrantz (1970) that compared memory functioning in amnesics and nonamnesics. In one study, a list of words was presented, followed by an explicit memory test (recognition). Faced with this test, which required them to consciously think back to the earlier episode, amnesics were relatively lost, recognizing far fewer words than nonamnesics. This finding came as no surprise. But testing retrieval with an implicit test yielded some surprising results. When their memory was probed indirectly with word stems or word fragments, amnesics demonstrated priming, just like nonamnesics. Amnesics were better able to complete stems and fragments that corresponded to words they had seen earlier *even though they could not consciously recollect many of those same words.* Clearly, the words were represented in long-term memory but were simply not retrievable with explicit memory instructions. This general pattern—equal performance between nonamnesics and amnesics on implicit memory tests—has been replicated in countless investigations, and the investigation of implicit, nonconscious manifestations of memory has been one of the most active frontiers of memory research.

As demonstrated by the previous study, one of the most fascinating things about implicit memory tests is that they seem to follow a different set of rules than do explicit tests. Over the years, study after study has demonstrated dissociations between implicit and explicit tests. As you read in Chapter 2 and have seen several times, a dissociation occurs when some variable influences performance in different ways, depending on how performance is measured. The study by Warrington and Weiskrantz (1970) revealed

Research Theme: Neuroscience

dissociative effects of amnesia on memory. The ability to remember explicitly is impaired in amnesics, while remembering implicitly is unaffected.

Dissociations between implicit and explicit memory are not limited to remembering in amnesics. These intriguing patterns have been revealed in many studies of nonamnesics. Let's look at a classic study by Jacoby (1983), one of the first studies to show such a dissociation. Jacoby had subjects encode common words in one of two different conditions. Let's say the target word was *cold*. In a *generate* condition, subjects were visually presented with an opposite (hot-???) and had to generate the target: COLD. In a *read* condition, subjects were visually presented with the target word alongside a row of x's (xxx-COLD). Note that in the generate condition, subjects never actually saw the word.

After encoding a series of words in one of these two conditions, subjects were given one of two different memory tests for the target words (*cold* in the present example). Half received a recognition test in which they had to determine whether each word was one of the targets from the encoding phase. This is an explicit test, because successful performance requires that subjects consciously think back and recollect what happened in the initial target episode. The other half received a perceptual identification task in which words were presented for an extremely brief duration (about 30 ms). The only thing subjects had to do was identify the word that had been presented. Performance on this task was measured in terms of priming, which we discussed earlier. In this case, the identification rate for nontargets was subtracted from the identification rate for targets. The expectation, of course, was that having encountered a word during the encoding phase would make the word easier to identify.

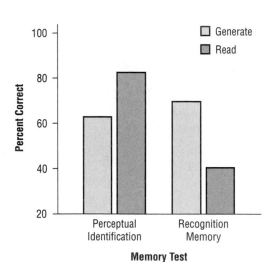

Figure 6.2 Results from Jacoby (1983), demonstrating a dissociation between implicit and explicit memory.

Adapted from Jacoby, L. L. (1983). Remembering the data: Analyzing interactive processes in reading. *Journal of Verbal Learning and Verbal Behavior, 22*(5), 485–508. Published by Elsevier. Used with permission from Elsevier and the author.

The results, presented in Figure 6.2, represent a classic dissociation. As you can see, the encoding conditions had converse effects on the two memory tests. Recognition (explicit memory) performance for phase 1 targets was best for subjects who had generated the words in response to an opposite. Identification (implicit memory) performance for phase 1 targets was best for subjects who had read the words in isolation. The dissociation between explicit and implicit memory tests demonstrated by Jacoby (1983) was only one of many. Early research comparing performance on explicit and implicit tests of memory revealed many other dissociations involving classic encoding and storage variables like levels of processing, visual encoding, organization, and retention interval.

Differences in brain processing that accompany implicit and explicit memory testing are also evident in investigations of online brain processing as reflected in event-related potentials. Paller, Hutson, Miller, and Boehm (2003) investigated these differences in a study of face memory. A number of reactions can occur when one views a face that one has previously encountered. One reaction is explicit recognition of the face as having been previously presented. This, of course, would be a case of explicit memory. A second possibility is more accurate or faster processing of the face with repeated viewing in the absence of recollection. This would be a case of implicit memory, reflected through priming. Paller (2004) notes that these two components of face processing are notoriously difficult to isolate from one another because when researchers want to look at the pattern of brain response produced along with perceptual priming, they can never be sure that the response doesn't reflect some component of conscious memory.

Paller and colleagues (2003) attempted to isolate implicit retrieval and remove any possible contribution of conscious (explicit) retrieval. During an encoding phase, they had subjects perform a difficult visual task on stimuli presented peripherally; as subjects were performing this task, a face was presented very briefly in the center of the screen, followed immediately by a random pattern to further mask its appearance. The purpose of this procedure was to isolate implicit retrieval (priming) in the absence of explicit retrieval (conscious recollection).

The results of the study indicated that the procedure had been effective. In the recognition test (an explicit memory test), subjects were no better than chance in deciding which faces had been presented earlier. However, in an implicit task—photo classification (in which subjects had to identify as quickly as possible whether a presented face was male or female), faces presented earlier were classified more quickly than those not presented earlier. This reflects implicit memory in the absence of explicit memory. In spite of the fact that subjects could not consciously recollect the faces, they were still faster at classifying the ones they had seen, relative to the ones they hadn't.

Next, Paller et al. (2003) collected event-related potentials from subjects in each of these retrieval conditions in order to determine the characteristic time course of processing for implicit and explicit retrieval. As it turned out, explicit retrieval (i.e., recognition) of faces was associated with positive ERPs that occurred in the posterior (i.e., rear) regions of the brain about 400 to 800 ms after the presentation of the stimulus, while implicit retrieval (i.e., priming) of faces was associated with negative ERPs that occurred in the anterior (i.e., frontal) regions of the brain about 200 to 400 ms after stimulus presentation. This difference between brain-processing topography and timing lends support to the notion that implicit and explicit retrieval involve different brain processes and/or systems. More recent work by Paller and his colleagues (e.g., Paller, 2004; Voss & Paller, 2006) lends further support to these distinctions.

> **Research Theme:**
> **Neuroscience**

Accounts of Explicit-Implicit Dissociations.   What factors might underlie these dissociations, in which different measures of memory seem to be playing by different rules? And what might these rules be? Two explanatory frameworks have emerged. According to the *transfer-appropriate processing account* (e.g., Roediger, 1990), dissociations between implicit and explicit memory tests occur because these tests typically depend on different sorts of processing. Implicit retrieval tests such as word-fragment completion, word-stem completion, or the identification task used in Jacoby's (1983) study are *data driven* in that they rely on reading and perceptual operations for successful performance. Explicit memory tests such as free recall and recognition are *conceptually driven* in that they rely on elaboration and organization for successful performance.

Performance on a given test will depend on how the material was processed at encoding. Successful performance will result if the encoding processes appropriately transfer to retrieval. Because implicit retrieval tends to be data driven, it will be aided by data-driven encoding processes. Explicit retrieval tends to be conceptually driven, so it will be aided by conceptually driven encoding processes.

Consider the dissociative effects of generation on implicit and explicit memory found by Jacoby (1983). According to the transfer-appropriate processing account, generating a target word in response to its opposite is a conceptually driven encoding process that will transfer better to a conceptually driven retrieval task like recognition. This explains why generated items were recognized better than read items; encoding and retrieval processes matched. Alternatively, reading is a largely perceptual (i.e., data-driven) process that should transfer well to a data-driven retrieval task like identification. Consistent with this prediction, priming in the identification task was higher for words that had been read, relative to words that had been generated. In sum, this account views the processing used at study and testing as the critical determinants of memory.

Let's consider the memory systems view of long-term memory that we briefly introduced at the beginning of the chapter. According to the memory systems view (e.g., Schacter, 1989; Squire, 1993, 2004; Tulving, 1983, 2002), LTM is not a unitary entity. Rather, it is made up of a number of subsystems. According to Squire (2004) the major distinction is between conscious forms of memory like retrieving memory for facts and events (**declarative memory**) and nonconscious forms of memory like priming and the learning of skills and habits (*procedural memory,* briefly discussed at the beginning of the chapter). These two types of LTM are mediated by different brain systems (Squire, 1993) with different neurological underpinnings. Because performance on explicit and implicit tests is based in different systems, these tests are affected by different variables. The dissociation between conscious and nonconscious forms of memory in amnesics suggests that the brain systems underlying these types of memory have been differentially affected by the associated brain damage. The structures associated with declarative memory have been damaged, but the structures underlying procedural memory have been spared.

Let's take a look at the distinction between these two memory systems. Declarative memory is the long-term memory system responsible for retention of factual information about the world, as well personally experienced episodes. It serves as the basis for performance on explicit memory tasks like recalling and recognizing that some event occurred earlier. Sometimes, knowledge based in the declarative system is informally described as "knowing that . . . " something is so. Greg *knows that* on August 30, 1982, he saw his first rock concert. He *knows that* the U.S. Declaration of Independence was signed on July 4, 1776. Do these examples sound familiar? You may recall that earlier in the chapter, we classified Greg's rock concert memory as an *episodic memory* and Greg's knowledge about the Declaration of Independence as a *semantic memory*. Some researchers consider episodic and semantic memory to be subsystems within declarative memory.

Whereas declarative information can be characterized as "knowing that . . . " something is the case, procedural memory can be characterized as "knowing how" to do something. Procedural memory in contrast to declarative memory is difficult to verbalize. Imagine you're teaching someone to tie their shoe. (Really, try it.) Chances are that you'd have a difficult time verbally describing the steps—so you'd probably demonstrate

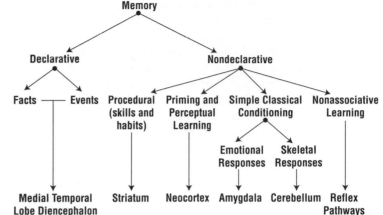

Figure 6.3 Memory systems.

From Squire, L. R. (2004). Memory systems of the brain: A brief history and current perspective. *Neurobiology of Learning and Memory, 82*(3), 171–177. Copyright 2004 Elsevier. Reprinted with permission from Elsevier.

it by going through the motions. Examples of procedural knowledge include skills (tying your shoe, typing, swinging a golf club), the priming involved in word-fragment completion, and the formation of simple associations (like a classically conditioned taste aversion). Results indicating that these forms of learning are spared in amnesia suggest that amnesia affects the declarative memory system but spares the procedural memory system.

So which explanation seems to provide a better account of what is currently known about memory? Although some researchers (e.g., Kelley & Lindsay, 1996; Tulving & Schacter, 1990) believe that the final answer may lie in some convergence of the two accounts, the notion that there are fundamentally different and discriminable memory systems seems to have carried the day (Squire, 2004). However, the complexities observed in decades of experiments comparing performance among various measures of memory have made it apparent that a simple two- or three-system view is not sufficient. Squire (1987, 2004) proposes the more complex grouping depicted in Figure 6.3. Also noted are the important brain structures and areas that seem to underlie performance on these tasks. Note that the primary distinction in this organizational scheme is between declarative (verbal) memories and nondeclarative (i.e., nonverbal) memories.

The areas critical for the formation of declarative memories—episodic and semantic memories in Tulving's (1983, 2002) scheme—are medial temporal areas as well as structures in an

Research Theme: Neuroscience ▶

area of the brain termed the *diencephalon*. The most critical structure in this area is the hippocampus, which appears to be important in indexing the "what, when, and where" of a given episode (Eichenbaum & Fortin, 2003). Recall that episodic memories in particular are distinguished by recollective detail of the sights, sounds, and other sensory details of the event. It's important to note that memories are not stored *in* the hippocampus, nor are they stored *in* any one area of the brain. As we discussed in Chapter 1, all knowledge—including the knowledge that comprises declarative memory—is thought to be represented in a distributed fashion. The retrieval of a given episode will involve the reactivation of areas that had been active during its encoding. The hippocampus is critical in the integrating of these sensory details into a coherent episode that can be assembled during later recall. Squire (2004) describes declarative memory as our model of the world, and what we know to be true and false about it. For example, "Greg was born in Cincinnati, Ohio" is a true statement, based on information represented by the structures and processes of the declarative memory system.

Nondeclarative forms of memory don't involve the verbal processing of consciously recollected facts or episodes. Squire (2004) notes that, in contrast to declarative memory, nondeclarative memory is expressed in terms of performance rather than in propositions that can be deemed true or false. As such, it includes quite a hodgepodge of reactions and associations. Expressions of memory based in this system are as simple as a classically conditioned association (remember Pavlov's dogs?), an emotional response (a heart flutter upon seeing an old crush), or an increase in the ability to read a word or complete a word fragment (as described earlier in the chapter). Though these specific manifestations of nondeclarative memory are based in different systems within the brain, they all have two things in common: They are nonconscious and they are expressed only through changes in behavior.

STOP *and* **REVIEW!**

1. What's the difference between a "remember" judgment and a "know" judgment?
2. True or false? Dissociations between explicit and implicit memory tests are observed only in amnesic subjects.
3. Implicit is to explicit as
   a. declarative is to procedural.
   b. procedural is to declarative.
   c. free recall is to word-fragment completion.
   d. conscious is to unconscious.

➤ Recognition is thought to rely on two possible sources. When we "remember" that an event occurred, this reflects conscious and effortful retrieval. If we just "know" that an event occurred, this reflects nonconscious, automatic memory retrieval. Remember and know judgments are differentially sensitive to encoding variables such as levels of processing.

➤ Implicit memory is reflected in priming. Many variables seem to affect explicit and implicit memory tests differently. For example, amnesia tends to impact explicit remembering more than implicit remembering. Dissociations are also observed in nonamnesics with standard encoding variables (e.g., stimulus generation) influencing explicit and implicit memory differently.

➤ According to the memory systems view of dissociations, implicit and explicit memory tests rely on different memory systems, and thus are influenced by different variables. Implicit memory performance is thought to be based in the procedural memory system, and explicit memory performance is thought to be based in the declarative memory system.

G L O S S A R Y

accessibility: the degree to which a piece of information can be recalled, given certain retrieval cues (p. 225)

amnesia: memory loss due to brain damage (p. 210)

availability: whether or not information is actually stored in memory (p. 225)

context-dependency effects: the finding that, given a particular encoding context, memory is better when retrieval reinstates that context (p. 227)

declarative memory: the conscious forms of memory, such as retrieving memory for facts and events (p. 242)

distinctiveness: the degree to which information is distinguished from other information in memory (p. 217)

distributed repetition: repeated presentations that are spread out over time (p. 211)

elaboration: the degree to which information is well specified, described, and/or related to other information in memory (p. 216)

elaborative rehearsal: the formation of links between material to be remembered and information already stored in memory (p. 214)

enactment effect: the finding that people are better at remembering action phrases (e.g., "hammer the nail") if they enact the activity rather than simply read it (p. 222)

encoding: the processes involved in the acquisition of material (p. 209)

encoding specificity principle: states that the retrieval of information in memory will be effective to the degree that the cues present at retrieval match the information that was present at encoding (p. 226)

episodic memory: the memory for personally experienced events that include contextual elements (p. 207)

explicit (direct) memory tests: memory tests that involve the conscious recollection of some specific event or episode from the past (p. 210)

implicit (indirect) memory tests: memory tests in which successful performance does not depend on conscious recollection of some specific event or episode from the past (p. 210)

incidental learning: conditions in which a memory test is not expected (p. 214)

individual-item processing: the degree to which we process information in terms of *individual* characteristics; aided by conditions that lead to distinctive processing (p. 219)

intentional learning: conditions in which a memory test is expected (p. 214)

levels-of-processing theory: a theory emphasizing the notion that memory depends on how information is processed at encoding (p. 216)

long-term memory (LTM): the permanent store of information (p. 207)

maintenance rehearsal: mental practice that consists simply of repeating information over and over (p. 213)

massed repetition: repeated presentations that occur closely together in time (p. 211)

material-appropriate processing: notion that the type of processing that one should emphasize in studying material for later retention depends on the nature of the material (p. 219)

method of loci: a mnemonic technique that involves relating each item to be remembered to a location along a well-practiced route or set of locations (p. 220)

mnemonic techniques: memory improvement techniques (p. 220)

organization: the degree to which incoming information is, or can be, structured (p. 218)

picture-superiority effect: the finding that concepts are more likely to be remembered if they are presented as pictures rather than as words (p. 221)

primacy effect: the finding that items at the beginning of a list are remembered better than items presented in the middle of the list (p. 206)

priming: the benefit gained in performance from having previously seen a word (p. 238)

procedural memory: the nonconscious forms of memory, such as priming and the learning of skills and habits (p. 209)

prospective memory: the ability to remember the activities and plans one has to perform in the future (p. 223)

recall: an explicit memory test in which subjects must retrieve information given relatively little information (p. 213)

recency effect: the finding that items presented at the end of a list are remembered better than items presented in the middle of the list (p. 206)

recognition: an explicit memory test in which subjects must discriminate items previously presented from new items (p. 213)

rehearsal: mental practice (p. 213)

relational processing: the degree to which we process information in terms of interrelationships; aided to the degree that incoming information affords *organization* (p. 219)

remember-know paradigm: a recognition task requiring subjects to indicate whether they truly remember (i.e., consciously recollect) that an event occurred or whether they simply know that it did (p. 235)

repetition: the presentation of an item more than once (p. 211)

retrieval: the processes that lead to the reactivation of a memory (p. 209)

retrieval cues: reminders; information that assists in the reactivation of stored information (p. 225)

retrieval failure: forgetting that occurs due to a lack of appropriate retrieval cues (p. 225)

retrospective memory: memory for past events (p. 221)

self-initiated retrieval: unique feature of prospective memory; a person has to initiate the retrieval of a memory without any cue (i.e., they must "remember to remember") (p. 223)

self-reference effect: material that is related to the self tends to be well remembered (p. 221)

semantic memory: the knowledge or information about the world that does not include contextual elements (p. 207)

serial position effect: the finding that memory for words in a list depends on their relative position (p. 206)

spacing effect: the advantage of distributed repetitions over massed repetitions (p. 211)

storage: the retention of a memory representation (p. 209)

testing effect: the finding that periodic retrieval of information is an effective means of improving long-term memory for that information (p. 232)

transfer-appropriate processing: the degree to which the processing performed at encoding maps onto the processes required at retrieval (p. 217)

unconscious plagiarism: wrongly taking credit for an idea when in reality one is implicitly remembering an idea from another source (p. 237)

von Restorff phenomenon: the finding that information that stands out from its context tends to be well remembered (p. 217)

word-fragment completion: an implicit memory test in which fragmented words are presented for completion (p. 237)

word-stem completion: an implicit memory test requiring subjects to complete a three-letter stem with the first word that comes to mind (p. 237)

7

Memory Distortions

How reliable are eyewitnesses to crimes, and how much stock should a jury put in their testimony? How common is it that people are wrongfully convicted because of mistaken testimony of an eyewitness?

Have you ever had a disagreement with a friend about how some event played itself out? The two of you are in pretty much complete disagreement, and with equal confidence. Both of you can't be right. How can memories that seem so real be mistaken?

It may seem obvious that we forget, given the incredible volume of information that we encounter every day. Forgetting may be annoying, but it probably seems like no big deal. It isn't like we create memories completely out of thin air . . . or do we?

What happens to memories of traumatic or particularly painful experiences? Was Freud right? Do we manage to push memories of these experiences out of consciousness? Or are they impossible to get out of our minds? Can we forget things if we want to forget them?

One of the joys of having two memory researchers in the house is the fact that we each think our memories are better than the other's, which sets the stage for what we fondly call "memory fights." Memory fights highlight a fundamental principle of memory: it's not perfect; in fact, sometimes it's far from it. How we remember a person, place, or event depends on a host of factors, many of which we discussed in Chapter 6. Memory is not a simple process of rote retrieval or replay; rather, it's largely a matter of reconstruction.

We remember (or reconstruct) past events with the help of fragmentary information, our own expectations and biases, and sometimes those of others.

STOP *and* THINK!

RECONSTRUCTING (AND DISTORTING?)

After you've been out with at least two friends (i.e., studying, going to dinner, going to a party), engage them in a conversation about what happened. Ask a range of questions, such as the following:

- What happened, in chronological order?
- Who was wearing what?
- Who said what?
- What were the context-specific details (i.e., where and how were you all sitting, etc.)?
- What were any distinctive events that occurred?

Then answer these questions:

- How complete and clear were the memories?
- How confident did the rememberers seem about their recollections?
- How were the recollections of your friends similar? How were they different?
- Did you start any "memory fights"?

The material in this chapter may seem a bit hard to accept, perhaps even a little threatening. It's hard for us to acknowledge that something that seems so real and tangible—our own personal history—is actually a rather fragile reconstruction that is subject to a host of distortions. These so-called **memory distortions** have become a hot topic in memory research.

The Sins of Memory

Memory researcher Daniel Schacter puts an interesting spin on the processes by which memory fails, calling them the "seven sins of memory," which evokes an image of the biblical "seven deadly sins (Schacter, 2001)." Although the sins of memory may not be deadly, they certainly are frustrating. And as you'll see in our discussions of eyewitness memory and so-called recovered memories of child abuse, these "sins" can have tremendous ramifications. According to Schacter, the sins of memory include **transience,** or the loss of information from memory with the passage of time; **absentmindedness,** which refers to problems with the interface between attention and long-term memory; and **blocking,** which is a failure in retrieving information stored in long-term memory. Schacter classifies transience, absentmindedness, and blocking as *sins of omission*—failures to bring something to mind. Two sins of omission have already been discussed: absentmindedness—the culprit responsible for action slips (Chapter 4)—and transience—forgetting (Chapter 6). Blocking will be discussed in the context of knowledge retrieval from semantic memory (Chapter 9).

The remaining four sins of memory are *sins of commission;* all of them involve the presence of unwanted or inaccurate memories (Schacter, 2001). **Misattribution** refers to a memory that is ascribed to the wrong source; you thought one of your friends said something when actually another friend did. **Suggestibility** occurs when someone is led to a false recollection, perhaps through leading questions or others' suggestions. The memory sin of **bias** refers to the influence of who we are—our beliefs, expectations, and desires—on what we remember. Finally, **persistence** refers to the continued (but unwanted) automatic retrieval of memories that we'd just as soon forget. This sin will be discussed in Chapter 8 (autobiographical memory). In this chapter, we focus on the three other sins of commission—misattribution, suggestibility, and bias.

STOP *and* **THINK!**

CONFESSING YOUR SINS

Attempt to spot the seven sins of memory, as discussed by Schacter (2001). You could do this in one of two contexts:

1. As you're going through this chapter, identify the sins (a) as sins of omission or commission and (b) as one of the specific types discussed by Schacter.
2. Keep a journal of memory errors. Once you become aware of a memory failure, log it as either a sin of omission or commission and then as one of Schacter's seven sins. Take note of when you are likely to fall victim to each of these sins and if any patterns emerge.

A classic early investigation of reconstructive memory processes was conducted by Carmichael, Hogan, and Walters (1932). These investigators presented subjects with ambiguous sketches, each of which could sensibly be interpreted as one of two objects. In Figure 7.1, the first sketch could be interpreted as a broom or a rifle; the second as barbells or eyeglasses; the third as the numeral 4 or 7. The twist was that subjects were given different labels for the presented objects. Half of the subjects were told that the pictures were of a broom, barbells, and the number 4; the other half were given the alternative labels—gun, eyeglasses, and the number 7. Later, memory was tested; subjects were to draw the figures they had seen. The results revealed that the label had a striking effect on what subjects remembered. In spite of the fact that all subjects had seen identical sketches, their retrieval sketches were quite different, depending on the label they had received. Gone were the

Figure 7.1 Figures presented by Carmichael et al. (1932), along with subjects' reproductions, given different labels for the items.

From Carmichael, L., Hogan, H. P., & Walters, A. A. (1932). An experimental psychology of the effect of language on the reproduction of visually perceived form. *Journal of Experimental Psychology, 15,* 73–86.

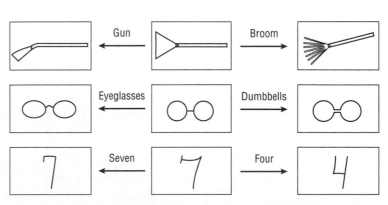

ambiguous-looking sketches that could be interpreted in one of two ways. Subjects' sketches depicted completely unambiguous renditions of the objects they had seen, renditions that were consistent with the encoded label. Subjects who were given the label "broom" sketched a broom; those who were given the label "gun" sketched a gun. The label biased the way the object was encoded and, as result, the way the memory was reconstructed.

An application of Carmichael and colleagues' results isn't hard to come by. Take the "memory fights" we just mentioned. Quite often, people disagree about some sequence of events because they have different labels (i.e., a biased view) for what happened or what was said. This (along with the results of the Carmichael study) is a clear example of the memory sin of bias (Schacter, 2001)—that is, when expectations and beliefs exert an undue influence on what is remembered.

STOP *and*THINK!

DRAWING FROM MEMORY

Try out the Carmichael and Hogan (1932) study on some acquaintances. Present each item on the list below. But for half of your subjects, present the picture with the left-hand label. For the other half, present the same pictures but with the right-hand label. After the list has been presented, have your subjects free recall the list in picture form. (It would be best if you could delay the test for as long as possible—at least 5 to 10 minutes, or days if possible.)

Verbal Labels	Stimulus Figures	Verbal Labels
curtains in a window		diamond in a rectangle
seven		four
ship's wheel		sun
hourglass		table
kidney bean		canoe
gun		broom
two		eight

Take a look at the pictures sketched by your subjects.

- How far did they deviate from the originals?
- Did the deviations reflect the bias implicit in the picture labels?

STOP *and* **REVIEW!**

1. Which of these is considered a memory "sin of omission"?
   a. absentmindedness
   b. misattribution
   c. persistence
   d. suggestibility

2. Suppose you had a strong memory of an event from childhood that you had seen many times in pictures. But then your parents informed you that you weren't even there when the event occurred. Explain what type of memory sin this might be and why.

➤ Memory is a reconstructive process that is subject to a host of distortions. The memory sins of omission refer to errors in which information is absent or forgotten. These include blocking (failures to bring something to mind), transience (the loss of information from memory), and absentmindedness (problems with the interface between attention and long-term memory).

➤ The memory sins of commission refer to the presence of unwanted or inaccurate memories and include misattribution (memory that is ascribed to the wrong source), suggestibility (leading someone to a false recollection), bias (the influence of who we are on what we remember), and persistence (continued automatic retrieval of unwanted memories).

Eyewitness Memory

Although the early work of Carmichael and colleagues (1932) served (in part) as a foundation for later work on the reconstructive nature of memory, the results lay relatively fallow due to the tremendous influence of behaviorism. The fragility of eyewitness memory was empirically investigated by some early psychologists, such as Hugo Munsterberg (often cited as one of the forefathers of applied psychology), but because behaviorism held sway, research on the fallibility of memory in this domain ebbed. As the "cognitive revolution" took firm hold, things began to change, as researchers began to discover the vagaries of eyewitness memory and the consequent implications. Consider cases of wrongful conviction, which are increasingly coming to light, given advances in DNA technology. Wells and Bradfield (1998) report that of the known cases in which people were wrongfully convicted by juries (and were later exonerated), mistaken eyewitness identification accounts for more of these wrongful convictions than all other causes combined. So it would seem that the concern over the accuracy of eyewitnesses' recollection is clearly well justified.

Countless investigations have been conducted to determine exactly which factors affect the accuracy of eyewitness recollection. One helpful way to organize the findings from this work is by using the tried-and-true distinction between encoding and retrieval introduced in Chapter 6. You'll recall that *encoding* refers to the processes by which information is acquired and stored—that is, the processes through which a memory representation is formed. *Retrieval* refers to the collection of processes that allow us to retrieve the memory representation, or perhaps more correctly, to *reconstruct* it. As stated in Chapter 6, distinguishing between encoding and retrieval factors is largely a matter of descriptive convenience; you can't really discuss one without considering the other. But for descriptive ease, we'll examine factors that are more intimately tied with encoding and storage, followed by those that are more likely to exert an influence on retrieval.

Encoding and Storage Factors

A number of factors influence eyewitness memory by impacting how the event is initially encoded. We'll term these *event-related factors*. Memories can also be profoundly affected (or infected, as it turns out) while in storage by what we'll term *post-event factors*.

Event-Related Factors.   As you can imagine, the accuracy of memory for a witnessed event—more specifically, a crime—depends upon a host of factors. Because these are relatively straightforward, we're not going to discuss them at length, but they do merit mention. The more obvious factors include the quality of the viewing conditions and the specific aspects of the event. Was it day or night? Were you a short or long distance away? What was your viewing angle? How long did the event last? Did you know you were witnessing a crime? Did the culprit wear a disguise? The influence of all of these factors is fairly intuitive. But the effects of the next variable we'll mention—emotional stress—isn't so intuitive.

Emotional Stress.   Our encoding of an event is also influenced by the emotional stress that is often a powerful component of a witnessed event. One way in which the effects of stress can manifest themselves is through a phenomenon termed **weapon focus.** The presence of a weapon can serve to focus one's attention quite narrowly, resulting in a lack of peripheral detail in the memory representation, although the central detail—the weapon—is remembered quite well (Cutler, Penrod, & Martens, 1987; Kramer, Buckhout, & Eugenio, 1989). In a review of the literature on the effects of emotional stress on eyewitness memory, Christiansen (1992) arrives at a conclusion consistent with this finding. Emotional stress narrows attention such that central details are processed more fully, at the expense of peripheral ones (Easterbrook, 1959). Emotional events also tend to be elaborated on later (i.e., as we "tell the story"), further benefitting memory for central details.

So the relationship between emotional stress and memory seems pretty straightforward: emotional stress helps memory for central details and harms memory for peripheral details. However, things are considerably more muddled than this when we consider the results of a more recent review by Deffenbacher, Bornstein, Penrod, and McGorty (2004) suggesting that a good deal of research indicates that stress harms the ability to remember crime-related details, including the central details. So what gives? Deffenbacher (1994) offers an intricate view, one that befits the complexity of emotion's effects. According to this view, cognitive and bodily reactions to stress can vary widely as a function of the event, and the precise nature of this reaction is critical for determining the quality of the resulting memory. One critical factor is the attentional mode that is present when the event occurs. The *arousal mode* is engaged when the observer is physiologically relaxed and the task requires simple perceptual intake. In this mode, novel, surprising, and informative events will receive the most attention, and will be remembered well. According to Deffenbacher et al. (2004), much of the research demonstrating the enhancement of central details in eyewitness memory would fit into this category.

The picture changes when we consider the second mode of attention, what Deffenbacher (1994) terms the *activation mode*. This mode is engaged when a person is experiencing high levels of both cognitive anxiety (worry) and physiological activation (bodily manifestations of anxiety). An interesting prediction from the model is a nonlinear relationship between physiological activation and memory under conditions of high cognitive anxiety. Under high levels of cognitive anxiety, increasing physiological arousal will lead to increasingly good memory, but only to a point. If physiological activation becomes too intense, it results in what Deffenbacher (1994) refers to as a catastrophic, discontinuous drop in performance. In other words, if someone is worried enough and is experiencing acute physiological arousal, their encoding of an event will suffer profoundly, even for the central details (Payne, Jackson, Ryan, Hoscheidt, Jacobs, & Nadel, 2006).

What would you remember if you were a witness?

Cross-Racial Identification.   One of the more intriguing factors that can influence eyewitness accuracy involves an interaction between the race of the observer and the race of the observed. Research on face recognition demonstrates that people are better at recognizing faces of their own race relative to faces of those of other races (Behrman & Davey, 2001; Bothwell, Brigham, & Malpass, 1989; Shapiro & Penrod, 1986). Although the effect of race has not been extensively studied in the context of eyewitness memory, some evidence indicates that race can be a factor in eyewitness identifications (e.g., Lindsay, Ross, Smith, & Flanagan, 1999; Shapiro & Penrod, 1986).

Post-Event Factors.   One fact about memory that will become increasingly obvious over the course of this chapter is that memory is not some fixed entity. Memory is a reconstructive *process* and therefore malleable. This process can be profoundly influenced by what are termed *post-event factors*—events that occur after the originally encoded event.

Misinformation.   The **misinformation effect** refers to the finding that misleading information presented between the encoding of an event and its subsequent recall influences a witness's memory. This corresponds to two of the memory sins discussed earlier. First, it reflects suggestibility—sometimes our recollections are unduly influenced by the prodding or expectations of others. Second, it's often an instance of misattribution, as witnesses get confused and misattribute misinformation to being part of the original event. By the way, this effect is also an example of a type of interference that we discussed in Chapter 4—retroactive interference. You'll recall that retroactive interference occurs when later information interferes with the ability to retain previously encoded information. This is precisely what happens with the misinformation effect. The misleading information works backward in time to distort memory for the original event.

The methodology used to investigate the misinformation effect is the granddaddy of paradigms for investigating memory distortion in eyewitness memory, having spurred over 30 years of research that is still going strong (see Loftus, 2005, for a review). This methodology is demonstrated in a classic study by Loftus, Miller, and Burns (1978). In the first phase of the study, subjects viewed a series of color slides depicting an auto accident. For half of the subjects, one of the slides depicted a car at a stop sign; for the other half, it was a yield sign. In the second phase of the experiment, 20 questions were asked about the slide sequence. Some subjects were asked, "Did another car pass the red Datsun when it stopped at the yield sign?" and others were asked, "Did another car pass the red Datsun when it stopped at the stop sign?" So half the subjects were misled, and the other half were given consistent information. A short time later, subjects were given pairs of slides, and were asked to pick the one that came from the original series. Subjects given consistent information in the questionnaire chose correctly 75% of the time; those who were misled by the questionnaire chose correctly only 40% of the time. Loftus et al. concluded that the misleading information altered subjects' versions of the events, leading to errant event recall.

STOP *and*THINK!

IMPLANT SOME MISINFORMATION

Be careful with this demonstration. See if you can implant a piece of misinformation. You'll want to take advantage of some of the memory principles you've read about. Pick an event that happened a while ago and one that you think your friends might be a little fuzzy on. Try and convince them of some detail that isn't true. (This, of course, assumes that you have a fairly good memory of the event in question!)

- Were you successful in your attempt?
- Why were you or why weren't you?
- What was it about the original event (and/or the misinformation) that made it particularly malleable or nonmalleable?

You may wonder whether small details such as those just discussed really matter; they seem fairly trivial. As Loftus (1979, 1992) notes, these details are anything but trivial and matter tremendously. A jury's perception of a defendant's guilt or innocence could turn on such a detail. If a witness remembers a mustache or a weapon when there was none, the wrong person may find themselves on the wrong side of prison bars.

Unconscious Transference.   Sometimes previous exposure to someone, either through a photo array in a police station or through a chance encounter, can make that person seem familiar at a later point, sometimes with near-tragic consequences. In her book *Witness for the Defense,* Loftus (1991) relates the story of Howard Haupt, who was charged with the kidnapping and murder of a child in Las Vegas. The crimes had occurred near a hotel where Haupt had been a guest. Several witnesses saw a man luring the boy from the hotel's video arcade and walking with him through the hotel. Haupt was wrongly identified as that man. Two explanations for this possible misidentification are possible. One explanation is termed photo bias, which we will discuss later. The other explanation is termed **unconscious transference,** which occurs when witnesses fail to distinguish between a target person (i.e., a criminal) and another person encountered at a different time whose face is also familiar (Loftus, 1976). This may have been at play in the Haupt case; witnesses did see Howard Haupt at the hotel where the crime took place. The witnesses may have seen his face as well as the kidnapper's face and assumed that the two people were one and the same. Therefore, when presented with his face at a later point in time, they identified Haupt as the kidnapper. (Due, in part, to Loftus's testimony assailing the reliability of the eyewitness identifications, Haupt was acquitted of the charges.)

An empirical demonstration of unconscious transference is seen in a study by Ross, Ceci, Dunning, and Toglia (experiment 1, 1994) in which subjects watched a film of teachers interacting with students. Near the end of the film, a female teacher, on a break, enters a cafeteria and is subsequently robbed by a male assailant. All subjects saw the same film, with one exception. In the transference condition, subjects saw a male bystander reading a book to children several minutes before the robbery. Subjects in the control condition did not see this bystander. After viewing the film, subjects were shown a lineup of five individuals—the bystander and four unfamiliar foils; subjects were asked whether the assailant was in the lineup and, if so, to identify him. The results from experiment 1 are presented in Table 7.1. Subjects in the transference condition were almost three times more likely than control subjects to identify the bystander as the assailant.

Table 7.1 Results of the Ross et al. (1994) Study

Condition	Experiment 1 Percentage of Subjects Choosing:		Experiment 2 Percentage of Subjects Choosing:	
	Bystander	Not in Lineup	Bystander	Not in Lineup
Transference	60.9	33.7	25.0	57.5
Control	21.9	64.4	21.9	64.4

From Ross, D. R., Ceci, S. J., Dunning, D., & Toglia, M. P. (1994). Unconscious transference and mistaken identity: When a witness misidentifies a familiar but innocent person. *Journal of Applied Psychology, 79,* 918–930. Copyright 1994 by American Psychological Association. Reprinted by permission.

In addition, control subjects were almost twice as likely as transference subjects to indicate that the assailant was not in the lineup.

Ross and colleagues contend that subjects in the transference condition believed that the assailant and the bystander were the same person seen at two different times. This assumption was supported by the fact that 66% of the transference subjects indicated that the assailant was seen in a context other than the cafeteria, and of those subjects, 95% indicated that he was seen reading a book to children (the bystander's activity). In contrast, only 4.1% of control subjects indicated that the assailant had been seen in a context other than the cafeteria. This seems to confirm that unconscious transference results from an inability to keep two memories separate from each other, resulting in a sort of "merged memory" in which the reading bystander and the assailant become one and the same. This is an example of the memory sin of misattribution—ascribing a memory to the wrong source (Schacter, 2001).

In experiment 2, Ross and colleagues directly tested this idea by telling transference subjects immediately before viewing the lineup that the assailant and the bystander were two different people. This instruction eliminated the unconscious transference effect. As you can see in Table 7.1, the results of experiment 2 indicate that transference and control subjects did not differ significantly in the percentage who indicated that the bystander was the culprit or in the percentage who indicated that the assailant was not in the lineup. Furthermore, the number of transference subjects who misidentified the bystander as the assailant was fewer in experiment 2 than in experiment 1. Therefore, it is possible to distinguish the two memories at the time of retrieval. However, the information needed for this distinction is not available in a real-world situation, and the likelihood of misidentifying an innocent bystander exists.

Photo Bias.   Perfect and Harris (2003) provide a specific example of unconscious transference known as **photo bias,** which refers to the increase in probability that a person will be recognized as the culprit due to previous exposure in a photo. Brown, Deffenbacher, and Sturgill (1977) were among the first to demonstrate this phenomenon. They had subjects view for 25 seconds each two groups of five individuals labeled "criminals"; they were told that later they might be required to identify the individuals. After viewing the criminals, subjects were exposed to 15 mug shot pictures. Some of the mug shots were of the original "criminals," and some were not. A week later, lineups were staged, and subjects had to determine whether each included one of the original 25 "criminals." There was a strong influence of mug shots on the selection of "noncriminals." Witnesses were more than twice as likely to incorrectly identify "noncriminals" who were included in the mug shots than "noncriminals" who were not viewed in these mug shots (20% vs. 8%). Obviously, presentation of the photos led subjects to have a vague familiarity with the faces that was then wrongly attributed to the original "crime."

Let's reconsider the Haupt case and its relationship to the phenomenon of photo bias. There is one fact that we left out when we told the story—at first, witnesses saw Haupt's picture in a photo array, yet he was never chosen as the culprit (Loftus, 1990). Subsequently, each witness was taken to Haupt's place of work; he was viewed in isolation and, hence, was the only choice. In this context he was identified by several witnesses as the man seen walking with the boy at the hotel months earlier. The problem with this identification should be obvious—witnesses had seen Haupt in the photo array; therefore, he was a familiar face. Their later recognition of him may have resulted from the misattribution of this familiarity—they decided that, because he was familiar, he must have been the person walking with the victim. This explanation is particularly compelling when you consider that no one identified him as the kidnapper in the original photo array.

Retrieval Factors

Eyewitness accuracy is not just a product of how events are encoded and stored. The way in which memory is queried also determines what will be remembered or, at least, what people are willing to report. Let's examine some of these factors.

Lineups.   Attempting to recall a witnessed event can be likened to a recall test. Little or nothing in the way of cues is presented, and the person must provide an accurate summary of what they witnessed. Attempting to identify which of several people committed a crime can be likened to a recognition test. When presented with a lineup of people (via either a photo array or a live presentation), a variety of factors can affect whether a choice is made and whether that choice is accurate. In other words, eyewitness identification is influenced by the specifics of the retrieval environment (for a review, see Wells & Olson, 2003).

Let's consider the four possible outcomes in a lineup situation. The first is an *identification failure*—the culprit (the person who actually committed the crime) is in the lineup, but the witness does not identify anyone in the lineup as the culprit. This is clearly a negative outcome, because the criminal goes back on the street. The second is a *correct rejection*—the culprit is not in the lineup, and the witness correctly states that the culprit is not there. The third is a *correct identification*—the culprit is in the lineup, and the witness correctly identifies the person. The fourth is an *incorrect identification*—a person other than the culprit is chosen from the lineup. This outcome is doubly negative and highly undesirable; the real criminal is still free, and the wrong person is accused of the crime.

The goal of a lineup is not to nab *someone;* the goal is to identify the person responsible for the crime. Put in the terms just discussed, lineups ought to be constructed in such a way as to maximize correct identifications and correct rejections and to minimize identification failures and incorrect identifications. Over the past two decades, a tremendous amount has been learned about the proper procedures for conducting lineups. These procedures are typically aimed at maximizing correct identifications (hence minimizing identification failures) and minimizing incorrect identifications (hence maximizing correct rejections).

Functional Size.   One way to assess the fairness of a lineup is to evaluate its **functional size** (Cutler & Penrod, 1995; Loftus, 1979). Imagine a lineup in which the suspect is 20 years old and rather seedy looking and the other five members are 30-something professionals in suits. Of course, the seedy individual will stick out like a guilty thumb. In this case, the lineup size is not really six; it's one. The functional size of a lineup is a reflection of the probability that any one person might be selected based just on how they look. To assess functional size, Wells and colleagues (1979) propose that one needs to look at nonwitnesses to the crime and who they choose from the lineup. If you think about it, someone who did not witness the crime should be equally likely to choose any of the people in the lineup as the culprit; the nonwitness is simply guessing.

In order to determine functional size, a simple formula is used: divide the number of nonwitnesses to a crime by the number of those nonwitnesses who choose the suspect. If there are four nonwitnesses and all of them pick the same suspect, the functional size of the lineup is 1 (4/4). This indicates an unfair lineup, because the same person is being chosen every time by individuals who didn't even witness the crime! The disproportionate rate at which the suspect was chosen could have been based only on the suspect's appearance, because a nonwitness has no other information on which to make the decision. To be a fair lineup, the functional size ought to be the same as the actual number of people in the lineup (4/1). All other things being equal, all members of the lineup should have an equal likelihood of being chosen.

Simultaneous vs. Sequential Lineups.

    A **simultaneous lineup** is what most people picture: lineup members are presented at the same time, and the witness must choose one. A **sequential lineup** presentation is the rarer case; lineup members are presented one at a time, and the witness must decide whether each of the lineup members is or is not the culprit. Investigations of both modes of presentation have indicated that sequential lineups are superior (Lindsay & Wells, 1985).

According to Wells (1993), sequential lineups are preferable to simultaneous ones due to the different strategies that the two invoke. Simultaneous lineups encourage witnesses to use a *relative judgment strategy* in which witnesses evaluate which of the lineup members most resembles the culprit they have in mind. Wells contends that this strategy encourages witnesses to pick someone. Sequential lineups, on the other hand, encourage an *absolute judgment strategy* in which witnesses are more likely to assess each individual in isolation, asking themselves, "Is this the one?" In addition to differences in judgment strategy employed, witnesses in a sequential lineup scenario are unaware of how many people are in the lineup; they never know if one more person might be coming and therefore will experience less pressure to pick someone. Also apparent are the effects that instructions can have on witnesses' choices or on their tendency to choose. Wells notes that when faced with a lineup, witnesses feel compelled to choose, increasing the chances of an incorrect identification. To combat this tendency, Wells suggests that witnesses be advised that the culprit may or may not be in the lineup.

Although research has borne out that sequential lineup procedures dramatically decrease the rate of false identification (Steblay, Dysart, Fulero, & Lindsay, 2001), there does appear to be a downside in that rates of identification in culprit-present lineups are also reduced. Ebbesen and Flowe (2002) contend that the reason for both of these outcomes is that sequential lineups raise the response criterion of the witness. You might remember the notion of response bias from our Chapter 3 discussion of perception. Response criterion basically refers to one's willingness to report the presence of a stimulus.

In this case, it refers to the willingness of the witness to pick someone. Ebbesen and Flowe's account is that sequential lineups cause an across-the-board conservative tendency. Witnesses are less likely to say yes when presented with a sequential lineup; this would have the effect of reducing both false identifications and correct identifications.

This analysis was supported by the results of a study by Meissner, Tredoux, Parker, and MacLin (2005). These investigators also employed a variation on the remember-know procedure discussed in Chapter 6 to assess the subjective experience associated with lineup identifications. Their results indicated that identifications from simultaneous lineups tended to be based more on feelings of familiarity rather than recollection, relative to identifications from sequential lineups. This is consistent with Wells's (1993) notion that identifications from simultaneous lineups tend to be based on a relative judgment, as witnesses attempt to pick the suspect who looks the most familiar.

In a review of sequential and simultaneous procedures, McQuiston-Surrett, Malpass, and Tredoux (2006) urge caution in rushing to a conclusion about which procedure is more appropriate. In their view, there needs to be more empirical research comparing the two procedures, as well as better theoretical accounts of the differences in identification patterns produced in simultaneous and sequential lineup procedures, before psychologists can advocate any particular identification procedure over another.

Lineup Distractors.   Finally, research indicates that the fairness of a lineup is also determined by how the distractors (i.e., the nonsuspects) are selected. Wells, Rydell, and Seelau (1993) compared lineups in which the distractors matched the appearance of the suspect to lineups in which the distractors matched a witness description of the culprit. Matching distractors in terms of suspect appearance has the potential to inadvertently provide information that witnesses may not have noticed, altering their memory for the culprit (e.g., "Gee, all of these people have a big nose; I didn't really notice, but I guess my mugger must have had a big nose"). In contrast, matching to a witness description of the culprit may allow for the exoneration of a nonculprit who has a noticeable feature that was not part of the description (e.g., "Well, I know it can't be that guy, because that guy has kind of a big nose; my mugger didn't have a big nose"). Consistent with this analysis, Wells and colleagues found that when lineup distractors were matched in terms of a culprit's description rather than the suspect's appearance, the correct identification rate increased and the incorrect identification rate decreased.

Eyewitness Confidence.

Witnesses who are extremely confident—who swear that their account is the way it happened—make compelling witnesses. Indeed, studies demonstrate that eyewitness confidence is a major factor in determining whether a witness has made an accurate identification (Wells, Olson, & Charman, 2002). But this begs an important question—is confidence a reliable indicator of memory accuracy? Here we revisit the concept of metacognition; are people good judges of what they know? A good deal of research demonstrates that the correlation between confidence and memory accuracy is rather weak. A review of the literature by Wells and Murray (1984) revealed the correlation to be only about 0.07. Clearly, the confidence with which a witness proclaims, "I'm sure that's the one who did it!" should be eyed with caution. Unfortunately, jurors are not always cautious in considering the testimony of eyewitnesses.

Juries tend to be swayed by confident eyewitnesses.

Research reveals that juries tend to overly believe witnesses, particularly confident ones (Cutler & Penrod, 1995). This exaggerated belief is even more disturbing in light of another finding—eyewitness confidence is malleable. When eyewitnesses are given confirmatory feedback about their eyewitness identification (e.g., "Yes, other people identified that person as well"), they become more confident about what they're reporting (e.g., Wells, Ferguson, & Lindsay, 1981; Wells & Luus, 1990).

As it turns out, however, the relationship between confidence and accuracy is quite complex. Certain variables *moderate* their relationship. It seems that sometimes, confidence *can be* a reliable indicator of accuracy. According to the **optimality hypothesis** (Deffenbacher, 1980), the relationship between confidence and accuracy is stronger to the degree that the encoding, storage, and retrieval of the event in question occurred under optimal conditions. For example, if a witness's viewing conditions were poor (e.g., dim lighting, poor viewing angle), then their confidence is not a good indicator of their memory accuracy; however, under better conditions (e.g., good lighting, clear view of the events), confidence is a reasonably good indicator of accuracy (e.g., Brigham, 1990; Cutler & Penrod, 1989).

Some have suggested that a related variable—speed of identification—might be a useful diagnostic in assessing eyewitness identification. Imagine the confident witness who sizes up the photo array or live lineup and, within just a few seconds, has made a confident choice. You might think this identification is more reliable than that of the witness who hems and haws and takes a much longer time to make their choice. Indeed, some research does point to the diagnosticity of identification time. For example, Dunning and Perretta (2002) suggest a "10–12 second rule"—that positive identifications made in that span of time typically turn out to be more accurate than ones made more quickly or more slowly. However, Weber, Brewer, Wells, Semmler, and Keast (2004) found the relationship to be much more variable, with the correct identification times ranging from 5 to 29 seconds. Their study revealed that the relationship between identification time and accuracy is so complex that it's probably of little practical use. However, Weber et al. did find an interesting combination of factors that proved highly diagnostic of correct identifications. It turns out that highly confident witnesses who make their identifications in about 10 seconds are strikingly accurate in their identifications. Information like this could prove useful to law enforcement personnel as they attempt to assess the accuracy of eyewitness identifications (Brewer & Wells, 2006).

Interview Techniques.   In Chapter 6, you learned that memory is critically dependent on the way in which memory is tested. Different results are obtained on recall and recognition tests and on tests of explicit and implicit memory. It should come as no surprise, then, that the way in which an eyewitness is "tested" (i.e., interviewed) has important ramifications for the completeness and accuracy of their report.

Hypnosis.   A popular assumption about memory is that everything is stored, and that given the right retrieval prompt or method, a memory will be "unlocked" and relayed accurately. You've already been presented with a good deal of evidence showing that this is simply not the case. A corollary to this common assumption is a belief that hypnosis can be used during retrieval as a way to reach and replay memories that are proving difficult to access. Research on hypnosis, however, provides no conclusive evidence that it reliably enhances memory (Smith, 1983). Hypnosis may lead to an increase in the amount of information reported, but this increase is both correct detail and fabricated detail (termed **confabulation**). The heightened suggestibility associated with hypnosis makes the rememberer more willing to label something as a memory; it also makes one highly susceptible to the suggestions of others. There are several deleterious consequences of this suggestibility. First, requests for further information may be met with compliance, even if the witness doesn't have anything else to report. Second, the suggestions to which the witness does respond may well become incorporated in their memory for the event (i.e., the misinformation effect; see Scoboria, Mazzoni, Kirsch, & Milling, 2002). Third, hypnosis often involves instructions to imagine the target event. As you'll read later, the simple act of imagining how events may have occurred can lead a person to be less certain whether they actually did (e.g., Hyman & Pentland, 1996). It's pretty much a consensus view that using hypnosis at retrieval is fraught with problems and should be avoided, particularly given that there's a better alternative.

The Cognitive Interview.   It's apparent that the reports and identifications offered by eyewitnesses can be distorted by a number of untoward influences. Concern over these influences led a group of researchers to develop the **cognitive interview technique** (Fisher & Geiselman, 1992). The cognitive interview has four primary features. First, there is an attempt to make the witness comfortable (e.g., by engaging in some relaxing and ice-breaking conversation at the beginning of the interview). Second, the witness is queried with *open-ended questions* (e.g., "Tell me what happened") that elicit answers with multiple pieces of information, rather than with *closed-ended questions* (e.g., "Where did the culprit put the money?") that elicit one specific piece of information and abbreviated answers. These latter types of questions are typical of police interviews. Third, the cognitive interview takes advantage of what we know about memory by implementing mnemonic instructions that can facilitate memory. For example, witnesses are encouraged to mentally reinstate the context of the encoded event and to try to recall the event from different perspectives and in different orders, using as many different retrieval pathways as possible (e.g., Anderson & Pichert, 1978). Both of these techniques take advantage of that tried-and-true principle from Chapter 6—encoding specificity (Tulving & Thomson, 1973). A fourth feature of the cognitive interview is allowing witnesses some freedom in exactly how they describe events (e.g., using sketches).

In many ways, the cognitive interview is like a hypnotic interview, but without the dangers of creating highly suggestible witnesses. For this reason, the cognitive interview has become the preferred technique (e.g., Wells, Malpass, Lindsay, Fisher, Turtle, & Fulero, 2000) and has met with good success. Compared to a standard police interview, the cognitive interview elicits anywhere from 35 to 75% more information, with no increase in incorrect responses (e.g., Kohnken, Milne, Memon, & Bull, 1999).

Witness Factors

Eyewitness memory doesn't vary just as a function of the event, or the conditions under which the event is experienced. It can also be influenced by characteristics of the person doing the encoding. One of the most thoroughly investigated of these witness factors is age.

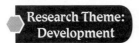

Children Eyewitnesses.   A fair amount of research on the topic of memory suggestibility and distortion has investigated these effects in children (e.g., Bruck & Ceci, 1997; Ceci & Bruck, 1993). The reliability of children's memories is of great concern when one considers the role that a child's recollection can play in investigations of child abuse. More often than not, the only people who know of the abuse are the perpetrator(s) and the victim(s). Given that the child is likely to be the only party who will cooperate with authorities in such investigations, the question of memory suggestibility is one of great importance. How accurate are children's memories for daily events, and for traumatic events? Are children more suggestible than adults? How can we tell when a child is relating accurate information from memory?

These questions came to the fore of cognitive developmental research when the 1980s and 1990s saw a number of high-profile cases in which allegations of child sexual abuse were made at a number of day-care centers across the country (e.g., the Little Rascals day-care center in North Carolina and the McMartin preschool in California). The allegations of abuse were based largely on the reports of children, often in response to direct questioning from parents and other authorities. Based on the records of these cases, there is good reason to believe that many of the allegations may have been false, produced through pressure, suggestive questioning, and the suggestible nature of the child witnesses. Given the potential dangers of relying on child witnesses in cases such as these, researchers redoubled their efforts to determine the factors that affect a child's recollections; the last 20 years have witnessed a tremendous amount of progress in this area.

Bruck and Ceci (1999; see also Bruck and Ceci, 2004) review some of the critical findings from studies of child suggestibility. One significant finding relates to **interviewer bias**—research evidence indicates that the accuracy of children's reports can be unduly influenced by interviewer beliefs about an event. Children seem to follow the lead of the interviewer and provide the information needed to support the interviewer's beliefs (e.g., Thompson, Clarke-Stewart, & LePore, 1997). Also, the style of questioning influences reporting accuracy. Children tend to be more accurate in answering open-ended questions (i.e., "Tell me what happened") than leading, closed-ended questions ("Tell me how you bumped your head") (Peterson & Bell, 1996). Sound familiar? The cognitive interview technique also advocates the use of open-ended questioning; it leads to better memory for adults, so it's not surprising that the same principle applies to children's recall as well.

Some believe that the pressures of reporting personal and embarrassing events such as sexual abuse may make the use of anatomically detailed dolls an effective interviewing aid. The reasoning seems sound—the use of dolls might make children more comfortable and allow them to overcome language and memory problems. Unfortunately, research indicates that the use of anatomically detailed dolls only creates more problems in reporting, particularly with younger children (Bruck, Ceci, & Francoeur, 2000). The use of dolls seems to be particularly suggestive if the interviewer uses leading questions. Bruck, Ceci, Francoeur, and Renick (1995) interviewed three- and four-year-old children who had undergone a medical examination; for some of the children, this included a routine genital exam. After the exam, children were given a doll and asked, "Show me how the doctor touched your genitals." Disturbingly, many of the children who had not been touched in the genital area nonetheless demonstrated such touching with the doll; and those who had been touched demonstrated extensive touching that had never taken place. Taken together, the findings reveal a host of suggestive influences on a child's memory. Importantly, Bruck and Ceci (1999, 2004) do point out that children can be accurate reporters of events if interviewed with caution, and without suggestive techniques.

Elderly Eyewitnesses.   Although not as much research has been conducted on eyewitnesses at the other end of the life span, there is a growing empirical literature on elderly adults as eyewitnesses. In Chapters 4 and 6, you read about some of the vagaries of cognitive processing and memory as we age, so it should come as no surprise that aging plays a role in the suggestibility of eyewitness memory. You may remember that elderly adults tend to perform more poorly, relative to younger adults, in situations that involve nonautomatic (i.e., controlled) processing, and self-initiated retrieval. Unfortunately, both of these conditions tend to be present in eyewitness memory situations, because these situations typically consist of effortful attempts to reconstruct a series of events. It also turns out that elderly adults have difficulty with another process critical to accurate remembering—the ability to pinpoint the source of an event (mentioned earlier in the context of unconscious transference). This leads elderly adults to be potentially suggestible witnesses, relative to younger adults (Hashtroudi, Johnson, & Chrosniak, 1989; Mueller-Johnson & Ceci, 2004). One encouraging finding is that the cognitive interview technique has been successful in improving the memory of elderly adults (Dornburg & McDaniel, 2006).

Research Theme: Development

An Applied Triumph

You may be amazed at the amount of information about eyewitness memory that's been amassed over the last 30 years, and what we've presented here is but a small snippet. You may also be wondering whether these research findings have had any systematic impact

To enhance accuracy of eyewitness memory, law enforcement officials should:

- Establish rapport with the witness
- Encourage the witness to volunteer information but not prompt the witness
- Ask open-ended questions but not ask leading questions
- Caution the witness against guessing
- Select the lineup fillers so that they fit the witness's description of the perpetrator
- Instruct witness that perpetrator may or may not be in lineup
- Avoid giving feedback to the witness after the lineup
- Use sequential, rather than simultaneous, lineups

Figure 7.2 Guidelines for the preservation of eyewitness memory.

Adapted from Wells, G. L., Malpass, R. S., Lindsay, R. C. L., Fisher, R. P., Turtle, J. W., & Fulero, S. M. (2000). From the lab to the police station: A successful application of eyewitness research. *American Psychologist, 55,* 581–598.

within the criminal justice system. In 1999, the U.S. Justice Department issued the first national guide for the collection and preservation of eyewitness evidence. As noted by Wells, Malpass, Lindsay, Fisher, Turtle, and Fulero (2000), psychological research (along with DNA-based exonerations and media pressure) played a large role in demonstrating the need for these guidelines and also provided the scientific foundation for their content. These guidelines (available for anyone to peruse) make many recommendations, some of which are listed in Figure 7.2. These guidelines seek to minimize leading eyewitnesses in their attempts to recall events and to ensure that lineup procedures maximize the probability of correct identifications while minimizing the probability of incorrect identifications.

STOP *and* **THINK!**

AVOIDING (MEMORY) SIN

Go to the following Web site (http://www.ncjrs.org/pdffiles1/nij/178240.pdf) and take a look at the new guidelines that psychologists helped put together. The guidelines are titled "Eyewitness Evidence: A Guide for Law Enforcement." Go through the guide and identify the contributions of experimental psychologists and how the contributions help to remedy some of the memory distortion problems discussed in this chapter.

STOP *and* **REVIEW!**

1. Describe the cross-racial identification effect.
2. Identify the post-event factors that can affect eyewitness accuracy.
3. The relationship between confidence and memory accuracy tends to be
   a. strong and positive.
   b. weak and positive.
   c. strong and negative.
   d. weak and negative.
4. What specific problem do the elderly have in reconstructing past events?

➤ Eyewitness testimony is fallible and is affected by many factors that operate at encoding/ storage, such as quality of viewing conditions and level of attention. The cross-racial identification effect refers to increased difficulty in discriminating among faces of another race relative to faces of one's own race. Emotional stress can narrow the focus of attention and lead to decreased recall of (particularly) peripheral details.

➤ A number of post-event factors can influence one's memory for an event. Exposure to misinformation increases the chances of misremembering. Memory for people we encounter can be altered by encounters with photos or other people. A number of retrieval factors influence eyewitness memory, especially issues surrounding lineups—how they are constructed, how the distractors are chosen, and the functional size of the lineup (each person must have an equal chance of being chosen by a nonwitness).

➤ Other retrieval factors include hypnosis, which can increase recall, but at the expense of increased confabulation. A high level of confidence turns out to be, at best, a relatively weak indicator of memory accuracy; however, it's a better predictor if viewing conditions are optimal. The cognitive interview technique implements principles of memory to enhance witness recall and minimize inaccuracy.

➤ Subject factors (i.e., age) can be influential in determining memory accuracy. Children are more suggestible than adults but can be reliable witnesses if interviewed without biased or leading questions. Elderly eyewitnesses are also suggestible, and seem to have particular trouble pinpointing the source of an event.

Illusory Memories

Research investigating the vagaries of eyewitness testimony leaves little doubt about the fragile nature of our reconstructions of previous events. It doesn't take much to tweak your memory for an event so that you remember seeing a Sprite can instead of a Coke can. Although this may seem somewhat disconcerting, maybe it's not surprising. But what may come as a surprise is the ease with which we can create a memory out of thin air.

Simple Events

Sometimes—more often than you might think—people can remember something that flat out did not happen. An ever-growing body of evidence studying the phenomenon of **illusory memory** (or **memory illusions** or **false memories**) has generally taken one of two basic tacks: one is a laboratory paradigm employing the basic list-learning approach discussed in Chapter 6. The other, partly in response to concerns of ecological validity, attempts to determine whether illusory memories can occur for everyday events like getting lost at a shopping mall. Let's look at the research from the laboratory paradigm.

The Deese-Roediger-McDermott (DRM) Paradigm.   Much of the recent focus on memory illusions stems from an investigation conducted by Roediger and McDermott (1995). These investigators scoured the periodical stacks in the library and then blew the dust off of a 1959 study by Deese, the subject of which was "particular verbal intrusions in list recall"—in other words, remembering words that had not occurred (i.e., intrusions) in presented lists. Subjects saw lists of related words like *doze, rest,* and *snore* that all related to

Rough	Sleep	Slow	Soft
smooth	bed	fast	hard
bumpy	rest	lethargic	light
road	awake	stop	pillow
tough	tired	listless	plush
sandpaper	dream	snail	loud
jagged	wake	cautious	cotton
ready	snooze	delay	fur
coarse	blanket	traffic	touch
uneven	doze	turtle	fluffy
riders	slumber	hesitant	feather
rugged	snore	speed	furry
sand	nap	quick	downy
boards	peace	sluggish	kitten
ground	yawn	wait	skin
gravel	drowsy	molasses	tender

Figure 7.3 Themed lists used in the illusory memory study of Roediger and McDermott (1995).

From Roediger, H. L., & McDermott, K. B. (1995). Creating false memories: Remembering words not presented in lists. *Journal of Experimental Psychology: Learning, Memory, and Cognition, 21,* 803–814. Copyright 1995 by the American Psychological Association. Reprinted by permission.

a theme word—in this case, *sleep*. But the theme word was never presented. In spite of this, it was often "remembered" by subjects. Does this effect sound familiar? In our discussion of prototypes in Chapter 5, we reviewed a study by Posner, Goldsmith, and Welton (1967) that bears a striking resemblance to the Deese study. In the Posner study, subjects were presented with dot patterns that were statistically generated distortions of a prototype. The parallel in the Deese study was words related to a particular theme. In the study by Posner and colleagues, the prototype itself was never presented, just as the theme word was never presented in the Deese study. In both studies subjects tended to confidently confirm that they had seen the never-presented item. In the Posner and colleagues study, this was the prototype dot pattern; in the Deese study, it was the never-presented theme word.

Roediger and McDermott (1995) replicated and extended the Deese study in an attempt to illuminate the nature of illusory memories. They adapted the Deese procedure in order to investigate false recognition as well as false recall. In experiment 2, all subjects were presented with a series of 15-word themed lists (a sample of the lists is presented in Figure 7.3), followed by an immediate test of recall. After all lists had been presented, subjects were given a recognition test that included the presented items and, more important, the nonpresented theme word for each of the lists. The recall and recognition results are presented in Figure 7.4. As you can see, illusory memories were quite common; the theme word was falsely recalled nearly half the time. Even more striking are the recognition results (the first two bars on the second graph); the theme word was falsely recognized at a level equivalent to correct recognition!

STOP *and* THINK!

ILLUSORY MEMORIES

Recruit some of your friends and give them the lists in Figure 7.3 (taken from Roediger & McDermott, 1995). You can either read the lists (without reading the theme word, of course) or present each of the items on separate index cards. After you've presented each of the lists, have your subjects recall all of the items. Take note of how often they recalled the themed word (i.e., how many illusory memories occurred). Also note how the number of theme word intrusions compares with other types of intrusions.

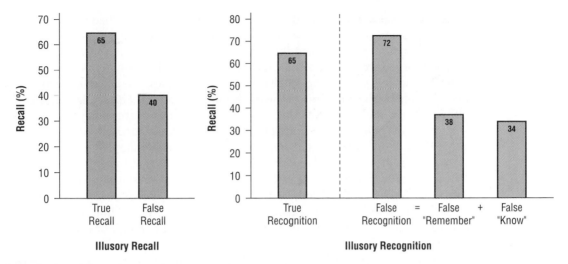

Figure 7.4 Results from Roediger and McDermott (1995).

From Roediger, H. L., & McDermott, K. B. (1995). Creating false memories: Remembering words not presented in lists. *Journal of Experimental Psychology: Learning, Memory, and Cognition, 21,* 803–814. Copyright 1995 by the American Psychological Association. Reprinted by permission.

Roediger and McDermott (1995) were also interested in investigating the *metamemory* accompanying these false memories—that is, a person's phenomenological experience when recognizing a word that has not occurred. To do this they used the remember-know judgment procedure discussed in Chapter 6. Recall that in this procedure, subjects are given an extra judgment task if they recognize an item as previously shown. After this decision, they must judge whether they remembered the occurrence of the item (complete with contextual details) or simply knew that the item occurred (but could recall no details of its presentation). Look again at Figure 7.4 (the last two bars on the second graph). Roediger and McDermott found that false recognition often was not simply a case of misattributed familiarity of the theme word. On more than half of the trials, subjects remembered (i.e., consciously recollected) that the word had occurred, when it actually had not. In other words, they had created a fairly detailed memory of the word's occurrence. Since this initial investigation, the basic list-learning illusory memory effect has been obtained using a wide array of conditions (see Roediger & Gallo, 2004, for a review and synthesis).

The finding that people can have vivid, recollective memories for an event that didn't happen is striking. Lampinen, Meier, Arnal, and Leding (2005) suggest that these vivid but mistaken memories are the result of a process they term *content borrowing*. Let's take a look at how this account explains the high proportion of "remembered false memories." According to this account, when subjects encounter the critical theme word, they have a strong sense of familiarity due to having seen the list of associates. This sense of familiarity leads to a search of episodic memory for evidence that would corroborate the theme word's appearance. During this search, details of the presentation of the actual list items can be mistakenly interpreted as evidence that the theme word had been presented. In other words, *content* is *borrowed* from the memory of another item's occurrence.

Lampinen et al. (2005) tested the notion of content borrowing by "borrowing" a tried-and-true research method from the domain of problem solving. As you'll see in Chapter 11, one way of assessing problem-solving techniques is to ask subjects to "think out loud" while they're attempting to work through a problem. This lends some insight into the strategies they might be using. Well, in a way, memory *is* problem solving, as we attempt to figure out whether something actually happened or not. Lampinen et al. employed the think-out-loud technique, asking subjects to supply verbal protocols (reports of what they were thinking) during encoding and retrieval as they partook in the DRM paradigm. In this way, the researchers could assess the basis on which subjects were making their recognition decisions, and evaluate whether content borrowing was going on. They provide the following example: One subject when encoding the word *sugar* noted that sugar was "fattening, but good." Then, during the recognition test, they were faced with the critical nonpresented lure *sweet*. The subject indicated that the word *sweet* had been presented on the list and noted that "I remember liking sweets but thinking they are going to make me fat." Apparently, the thought that had accompanied *sugar* was "borrowed" as evidence for the occurrence of the word *sweet*.

Their results supported the hypothesis—more than half of the recognition judgments made by subjects were accompanied by reports indicating that they were borrowing content from the encoding of other list items, as indicated by the think-out-loud protocols provided at encoding. Apparently, when we falsely remember, we are quite good at convincing ourselves of the veracity of our recollective feeling.

> **Research Theme: Neuroscience**

Neural Processing and False Memories.   Given that research into memory illusions is currently a hot topic, you shouldn't be surprised that it's recently been wedded to another hot topic—cognitive neuroscience. Over the last decade, researchers have been exploring the neural correlates and substrates of false remembering. Fabiani, Stadler, and Wessels (2000) provide some intriguing evidence that while our behavior and our judgment may be fooled by the presentation of a new but highly familiar item, our brain isn't. Apparently, brain activity during true and false recognition reveals some telltale differences. Real experiences seem to leave a "sensory signature" that can be used to differentiate between true and false memories.

Fabiani et al. begin with the assumption (as do other cognitive neuroscientists) that retrieval of information from memory involves the reactivation of the sensory information that was present at encoding. Because false memories are not associated with a sensory event (after all, they didn't occur), this reactivation cannot occur. Therefore, differences in brain activity between true and false memories should be evident in regions of the brain associated with the sensory experience of encoding the event. Previous research by Gratton, Corballis, and Jain (1997) revealed a potential way to pick up on these differences. In this study, Gratton et al. found that when a stimulus was encoded predominantly by one hemisphere of the brain, the ERP (event-related potential) response evoked by the stimulus during recognition was larger on that same side of the brain. In other words, if the word was predominantly encoded by the left hemisphere at study, then a stronger ERP response occurred in the left hemisphere during recognition.

Fabiani et al. (2000) applied this reasoning to true and false recognition and the ERP responses associated with each. In the study phase, list items from the laboratory-based illusory memory paradigm were presented to subjects. All words from a given associative list (e.g., the *sleep* list) were presented to the left or right of a fixation point (which meant they were processed primarily by the right or the left hemisphere, respectively). The encoding phase was followed by a recognition phase in which words were shown in the center of the display and ERP responses were recorded. Subjects were to judge whether each item was *old* or *new*. The recognition list included words presented earlier, the theme words, and unrelated control words that had not been presented earlier.

As is typically the case in investigations of illusory memory, subjects demonstrated high levels of false recognition; theme words were called *old* as frequently as were presented items. More importantly, the ERP responses differentiated between true and false recognition. ERP responses for the recognition of words that had actually been presented were lateralized; that is, a greater ERP response occurred in the hemisphere that had encoded the word than in the hemisphere that had not encoded it. No such differentiation was found in the ERP responses associated with false recognition. In those cases, the pattern of ERP responses was the same in both hemispheres. Fabiani et al. conclude that although people often can't distinguish between true and false memories in terms of conscious decisions (i.e., a recognition judgment), brain activity does yield some telltale signs that allow for this discrimination. Such "signatures" of false remembering have been obtained in a host of studies since (e.g., Bar & Aminoff, 2003; Okado & Stark, 2005; Slotnick & Schacter, 2004).

Complex Events

So it seems that we can be convinced that a single word was presented on a list when in reality it was never presented. Big deal! The events we experience in everyday life are more complex than a simple list of words. Surely we can't be convinced that entire life episodes occurred when in fact they didn't—or can we? As it turns out, false recall and recognition are not limited to remembering a single word after presentation of its associates. Recently, researchers have been able to induce subjects into falsely remembering entire complex events that are as detailed in some cases as an authentic memory.

Memory Implantation.   One of the first investigations to demonstrate such whole-sale false remembering was conducted by Loftus and Pickrell (1995). These investigators set out to determine whether they could induce subjects to completely fabricate a memory. The subjects were misled a bit; the study was ostensibly an investigation of childhood memories. With the help of a family member, the investigators discovered three actual experiences for which the subjects were likely to have genuine memories. The twist was that a fabricated experience (getting lost in a shopping mall) was added. The subjects were interviewed about all four events (three authentic, one not) and asked to write about the events in as much detail as they could remember. They then were interviewed twice about each of the events over the subsequent two weeks. During these interviews, family members "played along" with the researchers, attempting to draw out details about each of the events.

Have you ever been lost in a shopping mall? Are you sure?

Most of the time, subjects correctly reported that they recalled nothing about the fabricated event. But a significant proportion (25%) of the 24 subjects generated a false memory. Subjects' confidence in these memories and their level of detail wasn't quite as high as it was for memories of authentic events, but still, the memories were pretty convincing. How could an event that didn't happen become a fairly detailed and confidently held memory? Loftus, Feldman, and Dashiell (1995) offer some possibilities. Perhaps, unbeknownst to the family members, the person really had been lost, and the memory was authentic. A more likely possibility is that prompting and probing led subjects to (implicitly) use a "getting lost" schema in imagining what it must have been like. Combining this schematic information with specific information about known locations (e.g., a local mall) could lead to a fairly detailed, but false, memory episode.

Routes to False Memory.   It should be getting increasingly clear that it's pretty easy to manipulate memory. Have you ever wondered whether something happened or you only imagined it? Have seeing pictures or hearing stories about some event compromised your confidence that your memory of the event is actually your memory for the event, rather than your memory for the picture or story?

Imagination.   As we pointed out in our earlier discussion of hypnosis, it turns out that simply imagining that an event occurred increases the likelihood of someone remembering that it really did occur. This phenomenon has been termed **imagination**

Critical Events Presented to Participants

1. Got in trouble for calling 911
2. Had to go to the emergency room late at night
3. Found a $10 bill in a parking lot
4. Won a stuffed animal at a carnival game
5. Gave someone a haircut
6. Had a lifeguard pull you out of the water
7. Got stuck in a tree and had to have someone help you down
8. Broke a window with your hand

Figure 7.5 Have any of these events happened to you? Are you sure?

From Garry, M., Manning, C. G., Loftus, E. F., & Sherman, S. J. (1996). Imagination inflation: Imagining a childhood event inflates confidence that it occurred. *Psychonomic Bulletin and Review, 3,* 208–214. Reprinted by permission of the Psychonomic Society, Inc.

inflation: the finding that mental simulation of an event leads to an increase in belief that the event may have actually occurred.

One of the first studies to demonstrate this phenomenon was conducted by Garry, Manning, Loftus, and Sherman (1996). These investigators employed a three-stage procedure to demonstrate the memorial power of imagination. First, subjects were presented with events and were asked to rate the likelihood that these events had happened to them as children (see Figure 7.5). Two weeks later, subjects were asked to imagine that some of the low-likelihood events had really happened and to supply some detail about how the event might have played itself out. Finally, in a clever twist designed to get subjects to rate the childhood events again, the experimenters acted panicked and explained to the subjects that they had lost their original ratings. This allowed for a comparison of estimated event likelihood both pre- and post-imagination. This comparison yielded strong evidence of imagination inflation. When subjects rated the events for a second time, their ratings of event likelihood went up (i.e., inflated), but only for the imagined events.

Imagination inflation is a subtle effect; imagining how a fictional event could have happened makes one a little less certain that it didn't happen. This effect demonstrates that simply imagining an event is enough to plant the seed of a memory. One interpretation of the findings is that when subjects encountered the event in the second rating session, the events they had imagined seemed more familiar. However, this familiarity was misattributed to the possibility of a remote childhood memory rather than to the imagination session. In other words, subjects failed to pin down the source of the familiarity. As you're about to see, failure to ascertain correctly the source of an event memory lies at the heart of memory distortion.

Pictures and Stories. Two cherished practices for reminiscing about past events are looking over photographs and telling stories. Your hunch may be that these can have the same contaminating effect on later memory that imagination does. That hunch would be correct.

Lindsay, Hagen, Read, Wade, and Garry (2004) were interested in the effects on false remembering of viewing photographs. Their investigation involved a bit of an elaborate setup, similar to the Loftus and Pickrell (1995) study. Parents of the college student subjects (unbeknownst to the subjects themselves) were interviewed and asked to give accounts of two real events (from different grades in elementary school) that had involved their children. They were also asked to provide their child's school picture from the same years as the events they recounted.

Then it was the now-grown children's turn to participate. The experimenter read each of the parent-provided stories, along with a pseudo-event that had never happened (and the fact that it had never happened was verified by the parents). Half of the subjects were given the corresponding class picture before the story was read and were instructed to recall as much as they could, using mental reinstatement of context and imagery exercises. After this procedure, subjects made a number of ratings including the degree to which their memory experience resembled reliving the event and their confidence that the event really occurred. At the end of the session, subjects were told that the remainder of the experiment would focus on their ability to recall the oldest of the three memories (which happened to be the pseudo-event). They were encouraged to think about it using the procedures that the experimenters had taught them, and were given copies of the narrative (and the photo, for those in the photo condition) to assist in their recall. Four days later, they were brought back to the lab and were asked to recount the story of the pseudo-event and to make the same ratings.

Both interview sessions were tape-recorded and transcribed, and the transcriptions were coded by observers blind to the photo/no-photo manipulation. They were looking for evidence that subjects were experiencing actual full-fledged memories for the pseudo-event, fragmented images of the pseudo-event, or no memories or images for the pseudo-event. The judges placed each recall of the pseudo-event into one of these three categories based on their review of the transcript. The results of this analysis are presented in Figure 7.6. As you can see, the proportion of subjects reporting an actual memory was over twice as great in the photo condition, relative to the no-photo condition at immediate recall. After four days of imagining and looking at the photo, this difference became much more pronounced—the proportion of subjects in the photo condition reporting an actual memory was nearly three times the proportion in the no-photo condition! In fact, nearly two-thirds of the subjects in the photo condition reported having a memory of the pseudo-event! The ratings gathered from subjects converged with these data, confirming the memory-inducing power of simply viewing a class photograph.

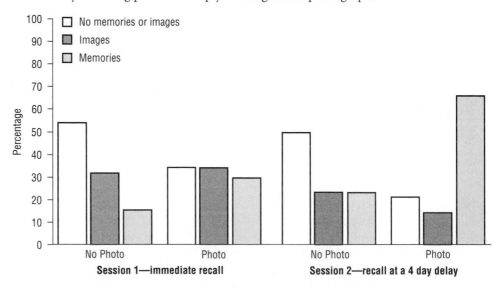

Figure 7.6 Results of the Lindsay, Hagen, Read, Wade, and Garry (2004) study.

Adapted from Lindsay, D. S., Hagen, L., Read, J. D., Wade, K. A., Garry, M. (2004). True photographs and false memories. *Psychological Science, 15*(3), 149–154. Published by Blackwell.

Which do you think would be more likely to induce a false memory—a photograph or a story? A study by Garry and Wade (2005) provided a direct comparison of these two conditions. They used a procedure similar to the one used by Lindsay et al. (2004), repeatedly interviewing subjects about recall of a few real events and a fictitious event. They supplemented these interviews and subject recall with either narrative descriptions (i.e., stories) or (doctored) photographs depicting the fictitious event. Their results were counterintuitive—narratives were actually much more likely to induce false memories than were photographs. Garry and Wayne suggest that narratives may be more effective in eliciting false memories because of their story-like nature. We tend to remember in story-like episodes rather than in momentary snapshots.

A Constructive Memory Framework

Dodson and Schacter (2001a) map out five stages necessary for the accurate encoding and retrieval of a memory—termed a *constructive memory framework*. Two of these processes characterize the encoding of an event. First, a *feature-binding process* occurs: all of the components of the encoded event—including the sights, the sounds, the people, and what they said—must somehow cohere into a unitized memory representation. Failure to bind the elements of an episode because of stress, emotion, lack of attention, or some other factor will result in disembodied memory fragments "floating around." Because of the disembodied nature of these fragments, their source is unclear. Second, the bound episodes must be kept separate from one another (*pattern separation*); otherwise, you'll confuse the sources of events. For example, if you repeatedly engage in the same activities or interact with the same friends at the same place, memory for these episodes will be difficult to separate; there are not enough unique features to differentiate the memories. Eventually, you may have just a memory of what generally happens when you and your friends go to your favorite hangout rather than a detailed memory of each occasion.

Three of the processes in the constructive memory framework operate at retrieval. Retrieval requires the use of a cue to get to the right memory—a process termed *focusing* (Norman & Schacter, 1996). A general retrieval cue like "hanging out with friends in the student union" wouldn't be very useful, because it fails to focus the memory search onto a unique episode. Something more distinctive about a particular episode (i.e., "the time the server spilled a cup of coffee on me") would better focus the memory search and hence serve as a more useful cue. The next process, called *pattern completion,* involves the successful reconstruction of the product from this focused search. But retrieval doesn't end here. After a pattern has been completed, a decision must be made. This stage, labeled *criterion setting,* involves discriminating true experiences from imagined experiences (i.e., "Did this really happen, or did I just imagine it?").

In order to decide whether a memory is the product of encoding an actual event or an imagined event, people rely on a number of factors, such as whether the memory includes perceptual detail or semantic vividness—in other words, how fully fleshed out the memory is. The more perceptually salient the memory is, the more likely it will be judged a true memory rather than an imagined memory. Criterion setting as the source of memory errors is evident in the effects of hypnosis on memory. The effects of hypnosis occur at retrieval, as the rememberer lowers the criterion for labeling a memory as valid. In hypnosis, criterion setting is influenced by the highly suggestible state of the rememberer.

The Importance of Source Monitoring.   The constructive memory framework highlights the importance of keeping memories (i.e., the source of each memory) differentiated from one another. Johnson (1988) characterizes **source monitoring** (the process of correctly identifying the source of remembered information) as a series of decisions. First, we must engage in **reality monitoring**—attributing the experienced memory to either a perceived external event or an internally generated event (i.e., event or imagination). If the memory is attributed to an externally perceived event, the source of the event must be determined ("Did I hear this in class? On the news? From a friend?"). The inability to distinguish between the sources of event memories is termed **source confusion** and represents a failure of the source-monitoring process. Another way of putting it is that we often *misattribute* our memories to incorrect sources. Some researchers (e.g., Johnson, Nolde, & Leonardis, 1996) go so far as to suggest that all memory errors (except for errors of omission) stem from source confusion. Indeed, confusion over the source of memories has been a recurrent theme in this chapter.

Many, if not most, of the problems in eyewitness memory are instances of source confusion. Let's reexamine two encoding factors—the misinformation effect and unconscious transference—in light of the notion of source confusion. After exposure to misinformation, witnesses fail to distinguish between the source of the misinformation and the source of the actual memory, blending them into one representation. The same blending process occurs in unconscious transference; a bystander and a culprit are assumed to be the same person due to a failure to remember the source of the encounters.

The illusory memories induced in laboratory experiments indicate a failure in the reality-monitoring phase of the source-monitoring process. Subjects fail to distinguish the internally generated target word (e.g., *sleep*) from the externally derived perceptual events (seeing the words *doze, rest, snore,* etc.). As Roediger and McDermott (1995) note, this failure is somewhat surprising, given that the illusory memories and the true memories differ in terms of the perceptual information they offer. The representations underlying illusory memories offer little or nothing in the way of perceptual characteristics, and so should be accurately labeled as "internally generated" and hence false. But source confusion remains, and illusory memories occur.

The effects of imagination, photos, and stories provide further examples of source memory confusion. As we noted in our discussion of the Garry et al. (1996) study, subjects became a little less sure about the nonoccurrence of a fictional event. This may have been because imagined events seem to share many of the characteristics of remote memories (Johnson, Foley, Suengas, & Raye, 1988). Both are fairly diffuse, making it difficult to distinguish between them (Garry et al., 1996) to arrive at the correct reality-monitoring decision. This problem in reality monitoring made subjects more willing to entertain the possibility that the fictional event was real. The same reasoning can be applied to the effects of narrative and photographs. These devices lead to quite vivid imaginings of events, even providing precise detail from an external source (as opposed to simply an internal simulation of the event). Upon repeated recall, it becomes increasingly difficult to distinguish between memories of the narrative or photo and memories of the event.

Enhancing Source Monitoring.   If source confusion is at the root of illusory memories, then enhancing source monitoring should serve to reduce them. This was the basic idea underlying a study by Hicks and Marsh (1999). They reasoned that if the source of the memories was a salient aspect of the encoding episode, then the memory representations would have complete and distinctive information regarding their source. In this context a potentially false memory would be scrutinized more closely because it would lack this distinctive source information and consequently would be less likely to be judged a true memory.

In order to make source information more salient, the investigators had subjects encode themed lists in one of two ways. In the two-source condition, half of the words in each list were spoken by the experimenter, while the other half were visually presented and followed by subject generation. (Subjects were to rearrange two letters: frgo—frog.) The source information in this condition was very distinct; one source was auditory and relatively passive (listening), while the other was visual and relatively active (generating). Therefore, false recall was expected to be low. In the one-source condition, the items on each list were read by the experimenter. Therefore, false recall was expected to be high due to the lack of distinctive source information. The results of the study are presented in Figure 7.7. As you can see, the level of false recall was quite high in the one-source condition. But in the two-source condition, false recall was reduced by nearly half. Sensitizing subjects to source by making it a salient dimension at encoding made it easier for subjects to use source information at retrieval. As a result, memories for nonpresented words were scrutinized more closely, and a lack of source information was interpreted as evidence that the item had not occurred.

In the same spirit, Dodson and Schacter (2001a) propose that false memories can be reduced by using what they term a **distinctiveness heuristic.** Basically, this is a retrieval strategy that's based on metamemory—people's knowledge of what a real memory should be like. If memories lack certain distinctive information that a rememberer assumes the memory ought to have, then the event is judged as new. This heuristic would come into play at the final stage of the Dodson and Schacter (2001b) constructive memory framework—criterion setting, or the process whereby we assess whether there's enough evidence of actual occurrence to label an event a memory.

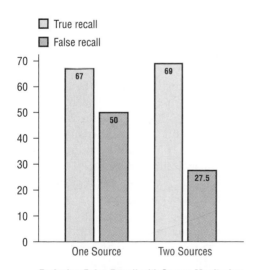

Reducing False Recall with Source Monitoring

Figure 7.7 Results from the Hicks and Marsh study (1999).

From Hicks, M., & Marsh, J. (1999). Attempts to reduce the incidence of false recall with source monitoring. *Journal of Experimental Psychology: Learning, Memory, and Cognition, 25,* 1195–1209. Copyright 1999 by the American Psychological Society. Reprinted by permission.

The reduction in false remembering shown by Hicks and Marsh (1999) is consistent with this view. When subjects had distinctive information related to source (two-source condition), false remembering was reduced. Also, Dodson and Schacter (2000b) provide additional evidence, comparing illusory remembering in conditions where subjects said words aloud or when they simply listened to the words. False remembering was less pronounced in the "say aloud" condition. According to the investigators, subjects in the "say aloud" condition had a higher criterion for judging an event as old at retrieval, relative to those who simply heard the words. Subjects expected to remember having said the words, and if this information was not part of the memory, the event was judged to be new. Although the distinctiveness heuristic may be effective in reducing illusory recall, it is far from being a panacea; as you've read, even illusory memories can include vivid detail that would lead one to judge the event as real. Nevertheless, the distinctiveness heuristic has proved to be an effective aid to avoiding false recall in a variety of empirical settings (e.g., Dodson & Hedge, 2005; Thomas & Sommers, 2005).

Social Influences and Constructive Remembering

Studies of illusory memories and imagination inflation involve compliance; subjects are asked to imagine events that occurred, complete with the requisite detail. In some studies, family members are recruited to help "sell" the story. These conclusions point to another source of memory errors—the social context in which remembering occurs. Although this may seem self-evident to the layperson who has had plenty of experience reminiscing with friends, memory research has just recently begun to reflect the fact that remembering (and misremembering) is quite often a social enterprise (e.g., Weldon, 2000).

Roediger, Meade, and Bergman (2001) found evidence for what they term the **social contagion effect.** The basic idea is that our memories can be "infected" by the memories of others. In this study, pairs of subjects were presented with household scenes (e.g., a kitchen). In the collaborative recall condition, members of the pair took turns recalling items from the scene. One subject was actually a confederate of the experimenter and deliberately engaged in false recall of several items. After the joint recall session, the non-confederate subject was tested alone and asked to recall as accurately as possible all of the items they had seen across all of the scenes. In the control condition, the subjects never participated in the collaborative recall; they recalled the items in isolation.

The results of the isolated recall provide clear evidence of infection; false recall was nearly four times greater in the collaborative recall condition relative to a control condition. Additionally, the social contagion effect was stronger when the confederate falsely remembered items that were consistent with the presented scenes (e.g., a hair dryer in a bathroom) than when they were inconsistent (e.g., a toaster in a bathroom). The finding fits well with the idea that providing distinctive source information reduces illusory memories. Think about it: Wouldn't you be likely to remember something as strange as a toaster in a bathroom? If subjects were unable to access this distinctive information, then the item would be correctly rejected as new.

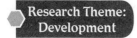
Research Theme: Development

An unsettling demonstration of the role that social forces can play in false remembering comes from a study by Principe, Kanaya, Ceci, and Singh (2006). They were interested in how rumors might lead to false memories in preschoolers. The experimenters staged a magic show for four different groups of children, ages 3 to 5. During the show, the magician tried but failed to pull a rabbit from his hat. At this point, the four groups of preschoolers were exposed to different sources of information. In the *overheard* condition, the preschoolers were exposed to a conversation among adult confederates in which it was alleged (i.e., rumored) that the magician failed because the rabbit had escaped and was now eating carrots in one of the classrooms. In the *classmate* condition, the children did not hear the rumor conversation firsthand, but were classmates of those who did hear it. In the *control* condition, the children neither heard the rumor nor were classmates with anyone who heard the rumor. Finally, in the *witness* condition, children did not hear the rumor about the rabbit, but they did experience the event suggested by the rumor. That is, they actually witnessed a rabbit eating carrots in one of the classrooms. This group served as a baseline recall condition that would allow for a comparison between recall of the actual event and recall in the other conditions in which the event was not witnessed.

After the first phase involving the magic show, children were interviewed with either neutral (e.g., "Tell me about the day the rabbit visited your school") or suggestive ("What did the rabbit eat when he got loose in your school? Did he eat carrots or lettuce?"). Then, during a final interview, the children who had reported the rabbit incident in their initial interview were asked the critical question—whether they saw the rabbit "with their own eyes" or had simply heard about it from someone else. In design terms, then, the study employed a 4 × 2 design, with two independent variables. Both of these variables would be considered experimental context variables. One was the condition in which preschoolers heard about the target event (overheard, classmate, control, or witness). The other was the type of interview preschoolers experienced after the event (neutral or suggestive). The dependent variable was their answer to the critical question: Did they actually see the rabbit?

The results can be seen in Table 7.2, which shows the proportion of children in each condition who answered the critical question in the affirmative—that yes, they had actually *seen* the rascally rabbit. In the witness condition, every child correctly reported that they had indeed seen the rabbit. The noteworthy findings are the alarmingly high levels of false reporting in the other three conditions, particularly in the suggestive interview condition. After this type of interview, nearly three-quarters of children reported that they had seen the event, when they had only overheard a rumor first- or secondhand. Even in

Table 7.2 The Proportion of Children Who Reported Seeing the Target Event in Principe, Kanaya, Ceci, and Singh (2006) as a Function of Rumor Condition and Type of Interview

		Interview Type	
		Neutral	**Suggestive**
Rumor Condition	Witness	1.0	.92
	Overheard	.38	.70
	Classmate	.68	.78
	Control	.00	.23

From Principe, G. F., Kanaya, T., Ceci, S. J., & Singh, M. (2006). Believing is seeing: How rumors can engender false memories in preschoolers. *Psychological Science, 17*(3), 243–248. Blackwell. Adapted with permission.

the neutral interview condition, a good number of the children reported seeing the event. These findings have important implications for the evaluation of children's memory reports. First, they demonstrate once again the danger of suggestive questioning, as discussed earlier. Second, they provide another powerful demonstration of the role that social factors play in misremembering.

STOP and REVIEW!

1. True or false? The false memories found by the DRM paradigm were more likely to be associated with familiarity-based judgments than with recollection-based judgments.
2. Describe the phenomenon of imagination inflation.
3. Name the five stages of the constructive memory framework.
4. If one can recall a piece of distinctive information as an element of a memory, then
   a. the memory is likely to be illusory.
   b. the memory is likely to be true.
   c. this doesn't really tell us anything about the veracity of the memory.
   d. the memory is more likely to be affected by social contagion.

➤ Memory illusions involve the creation of a memory for an event that did not happen. High levels of false recall and false recognition have been found in the laboratory using lists of words created around a theme word that is never presented (DRM paradigm). False recognition was found to be based on a recollection-based judgment rather than a familiarity-based judgment. Some neuroscientific research indicates that it may be possible to tease apart a real from an illusory memory.

➤ False memories can also be induced for everyday events, such as being lost. These memories are the product of leading questions and imagining how events might have occurred. Research has demonstrated a phenomenon termed *imagination inflation*, which refers to the idea that imagining how an event may have occurred increases the feeling that it really did.

➤ A constructive memory framework proposes that five stages are necessary for accurate memory reconstruction: feature binding, pattern separation, focusing, pattern completion, and criterion setting. Also important to memory reconstruction is the process of source monitoring, which involves correctly identifying the source of remembered information.

➤ The distinctiveness heuristic assumes that if a memory lacks distinctive information that a rememberer assumes the memory ought to have, then the event should be judged as new. The social contagion effect refers to the fact that memories can be affected/infected by others.

The Recovered Memory Controversy

The issue of the accuracy and inaccuracy of memory lies at the heart of a fierce debate that raged throughout the 1990s and still provokes strong feelings today, although the deep divide may be closing a bit. At the center of the controversy lies the question of repressed, and subsequently recovered, memories that typically involve childhood sexual abuse. The early 1990s saw a rapidly growing number of these cases. These claims, coupled with research demonstrating the reconstructive nature of memory, have caused grave concern in the psychological community regarding the validity of **recovered memories.** The recovery of a *repressed memory* has the potential to completely devastate a family; that this devastation would occur as the result of a recovered memory that is false seems particularly tragic. In response to the increasing number of recovered memory cases, experimental and clinical researchers have intensified their investigations into the nature of illusory memories and the nature of memory for trauma (for reviews, see Kihlstrom, 2004; Loftus & Davis, 2006; McNally, 2003).

The notion of **repression** stems from Sigmund Freud's psychoanalytic approach to personality and psychotherapy. You're probably familiar with Freud's claims; the most relevant for present purposes is Freud's contention that traumatic memories are submerged in the unconscious. Although these repressed feelings and memories are unavailable to consciousness in any direct way, they do manifest themselves, most notably through problems in adjustment and behavior. Freud's notion of repression has become the centerpiece for some approaches to psychotherapy; these approaches champion the liberation of repressed memories as the road to recovery.

Some confusion exists regarding exactly what is meant by repression. Freud himself wasn't consistent in his application of the term. As Lindsay (1998) notes, scholars have differed widely, and sometimes wildly, about the specific meaning of repression. At one extreme (the *special mechanism view*), suggests the existence of a special mechanism, unlike any memory mechanism we've discussed to this point, whereby memories for traumatic events are encapsulated in a more or less complete and accurate form. At some later point, the memories return. Less extreme versions of this view might allow for some forgetting and error in the repressed memory but would retain the notion of a specialized mechanism whereby a memory is repressed, stored, and recovered.

Most memory researchers are skeptical of the special mechanism view, and for good reason. As Roediger and Bergman (1998) note, several elements of it fly in the face of over a century of experimental research on the basic workings of memory. Therefore, memory researchers are likely to adopt another quite different view of repression. According to what might be termed the *ordinary forgetting view* (Lindsay, 1998), memory for trauma is nothing special; we forget traumatic events according to the same rules whereby we forget joyous or run-of-the-mill events. For example, an individual who has experienced a traumatic event may choose not to think about it; after a substantial period of time in which the memory is unrehearsed, the memory becomes less retrievable. And any memory, even if it is rehearsed, is subject to the ravages of time and interference. Most memory researchers adopt some version of this ordinary forgetting view and attempt to account for repressed memories in these terms.

To avoid the Freudian associations with the term *repression,* a number of alternatives have been proposed, *recovered memories* being the most common. But this term has its own problems, as noted by Lindsay (1998); most take it to mean "repressed and then recovered memories." Also, the very words *recovered memory* imply that the memory is an accurate one, when it's evident that this is not always the case. Lindsay proposes the term *recovered memory experience* to emphasize that the subjective experience of the rememberer is the phenomenon that needs to be analyzed.

As Schooler (1994) points out, resolving the controversy over the validity of recovered memory experiences requires an answer to two basic questions: First, is it possible to completely forget and subsequently recover memories for traumatic events? Second, can false memories for traumatic experiences be fabricated? We'll use these questions to guide our discussion of the controversy.

Can We Completely Forget and Recover Traumatic Events?

At the center of recovered memory claims is the idea that traumatic events are often forgotten. Several researchers who have gathered retrospective reports of abuse victims (e.g., Briere & Conte, 1993; Herman & Schatzow, 1987) report that clients often go through extended periods in which the abuse is forgotten. However, as Schooler (1994) and others note, this research is rife with problems in interpretation. First, the events cannot be definitively corroborated; neither can it be ascertained exactly how the respondents interpreted the questions. Also, the fact that abuse experiences were forgotten for a period of time does not necessarily mean that they were completely inaccessible.

Williams (1994) took a more direct route to corroborating cases of lost traumatic memories, finding individuals who had been admitted 17 years earlier to sexual abuse clinics and interviewing them about their current knowledge of the experience. Of the 129 women she managed to interview, a substantial portion (38%) had no memory of the incident for which they had been admitted. Although this finding does provide more compelling evidence for the forgetting of sex-related trauma than do the retrospective reports discussed above, it is subject to some interpretational limitations of its own. The majority of those who reported forgetting did recall other episodes of abuse; so the particular episode that was the subject of the research may simply have been confused with others (recall that a common cause of memory failure is source confusion). But compellingly, disregarding these individuals still left 12% who reported that they had never been sexually abused when they actually had been.

So, substantial forgetting of traumatic events can happen, but this seems to be the exception rather than the rule. A great deal of research indicates that children often have quite intact memories for a variety of nonsexual traumas, such as kidnapping (Terr, 1979), sniper attack (Pynoos & Nader, 1989), and emergency room treatment (Howe, Courage, & Peterson, 1994). Findings that reveal relatively intact memories for these events stand in stark contrast to claims of massive repression of childhood sexual abuse. But, on the other hand, there are some informative differences between the traumas listed above and sexual abuse. As Schooler (1994) points out, the traumas listed above all relate to single instances that could be discussed with relatively little embarrassment. Neither of these conditions typically characterize childhood sexual abuse. And in fact, one study that does approximate some elements of sexual abuse in its involvement of an embarrassing and painful event (urinary tract catheterization) does lend some support to the notion that such events might be more subject to forgetting (Goodman, Quas, Batterman-Faunce, Riddlesberger, & Kuhn, 1994).

In addition, some theorists contend that the encoding and storage of particularly traumatic events may differ in important ways from the encoding and storage of more mundane events (e.g., Spiegel, 1994; van der Kolk, 1994), although the mechanisms have not yet been well specified. Basically, these views contend that the storage of particularly traumatic events can be fragmented; the elements of these memories remain unintegrated. Remember the constructive memory framework, which states that in order for a memory to be accurately retrieved, the components of the encoded event must be bound together. Stress and emotion, like that associated with a traumatic event, could interrupt this feature-binding process. Therefore, recall would be difficult and should (and does) occur in the form of nonverbal fragments—as images, sights, or sounds. But these accounts fail to explain how such fragmented memories could serve as the basis for an integrated, detailed memory (Roediger & Bergman, 1998).

Physiological evidence seems to support the idea that the encoding of intensely stressful events (i.e., traumatic events) is different from that of nonstressful events. Explicit recall 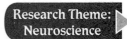 involves brain structures in and around the medial temporal lobe, including the amygdala and the hippocampus (Nadel & Jacobs, 1998). Each area is responsible for different aspects of explicit memory. In addition, each area is affected in a characteristic manner by traumatic events, with concomitant effects on explicit memory for those events. Nadel and Jacobs (1998; see also Payne, Nadel, Britton, & Jacobs, 2004; Payne, Jackson, Ryan, Hoscheidt, Jacobs, & Nadel, 2006; Shors, 2006) provide a useful synthesis of the evidence, spelling out the role of each set of structures in forming memories of traumatic events. The amygdala seems to be essential for remembering emotionally charged events. The hippocampus seems to be the structure responsible for "putting it all together," allowing for the consolidation of each element of the memory into a coherent episode (i.e., the feature-binding process).

Trauma has complex and varying effects on brain structures. For example, high levels of stress enhance the functioning of the amygdala but disrupt the functioning of the hippocampus. Jacobs and Nadel (1998) suggest that the differential effects of stress on these structures account for some of the oddities of memories for trauma. For example, victims sometimes fail to recall the context of the event but can vividly recall how they felt (the emotions surrounding the event). Because the stress has enhanced the functioning of the amygdala and interfered with the functioning of the hippocampus, memory for the traumatic event demonstrates a predictable pattern of strength and weakness: memory in the form of feelings or mood states is enhanced, while memory in the form of a coherent episode is poor.

So the issue may be one of poor encoding rather than of forgetting. Therefore, caution should be taken when considering the issue of "recovery"; because the elements of the memory are not fully integrated at encoding, there is no coherent representation to retrieve. Therefore (literally), the memory has to be "pieced together." As Nadel and Jacobs (1998) point out, the narratives that are woven around these memory fragments are likely to be a joint product of several sources, including real emotional fragments from the experience as well as inferences, guesses, and suggestions from other sources—all of which may well feed the memory distortion processes we have discussed in this chapter.

Corroborated Cases of Recovered Memories.   Much of the evidence for the reality of recovered memories is anecdotal and based on uncorroborated case studies.

However, there are a number of corroborated cases that lend some valuable insight into the conditions associated with valid memory recovery (e.g., Gleaves, Smith, Butler, & Spiegel, 2004; Schooler, Bendiksen, & Ambadar, 1997). Schooler et al. outline four such cases and note several themes that the memory recoveries seemed to have in common. First, the cues present in the recovery situation corresponded to elements of the originally encoded experience (consistent with the encoding specificity principle discussed in Chapter 6); that is, the memories were triggered by a retrieval cue that reinstated some aspect(s) of the encoded experience. Another aspect of recovery was that it tended to occur very suddenly and was accompanied by extreme shock and emotion. Finally, if the memory was not always forgotten (i.e., it had been previously reported to others), there was evidence that the experience was interpreted differently at the time of "recovery" than it had been previously. In two of the corroborated cases, the rememberers were shocked to find out they had previously related the abuse incident to their husbands. That is, they believed they were completely unaware of the memory, but corroborating evidence demonstrated that they were aware of it. Schooler and colleagues label this a "forgot-it-all-along effect," suggesting that because the recovered memory "packs such a punch," the rememberer assumes that it must have been completely forgotten. Recall that a feeling of familiarity is interpreted as evidence that an event is "old." In this case the stunning lack of familiarity is taken as evidence that the event had never been remembered, when perhaps it had.

This intriguing effect has now been empirically demonstrated in a variety of contexts (e.g., Joslyn, Loftus, McNoughton, & Powers, 2001; Merckelbach, Smeets, Geraerts, Jelicic, Bouwen, & Smeets, 2006), indicating that one's *lack* of memory can't even be taken as evidence that a memory is long forgotten. So how is this relevant to the recovered memory debate? As Geraerts, Arnold, Lindsay, Merckelbach, Jelicic, and Hauer (2006) note, it could be the case that abuse victims underestimate their prior recollections of the abuse, which leads to a false impression that they had repressed the memory. Indeed, Geraerts et al. found that the tendency to underestimate previous remembering (as in the forgot-it-all-along effect) was greater for individuals who had previously reported repressed memories of abuse, relative to individuals with continuous memories of their abuse and individuals with no history of abuse.

Can False Memories for Traumatic Events Be Created?

This is a tough question to answer directly. It would be unethical to attempt to implant false memories of traumatic events such as sexual abuse. But it is quite evident that we can be fairly easily convinced that something happened even though it really didn't. Clearly, under any circumstances, memory is a reconstructive enterprise. This is especially the case in the highly suggestive context that characterizes some therapeutic techniques.

Memory Work and Suggestive Influences in Therapy.   The research we've discussed on false memories has led to great concern about the risk of false memory creation in the therapeutic context, where some of the factors conducive to false remembering can be present. First, the therapeutic context itself is suggestive, as the client will tend to trust the expertise of the therapist and be open to therapeutic suggestion. In addition to the

Some fear that the therapeutic setting has the potential to increase memory suggestibility.

general suggestibility of this context, some therapeutic approaches involve what is sometimes termed *memory work*—elaborate attempts to retrieve memories using methods that include repeated imagining, hypnosis, and group attempts to retrieve memories. As you've read, imagining (Goff & Roediger, 1998; Hyman & Pentland, 1996), hypnosis (Scobria, Mazzoni, Kirsch, & Milling, 2002), and social conformity pressures (Roediger, Meade, & Bergman, 2001) are three factors that heighten the likelihood of forming illusory memories.

By no means is anyone implying that these suggestive techniques are used by all therapists. But given the devastating potential of a false memory of childhood abuse, any usage of these techniques may be too much. So how commonly are they used? A number of studies have surveyed clinical practitioners to ascertain their beliefs and practices. For example, Poole, Lindsay, Memon, and Bull (1995) surveyed a random sample of licensed clinicians in the United States and Britain about their beliefs and practices. A majority of the therapists (over 70%) reported using at least one memory-recovery technique (i.e., imagining, hypnosis, dream interpretation), and approximately 25% of those therapists used a combination of such techniques along with suggestions that placed an emphasis on the importance of recovering memories (i.e., telling clients that memory recovery was necessary for therapy to be effective).

These figures seem to indicate widespread use of memory-recovery techniques. However, a criticism of the Poole and colleagues (1995) study is that the survey did not distinguish between techniques used with clients who always remembered their abuse and those who had no previous memories of abuse. Surely, the techniques are more dangerous with the second group than the first group. A survey by Polusny and Follette (1996) asked clinicians to report which memory-recovery techniques they used with clients who reported no memories of abuse but whom the clinician strongly suspected had been abused. Suggestive techniques (e.g., hypnosis) were cited by 20% to 35% of the therapists, depending on the particular technique. So it seems that a substantial minority of therapists do employ techniques that enhance the likelihood of false remembering when they suspect child sexual abuse. However, Courtois (1997) points out that the survey also revealed that very few respondents indicate childhood sexual abuse as a focus of their therapy; so these techniques would come into play relatively infrequently. Still, there are potential dangers in using these techniques when they do come into play.

Self-Help Books and Checklists.   Suggestive influences also exist outside of the therapeutic context. Skeptics of recovered memory have expressed considerable concern about self-help books designed to aid in the recovery of childhood sexual abuse. These books include highly suggestive statements. For example, in *The Courage to Heal* (Bass & Davis, 1988), the authors state

> If you are unable to remember any specific instances . . . but still have a feeling that something abusive happened to you, it probably did. . . . If you think you were abused, and your life shows the symptoms, then you were. (p. 21)

and offer advice for recovering memories, such as

> If you don't remember what happened to you, write about what you do remember. Re-create the context in which the abuse happened even if you don't remember the specifics of the abuse yet. . . . Often when women think they don't remember, they actually remember quite a lot. (p. 83)

In addition to these sorts of suggestive statements and advice, many recovery books include checklists of symptoms that allegedly serve as indicators of previous abuse; however, these checklists are not derived or validated in any systematic manner, and the "symptoms" are so vague and nonspecific that they could apply to anyone. For example, Bass and Davis suggest that affirmative answers to the following questions may be suggestive of previous abuse:

> Do you feel different from other people? . . . Do you have trouble feeling motivated? . . . Do you feel you have to be perfect? . . . Do you have trouble expressing your feelings? . . . Do you find that your relationships just don't work out? . . . Do you find yourself clinging to the people you care about? (p. 35)

Coupling this list with such assertions as, "If you think you were abused and your life shows the symptoms, then you were" has tremendous suggestive potential (Kihlstrom, 1998). These books undoubtedly offer great comfort to those who vividly remember and suffer the effects of childhood sexual abuse. But for a reader who has no memories but is beginning to explore the possibility, such suggestions pose a serious risk of eliciting a false memory.

STOP *and* THINK! ─────────────────────────

SCRUTINIZING SELF-HELP

Take a trip to the local bookstore and peruse some of the books in the self-help/recovery sections. You could also surf the Internet and look for Web sites devoted to these issues.

- Do these books and Web sites feature general symptom checklists?
- Do they discuss any memory-recovery techniques that may lead to memory distortion?
- Are any caveats about these techniques mentioned?
- Do they specifically mention the issue of false memories?
- How do they deal with the possibility?

Converging Evidence of False Recovered Memories.   Although there is no direct experimental evidence of false trauma memories being implanted, there are several converging lines of evidence that suggest that this does occur (Schacter, Norman, & Koutstaal, 1997). First, many clinical practitioners have reported clients recovering memories of satanic ritual abuse (e.g., Wakefield & Underwager, 1994); however, these instances are never corroborated, and extensive investigations by law authorities continually fail to find evidence of satanic abuse (e.g., Nathan & Snedeker, 1995). Recovering memories of other experiences involving highly unlikely events (e.g., being abducted by aliens) would also seem to be evidence for memory implantation (Schacter, Norman, & Koutstaal, 1997). The reality of false memory implantation is also suggested by the existence of significant numbers of *retractors*—individuals who recover memories of abuse but later recant their reports (e.g., Nelson & Simpson, 1994).

Finally, the research we've discussed throughout this chapter constitutes a third line of evidence that memories can be implanted. Consider the range of events for which memories have been implanted or judgments of possible memories inflated: being lost in a mall (Loftus & Pickrell, 1995), spilling a punch bowl at a wedding reception (Hyman & Pentland, 1996), being hospitalized overnight (Hyman, Husband, & Billings, 1995), and witnessing demonic possession as a child (Mazzoni, Loftus, & Kirsch, 2001). Although these false memory experiences are certainly not on a par with sexual abuse, to dismiss their significance completely would seem reckless (Lindsay, 1998).

What Constitutes Valid Evidence?

One reason that common ground has been so difficult to reach in the debate over recovered memories relates to the fundamental differences over what constitutes good evidence. The databases that clinicians and memory researchers rely on to make their arguments are quite different. Clinicians base much of their argument for the validity of recovered memories on their interactions with clients and other evidence in the form of case studies and interviews. But because these sources of data are descriptive and thus subject to various self-report biases, experimental psychologists are reluctant to draw definitive conclusions from them. But the database emphasized by memory researchers—the extensive data demonstrating our propensity toward illusory memories—leaves many clinicians unmoved. They point out that illusory memories are, in large part, laboratory contrivances that don't generalize to the real-world issue of how it is that we store and retrieve memories for trauma.

As you can see, it's pretty clear from the preceding discussion that the answer to both of Schooler's (1994) questions is yes. Entire episodes of one's life can be completely forgotten for a period of time; further, there is evidence that such forgetting may be more severe for more painful and/or embarrassing circumstances. Also, there seems to be a significant number of recovered memory experiences that can be corroborated. On the other hand, it is just as clear that memories for entire events can be created, particularly in circumstances that involve imagining, hypnosis, and/or conformity pressures—all of which can be present in the therapeutic setting.

Given the affirmative answers to these questions, the issue becomes one of discrimination: How can we tell when a recovered memory experience is valid (i.e., the event really happened) and when it is not? Memory researchers tend to be most skeptical of memories that emerge from therapeutic interactions involving suggestive memory techniques, particularly when the client entered therapy for nonspecific reasons not related to sexual abuse. Recall that the corroborated cases reported by Schooler, Bendiksen, and Ambadar (1997) involved sudden remembering, cued by an event that shared characteristics of the original abuse.

The APA's Position on Recovered Memory

In the midst of the controversy over the validity of recovered memory experiences, the American Psychological Association appointed a special working group to review the scientific literature on memory and abuse experiences and to identify future research and training needs relevant to evaluating recovered memory experiences. The working group was composed of prominent researchers and clinicians who represented a range of views on the reality of recovered memory experiences; their final report was published in 1998, and although that was some time ago and much more research has been done, the points of agreement and disagreement have not changed (see Table 7.3). Meanwhile, research presses on to further specify the nature of memory for trauma.

Table 7.3 Points of Agreement and Disagreement from the APA Working Group on Memories of Childhood Sexual Abuse (APA, 1998)

Points of Agreement	Points of Disagreement
• Controversies regarding adult recollections should not be allowed to obscure the fact that child sexual abuse is a complex and pervasive problem in America that has historically gone unacknowledged.	• How constructive is memory?
	• How accurately can events be recalled after extended delays, and what mechanisms that might underlie such remembering?
• Most people who were sexually abused as children remember all or part of what happened to them.	• Are memories of traumatic events "special"?
	• How relevant is basic research on memory and development for understanding the recall of stressful events?
• It is possible for memories of abuse that have been forgotten for a long time to be remembered.	• What rules of evidence should guide hypothesis testing about the consequences of trauma and the nature of remembering?
• It is also possible to construct convincing pseudomemories for events that never occurred.	• How easy is it to create pseudomemories by suggestion, both within and outside of therapy? How often does it occur?
• There are gaps in our knowledge about the processes that lead to accurate and inaccurate recollections of childhood abuse.	• How easy is it to distinguish "real" memories and pseudomemories, in the absence of external corroborative evidence?

STOP *and* REVIEW!

1. True or false? Most memory researchers adopt a normal for-getting view of the failure to remember traumatic events.
2. Which of these is **not** a common theme in corroborated cases of recovered memories?

   a. surprise
   b. context reinstatement as a trigger for the memory
   c. gradual emergence of the memory
3. Describe one piece of evidence that indicates the possibility of implantation of false memories for traumatic events.
4. Why has it been difficult to establish the criteria for what constitutes a true and a false repressed memory?

➤ The existence of repressed and subsequently recovered memories has been an issue of much debate. Some believe that there is a special mechanism responsible for the forget-ting of traumatic events; most memory researchers adhere to a normal forgetting view—traumatic events are forgotten according to the same rules whereby any event may be forgotten. Forgetting childhood sexual abuse is the exception rather than the rule.

➤ Some research indicates that encoding traumatic events is different from encoding non-traumatic events. Memory in the form of feelings and images is enhanced; however, memory in the form of a coherent episode is poor. "Recovery" of such memories is recon-structive and subject to the influences discussed throughout this chapter. Corroborated memories of abuse seem to appear suddenly, in a context that reinstates some aspect of the abuse situation, and tend to be accompanied by great surprise.

➤ Research suggests that it is possible to implant false memories of traumatic events. One piece of evidence is the existence of retractors (individuals who recover memories of abuse but later recant their reports). Self-help books and therapeutic approaches that focus on memory recovery can provide a suggestive environment that may lead to the creation of memories of childhood sexual abuse.

➤ Current concern is focused on distinguishing between true and false memories of abuse. Common ground between clinicians and experimental researchers has been difficult to find due to differing views on what constitutes good evidence. Memory researchers value well-controlled basic studies of memory and are less persuaded by descriptive evidence, such as case studies. Clinical researchers tend to show the converse pattern of bias.

GLOSSARY

absentmindedness: a lack of attention resulting in long-term memory distortion (p. 248)

bias: the influence of our beliefs, expectations, and desires on what we remember (p. 249)

blocking: a failure in retrieving information stored in long-term memory (p. 248)

cognitive interview technique: an interview proce-dure that incorporates practices known to maximize the chances of complete and accurate memory (p. 261)

confabulation: the introduction of inaccurate detail to memories (p. 261)

distinctiveness heuristic: a rule of thumb used to determine whether a retrieved memory is real; the rememberer assesses whether enough detailed information is present in the memory to deem it true (p. 275)

functional size: a reflection of the probability that any one person might be selected based solely on how they look; a fair lineup has a functional size equivalent to the number of people in the lineup (p. 257)

illusory memory (memory illusions or **false memories):** the remembering of events that never occurred (p. 265)

imagination inflation: the finding that mental simulation of an event leads to an increase in belief that the event may have actually occurred (p. 270)

interviewer bias: the beliefs and expectations of someone querying the memory of another individual, which can lead to errant memory reports (p. 262)

memory distortions: errors in remembering (p. 248)

misattribution: ascribing a memory to the wrong source (p. 248)

misinformation effect: the influence on the witness's memory of misleading information presented between the encoding of an event and its subsequent recall (p. 254)

optimality hypothesis: the idea that the relationship between confidence and accuracy is stronger to the degree that the encoding, storage, and retrieval of the event were optimal (p. 260)

persistence: the continued (but unwanted) automatic retrieval of memories that we'd prefer to forget (p. 249)

photo bias: the increase in probability that a person will be recognized as the culprit due to previous exposure (e.g., a lineup or photo array) (p. 256)

reality monitoring: a decision regarding whether a memory corresponds to either a perceived external event or an internally generated event (p. 274)

recovered memories: the return of memories that have previously been forgotten (p. 279)

repression: the Freudian notion that anxiety-provoking thoughts and memories are blocked from consciousness (p. 279)

sequential lineup: a lineup in which the witness must choose from lineup members presented one at a time (p. 258)

simultaneous lineup: a lineup in which the witness must choose from lineup members presented at the same time (p. 258)

social contagion effect: the finding that a person's recall in a collaborative setting can be affected by others' recall (p. 276)

source confusion: the inability to distinguish between the sources of event memories (p. 274)

source monitoring: the process of correctly identifying the source of remembered information (p. 274)

suggestibility: the malleability of memory to leading questions or others' suggestions (p. 249)

transience: the loss of information from memory with the passage of time (p. 248)

unconscious transference: what happens when witnesses fail to distinguish between a target person (i.e., a criminal) and another person encountered at a different time whose face is also familiar (p. 255)

weapon focus: the tendency for the presence of a weapon to focus attention narrowly, resulting in a lack of peripheral detail in the memory representation (p. 252)

8

Remembering
the Personal Past

Why do people remember such precious little information from their early childhood? In fact, we're willing to bet that you remember not a thing from before you were age 3 or 4. A good deal of important stuff happens early in life, so why is memory for this period so poor?

Why is it that smells pack such a punch when it comes to memory? The smell of burning firewood reminds you of a great night around a campfire; the smell of baking cookies transports you to Christmases past. Is it really true that smells lead to more complete and vivid memories?

Did you ever wonder, as you relate the story of some event from your life, whether it actually is just a story? Obviously, the event happened to you in some form but it feels almost as if you're making it up, or reconstructing it as you tell it, rather than "grabbing it whole." What's going on?

Why do certain events seem as clear as if they happened yesterday? Your memory for the September 11 terrorist attacks probably seems like a crystal-clear moment, fixed forever in time. What gives rise to these memories, and do we ever forget something like that?

Everyday Memory

When we tell people that we teach psychology, this information elicits knowing glances or furrowed brows, or, worse yet, comments like, "Ohhhh . . . going to analyze me, huh?" We quickly inform these new acquaintances that no, we don't really care about their problems (in a clinical sense, at least); we do memory research. This triggers an entirely different (and at times, equally frustrating) set of questions and comments, such as, "Why do I have such a terrible memory for my childhood?" or "I'll never forget what I was doing when I heard that Princess Diana was killed" or "Why do I remember things differently than my spouse?" Why should we, as memory researchers, find these questions about memory frustrating? Because, until fairly recently, we haven't had very good answers to these questions. These questions are partially answered by material discussed in Chapters 6 and 7. But there is something unique about these questions, something that goes unaddressed by the material presented in Chapters 6 and 7. These questions refer to one's personal experience and use of memory in an everyday context. As such, they aren't fully addressed by much of the memory research discussed thus far.

Neisser's Challenge: Ecological Validity and Memory Research

As you've no doubt noticed, cognitive psychology research is quite elegant: every confounding variable is anticipated and controlled, and each aspect of responding is carefully and precisely measured. To put it in terms of a concept introduced in Chapter 2, the *internal validity* of cognitive research is nothing short of impressive. Cognitive psychology no doubt owes to behaviorism a debt of gratitude on this score; behaviorist challenges to the notion of scientifically analyzing mental processes (as defined by structuralists and functionalists) meant that any new approach to the study of cognition would have to live up to extremely high methodological standards. Cognitive psychology has more than answered the challenge.

But while saluting the incredible progress cognitive psychology has made in establishing an empirical base, many would say that it has come at a cost. Often, the *ecological validity* of cognitive psychology research has fallen well short of impressive. There exists a natural tension between the internal validity and the ecological validity of any research enterprise. You trade off one to get more of the other; more controlled is less natural, and vice versa. Take memory, for example; a great deal of the research in the first three decades of experimental work on memory fit a pretty standard pattern. Word lists carefully constructed to control for the effects of various extraneous variables were presented under precisely controlled conditions, and subject memory was tested with a number of standard laboratory memory tasks, like free recall or recognition. But one might argue that the number of words you can recall from a list of 48 concrete and abstract words presented for four seconds each doesn't tell you that much about why you can't remember events from your life that occurred before age 3. The emphasis in memory research (and cognition research in general) has always been on internal validity, often at the expense of ecological validity.

In an important address to cognitive psychologists in 1977, Ulric Neisser delivered a blistering critique of the memory research that had accumulated in the first quarter-century

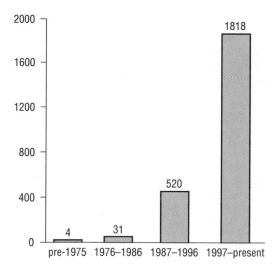

Figure 8.1 Cumulative number of citations from PsychINFO including the keywords of either *everyday memory* or *autobiographical memory*.

of cognition research, a critique that was directed at the emphasis on internal validity. According to Neisser (1978), "If X is an interesting or socially significant aspect of memory, then psychologists have hardly ever studied X" (p. 4). These were fighting words, to say the least. Neisser was basically saying that the first 30 years of memory research had been boring and trivial. Neisser went even further, claiming that although firm empirical generalizations about memory had indeed been made, most of these generalizations "are so obvious that every 10-year-old child knows them anyway (p. 4)". Extremely harsh words, perhaps, but many cognitive psychologists took them to heart. Since Neisser's address, there has been a veritable explosion of research on what might be considered "everyday" memory. The explosion is evident in the chart in Figure 8.1, which plots the combined number of citations found in the psychology research database PsychINFO, using the search terms "everyday memory" and "autobiographical memory." Up until 1986, only a few dozen psychology articles were directed at issues of everyday memory. Since then, there have been over two thousand investigations of these phenomena. The fact that you're reading an entire chapter devoted to everyday memory is another testament to this incredible trend; most cognitive psychology textbooks devote only subsections of chapters to everyday memory topics like childhood amnesia and flashbulb memory.

Everyday Memory Research: Bankrupt?   Not everyone jumped on Neisser's bandwagon. In an influential countercritique, Banaji and Crowder (1989) decried what they termed the "bankruptcy of everyday memory," objecting strongly to most of Neisser's claims. They drew an analogy between the psychologist who conducts well-controlled basic laboratory research on memory and the chemist who does controlled experimentation on the properties of yeast in order to establish why bread dough rises. In their view, the precisely controlled experimentation of the chemist is a more sensible approach and is more likely to yield meaningful results than "loitering in professional bakeries and taking careful notes" (p. 1187). They add that memory psychologists should not be embarrassed or frustrated when faced with questions that can't really be answered by basic research. "What other science," they ask, "has established that its students should decide on the importance of questions by checking first with Aunt Martha?" (p. 1187). Banaji and Crowder argue that in everyday memory contexts (such as attempting to remember events from one's life), the uncontrolled factors are so numerous that generalizability of the results is limited, not increased. Banaji and Crowder assert that the emphasis on internal validity in investigations of memory is entirely appropriate and is likely to be the road to truly generalizable principles of memory function.

Striking a Middle Ground. Following Banaji and Crowder's (1989) critique, a number of researchers came to the defense of everyday memory research (e.g., Conway, 1991) and/or emphasized the value of both laboratory and everyday approaches (e.g., Loftus & Ketcham, 1991; Tulving, 1991). Tulving (1991) makes the important point that memory research is not a "zero-sum game" (i.e., someone must win, and someone must lose); forsaking everyday memory research for a basic laboratory approach, or vice versa, would be "throwing the baby out with the bath water." Both approaches can be quite valid and generalizable, and both approaches should be employed to discover the principles of memory function.

Since the opening salvos of the everyday memory debate, the dust has settled, and to no one's surprise, both laboratory and everyday approaches to the study of memory are still standing. And both approaches are probably the richer for the exchange. Laboratory psychologists are more sensitive to issues of ecological validity, and everyday memory researchers are more sensitive to issues of precision and control (i.e., internal validity). In this chapter, we'll review some of the discoveries that have been made by researchers investigating issues of everyday memory, so you'll be well informed in your conversations with "Aunt Martha."

STOP *and* **REVIEW!**

1. Discuss Neisser's criticism of traditional memory research.
2. What is the relationship between ecological and internal validity?
3. Which of the following accurately describes the current state of research in memory?
   a. Everyday approaches are the sole focus of memory research.
   b. Laboratory-based approaches are the sole focus of memory research.
   c. Both everyday approaches and laboratory-based approaches are used in memory research.
   d. Memory researchers are concerned with internal but not ecological validity.

➤ Neisser delivered a critique of this laboratory-based approach to memory research, claiming that it was boring, noninformative, and not very generalizable to everyday life. In answer to his challenge, recent years have witnessed an astounding increase in the number of studies devoted to the investigation of everyday memory.

➤ Traditional laboratory-based memory research is high in internal validity (experimental control), but quite low in ecological validity (generalizability to the real world). There is a tension between internal validity and ecological validity. You must trade off one to get more of the other.

➤ Not everyone agreed with Neisser's critique, arguing that controlled, laboratory-based memory research is more likely to yield meaningful and generalizable results than everyday memory research. Others argued that both approaches to memory research are valuable. Currently, both types of research programs are quite active.

Autobiographical Memory: Basic Issues and Methodology

The most popular topic of investigation within the realm of everyday memory has no doubt been autobiographical memory (AM), or memory for the experiences that comprise a person's life story, or *autobiography*. It's somewhat surprising that it took cognitive psychology so long to mine this important area of research. A person's past history is at the core of their identity. It shouldn't surprise you to learn, then, that autobiographical memories are as varied as the people who produce them. Given this level of complexity and individual variation, perhaps it isn't so surprising that it took cognitive psychology so long to explore this area. As you'll see, a host of variables affect the form and quality of autobiographical memories, including emotion, developmental stage, gender, and the cultural background of the rememberer.

Memories vs. Facts

On reviewing some of the early research on autobiographical memory, Conway (1990) provides a useful distinction between an **autobiographical memory** and an **autobiographical fact** (see also Brewer, 1986); the characteristics of each are presented in Table 8.1. For your authors, an example of an autobiographical memory would be the events that took place on our wedding day. An example of an autobiographical fact would be the knowledge that we have two cats. Both of these are autobiographical in the sense that they are part of our life story, but they are very different from each other. Both autobiographical memories and facts are high in self-reference; they are both closely related to our personal identity; and they both will likely last for years—we're not likely to forget our wedding day or the fact that we own two cats.

But that's where the similarities between autobiographical memories and facts end. Autobiographical memories feature an experience of remembering. When either of us thinks of our wedding day, a sort of "reliving" experience occurs: we can see, hear, and feel the sights, sounds, and emotions that occurred on that day. No such reliving experience occurs when we think of the fact that we have two cats. It's just something we know about our lives. Another difference is that autobiographical memories quite often feature an

Table 8.1 Characteristics of Autobiographical Memories and Autobiographical Facts

	Autobiographical Memories	Autobiographical Facts
Experience of remembering	Always present	Rarely present
Personal interpretation	Frequent	Rare
Truthfulness	Variable	High
Context-specific sensory attributes	Always present	Rarely present
Self-reference	High	High
Duration of memory	Years	Years

From Conway, M. A. (1990). *Cognitive models of memory.* Cambridge, MA: MIT Press. Reprinted by permission.

interpretation on the part of the rememberer. We each have our own interpretation of and reaction to the events of our wedding day. However, we have no personal spin on the fact that we own two cats; we just do. Related to this difference is the notion of veridicality: Are autobiographical memories and facts "true"? Consistent with the idea that autobiographical memories are often subject to interpretation, it should come as no surprise that their "truth" can be quite variable. After all, as you learned in Chapter 7, our memories don't function as videotape recorders. Autobiographical facts fare much better on the dimension of truth; the facts that you know about your life are more or less "true," unless you're suffering some sort of psychopathological break with reality.

Let's consider the distinction between autobiographical memories and facts in light of another well-worn memory distinction: Tulving's (1983) distinction between *episodic* and *semantic* memories (discussed in Chapter 6). Recall that episodic memories are memories for personally experienced events that can be tied to a specific time and place, while semantic memories refer to knowledge or information about the world that is not tied to any specific contextual information like time or place. Autobiographical memories would be considered episodic memories in that they are essentially relived personal experiences that are rich in contextual detail. Autobiographical facts would be considered semantic memories in that they refer to simple, context-free knowledge of one's own personal world.

Linton (1975), in a self-study of her own memory, found that some memories undergo a transition from specific episodic memories (i.e., autobiographical memories) to more generic semantic memories (i.e., autobiographical facts). For example, think about your memories about college. When you started college, no doubt you remembered every day

An autobiographical memory (our wedding day) and an autobiographical fact (we have two cats).

as its own distinct event (autobiographical memory) for about a week or so, after which you began to form more general semantic memories about the types of things that happen in college (autobiographical facts). This transition from specific-event memories to more general representations of repeated events is a common theme in much of the work on autobiographical memory. You'll read more about these sorts of general knowledge representations in Chapter 9. Our discussion in this chapter will focus primarily on autobiographical memories rather than autobiographical facts.

STOP and THINK!

PERSONAL FACTS AND MEMORIES

In Chapter 6, you generated both episodic and semantic memories and compared their characteristics. Try the same exercise, but this time for autobiographical memories and autobiographical facts:

- Come up with an example of an autobiographical memory and an autobiographical fact.
- Examine Table 8.1, which summarizes the key distinctions between these two types of memory.
- Assess the distinction between these types of memory by analyzing your examples. For each example, evaluate whether or not it fits each of the characteristics listed.
- Note how autobiographical memories and autobiographical facts are distinct.

Methods of Investigation

Traditional studies of memory like the ones discussed in Chapter 6 are, in many ways, quite different from the ones we'll be discussing in this chapter. Typically, in these traditional sorts of studies, some type of material is presented during an encoding phase; then at some later point in time, memory for this information is tested, and the completeness and accuracy of the memory are assessed. Autobiographical memory research differs in significant ways from this model. First, no event is presented; the memories being assessed are for events that have happened, sometimes long ago and always out of the control of the experimenter. Second, accuracy of autobiographical memory can be difficult to assess. Who holds the right answer about what happened in the past? Even attempts to corroborate memories by talking to other people who experienced the same event are subject to that person's interpretations, biases, and just plain old forgetting.

Because there is no real way to control the events being remembered or to judge the accuracy of those memories, autobiographical memory researchers focus on aspects that can be assessed, such as the age of the recalled memories, their vividness and detail, their emotional intensity, and how these characteristics differ systematically across different groups of people (men and women, young and old, East Asian and European). And, in spite of the difficulties involved, a number of studies have been successful in evaluating the accuracy of autobiographical memories.

A number of methods have been developed to investigate recall of life episodes. Targeted event recall requires the recall of specific events or well-defined periods from one's life and can allow for some assessment of memory accuracy. Often, corroborating information about the target event exists, either through the public record (in the case of memory for news events) or through family members (in the case of memory for major life events). However, evaluation of memory accuracy is limited by the completeness and accuracy of the corroborating source—be it public accounts or your Aunt Martha.

Most autobiographical memories recalled by the targeted event recall technique would be things that stand out in a person's life. The **diary technique** allows a broader range of memories to be sampled—both the mundane and the distinctive. In this technique, the subject keeps a running record of events that occur in daily life; in other words, an event diary is kept and, at some point, is used to query memory. In addition, the diary technique allows for firmer conclusions about memory accuracy. The remembered events can be verified as having occurred because they were recorded and dated as they occurred (or immediately after). Therefore, diary studies have been the primary vehicle for understanding the processes by which we date our autobiographical memories or place them correctly in time.

Another technique for eliciting autobiographical memories involves a sampling procedure similar to the cued-recall test you read about in Chapter 6. In the cue word technique, subjects are presented with many word cues. They are asked to retrieve an autobiographical memory associated with each word and to write a short description of it and date the event. The use of this technique allows the researcher to assess something we're about to discuss in great detail: the autobiographical memory retention function—the distribution of personal episodic memories across the life span.

STOP *and* REVIEW!

1. Explain the difference between an autobiographical memory and an autobiographical fact.
2. Briefly describe the diary technique for investigating autobiographical memory.
3. True or false? The cue word technique for investigating autobiographical memory allows researchers to assess the recall of events from different points in the life span.

➤ Autobiographical memory (a type of episodic memory) refers to one's memory for their life experiences. An autobiographical fact (a type of semantic memory) refers to a piece of general knowledge about oneself. Memory for events seems to undergo a transition from episodic to semantic. Initially, experiences are recalled as distinct episodes. With a great deal of repetition, memory for these events becomes general knowledge.

➤ A number of methods are used in the study of autobiographical memory. In the targeted event recall technique, specific questions about a particular event or period from one's life are asked. The diary technique requires the subject to record a number of events each day for a span of time, and memory for these events is tested later.

➤ In the cue word technique, word cues are presented and subjects must recall an autobiographical memory in response to each. This technique allows researchers to assess the autobiographical memory retention function, the distribution of personal memories from across the life span.

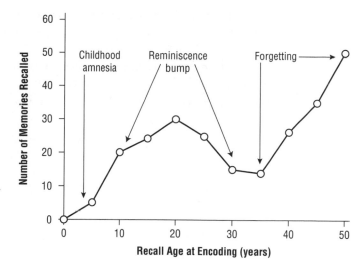

Figure 8.2 Autobiographical memories retrieved as a function of life period.

From Anderson, S. J., & Conway, M. A. (1997). Representations of autobiographical memories. In M. A. Conway (Ed.), *Cognitive models of memory* (pp. 217–246). Cambridge, MA: MIT Press. Reprinted with permission.

The Autobiographical Memory Retention Function

Rubin, Wetzler, and Nebes (1986) conducted an extensive study attempting to investigate the shape of the memory function across the entire life span. Their analysis included subjects ranging in age from 18 to 76. The complete memory function is presented in Figure 8.2. What you see plotted is the number of memories recalled from each period of life. Note the peaks and valleys of this retention function. These researchers observed that these patterns are indicative of three basic phenomena. First, there are very few memories from the early years of life and almost none before the age of about 3—a phenomenon typically termed **childhood amnesia.** Second, there is a disproportionately great number of memories from ages 10 to 30—a phenomenon termed the **reminiscence bump.** Third (and evident only for the older subjects), there is a standard forgetting curve for information that occurs in the last 20 years. Most of the information recalled by older adults is for events that have happened recently. The specifics of this retention function have occupied autobiographical memory researchers' attention over the past 15 years and will be discussed in much of this chapter.

STOP *and* THINK!

CUING YOUR PAST

For each of the following, try to recall a specific autobiographical memory. For each one you recall, write a brief (fewer than 10 words) description:

bananas
lake
grass
bubble
toast

For each of the memories you've generated, take note of

- whether it's an autobiographical fact or an autobiographical memory
- how old you were when the event occurred
- whether your memory is positive or negative emotionally

Plot the five memories you recalled as a function of your age at the time of the memory and evaluate them in terms of the autobiographical retention function. Were the following key components of this function evident?

- lack of early childhood memories (childhood amnesia)
- many recent memories and fewer earlier memories (forgetting function)
- more memories between ages 10 and 30 (reminiscence bump)

Childhood Amnesia

Look again at the first part of the retention function shown in Figure 8.2 (p. 297)—memories for events from the first decade of life. What you see is a precipitous drop in the number of memories reported before the age of 10 and a complete lack of any memories at all before the age of 2 or 3. The paucity of memories from the first few years of life has been termed *childhood amnesia* (or, less commonly, *infantile amnesia*). This finding has been recorded by many researchers, using a variety of methods. We should make note of the terminology we'll be using in this section. Researchers often speak of "the emergence (or development of) autobiographical memory" or "the offset of childhood amnesia." These two phrases can be considered synonymous; they describe exactly the same process. As the amnesia of childhood is lifted, autobiographical memory emerges. We'll be using both of these phrases in our discussion.

Investigating memories for early childhood presents a formidable methodological challenge. One big problem is that there is no way to check on the accuracy of what is reported. In other words, in studies in which subjects attempt to remember events from their childhood, there are no guarantees that subjects are truly remembering the events. Think of the big events you may remember from your childhood. Can you determine if these memories are real or not? Perhaps what you're remembering is someone else's description of the event or the pictures you've seen since.

STOP *and* THINK!

CHILDHOOD AMNESIA

Think back to the earliest memory you can retrieve from your life. Once you've retrieved this memory, note the following things about it:

- How old were you when the event occurred?
- Is the memory general (an autobiographical fact) or specific (an autobiographical memory)?
- How vivid is the memory?

- Is the memory emotionally positive or emotionally negative?
- To what degree do you think the memory has been influenced by later rehearsals (retellings, pictures, etc.)?
- Can anyone corroborate your memory?
- If so, does their recollection match yours?

To avoid some of the pitfalls of faulty and subjective autobiographical recall, one research strategy involves asking subjects about salient events from their childhood that can be corroborated. For example, Usher and Neisser (1993) asked subjects to recall a number of critical events from their childhood that were documented and that could be checked with relatives and records. The events included birth of a sibling, a family move, the death of a family member, and a hospitalization. In addition, they were asked how frequently and recently they had rehearsed (i.e., thought about) the event and whether they had been exposed to pictures of it. Memory was tested with a set of questions asking basic information about each of the events.

The results are summarized in Figure 8.3. The figure plots recall scores for each of the events as a function of the age when it was experienced. The typical retention pattern for early childhood events was obtained: relatively poor memory before the age of 5. In addition, the offset of childhood amnesia occurred at different times, depending on the particular event. Memories for the birth of a sibling and hospitalization went further back than memories for a death or a family move. Hospitalization may be well remembered because it is such a distinctive, involving, and frightening event—a combination that makes the event unforgettable (Usher & Neisser, 1993). The birth of a sibling may be memorable because it becomes the first installment of a story that will be told again and again— in other

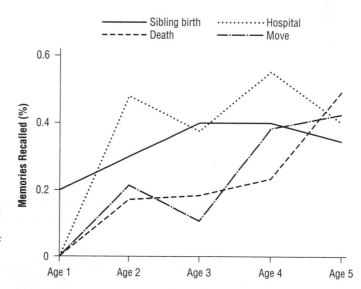

Figure 8.3 Results from Usher and Neisser (1993).

From Usher, J. A., & Neisser, U. (1993). Childhood amnesia and the beginnings of memory for four early life events. *Journal of Experimental Psychology: General, 122,* 155–165. Copyright 1993 by the American Psychological Association. Reprinted with permission.

words, the story receives a great deal of rehearsal. This explanation provides a preview of one explanation for autobiographical memory development that you'll be reading about shortly—an account that cites language development as a major factor.

You might imagine that there would be a relatively straightforward relationship between rehearsal of these salient events (in the form of family stories, photographs, etc.) and their later recall. Not so; the relationship is actually quite complex. The effect of rehearsal depended on the child's age at the time of the experience. If the child was three years old or younger at the time of the event, family stories and photographs actually led to fewer memories than if the child was 4 or 5; in this case, family stories and photographs tended to make the memories stronger. Usher and Neisser suggest that a two- or three-year-old's memory may be relatively fragile and that their memories may be easily confused with stories and photographs. (Remember the idea of source confusion presented in Chapter 7.) The more of these that are present, the more obscured the actual memory becomes. But since a four- or five-year-old's memory may be less tenuous, these rehearsals are probably beneficial.

Explanations for the Offset of Childhood Amnesia.   At some level, the very existence of childhood amnesia is baffling. Many important and exciting things are happening during our first couple of years of life. Why is it that we can't retain any of it? When do we start "writing our life stories" cognitively? A number of factors have been implicated in the emergence of autobiographical memory. Some accounts emphasize neurological development, attempting to map the development of brain subsystems to the development of autobiographical memory. Other accounts take a more psychological tack, attempting to explain the development of autobiographical memory as a function of the development of language, or alternatively, as a manifestation of the development of a "self."

Brain Development.   One possible source of the memory deficits that characterize childhood amnesia is the immaturity of the developing infant brain. Perhaps the neurological structures that subserve the complex processing that leads to autobiographical memories are not fully developed; hence, early memories are not formed. In young organisms, the hippocampal areas of the forebrain, critical for the formation of new long-term memories, are underdeveloped (Nadel & Zola-Morgan, 1984; Squire, 1987). Also, the prefrontal cortex undergoes rapid development at around age 1, with a coincident improvement in the proficiency with which certain cognitive tasks are performed (e.g., Diamond & Doar, 1989). The development of a capacity for autobiographical memory would be limited to the extent that it is subserved by these brain areas. (Bauer, 2004, provides a useful and detailed overview of the establishment of explicit memory processes in the first two years of life.)

This physiological approach to explaining childhood amnesia also seems to fit with some findings on people who have suffered damage to the hippocampus. As discussed in Chapter 6, patients who have suffered such damage often show a dissociation in memory abilities. They are unable to effectively store (or perhaps retrieve) events that have been recently experienced, yet they show preserved ability to learn, and they retain many perceptual and cognitive skills (e.g., Squire & Zola-Morgan, 1988). This view contends that memory is not one thing but actually several different subsystems. (You'll remember this argument from Chapter 6 regarding the corresponding distinction between declarative and procedural memory.) So how might this apply to childhood amnesia? An early suggestion (Bachevalier & Mishkin, 1984; Schacter & Moscovitch, 1984) was that infant memory may obey a similar dissociation. Basically, infants have an early developing procedural system that allows them to succeed on relatively simple memory tasks—like forming associations between events and remembering how to perform tasks such as walking, talking, eating, and so on—and a later-developing declarative system that serves as the basis for more complex memories. This later-developing system serves as the basis for autobiographical memories.

Even if this distinction were correct (and many believe it to be, at best, oversimplified), it would explain childhood amnesia only for events that occur extremely early in life. As we've seen, childhood amnesia extends to ages 3 or 4. Neurological underdevelopment wouldn't be able to explain childhood amnesia for those events that occur relatively late in toddlerhood. Complicating the picture even more is that children themselves do not show childhood amnesia. In other words, little kids (ages 2 to 3) can remember things that happened when they were even littler kids (e.g., ages 1 to 2) (Fivush, Gray, & Fromhoff, 1987). Think about it—a three-year-old can relate something that happened when they were 18 months old, but when 20 years old, their retrieval of this event is extremely unlikely. The fact that they could retrieve it when they were three years old suggests that the basic brain "machinery" is in place, which casts doubt on a purely neurological account of childhood amnesia.

Development of Language.

One of the more popular accounts for childhood amnesia cites developing language skills as the critical factor in the emergence of autobiographical memory. In one of the earlier accounts of the emergence of autobiographical memory, Pillemer and White (1989) suggest that autobiographical memory develops pretty much in lockstep with the development of language. In other words, children begin to remember events from their lives as soon as they are capable of describing these events with language. It makes sense, then, that the emergence of autobiographical memory would mirror the highlights in language development. Children make the most dramatic linguistic strides between ages 2 and 4 (at least in terms of verbal expression), so this is when they start verbally recounting their experiences; in other words, this is when they start developing autobiographical memory.

The importance of language in autobiographical memory has been found in a number of studies demonstrating consistent differences in *narrative style*—the way

> **Research Theme:**
> **Individual Differences**

that families reminisce about, or narrate, past events (Fivush, 1991; Reese & Fivush, 1993). When conversing with their daughters, parents tend to adopt what is termed an *elaborative style;* this consists of long and richly detailed discussions of past events. When conversing with their sons, parents are more likely to adopt what is termed a *pragmatic style.* A pragmatic style of reminiscing is more succinct and contains less detail and elaboration. The style of reminiscing influences the quality of childhood memories; children of elaborative parents have better elaborated accounts of past events than do children of pragmatic parents. Given that this difference between elaborative and pragmatic styles is linked to the sex of a child, it's not surprising that Davis (1999) found evidence for female superiority in autobiographical recall. This difference in narrative style could underlie one's ability to relate in fact, past events in great detail.

In fact, Nelson (1993) cites language as the critical factor in the development of autobiographical memory, claiming that autobiographical memory emerges as parents begin to engage in memory talk with their children. Parents play an active role in guiding and shaping a child's view of "what happened." They serve as "play-by-play announcers," pointing out what was important, how it happened, and why it happened. As events are discussed and recounted, the child begins to build a generic event memory for events that are often repeated (e.g., trips to the zoo) and also, with more unique events, begins to build the autobiographical memory system.

Development of a Cognitive Self.   Not all believe that language is the critical variable in the emergence of autobiographical memory. Howe and Courage (1997; see also Howe, Courage, & Edison, 2003) believe that while language is critical to the expression of stored experiences, it is not the same thing as the stored experiences. In other words, the symbols used to express what happened yesterday are just that—symbols. Just because an 18-month-old child doesn't have the linguistic skill to tell the story of what happened yesterday doesn't mean they don't have a sophisticated notion of what happened yesterday. Language is the most powerful means for expressing experience, but it doesn't determine whether the event is remembered. So what is the critical factor in the offset of childhood amnesia?

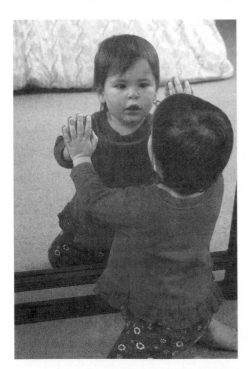

According to Howe and Courage, it is the development of the sense of self. A *sense of self* (or self-concept) refers to one's knowledge that one is a person with unique and recognizable characteristics, and that one thinks and knows things about the world and can serve as a causal agent. This developing sense of self becomes an important organizer of autobiographical experiences. Given that autobiographical memory is basically the knowledge of oneself and one's experience, it makes sense that children don't really demonstrate autobiographical memory until they have a sense of themselves as independent entities. Howe and Courage view language as the mechanism by which autobiographical memories are "let out," not the basis for their development.

Social-Cognitive Development.   So where do we stand? There is no doubt that the emergence of autobiographical memory involves a complex interplay between the developing brain, the use of language, and the child's developing sense of who they are (or indeed, *that* they are *someone*). Nelson and Fivush (2004) attempt to weave these disparate strands of explanation together in their *social-cognitive account* of the emergence of autobiographical memory. They place a particular emphasis on the notion of

One's development of a sense of self plays an important role in autobiographical memory.

emergence. In their view, too much of the discussion of autobiographical remembering has focused on *the point* at which such remembering begins, implicitly making the assumption that there is such a point. Assuming that there is some type of barrier to childhood memories that, once removed, allows for their formation is overly simplistic. Rather, autobiographical remembering is a complex ability that emerges as a number of abilities and contextual factors coalesce.

What are the factors critical to autobiographical memory development, according to the social-cognitive view of Nelson and Fivush? Obviously, the basic explicit memory abilities must be in place, and they seem to be by the time a child is 2 years of age (Bauer, 2004). Language then takes on a prominent role; over time, a developing understanding of *narrative* (i.e., the notion of a meaningful story) enables children to encode events in a richer and more complex manner than had been possible before. The child begins to encode episodes in their life as part of a coherent and meaningful story—the beginning story of their life. In addition, they're engaging in more *memory talk* with adults. As noted earlier in our discussion of the Davis (1999) study, this type of interaction is key in setting the stage for the ability to remember personal events.

Another important factor discussed by Nelson and Fivush is a developing consciousness about the past; children don't really have a sense of themselves across time (i.e., a sense that they have a past self that's connected to their present self) until they're about four years old (Povinelli, Landry, Theall, Clark, & Castille, 1999). This sense of "extended consciousness" is critical to autobiographical memory. This notion may remind you of our earlier discussion of the importance of a sense of self to the development of autobiographical memory. While Nelson and Fivush acknowledge the importance of the self concept, they consider it to be only one of a host of factors that play a role in autobiographical memory's emergence. A related factor is what is commonly termed a *theory of mind,* which refers to a child's understanding that they have a unique set of beliefs, desires, and knowledge that is inaccessible to others.

Nelson and Fivush's social-cognitive view predicts that there should be differences in the emergence of autobiographical memory as a function of culture, to the extent that different cultural backgrounds feature differences in factors like memory talk, reminiscing about the past, and the development of a self-concept. Indeed, there is an increasing body of research demonstrating such differences (e.g., MacDonald, Uesiliana, & Hayne, 2000; Wang, 2004).

Research Theme: Culture

MacDonald, Uesiliana, and Hayne investigated whether differences in early narrative style and interaction might influence the offset of childhood amnesia. This study compared New Zealanders of varying cultural origins: native New Zealanders, New Zealanders of European descent, and New Zealanders of Asian descent. Native New Zealanders (the Maori) have a particularly strong sense of cultural identity and place a strong emphasis on oral tradition, passing down richly descriptive accounts of the past. Based on this characteristic of the Maori people, the researchers hypothesized that the estimated offset of childhood amnesia would occur at a relatively young age. And, given the relatively sparse narrative style of Asian parents and children, the authors expected to find a relatively late offset of childhood amnesia for subjects of Asian origin, with subjects of European origin somewhere in between. The procedure they employed was simple; subjects were asked simply to recount and date their earliest personal recollection.

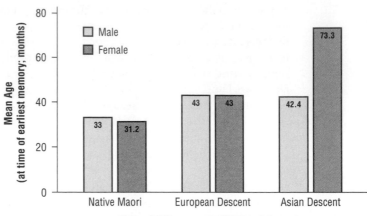

Figure 8.4 Results from MacDonald, Uesiliana, and Hayne (2000).

From MacDonald, S., Uesiliana, K., & Hayne, H. (2000). Cross-cultural and gender differences in childhood amnesia. *Memory, 8,* 365–376. Copyright 2000. Reprinted by permission of Psychology Press, Ltd.

The results are presented in Figure 8.4; as you can see, differences in earliest recollections fit the predictions nicely. As predicted, the age of the earliest reported memories was oldest for the Maori New Zealanders; in other words, they recalled events from earlier in their development than the other two groups. Asian subjects reported significantly later recollections; particularly striking is that this finding was localized in women of Asian descent. This sex difference had not been found in an earlier study of Korean children (Han, Leichtman, & Wang, 1998), suggesting variation within Asian cultures themselves. (The Asian students in the MacDonald and others' study were primarily Chinese.)

Research Theme: Individual Differences

Why did women of Asian descent show such strikingly late personal recollections? MacDonald et al.'s account is consistent with the social-cognitive view of Nelson and Fivush (2004). MacDonald et al. speculate that the long history of socialization differences between men and women in China, a culture that favors men economically and socially, has led to a greater emphasis on the personal experiences and accomplishments of men. As a result, Chinese men have a better developed sense of self than do Chinese women. In light of Howe and Courage's (1997) account of childhood amnesia, it's not surprising that this difference in development and elaboration of the self would lead to differences in the development of autobiographical recall and the offset of childhood amnesia.

The Reminiscence Bump

What an odd title for a section! It sounds like a new dance that cognitive psychologists are doing. But actually, the reminiscence bump refers to another distinctive aspect of the retention function that people show for the memories from their lives. Namely, people recall a disproportionately greater number of memories for events that occur between the ages of 10 and 30 (see Figure 8.2, p. 297). Can you think of why this might be the case? Many of the events that occur in this period are "firsts," and many would be considered life milestones: first kiss, first date, first job, first year of college . . . the list goes on. These events serve as signposts in the stories of our lives. They're salient, distinctive, and important, so it's no wonder that they're well remembered.

This explanation sounds pretty reasonable until you consider some findings from a study by Rubin, Rahhal, and Poon (1998). These researchers reviewed evidence that demonstrates a reminiscence bump not only for personally experienced events (i.e., autobiographical memories), but also for autobiographical facts like the things that people prefer (e.g., movies, books, and music) as well as the events that people think are important or significant historically (like World War II or President Kennedy's assassination). For example, in a study by Holbrook and Schindler (1989) subjects across a wide range of ages were asked to rate how much they enjoyed excerpts from songs that had been popular at different times from the 1930s to the 1980s. People showed a marked preference for songs that were popular when they were between the ages of 10 and 30. In a similar study, Larsen (1996) had older adults (average age 68) recall a particularly memorable reading experience. Books that were particularly memorable tended to have been read between the ages of 10 and 40. Schulster (1996) reported a similar effect for memorable films.

Not only do personal preferences seem to exhibit this "bump," but so do general semantic memories; things we learn in early adulthood are remembered best. Rubin, Rahhal, and Poon (1998) gave subjects multiple-choice tests of their general knowledge for information learned at different times throughout their life span. These included questions about the Academy Awards, the World Series, and current events. As you can see in Figure 8.5, the reminiscence bump was evident. People knew much more about events that had happened in their early adulthood than during any other period. (Recent events were also remembered fairly well, as you can see.)

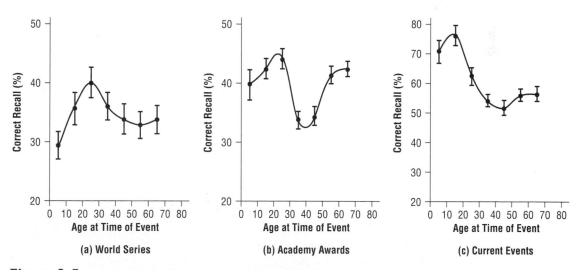

Figure 8.5 Results from Rubin, Rahhal, and Poon (1998).

From Rubin, D. C., Rahhal, T. A., & Poon, L. W. (1998). Things learned in early adulthood are remembered best. *Memory and Cognition, 26*, 3–19. Reprinted by permission of the Psychonomic Society, Inc.

These authors suggest a variety of explanations, any or all of which could play a role. First, it may be that the memory mechanisms described in Chapter 6 favor the retrieval of events from early adulthood because of their importance and distinctiveness. According to this view, these events are thought of (i.e., rehearsed) often due to their importance and are not subject to much interference because of their distinctiveness. A second account might claim that because our cognitive abilities and brain function are at their peak in early adulthood, things experienced during this period are remembered best. A third explanation lies in the notion of identity formation. As you know from experience, the period from adolescence to early adulthood is a critical time for the formation of an individual's identity (Erikson, 1950). So events that occur during this critical period will be the most defining ones, the ones that are most often recounted and incorporated into one's life story.

A review by Habermas and Bluck (2000) fits nicely with this third view. The article, cleverly titled "Getting a Life: The Emergence of the Life Story in Adolescence," points out that the cognitive tools a person needs to *construct* a coherent life story, as well as the social and motivational reasons one needs to *have* a life story, both develop during adolescence. So in some ways, early adulthood is the beginning of the life story. It's no wonder, then, that both personally experienced events and general knowledge learned during this time are so memorable. This analysis provides an interesting parallel to the *cognitive self* explanation for the offset of childhood amnesia. Just as childhood events are encoded more memorably when we've developed a sense *that* we are, later life events are encoded more memorably when we've developed a sense of exactly *who* we are.

Earlier, we discussed how the social-cognitive view predicts variation in autobiographical remembering as a function of cultural variables. This might lead you to believe that there would be cross-cultural variation in the reminiscence bump. Indeed, this is what Conway, Wang, Hanyu, and Haque (2005) hypothesized as they set out to compare life span recall of groups from five different countries (Japan, China, Bangladesh, England, and the United States). Their reasoning was that in Western cultures (e.g., England and the United States), people tend to have a sense of self that is characterized by *independence*—an orientation toward the individual, rather than the group. Because of this orientation, individuals in Western cultures tend to feature an early establishment of a coherent identity and corresponding autobiographical history. By contrast, those in Eastern cultures (e.g., Japan, China, Bangladesh) have a sense of self that is more *interdependent*—an orientation toward relations with others, rather than simply toward the individual themselves. This orientation, which is less focused on the self, leads to a later emergence of a coherent identity and unique autobiographical history.

Based on this analysis, Conway and colleagues predicted that the reminiscence bump—the period of rich and elaborated memories that corresponds to the development of one's personal identity—would be later for individuals from Eastern cultures, relative to those from Western cultures. To test this idea, the researchers collected memories from individuals in the five countries mentioned and plotted life span retention functions for each. The surprising results are presented in Figure 8.6. As you can see, there was *no* cultural variation in the placement of the reminiscence bump! For each culture studied, the bulk of autobiographical memories recalled were for events that occurred between about

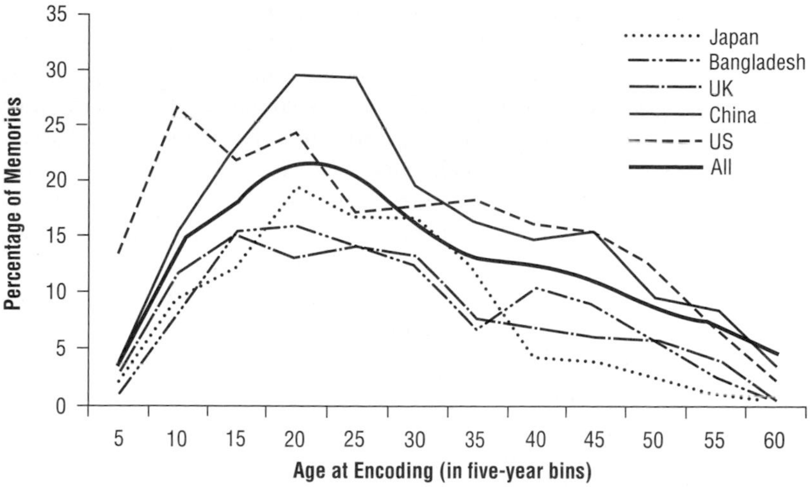

Figure 8.6 Cross-cultural comparison of life span recall curves from Conway, Wang, Hanyu, and Haque (2005).

From Conway, M. A., Wang, Q., Hanyu, K. & Haque, S. A. (2005). Cross-cultural investigation of autobiographical memory: on the universality and cultural variation of the reminiscence bump. *Journal of Cross-Cultural Psychology, 36*(6), 739–749. Sage Publications. Reprinted with permission.

15 and 30 years of age. Based on this seeming universality of the reminiscence bump, the authors suggest that the formation of autobiographical memories in the service of a personal identity might be dictated more by internal factors tied to brain development rather than by external factors that vary among cultures.

Conway and colleagues did find that some other aspects of autobiographical remembering varied as a function of culture. If you look again at Figure 8.6, you'll notice that U.S. subjects had more memories from the early years, consistent with the view that they have an early developing sense of self. Also, the researchers classified each of the memories recalled by the subjects in terms of theme. *Personal-theme* memories were those that involved primarily the individuals themselves. *Social-theme* memories involved collective activities of groups such as family, friends, and coworkers. Consistent with the cultural differences we've been discussing, U.S. subjects were more likely than their Chinese counterparts to relate personal-theme memories, and less likely to relate social-theme memories.

Forgetting

Let's go back to our favorite figure—the retention function for autobiographical memory across the life span (Figure 8.2, p. 297). We've already discussed two of the three components that characterize this function—childhood amnesia and the reminiscence bump. The third characteristic of this function is forgetting—as we might expect, given what we know about memory. For the period immediately preceding recall, there is a pretty standard forgetting curve: recent events are remembered fairly well, but recall falls off pretty quickly for events that aren't as recent. Wagenaar (1986) found that memory dropped from nearly 75% correct to less than 33% correct over a four-year period. You'll note that this is the same pattern of forgetting found in countless studies of memory, beginning with Ebbinghaus's classic self-study (discussed in Chapter 1).

It's not too difficult to come up with some general reasons for autobiographical memory forgetting. As you've seen in Chapter 6, the causes of forgetting are many. Probably the most common cause of autobiographical forgetting is a simple lack of rehearsal; if events are not thought about or discussed (i.e., rehearsed), the corresponding memory representation will be, at best, transient and, at worst, nonexistent. There is also an incredible potential for interference between autobiographical episodes; one need only think of all of the events that have occurred over the past month and how hard it is to retrieve one event in the face of the others; most events don't really stand out. This relates to another likely cause of AM forgetting; many of the daily events in which we partake are routine; every day, we get up, eat breakfast, go to work or school, and so on. When events are this regular and routine, they blend together. Recall what happens when events are repeated, as noted by Linton (1975): repeated episodes lose their individualized character, transitioning from autobiographical (episodic) memories to autobiographical facts (personalized semantic memories).

STOP *and* **REVIEW!**

1. Describe the three basic components of the autobiographical memory function.

2. Two critical determinants of autobiographical memory—language, and a sense of self—reach a critical stage of development at around age:

  a. 1

  b. 2

  c. 3

  d. 4

3. Why does the reminiscence bump occur?

➤ Autobiographical memories retrieved throughout the life span follow a predictable pattern. First, there is a forgetting function, as many memories are retrieved from the last several years before the age of recall. Second, there is a disproportionate number of memories recalled from between the ages of 10 and 30 (the reminiscence bump), and third, relatively few memories are recalled from early childhood, and none before the age of about 3 (childhood amnesia).

➤ Possible reasons for the lack of early memories and the eventual emergence of autobiographical memory include a lack of maturity of the brain before the age of 1. The most important factors in the emergence of autobiographical memory seem to be the large strides in language development and the development of the self that occur at around age 2.

➤ The reminiscence bump probably results in part from the distinctiveness of the events occurring within that particular time period. Forgetting of autobiographical memories occurs as the joint result of lack of rehearsal and interference among memories.

Factors Affecting Retrieval
of Autobiographical Memories

There is little doubt that much autobiographical memory forgetting is the result of retrieval failure; information about our experiences is available to be retrieved, but we need the right cue to access it (recall the availability/accessibility distinction discussed in Chapter 6). Everyone has had the experience of having "forgotten" memories come flooding back when revisiting some location, event, or person. This phenomenon is basically the autobiographical memory version of a context-dependency effect we talked about in Chapter 6. The representations of autobiographical memories are no doubt richly detailed and elaborated; these elaborations can serve to make the memory easier to access at retrieval, should the retrieval environment reactivate some of these elaborations.

Encoding Specificity in Autobiographical Memory

A context-dependency effect is an example of the powerful memory principle (discussed in Chapter 6) termed *encoding specificity*. According to this principle, memory will be successful to the degree that the cues present at retrieval match the way the event was encoded. Marian and Neisser (2000) developed an intriguing test of this idea for autobiographical memory. Their research subjects were bilingual individuals who were fluent in Russian and English. Each was a student at a U.S. university and had emigrated from Russia around a decade earlier. So their autobiographical memories included events that occurred when they lived in Russia and events that had occurred since their arrival in the United States.

Marian and Neisser's method was disarmingly simple. They interviewed each subject using the cue word method described earlier to elicit autobiographical memories. Here's the

Research Theme:
Culture

catch: half of the cue words were presented in Russian, and half of the cue words were presented in English. Can you see where this is going? Marian and Neisser (in line with the encoding specificity principle) hypothesized that autobiographical memories would be especially accessible if the language of retrieval matched the language of encoding. So when subjects were interviewed and presented with cue words in Russian, they should have recalled more "Russian memories" (defined as an event in which the only language used by anyone involved was Russian). The parallel prediction was made for the English interview and cue condition. The results, presented in Figure 8.7a, confirm the prediction neatly.

Marian and Neisser explain their result by noting the inherently linguistic nature of autobiographical memories (discussed earlier in the context of the offset of childhood amnesia). Memories are not only expressed through language but also include language as a fundamental feature of the encoded event. When this salient feature is presented again at retrieval, the entire memory representation is more likely to become active.

If you're particularly interested in experimental design, a thought may have occured to you as you read about this study. The retrieval procedure used by Marian and Neisser involved the entire interview, which was conducted either in Russian or English.

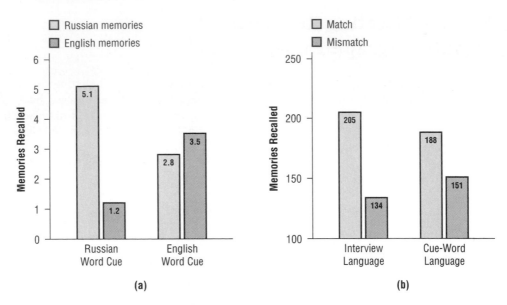

Figure 8.7 Results from Marian and Neisser (2000).

From Marian, V., & Neisser, U. (2000). Language-dependent recall of autobiographical memories. *Journal of Experimental Psychology: General, 129,* 361–368. Copyright 2000 by the American Psychological Association. Reprinted by permission.

In addition, the cue words were presented in the corresponding language (e.g., in the Russian interview, Russian cue words were presented). This raises an interesting question: What was more important in producing the language-dependent recall—the Russian (or English) cue words or the ambience (or feeling) created by the Russian (or English) interview?

This question was tested in a second study in which Marian and Neisser separated the effects of cue word and interview ambience by adding two conditions to the mix. In addition to conditions in which they interviewed and cued in the same language, they added conditions in which the interviewing was done in one language while cues were presented in the other. For instance, the interaction with the subjects might occur entirely in Russian except for the presentation of the cue words, which would occur in English. By adding these conditions, Marian and Neisser hoped to determine which aspect of the retrieval environment was more critical for recall.

The results are presented in the Figure 8.7b. This figure presents the number of autobiographical memories recalled by subjects as a function of whether the language in which the memory had been encoded matched or didn't match the language of the cue word, and whether the language in which the memory had been encoded matched or didn't match the language of the interview. As you can see, a mismatch of either type led to lower levels of recall, but the effect of the interview (ambient) language seems to be the more important factor. Marian and Neisser explain this result by appealing to the notion of a *language mode*. As they point out, using a certain language doesn't just involve saying specific words; it involves a more general way of thinking that is specific to that language. This *state of mind* is distinctive and will likely serve as an effective cue if present at retrieval (i.e., facilitate the *focusing stage* of the constructive memory framework discussed in Chapter 7). The Marian and Neisser (2000) study reveals that retrieval of life experiences obeys a tried-and-true principle of memory—the encoding specificity principle. But other than the general cue that context provides, what other guides do we have for autobiographical memory retrieval? How are autobiographical memories organized and accessed?

Retrieval Cues for Autobiographical Memory

We've seen that the principle of encoding specificity applies to the retrieval of autobiographical memories. What other cues serve as useful triggers for autobiographical memories? Suppose your authors wanted to recall an episode from a visit to Toronto in the summer of 2001. Given the following set of W questions (what? when? where? who?) used in a study by Wagenaar (1986), which do you think would serve as the best cues for memory retrieval?

- What comprised the memory (our visit to Niagara Falls)
- When the event occurred (June 25, 2001)
- Where it occurred (at a restaurant)
- Who was involved (Greg and Bridget)

Well, *what* do you think? "What" served as the best memory cue. The "when" cue was the least helpful. So the cue "our trip to Niagara Falls" will lead to quicker and better recall of that particular event than will "June 25, 2001."

These results are consistent with those found in a diary study by Brewer (1988). He found that location ("where") and time ("when") were poor cues for retrieval, but actions ("what") were good cues for retrieval. Once again, this makes sense; in trying to remind a friend of an incident at a restaurant, it would be more effective to say, "Remember the time you won $150 playing pull tabs" than "Remember that time at Ol' Mexico?" This second cue will be relatively ineffective, particularly if going to Ol' Mexico is a repeated event. This result seems to indicate that the repetition of events leads to poor episodic memories (i.e., autobiographical memories), which replicates the result found in Linton's (1975) self-study indicating that event repetitions lead to a transition from specific episodic memories (i.e., autobiographical memories) to more general semantic memories (i.e., autobiographical facts).

Odors as Cues to Autobiographical Memory.   When we discuss autobiographical memories in class or with friends, the question of whether odors are especially strong memory cues invariably arises. Everyone has had the experience of a vivid memory leaping into consciousness in the presence of a distinctive odor. The most famous example of this is a literary one, from Marcel Proust's *Swann's Way* (1922/1960):

> I raised to my lips a spoonful of the tea in which I had soaked a morsel of the cake. No sooner had the warm liquid, and the crumbs with it, touched my palate than a shudder ran through my whole body, and I stopped, intent upon the extraordinary changes that were taking place. . . . I was conscious that it was connected with the taste of tea and cake, but that it infinitely transcended those savours. (p. 58)

What did *you* do on June 25, 2001?

What Proust experienced was the apparent power of odors to elicit memories that are especially old and vivid; this has been termed the **Proust phenomenon** (Chu & Downes, 2000). Proust's anecdote provides a powerful description of the power of olfactory cues. But anecdotes are poor evidence, so Chu and Downes (2000, 2002) set out to put the Proust phenomenon to the empirical test. Chu and Downes (2002) used a straightforward cuing procedure to compare the effectiveness of odors and verbal labels in eliciting autobiographical recall. They gave subjects an odor-label cue (e.g., the word *ginger*), and asked them to recall an autobiographical memory. Once they had one in mind, they described it and rated it on a number of different scales including pleasantness, vividness, uniqueness, and personal significance. They were then asked to pursue the memory further, and this is where the critical comparison came in. Some of the subjects were re-presented with the odor label, and were asked again to describe and rate the memory. Other subjects were presented with the actual odor (ginger, in this example) and like the other group, were asked to describe and rate the memory again. Chu and Downes (2002) were interested in how this second recall would differ from the first. The anecdotal evidence suggested that odors would prompt more vivid and detailed memories than the corresponding verbal cue.

It turns out that, as the authors quip in the title of their article, "Proust nose best." Odors did indeed turn out to be more powerful cues for autobiographical memories. When the second recall was cued by the odor rather than a second presentation of the odor label, subject ratings of the personal nature of the memory, its vividness, and its pleasantness all increased significantly. When the second recall was cued by the odor label rather than the odor, those ratings barely budged. In addition, the researchers measured recall detail by analyzing the words subjects used to describe the memories in their verbal reports. This analysis provided converging evidence for the effectiveness of odors as cues; subjects used more words to describe odor-cued memories relative to memories cued verbally (i.e., the odor label).

STOP *and* THINK! ──────────────────

WHAT'S THAT SMELL?

Do some personal introspection about odors and memories and then answer the following questions:

- Are there any smells that cue particularly strong memories for you?
- What are these smells, and what are the accompanying memories?
- Are these memories especially vivid?
- Are the memories from especially early in life?
- Do any of the memories share a common theme?

If you're having trouble coming up with odor-cued memories, try to think of memories that you associate with these odors:

- a hospital or nursing home
- fresh-baked cookies
- bread baking
- perfume
- gasoline

So why are odors such effective cues? Chu and Downes (2002) present a couple of possibilities. One involves the proximity of the sensory area for olfaction to mechanisms important to memory—more specifically, areas near the amygdala and hippocampus. Due to this proximity, Chu and Downes speculate that the olfactory areas may be especially likely to influence the memory-related processing of the amygdala. We'll discuss another possible reason for the effectiveness of odors as cues in the next section, as we consider a leading theory of autobiographical memory construction.

The Self-Memory System

We've seen that autobiographical memory involves effortful reconstruction, rather than rote retrieval. Furthermore, we've seen in this chapter and the last that memory can be profoundly influenced by a host of factors ranging from cuing conditions and context to one's personal goals, motivations, or biases. In line with this general idea, Conway and his colleagues (Conway, 2005; Conway & Pleydell-Pierce, 2000; Conway, Singer, & Tagini, 2004) have developed a model of autobiographical memory termed the **self-memory system.** According to this approach, autobiographical memories are not retrieved as whole episodes. Rather, they are *reconstructed* from an autobiographical knowledge base in the service of higher-level plans and goals. Consistent with the workings of memory that you've read about to this point, autobiographical memories are personal interpretations of life events, and not necessarily veridical records of these events.

The self-memory system includes two components. One component is termed the *autobiographical memory knowledge base.* Based on research investigating the effect of various sorts of cues on the speed and ease of access to autobiographical memory (Anderson & Conway, 1993; Conway & Bekerian, 1987), Conway and colleagues propose that autobiographical memory knowledge is organized hierarchically, with three distinct layers of knowledge (see Figure 8.8).

The first layer is *lifetime periods,* substantial slices of our lifetime that are characterized by specific goals, plans, or themes (e.g., the authors' years in graduate school at Purdue). Also, within a given lifetime period, autobiographical knowledge is organized into different thematic categories, such as academic experiences and relationships. The second layer of knowledge is *general events,* a more specific representation of particular events that occurred over the weeks and months that make up each lifetime period. For

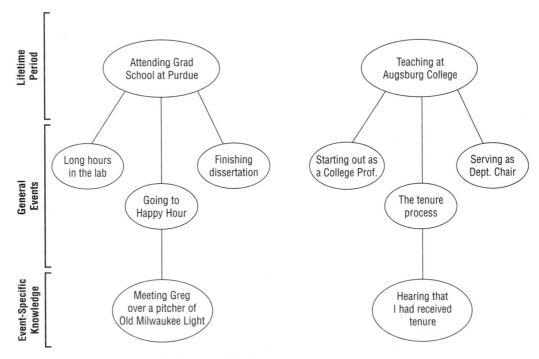

Figure 8.8 Conway's hierarchical model of autobiographical retrieval.

Adapted from Conway, M. A. (1995). Autobiographical knowledge and autobiographical memories. In D. C. Rubin (ed.) *Remembering our past: Studies in autobiographical memory.* New York: Cambridge University Press. Adapted with permission from Cambridge University Press and the author.

We tend to remember memories in terms of certain lifetime periods—for instance, your authors remember their years at Purdue.

example, Greg remembers all the times he shot pool at Locomotives, a local dive in West Lafayette, Indiana (and Bridget remembers watching him!). Knowledge at the general-event layer can be used to access information at the third layer of storage, *event-specific knowledge*. At this layer are sensory-perceptual details that can be used to construct a specific memory. For example, we remember the particular Friday afternoon happy hour when we met each other for the first time over a pitcher of Old Milwaukee Light (how romantic!). This type of cognitive organization should sound familiar. Do you recall the idea of levels of categorization (superordinate level, basic level, and subordinate level) discussed in Chapter 5? It seems that autobiographical memories are organized in much the same way.

According to this model, autobiographical remembering involves a process of retrieval from the autobiographical memory knowledge base that proceeds from general to specific layers. The construction of an autobiographical memory takes place "on the spot." Cognitively, this means that we use working memory processes to generate a memory that is consistent with current *task demands* and goals. These task demands and goals are maintained by the second component of the self-memory system, the *working self*. The working self is basically your representation of, well, . . . *you*. It includes your current goals, as well as knowledge about your own values, attitudes, and beliefs. An interesting implication of this reconstructive model of autobiographical memory is that it's possible (even likely) that someone would remember the same event differently on two different occasions, depending on those values, beliefs, or goals.

The self-memory system model (in particular the notion of an autobiographical memory database from which we build memories) fits quite nicely with a number of findings from investigations of autobiographical memory. First, a study by Barsalou (1988) had subjects generate specific memories of what they had done over their summer vacations. In spite of instructions to be specific, over 60% of the memories that the subjects generated were general memories like, "I read a lot" or "We went to the beach."

This suggests that rather than directly accessing specific memories, people sample from general knowledge of the period—specifically, the intermediate level (Conway, 1996). It's interesting to note here that this is the same level at which people tend to access categories—instead of thinking of "animals" (superordinate level) or "fat Tabby who loves Pounce treats" (subordinate level), we think "cat" (basic—intermediate—level). Second, Conway and Bekerian (1987) found that recalling from a given lifetime period led to substantial priming effects in recalling other events from that same period, which would be expected if life events were categorized as proposed in the model. Third, retrieval of autobiographical memories is typically a slow and effortful reconstruction rather than a rapid retrieval of facts. For example, it will take you longer to reconstruct what you did last June than it will to retrieve the colors of the rainbow or the 12 months of the year. Finally, the model's proposal that autobiographical memories are constructed "on the fly," and therefore can vary depending on the retrieval circumstances, is consistent with the fact that autobiographical memories can be variable across multiple recalls.

Let's return to the Chu and Downes (2002) finding that smell serves as an especially potent cue for autobiographical memory. One explanation for its potency relates to Conway's multiple levels of autobiographical knowledge and retrieval. According to Conway (1992), sensory cues such as smell are capable of bypassing the usual reconstructive process of autobiographical memory construction and making direct contact with information at the most specific level—event-specific knowledge. This is consistent with the fact that memories cued by smell don't seem reconstructed at all—they seem to present themselves immediately and completely to your conscious experience.

STOP and THINK!

RECONSTRUCTING AUTOBIOGRAPHICAL MEMORIES

Try and remember any event that relates to

- summer vacations
- Christmas
- final exams

Take special note of the reconstruction process that you go through:

- Does this process match the autobiographical retrieval process as outlined by Conway?
- Was this reconstructive process rapid or slow?
- Do your memories seem to be hierarchically organized?

Try and fit the elements of your memory within the framework laid out in Figure 8.8.

The Brain and Autobiographical Remembering. Conway and his colleagues (Conway & Pleydell-Pearce, 2001; Conway, Pleydell-Pearce, & Whitecross, 2001; Conway et al., 1999) have cast some light on the brain processes underlying the construction of an autobiographical memory. Conway and Turk (1999) elaborate on the model of autobiographical memory construction derived above and attempt to relate the processes in their constructive model to cortical areas in the brain. Previous research on brain activity during episodic memory retrieval revealed a number of consistent findings. One you may remember from Chapter 6: recall the HERA (hemispheric encoding/retrieval asymmetry) model proposed by Nyberg, Cabeza, and Tulving (1996). These researchers found that the retrieval processes used during memory tasks, such as free and cued recall, involve extensive right-hemisphere activation and relatively little left-hemisphere activation (in contrast to encoding, which revealed the opposite pattern).

Conway and Turk (1999) were interested in any possible differences between the rote-type recall of episodic memories that characterizes a laboratory memory task and the constructive recall that characterizes autobiographical memory. They had subjects perform two different memory tasks while they were being PET scanned. One was a standard paired-associate task in which subjects memorized word pairs and were asked to recall the second member of the pair, given the first. The other task was to generate specific autobiographical memories in response to presented cue words. To verify that they had indeed generated a memory, subjects gave a one-word description to the experimenter.

The scanning results featured some interesting surprises. Markedly different patterns of activation characterized the paired-associate and autobiographical-memory-generation tasks. Activity during the paired-associate test mirrored earlier findings of Nyberg and others (1996): increased activation in the right hemisphere, particularly temporal and prefrontal regions. However, activity during autobiographical memory generation featured prominent and intense activation in the left hemisphere, particularly in the frontal regions. Conway and Turk consider this left-hemisphere activation a "distinguishing feature" of autobiographical memory recall and propose that it reflects the operation of a self-memory system located in the left frontal areas. Converging evidence for this suggestion comes from brain-imaging studies of the self-reference effect (discussed in Chapter 6), which have revealed extensive left-hemisphere activation (Craik et al., 1999). More recent work (e.g., Addis, Wong, and Schacter 2007) has gone further to specify the precise brain mechanisms involved in the recall of autobiographical memories. These areas include medial regions of the prefrontal cortex and the medial temporal regions, in particular regions around the hippocampus. This makes sense, because as you'll recall, these regions are critical in the formation and retrieval of episodic memories.

Involuntary Autobiographical Memories

The research described in this chapter has dealt almost exclusively with effortful and *conscious* retrieval of autobiographical memories—cases in which people actively seek to reconstruct  a memory from their past. But that's not always the way autobiographical memories are retrieved; quite often, memories enter consciousness without any effort or deliberate search. In fact, these unconsciously cued memories comprise a fair number of the autobiographical memories that we experience on a daily basis (e.g., Brewin, Christodoulides,

& Hutchinson, 1996). But these memories have not been the subject of much investigation, for reasons that may be apparent: involuntary memories are just that—involuntary; therefore, neither the rememberer nor the experimenter can exert control over their appearance. This makes them difficult to study in a systematic manner. They have, however, long been of interest in a clinical setting; those who suffer from post-traumatic stress disorder (PTSD) often experience intrusive, frightening, involuntary recollections (Christiansen, 1992).

Berntsen (1996, 1998) performed a series of investigations to compare the characteristics of voluntary and involuntary memories. To study involuntary autobiographical memories, Berntsen (1996) had subjects record two involuntary memories a day in a diary. Then, in a follow-up study (Berntsen, 1998), cue words derived from the previously collected diaries were used (with a different sample of subjects) to elicit voluntary autobiographical memories. Berntsen compared voluntary and involuntary memories on a number of key variables: level of specificity, emotional intensity, amount of rehearsal, and event recency.

The investigation revealed differences between involuntary and voluntary memories. Perhaps the most striking was the level of specificity of the memories; nearly 90% of the involuntary memories were of specific events. The number of specific memories voluntarily recalled in response to cues was just over 60%, so it seems that voluntary memories are more likely than involuntary memories to be generic descriptions of events (i.e., from the intermediate level of the autobiographical knowledge base, as described above). Involuntary memories tended to have received less frequent rehearsals relative to voluntary memories. In addition, involuntary memories were more likely to show a **Pollyanna effect,** with a predominance of positive memories recalled (an exception to this general rule can be seen in cases of psychological disorders such as PTSD, in which involuntary memories are negative). Involuntary memories tended to be of more recent origin than voluntary memories, contrary to popular folklore (e.g., Salaman, 1970). Finally, Berntsen and Hall (2004) added one more layer to the analysis of involuntary autobiographical memories by focusing on these memories' accompanying phenomenological qualities—in other words, how involuntary autobiographical memories feel on a subjective level. Berntsen and Hall found that involuntary memories, relative to voluntary memories, seem to involve a more intense "reliving" of the original experience, replete with vivid recollection of the emotions and sensations experienced.

Based on what seem to be fairly salient differences between involuntary and voluntary memories, particularly in their levels of specificity and the way in which they're retrieved, Berntsen (1998) proposes that there may be two different systems for autobiographical memory retrieval. The hierarchical autobiographical knowledge base described above is the system used in voluntary searches of autobiographical memory and is likely to yield general (intermediate-level) autobiographical memories. A second system might serve as the basis for the spontaneous retrieval of highly specific and unique episodes, which are cued by particular situations. So according to this (speculative) view, involuntary memories are not reconstructed; they are more or less directly retrieved as episodes. Whether this added complexity to the proposed processes involved in autobiographical memory retrieval is warranted awaits further empirical test.

STOP *and* THINK!

WHAT POPS INTO YOUR HEAD?

For the next week or so, keep a running diary of memories that just seem to "pop into your head" for no apparent reason (that is, involuntary memories). Jot down a short description of each memory. After you've accumulated a number of these memories, evaluate them to determine if they show the same characteristics revealed in Berntsen's (1996) study.

- Do your involuntary memories tend to be recent?
- Do your involuntary memories tend to be positive?
- Do your involuntary memories tend to be specific rather than general?

STOP *and* REVIEW!

1. The most effective cue for retrieving an episode appears to be which of these "W questions"?
   a. what happened
   b. where something happened
   c. when something happened
   d. who was present
2. True of false? Odors are effective retrieval cues for autobiographical memories.
3. Name the three levels of the autobiographical memory database, according to the self-memory system model.
4. Name two characteristics that differ between involuntary and voluntary autobiographical memories.

➤ The reconstruction of autobiographical memories is subject to the encoding specificity principle. Re-presenting linguistic context leads to enhanced recall of memories. Aside from context, the best cues for autobiographical memories tend to be hints about what happened in a specific episode, rather than where or when it happened, or with whom.

➤ The Proust phenomenon refers to the famous author's anecdotal report of the unique power of olfactory (odor) cues in eliciting memories. Consistent with this anecdotal evidence, odors do serve as effective cues for autobiographical memories.

➤ According to the self-memory system model of autobiographical memories, autobiographical remembering is a reconstructive process based on three different levels of knowledge (lifetime periods, general events, and event-specific knowledge). Neuroscientific evidence regarding the construction of autobiographical memories reveals a progression from left-frontal activation to right-hemisphere temporal and parietal activation.

➤ Research on involuntary autobiographical memories reveals a number of distinguishing features. Involuntary memories tend to be more recent and more positive, and involve a more intense "reliving" of the original experience than do voluntary autobiographical memories.

Emotion and Autobiographical Memory

Of all the influences on our life's memories, perhaps none is so evident as emotion. Many of the events we remember are emotionally charged: your first kiss; hearing a startling piece of news, good or bad; the time you won the spelling bee (actually, we both came in second—sniff); your favorite team winning the World Series or your college winning the NCAA basketball championship. The impact of emotion on autobiographical memories has been a focal point of investigation and, as we'll see, a source of some controversy. A number of studies have attempted to determine how we remember autobiographical experiences associated with particular emotions. In one early study, Robinson (1980) used the cuing technique, asking people to retrieve memories in response to emotion-word prompts such as *angry*. The study revealed that emotional experiences are associated with shorter retrieval times than nonemotional experiences, implying that emotional events enjoy heightened accessibility in memory. Let's now turn to a discussion of the autobiographical memories that are among the most accessible ones you have.

Almost everyone will remember vividly the circumstances in which they heard about the tragic events of September 11, 2001.

Flashbulb Memories

No doubt one of the most interesting and well-documented forms of emotional memory is **flashbulb memory**—a detailed, vivid, and confidently held memory for the circumstances surrounding when you first heard some startling bit of news. Our parents will never forget what they were doing when they heard the news of John F. Kennedy's assassination; we'll never forget what we were doing when we heard about (or saw) the explosion of the space shuttle *Challenger*. And none of us will ever forget what we were doing when we heard that two airliners had hit and toppled the World Trade Center towers. Memories for when you heard the news of a surprising event are striking in their degree of detail and vividness, and therefore we'd swear to their accuracy. Indeed, the term *flashbulb* implies that the events are brief in duration, surprising, and lead to photograph-quality memories. As you'll see, there is some truth to these assertions.

Characteristics of Flashbulbs.   The defining research on flashbulb memories was reported by Brown and Kulik (1977). They asked adults to report their memory for when they heard about the assassinations of John F. Kennedy, Martin Luther King, Jr., and Malcolm X, among others. One of the most striking things to emerge from their investigation was the consistency in the types of information reported about these memories. The flashbulb memories that people reported tended to include five categories of information: *location* (where they heard), *activity* (what they were doing), *source* (who told them), *emotion* (how they felt emotionally when they heard), and *aftermath* (what they did next). Figure 8.9 presents two accounts of the space shuttle *Challenger* explosion taken from subjects in an investigation by Neisser and Harsch (1992). Note that both accounts include each of the five components of a flashbulb memory.

STOP *and* THINK! ━━━━━━━━━━━━━━━━━━━━━

IS IT A FLASHBULB?

Try to retrieve a flashbulb memory. Once you have, see whether it includes the components that typically characterize these memories:

- who told you
- where you heard
- what you were doing when you heard
- how you felt
- what you did next

Then answer these questions:

- Is this memory personally relevant to you in any way?
- What factors do you think have led to its vividness?

Flashbulb Account A

"When I first heard about the explosion I was sitting in my freshman dorm room with my roommate and we were watching TV. It came on a news flash and we were both totally shocked. I was really upset and I went upstairs to talk to a friend of mine and then I called my parents."

Flashbulb Account B

"I was in my religion class and some people walked in and started talking about [it]. I didn't know any details except that it had exploded and the schoolteacher's students had all been watching which I thought was so sad. Then after class I went to my room and watched the TV program talking about it and I got all the details from that."

Figure 8.9 Two sample accounts of the *Challenger* explosion (from Neisser & Harsch, 1992).

From Neisser, U., & Harsch, N. (1992). Phantom flashbulbs: False recollections of hearing the news about *Challenger*. In E. Winograd & U. Neisser (Eds.), *Affect and accuracy in recall: Studies of "flashbulb" memories* (pp. 9–31). New York: Cambridge University Press. Reprinted by permission of Cambridge University Press.

What Produces a Flashbulb?   What accounts for the seeming clarity, accuracy, and vividness of these memories? Early in the investigation of flashbulb memories, Brown and Kulik (1977) proposed that any event that is particularly surprising and consequential (such as the assassination of a leader) receives prioritized processing in the brain, almost as if the memory of the event was "seared in" by a special brain mechanism. This account is typically termed "Now Print!" Such a mechanism would have high adaptive value; an organism that can remember consequential past events is more likely to adapt to changing conditions. Brown and Kulik also proposed that the more consequential the event, the more rehearsal it receives. People think about the event frequently and relate it to others, which leads the memory to be more detailed.

This mechanism leads to one of the central questions about flashbulb memories—their accuracy. Subjectively, flashbulb memories seem so clear, but how accurate are they? And how do flashbulb memories hold up over time? Research has provided mixed results. Early studies indicated that such memories were highly accurate; Pillemer (1984) found that subjects' memories for the 1982 assassination attempt on former president Ronald Reagan included many accurate details two months after the event and that seven months later, they had lost very little of that detail. But a number of studies of people's recollections for hearing about the space shuttle *Challenger* explosion gave researchers some pause. McCloskey, Wible, and Cohen (1988) found that these recollections were not astoundingly accurate; only a little over half of the accounts were consistent across two tests given one week and nine months later.

One of the most striking examples of inconsistency was provided by Neisser and Harsch (1992). Look back at the accounts of the space shuttle *Challenger* explosion in Figure 8.9. We mentioned that these were two different accounts, but we left out the interesting fact that these accounts are from the same person. Neisser and Harsch found evidence for what they termed *phantom flashbulbs*. The day following the tragedy, the researchers gave a questionnaire to subjects regarding the circumstances under which they first heard the news (account B). Two and a half years later, subjects were once again given this questionnaire (account A). Much to Neisser and Harsch's surprise, there were many serious errors in reporting (although many accounts were correct as well). Even showing the subjects their original (day-after) recall protocols failed to bring the memories back! And even when interviewed six months after this point in time, these erroneous accounts remained consistent.

What mechanisms account for such striking inconsistencies and misplaced confidence? One trend in the misremembrances was a phenomenon termed *TV priority* (Neisser & Harsch, 1992): many of the mistaken recollections were associated with subjects having heard about the event on television. The researchers suggest that these mistakes likely arose in several ways. Subjects no doubt watched a good deal of follow-up news reports on the tragedy; the image of the space shuttle going up in flames was widely and repeatedly broadcast; indeed, one still sees it occasionally replayed today. Perhaps most interesting of all, Neisser and Harsch propose that people have a schema for hearing about disaster news, a schema that includes having watched TV coverage. For example, how many of you heard about the World Trade Center attack on TV? Given the prominence of TV in our culture, this is the avenue by which we most frequently hear about disasters. Therefore, it isn't surprising that a later reconstruction of how one first heard a piece of news would include a memory of having seen it on TV. Another type of error observed was the *time slice error*—subjects vividly recalled an occasion on which they heard about the event. And indeed, it may have been an instance of hearing about the event, but it wasn't the first instance. So subjects remembered the wrong "slice" of time. To use a term from Chapter 7, this is a *failure in source monitoring* (failing to correctly attribute the source of a memory).

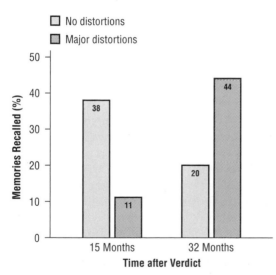

□ No distortions

□ Major distortions

Accuracy and Distortion in Flashbulb Memories

Figure 8.10 Results from Schmolck, Buffalo, and Squire (2000).

From Schmolck, H., Buffalo, L. R., & Squire, L. R. (2000). Memory distortions develop over time: Recollections of the O. J. Simpson trial verdict after 15 and 32 months. *Psychological Science, 11,* 39–45. Copyright 2000 by Blackwell, Inc. Reprinted by permission.

So it seems that the evidence is mixed regarding the accuracy and durability of flashbulb memories. A number of studies (e.g., Christiansen, 1989; Pillemer, 1984) have found these memories to be more accurate than the typical memory, while other studies (e.g., Bohannon & Symons, 1992; Neisser & Harsch, 1992) have found a fair amount of distortion in these memories. A study by Schmolck, Buffalo, and Squire (2000) pinpointed one possible source of the discrepant findings. The authors noted that studies that found more distortion typically featured a longer delay between the event and recollection; studies with shorter delays demonstrated less distortion and better overall recollection. They tested this observation by investigating students' flashbulb memories for the O. J. Simpson trial verdict. These quick-thinking researchers, who knew a flashbulb memory when they encoded one, tested students three days after the verdict was announced, and then again 15 or 32 months later. Their results (see Figure 8.10) indicated a powerful interaction of delay with both accuracy and distortion. At the 15-month delay, 38% of the recollections showed no real distortions, with only 11% containing significant distortions. However, at the 32-month

What were you doing when O. J. Simpson was declared not guilty?

delay, only 20% of the recollections were without distortions, and nearly half included major distortions. In accordance with what you read in Chapter 7 about false memories, even flashbulb memories can show significant distortions, given a long retention interval.

Based on studies like these, the current view on the formation of flashbulb memories is that for the most part, flashbulb memories can be accounted for by appealing to some of the well-known factors that have been shown in countless laboratory studies to influence memory: degree of rehearsal, distinctiveness, and salience or personal relevance. Each of these factors leads to well-formed memories of any event. But Schooler and Eich (2000) suggest that while these usual memory mechanisms can account for the formation of flashbulbs, the operation of these basic mechanisms is somehow supplemented and/or intensified by emotion. The nature of emotion's effect is still unclear; it may alter the initial encoding of the event, or it may enhance the likelihood that the event is rehearsed on a later occasion.

It is also important to note that even if flashbulbs are phenomenologically "special" in their seeming vividness and detail, they are not special in one respect: They involve the same reconstructive memory processes, and hence the distortion, that characterize any other memory. But even in the face of significant distortion, the degree of vividness and clarity that characterizes flashbulb memories does seem to distinguish them from other episodic memories. So in answer to the question, "Are flashbulbs a special type of memory?", most memory researchers would probably answer, "Yeah, sort of." Or perhaps with a little more attention to grammar, they'd say, "Flashbulb memories are 'special, but not that special'" (Christiansen, 1989).

Memories of 9/11.   Certainly some of the most powerful memories formed in the past decade are those related to the horrific events of September 11, 2001. Memories of the terrorist attacks on New York and Washington, D.C. would almost certainly qualify as flashbulb memories; you most likely remember information from all of the standard categories that define a flashbulb memory. But never have so many people felt so personally about a public event. The families of thousands of people were directly impacted by the attacks, and millions of people around the country (not to mention around the world) suffered from anxiety and stress in the attacks' wake. A number of investigators (e.g., Pezdek, 2004; Schmidt, 2004) have looked at people's memory for the events of that day to gain some insights on how we process and remember public events of an extremely stressful nature.

Pezdek (2004) investigated memory for the attacks in subject groups who varied in their physical (and, quite likely, emotional) proximity to the attacks—college students in Manhattan, California, and Hawaii. Her view was that the differing levels of distress experienced by these subjects would lead to corresponding differences in memory. She was also interested in contrasting two different sorts of memory—*event memory* for the specifics of the attacks (e.g., what time did the first plane hit the WTC towers?), and *autobiographical memory* for the circumstances in which people heard news of the attacks (e.g., who told you of the attacks?). To understand why she contrasted these particular types of memory, let's consider Neisser, Windgrael, Bergman, Schreiber, Palmer, and Welden's (1996) narrative hypothesis of flashbulb memories. According to this view, stressful events (e.g., flashbulb events) are likely to be transformed into "narrative constructions"—stories—that are repeatedly told. These repeated tellings function as rehearsals and lead to vivid and detailed recollection. This is where the distinction between event memory and autobiographical memory comes in.

According to Pezdek's extension of the narrative hypothesis, the stress of an event will improve memory for whatever aspects are being closely monitored. Consider the different subject groups tested by Pezdek; the subjects in Manhattan were no doubt extremely upset and stressed about the unfolding events, and were paying close attention to them. Therefore, the stress they experienced would most likely improve their event memory. By contrast, observers elsewhere (including the California and Hawaii samples) were no doubt upset, but were likely more focused on talking to others about the news. They and their families were in no immediate danger, in contrast to the Manhattan sample. Therefore, the stress they experienced would most likely improve their autobiographical memory for the personal circumstances surrounding how they heard about the event. Pezdek tested her hypothesis by surveying students seven weeks after the attack. She asked them questions about the events of September 11, 2001, and their personal recollections of how they had experienced the day. The results fit the hypothesis nicely. Subjects from Manhattan remembered the events surrounding the attacks with greater accuracy than did subjects in the other two samples. In contrast, the autobiographical memories of the New York sample were more sparse than those of the California and Hawaii samples.

Pezdek also found some interesting evidence of reconstruction. Nearly three-quarters (73%) of all subjects reported that they had seen videotape of the first plane hitting the WTC towers. In reality, this memory must have been a reconstruction because this event was not filmed. Also, a significant number (61%) falsely reported that the first WTC tower had collapsed prior to the attack on the Pentagon. As was the case with the phantom flashbulbs discussed earlier, these are sensible errors. Given the extensive TV coverage of the events in subsequent weeks, it would seem sensible (even obvious) to assume that one had seen video of the first plane's attack. The misalignment of the WTC towers' collapse and the Pentagon attack likely resulted from a clustering of the events in New York, which led to an underestimation of the time that intervened between the attack on the WTC towers and their subsequent collapse. Other studies have also demonstrated that even the unforgettably tragic characteristics of an event like the 9/11 attacks are not impervious to forgetting, although the certainty with which we hold our memories seems relatively unshakeable (e.g., Talarico & Rubin, 2003).

Effects of Mood on Remembered Events

A second area of investigation that lies at the crossroads of emotion and memory is the relationship between mood and the types of memories people recall. If we're in a sad mood, do we recall sad experiences? Might such a link be at the root of psychological disorders like depression?

Mood Dependence.   A great deal of the research on the interplay between mood and memory has focused on one phenomenon. **Mood-dependent memory** refers to the finding that retrieval of a previously encoded event is enhanced when the mood experienced at retrieval matches the mood that was present at encoding. Sound familiar? It should; the principle of mood dependency is conceptually quite similar to Tulving's encoding specificity principle, discussed in Chapter 6. This phenomenon would seem to have some important ramifications for mood disorders. If one is depressed, does this lead to enhanced retrieval of negative autobiographical memories? And does this inclination, in turn, deepen depression?

Depression and Autobiographical Memory Recall.   The interplay between mood and memory has important implications for the treatment of depression. As we've seen, people often tend to recall events that are congruent with their current mood; as you might expect, people suffering from depression are likely to retrieve negative memories. Indeed, this is the case for both traditional laboratory materials, such as words and stories, and for autobiographical experiences (e.g., Williams & Scott, 1988). The bias is also evident in speed of retrieval; depressives are faster at retrieving negative events from memory and slower at retrieving positive events, relative to nondepressed controls. This *preferential treatment* for negative experiences can both worsen depression and impair one's attempt to overcome it. (See Blaney, 1986, for a review of the relationship between affect and memory.)

Another possible reason for this dominance of negative autobiographical recall, and for its continuing hold on those suffering from depressive disorders, is a tendency for depressives to be overly general in autobiographical recall (Williams, 1996). For example, if asked to recall an academic failure from college, a nondepressed individual may recall that they really struggled on their midterm in biology. In contrast, in response to the same prompt, a depressed individual might remember that last semester was a complete disaster. Stated in terms of the self-memory system model of autobiographical memory, depressives recall events from the higher (more general) level of the autobiographical knowledge hierarchy.

Research indicates that the relative inability of depressed individuals to be specific in remembering past events leads to a number of memory deficits. For instance, lack of specificity in their remembering has been linked to their inability to solve present problems (Evans, Williams, O'Loughlin, & Howells, 1992). This makes sense; if people are unable to remember previous problems, along with the specifics of how the situations were resolved, then current problems will be more difficult to master. Lack of specificity in autobiographical memory also affects our perceptions of the future. Williams, Ellis, Tyers, Healy, Rose, and MacLeod (1996) found that suicidally depressed patients' lack of specificity about the past was associated with an inability to imagine future events. Based on this, depressed individuals will have trouble imagining in any specific and concrete way how things might get better in the future. This deficit in future problem solving makes depression that much harder to overcome.

STOP *and* **REVIEW!**

1. What is a flashbulb memory?
2. What are the five types of information typically included in a flashbulb memory?
3. True or false? The September 11 attacks were so jarring that flashbulb memories for that day are especially accurate.
4. Mood-state dependence refers to
   a. the fact that people tend to remember events when the retrieval mood is the same as the original encoding mood.
   b. the fact that people tend to retrieve events that match their current mood.
   c. the finding that depressed people tend to retrieve overly general memories.
   d. the general finding that mood and emotion influence autobiographical memory.

➤ Emotion has a number of powerful influences on autobiographical memory and is thought to play an important role in flashbulb memories, which are detailed, vivid, and confidently held memories for the circumstances surrounding when a person first heard some startling bit of news.

➤ Flashbulb memories tend to include information about who told you about the event, where you were, what you were doing, how you felt, and what you did after you heard. Despite their vividness, these memories are subject to forgetting, as revealed by findings of phantom flashbulbs, confident and vivid recall that is wholly inaccurate.

➤ Memories for the terrorist attacks of 9/11 fit the profile of a flashbulb memory, although different patterns of memory have been found for individuals with different levels of involvement in the events of that day. Memories for these attacks also show evidence of distortion, like any other memory.

➤ Mood-state dependence refers to the fact that recall is better when mood at retrieval matches mood at encoding. Mood-congruent and overly general recall seem to play an important role in depression.

Conclusion: Functions of Autobiographical Memory

What is the importance of autobiographical memory? What are its functions? Bruce (1989) distinguishes between two senses of the word *function*. One sense is that of *adaptive significance:* Why would some set of memory processes have evolved in a particular way? Is there something adaptive about having strikingly vivid memories of newsworthy events, as in the case of flashbulb memories? Bruce also refers to another sense of function—*real-world usefulness:* What good is this type of memory to our daily living? Pillemer (1992, 1998) offers some compelling answers to these questions. According to his view, autobiographical memories serve three important functions: communicative, emotional, and directive.

Communicative Function

Autobiographical memory serves a *communicative function.* A significant part of the conversations we have with others involves telling them personal stories relevant to the topic at hand. Specific autobiographical memories are especially powerful in this regard. Relating details of personally experienced events makes our communications seem more truthful and believable and tends to make them more persuasive (Pillemer, 1992). Relating detailed autobiographical memories also allows us to connect emotionally with others in an intimate and immediate way. What would provoke a stronger reaction in you—a friend telling you that they came from a tough background, or the same friend telling you that her parents had divorced when she was 4, she had battled and overcome cancer when she was 10, and she was suspended in high school for underage drinking? Clearly, more detailed and personal memories offer you a greater sense of intimacy and a stronger connection with your friend. You will likely also feel empathetic and relate a similarly detailed and personal story of your own.

Emotional Function

According to Pillemer (1998), autobiographical memory also serves an important *emotional function* in that it helps us organize, reflect on, and think through important life events. Most approaches to psychotherapy place a good deal of emphasis on the connection between one's personal memories and one's psychological functioning. As you read earlier, the inability of many depressives to recall the specifics of memories deters their ability to solve current problems and to imagine a better future. According to some (e.g., Herman, 1992), recounting one's personal memories of trauma in detail is critical for recovery. But it's also important to note that the vivid reliving of trauma is not always associated with positive consequences, as in the case of post-traumatic stress disorder.

Directive Function

Finally, Pillemer (1998) notes what he terms the *directive functions* of autobiographical memory. Remembering personally experienced events in detail can help direct future behavior. For example, there may be important events from your life in which you really "learned your lesson"—when you mistakenly trusted someone, when you failed to plan ahead, when you were needlessly worried about something. Recollecting events of this sort can serve to change future behavior. Pillemer relates an especially relevant example, an English major's recollection in college that was critical in shaping her career aspirations:

> My first Shakespeare class . . . would have to rank as one of my most influential experiences, since it started me on the life I'm following now (graduate school in Elizabethan literature). But the memory I have from that class is very small and tight. . . . I remember the first day best. I was fascinated by the easy way [the professor] roamed through Shakespeare, by just the amount of knowledge that he had. He seemed to know everything. In fact, after class, I asked him if he could identify a quote I had found about fencing, "Keep up your bright swords, for the new dew will rust them." Immediately, he said "Othello, Act 1, Scene 2, I believe." Which turned out to be exactly right. I wanted to know a body of literature that well. I'm still working on it. (Pillemer et al., 1996, p. 330)

Clearly, this student's memory of this specific encounter with her English professor served an important directive function.

One final point about the functions of memory outlined by Pillemer (1998): none of these functions is completely dependent on memory accuracy. In other words, for autobiographical memory to serve us in communication, in emotional adjustment, and in life direction, it isn't always critical that we remember events correctly. As Pillemer states, "From a functionalist perspective, it is permissible and often valuable to view personal event memory as a belief system rather than a mechanistic entity filled with traces that are objectively true or false." In other words, autobiographical memory serves us well, even if it's far from 100% accurate.

STOP *and* REVIEW!

1. Name and briefly describe the 3 functions of autobiographical memory.
2. True or false? Autobiographical memory's function doesn't really depend on autobiographical memory accuracy.

➤ The communicative function of autobiographical memory is to allow for emotional connection with others, and to afford our communications with them more credibility and believability. The emotional function of autobiographical memory is to help us organize, reflect upon, and think through important life events. The directive function of autobiographical memory relates to the ways in which personal recollection can serve as life lessons, helping to direct our lives in certain ways.

➤ The functions of autobiographical memory don't really depend on memory accuracy.

GLOSSARY

autobiographical fact: the general (context-free) knowledge about oneself and one's personal history (p. 293)

autobiographical memory: the memory for the specific experiences that comprise a person's life story (p. 293)

childhood amnesia: the inability to recall events from one's life that occurred before the ages of 3 or 4 (p. 297)

diary technique: a method for investigating autobiographical memory in which the subject keeps a running record of events that occur in daily life (p. 296)

flashbulb memory: a detailed, vivid, and confidently held memory for the circumstances surrounding when you heard some startling bit of news (p. 321)

mood-dependent memory: the finding that retrieval of a previously encoded event is enhanced when the mood experienced at retrieval matches the mood present at encoding (p. 326)

Pollyanna effect: the tendency to recall positive autobiographical memories more easily than negative ones (p. 318)

Proust phenomenon: the apparent power of odors to elicit memories that are especially old and vivid (p. 312)

reminiscence bump: the disproportionately greater number of life memories that can be recalled from the ages of 10 to 30 (p. 297)

self-memory system: a theory proposing that autobiographical memories are *reconstructed* from an autobiographical knowledge base in the service of higher-level plans and goals (p. 314)

9

Knowledge Representation and Retrieval

You may have noticed that when you're thinking of certain categories or concepts (e.g., fruits, types of furniture, gemstones), certain examples of these categories seem to be more readily available than others. Moreover, thinking of a specific concept (e.g., "diamond") triggers a host of associations (e.g., ring, expensive, marriage proposal, etc.). What accounts for this aspect of knowledge?

How much of what we learn in school do we actually retain? On what factors does this retention depend? Are there ways to go about ensuring better long-term retention of what we learn in school?

What's going on when some piece of information is on the "tip of your tongue"? What underlies that frustrating experience, and why does it seem to be so common in the case of people's names?

Thinking often involves conjuring up a sort of mental picture. You do it all the time when you review events from your past, when you imagine the events of the future, or when you're simply jotting down some directions you're being given. Is this thinking truly visual? Are you seeing, or simply imagining? Might these two be the same?

The preceding three chapters have dealt primarily with the phenomena of episodic memory—our recollection of previous events, complete with contextual details. Indeed, this is memory as we experience it day to day. However, conscious recollection of previous events is only a portion of the long-term memory picture. In fact, one could make the argument that most remembering doesn't involve the conscious recollection of episodes. Consider everyday tasks like getting up, dressing, driving to school, and fixing dinner. You could conceivably accomplish all of these without recalling previous events or episodes from your past. But you could not accomplish any of these tasks without procedural memory (memory for how to do things, discussed in Chapter 6) or remembering (i.e., knowing) what a toothbrush, shower, car, or hamburger is. The database of general knowledge that enables our successful interaction with the world around us is termed **semantic memory.** In contrast to episodic memory, semantic memory is typically devoid of any context; you don't recollect the first time you heard about or used a toothbrush or a car; you just know what they are. You might think of semantic memory as a mental dictionary in which you look up (i.e., retrieve) concepts during cognitive processing. In addition, semantic memory serves as a mental encyclopedia that houses important facts, historical information, and the like.

Cognitive psychologists have investigated a number of important issues regarding semantic memory, or what is sometimes simply termed *knowledge:* How is knowledge organized? How is knowledge retrieved? What is the best way to describe how knowledge is represented—in terms of lists of features, networks of facts, or some other representational mode? Do we have multiple forms of representation—for example, both a verbal representation of the word *robin* as well as an imaginal mode of representation that allows us to visualize a robin?

The material we'll discuss in this chapter is a bit different from the ground already covered. You may have noticed that we've tried to emphasize cognitive processes within applied settings—the everyday situations you "think your way through." The findings and phenomena we'll be discussing in this chapter are decidedly nonapplied, and the issues that are addressed by these findings are, for the most part, theoretical. The fact that you agree with the statement "A robin is a bird" more quickly than "A penguin is a bird" doesn't have any particular ramifications for your everyday life, but differences like these are quite informative, giving us an idea of how our knowledge is organized and accessed.

Another frustration you might experience with this chapter is that the topics and ideas covered are quite disparate, and seem to lack a common thread. But think about it: the same thing could be said of all of the information you know, which ranges from your 50,000-word vocabulary, along with knowledge of connections among those words, to all of the concepts you've learned in your dozen or so years of formal education to all of the trivial nonsense you've absorbed from popular culture to . . . well, you get the idea. There is no one theory or experimental paradigm that successfully captures or explains the vast array of knowledge that you're able to access and retrieve. As you'll see, however, some themes do emerge, most notably the notion of a network architecture for describing interrelationships among words and ideas.

Representing and Retrieving Words and Associates

One of the most important facets of our semantic memory is our vast knowledge of word concepts. Without this knowledge, we would be rendered incapable of thinking and incapable of using the language processes discussed in Chapter 10.

Word Representation and Retrieval: The Mental Lexicon

One way of conceptualizing our general knowledge of words is in terms of a **mental lexicon,** a term researchers use to refer to our mental dictionary. The process by which a word is activated within the lexicon is termed **lexical access.** The process of lexical access is often investigated by using a **lexical decision task,** which involves deciding whether or not a presented letter string (i.e., BRUF) is a word. *Speed,* not accuracy, is the variable of primary interest. Using this task, researchers have found evidence of *priming* in semantic memory. As you read in Chapter 6, priming refers to a benefit in memory performance from previous exposure to some item. To investigate priming in semantic memory, a word (typically termed the *prime*) is presented before the letter string (typically termed the *target*). The prime is either related or unrelated to the target. **Semantic priming** refers to the benefit in lexical decision (an increase in RT) that occurs as a function of the prime. For example, people identify that the target "robin" is a word faster if it is preceded by the prime "bird" than when the target is presented alone or preceded by an unrelated prime (e.g., "weapon").

Factors Affecting Lexical Access.   As the phenomenon of semantic priming would suggest, it turns out that a variety of factors affect lexical access. One of the most robust factors affecting lexical access is word frequency, which refers to how commonly a word occurs in one's day-to-day encounters. High-frequency words (e.g., *house*) are more easily and quickly accessed than low-frequency words (e.g., *bungalow*). In a divided-attention study that investigated lexical access, Foss (1969) had subjects perform a task in which they had to detect basic speech sounds (termed *phonemes;* you'll find out much more about them in Chapter 10). They were to listen for a target phoneme (e.g., the sound of a "g") while attempting to comprehend a speech passage. The targets immediately followed either low-frequency or high-frequency words within the passage. Detection times for the target phonemes were longer when the phonemes followed low-frequency words, relative to when they followed high-frequency words. Foss concluded that phoneme detection was slower in this condition due to the increased mental effort required to access low-frequency words.

Another factor that affects lexical access is *lexical ambiguity,* which occurs when a word with two possible meanings (e.g., *bank*) is encountered. This raises several interesting questions with regard to lexical access: Do ambiguous words have two separate representations in semantic memory? Are both representations activated, or is only the one relevant to the particular context activated? An early study by Foss (1970) suggested that the first scenario is the case. The study used a phoneme-monitoring task; subjects listened for target phonemes that appeared immediately after (1) words with only one possible meaning, or (2) words with two possible meanings. Foss found that subjects were slower in detecting phonemes that followed ambiguous words, ostensibly because the ongoing disambiguation of the word delayed the detection of the subsequent phoneme. This suggests that all meanings of ambiguous words are activated, at least temporarily; context then leads to disambiguation of the word. Later research has muddled the picture a bit, revealing quite a complex relationship between the particular nature of the ambiguous word and the nature of the disambiguating context.

The Bilingual Lexicon.   Bilinguals, individuals who are fluent in two (or more) languages, make an interesting case for questions of lexical access. How are concepts represented in bilingual individuals' brains? To put it in concrete terms, when a Spanish-English bilingual sees a cat, how many representations are activated? Is a single word stored as one general representation or as two distinct language-specific representations? The answer seems to be "both." Some findings indicate equivalent performance regardless of the language in which words are presented. For example, in an investigation of bilingual semantic memory, Caramazza and Brones (1980) had Spanish-English bilinguals decide whether a presented concept (e.g., "gun") was a member of a more general category (e.g., "weapon"). In this study, it didn't matter whether or not the language of the presented word matched the language of the presented category name. This suggests that a general representation of the concept is being activated. This general activation facilitates either language's form of that concept.

However, Kirsner, Smith, Lockhart, King, and Jain (1974) found that priming in a lexical decision task was not as strong when cross-language equivalents were used as primes, relative to when a word was repeated in the same language. In other words, "miedo" was not as good a prime for "fear" as was the word itself; "fear-fear" led to faster RTs than "miedo-fear." Note that there should be no difference between these conditions if both "fear" and "miedo" lead to the activation of one general (nonspecific language) representation.

Many researchers adopt a hybrid view (Taylor & Taylor, 1990). If words are concrete (*dog*), high in frequency (*book*), or cross-linguistic cognates of one another (i.e., they have similar sound properties in both languages, like *flauta* and *flute*), they tend to be accessed via a common representation. Conversely, words representing concepts that are abstract (*fear*), low in frequency (*unicorn*), or noncognates (*mesa* and *table*) tend to be accessed via separate representations for each language.

Models of Word Recognition

The Logogen Model.   A handy way to conceptualize lexical access from a mental lexicon was provided by Morton (1969, 1979), who proposed the **logogen model.** According to this model, a logogen is the basic unit of representation for a word. Each logogen has a baseline level of activation. As words are encountered, their corresponding logogens accumulate evidence. For example, let's take the word *book*. When the "b" sound in this word is encountered, activation of all logogens with this feature increases. Each logogen has a *threshold* of activation, or a critical point at which accumulating evidence will trigger recognition of the word. So once the accumulation of evidence for the word *book* reaches a critical level, recognition of the word will occur.

The logogen model can account fairly easily for the effects of word frequency, as discussed above. The basic assumption is that every time a logogen is activated, its threshold for activation is lowered. Therefore, words that appear frequently in the language are going to have reduced thresholds for recognition relative to words that appear less frequently. Context can aid in the recognition of a word by increasing its activation level. The word *library* is likely to increase the activation of the related concept "book," enhancing its recognition.

Interactive Activation Model.   Another influential model of word recognition, termed the **interactive activation model** (McClelland & Rumelhart, 1981), builds on the basic structure put forth in the logogen model. According to the interactive activation model, words are represented in our lexicon at three different levels: as sets of features, as groups of letters, and as whole words. This model uses a connectionist approach. (See Figure 9.1.) We discussed the fundamental assumptions of this approach in Chapter 1. One of the key assumptions is that cognitive processes occur largely in parallel. According to the model, combining this parallel processing assumption with our representations of words means that each type of information about a word is analyzed simultaneously, and information about the word's identity accumulates. That is, when you read the word *chair*, analysis of the component features of the letters, the letters themselves, and the word pattern converges to allow for identification of the word. Not only that, the analysis on each level influences the analysis at other levels. The connectionist

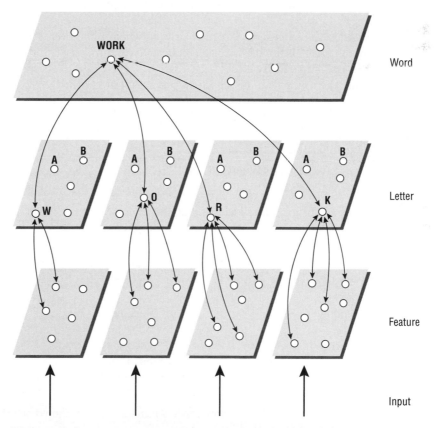

Figure 9.1 Interactive activation model of word recognition.

From McClelland, J. L. (1985). Putting knowledge in its place: A scheme for programming parallel processing structures on the fly. *Cognitive Science, 9,* 113–146. Copyright 1985 Cognitive Science Society. Reprinted with permission.

WORK ⟶ **K**
         D

ORWK ⟶ **K**
         D

Figure 9.2 Display used in studies of the word-superiority effect. The word on the left is presented very quickly, followed by a choice of two letters. The subject is to respond with which letter appeared in the under-lined position.

From Reicher, G. (1969). Perceptual recognition as a function of meaningfulness of stimulus material. *Journal of Experimental Psychology, 81,* 275–280. Published by the American Psychological Association. Reprinted with permission.

approach provides a realization of a distinction we've discussed several times already—bottom-up and top-down processing. In this model, the two interact and converge on a solution.

An important demonstration of the interaction between top-down and bottom-up processing in word recognition was provided in a classic study by Reicher (1969). Reicher was interested in the effects of different contexts on the recognition of letters. In his study, subjects were briefly presented with letter strings that either did or did not form a word (e.g., WORK or OWRK, respectively). Following a rapid display of such a letter string, subjects were queried about the component letters, as depicted in Figure 9.2; two alternatives were presented, and subjects were required to pick the one they had just seen. Reicher found that identification was easier if the letter had been presented in the context of a word, relative to when it had been presented in the context of a nonword. This finding has been replicated in a number of studies, and has been termed the **word-superiority effect** (e.g., Krueger, 1992). The word-superiority effect demonstrates the importance of top-down processing in knowledge retrieval.

STOP and THINK!

TESTING WORD SUPERIORITY

Recruit two friends and have them identify the underlined letter in each letter string as quickly as possible. Have one friend do this for list 1 and one friend do this for list 2.

List 1	**List 2**
house	ohesu
tiger	rtgie
television	tievesinol
daisy	yasid
window	nwiodw
book	obok
couch	cuhco
paper	epapr
shirt	tihrs
road	aodr

According to the word-superiority effect, which list of letters should be identified more quickly? Is this what you found?

Do We Rceoginze Wrods as a Wohle? No, that heading you just read wasn't a typo—the misarrangement of the letters was deliberate. And the fact that you probably

Table 9.1 Results from the Rayner, White, Johnson, and Liversedge (2006) Jumbled-Word Study (Fixation Times per Word in Milliseconds and Reading Rates in Words per Minute for Each of the Transposition Conditions)

Transposition Condition	Fixation Time (ms)	Reading Rate (wpm)
Normal text		
The boy could not solve the problem so he asked for help.	236	255
Internal letters transposed		
The boy could not slove the probelm so he asked for help.	244	227
Ending letters transposed		
The boy could not solev the problme so he asked for help.	246	189
Beginning letters transposed		
The boy could not oslve the rpoblem so he asked for help.	259	163

Adapted from Rayner, K., White, S. J., Johnson, R. L., & Liversedge, S. P. (2006). Raeding wrods with jubmled lettres: There is a cost. *Psychological Science, 17*(3), 192–193. Published by Blackwell, Inc. Adapted with permission from the author.

barely missed a beat in reading them is yet another testament to the power of top-down processing in word recognition. You may have seen this demonstration before; some years back, there was a report of a (as it turns out, apocryphal) study of word recognition being conducted at Cambridge University showing that jumbled words can be easily recognized (see http://www.mrc-cbu.cam.ac.uk/~mattd/Cmabrigde/). The proposed explanation in the "research article" was that only the first and last letters of a word need be processed for word recognition to occur.

That, of course, is a dramatic oversimplification. It's doubtful that we would recognize *ehnlpeat* as *elephant*. Indeed, a subsequent discussion of the phenomenon by Rayner, White, Johnson, and Liversedge (2006) adds some pretty important qualifications to the basic phenomenon of our sometimes striking ability to recognize jumbled words. As it turns out, not all letter jumblings are created equal (as anyone who works the daily newspaper puzzle, the Jumble, can attest!). Rayner and his colleagues assigned subjects to one of four conditions, each of which required subjects to read 80 sentences. In a control condition, the sentences were left intact. In the three experimental conditions, a few of the words in each sentence were transposed in one of three ways: internal letters only, beginning letters only, or ending letters only. Performance was measured by assessing fixations on the words (or wrods), and by a measure of how many words could be read in one minute.

The results, presented in Table 9.1, demonstrate that although jumbled words can be recognized, it comes at a cost. As you can see in the first column of Table 9.1, fixation times were longer for the words with transposed letters, particularly when the transpositions involved beginning letters. An analysis of reading time (measured in words per minute) revealed a parallel effect, as depicted in the second column of Table 9.1. When transpositions were present, fewer words were read per minute, and the decreased rate varied systematically with the type of transposition. Internally transposed letters proved the least problematic, and initial-letter transposition was the most problematic. Although these findings provide more evidence of the importance of top-down processing in word recognition, they also underscore the limits of such processing. Clearly, a word cannot be recognized solely on the basis of context. Some data need to be present; the letters in a word and their respective positions are critical for word recognition (cf. Grainger & Whitney, 2004).

STOP and THINK!

REOGCNZIING JMULEBD WRODS

For this exercise, you'll do your own version of the jumbled-word study conducted by Rayner, White, Johnson, and Liversedge (2006). Recruit some friends, and test them in each of the four conditions presented below. Have them read each sentence in succession; tell them that some of the sentences may contain misspellings but that they should try to ignore them and read the sentences so that they make sense. Your dependent variable will be reading speed, in seconds. To obtain this, add together the times (in seconds) that it took each friend to read the three sentences (i.e., find one total time). Then, divide this time by the total number of words (35). How does the reading-time data compare to the pattern of results found by Rayner et al.?

Intact

John had three papers to write, so he spent most of the month in the library.
Psychology is the scientific study of mental processes and behavior.
Greg had his laptop computer stolen from the car.

Beginning Letters

John had three appers to rwite, so he psent most of the omnth in the ilbrary.
Psychology is the csientific study of emntal rpocesses and ebhavior.
Greg had his alptop ocmputer tsolen from the car.

Ending Letters

John had three papesr to wriet, so he spetn most of the monht in the librayr.
Psychology is the scientifci study of mentla processse and behaviro.
Greg had his laptpo computre stolne from the car.

Middle Letters

John had three paeprs to wrtie, so he spnet most of the motnh in the ilbrary.
Psychology is the sceintific study of mnetal procseses and beahvior.
Greg had his lpatop copmuter stloen from the car.

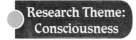

Research Theme: Consciousness

Is Word Recognition Automatic? The Stroop Effect. A central question about word recognition is whether it occurs automatically. As you read in Chapter 4, automatic processes (relative to control processes) are less open to conscious control, less likely to involve intention, and more attentionally efficient. Perhaps the most celebrated piece of evidence for the automatic recognition of words is termed the *Stroop effect*. First demonstrated by J. Ridley Stroop (1935), the **Stroop effect** refers to the finding that the ability to name the ink color in which a word is printed is inhibited if that word is the name of a conflicting color. For example, if the word *red* is printed in *blue* ink, it's quite difficult to name the ink color (blue) without suffering some interference. How does this demonstrate automatic processing? One common explanation for the effect is that reading is an automatic process; as stated earlier, it's obligatory—you can't *not* do it. Therefore, the ability to name the ink color of the word suffers tremendous interference because you are automatically reading a color word that conflicts with the ink color. It is important to note that this effect is not limited to the traditional task of naming color words. Words that arc closely associated with a given color can also have an inhibitory effect on naming a conflicting color (e.g., if the word *grass* is written in *red*, it's very difficult to name the color *red* without first thinking of *green* because grass is green; Klein, 1964).

STOP *and* THINK!

STROOPING

Try these variations on the Stroop task. Find a friend to take part in each version.

Version 1: For each of the two lists, have your friend name the number of characters in each grouping as quickly as possible. Test the list separately, and time how long it takes your friend to finish each of the lists.

List 1	List 2
FFF	222
GGGGGGG	8888888
PPPPP	66666
VVVVV	555555
JJ	33
DDDDD	44444
NN	11
LLLLLL	777777
SSSSSSSS	99999999

Version 2: Treat each of the following as "cards." The subject's task is to say the position of each word on the card using one of these four labels: *up, down, right,* or *left.*

List 1

List 2 (control)

- How did your subject's reaction time for the lists vary with the type of list?
- What two processes seem to be competing with each other?
- Can you map these versions of the Stroop effect onto the traditional version (color naming)?

Work on the Stroop effect by Besner and his colleagues (Besner & Stolz, 1999; Besner, Stolz, & Boutilier, 1997) casts some doubt on the automaticity interpretation of the Stroop effect. Besner, Stolz, and Boutilier (1997) tested this interpretation with a disarmingly simple task. Subjects were presented with a word in the center of a computer screen. Either one letter of the word (randomly chosen) was colored, or the whole word was colored. Subjects' task was to name the color they saw—of the entire word or the single letter. Note that according to the automaticity interpretation of the Stroop effect, there should be equal interference in both conditions because in both conditions, subjects should be automatically drawn to reading the word. However, Besner and colleagues found the Stroop effect to be greatly reduced in the letter condition.

Besner and his colleagues (1997) have an account of the Stroop effect that is markedly different from the over 500 articles that chalk the Stroop effect up to the automatic reading of words. These researchers claim that the Stroop effect is an instance of a *mental set*. Mental set refers to our tendency to revert to well-practiced and routine mental processes when faced with a cognitive task. We'll be talking more about mental set in Chapter 11. But in the present example of the Stroop effect, subjects fall into a familiar mental set when faced with a word—they read it. But they don't *have to* read it, as the automatic reading view suggests. Give them an alternative mind-set (i.e., search the letter strings for the colored letter), they are able to disregard the typical mind-set and not read the word, contrary to what the automaticity view would predict. Although word recognition may not be automatic, there is no doubting the incredible speed and efficiency that characterizes word retrieval in most circumstances.

Difficulties in Word Retrieval: Tip-of-the-Tongue Phenomenon.

Although word retrieval is generally fast, there are painfully notable cases in which knowledge retrieval is characterized by lack of speed and inefficiency. Quick! Name the person depicted in the photo. Having some trouble? Name last year's winner of the Best Picture Academy Award. Not so easy? It's very likely that at least one of these queries led to a difficulty in word/knowledge retrieval termed the *tip-of-the-tongue phenomenon*.

The tip-of-the-tongue (TOT) phenomenon (Brown & McNeill, 1966) occurs when we're fairly certain that we know the word we want to say but can't come up with it—the word is "on the tip of the tongue." Given stronger retrieval cues—for example, the choices *Matt Damon, Josh Hartnett,* and *Tobey Maguire*—the

Is his name on the tip of your tongue?

answer may now be apparent (Tobey Maguire). Retrieval blocks are another demonstration of the fundamental distinction between availability and accessibility that we discussed in Chapter 6. The mind's failure to offer a piece of knowledge doesn't mean that the knowledge isn't there—it may be *available* in your general knowledge store, but temporarily *inaccessible* given the retrieval cues.

Tip-of-the-tongue experiences are intriguing to researchers because they provide a rare window into the process of knowledge retrieval, allowing for insights about both language and our ability to monitor our own thought processes. Brown (1991) likens the TOT experience to "slow-motion photography" of the retrieval process. However, TOT experiences are difficult to investigate empirically because they occur spontaneously and are difficult to control. Researchers generally take one of two tacks. One is to have subjects keep a running diary of these experiences, noting their characteristics. The other is to try and induce TOTs by asking general knowledge questions that are in a middle range of difficulty and seizing on the ones that produce the TOT state.

How often do TOTs occur? In a review of the literature, Brown (1991) reports that, although the estimates range across different studies, naturally occurring TOT experiences happen a few times a week, on average. In laboratory studies, TOTs are induced for about 10 to 20% of the questions asked by experimenters. Some evidence, most of it anecdotal, suggests that TOTs may be more likely to occur under conditions of stress (e.g., Brown, 1991; Cohen & Faulkner, 1986). In a similar vein, Brown and McNeill (1966) reported that emotional agitation was a notable correlate of TOTs.

You probably know from your own TOT experiences that your consciousness is often bombarded by (wrong) alternatives. But these alternatives aren't random; they are related to the target word. Investigations of the specific characteristics of these wrong alternatives have yielded some intriguing regularities. Quite often (anywhere from 50 to 75% of the time), people successfully guess the first letter of the target (e.g., Brown & McNeill, 1966; Koriat & Lieblich, 1974). Interestingly, the final letter position is also frequently recalled at a level higher than chance. This provides an intriguing parallel to the serial position effect discussed in Chapter 6—another case of how the salience of primacy and recency impacts cognitive processing. Research indicates that during TOT states, people often think of words that are similar in sound or meaning to the desired word (Cohen & Faulkner, 1986; Reason, 1984). In addition, the syllabic structure of wrong alternatives is similar to the desired word (Lovelace, 1987). These regularities in the orthographic (physical) structure of wrong alternatives provide a hint that the organization of semantic memory is in some part based on the physical structure of words (Collins & Loftus, 1975).

STOP *and* **THINK!** ━━━━━━━━━━━━━━━━━━━━━━━

PLACING INFORMATION ON THE TIP OF THE TONGUE

This exercise will give you some idea of how TOT research is conducted. Recruit a couple of friends and try to induce TOTs by asking them some trivia questions. (You can make these questions up based on what you know or get some questions from a trivia game you may have handy.)

1. Read each question, and give subjects 5 or 10 seconds to answer it.
2. For each question they can't answer, ask them if the answer is on the tip of their tongue.
3. If it is, ask them to verbalize any possibilities that come to mind and record them.
4. Note whether the possibilities generated seem to resemble the actual answer in terms of sound and/or meaning.

A question of central interest to researchers is the nature of the cognitive processing that precedes TOT resolution. Is the answer obtained after an active and effortful search process, or is it more likely that the answer spontaneously "pops up" in the absence of any conscious retrieval effort? Some studies (e.g., Burke, MacKay, Worthley, & Wade, 1991; Reason & Lucas, 1984) report that answers "pop up" anywhere from 25 to 50% of the time. Norman and Bobrow (1979) propose that spontaneous solutions occur because of nonconscious processes that continue working toward the resolution of a TOT even when it isn't currently in consciousness. You'll read about a similar phenomenon in Chapter 12 called *incubation*. However, to trigger these processes, an initial period of sustained conscious effort (e.g., generating possibilities) is necessary. It is also possible that the TOT may resolve during an effortful memory search, by a cue from some environmental stimulus, or by looking up the answer.

STOP *and* THINK!

DEAR DIARY . . . I HAD A TOT EXPERIENCE TODAY

Now you'll be using the other method for analyzing TOTs—a running diary. Keep track of when you experience TOTs, and take note of these questions:

- What type of information tends to be the subject of a TOT?
- What is your state of mind before and during your experience of a TOT?
- What are the characteristics of any wrong alternatives you generate while in the TOT state?
- How does a TOT resolve—via a pop-up or deliberate effort?
- How long does it take to resolve?

Research Theme: Development   In Chapter 6 we discussed some memory differences between older and younger adults. One such difference is that older adults have more difficulty with tasks to the degree that the tasks require self-initiated retrieval. For example, free recall is more likely than recognition to reveal age-related deficits because in free recall, almost no retrieval support is given. Rememberers are left pretty much to their own devices in attempting to drive retrieval. This isn't the case in recognition, in which the answer is actually presented, and need only be recognized.

How does this brief review relate to the tip-of-the-tongue phenomenon? Situations that give rise to TOTs are best likened to recall; a question is posed, and a person must retrieve the answer. Given the age deficits observed in free recall, it shouldn't surprise you to learn that there are also age-related differences in the TOT experience. Elderly adults are more likely to experience TOTs, relative to younger adults. In fact, Burke, MacKay, Worthley, and Wade (1991) found that middle-aged adults reported significantly more TOT experiences than younger adults (1.4 per week vs. 1.0 per week), while the oldest group reported still more, 1.7 per week. Burke and colleagues also found that TOTs take longer to resolve in older subjects, and that active strategies like generating possible answers are more characteristic of younger subjects. Older subjects are more likely to experience spontaneous "pop-ups" of the answer.

What do age differences in the TOT experience tell us about cognitive processing? Interpretations of the tip-of-the-tongue experience, and of the age differences that are so often found, have fallen into two distinct camps. One perspective views TOT experiences as a linguistic phenomenon, placing special emphasis on what the experiences tell us about the retrieval of words from semantic memory. The other perspective emphasizes the phenomenology, or subjective experience, of the TOT state, and what it tells us about cognition.

Linguistic Accounts.   A detailed linguistic account of the TOT experience is offered by Burke and Shafto (2004). The basic idea behind their **transmission deficit hypothesis** is that the elevated rate of TOTs in older adults results from decreased efficiency in the connections between the different levels of representations for words. Most views of language production (a process we'll examine a bit more in Chapter 10) propose that words are mentally represented by sets of "nodes" at two different levels. At the semantic level are *propositional* nodes that represent complex relationships (e.g., properties of the concept the word represents, associated words, etc.) and *lexical* nodes that represent words and their meanings. At the phonological/orthographic level are syllable nodes and phonological nodes that represent information about word pronunciation (i.e., phonology) and spelling (i.e., orthography).

Word production begins when the semantic representation of a word is activated; activation spreads from the propositional nodes to the lexical node that best matches the propositional information that has been activated. Then the phonological information corresponding to this lexical representation is activated, leading to word production. Tip-of-the-tongue experiences occur because of incomplete activation at the phonological level. According to the transmission deficit hypothesis, TOTs are more likely in older adults relative to younger adults because in older adults the connections between the semantic and phonological levels of representation have become weakened. This weakening occurs due to advancing age as well as to infrequent or nonrecent retrieval of the representations (MacKay & Burke, 1990).

Metacognitive Accounts.   While linguistic accounts view TOT experiences as informative linguistic failures that provide a glimpse into the processes of language production, an alternative account of TOT experiences views them as instances of metacognition. Metacognition refers to our awareness of our own cognitive processes. It could be summarized simply as "thinking about thinking."

Indeed, research into the TOT experience has proved to be an important inroad to metacognition. One of the trademark characteristics of the TOT state is what has been termed a *feeling-of-knowing* judgment—we feel quite confident that we know the information. Is this feeling accurate? When researchers collect feeling-of-knowing judgments from someone experiencing a TOT, they can test metacognitive accuracy by having that person attempt to pick out the answer, given some choices. If feelings of knowing are accurate, people should be able to pick out the answer at a level above chance, and this is indeed the case. When people report that they would recognize an answer that is currently on the tip of their tongue, it turns out that the answer really is available the majority of the time (see Nelson, 1984, for a review).

Schwartz and his colleagues (Schwartz, 1999, 2002; Schwartz & Frazier, 2005) view tip-of-the-tongue states as important and informative phenomenological experiences. Basically, this state lets us know two important pieces of information—first, that the information is indeed stored in semantic memory, and second, that it is on the verge of being retrieved. So, rather than focusing on the generation of wrong alternatives and what that generation might indicate about language, this camp focuses on the subjective experience of the TOT per se.

For example, Schwartz (2001) was interested in whether a person uses a TOT state in order to control retrieval decisions; if one experiences a TOT, they know they know the word, and will therefore spend more time attempting to retrieve the information than they would if they were not experiencing the state. Notice that in this case, the TOT experience and its role in thinking is of central interest. Schwartz and Frazier (2005) tie research on TOT experiences to other metacognition research showing that older subjects monitor their memory just as well as younger adults, indicating that metacognition may be impervious to the effects of aging. Similarly, if TOT experiences are viewed as instances of metacognition, then the increase in TOTs with age could be viewed as an especially effective monitoring of one's own cognition. The increasing instances of retrieval failure in older adults is accompanied by increased sensitivity to these failures in the form of TOT experiences.

Words Connecting with Words: Semantic Networks

Let's now turn to some ideas about how words are represented in the context of other words. As we hinted at in our discussion of the mental lexicon, relationships among words play a key role in words' recognition. These relationships are most often captured in terms of the notion of a semantic network. In general, semantic network approaches propose that knowledge is stored in the form of associative networks in which concepts are represented by *nodes* (a concept quite similar to Morton's notion of logogens); nearby nodes correspond to related concepts or features of a given concept.

Basic Methodology.   A **category verification task** can be used to determine how we access categorical knowledge. In this task, subjects are asked to verify or deny simple statements like "A penguin is a bird" or "A robin is a bird" as quickly as possible. A **feature verification task** is used to assess how the *features* of categories are stored and accessed. Subjects are asked to verify or deny sentences like "A cat has pointy ears" or "A cat has skin."

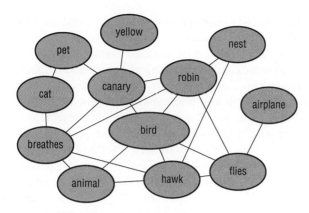

Figure 9.3 A semantic network.

As you might suspect, accuracy is not really of concern in these studies; in general, these questions are relatively easy, and people almost never make mistakes unless they're trying to answer too quickly (recall the speed-accuracy trade-off discussed in Chapter 2). *Speed* is the more informative dependent variable in studies of category and feature verification. The fact that subjects consistently verify "A robin is a bird" more quickly than "A penguin is a bird" tells us something about how knowledge is organized—in some way, *robin* is more tightly connected with the more general concept "bird" than *penguin* is. In addition, the fact that we tend to verify "A cat has pointy ears" faster than a "A cat has skin" tells us something about the *proximity* of these features to the concept "cat." So let's take a look at some general theoretical notions that have been suggested to account for the way we retrieve words and their associates.

Consider the example presented in Figure 9.3. As you can see, like concepts are "close to" one another, as are a given concept's features. It's important to note that within these models, the phrases "close to" and "nearby" are in the colloquial sense; that is, the concept "robin" is figuratively close to the concept "bird." Another important clarification—this type of model is *not* the same (indeed, it's quite different from) the *neural* network approaches to knowledge and cognition that we've discussed elsewhere. The networks we're about to discuss are not based on brain structure, as are neural networks (although you might consider the two approaches kindred theoretical spirits). In neural network models, the representations (nodes) correspond to neurons, and the connections between the nodes correspond to the complex interconnections between neurons that form neural networks. In the neural network approach, these nodes and links are not specifically dedicated to particular words and characteristics—that is, there is no neuron that corresponds to "robin" and no neural connection that connects this concept to a neuron for "bird."

In contrast, the nodes in semantic network models *do* correspond to specific concepts (i.e., "tree"), and the links between these nodes do correspond to relationships among concepts (i.e., "tree" would be connected to "leaves"). These sorts of metaphorical networks provide a convenient way to describe and represent the relationships among concepts. Knowledge retrieval is described within the framework offered by these models as a process of traversing the nodes by gliding along the associative links.

As we just noted, however, the neural network and semantic network approaches are similar in at least one basic way. Both architectures rely on the concept of excitatory connections between representations as a way of explaining knowledge activation and retrieval. As you'll see, semantic network models posit spreading activation, a process whereby the activation of one node spreads to other, related nodes. Neural network models posit a similar mechanism whereby activation of one node or network can lead to the activation (or inhibition) of other nodes or networks. So the two approaches are not without their similarity.

Hierarchical Network Model.   Collins and Quillian (1969, 1970) proposed the first semantic network model, the **hierarchical network model.** The model's name highlights the major structural assumption of the model—that concepts are organized hierarchically, with specific concepts nested within more general ones. This should sound familiar; we discussed these levels of categorization in Chapter 5. Figure 9.4 provides a graphic depiction of the model. As you can see, three levels are represented (corresponding to the levels of categorization discussed in Chapter 5). Nodes at the superordinate level represent the most general concepts (i.e., "animal"); nodes at the basic level represent more specific categorical subsets (e.g., "bird"); nodes at the subordinate level represent even more specific concepts (e.g., "duck"). Attached to each of these *concept nodes* are particular features of the concepts (e.g., white, quacks, thinks we should buy AFLAC insurance), termed *feature nodes*.

So how does the model work? Verification of statements about category membership (e.g., "A bird is an animal") activates the node corresponding to the concept "bird"; from there, a spread of activation moves to linked concepts and features in the network. The activation of the basic-level concept "bird" will eventually get to the associated superordinate-level concept "animal," leading to an affirmative response.

These network dynamics lead to a straightforward prediction: it should take longer to traverse the links from a subordinate-level concept (i.e., "duck") to a superordinate-level

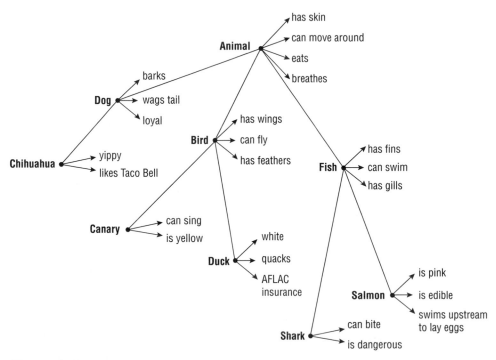

Figure 9.4 A hierarchical knowledge network.

From Collins, A. M., & Quillian, M. R. (1969). Retrieval time from semantic memory. *Journal of Verbal Learning and Verbal Behavior, 8,* 240–247. Copyright 1969, Elsevier Science (USA). Reprinted by permission.

concept (i.e., "animal") than to do the same from a subordinate-level concept to a basic-level concept (i.e., "bird"). This prediction, as it turns out, is a pretty consistent finding termed the **category size effect.** As you can see in the bottom line of Figure 9.5, people are quicker to verify a concept as a member of a smaller category ("bird") than they are to verify the concept as a member of a larger category ("animal"). The hierarchical model neatly accounts for this effect.

STOP *and* THINK!

TESTING THE CATEGORY SIZE EFFECT

Recruit a couple of willing subjects, and present them with the following sentence verification task.

1. Give them the items from each list below (test each list separately).
2. Have them respond "true" or "false" to each statement as quickly as possible.
3. Record the time it takes them to complete each of the lists.

List 1	List 2
A bird is an animal.	A robin is a bird.
A canary is a living thing.	A cactus is a plant.
A cactus is a tool.	A canary is a dog.
A tiger is a vehicle.	A vehicle is a living thing.
A poodle is a dog.	A banjo is a musical instrument.
A bat is a living thing.	A cat is a vehicle.
A chair is a living thing.	A tree is a living thing.
A banjo is an animal.	A piano is an animal.

List 1 involves traversing a total of 14 category levels across all of the items, while list 2 involves traversing a total of only 8—one per item.

- Did list 1 take a longer time to complete than list 2?
- Did your subjects demonstrate the category size effect?

Another feature of the hierarchical network model is a certain "thriftiness" in the way information is stored, a characteristic that Conrad (1972) terms **cognitive economy.** Cognitive economy means that the feature information of a concept is stored in the highest possible level of representation. Take the concept "bird" and the feature "has skin"; according to the principle of cognitive economy, the "has skin" feature is stored nonredundantly and at the highest possible place in the network. In other words, "has skin" will be stored at the level of "animal," and verification of the statement "A canary has skin" will require traversal from the subordinate level ("canary") to the basic level "bird" to the superordinate level ("animal"). This feature of the model makes good sense; it does seem absurd to assume that the feature "has skin" would be stored with every single animal in the network. It makes more sense to assume economical storage. Collins and Quillian (1969)

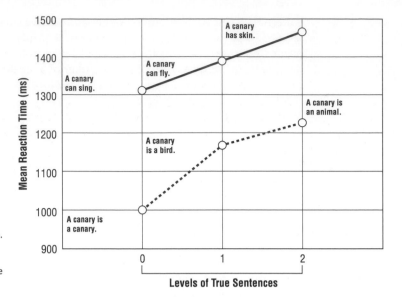

Figure 9.5 Early findings from studies of category verification, demonstrating a category size effect along with verification findings consistent with the assumption of cognitive economy.

From Collins, A. M., & Quillian, M. R. (1970). Does category size affect reaction time? *Journal of Verbal Learning and Verbal Behavior, 9, 432–438.* Copyright 1969, Elsevier Science (USA). Reprinted by permission.

found support for their assumption by comparing feature verification reaction times (RTs) for statements that required participants to traverse 0, 1, or 2 levels in the hierarchical network (see the top line in Figure 9.5). The RT findings perfectly paralleled the findings from category verification. The more distant the feature was from the target concept, the longer it took to verify the target-feature relationship.

The idea of cognitive economy also describes the first assumption of the model that we discussed—the hierarchical organization of subordinate-, basic-, and superordinate-level categories that predicts the category size effect. The links between these concept levels are organized economically; rather than have three links between the concepts "canary," "bird," and "animal" ("canary-bird," "canary-animal," and "bird-animal"), only two links are necessary ("canary" to "bird" and "bird" to "animal"). The fact that a canary is an animal can be inferred from this more economical system of links.

Problems for the Hierarchical Network Model. Alas, although the early research returns provided some support for the existence of hierarchically organized knowledge networks, problems began to arise. One weakness relates to a question that may have occurred to you. Up to this point, we've considered only cases where statements are true. What happens in the case of false statements, like "A bird meows"? It turns out that RTs for false statements parallel those of true statements. However, the explanation for this result isn't as clear. It seems silly to assume that "does not meow" would be stored as a feature of "bird" (particularly in light of the cognitive economy principle).

Collins and Quillian (1969) proposed several accounts of falsification RTs. According to the *contradiction hypothesis,* false responses require that a contradiction be found between the information in the hierarchical knowledge network and what the statement claims. So the statement "A canary is green" would lead to a search of memory that would turn up the fact that canaries are yellow, and the presented statement would be rejected. This hypothesis leads to exactly the same prediction for falsifications as for verifications: the more distance that must be traversed in the network, the longer it should take to find a contradiction. For example, the statement "A bird meows" requires movement from the basic-level concept node to a feature node at the same level. This should lead to a quicker falsification time than for "A canary meows" because in this case, the knowledge search would need to move from the subordinate-level concept node to a basic-level feature node. Unfortunately, the results of the study by Collins and Quillian contradicted their prediction: the RT increase was negligibly small and in the opposite direction! That is, it took a longer time to reject "A bird meows" than it did to reject "A canary meows." Collins and Quillian provide some alternative accounts of falsification processes, but they are quite complex and don't account all that well for the data. So falsification results continue to be a bit of a problem for the hierarchical model (Chang, 1986).

Another problem with the model relates to one of the cornerstone findings that supports it, the category size effect. It turns out that this effect depends on how stimuli are constructed. Rips, Shoben, and Smith (1973) found evidence of a *reverse category size effect*. They compared two conditions in which the hierarchical category structures were slightly different. The first condition was the traditional category structure (e.g., "collie"–"dog"–"animal"). The other condition used a less traditional category structure (e.g., "dog"–"mammal"–"animal"). According to the hierarchical network model, the verification of category membership should take the longest as you move from smaller to larger categories, regardless of condition. However, the researchers found an interesting interaction: a category size effect was found for the traditional category structure, but the nontraditional category condition yielded a reversal of the effect (e.g., "A dog is a mammal" was verified more slowly than "A dog is an animal"). Clearly, this finding is problematic for the hierarchical network model. Can you think of what may have led to this violation of the hierarchical network model's prediction? Although "mammal" may be a smaller category than "animal," it is not as familiar. Less familiar concepts lead to slower verification. This leads us to another finding that proves even more problematic for the hierarchical network model, the typicality effect. This effect seems to pound an empirical nail in the coffin of the hierarchical network approach. The **typicality effect** refers to the finding that speed in verifying category membership depends on how typical the instance of the category is. For example, people are quicker to verify that "A robin is a bird" relative to "A penguin is a bird," because "robin" is a more typical or familiar example of the category. Put in terms of a concept from Chapter 5, the category membership of prototypes is verified more quickly than that of nonprototypes. Why is this finding problematic for the hierarchical network model? Because the model says nothing about certain category members having prominence or primacy over others. Canaries, robins, owls, egrets, and flamingos are all birds, and all should be verified as such with equal ease. But, in reality, certain category members serve as better examples than others and are retrieved more easily.

The Feature Comparison Model. Semantic networks may provide a sensible approach to modeling how we access and retrieve information, but there are other possible architectures. Based on some of the problems encountered by the hierarchical network

Which of these is a "better" bird?

model, Smith, Shoben, and Rips (1974) proposed a **feature comparison model** that was decidedly different. Rather than a complex interrelated network of concepts, knowledge consists of a set of descriptions, or what might be termed *feature lists*. So, concepts are not nodes in a network but sets of semantic features that reflect the meaning of the concept.

An important assumption of the model is a distinction between two types of features. **Defining features** are those that are essential to the meaning of the concept. **Characteristic features** are those that are not essential; sometimes, these are termed *accidental features*. Smith, Shoben, and Rips (1974) propose that the features of any given concept can be classified along a continuum from defining to characteristic. For example, defining features for the concept "bird" might be that it has wings and two legs; characteristic features might be that a particular bird is yellow in color or may be kept as a pet. When we make categorization decisions, defining features are given more weight; when it comes right down to it, these are the features that *are* the concept.

The feature comparison model proposes that information retrieval in response to a categorization query is either a one- or two-stage process, depending on the nature of the target concepts. Take a look at a sketch of the model presented in Figure 9.6. When a query is presented, the feature lists (both defining and characteristic) that correspond to the two concepts are retrieved, and an overall comparison is made. If this rough comparison yields a great deal of overlap ("A canary is a bird") or almost no overlap ("A canary is a weapon"), a *quick true response* or *quick false response,* respectively, will be elicited. These types of decisions are made relatively quickly, because a one-stage rough comparison of features yields enough evidence for the decision.

How about the case in which less typical instances of a category are presented, as in the case of "A penguin is a bird"? In this case, the stage 1 comparison will yield some

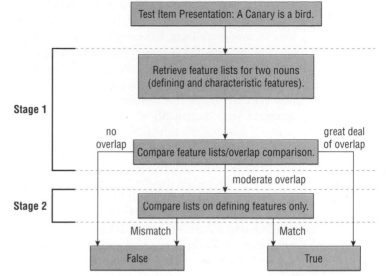

Figure 9.6 Steps involved in category/feature verification, according to the feature comparison model.

From Smith, E. E., Shoben, E. J., Rips, L. J. (1974). Structure and process in semantic memory: A featural model for semantic decisions. *Psychological Review, 81,* 214–241. Copyright 1974 by the American Psychological Association. Reprinted by permission.

overlapping features but also many nonoverlapping features. In cases where feature lists yield a moderate amount of overlap, a second decision stage is necessary. In the stage 2 comparison, only the defining features are compared: When it comes right down to it, is a penguin a bird? This comparison will yield a match, and the statement will be confirmed. But because of the additional processing stage, judging these less typical category instances takes more time.

The astute reader (this means you) may have noticed that the last two paragraphs redescribe the typicality effect—and, indeed, one of the major accomplishments of the feature comparison model is that it easily accounts for this effect. Typical instances of a category are verified more quickly because they overlap more with the general category concept. Another strength of this model is that it explains what is sometimes termed the **false relatedness effect,** an effect that cannot be easily explained by the hierarchical network model. Falsification RTs take longer when two concepts are somewhat related (i.e., "A robin is a tree") than when the two concepts are not at all related (i.e., "A robin is a brick"). According to the feature comparison model, the brick-robin comparison would yield no overlapping features, leading to a quick falsification. The tree-robin comparison would yield some overlapping features (i.e., living thing) and thus would lead to slower falsification RTs. Implicit in the preceding points is another strength of the feature list model: it provides a more elegant account of falsification RT data (Smith, Shoben, & Rips, 1974).

Problems for the Feature Comparison Model. In spite of its successes, the feature comparison model (in its simpler forms) runs into a number of significant problems. For one thing, it doesn't really account for the category size effect. Consider the comparison between "A penguin is a bird" (small category) and "A penguin is an animal" (large category). Verification of the second takes longer than varification of the first.

However, the feature list model makes the opposite (and wrong) prediction. For both queries, a stage 2 analysis is likely: both penguin-bird and penguin-animal are likely to lead to moderate feature overlap. In stage 2, only defining features are compared, and smaller categories have more defining features than larger ones. Therefore, smaller categories would be associated with longer reaction times, which is exactly the opposite of what happens. In addition, the model doesn't really provide a mechanism whereby feature statements (i.e., "A canary is yellow") are verified or falsified. It would seem that assessing such statements would involve comparing the feature list for the concepts "canary" and "yellow things," which doesn't seem very plausible. The only feature on the list for "yellow things" would be "is yellow."

Another problem with the model is its reliance on the distinction between defining and characteristic features. As we noted in our discussion of the classical view of concepts in Chapter 5, it's quite difficult to specify which features of a concept are truly essential. Smith, Shoben, and Rips (1974) do propose that this variable is a continuum rather than a dichotomy, but it's still not clear where defining features leave off and characteristic features start. Also, the processing stages outlined in the model (see Figure 9.6) implicitly assume a dichotomy between these types of features; a stage 2 decision requires that the comparison be between defining features.

It's difficult to evaluate which of these two approaches (hierarchical network model and feature comparison model) is more successful. Indeed, as Chang (1986) points out, the findings that support one approach turn out to be the Achilles' heel for the other. The hierarchical network model predicts category size effects but cannot account for effects of typicality; conversely, the feature comparison model can easily account for the effects of typicality but has trouble handling category size effects. More recent data haven't done much to resolve the issue. But one thing is certain: the architecture espoused by the hierarchical network model—that of an associative network—has become part and parcel of several influential accounts of knowledge representation and cognitive processes in general.

The Spreading Activation Model.   In response to some of the difficulties encountered by the hierarchical network model (in particular, the typicality effect), Collins and Loftus (1975) propose an extensive revision, termed the **spreading activation model** (although the original hierarchical model also proposed a spread of activation). This theory makes a number of assumptions about the representation of knowledge in addition to the central assumption that concept nodes are linked in an associative network. But unlike the original Collins and Quillian (1969) model, associations are not strictly hierarchical. In fact, the links that connect concepts represent a wide variety of relationships. As you can see in the network pictured in Figure 9.7, the relationships include category membership (violets to flowers), property to concept (red to sunrises) relationships, and more subtle relationships like those between street-ambulance and house-fire.

Collins and Loftus (1975) propose a number of processing assumptions. When a given concept is presented, the corresponding node is activated, and the activation spreads out to other concepts in the network. The strength of activation decreases as a function of time, distance, and the number of concepts activated: the more concepts that are activated, the less activation any one concept receives. Finally, the activation that reaches any concept node is summed up, and if the activation passes some threshold value, that concept will be activated.

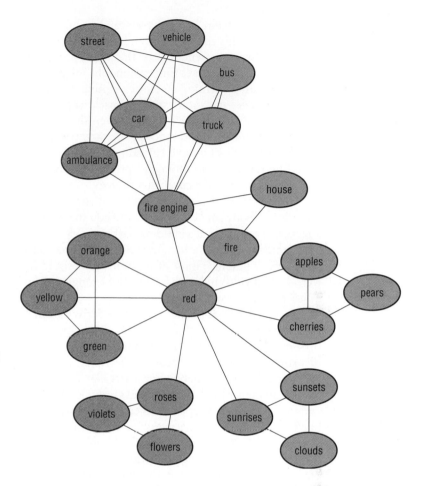

Figure 9.7 A sample of a knowledge network according to the Collins and Loftus spreading activation model.

From Collins, A. M., & Loftus, E. F. (1975). A spreading-activation theory of semantic processing. *Psychological Review, 82,* 407–428. Copyright 1975 by the American Psychological Association. Reprinted by permission.

The spreading activation model provides a straightforward account of semantic priming. Priming will result when a concept like "cherry" is activated beyond a threshold level. So consider what happens in the network when a prime (e.g., "red") is presented. Presentation of the word *red* activates that concept, and the activation spreads out from there; concepts receiving activation would no doubt include "orange," "fire," and, of course, "cherry." The activation gives these concepts a "head start" toward the threshold that needs to be reached for identification. So when the word *cherry* is actually presented, the responder is almost ready (primed and ready, as it were) to verify it as a word.

Is Priming Automatic? One of the assumptions about spreading activation is that it occurs automatically. Recall the characteristics of an automatic process (discussed in Chapter 4):

Research Theme: Consciousness

automatic processes occur without intention, are not subject to conscious control, and consume little in the way of mental resources. Conversely, controlled processing is intentional, deliberate, and takes mental effort. In a classic study, Neely (1977) sought to tease apart the automatic and controlled components of semantic priming within semantic networks.

Neely's procedure utilized a lexical decision task in which a word prime preceded a target. Within this context, Neely manipulated **stimulus onset asynchrony (SOA),** the time lag between presentation of the prime and presentation of the target. Given that spreading activation takes time, you might imagine that some SOAs would be too short for it to occur, preventing semantic priming. Conversely, if SOA is long, spreading activation will fade, and some type of conscious preparation will need to take over. Think about it: if you get the word *bird* and then sit there for three seconds, you're going to be plenty ready for the appearance of the target *robin.* Any semantic priming you get will not be the result of simple spreading activation. So effects that occur at short SOAs would be reflective of automatic spreading activation; effects that occur at long SOAs would be reflective of a conscious strategy.

Neely added a twist to the traditional semantic priming procedure. Subjects received the primes "body" or "building," but when they saw the prime "body," they would actually receive the name of a building part on most trials. Therefore, on receiving this prime, they should shift their attention accordingly. The converse would be true when they saw the prime "building"; most of the time, this would be followed by a body part. Primes were separated from targets by durations ranging from quite short (250 milliseconds) to quite long (2,000 milliseconds).

Some interesting predictions can be derived from Neely's procedure and the assumption of automatic spreading activation. Consider the body-building part condition; when presented with the prime "body," automatic spreading activation will lead to temporarily increased availability for words like *heart, leg,* and so on. But there will be no automatic spreading activation for building parts like *door* or *window;* these are distant from one another in the semantic network. But given a long enough pause between the prime "body" and the target "building part," subjects might shift their attention to expect a building part. So, "body" could be an effective prime for a building part if subjects have time to shift their attention. The more time they have, the more semantic priming there will be.

Even more intriguing predictions can be derived for trials in which subjects received targets that were unexpected. Recall that *body* indicated that a building part was going to be presented on most trials. On some trials, Neely threw subjects a curve, presenting them with an unexpected target; instead of getting a building part, they actually got a body part like *arm.* These trials led to a unique prediction. At short SOAs, it doesn't really matter what subjects expect, because spreading activation is nonconscious and will result in semantic priming for related items but not for unrelated items (i.e., "body" will prime the response to "arm"). But at the long SOAs, spreading activation is done, and strategy takes over as subjects wait for the category not designated by the prime. When they get a related word, rather than being aided by the prime, they should be hampered by it (i.e., "body" will inhibit the response to "arm").

The results are presented in Figure 9.8. This graph presents the results for two of the critical conditions in Neely's study. The solid line is from the unexpected-related target condition. These are trials in which the subjects were told to shift their category expectation when they saw the prime (e.g., if they saw "body," they should expect a building part), but then unexpectedly were given a word that actually was semantically related to the prime. The dotted line is from the expected-unrelated target condition. These are trials in which the subjects were told to shift their category expectation when they saw the prime (e.g., if they saw "body,"

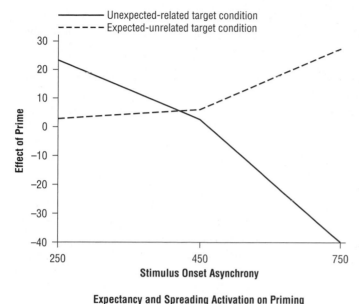

Expectancy and Spreading Activation on Priming

Figure 9.8 Results from Neely's (1977) study.

From Neely, J. S. (1977). Semantic priming and retrieval from lexical memory. Roles of inhibitionless spreading activation and limited-capacity attention. *Journal of Experimental Psychology: General, 106,* 226–254. Copyright 1977 by the American Psychological Association. Reprinted by permission.

they should expect a building part) and, as they expected, given a word that actually was semantically unrelated to the prime. The means are laid out in terms of whether the primes in each of these two conditions led to facilitation or inhibition in deciding about the target word. These facilitation and inhibition scores were computed by comparing RTs in these prime conditions to conditions where the string xxxxx was presented as a prime. If a prime led to faster RTs than xxxxx, then there was facilitation; if slower, then there was inhibition.

As you can see, this is a beautifully elegant, if extremely complex, design. The results confirmed Neely's suspicions about the role of automatic spreading activation and strategic control in priming. Let's examine the graph. In the expected-unrelated target condition, the prime "body" facilitated the building part target but only at long SOAs. The expectation of a building part target, given "body" as a prime, is a conscious and strategic process that takes time to develop. Now let's look at the unexpected-related target condition. Here we see precisely the opposite pattern. At short SOAs, subjects couldn't help but be facilitated by "body" as a prime preceding a body part target because of automatic spreading activation. But if more time was allowed for the strategic expectation to be implemented (seeing "body" and expecting a building part), then automatic spreading activation would be gone, and the clash between the expectation and the presentation of a related word would actually inhibit responding. Neely's results seemed to demonstrate the automatic and nonconscious nature of spreading activation and also that strategic and conscious processes play an important role in the activation of semantic networks.

However, later research (Stolz & Besner, 1999) indicates that this presumably automatic spreading activation is subject to attentional control. Priming can be prevented if a secondary task is sufficiently demanding to tie up attentional resources. Stolz and Besner (1999) conclude that spreading activation is not automatic, despite what Collins and Loftus (1975) originally proposed. However, Stolz and Besner make an important distinction between automatic and nonconscious processing:

> Consciousness need not result in control of processing, and control need not imply consciousness, contrary to the long-standing claim in the psychological literature that there is a strong dependency between consciousness and control (and non-consciousness and lack of control). (p. 64)

In other words, consciousness doesn't necessarily imply control, and nonconsciousness does not necessarily imply lack of control. Spreading activation could be both under strategic control and also nonconscious.

Representing and Retrieving Propositions.   As you'll read in the next chapter, knowledge retrieval is at the heart of language use. We need to be able to select the appropriate concepts during language production and decipher the concepts we receive during language comprehension. Although the previously discussed models proposed to explain the representation of knowledge are fairly successful in providing a simple model of knowledge retrieval, they are clearly limited by their simplicity. This simplicity has allowed for clear tests of basic assumptions and has generated a great deal of fundamental data that has formed the basis for other theories of knowledge representation.

Anderson (1974, 1982) proposes a different type of network model of general knowledge centered not on simple noun concepts but on propositions. A **proposition** is the smallest unit of knowledge that can stand alone and be declared true or false. More specifically, it's a mental representation of the relationship among people, objects, actions, and events—as Kosslyn (1994) puts it, "a mental sentence." But propositions aren't really words themselves; as McNamara (1994) notes, "They are best thought of as ideas that can be put into words." They're the abstract representations underlying what we think and say. For example, "The sky is blue" is a simple statement of the relationship between the sky and one of its well-known properties and as such will be stored in semantic memory. A more complex idea such as "The sky was blue, so Greg and Bridget bought some food and

A complex scene that can be represented as simple propositions.

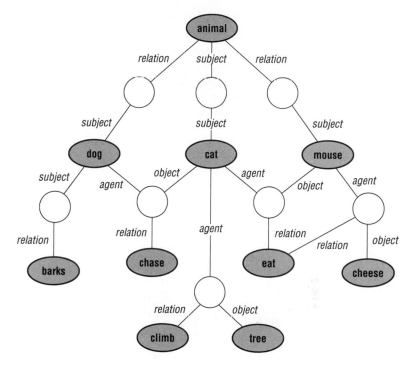

Figure 9.9 Dog/cat/
mouse network.

From McNamara, T. P. (1994).
Knowledge representation. In R. L.
Sternberg (Ed.), *Thinking and problem
solving* (pp. 81–117). New York:
Academic Press. Reprinted by permission.

went for a picnic by lake number 8,679" (in our home state of Minnesota, the "land of
10,000 lakes") would be stored in terms of its component propositions.

According to Anderson (1976), knowledge is represented in the form of
propositional networks, which are constructed from the facts and relationships we learn
and experience. Figure 9.9 depicts a propositional network that corresponds to knowledge of those legendary adversaries, dogs, cats, and mice. You'll note that this network is
similar but more complex than those proposed earlier. There are nodes that correspond
to the major players within this knowledge scenario (i.e., dogs, cats, and mice) as well as
links that connect these nodes and specify the nature of the relationship between the
concepts (dogs bark at cats, cats chase mice, etc.).

STOP *and* THINK!

SEMANTIC NETWORKS

Consider the following concepts:

dog   birthday   ocean   clothing   vegetable

For each concept:

1. Come up with a "minisemantic network" by generating five or six associated concepts
   and connecting them via arrows.

2. Look at the relationships that hold among the given concept and all the ones you generated.

- Are the generated concepts properties of the given concept?
- Are they properties of other members of the same category?
- Or are the relationships more complex, as might be described by the propositional network theories?

One phenomenon that supports the propositional network view is called **mediated priming.** Given that it is a network approach, the propositional view predicts that concepts prime other concepts in the network and that the amount of priming depends on the degree of their separation. So two concepts that share a proposition, like "mouse" and "cheese," will prime each other. The concepts of "cat" and "cheese" will show less priming because they are more distantly related; they're separated by a proposition: "Cats chase mice" and "Mice like cheese." Even less priming will be observed between "dog" and "cheese," because yet another proposition separates these concepts: "Dogs chase cats," "Cats chase mice," and "Mice like cheese."

Are dogs related to cheese?

This phenomenon has been observed in a number of studies (e.g., Balota & Lorch, 1986; McNamara & Altarriba, 1988). McNamara (1992) investigated the relationship between distance in a propositional network and speed of information access. Distance was defined as the number of associations that separate a prime and a target in memory. For instance, consider these primes and targets: "mane" and "lion," "lion" and "tiger," and "tiger" and "stripes." Based on these connections, one might expect to find mediated priming of "mane" on "stripes." But because activation weakens as it spreads, the mediated priming effect will be weaker than the classic priming effect demonstrated by Neely (1977) and many others. Also, as the number of mediators increases, spreading activation will fade, and priming will fail to occur.

To test the limits of spreading activation and investigate the phenomenon of mediated priming, McNamara (1992; McNamara & Altarriba, 1988) needed information about associative relationships in memory. To gather this basic information, subjects were given single words and asked to generate associates. From these responses, associative chains were constructed (e.g., dog–cat–mouse–cheese) such that successive pairs were directly associated (e.g., dog-cat), but nonsuccessive pairs (e.g., dog-mouse) were not. This ensures that any priming effect is due to the mediation of some intervening concept rather than a direct link. After construction of these chains, priming in lexical decision tasks was assessed. Subjects received prime-target pairs that differed in distance. Consistent with the predictions derived from the propositional networks generated by subjects, the amount of priming was a systematic function of the distance between concepts. The demonstration that one concept can prime an ostensibly unrelated one has proved to be a robust finding (e.g., Livesay & Burgess, 2003), and provides strong evidence for the spread of activation through a propositional network.

Another phenomenon that supports the idea of a propositional network is termed the *fan effect*. The **fan effect** refers to the finding that as more and more facts are learned about some concept, the ability to quickly and easily retrieve any one of those facts decreases, almost as if our knowledge representation resources have been spread too thin. Anderson (1974) investigated the fan effect in a series of studies in which subjects learned sets of (experimenter-generated) "facts" expressed as simple propositions like those listed in Figure 9.10. Subjects studied a set of facts about people in locations; the number of people and locations ranged from one to three. After memorizing the set of facts, subjects were required to make rapid recognition decisions about presented facts. During this recognition phase, facts presented earlier (termed *targets*) were mixed with facts that included names and locations from the first phase but in novel combinations (termed *foils*). Each target sentence and foil sentence varied in the number of facts that had been associated with its respective person and location.

Sound a bit confusing? It is. But look at the sample materials in Figure 9.10. Take the target sentence "The hippie is in the park." (Yes, that's right . . . a "hippie"; keep in mind the experiment was done in 1974.) This sentence was presented during the first phase and again during the recognition phase. If you take a look, both the person word *hippie* and the location word *park* appear in three other target sentences. Now look at the target sentence "The debutante is in the bank"; the person word and the location word appear only once. Based on the propositional network model and its

The *hippie* is in the *park*.
The captain is in the church.
The fireman is in the cave.
The *debutante* is in the *bank*.
The captain is in the **park**.
The fireman is in the church.
The **hippie** is in the cave.
The fireman is in the **park**.
The **hippie** is in the church.

Figure 9.10 Example propositions like those from Anderson's (1974) study of the fan effect.

From Anderson, J. R. (1974). Retrieval of propositional information from long-term memory. *Cognitive Psychology, 6,* 451–474. Copyright 1974, Elsevier Science (USA). Reprinted by permission.

A hippie and a debutante.

assumption of spreading activation, Anderson (1974) predicted and found a fan effect. The more propositions (i.e., facts) to which a person or location belongs, the longer it will take to recognize or reject a sentence that contains those persons/locations. That is, because the concepts "hippie" and "park" are each connected to three facts, they will take longer to recognize than "debutante" and "bank," which are connected to only one fact each. Simply put, the more facts you know about something, the more difficult it is to retrieve any one of those facts. Anderson's explanation for this phenomenon is based on the concept of competition between propositions and their respective components (Anderson, 1974; Anderson & Reder, 1999). Different pieces of knowledge compete for limited capacity; the more that compete, the less activation that any one gets, an account termed *response competition.*

Response competition is not the only mechanism that can explain difficulties in retrieving knowledge from propositional networks. Some researchers (e.g., Anderson & Bell, 2001) propose an additional mechanism termed *response inhibition.* According to this view, when we attempt to retrieve a piece of knowledge, other knowledge is activated as well. This ancillary activation inhibits the retrieval of the information that we want (Anderson, Bjork, & Bjork, 1994). Simply put, the process of retrieving a piece of information can serve to inhibit the ability to retrieve other pieces of information. In the case of the fan effect, retrieving a fact (i.e., the hippie is in the park) actively suppresses other facts about the hippie and other facts about the park. This inhibition makes the concepts more difficult to retrieve on subsequent attempts.

Both accounts of the fan effect chalk the effect up to some type of attentional limitation. According to the response competition view, propositions compete for limited capacity. According to the response inhibition view, attention is too broadly distributed, and unwanted information is activated along with targeted information. The notion of a fan effect being the product of limits in attention fits well with the finding that working memory capacity modulates the fan effect. You'll recall the notion of working memory as the ability to control attention, discussed in Chapter 4. Bunting, Conway, and Heitz (2004) assessed the relationship between working memory capacity and fan-related interference and found high-WM capacity subjects to be less vulnerable to fan effects than were low-WM capacity subjects.

1. What is the mental lexicon?
2. The Stroop effect is often taken as evidence that
    a. color naming is superior to word reading.
    b. word reading is an automatic process.
    c. color names are particularly hard to read.
    d. we are able to read jumbled letters.
3. True or false? Older adults are more likely to experience a TOT state than are younger adults.
4. Give one finding that presents a problem for the hierarchical network model.
5. What is the major difference between the hierarchical network model and the spreading activation model?
6. Define the fan effect.

➤ Semantic memory can be defined as our database of general knowledge about the world. One aspect of semantic memory is the mental lexicon, the set of words we know. Access to the mental lexicon is assessed with a lexical decision task, and can be influenced by a number of variables including word frequency and the presentation of related words. Models of word recognition include the logogen model and the interactive activation model.

➤ Reading words with jmubeld lteters is possible, but does incur a cost to reading speed. The Stroop effect refers to the interference that results when a color word is printed in a conflicting color. Although many interpret this as evidence of word reading's automaticity, others believe it to be the result of a mental set we have when encountering words.

➤ Tip-of-the-tongue experiences refer to instances in which we have difficulty retrieving a piece of knowledge along with a strong feeling of knowing. Older adults are much more susceptible to TOTs than are younger adults. Linguistic accounts of TOTs, such as the transmission deficit hypothesis, emphasize what these states tell us about linguistic processing. Metacognitive accounts of TOTs emphasize the subjective experience of TOTs, and how they are used to guide knowledge retrieval.

➤ The hierarchical network model assumes an associative network of concepts and features that are organized hierarchically and economically. This model predicts the category size effect but runs into trouble with falsification RTs, reverse category size effects, false relatedness effects, and typicality effects. The feature list model represents concepts as sets of defining and characteristic features. The strengths of the feature list model (explanations for the typicality effect, the false relatedness effect, and falsification RTs) are undermined by its weaknesses (inability to explain the category size effect and no mechanism for feature verification).

➤ The spreading activation model is a nonhierarchial network model that represents categorical knowledge in an associative network of nodes representing various relationships. The model proposes spreading activation that decreases with time, distance, and total activation. The model is supported by the semantic priming found in lexical decision tasks.

➤ A propositional network consists of nodes that correspond to major concepts within a knowledge scenario and links that connect these nodes and specify the nature of the relationship between the concepts. Mediated priming (priming that extends over more than one link in a knowledge network, with decreasing strength) and the fan effect (difficulty in retrieving facts about a concept as more facts are known) support propositional models. The inhibition observed in the fan effect can be attributed to response competition or response inhibition.

Representing and Retrieving Everyday Knowledge

Our semantic memory doesn't consist simply of noun concepts and their corresponding features or of abstract statements of relationships espoused by the propositional network approach. Semantic memory also includes information about people we've encountered throughout our lives (like their names and faces), what we've learned through our years of formal education (did you realize you're in the 15th grade or so?), our knowledge of facts and the trivia that relate to our interests and hobbies—the list goes on.

These particular categories of knowledge have not received nearly as much theoretical and empirical attention as have simple noun concepts like "bird." This is primarily due to the relative uniformity in people's representations and definitions of simple concepts;

How do we represent knowledge of everyday concepts like books or music?

this uniformity allows for experimental manipulation and control. Control is much more difficult in investigations of knowledge that is likely to differ widely among individuals. Although everyone knows what a book is, Bridget is one of the few people who can list all of the thrillers written by Mary Higgins Clark. These sorts of detail comprise a great deal of our knowledge.

We are faced once again with the notion of *ecological validity*—the study of cognition in its everyday forms. The empirical study of autobiographical memory (discussed in Chapter 8) was one answer to Neisser's (1978) call to arms for more ecologically valid research within the domain of episodic memory. In this section, we'll examine some of the answers from the domain of semantic memory.

Knowledge Learned through Formal Instruction

Much of the knowledge you carry around in your head is information you learned in school. A number of researchers—most notably Bahrick and associates (Bahrick, 1984, 2000, 2005; Bahrick & Hall, 1991; Bahrick, Hall, & Berger, 1996)—have investigated the characteristics and dynamics of this sort of knowledge. Such research presents significant methodological challenges. Since the researcher is interested in the long-term maintenance of knowledge over time, time becomes an important variable. As you know, the retention interval (the amount of time that passes between encoding and retrieval) has been one of the classic variables in memory research since the pioneering work of Ebbinghaus (discussed in Chapter 1). But in contrast to traditional work on episodic memory, research on the maintenance of semantic memory requires the assessment of retention after intervals of years.

Foreign Language Vocabulary.   Systematic research on the retention of information learned in school pretty much began with Bahrick's investigations of how we retain

Do you remember what you learned in school?

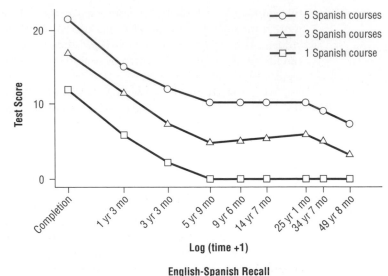

Figure 9.11 Knowledge of Spanish learned in high school over the life span.

From Bahrick, H. P. (1984). Semantic memory content in permastore. Fifty years of memory for Spanish learned in school. *Journal of Experimental Psychology: General, 113*, 1–29. Copyright 1984 by the American Psychological Association. Reprinted by permission.

foreign language vocabulary. In these classic studies (Bahrick, 1979, 1984), the subjects were individuals who had learned Spanish in either high school or college from 1 to 50 years earlier. Subjects were administered various tests to assess their knowledge of Spanish, including reading comprehension, vocabulary recall and recognition, and grammar. A background questionnaire was also included to take stock of any important differences among subjects other than age. These factors included the level of original language training, grades received, and the amount of rehearsal since the language was originally learned (i.e., continuing to read, write, or speak Spanish).

A sample of Bahrick's findings for recall of a Spanish word, given its English equivalent as a cue, is presented in Figure 9.11. A number of things are apparent at first glance. There's a pretty standard forgetting curve; information is lost early in the retention interval, but this loss levels off later. But even after 25 years or more, subjects still retained a fair amount of information. More important, however, this long-term retention was dependent on the degree of initial learning. Those with only a year of Spanish forgot everything relatively quickly. And not surprisingly, the people with more training showed better overall retention.

Permastore.   Based on his findings, Bahrick (1984) proposes what might be considered a subcategory of long-term memory, which he terms *permastore*. **Permastore** is the store of knowledge that has been learned so thoroughly (i.e., overlearned), that its storage is essentially permanent; we won't forget it. It is important to note that even though this definition seems to indicate that permastore is a location in memory, memories, as you know, are not stored in given locations in the brain. The concept of different memory stores is a holdover from information-processing terminology and is descriptive only.

Given the results from the recall of Spanish study, Bahrick proposes that the amount of information in permastore varies with a number of factors, including the level of initial learning, the grades received, and the way in which memory is tested. Surprisingly, it seems that a large amount of information can reside in permastore even if it receives a minimal amount of subsequent rehearsal after initial learning. Most of Bahrick's subjects engaged in very little rehearsal during the retention interval; in spite of this, large amounts of information were available for retrieval 25 or more years later. One other intriguing note about permastore: based on some more subtle aspects of his data, Bahrick (1984) contends that the transition of information to permastore is discrete rather than continuous. Information is not encoded semipermanently; it's either in permastore, or it's not. (And if it's not, it will be lost from long-term memory unless it receives additional learning trials.)

Math.   Bahrick and Hall (1991) investigated the retention of material from high school algebra. Subjects in the study had all taken algebra, but only some of them had subsequently enrolled in college-level mathematics. As in the earlier studies (e.g., Bahrick, 1984), Bahrick and Hall took stock of important factors such as level of performance in high school algebra, subsequent rehearsals of the material, and scores on the Scholastic Aptitude Test (SAT). The results of this study were intriguing; although factors like SAT scores and grades did relate to overall levels of performance, they were relatively unimportant in predicting the maintenance of knowledge over time. The only really good predictor of knowledge maintenance was the time period over which the material was initially learned. Material learned over the course of a longer period persisted for decades; the same material learned over a shorter period of time vanished relatively quickly (Bahrick & Hall, 1991).

Cognitive Psychology.   Appropriately enough, one investigation of information learned through formal instruction focuses on the very class you're currently enjoying—cognitive psychology! Conway, Cohen, and Stanhope (1991) examined retention of knowledge acquired in a cognitive psychology class taught over the course of one year at the Open University (located in England). The cognitive psychology course was highly structured, allowing for a systematic assessment of retention for different sorts of information, such as basic research methods, researcher names, theoretical concepts, and empirical findings. In addition to testing retention, the researchers also assessed subject confidence regarding what they had learned.

The findings (some of which are presented in Figure 9.12) reveal the classic forgetting curve: a great deal of forgetting occurs in the period immediately following completion of the course. As you might expect, the speed of forgetting is greater when retention is measured with recall relative to when it's tested with recognition (consistent with the findings from episodic memory presented in Chapter 6). You're much more likely to recognize the names and concepts you're learning in class than you are to recall them. Conway and colleagues also observed more rapid forgetting of names than of facts, a testament to the difficulty of retaining names. Names serve as a sort of arbitrary, disconnected label for a person; they don't really have semantic associates and thus are particularly difficult to retain. We'll have more to say about the retrieval of names shortly. Although the rapid forgetting is unfortunate, take heart! As you can see, retention of names and concepts stays well above chance for over 10 years, demonstrating that much of the material qualified as permastore.

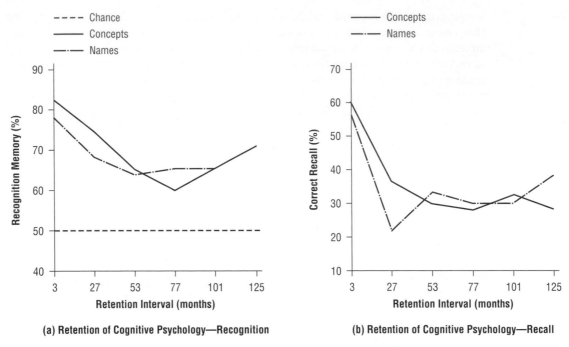

Figure 9.12 Retention of knowledge learned in a cognitive psychology class.

From Conway, M. A., Cohen, G., & Stanhope, N. (1991). On the very long-term retention of knowledge acquired through formal education: Twelve years of cognitive psychology. *Journal of Experimental Psychology: General, 120,* 395–409. Copyright 1991 by the American Psychological Association. Reprinted by permission.

Particularly compelling to the authors was the sturdiness of what subjects had learned about research methods. Retention of knowledge about general research methods showed no decline over the retention interval! Conway and colleagues offer a couple of reasons for the persistence of these particular concepts. First, the cognitive psychology course in question was a methods course, leading to more exposure to, and hands-on practice with, research methods. In addition, because research methods are covered in a number of psychology courses, they enjoy the benefit of spaced repetition. It's informative, at this point, to make a connection between the persistence of information learned about research methods and the Ebbinghausian notion of savings in relearning. You'll recall (from Chapter 1) that savings refers to the benefit we gain from having learned material previously. It's much easier to learn something in a second and third encounter, particularly if those encounters are sufficiently spaced out.

The confidence ratings collected by the researchers revealed some intriguing patterns. Recall from our previous discussion of distortions in eyewitness memory (Chapter 7) that confidence is not always a very good indicator of memory accuracy. This weak relationship characterized knowledge of cognitive psychology as well; there was only a weak relationship between confidence and accuracy on the knowledge test. Also intriguing was the relationship between the grade achieved in the course and confidence; people who obtained top grades in the course were no more confident in their knowledge than were students who obtained lower grades in the course (all received at least a passing grade). Also, confidence ratings fell throughout the retention interval, reflecting subject understanding that memory tends to decline with an increasing retention interval—another example of metamemory.

The fact that subjects reported a good deal of knowledge even in the absence of much confidence suggests that much of what they retained could be classified as implicit memory 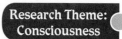 (Conway, Cohen, & Stanhope, 1991). You'll recall from Chapter 6 that implicit memory is reflected in changes in performance not accompanied by conscious recollection. In this study, subjects didn't consciously recollect the knowledge they were expressing on the test; if they had consciously recollected their knowledge, they would have been more confident in their performance on the test. The fact that they performed fairly well even in the absence of confidence suggests that they weren't really basing their answers on conscious recollection.

Educational Implications.   Research on the retention of knowledge learned through formal instruction has some serious implications for how information should be taught and retaught and provides a further demonstration of a powerful encoding principle discussed in Chapter 6. Recall the notion of spaced repetitions: studying material at spaced intervals over a period of time leads to better retention than learning the same information through closely spaced repetitions over a shorter interval. The evidence just discussed demonstrates the benefits of spaced practice but on a much grander scale. The most important factors in later retention seem to be the level of original learning and the length of time over which the learning takes place. Material that is repeatedly retrieved is better remembered than material that is not (even if the latter material was learned extremely well).

These conclusions have important educational implications. One aim of education is to instill knowledge; wouldn't it be nice if that knowledge were to remain in long-term memory rather than be forgotten the day after a test is taken? Based on the results from studies of knowledge maintenance, Bahrick (2000; Bahrick & Hall, 1991) offers some recommendations (some of which you may not like!). For example, let's consider the unpopular cumulative final. Bahrick's research indicates that you will have a better chance of retaining course-related information if the professor asks you to repeatedly rehearse the information over the entire semester in preparation for a cumulative final.

People's Names

Because we are experts in memory, the most common complaint we hear from family and friends is their inability to remember names. Retrieving names is the final stage of a process we discussed in Chapter 5—face recognition. Since we've already discussed the recognition of faces, in this brief section we turn specifically to the issue of name representation and retrieval and why names prove especially difficult to remember.

Hanley and Cowell (1988) conducted a study that highlighted the special difficulty in retrieving people's names. Subjects were presented with familiar faces and asked to recognize them as familiar, provide biographical information about them, and, finally, name them. The pattern of errors was quite revealing; in many instances, people could recognize that a face was familiar but couldn't provide any biographical information about the person or name the person. Other times, subjects could recognize the face as familiar and provide some biographical information but could not name the person. And, revealingly, the converse was almost never true; it was almost never the case that the name was retrieved in the absence of any other information about the person.

These results indicate a gradient of difficulty in the processes of person recognition, with the most difficult task being name retrieval. Young, Ellis, and Flude (1988) provided converging evidence for the notion of a difficulty gradient using a reaction time (RT) task. The RT for recognizing a face as familiar is reliably faster than the RT for retrieving biographical information about the person; and this RT is faster than the RT for retrieving the name. Based on this evidence, some propose that the retrieval of names and the retrieval of biographical information comprise different processes and stages within a person-recognition system.

Two theories have been offered to explain why the retrieval of a person's name is more difficult than the retrieval of other information about that person. The Bruce and Young (1986) model proposes a serial process for accessing information about a person. First, a face must activate a face recognition unit (FRU)—a stored representation of that face in memory. If activated, the person is recognized as familiar. Next, the FRU must activate the person identity node (PIN), which stores biographical information about the person. If activated, this biographical information becomes available. Next, the PIN must activate the terminal node, which stores the name of the person. This model accounts for the finding that names are retrieved slower than other information about a person; name retrieval is the last node activated in the system. It can also explain why a name is some- times not remembered while other information about the person is; information about the person must be retrieved before the name can be retrieved. Therefore, a name will never be activated in the absence of information retrieval about the person.

In contrast to the serial nature of the Bruce and Young (1986) model, the *interactive activation and competition (IAC) model* (Burton & Bruce, 1992) proposes that parallel processes allow us to access names. The IAC model assumes that there are separate FRUs (stored representations of faces), PINs (which in this model are multimodal general rep- resentations of people), and semantic information units (SIUs). An SIU contains both biographical information and names; there is no separate representation for names. In addition, the activation and retrieval process is parallel, not serial. So the face of David Letterman will simultaneously activate his PIN, his FRU, and his SIU. His SIU will include "talk show host," "from Indiana," and the name "David Letterman." "Talk show host" will also be linked to the Jay Leno PIN, and "from Indiana" will also be linked to the Larry Bird PIN. But the name "David Letterman" will be linked only to the David Letterman PIN (see Figure 9.13).

Superior access to biographical information like "talk show host" and "from Indiana" relative to the name "David Letterman" can be explained by a faster buildup of activation for his biographical information relative to his name. For example, when we encounter the funniest man in late-night TV, activation spreads from the David Letterman PIN to "talk show host" and "from Indiana" back to the David Letterman

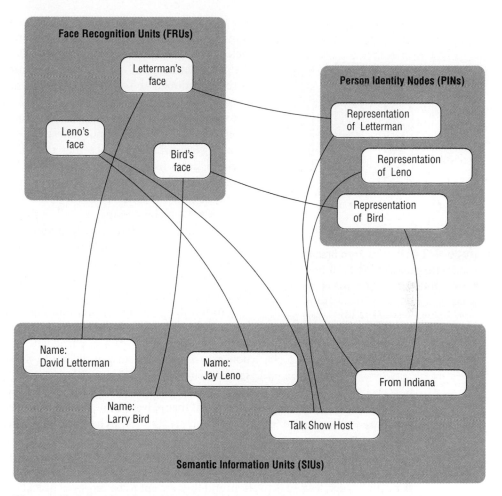

Figure 9.13 A portion of the knowledge network representing names and faces, according to the interactive activation and competition (IAC) model.

Adapted from Burton, A. M., & Bruce, V. (1993). Naming faces and naming names: Exploring an interactive activation model of person recognition memory. *Memory, 1,* 457–480.

PIN, but also to the Jay Leno PIN and the Larry Bird PIN, respectively. The David Letterman PIN and the Jay Leno PIN will reactivate "talk show host," and the David Letterman PIN and the Larry Bird PIN will reactivate "from Indiana." But the name "David Letterman" receives activation only from the David Letterman PIN specifically. So over time, nodes that refer to more general pieces of biographical information (e.g., "from Indiana" and "talk show host") will receive more activation than the person's name, which is completely unique and corresponds only to that person. Due to this faster buildup of activation, biographical information will be in a state of higher activation than will a specific name and hence will be more retrievable.

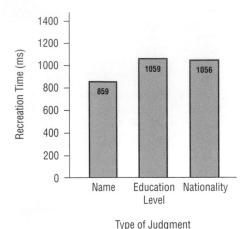

Figure 9.14 Results from Brédart, Brennan, Delchambre, McNeill, and Burton's (2005) study of name recognition.

From Brédart, S., Brennen, T., Delchambre, M., McNeill, A., & Burton, A. M. (2005). Naming very familiar people: When retrieving names is faster than retrieving semantic biographical information. *British Journal of Psychology, 96*(2), 205–214. Adapted with permission from the author and with the kind permission of the British Psychological Society.

The parallel approach to name retrieval receives some solid support from a study by Brédart, Brennan, Delchambre, McNeill, and Burton (2005). They reasoned that it might be possible to reverse the commonly found effect (mentioned above) that names are more difficult to retrieve than biographical information. You'll recall that this effect is one basis for supposing that name retrieval is a serial process. Brédart and colleagues subscribe to the parallel view, which assumes that the difficulty of name retrieval stems from the fact that names have chronically lower levels of activation, as described above. They reasoned, however, that not all names have such low levels of activation. One's own name, as well as the names of family members and close friends, are frequently activated, so one might suspect that they would be at a chronically high level of activation, just waiting to be recognized. In fact, one might expect the activation of the name to exceed the activation of other biographical information.

To test this hypothesis, Brédart et al. (2005) asked colleagues in the same psychology department who had known each other for several years to participate in a face recognition experiment. The task was simple; subjects were presented with one of three different cue words—*name*, *educational level*, or *nationality*. Immediately following the cue, they were presented with a picture of themselves or one of their coworkers. The results are presented in Figure 9.14. As you can see, the researchers' hypothesis was supported. Contrary to previous findings, and to the assumptions of the serial model of name retrieval, retrieval of names was significantly *faster* than the retrieval of biographical information. This finding fits quite nicely with the notion that extremely familiar names rest at a relatively high level of activation, and thus are apt to be retrieved quickly and easily.

Songs

Given the omnipresence of music in our daily lives, it's surprising that we don't know more about the processes involved in remembering song lyrics. Knowing the lyrics to songs is truly a prodigious feat of semantic memory. Think of your favorite musical artist and then recall everything you know by and about them. Chances are, it's a vast amount of information. In Greg's case, his favorite group is the Beatles, and his knowledge of their songs is extensive. What accounts for the fact that he can sing any lyric from any of their hundreds of songs? How are these songs stored in Greg's memory, and what allows for their rapid and easy retrieval?

Not too many studies have investigated memory for music, but there are some notable exceptions. Coincidentally, one of them is cleverly titled "Memorabeatlia," and as you may expect, it examines memory for songs and lyrics using Beatles tunes. Hyman and Rubin (1990) were interested in discovering the cuing relationship between song titles and song lyrics and the variables that dictate knowledge of melodies and lyrics. One

Whose song lyrics do you know perfectly?

obvious difference between memory for words and stories and memory for songs is that memory for songs is exact (verbatim); memory for stories is not. What accounts for the absolute precision in the recall of songs? Hyman and Rubin addressed this question by analyzing cued recall of Beatles song lyrics, noting which lines of a song tended to be recalled particularly well and which lines served as the best cues for song titles. Subjects performed one of two straightforward tasks: (1) lyric recall, in which they were given the title and the first line for 64 Beatles songs and were asked to write as many of the lyrics as they could for each, or (2) cued recall, in which they were given one line from a Beatles song and asked to write the title, first line, and one other line from the song.

So what factors were related to knowing any given line from a song? The recall data revealed a number of predictors. A line was more likely to be recalled to the degree that it was repeated, shared words with the title, and occurred early in the song (more evidence of the ubiquitous nature of the primacy effect discussed in Chapter 6). The cuing data revealed one major predictor for the recall of a song title: not surprisingly, song titles were most likely to be recalled when the presented line shared words with the title. Analysis of errors in the recall of lyrics revealed some interesting regularities. Subjects were rather poor at remembering lines; only about 20% of lines were recalled correctly. However, when a line was recalled, it was recalled verbatim. And even though subjects couldn't remember most lines verbatim, the mistakes in recall preserved information from the correct lyric. Specifically, inaccurately recalled lyrics tended to preserve the meaning, rhyming, and rhythm of the correct line. Hyman and Rubin (1990) concluded that the organization of semantic memory is not based solely on meaning; the physical structure of information is also important.

This finding also relates to the issue of how melody and lyrics are represented in memory. The fact that misrecalled lyrics maintain the rhythm of the melody provides some evidence that the two may be represented as a unit. You may have found this to be true when you think about your knowledge of music. To remember lyrics, you may need to hum the accompanying melody to yourself. The notion that melody-lyric integration underlies our knowledge of music is consistent with the results of a study by Peretz, Radeau, and Arguin (2004). These researchers used a priming methodology to investigate whether lyrics and melodies would prime one another. They used familiar songs (e.g., "Frere Jacques," "My Bonnie Lies Over the Ocean," "Happy Birthday"). Lyric primes consisted of spoken words from the song, while melody primes consisted of the song melody sung with only the sound "la." The researchers used a priming procedure in which subjects listened to a lyric or melody prime presented in one ear of a set of headphones. Immediately after the presentation of the prime, the subjects heard the target (either a whole line of lyrics or a whole segment of the melody) and had to determine as quickly as possible whether it was from a familiar song. Consistent with the notion of melody-lyric integration, subjects showed significant priming between spoken lyrics and hummed (or "la'd") melodies, indicating that music and lyrics are represented together in semantic memory.

STOP *and* THINK!

LYRIC KNOWLEDGE

If you're a music fan, try to generate the lyrics to some of your favorite songs. You might try to do this under a few different conditions:

1. Try to recall the lyrics.
2. Try to recall the lyrics while mentally playing the melody.
3. Try to recall the lyrics as you're listening to the song.

Reflect on the differences between 1, 2, and 3. Look at your pattern of errors.

- Were there any differences between them in terms of ease of recall?
- Did they fit with the findings discussed in the chapter?
- Did the patterns of errors differ among the conditions?

STOP *and* REVIEW!

1. Transition to permastore
   a. is more likely if learning occurs over a short period of time.
   b. depends on the level of initial learning.
   c. depends on the type of material being learned.
   d. is more likely if the material is in a foreign language than if it is math.
2. Describe the gradient of difficulty in retrieving information about a person.
3. True or false? Research on the memory for songs indicates that the melody and lyrics are retrieved as separate units.

➤ For reasons of ecological validity, research on semantic memory has expanded into areas of real-world knowledge. Study of knowledge learned through formal education (foreign language vocabulary, math, and cognitive psychology) has suggested a type of long-term memory termed *permastore*. Information becomes permastore in an all-or-none manner, and whether it does depends on the level of initial learning and the length of time over which learning takes place (spaced repetitions over a long period of time are best).

➤ Studies on memory for names indicate that names are particularly difficult to retrieve. There is a gradient of difficulty in person-recognition tasks. Recognizing a face as familiar is least difficult, while name retrieval is most difficult. Researchers have proposed models of name retrieval that emphasize either serial or parallel processing of person information.

➤ People are rather poor at remembering lines from songs; lines that are recalled are usually recalled verbatim. Also, inaccurately recalled lyrics tend to preserve meaning, rhyming, and rhythm, indicating that semantic memory organization is sensitive to meaning and the physical structure of information. Research also indicates that the melody and lyrics are stored together and retrieved as one unit.

Analog Representation

All of the topics discussed thus far have focused on information that is verbal in nature: the information is represented by letters and words. All of the experiments assessing the retrieval and maintenance of this knowledge were conducted using verbal stimuli and verbal responses. However, there's another major body of research and theory that examines knowledge representation of a different form. Rather than answer the question, "Does a robin have wings?", simply imagine a robin. Are you bringing to mind a visual image? A good deal of research evidence points to the prominence of imaginal forms of representation; these are sometimes referred to as *analog representations,* because the nature of the imaginal representation corresponds to (i.e., is analogous to) the real-world object. In other words, the robin you just visualized corresponds in some fundamental ways to an actual robin.

The Study of Visual Imagery

The question of whether *imaginal representations* exist and whether they serve any important information-processing purpose has been a center of controversy since the inception of cognitive psychology. In fact, this question dates back to psychology's forebearers in philosophy. A number of philosophical questions about mental images have been at the center of this debate: Does mental imagery exist? Do we regularly think in the form of mental images? Do mental images serve a purpose, or are they simply by-products of nonimaginal thinking? We should note here that our discussion will focus on visual imagery, given that it's the most investigated and arguably the most salient. However, there certainly are other forms of mental imagery; it's not difficult to mentally conjure up your favorite song and "hear" it or to imagine the feel of a cool breeze or the smell of bread being baked.

Just like all aspects of cognition, the experience of a visual image is impossible to observe directly; people can't project onto a screen the images they experience. To make mental images "visible," cognitive researchers have developed some creative methods.

Mental Rotation.   Shepard and Metzler (1971) developed a method that has served as one of the blueprints for empirically investigating the properties of visual images. The task

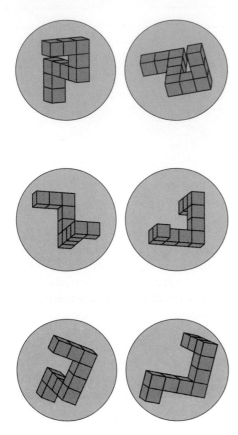

Figure 9.15 Stimuli used by Shepard and Metzler (1971) in their study of mental rotation.

From Shepard, R. N., & Metzler, J. (1971). Mental rotation of three-dimensional objects. *Science, 171,* 201–203. Copyright 1971. Reprinted by permission of the American Association for the Advancement of Science.

they developed is termed the **mental rotation task.** Take a look at Figure 9.15: the pairs of figures are similar, but they differ along an axis of rotation. The figures on the right have been rotated 45° relative to the ones on the left. If asked whether the two figures are the same or different (except for the degree of rotation), how would you make the decision? Shepard and Metzler speculated that a process of mental rotation (using imagery to manipulate one image to match the orientation of the other) underlies this decision and that the decision would take a measurable amount of time to make.

They presented subjects with a series of pairs like those in Figure 9.15; for each pair, a simple "same" or "different" judgment was required. The members of the figure pairs differed from each other by varying degrees of rotation, from 0° (same orientation) to 180° (mirror image). The results, presented in Figure 9.16, are about as perfect as you'll ever see. As the degree of rotation increased, so did RT for the same-different judgment. Not only that, the increase was incredibly consistent across varying degrees of rotation, almost as if each degree of rotation added a constant amount of time to the decision process. Shepard and Metzler interpreted their results as evidence that the task was accomplished by mentally rotating one of the figures until its orientation matched the other. Then the rotated figure (a visual image) was compared to the standard figure, which was still physically visible. Some support for this interpretation comes from the subjects in the study, who reported that they accomplished the task by mentally rotating the image. While this is introspective evidence and far from conclusive, it does provide converging evidence for Shepard and Metzler's interpretation.

This classic investigation served to define much of imagery research. Researchers scrambled to replicate and extend Shepard and Metzler's results. And replicate they did; the basic pattern of results was repeated across a wide variety of materials, including rotations in three-dimensional planes (Shepard & Metzler, 1971), polygons (Cooper, 1975), and body parts (Cooper & Shepard, 1975; Parsons, 1987).

A different approach to investigating the properties of visual images and whether they function as analogs to visual perception was undertaken by Kosslyn and colleagues in a series of investigations that have spanned two decades (e.g., Kosslyn, Chabris, Marsolek, & Koenig, 1992; Kosslyn, Murphy, Bernesderfer, & Feinstein, 1977; Kosslyn, Reiser, Farah, & Fliegel, 1983). Throughout this span, Kosslyn has employed a variety of clever tasks to further illuminate how we process and use visual images.

Image Scanning. In a classic investigation of imagery processes, Kosslyn, Ball, and Reiser (1978) sought to determine whether we scan mental images in the same way we might scan a picture that's physically present in front of us. Subjects in this study were

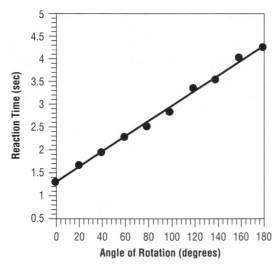

Figure 9.16 Results from Shepard and Metzler (1971).

From Shepard, R. N., & Metzler, J. (1971). Mental rotation of three-dimensional objects. *Science, 171,* 201–203. Copyright 1971. Reprinted by permission of the American Association for the Advancement of Science.

presented with the map pictured in Figure 9.17, depicting a fictitious island (could it be Gilligan's?). They were instructed to memorize it along with some of its designated features. After committing the map to memory, they performed an *image-scanning task* in which they were asked to form a visual image of the map and focus on a particular location (e.g., the hut). Then they were presented a location that either was or was not on the map. Their task was to scan from the original location to the named location (if this location was on the map) and press a button when they got there. Figure 9.18 presents the scanning time for all possible pairings of the seven locations on the map. What you see is strikingly similar to the mental rotation results: a nearly linear increase in RT with increasing map distance. Once again, it seems that visual images are analogous to their physical counterparts; mental maps seem to retain the spatial relationships that characterize their physical analogs.

STOP *and* THINK!

MENTAL TRAVEL ACROSS CAMPUS

This mental scanning demonstration will take a little bit of advance preparation. Sit down with a campus map and find pairs of locations on the map that represent a range of distances (i.e., two locations that are relatively close or relatively far apart, and some that are a moderate distance from one another). Once you've got these pairs set, recruit a few friends for a mental map-scanning study. You'll need some sort of stopwatch to record response times.

1. Have them form a mental image of campus (perhaps even giving them the map at first to "fix" the image).
2. Then ask them to imagine a dot starting at one location and ending at the second location in the pair.
3. When they "arrive" at the second location, they should say "stop," and you should record the scanning time.

Then answer the following questions:

- Did you find the predicted relationship between the distance to be scanned and response time?
- Did subjects have any trouble performing the task?
- Did they feel that they were using a visual image to accomplish it?
- Did subjects have any sense of what you were doing and why?
- Do you think there was any sort of expectancy bias at work?

Figure 9.17 Fictional island shown to subjects in the Kosslyn, Ball, and Reiser (1978) study.

From Kosslyn, S. M., Ball, T. M., & Reiser, B. J. (1978). Visual images preserve metric spatial information: Evidence from studies of image scanning. *Journal of Experimental Psychology: Human Perception and Performance, 4,* 47–60. Copyright 1978 by the American Psychological Association. Reprinted by permission.

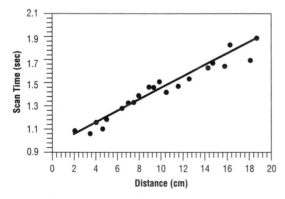

Figure 9.18 Image-scanning data reported by Kosslyn, Ball, and Reiser (1978).

From, Kosslyn, S. M., Ball, T. M., & Reiser, B. J. (1978). Visual images preserve metric spatial information: Evidence from studies of image scanning. *Journal of Experimental Psychology: Human Perception and Performance, 4,* 47–60. Copyright 1978 by the American Psychological Association. Reprinted by permission.

Methodological Problems? Some (Pylyshyn, 1981; Richman, Mitchell, & Reznick, 1979) have argued that the results of image-scanning studies are not the result of using imagery but the result of **task demands**—people's tacit knowledge regarding the behavior of objects in space. Because people know that it takes time to travel across any kind of space, this knowledge implicitly (and possibly unconsciously) guides their responding. For longer distances, people respond more slowly; for shorter distances, more quickly. Kosslyn (1994) cites a number of studies that undermine this task demands explanation (Finke & Pinker, 1982, 1983; Pinker, Choate, & Finke, 1984) but agrees that people do have control over some of the processes involved in image scanning (e.g., speed of scanning) but not others (e.g., the effects of scanning over variable distances). According to Kosslyn, this issue has never been successfully resolved, because it is difficult to determine definitively whether or not knowledge and expectations unconsciously dictate behavior in imagery experiments. As a result, researchers have moved on to empirical questions that are more tractable.

Image Inspection. Another task used by Kosslyn to investigate the properties of visual images is an *image inspection task*, which involves the inspection of mental images in order to pick out details. In this type of experiment, subjects are asked to imagine a rabbit next to either an image of an elephant or an image of a fly. Why these odd pairings? Kosslyn speculated that this would affect the size of the rabbit image. In the first condition, the rabbit would be relatively small, and details would be difficult to pick up in the image, as in Figure 9.19a. By contrast, in the second condition (Figure 9.19b), the rabbit would be relatively large, and details would be easier to pick up in the image.

In the Kosslyn (1975) study, after subjects imagined the "target animal" (e.g., rabbit) next to the "context animal" (e.g., fly or elephant), they were then presented a feature (e.g., whiskers) and

Figure 9.19 Figures used by Kosslyn (1975) in his study of image comparison and perception of image detail.

From Kosslyn, S. M. (1975). Information representation in visual images. *Cognitive Psychology, 7,* 341–370. Copyright 1975, Elsevier Science (USA). Reprinted by permission.

(a)

(b)

were asked to determine as quickly as possible whether the target animal possessed that feature. They were told to determine this by searching for the feature within their visual image. The results were clear-cut: when target animals were imagined next to a large context animal, subjects' response time was longer than when the target animal was imagined next to a smaller context animal. Once again, the findings indicated that visual images are analogous to pictures; scrutinizing the details of a small image is relatively difficult, just as scrutinizing the details of a matchbook-sized picture would be.

The Imagery Debate

The results from studies of mental rotation, image scanning, and image inspection would, on the face of it, seem to provide fairly compelling evidence that we are indeed capable of visual imagery and that imagery is a useful mode of processing that functions in a matter analogous to actual visual perception. However, this contention is controversial. Let's consider each side of this debate in more detail.

The Functional Equivalence View.   The way we manipulate, scan, and form images seems to mirror the way we manipulate, scan, and draw real pictures. In other words, images serve as depictions, or analogs, of actual physical objects and layouts. Visual images retain the characteristics of the scenes or layouts they depict. This view of the similarity between visual images and actual percepts has been termed the **functional equivalence view**—that is, images and transformations of images are functionally equivalent to percepts of real physical objects and their transformations (Finke & Shepard, 1986). According to this view, when someone gives you directions, your processing is analogous to a map sketched on a piece of paper, and your scanning and manipulation of the map are analogous to the inspection and rotation that you might engage in with a map that you're holding in your hands.

Cooper and Lang (1996) reviewed several versions of the functional equivalence view. Weaker versions of this view contend that there are parallels between the processes involved in visual imagery and visual perception—that is, there are some notable similarities between them. Moderate versions (e.g., Kosslyn, 1981) argue for a much closer correspondence between visual images and perceived objects. According to this moderate view, the processes whereby we construct, manipulate, and scan mental images are closely analogous to, rather than loosely associated with, the way we would draw or construct, manipulate, and inspect perceived objects. This moderate view is consistent with the results from the studies of mental rotation, scanning, and inspection just discussed.

The strongest version of the functional equivalence view holds that images and percepts are generated by the same underlying mechanisms as visual perception. In Chapter 4, you read about the visuo-spatial sketchpad component of working memory. According to a strong version of the functional equivalence view, the operation of this sketchpad is akin to the operation of vision. Evidence supporting this view comes from studies of selective interference. For example, in a classic study by Brooks (1967), subjects were to imagine a block letter F and, while holding it in mind, perform a conjoint task that was either visual or auditory. The findings demonstrated selective interference: holding a visual image in mind interfered with the performance of the visual task but did not interfere with the performance of the auditory task. This selective pattern of interference suggests that imagining and perceiving share similar mechanisms.

The Propositionalist View.   Although the findings from studies of imagery seem quite persuasive on their face, some (e.g., Anderson, 1978; Pylyshyn, 1973, 1981, 2004) contend that it is unnecessary to postulate analog representations to account for these findings. In other words, one need not refer to the existence and operation of visual images to explain the results from studies of mental rotation and scanning. These researchers espouse what has typically been termed the *propositionalist view,* asserting that we need only postulate one type of knowledge representation—propositions—to account for cognitive processing in all situations, including those that ostensibly involve visual imagery. Thinking in terms of these "mental sentences"—statements of the relationships between objects—would yield results like those obtained in studies of visual imagery. When someone gives you directions to get to their house, you may have an *experience* of a visual image that corresponds to the directions being given, but you're not using this mental image to accomplish anything; the images are *epiphenomenal,* a by-product of thinking about the propositional relationships embedded in the instructions being given. So for the sake of parsimony, or theoretical thriftiness, propositional theorists postulate that propositions are the only mode of representation and processing. But you'll recall that the evidence for the processing of visual images is pretty compelling. What explanations for these phenomena have been offered by the propositional theorists?

Let's look at the mental scanning studies. Propositional theorists (e.g., Pylyshyn, 1981) argue that subjects memorize the spatial relationships between objects. These spatial relationships are represented in terms of linked propositions: objects far apart in the space would be far apart in the list of propositions, and objects close together in the space would be close together in the list. Consequently, systematic increases in reaction time reflect the amount of time needed to move through the list of propositions: the more propositions, the longer the reaction time.

Neuroscientific Evidence. To an extent, the questions of whether visual images are truly visual and whether they serve a purpose in representation and processing remain philo-sophical ones that can't be definitively answered by empirical data. Whatever the result, a propositional theorist could always argue that only knowledge of concepts and the rela-tions between them (i.e., propositions) are used for processing. Yes, people experience visual imagery, and, yes, they think they're using images to answer questions. But ulti-mately, decisions and judgments are based on propositional knowledge. However, neuro-science research has revealed compelling parallels between visual perception and visual imagery, leading many researchers to conclude that the underlying processes are quite similar—that when we're engaged in visual imagery, we are, in a manner of speaking, "seeing." According to Kosslyn (2005), the use of neuroimaging techniques has constituted a whole new phase in the imagery debate, the first phase being the cognitive processing and behavioral studies just discussed.

Research Theme: Neuroscience

Behrmann (2000) describes visual imagery as "perception in reverse." In visual per-ception, an externally presented stimulus leads to processing in the visual cortex, and this processing in turn activates the long-term representation of that stimulus in memory. Say you're at the zoo, admiring the tigers at the cathouse (the Cincinnati Zoo indeed has this unfortunately named enclosure). The visual stimulus (tigers, in this case) stimulates retinal processing, and ultimately, the processing in the visual cortex that leads to activa-tion of the appropriate long-term representation, which in turn allows you to name the animal and behave accordingly (i.e., don't try and pet it). In visual imagery, the sequence proceeds in the opposite direction. Activation of a long-term representation (e.g., of the same tiger) leads to the activation of areas responsible for vision. Of course, Behrmann's analysis depends on whether the same neural substrates underlie both visual imagery and perception.

Suggestive evidence that visual perception and visual imagery share common brain mechanisms comes from a couple of sources. First, brain-damaged individuals who have deficits in visual perception often show parallel deficits in visual imagery. Bisiach and Luzzatti (1978) found that patients with visual neglect (an attentional disorder in which an entire side of space is ignored) show neglect in their visual images as well as in their visual perceptions. However, other findings have revealed visual perception deficits with no corresponding problems in visual imagery. So although there may be some shared mechanisms between the two, the mechanisms aren't identical. A second line of evidence for a perception-imagery brain parallel comes from studies of brain imaging. These studies show that the brain areas active during visual imagery tasks are in large part the same ones used during visual perception (see Kosslyn & Thompson, 2003, for a review).

Currently, there is still a good deal of rancor and debate surrounding the experience and possible use of mental images in our day-to-day cognition (e.g., Kosslyn, 2005; Pylyshyn, 2002, 2003, 2004; Reisberg, Pearson, & Kosslyn, 2003). But for many, the debate seems to be over; visual imagery is a unique representational and processing sys-tem with specific functions, and research continues into those functions and neurolog-ical underpinnings.

STOP and REVIEW!

1. True or false? Mental rotation times are shorter the more difference there is in the degree of rotation of two stimuli.
2. Explain how the results of image-scanning experiments might arise from demand characteristics.
3. Describe the differences between the propositionalist view and the functional equivalence view of results from mental imagery studies.

➤ A good deal of evidence suggests that an imaginal form of representation exists in addition to verbal representations. Research with mental rotation tasks has found that the greater the degree of rotation between two figures, the longer it takes to determine if the figures are the same or different.

➤ Research with image-scanning tasks has found that the farther apart two objects are in an imaginal representation, the longer it takes to scan from one to the other. Some have argued that these findings may have resulted from task demands (subjects manipulate their responses in line with what they perceive to be the expected finding), but the issue has not yet been conclusively resolved. Research with image inspection tasks has found that the smaller the visual image, the harder it is to identify features of that image.

➤ According to the functional equivalence view, processes underlying visual imagery are similar to those underlying visual perception; images are analogs of actual physical objects. Propositional theorists claim that the processes can be explained in terms of propositional knowledge. A definitive empirical answer to the debate has been difficult to achieve. Neuroscientific studies of imagery lend support to the functional equivalence view, revealing that visual imagery shares brain mechanisms with visual perception.

GLOSSARY

category size effect: the finding that it takes longer to verify or deny membership in a large category than it does to verify or deny membership in a small category (p. 347)

category verification task: a task used to assess semantic memory structure in which subjects are asked to verify or deny statements about category membership (p. 344)

characteristic features: those characteristics that are often present but not essential to the identity of a concept (p. 350)

cognitive economy: the idea that feature information in semantic networks is stored nonredundantly at the highest possible level of representation in the network (p. 347)

defining features: those characteristics that are essential to the identity of a concept (p. 350)

false relatedness effect: the finding that falsification RTs take longer when two concepts are somewhat related than when the two concepts are not at all related (p. 351)

fan effect: the finding that as more and more facts are learned about some concept, the ability to quickly and easily retrieve any single one of those facts decreases (p. 359)

feature comparison model: a model positing that a concept is represented as a set of descriptions, or "feature lists" (p. 350)

feature verification task: a task used to assess semantic memory structure in which subjects are asked to verify or deny statements about the features of concepts (p. 344)

functional equivalence view: the view that mental images share properties with their physical analogs and are accessed and manipulated in a similar way (p. 377)

hierarchical network model: a model positing that concepts are organized hierarchically, with specific concepts nested within more general ones (p. 346)

interactive activation model: a model of word recognition proposing that words are represented in our lexicon in terms of features, letters, and whole words; recognition results from simultaneous activation at all three levels (p. 335)

lexical access: process by which a word is activated within the lexicon (p. 333)

lexical decision task: the process of deciding whether or not a presented letter string (i.e., BRUF) is a word (p. 333)

logogen model: a basic model of word representation and activation that proposes that words are represented by nodes, or *logogens*, that vary in activation (p. 334)

mediated priming: the finding that the amount of priming between two concepts in a semantic or propositional network will depend on the degree of their separation (p. 358)

mental lexicon: our general knowledge system of words and their characteristics (p. 333)

mental rotation task: a task that involves judging whether two presented figures match in orientation (p. 374)

permastore: the store of knowledge that has been learned so thoroughly that its storage is essentially permanent (p. 364)

proposition: the smallest unit of knowledge that can stand alone and be declared true or false (p. 356)

propositional networks: networks of propositions constructed from the facts and relationships we learn and experience (p. 357)

semantic memory: the database of general knowledge that enables our successful interaction with the world around us (p. 332)

semantic priming: the benefit in lexical decision (an increase in RT) that occurs as a function of receiving a semantically related prime (p. 333)

spreading activation model: a nonhierarchical network model that posits links of varying types among related concepts in semantic memory and assumes spread of activation during knowledge retrieval (p. 352)

stimulus onset asynchrony (SOA): the time lag, in a semantic priming task, between presentation of the prime and presentation of the target (p. 354)

Stroop effect: the ability to name the ink color in which a word is presented is inhibited if the word happens to name a conflicting color (p. 338)

task demands: the features of the task that lead subjects to form expectations about what should and should not occur, thus biasing their responding (p. 376)

tip-of-the-tongue (TOT) phenomenon: a block in retrieval accompanied by a strong feeling of knowing (p. 340)

transmission deficit hypothesis: the theory proposing that the elevated rate of TOTs in older adults results from decreased efficiency in the connections between the different levels of representations for words (p. 343)

typicality effect: the speed in verifying category membership is faster for typical members of a category relative to less typical members (p. 349)

word-superiority effect: the finding that letters are more easily identified if presented in the context of a word, relative to when they're presented in the context of a nonword (p. 336)

10

Language

How in the world do infants learn language? They come into the world with no knowledge of it whatsoever, and by the time they're just a few years of age, they know hundreds of words and are stringing them together pretty accurately. What are some of the factors that underlie language learning and language use?

Why do people who speak a foreign language talk so fast? Why would anyone (in this case, your second author, in a conversation about baseball) ever hear, "The Mets beat Philly again" as "You must be silly again"?

You've no doubt embarrassed yourself with some type of speech error, or "Freudian slip," to use the better-known term. What factors underlie these slips of the tongue? Are they really windows into a person's unconscious mind, or is there a more mundane explanation? Does motivation play any role?

Can animal communication be considered a form of language? Can we "grunt and squeak and squawk with the animals," as Dr. Dolittle aspired to do? You've probably heard or seen cases of chimps using sign language or other language-like systems—are they using and understanding language in the same way you are?

Language: Basic Principles

Perhaps our most impressive and important cognitive achievement as human beings is language—the intricate symphony of representations and processes that allows us to communicate our thoughts to others. Indeed, Pinker (1994c) esteems language as "the jewel in the crown of cognition." Like the proverbial jewel, language is in many ways the culmination of all of our cognitive processes; in fact, it quite often serves as the means through which cognitive processes are revealed. And, like a jewel, language is arguably the most beautifully complex and valuable aspect of cognition. Where would we be without the ability to tell others what we know, think, and understand or to comprehend this information when expressed by others? Indeed, the mere fact that *language* can be meaningfully referred to as a *jewel* in a *crown* attests to its own power and flexibility.

The ease with which we acquire and use language is amazing, considering what is involved. We take our language ability for granted, rarely giving it a second thought. In this chapter, we'll take a closer look at some of the basic features of language. We'll also examine a number of the "instruments" in the "symphony"—the basic cognitive processes that we've discussed in earlier chapters, such as pattern recognition, working memory, and knowledge representation, all of which are critical to language.

Cognitive psychologists certainly do not have a monopoly on the investigation of language. Cognition researchers investigate what would be termed *psycholinguistics*—the psychological processes involved in using language, as reflected in processes as varied as speech perception and reading and comprehending the ideas in this textbook. Psycholinguists are also interested in exactly how we execute our language abilities, or **linguistic performance.** Psycholinguistics is related to another field known simply as *linguistics.* Linguists would not be particularly interested in the exact mechanisms by which speech is perceived or misperceived, nor would they be interested in why a person said, "Oh my gooshness" instead of "My goodness!" (real-life speech error generated by one of our students). These are psychological questions and issues of precisely how language plays itself out. Linguists would be interested in language in its pure form—the rules that define it and our knowledge of those rules. This (relatively) pure knowledge of language and its rules is termed **linguistic competence.** In the following pages, we will be concerned primarily with psycholinguistics and the cognitive processes that combine to allow for our seamless ability to speak, read, write, and understand.

Words and Rules

First, let's define what we mean by a language. We'll begin with a relatively simple definition. **Language** can be defined as a set of symbols and principles for the combination of those symbols that allow for communication and comprehension. Linguist Stephen Pinker (1999) sums it up neatly in the title of his book on language: *Words _and_ Rules* (emphasis added). Your ability to read and understand this textbook is based entirely on your knowledge of the words you're reading as well as your (mostly implicit) understanding of the rules that dictate how they may be combined.

One obvious characteristic of language is that everything to which we refer is symbolized by a word. This is a simple, but stunning, fact when you consider the tens of thousands of these symbols that you know and the relative ease and speed with which you retrieve them; naming an everyday object takes well under one second. All the words a person knows comprise their *mental lexicon,* or mental dictionary. Your mental lexicon is a significant part of semantic memory, the general knowledge store that we introduced in Chapter 6 and examined in detail in Chapter 9. Each representation in the mental lexicon is thought to include more than just a representation of word meaning. It includes other information that we know about a word, such as its sound, its written form, and the roles it can take on in a sentence (e.g., noun, verb, etc.). We'll be returning to the mental lexicon at several points in our subsequent discussion.

Obviously, language doesn't consist simply of all the words we know thrown together in whatever grouping we please. If we were to say, "Walked me in cat front of the just," you would probably wonder whether we should be coauthoring a textbook. But if we were to simply rearrange these words—"the cat just walked in front of me"—you would have no confusion. Along with the words we use to represent objects, ideas, and actions are rules that govern how these symbols may be combined. The term commonly used to describe these rules is **grammar.** Although grammar is often used to describe the arrangement of words in sentences and words in paragraphs, it's actually a more general term referring to the rules for combining *any* unit of language, be it a sound, word, or sentence.

Design Features of Language

One framework that has proved useful in capturing some of the major characteristics of language was proposed by Hockett (1960), who delineated a number of **design features** shared by many (in some cases, all) languages. A complete list of these characteristics is presented in Table 10.1. In scanning the list, you might find that some of the design features seem to be more at the core of what language is. Think back to the distinction we made in Chapter 5 between characteristic features and defining features of a concept. This distinction can be loosely applied here. Certain design features of language seem to be more defining—that is, they seem to be central to what language truly is (Harley, 1995). Let's consider a few of these design features.

Language is not simply a group of sounds or marks on a piece of paper. These sounds and marks mean something. This aspect of language is termed **semanticity**—that is, the symbols of language refer to meaningful aspects of the real world. In addition, the symbols of language exhibit **arbitrariness**—that is, they (typically) in no way represent the concepts to which they refer. There's no reason that these particular shapes—C–A–T—should be used to denote a little four-legged furry thing that says "meow." This little furry thing could have just as easily been called a frog. Although this arbitrariness makes learning the symbols of language a formidable task, it also affords language tremendous power: theoretically, any symbol can be used to represent anything. Although arbitrariness is the general rule, there are exceptions. You may have noticed one such exception in the earlier sentence—*meow.* This word actually does bear some resemblance to the real-world features it represents. Also, some languages (American Sign Language, for one) do include symbols with a close correspondence to the named concept or feature.

Language has the power to transport us beyond the present place and moment. We can talk about what we're going to do tomorrow or what we did yesterday as easily as we

Table 10.1 Design Features of Human Languages

Design Feature	Description
Vocal-auditory channel	Auditory reception of voice message
Rapid fading	Disappearance of message over time
Broadcast transmission and directional reception	Hearing of message by anyone within earshot; locating by direction
Interchangeability	Reproduction of linguistic message by the receiver
Total feedback	Complete understanding of what has just been said
Specialization	Communication is only purpose of speech transmission
Semanticity	Specific meanings of language sounds
Arbitrariness	Little or no connection between linguistic symbols and what they represent
Discreteness	Language symbols are categorical, not continuous
Displacement	Communication of ideas that are remote in space and time
Productivity	Infinite number of messages can be formed
Traditional transmission	Teaching and learning of "detailed conventions" of language
Reflectiveness	Thinking about and communication about language
Prevarication	Deceptive use of language
Duality of patterning	Combining the same limited number of linguistic symbols (i.e., simple sounds and letters) in different ways (e.g., *cat, act, tack*)

Adapted from Hockett, C. F. (1960). The origins of speech. *Scientific American, 203,* 89–96.

can talk about things in the present. In other words, language allows for **displacement** in time. Language also allows for displacement of another sort—the creation of alternate realities through deception. In other words, we can lie. This design feature is termed **prevarication.** The flexibility of language is also evident in the design feature of **reflectiveness.** Language allows us to communicate about the very topic of language; in other words, we can use language to reflect on language, which is what we're doing in this chapter. Perhaps the most important design feature is **productivity.** From the vast array of symbols (words) available and rules for their combination, an infinite array of new messages can be formed. It's sort of mind-boggling when you consider that virtually every statement you utter is new; you've never said it exactly that way before. This versatility is the product of a productive system of words and rules.

STOP and **THINK!**

LOOKING AT LINGUISTIC UNIVERSALS

Take a look at the design features of language listed in Table 10.1.

1. Pick out the ones you feel are most important to and/or most defining of human language and think about why they are.
2. Of these, pick one or two that are the most important.
3. Look at the ones you consider less important and think about why they are.

Is Language Modular?

One oft-encountered theoretical question that arises in the field of psycholinguistics is the degree to which language is modular. A **modular view** holds that language is made up of a unique set of abilities and capacities that cannot be reduced to or explained solely in terms of other cognitive processes. According to this view, language is special. Correlaries to the modular view are that language is species specific (only humans possess the module) and innate (the module is present from birth). The **nonmodular view** contends that language perception, production, and comprehension are the joint product of the cognitive processes we've been discussing throughout the text. The debate is largely a philosophical one; no experiment can provide a definitive answer to the question. Nevertheless, it is an argument that bears importantly on many aspects of language, as you'll see throughout our discussion. Indeed, debates about modularity of processing are raging along many fronts in cognitive psychology (see Barrett & Kurzban, 2006).

Let's take a look at a sample investigation that addresses the question of modularity, within the context of a unique form of linguistic processing—the linguistic processing that occurs within the context of music. Researchers have become increasingly interested in the parallels between music and language processing (e.g., Patel, 2003; Peretz & Zatorrre, 2005). The two do seem to have inherent similarities; in fact, you might say that while language is "words and rules," music is "notes and rules."

Research Theme: Neuroscience

Some of the research that bears on this conclusion has been done using event-related potentials (ERPs). You'll recall that ERPs are derived from electroencephalographs (EEGs), which assess the gross electrical activity of the brain. One finding from ERP research on the processes of language is an N400 wave, termed the *N400* because it's characterized by a negative-voltage brain wave that peaks about 400 milliseconds after the onset of a word (Gazzaniga, Ivry, & Mangun, 1998). The N400 is particularly sensitive to the semantic dimension (i.e., the meaning) of language (Kutas & Hillyard, 1970); a particularly strong N400 occurs after the presentation of a semantically incongruous word ("He spread the warm bread with *socks*"). There is a musical "cousin" to the N400 wave: the P600—a positive-voltage brain wave that peaks around 600 milliseconds after the presentation of a musically incongruous ("wrong") note.

Besson, Faita, Peretz, Bonnel, and Requin (1998) were interested in what happens when semantic incongruity (the wrong words) meets musical incongruity (the wrong notes). In their investigation (cleverly titled "Singing in the Brain"—get it?), they presented opera excerpts to professional musicians from the Marseille (France) opera under three different conditions: (1) the passage had the correct words throughout but ended on an incongruous word; (2) the passage had the correct notes throughout but ended with an incongruous note; and (3) the passage ended with both an incongruous musical note and an incongruous word. They were interested in whether the ERPs produced in response to the semantic incongruity would be affected by the musical context, and vice versa.

The nonmodular view suggests that the processing of the semantic (lyrics) and musical (notes) aspects of vocal music is affected by each other. Consequently, the associated N400 response (to semantic incongruity) and P600 (to musical incongruity) brain waves should deviate from the normal shape observed when each is presented in isolation. On the other hand, the modular view would suggest that these aspects of vocal music are processed independently of one another, so there should be no interaction apparent in the brain processing of lyrics and musical notes. As a result, the standard N400 and P600 brain waves should be observed.

The simple effects replicated those of earlier studies. Incongruous words, even in the context of music, led to an N400 response; incongruous notes, even when attached to words, led to the standard P600 response. Most relevant to the question of modularity is the finding that when a passage featured both types of incongruity, the resulting brain response was not some "average" of the N400 and P600 responses. Instead, the response to this "double violation" was a standard N400 and a standard P600, indicating that the processing underlying each violation was separate. Thus, the online cortical processing of music and words seems to be at least partially independent, suggesting to the authors that "the exquisite unity of vocal music" (Risset, 1991, p. 497) arises, in part, from separate processing centers, as the modular view would predict.

Levels of Analysis

As you may have already gathered, language in some way or another involves an elaborate orchestration of all of the cognitive processes we've discussed thus far. Presenting a representative sample of this research is, quite frankly, a daunting task. Fortunately, the very nature of language provides a ready-made organizational rubric—its hierarchical structure—that we'll use to survey the field. Language can be analyzed on a number of different levels, each of which features its own set of methodologies, empirical findings, and theoretical issues. At a molecular level, language involves the analysis of the small bits of information that we know as letters and speech sounds. The next level in the hierarchy is made up of words: How are words represented and accessed in semantic memory during language comprehension and production? Next, one must consider the syntactic and semantic rules that nonconsciously guide our ability to form sentences. In this chapter we will traverse this hierarchy.

STOP *and* **REVIEW!**

1. Words are to rules as
   a. communication is to comprehension.
   b. comprehension is to communication.
   c. mental lexicon is to grammar.
   d. grammar is to lexicon.
2. Name and define three of language's design features.
3. True or false? The modular view proposes that the mechanisms used by language are used for nothing else *but* language.
4. Describe the difference between linguistics and psycholinguistics.

➤ Language can be defined as a set of symbols and principles for the combination of those symbols that allows for communication and comprehension—a system of words and rules. The words comprise the mental lexicon, while the rules are implicit in a language's grammar.

➤ The design features shared by many languages include semanticity—the symbols of language refer to meaningful aspects of the real world; arbitrariness—symbols do not represent the concepts to which they refer; displacement—the power to refer to the past and future; prevarication—the creation of alternate realities through deception; reflectiveness—the ability to communicate about language; and productivity—an infinite array of messages that can be formed.

➤ The modular view contends that language relies on special mechanisms devoted to nothing else, while a nonmodular alternative views language as the joint product of the cognitive processes used for other thinking tasks. Neurological research on the processing of singing indicates at least partially independent processing of words and tunes.

➤ Psycholinguistics involves the study of linguistic performance, or how humans use language. Linguistics involves the pure study of language structure and linguistic knowledge. Language is hierarchically structured. The basic units are sounds and letters, which combine to form words. Syntactic and semantic rules are used to combine words into sentences.

Speech and Spoken Word Recognition

We now begin our trek up the language hierarchy for spoken language. Understanding spoken language could be considered an exercise in auditory perception and pattern recognition. First, sounds must be registered in the auditory system (perception); subsequently, these sounds must activate representations of the corresponding concepts in semantic memory (pattern recognition).

A great deal of research has investigated the basic components of speech and how they are perceived, as well as how a given string of speech sounds is identified as a word. Recall the distinction between bottom-up processing and top-down processing discussed in Chapter 3. Bottom-up processing refers to the identification of a pattern based on the component data. But as you'll see, speech perception and recognition involve more than just the compilation of speech data. Understanding speech involves extensive top-down processing whereby we use everything but the data to aid in pattern recognition. Speech signals are quite often unclear or imperfect; therefore, we must rely on surrounding information or previous knowledge to disambiguate the signal.

Phonology

Let's start with bottom-up processing and take a look at the "data" that comprise spoken language. **Phonology** refers to the analysis of basic speech sounds. Given that most of us have more experience working with visual language processing (processing written letters) than we do in analyzing basic speech sounds, let's start with a visual analogy. Consider the visual identification of the letter *A*. It always has the same component features (more or less) in approximately the same arrangement, regardless of the particular word in which it is embedded. But the sound of an "A" in a spoken word has different component features depending on the context. For example, the "A" sound in *cat* is different when a person

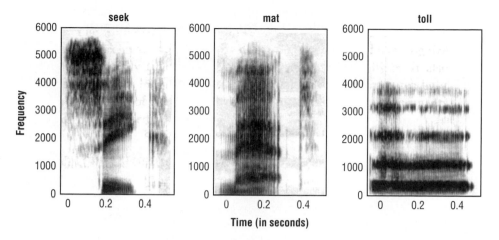

Figure 10.1 Sound spectrograms for several different words.

From Denes, P. D., & Pinson, E. N. (1993). *The speech chain.* New York: Freeman. Copyright 1993 by W. H. Freeman and Company. Reprinted by permission.

from the East Coast, the Deep South, or England says it. Each of these people speaks with a different accent, so the "A" sound is not the same. How can that be? In order to understand this, we have to look at the actual physical sounds that make up words.

The acoustic structure of a speech signal can be viewed with the use of a *sound spectrograph,* which, when presented with a speech signal, yields a *sound spectrogram.* The spectrogram plots what are basically bursts of energy (sound waves of differing frequency) that result from speech. Sample sound spectrograms for several different words are presented in Figure 10.1. The vertical axis represents frequency, and the horizontal axis represents time. Intensity of the auditory signal is represented by the darkness of the frequency bands. The particular physical stimulus elicited by speech is different, depending on factors such as rate, stress, intonation, accent, and surrounding sounds.

Phones and Phonomes.   Because some variations in the speech signal are due to purely physical properties of the speech waveform, the smallest unit that we need to identify must be defined by the acoustic properties of a sound. This segment of speech is called a **phone.** For example, the *o* in *boat* spoken by a Minnesotan is physically different from the *o* in *boat* spoken by a New Yorker. The two sounds are phonetically different from each other; they represent two different phones. However, such phonetic (physical sound) differences do not change the meaning of a word: an *o* is an *o* no matter who says it. Therefore, we need another term—**phoneme**—to refer to categories of speech sounds that are clearly different and that change the meaning of a spoken signal. For example, the phonemes /b/ and /p/ (// indicate the sound, apart from spelling) yield quite different concepts when combined with the segment *-ig.* The phonemes of American English are listed in Table 10.2. These phonemes can be categorized as consonants or vowels. It's important to note that the number of phonemes in a word doesn't necessarily correspond with the number of letters. Some phonemes are represented by a pair of letters (e.g., /sh/). Try to identify the number of phonemes in the word *boat.* Is it four? Or three?

Table 10.2 The Basic Sounds of English

Vowels	Consonants	
ee as in *heat*	*t* as in *tee*	*s* as in *see*
i as in *hit*	*p* as in *pea*	*sh* as in *shell*
e as in *head*	*k* as in *key*	*h* as in *he*
ae as in *had*	*b* as in *bee*	*v* as in *view*
ah as in *father*	*d* as in *dawn*	*th* as in *then*
aw as in *call*	*g* as in *go*	*z* as in *zoo*
u as in *put*	*m* as in *me*	*zh* as in *garage*
oo as in *cool*	*n* as in *no*	*l* as in *law*
o as in *ton*	*ng* as in *sing*	*r* as in *red*
uh as in *the*	*f* as in *fee*	*y* as in *you*
er as in *bird*	*θ* as in *thin*	*w* as in *we*
oi as in *toil*		
au as in *shout*		
ei as in *take*		
ou as in *tone*		
ai as in *might*		

From Denes, P. D., & Pinson, E. N. (1993). *The speech chain.* New York: Freeman. Reprinted by permission.

Remember that phonemes are sounds, and sounds don't necessarily correspond one to one with letters. Boat has three phonemes: /b/, /oa/, and /t/.

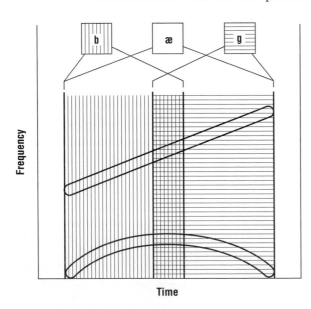

Figure 10.2 Coarticulation—the sound of each phoneme is influenced by surrounding phonemes.

Speech perception is quite a difficult task. Speech sounds are present only briefly and, as we just noted, can vary widely from speaker to speaker. They differ in what are termed **suprasegmental factors**—aspects of the speech signal such as rate, stress, and intonation—over and above the actual phonemes. In addition to differences produced by suprasegmental factors, any given phoneme within a word is affected by surrounding phonemes. The *a* in *cat* sounds different from the *a* in *bad,* because the *a*'s are surrounded by different phonemes. This poses a significant problem for the perceptual system. How do we perceive a given phoneme as the same when it is uttered by different speakers or in two different contexts?

The fact that a given phoneme sounds different depending on neighboring phonemes is termed **coarticulation;** phonemes are, to some extent, articulated together (see Figure 10.2). In spite of this, we perceive more-or-less identical

/a/ sounds in the words *cat* and *bad*. In other words, the perception of phonemes is *invariant* across different contexts. Although coarticulation does make it a bit of a challenge to perceive phonemes as invariant, it does aid word recognition by hinting at what sounds are coming next. As Harley (1995) points out, the fact that the phoneme /b/ in *ball* and *bull* is articulated differently provides information about what is coming next, thereby facilitating recognition of later phonemes.

The invariance in perceiving phonemes in spite of their different acoustic properties is the result of a fundamental characteristic of speech perception termed *categorical perception*. **Categorical perception** refers to our tendency to perceive phonemes in a relatively broad (i.e., categorical) fashion; we don't discriminate between subtle shadings in the way a particular phoneme sounds. This would seem to solve the problems associated with coarticulation. Each phoneme represents a distinct category; any particular variation of one of these phonemes is still placed firmly into the appropriate category. Have you ever wondered why it is so hard to understand a nonnative speaker of English when they are trying to speak English? The reason involves categorical perception—their pronunciation of English phonemes is too phonetically different to be placed within our English phoneme categories. So we have trouble deciphering the phonemes, which leads to trouble in figuring out the words, which leads to . . . well, you get the idea.

Consider a classic demonstration of this phenomenon by Liberman, Harris, Hoffman, and Griffith (1957). These researchers used a speech synthesizer to produce and present speech sounds that differed along a continuum (*b–d–g*). In spite of the continuous variation in the speech signals presented, subjects did not classify the sounds continuously. Rather, they placed the sounds into three distinct categories corresponding to the phonemes /b/, /d/, and /g/. They didn't hear *b*-ish *g*'s or *g*-ish *d*'s.

How Do We Perceive Speech Sounds?   The results from studies on categorical perception indicate that we may sort tremendously varied speech sounds into a much smaller number of simple phoneme categories (later we'll discuss some work that casts doubt on this phenomenon). But how do we accomplish this? Given the complexities involved in the perception of speech and the relative ease with which we accomplish it, some theorists believe that speech perception is "special," involving mechanisms that are devoted to *nothing but* speech perception. Does this type of argument sound familiar? It's exactly the type of argument that's offered for language being modular. Here, we revisit the issue of modularity within the context of speech—is there a speech perception module? To what degree is speech perception a special ability or just another instance of auditory perception? Several explanations for the intricacies of speech perception have been proffered and are reviewed by Diehl, Lotto, and Holt (2004). Here is a brief survey of two.

Motor Theory: The "Speech Is Special" View.   The **motor theory of speech perception,** proposed by Liberman and colleagues (e.g., Liberman, Cooper, Shankweiler, & Studdert-Kennedy, 1967), posits a close link between the mechanisms we use to articulate speech and our perception of speech. Basically, implicit knowledge about how speech sounds are articulated aids in our perception of those same sounds when we hear them. For example, we have implicit knowledge about coarticulation and how it confuses the mapping from acoustic signal to the phonemes intended by the speaker; this tacit knowledge of articulation allows us to decipher the spoken message (Miller, 1990). This approach is sometimes termed the *motor theory* because it contends that the basic representations we use for speech perception are the articulatory mechanisms that we use to produce the sounds when we speak. In other words, speech perception and speech production rely on the same specialized representations (Liberman & Whalen, 2000). Two other important principles follow. First, because only humans possess the mechanisms necessary for speech, only humans are capable of understanding speech. Second, speech perception is innate; infants are born equipped with the representations that allow for speech perception and production.

The argument that speech perception involves a specialized module is consistent with a number of observations, most of which relate to the ease of speech perception in spite of a supposed lack of correspondence between the physical speech signal and the phonemes that need to be identified from within it (i.e., coarticulation). The phoneme /a/ always has different phonetic features, depending on the context in which it's embedded, so there's really nothing for the perceptual system to "grab hold" of in order to identify it. Therefore, speech perception must rely on a special mechanism— categorical perception. Categorical perception is an important aid to speech perception, given the variability of a phoneme in different contexts. It is also unique in comparison to other forms of perception, which demonstrates that we are able to make relatively fine discriminations, not just categorical ones. Thus, speech perception does seem to be special.

Another argument for a specialized speech processor is the breathtaking speed apparently necessary for the perception of speech. Phonemes occur at a rate of around 10 to 20 per second. Our normal perceptual mechanisms are simply not capable of making so many discriminations in such a short period of time. To decode these rapid-fire speech stimuli, a special mechanism is needed.

Auditory Theory.   A nonmodular approach to speech perception contends that speech perception is just another exercise in auditory perception and pattern recognition. The basic mechanisms that accomplish these tasks are the same ones we use to decode speech. No special mechanism is necessary (e.g., Massaro, 1994). And because other species have auditory systems similar to our own, the ability to perceive speech sounds should not be unique to humans. An example of this approach is the **auditory theory of speech perception** (Miller, 1990).

In support of the auditory theory of speech perception, Massaro (1994) systematically counters each of the arguments outlined above for the special status of speech perception. Recall the argument that there are really no discernible physical features that define a given phoneme, because phonemes differ so widely with context. Massaro points out that this is a problem for speech perception only if the basic unit of perception is a phoneme, and there is good reason to believe that this isn't the case. If the perceptual units of analysis for speech are syllables (which may involve as many as three or four phonemes in combination), then the problem of invariance is not nearly as much of a problem. This also deflates another argument for the speech-is-special theory, the unmanageable speed of speech input. If the basic unit of speech perception is a cluster of phonemes, then we wouldn't need to process 10 to 20 units per second; it would be more like 5 to 10 units, which is more within the range of normal perceptual abilities.

Massaro also takes issue with the assumption that we perceive speech sounds categorically, contending that this assumption is simply wrong. As it turns out, categorical perception is more evident with consonants than with vowels (Repp, 1984). Also, research on how we perceive and recognize speech sounds has revealed that although people have the experience of categorical perception, we are actually capable of more fine-grained distinctions than previously thought. This relates to a distinction we made in Chapter 3. Recall our discussion of consciousness and the effects of subliminal primes on responding and that although people reported not seeing subliminal primes, their forced-choice responses indicated that they had processed the primes. The same thing happens in speech perception. People report not hearing differences between phoneme categories, but a more fine-grained analysis of processing reveals that they can make subtle distinctions (Massaro, 1994).

Finally, the speech-is-special argument contends that the speech perception module exists only for humans, since the module is linked directly to the ability to speak. But some research indicates that nonhumans can perceive speech. For example, Kleunder, Diehl, and Killeen (1987) found that quail (of all things!) were able to distinguish among different phonemic categories. So aspects of the auditory (speech) signal itself must provide information that allows for successful perception.

In spite of strong counterarguments, the speech-is-special view is still alive and well. Trout (2001, 2003) takes serious issue with the implications of the finding just mentioned—that nonhumans can perceive speech—and notes that "mere behavioral similarities come cheap." Just because an elephant can be taught to walk on two feet does not mean that the elephant is using the same mechanisms as humans, nor does it mean that humans do not have special mechanisms for their 2-footed gait. Trout also notes that the ability of animals such as the quail mentioned above demonstrated categorical perception only after thousands of trials of specific training. So the fact that quail can mimic some aspects of speech perception does not necessarily mean they're doing it the same way humans do.

Liberman and Whalen (2000) argue persuasively for the speech-is-special view, pointing out a number of characteristics of speech processing that aren't addressed by the auditory perception account. One rather compelling argument is what Mattingly and Liberman (1987) term the *requirement for parity*. Those involved in any communication exchange must have knowledge of "what counts"—and what doesn't count—as part of the communication system. Consider an example discussed by Liberman and Whalen. A sniff and the phoneme /b/ are both auditory percepts, but clearly only the latter is a speech signal. How do the speaker and the listener both know this? How did one category of auditory percepts (phonemes, like /b/) achieve phonological significance whereas others (e.g., sniffs) did not? The auditory perception view doesn't really provide an answer. But for the speech-is-special view, phoneme perception is unique and directly tied to phoneme production—our knowledge of what counts as speech is built into the language system.

Another provocative possibility for explaining the link between the perception and production of speech (Arbib, 2003; Fowler, Galantucci, & Saltzman, 2003) lies in the recent discovery of **mirror neurons,** neurons that appear to react the same way when perceiving an act and when performing the act. These neurons are thought to provide a basis for the imitation and copying of actions simply by watching the actions. According to Trout (2003), mirror neurons may provide the "common code" or link between speech perception and speech production that is proposed by advocates of the notion that speech is special.

Research Theme: Development

Phoneme Boundaries.   Special or not, there's no doubting the fact that speech perception is really *good*—efficient, accurate, and relatively impervious to variations in the particular characteristics of the speech signal. This fact is true regardless of where or to whom you were born. Eventually we understand and produce the language spoken in our home. This is truly amazing when you consider that the set of phonemes that define a given language shows tremendous variation cross-linguistically. Some languages have phonemes and phonemic boundaries that are nonexistent in other languages. For example, native speakers of Japanese have trouble discerning between the phonemic segments /l/ and /r/ because in Japanese, these two belong to the same underlying category. The development of language-specific phoneme boundaries occurs early in infancy; some evidence indicates that phonemic tuning is already under way as early as six months of age (Kuhl, Williams, Lacerda, Stevens, & Lindblom, 1992). And not only do infants seem to "tune in" to phonemic differences that are relevant to their language, they also seem to "tune out" differences that are not relevant (Bates, Devescovi, & Wulfeck, 2001). That is, there seems to be a process of suppression in speech perception that eliminates nonnative phoneme contrasts from the perceptual repertoire. Some speculate that this *learned inhibition,* as Bates and colleagues (2001) term it, may be part of the reason that adults can't seem to learn a second language without an accent (McClelland, Thomas, McCandliss, & Fiez, 1999).

Motherese.   The fact that infants tune in phoneme-relevant distinctions and tune out phoneme-irrelevant distinctions prompts an important question: How are infants able to make out the basic sounds that form the basis for language? Deciphering the basic sound elements of a language is one of the many bewildering perceptual tasks faced by infants. Intuitively, it seems obvious that they gain this knowledge from experience—by listening to adult speakers of their respective languages. If you've ever spoken to a baby, you've no doubt done so in an exaggerated, drawn out, sweet, and slow voice. The manner in which speech is delivered to infants has been dubbed **motherese,** and it seems to substantially aid infants' speech processing. Research shows that across cultures, adult speech to infants is higher-pitched, has exaggerated "ups" and "downs" in pitch, and has a slower cadence (Fernald & Simon, 1984). Also, infants show a marked preference for this type of speech relative to normal adult speech (Fernald, 1985).

Motherese aids in the perception of individual phonemes by exaggerating their critical features. This contrasts with typical adult speech, which has poorly formed and articulated consonant and vowel phonemes. Kuhl and colleagues (1992) assessed natural language input of mothers to children in the United States, Russia, and Sweden and found that in all spoken languages, vowel sounds are more (in the authors' words) "acoustically extreme" and "stretched out." The modifications that adults lend to the speech signal provide useful information about basic speech sounds that are exploited by the infant's rapidly developing perceptual system (Kuhl et al., 1992).

In a provocative account of the role of motherese in the evolution of language, Falk (2004) proposes a "put the baby down hypothesis"—the notion that motherese was an adaptation that served as a partial basis for present-day language expression. Her proposal is that early in the evolution of language, mothers would often have to cease holding their babies and put them down occasionally, as they carried out their daily tasks. To keep the babies content, they would engage in "prosodic," or song-like, vocalizations. This behavior would certainly have had selective value, and according to Falk, it formed a partial basis for the emergence of modern language. More specifically, it may have been the basis for the importance of tone in listening to and interpreting language. This tone and prosody is the defining characteristic of motherese and no doubt plays an important role in the learning of words and word boundaries, a process that we'll discuss a bit later.

STOP *and* THINK!

MOTHERESE

This exercise requires access to a baby, perhaps a niece or nephew, or your own (although it would be much easier to observe someone else engaging in motherese). Eavesdrop on the way the adult caregiver talks to the infant, noting specific characteristics of the speech.

- How do these characteristics compare to the adult's normal mode of speech?
- How are phonemes exaggerated?
- Which phonemes seem to be more exaggerated?
- Are word boundaries emphasized?

The Importance of Context.   At the beginning of this section, we discussed the issues of bottom-up processing and top-down processing. Thus far, we have been discussing primarily bottom-up processing—the identification of a pattern based on information that is part of the pattern (i.e., data in the form of speech sounds). But as we noted, speech perception also involves top-down processing—the use of context and/or previous knowledge to disambiguate a messy signal. A particularly compelling demonstration of the role of context comes from a classic study by Warren (1970) in which subjects were presented with one of these four sentences.

1. It was found that the *eel was on the axle.
2. It was found that the *eel was on the shoe.
3. It was found that the *eel was on the orange.
4. It was found that the *eel was on the table.

The presented sentences were completely identical except for the last word in the sentence. A coughing sound was spliced into the tape (at the point where the asterisk is) for each sentence. You can probably anticipate the result; subjects restored the missing phoneme, but exactly which phoneme depended on the particular semantic context. This finding has been dubbed the **phonemic restoration effect** and serves as a testament to the importance of top-down processing—the role that previous knowledge and context play in processing and identification.

Morphology

If speech perception involved only the perception of basic sounds, this would be a very short chapter. But speech is made up of words that are combinations of phonemes. So we need to climb up one more step in the language hierarchy—to morphology. The system of rules by which we combine phonemes into words and manipulate and change words to produce different shades of meaning is termed **morphology.**

A **morpheme** is the smallest unit of language that carries meaning; it may refer to a single word (e.g., *tree*) or to a prefix or suffix that changes the precise meaning of the word (e.g., the *s* in *trees*). Word morphemes are termed **free morphemes** because they may stand alone; prefix or suffix morphemes are termed **bound morphemes** because they must accompany (i.e., they must be bound to) a free morpheme in order to stand alone. Let's consider the word *unprepared.* How many morphemes does this word have? It has three: *un* (bound morpheme; negates the verb); *prepare* (free morpheme); and *ed* (bound morpheme; indicates past tense).

"Morphing" Words: Two Systems?   What happens when we change the form of a word? How does *mouse* become *mice?* How do we go from a *word* to a bunch of *words?* In the latter case, we have an example of a regular transformation (add *-s* to make something plural); in the former, an irregular transformation (*mouse* to *mice*). Pinker (1990, 1991) proposes that making these transformations relies on two separate systems. First, for regular forms, we have a system of rules that is implemented to make the appropriate transformations. Second, for irregular forms we have an associative system whereby regular-irregular pairs (*mouse-mice*) are simply committed to memory and used to retrieve each other.

It is important to note that not all researchers are convinced that successful word morphing requires two distinct mechanisms, instead proposing a single mechanism view (see Haskell, MacDonald, & Seidenberg, 2003). However, there is a substantial amount of evidence supporting the two-system view. Pinker (1991) notes a number of dissociations that support the existence of two systems for morphing words. One interesting dissociation occurs in children as they learn the words and rules of language. At about age 3 or so, children begin to make mistakes termed **overregularizations**—the child extends a grammatical rule too far, treating an irregular form as regular (e.g., adding *-ed* to *go* to come up with the past tense *goed*). The funny thing is, *before* this point, children tend to use *correct* irregular forms (i.e., they say *went*, not *goed*). As children begin to apply the rules of language (e.g., adding *-ed* to indicate that an action took place in the past), they start making mistakes that they've never made before. As the child gets older, they get better at discerning when the rule applies, and when it doesn't, and add *-ed* (or not) accordingly. This rather odd sequence of doing it right, doing it wrong, and doing it right again suggests that two systems are at play, and occasionally in conflict (Pinker, 1991).

Some neuroscientific evidence fits with this view as well. Ullman, Corkin, Coppola, Hickok, Growdon, Koroshetz, and Pinker (1997) found that different brain areas are active dur-

ing the processing of regular and irregular word forms. Based on their findings, Ullman et al. propose that the associative mechanism used for irregular forms is a manifestation of the declarative memory system, while the rule-based mechanism used for regular forms is based in the procedural system. You'll remember these two memory systems from our discussion in Chapter 6. Recall that declarative memory refers to "knowing that . . ." something is the case and describes our knowledge of facts, while procedural memory refers to "knowing how . . ." to perform some skill or habit. In the present context, declarative knowledge refers to our "knowing that" *mice* is the irregular plural of *mouse*, while procedural knowledge refers to "knowing how" to add *-s* to *house* to make it plural.

Recognizing Spoken Words. The rules for combining phonemes into words/ morphemes is primarily a production issue. What about the processes by which we perceive/recognize these words? Several theories for the recognition of spoken words have been proposed. Most accounts assume an interaction between bottom-up processes, which involve the analysis of the physical characteristics of the speech signal, and top-down processes, which bring context and expectation to bear on the recognition process (e.g., McClelland & Elman, 1986; Norris, 1994).

Cohort Model. A leading account of spoken word recognition is provided by the **cohort model** of Marslen-Wilson and colleagues (Gaskell & Marslen-Wilson, 2001; Marslen-Wilson & Welsh, 1978; Warren & Marslen-Wilson, 1988). According to this theory, speech perception starts with the first sound uttered by the speaker. With the appearance of that first phoneme, a cohort of possible matches is activated in long-term memory. Say the word in question was *boat;* according to the cohort model, the recognition process begins with the phoneme /b/, which activates *boat, bow, boast, bring, bug, bat, Beelzebub*—any concept starting with that phoneme. But as you know, one phoneme is quickly followed by another (in this case, /oa/). At that point, the cohort of possible matches is whittled down further—*bug, bat, bring,* and *Beelzebub* would drop out as candidates. Eventually, the recognition process settles on the only candidate that remains standing.

The cohort model is supported by a number of findings. For example, it turns out that speed of recognition is strongly influenced by the number of words to which a target word is phonologically similar (e.g., Goldinger, Luce, & Pisoni, 1989). Another interesting finding comes from a study by Allopenna, Magnuson, and Tanenhaus (1998). In this study, subjects were given spoken instructions that involved interacting with simple objects (e.g., "Pick up the beaker; now put it beneath the diamond"). Also present were distractor items that were selected to share a phonological cohort with the critical items. For example, distractors in the present case would include a *beetle* and a *speaker,* both phonologically similar to *beaker.* Eye movements were monitored as they followed these instructions. In line with the predictions of the cohort model, subjects glanced at the distractor items as they were listening to the spoken instruction (i.e., upon hearing the first segment of *beaker,* they would glance at the *beetle*).

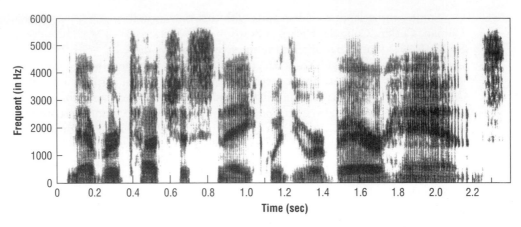

Figure 10.3 Speech spectrogram for the spoken sentence "Never touch a snake with your bare hands." Note the lack of discernible boundaries.

From Liberman, A. M. (1970). The grammars of speech and language. *Cognitive Psychology, 1,* 301–323. Copyright 1970, Elsevier Science (USA). Reprinted by permission.

One problem with the cohort model is that it places special importance on discerning the initial phoneme of a given word. As you'll see, this is no mean feat; speech is so continuous that it can be difficult to discern where one word ends and the next one picks up. Other models of speech recognition (e.g., McClelland & Elman, 1986; Norris, 1994) loosen this sequential restriction of the cohort model but retain the notions of gradual and interactive (top-down and bottom-up) activation leading to word recognition.

Discerning Word Boundaries.   As you read in the section on phonology, the fact that individual sounds in a word run together poses a significant problem for the speech perception system. The same problem arises when we need to segment these sounds into words. Identification is not a simple matter of identifying the blank spaces in the acoustic signal. Take a look at the spectrograph in Figure 10.3. You'll notice a pretty weak relationship between the breaks in the speech signal and the breaks between the words themselves. In other words, the "data" of the acoustic signal provide limited information regarding word boundaries. But you know from personal experience that understanding the component words of an utterance is (phenomenologically) a trivial matter. Mattys, White, and Melhorn (2005) note that researchers have taken two tacks in tackling this segmentation problem. One is what might be termed a *bottom-up approach,* emphasizing the physical data themselves.

Bottom-Up Factors.   Evidence indicates that we are able to use factors such as the stress patterns of words and the rhythms of speech to distinguish among the words of a spoken sentence. One factor is **phonotactic knowledge,** which refers to sensitivity to the rules that govern phoneme (i.e., sound) combinations in different languages. For example, the phonemes /t/ and /zh/ are never combined in English. Similarly, the phoneme /h/ as in *harp* often starts a word but never ends one. Sensitivity to these types of constraints helps listeners discern words and word boundaries. Another bottom-up factor is *metrical segmentation* (Cutler & Carter, 1987), which refers to the notion that the segmentation of words is dependent on the phonology of the particular language. For example, in English the important (content) words in a sentence are much more likely to start with what is termed a *strong* syllable (one that contains a *nonreduced* vowel sound, like the initial vowel sounds in *eagle, candor, bacon*—a *short* or a *long* vowel sound), and end with a *weak* syllable (a *schwa* sound, like *uh*—the second vowel sounds in each of the aforementioned words). Based on this, our perceptual systems are "tuned" to detect word boundaries when a strong syllable is encountered (Vroomen, van Zon, & de Gelder, 1996). In line with this idea, Cutler and Butterfield (1992) found that listeners showed strong tendencies to mistakenly insert word boundaries before strong syllables, and to mistakenly delete word boundaries before weak syllables.

Implicit Learning of Word Boundaries.   Some fascinating research by Saffran and colleagues (e.g., Saffran, Aslin, & Newport, 1996) suggests that statistical regularities present in speech sequences can be exploited to discern word boundaries. Some syllable combinations are more likely to appear within a word, while other syllable combinations are more likely to appear between words than within them. For example, in the phrase "pretty baby," the syllables *pre* and *ty* are more likely to occur within a word than are *ty* and *ba*. Therefore, after constant exposure to speech, word boundaries will tend to be placed between *ty* and *ba* rather than between *pre* and *ty*. And, surprisingly, it seems that exposure need not be all that constant; infants are powerful little statisticians who pick up on these sorts of statistical properties of the speech signal quite easily.

STOP *and* THINK!

FINDING PROBABILISTIC CONSTRAINTS

Look at any paragraph or two from this (or any other) chapter.

1. Analyze the syllable boundaries that occur within words.
2. Compare these boundaries to the ones that occur between words.
3. Note any systematic differences in these two types of syllable transitions.

Saffran, Aslin, and Newport (1996) for a period of two minutes presented infants with a continuous speech stream composed of four different three-syllable non-sense words strung together in random order. The infants heard something like *bidaku/padoti/golabu/bidaku* (slashes inserted to indicate experimenter-defined words). The stream was presented continuously, with no breaks whatsoever. The only cues to the experimenter-defined words were the differences in transitional probabilities between pairs of syllables within and between words. Some syllable pairs (*da* and *ku*) were more likely to occur within rather than between the experimenter-defined words, and some syllable pairs (*ku* and *pa*) were more likely to occur between rather than within the experimenter-defined words.

To find out whether the infants had learned the experimenter-defined "words" after this brief two-minute exposure, the infants were presented with two different types of test trials: (1) the previously defined "words" extracted from the two-minute stream the infants listened to, or (2) new experimenter-defined words containing the same syllables but in new combinations. Infants could control their listening time by staring or not staring at a blinking light. If the infant stared at the light, the same sequence was continually presented. If the infant stopped staring at the light, a new sequence was presented.

Let's take a few minutes to describe this method. Infants prefer novelty and will alter their behavior to gain access to novel events. So if the infants had picked up on the experimenter-defined "words" during the initial two-minute sequence, they should then prefer to listen to some other sequence during the test phase—that is, stimuli of type 2. If, on the other hand, they had not picked up on the experimenter-defined "words" and had essentially been listening to a string of syllables for two minutes, they should show no difference in preference for test stimuli of type 1 and 2. Both are simply strings of the syllables they had heard earlier and are equally boring. Infants' listening times indicated a preference for novelty—that is, they preferred to listen to the test sequences of type 2—the same syllables, but in new combinations. This indicates that they recognized the test sequences of type 1 as sequences they had heard before. During the two-minute encoding sequence, these infants had extracted the experimenter-defined "words"!

Saffran, Aslin, and Newport underline how striking this finding is. Infants were able to pick up on word boundaries after only two minutes of exposure to a speech signal that basically had no cues—no pauses, no intonation, no variations in contour . . . nothing. This ability to pick up on phonemic boundaries effortlessly and automatically serves as a powerful tool in word learning (Werker & Yeung, 2005).

Top-Down Factors.   So, learning the statistical properties of syllables within and across word boundaries is one important factor that aids the segmenting of speech, which in turn helps infants learn words. But another approach to speech segmentation flips the equation around, emphasizing that knowledge of words is what helps us segment speech (e.g., Norris, 1994). Knowing the words of a language no doubt enhances your ability to extract them when listening to a fluent stream of speech.

Consider an example from Mattys et al. (2005): Suppose you heard the following stream of phonemes: /hē kōld imēdēətlē/—for the less phonologically able among you, that's the phonetic spelling of "He called immediately." It's easy to see that the segmentation of the stream into those three words is influenced by our knowledge of those words. In terms of our mental lexicon, that's the only parsing that works. Now consider what would happen if you had little or no familiarity with a language. Have you ever listened to a person engaged in the fluent speaking of a language other than English? It sounds like they're talking a mile a minute, but really, this is a sort of illusion induced by your lack of familiarity with the language. Because you have only minimal (or no) knowledge of the words in that language, parsing them is nearly impossible.

Even with knowledge of the statistical properties of words, and knowledge of the words within our own language, the perception of word boundaries remains a challenging perceptual task. Let's consider a visual analog. How would you segment the following stream of letters into words?

THEREDONATEAKETTLEOFTENCHIPS

There are multiple interpretations: "There Don ate a kettle of ten chips"; "The red on a tea kettle often chips"; "There donate a kettle of ten chips." Just like the above example, speech is a continuous stream of information, and we must impose boundaries. Often we make mistakes; misheard word boundaries have been dubbed **mondegreens.** Song lyrics are fertile ground for mondegreens. (How many times have you heard someone say, "I can't understand the lyrics"?) We are not used to hearing language set to music; in some cases, it's almost like listening to a foreign language. One well-known musical mondegreen involves the butchering of a Jimi Hendrix classic in which one line of the song is heard as "'Scuse me while I kiss this guy." When the "data" for bottom-up processing are distorted or ambiguous (as they often are in sung lyrics), we apply our knowledge of words and make our best guess (which is often wrong). Top-down processing is playing a prominent role in the present example; "kissing a guy" fits with our previous knowledge a little better than "kissing the sky." Top-down processing could quite often lead to the successful resolution of ambiguous lyrics in a couple of ways. First, extensive experience with a given artist or type of music is likely to "fine-tune" our ability to process the "acoustic signals" produced. Second, knowing what someone is singing about—be it love, money, or the weather—is likely to aid recognition and segmentation.

STOP *and* **THINK!** ——————————————

ANNA LIZING MISS HURD LYRICS

Monitor your conversations in the coming weeks for mondegreens, or misheard speech.

1. Interview some friends to see if they have any examples of misheard song lyrics.
2. Look at the misheard speech and/or song lyrics, and evaluate ways in which boundaries were misheard.
3. Analyze the failures of bottom-up processing and the role of top-down processing involved in mishearing the speech signal.

STOP *and* REVIEW!

1. Define motherese.
2. True or false? The motor theory proposes that speech perception occurs via specialized mechanisms.
3. Morphology refers to
   a. our ability to detect word boundaries in fluent speech.
   b. our tendency to fill in missing speech sounds.
   c. analysis of the meaningful units of a language.
4. What is a mondegreen?

➤ Phonology refers to the analysis of the basic sounds of spoken language. Coarticulation refers to the fact that the nature of phoneme transmission varies depending on neighboring phonemes. Categorical perception refers to our tendency not to discriminate between subtle shadings in the way a particular phoneme sounds. Motherese refers to the exaggerated, musical way adults communicate with infants, and aids infant processing of speech.

➤ According to the motor theory of speech perception, the same mechanisms and representations underlie speech production and speech perception. According to the auditory theory, speech perception is the product of "regular" auditory perceptual processes. According to the cohort model of word recognition, spoken words are recognized by activating the entire set of possible words based on the word's initial sound, with a subsequent narrowing of the candidate set as more of the word is perceived.

➤ The phonemic restoration effect refers to our tendency to fill in missing speech sounds that fit within the semantic context. Morphology refers to an analysis of the meaningful units of language. Identification of word boundaries is a perceptual challenge because of the weak relationship between breaks in the speech signal and breaks between words. Word boundaries can also be identified via statistical regularities in speech and via our knowledge of words.

➤ The ambiguity of speech sequences leads to mondegreens (misheard word boundaries). When the speech signal is distorted or ambiguous, we apply our knowledge of words and make our best guess, which is often wrong. The importance of top-down processing is also observed when we have difficulty parsing words in a foreign language because of our lack of familiarity.

Reading and Visual Word Recognition

Just as speech perception involves the formulation of meaning from an inherently meaningless stimulus—air displacement in the form of sound waves—reading involves the formulation of meaning from little squiggles of different shapes, sizes, and spacings on a sheet of paper or similar medium. It's truly a wonder that we so quickly and effortlessly afford such a stimulus meaning. In the last four or five decades, a legion of researchers have amassed a great deal of information about the processes involved in reading and what happens when these processes go astray.

What processes are taking place during reading?

Eye Movements

The processing of information during reading starts when the eyes take in the printed page. This being the case, the movements of the eyes across the printed page have been a primary focus of reading research. As you'll see, the consistencies in the speed and pattern of our eyes' trek through a written passage, along with the variables that influence these consistencies, can reveal much about the underlying mental processes.

Saccades and Fixations.   If you think about how your eyes move as you scan across a page of this book, you may think that your eyes scan smoothly across the page from left to right, then back again. This impression is mistaken. Your eyes actually move in a series of stops, pauses, and starts, termed *saccades* and *fixations.* **Saccades** are the discrete movements that our eyes make from one point to another when we're reading, taking in a visual scene, or searching for an object (Rayner, 1998); they occur continually. The saccades we make during reading are typically six to eight letters in length and take about 20 milliseconds. During saccades, we seem to take in little or no visual information, a phenomenon termed **saccadic suppression** (Matin, 1974); indeed, eye movements occur with such velocity that if we did take in information, it would probably register as a blur. It's not completely clear whether or not cognitive processing is suppressed during saccades; the empirical jury is still out on this issue. In between saccades are **fixations** in which the eyes pause briefly to take in information. Fixations typically last anywhere from 200 to 300 milliseconds. The length depends on the nature of the reading task, be it silent reading, reading aloud, or reading music. Consecutive fixations in the same spot are sometimes labeled **gazes;** the summed duration of these gazes (i.e., **gaze duration**) is another dependent variable in the study of reading.

The pattern of fixations, gazes, and saccades can be seen in Figure 10.4, which presents eye-fixation data, along with the text that was being read (from Rayner & Pollatsek,

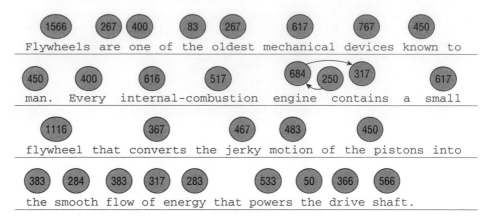

Figure 10.4 Length of eye fixations on words in a passage of text.

From Just, M. A., & Carpenter, P. A. (1987). *The psychology of reading and language comprehension.* Boston: Allyn and Bacon. Copyright 1987 by Pearson Education. Reprinted by permission of the publisher.

1989). You'll note a number of interesting characteristics of eye fixations and eye movements. First, some words are fixated twice and some not at all. Notice how content words, like *devices* and *combustion,* receive more gaze time than do function words like *and* and *that;* sometimes, these function words are not fixated at all. About 80% of content words and only 40% of function words are fixated. Also, the more unfamiliar a word (e.g., *flywheel*), the longer the fixation. Overall, approximately 65% of the words in a given text are fixated; this proportion varies with content and with the characteristics of the reader.

Word Skipping.   What leads a reader to skip certain words? One factor is how predictable a word is based on the context; words that are highly constrained (i.e., the word is about the only one that would make sense, given the context) are more likely to be skipped than words that are less constrained (Balota, Pollatsek, & Rayner, 1985). In addition, high-frequency words are more likely to be skipped than low-frequency words (Rayner & Well, 1996). The variable that most strongly determines whether a word will be skipped is word length (Brysbaert & Vitu, 1998). Short words (e.g., *an, the*) are much more likely to be skipped relative to longer words (e.g., *flywheels, devices*). This makes sense; shorter, more predictable words don't carry very much of the meaning in text, so spending too much time on them would be inefficient.

STOP *and* THINK!

READING FROM THE TOP DOWN

Have two of your friends read this passage:

In the previous chapter, we sketched some of the basics of language, such as its basic definition, major components, and fundamentals of speech perception. Although language is first and foremost a spoken medium, it takes only a moment's thought to consider its many different expressions. After all, we're not talking to you about cognitive psychology; we've written this text, and you're reading it— and not only that, but understanding it. After you learn about cognitive psychology, we're sure that you'll be so excited by it that you'll engage your classmates in conversation about it.

Tell one of your friends to count the number of f's in this passage. Have the other friend count the number of m's. There are 11 of each, but the f's tend to be in shorter, more predictable words that are likely to be skipped during reading. See if your friends' letter counting fits this pattern.

Regressive Saccades.   In Figure 10.4 you'll also notice that on occasion, the eyes move backward; these backward movements are termed **regressive saccades,** and they constitute about 10 to 15% of all saccades. These occur when a reader makes a saccade too long and has to backtrack, or if a word is particularly difficult to decipher. Regressive saccades may even occur within a word (Rayner, 1998). Good and poor readers differ in the "quality" of their regressive eye saccades. Good readers are better at regressing back to exactly where they encountered a problem; in contrast, poor readers must do more backtracking in order to zero in on where they had a problem (Murray & Kennedy, 1988). Based on the poorly placed eye movements of poor readers, you might be tempted to jump to the conclusion that poor reading is caused by inefficiency of eye movements. Indeed, this is what many reading specialists believed decades ago. As a result, many programs were designed to train eye movements in the hope of improving reading. Unfortunately, later research showed that inefficient eye saccades and fixation patterns are a symptom, rather than the cause, of poor reading. As a result, these programs proved to be unsuccessful (Tinker, 1958).

Perceptual Span.   You may have noticed that when you read, your eyes basically "look ahead." The amount of text that the eyes can cover effectively to either side of a given fixation is termed **perceptual span.** For the English alphabet, perceptual span is about 3 characters to the left and 15 or so characters to the right of any given fixation (McConkie & Rayner, 1976). Interestingly, the characteristics of the perceptual span differ depending on the writing system (i.e., the orthography) of the language in question. For Hebrew, which is read from right to left, the perceptual span is a mirror image of English; 3 characters to the right and about 15 to the left of fixation. Another interesting fact about the perceptual span is that it differs with the difficulty of the material. Your reading span for this text is quite likely shorter than that for reading lighter material, like the Mary Higgins Clark books that Bridget loves to read.

How are we influenced by what falls slightly out of fixation but is still within the perceptual span? Such information is termed *parafoveal* (because it falls outside of the fovea—the point of central focus). Evidence indicates that parafoveal information aids in lexical access; in other words, getting the first few letters of the next word aids the word recognition process. Parafoveal information also allows the reader to detect word length and where word boundaries are (a decidedly easier task than deciphering word boundaries in spoken language!) so that the reader knows where to look next (e.g., Rayner &

Morris, 1992). The detection of word length allows for the identification and skipping of short function words (Blanchard, Pollatsek, & Rayner, 1989), which makes reading the fast and efficient process that it is in most circumstances.

Visual Word Recognition

Now that you have a basic understanding of the mechanics of reading, let's take a step up in the language hierarchy. Previously, this involved moving from sounds to spoken words; here, we move from letters to written words. It's obvious that the look of a written word—its **orthography**—is an important factor in its visual recognition. The view that orthography provides the major route to word recognition is termed the **direct-access view.** Words are recognized by using the written label to access the appropriate semantic memory representation directly. Labeling this the "direct" view implies that there must also be an "indirect" view. Indeed there is. The **indirect-access** (or **phonological**) **view** of word recognition proposes that word recognition goes through the phonological representation of the word prior to the word's identification. In other words, visual recognition of the word *apple* as a sweet, red thing you pick off trees in the fall involves the activation of the word's sound. This view might remind you of the motor theory of speech perception that we discussed earlier—the view that the recognition of speech is aided by one's own knowledge and experience with the articulation of speech. Although it may seem a bit counterintuitive, the indirect-access view has a good deal of support. It seems that even when we are silently looking at a printed word, the "road to recognition" appears to go through the word's phonological characteristics.

STOP *and* THINK!

RECONSIDERING READING

Carefully read a randomly chosen passage from this text, and observe whatever difficulties you might have. What is the source of the difficulties? How did your reading processes attempt to deal with these difficulties (i.e., did you backtrack, etc.)? As you were reading, was there any evidence that you used the auditory route to word recognition (i.e., sounding words out)?

Now pick up a newspaper or magazine and carefully read a passage from it. Did you have less trouble reading this? Did you read it more quickly?

Now have a friend read the two passages (be sure they are about the same length). Which one did they read more quickly?

Cognitive psychologists, ever resourceful, have come up with a novel way to investigate the issue of direct versus indirect access—by analyzing the visual recognition of homophones. Homophones are word pairs with the same component sounds but different spellings and different meanings (e.g., *reed* and *read*). A study by Van Orden (1987) took advantage of the ambiguity of homophones to conduct a test of phonologically mediated (indirect) access to semantic memory during word recognition. In this study (experiment 1), subjects were presented with a category verification task; a category name (e.g., "*flower*") was followed by one of three types of stimuli: a member of the category (e.g., *tulip*), a homophone of a member of the category (e.g., *rows*, which is a "phonological replica" of *rose*), or a word orthographically similar to a member of the category (e.g., *robs*, which has orthography similar to *rose*). The task was to indicate as quickly as possible if the word was a member of the category. If access is direct, then *rows* and *robs* should have both caused problems, because they're visually similar to *rose*. If identifying a word involves activation of a phonological code, however, there should have been a good deal of misclassification of *rows* and other homophones as being members of the stated category (e.g., "flower"). In line with this prediction, subjects made categorization mistakes nearly 20% of the time for homophones but only 3% of the time for orthographically similar words; it's almost like homophones are "pseudomembers" of a category. This suggests strongly that word recognition involves access to sound.

Even more compelling evidence comes from research employing pseudohomophones. A pseudohomophone is a made-up word that sounds like a real word (e.g., *brane* for *brain*). Luo, Johnson, and Gallo (1998) tested whether pseudohomophones might show effects of semantic relatedness. In other words, would *chare* (mistakenly) be viewed as related to *table* because it sounds identical to *chair*? If access to the mental lexicon is direct (i.e., not phonologically mediated), then you might expect that the pair *table-chare* would be easily classified as unrelated. If such access is mediated by phonology, however, then it is likely that such pairs would lead to more errors and/or a slower RT in judgments of semantic relatedness.

The results are presented in Figure 10.5; as you can see, pseudohomophones led to more errors and slower RTs, suggesting that access to the mental lexicon involves phonological information. Many researchers favor what is typically termed a **dual-route view**

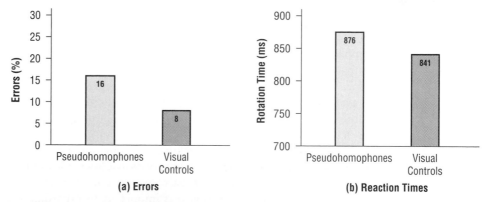

Figure 10.5 Results from Luo, Johnson, and Gallo (1998).

From Luo, C. R., Johnson, R. A., & Gallo, D. A. (1998). Automatic activation of phonological information in reading: Evidence from the semantic relatedness decision task. *Memory and Cognition, 26,* 833–843. Reprinted by permission of the Psychonomic Society, Inc.

of word recognition (Coltheart, Rastle, Perry, Langdon, & Ziegler, 2001), proposing that word recognition can proceed by either a direct (visual label only) route or an indirect (visual label plus phonological representation) route.

Teaching Reading.   As you've seen, cognitive researchers have amassed a wealth of data on the processes that underlie word recognition. So of course their research findings provide a critical database that can be used to address an important educational question: What's the best method for teaching children to read? Educators have wrestled with this question for decades, and a clear answer has finally emerged from research on reading. Before we give away the answer, let's review the reading techniques that have been used. The **whole-word approach** involves the rote learning of words, which children eventually learn to recognize with a quick glance. Basically, children are taught to apprehend whole words at a time; you can think of this as a top-down approach. The bottom-up alternative to this approach is termed the **phonics approach,** which involves sounding words out by noting the correspondence between the component letters and their sounds. This technique runs into problems when there is an irregular mapping of letters to sounds (which happens quite often in English).

Because of these problems with the phonics approach, some espouse a **whole-language approach.** This approach is in the spirit of the whole-word approach but is even broader in its application of top-down elements. In this approach, young readers are given engaging things to read on their own and are encouraged to guess at new or unfamiliar words by using illustrations, context, and story line. They are also encouraged to make up their own stories. Basically, the aim of the whole-language approach is to make reading and reading instruction fun. The approach is almost antiphonics. According to the whole-language approach, the mechanics of sound-to-letter mappings should not be taught explicitly, and a child should not be corrected when they mispronounce a word, because they will eventually arrive at the correct usage and pronunciation of the words on their own.

In a review of these three methods for reading instruction, Rayner, Foorman, Perfetti, Pesetsky, and Seidenberg (2001) provide ample evidence for a clear winner . . . the phonics approach. As you read earlier, a great deal of research indicates that reading involves access to the phonological representations of words. Rayner and colleagues point out that this is the case even for highly skilled readers. Therefore, it appears that learning letter-to-sound correspondences (i.e., developing what is termed *phonological awareness*) is vitally important to reading instruction. This turns out to be the case even in languages that differ markedly from English. McBride-Chang and Kail (2002) found the same relationship in a study of Chinese toddlers learning to read Chinese characters.

The evidence supporting this assertion is overwhelming; recent reviews of the evidence by the National Reading Panel and the National Research Council clearly demonstrate the superiority of the phonics approach over the other two approaches in producing higher reading achievement. However, it is important to note that not all researchers have arrived at the conclusion that phonological awareness is *causally* linked to reading skill. Castles and Coltheart (2004) note that the evidence supporting such a link is correlational in nature. And, as the critical thinking mantra goes, "Correlation does not equal causation." It may be the case that children who start reading early develop better phonological awareness, or that some third variable supports both phonological awareness and reading skill.

STOP *and* **REVIEW!**

1. Saccade is to fixation as
   a. information intake is to no information intake.
   b. jump is to pause.
   c. progressive is to regressive.
   d. familiar is to unfamiliar.
2. Distinguish between the direct- and indirect-access views of word recognition.
3. True or false? Reading research indicates that the phonics approach is more effective than the whole-word or whole-language approaches.

➤ When we read, our eyes move across the page in a series of jumps and pauses termed *saccades* and *fixations.* During saccades, little or no visual information is taken in (saccadic suppression). During fixations, we take in text information. Content words receive more gaze time than do function words. The more unfamiliar the word, the longer the fixation. Highly constrained words, high-frequency words, and short words are most likely to be skipped. Saccades can be regressive.

➤ Perceptual span is about 3 characters to the left and 15 or so characters to the right of any given fixation for the English alphabet. Perceptual span is shorter the more difficult the material. According to the direct-access view, words are recognized by direct access to the word's representation. The indirect-access (phonological) view proposes that word recognition involves phonological activation. Dual-route views state that access can be direct or indirect.

➤ Research on teaching reading indicates that the phonics approach (teaching letter-to-sound correspondence) is much more effective than the whole-word or whole-language approaches.

From Words to Sentences: Syntax and Semantics

Consider the following sentence: "The crowd booed the referee after his terrible call." It's clear that when we read (or listen), we implicitly understand not only the meaning of the individual words in the sentence, but also the structure of the sentence: the subject (*The Crowd*), the object (*the referee*), and the connecting verb (*booed*). We understand each of these components and their interaction—the "who is doing what to whom," if you will. How do we arrive at this understanding? You no doubt have the intuition that it depends on a number of different factors: we must (1) successfully recognize each word in the sentence, (2) discern the grammatical structure of the sentence, and (3) form a representation of the meaning expressed by the sentence. In other words, sentence comprehension involves analysis at the word (discussed early in this chapter), syntactic, and semantic levels. However, the essence of language lies not in individual words, but in the combinations of particular words that we assemble to convey some particular meaning. The term **syntax** refers to the set of rules that specify legal combinations of words within a given language. **Semantics** refers to the rules governing the effective transmission of meaning.

Transformational Grammar

Let's take a closer look at one of the defining characteristics of language—the system of rules that allows one to take a finite set of symbols and produce an infinite array of sentences. You may remember from Chapter 1 that it was linguist Noam Chomsky's revolutionary ideas about the mental representation of rules for language that provided what may have been the most devastating blow to the behaviorist account of complex behavior. Chomsky argued convincingly that the breathtaking variety and creativity demonstrated by speakers of any language could not be accounted for by the simple mechanisms of imitation, positive reinforcement, and stimulus-response chaining. To Chomsky, it was inconceivable that such a simple, highly constrained mechanism could be at the root of language, with its infinite flexibility, novelty, and creativity. To account for the powerful design features of language, there must be a complex system of rules that allows for virtually infinite combinations of the symbols of language. Another piece of "thought evidence" for this view is that children say things that adults never say (e.g., "Look at the mouses") and make mistakes in grammar that adults never make (e.g., "I goed to the bathroom"). For Chomsky, this implies that they are applying stored rules (rules that are represented physiologically from birth) to the symbols of language.

Syntactic rules are at the heart of Chomsky's linguistic theory. According to Chomsky, we are born with an implicit sensitivity to sentence structure and the rules of syntax. When this implicit sensitivity is engaged by spoken language, it begins to develop rapidly in the absence of any formal "teaching." Chomsky's approach to how we engage in language is termed **transformational grammar.** Although the theory is not generally considered a complete model of language, it revolutionized the way language was viewed when it was first proposed and pretty much single-handedly established the field of psycholinguistics. At the heart of Chomsky's approach to language is the notion that language is based on rules. These rules apply to syntactic structure of sentences, and we have implicit knowledge of these rules. And because these principles apply regardless of which particular language one is speaking about, Chomsky's approach is often termed **universal grammar.**

A central component in any rule-based (i.e., grammar-based) description of language is the notion of *phrase structure*. Intuitively, it is usually a pretty simple matter to break a sentence down into its component phrases, termed **constituents.** Consider how you would break up the following sentence: "The engaging professor entertained the class." (No doubt this sentence describes your usual experiences in class!) Chances are you'd break the sentence into two major phrases, or constituents—a noun phrase ("The engaging professor") and a verb phrase ("entertained the class"). Each of these constituents can in turn be broken down into still smaller parts. The noun phrase consists of an article (*The*), an adjective (*engaging*), and a noun (*professor*); the verb phrase consists of a verb (*entertained*) and an object phrase (*the class*). Why the painstaking analysis of this sentence? We want to demonstrate the notion of phrase structure and to make it clear that we all have some intuitive notion of phrase structure rules—the rules that define the fundamental components of a sentence, the types of words that typically comprise these components, and the ways these words may be arranged.

STOP *and* THINK!

CONSIDERING CONSTITUENTS

In order to realize the "psychological reality" of how we perceive sentences in terms of constituents, go to any random paragraph in the text, pick out a few sample sentences, and break them into their constituents.

The idea that we use phrase structure rules to generate and comprehend sentences seems plausible, but before long, this concept runs into problems. Consider the following sentence: "The shooting of the hunters was terrible." If you examine the sentence for a moment, you'll notice that the meaning is ambiguous. Does it mean that the hunters couldn't hit the broad side of a barn? Or could it be that somebody shot the hunters? Breaking the sentence down into its constituents doesn't help: "The shooting of the hunters" . . . "was terrible." The ambiguity remains. So a theory of grammar based only on phrase structure rules seems to lack something.

Surface Structure and Deep Structure.   Based on the inadequacy of phrase structure in describing how a sentence like this can be formulated or understood, Chomsky had the critical insight that sentences must exist at two levels—both as an idea and as a concrete representation of that idea. He termed these *deep structure* and *surface structure*, respectively. The **deep structure** of a sentence conveys its meaning. The **surface structure** of a sentence is the particular phrase ordering used to convey that meaning. The sentence "The shooting of the hunters was terrible" is an example of *deep-structure ambiguity;* in spite of the single surface structure, the sentence has two possible deep structures.

Two other scenarios make it apparent that phrase structure rules are insufficient for describing an understanding of language. Consider these sentences:

The professor is easy to please.
The professor is eager to please.

Although neither of these are necessarily true of any of your professors, note that describing the sentences in terms of phrase structure doesn't differentiate between them. Once again, the distinction between surface structure and deep structure is critical; while the phrase structures are nearly identical, the deep structures are quite different. Finally, consider these two sentences:

> The professor graded the tests.
> The tests were graded by the professor.

In this case, phrase structure rules make the sentences seem radically different; the noun phrase in one is the verb phrase in the other, and vice versa. But it's easy to see that these sentences are expressing identical ideas. In Chomsky's terms, these sentences have different surface structures but identical deep structures. According to the theory of transformational grammar, we use the rules of phrase structure to generate the underlying idea, or deep structure, of the sentence. Then we apply *transformational rules* to the deep structure to generate a surface structure that conveys the intended meaning.

Sentence Parsing

Chomsky's distinction between the surface structure and the deep structure of language highlights the important interaction between meaning and the physical structure of sentences (spoken or written) in our comprehension. We implicitly use our knowledge of grammar to comprehend sequences of words through a process termed **parsing.** Parsing usually occurs so seamlessly that we don't even notice we're doing it. How is it accomplished? How are the components of a sentence recognized and combined? Does the syntactic (i.e., structural) analysis of a sentence have to be computed before we compute the meaning of a sentence, or is meaning computed along with syntax?

The Importance of Syntax.   According to some views of sentence parsing, syntax is central. Put in terms of a concept we introduced earlier, we parse sentences according to their phrase structure. Word order (i.e., surface structure) helps the reader determine the phrase structure and thus serves the primary role in sentence comprehension. For example, sentences with a noun-verb-noun (i.e., subject-verb-object, or SVO) phrase structure are quite common in English, so the tacit assumption of a reader would be that sentences fit this general structure; this assumption helps guide parsing.

The Garden-Path Approach.   One approach to parsing is termed the **garden-path approach** (e.g., Frazier & Rayner, 1982) because it assumes that the reader follows a simple, word-by-word path through the sentence, attempting to fit each word within the assumed syntactic structure. Consider this sentence: "The professor argued the student's position passionately." If we (as English speakers) parse this sentence according to the garden-path approach, we will assume that it fits a standard SVO (subject-verb-object) structure. You might imagine a representation of this sentence that includes two major "nodes" corresponding to each of the sentence constituents: the noun phrase ("The professor") and the verb phrase ("argued the student's position passionately").

Noun Phrase		Verb Phrase	
Verb Phrase	Verb	Noun Phrase	Adverb
The professor	argued	the student's position	passionately.

According to the garden-path approach, as we read we assume the simplest syntactic structure and then revise this assumption if it proves to be wrong. For example, when we read the sentence above, we make the simplest possible assumption about its syntax; we assume that the phrase "the student's position" is the object of the just-encountered word "argued." This type of simplifying assumption makes sense when one considers the limited capacity and time pressures faced by the human information processor.

Let's get a little more specific. The garden-path approach assumes that we use two different heuristics, or rules of thumb, to parse a sentence. One heuristic is termed *minimal attachment.* This principle states that one does not assume that the syntax of the sentence is more complicated than it probably is. For instance, we could assume that the phrase "the student's position" starts a whole new sentence embedded within the main sentence. However, we do not make this assumption. Another way to look at it is that as readers, we are parsimonious (i.e., minimal) about assuming new phrases. A second heuristic that converges on this interpretation of the sentence is the principle of *late closure.* According to this principle, we try to attach each word that we encounter to the phrase that's currently being processed. In this case, "the student's position" is assumed to be part of the verb phrase.

If our syntactic analysis proceeds down the garden path as just described, then we would have a problem with this sentence: "The professor argued the student's position was indefensible." Did you stumble over this sentence? Initially, it seems that the professor is arguing the student's position, but when we encounter the word "was," the interpretation of the sentence must change. The professor is arguing against the student's position. This is termed a garden-path sentence.

Garden-path sentences provide strong evidence for the garden-path model of parsing proposed by Frazier and Rayner (1982). According to this model, when this sentence is read, "the student's position" will be placed within the verb phrase that starts with the word "argued," because of the principles of minimal attachment and late closure. However, when we encounter the word "was," this interpretation is rendered invalid; at this point, a new syntactic interpretation is constructed. Studies of online reading behavior confirm the difficulty readers have when they encounter garden-path sentences; these sentences are associated with longer reading times, longer fixations, and more regressive saccades (Frazier & Rayner, 1982). The difficulty in processing garden-path sentences seems quite general; even blind readers of Braille show regressive movements to cope with the ambiguity these sentences create (Mousty & Bertelson, 1992). The difficulty encountered in garden-path sentences supports the notion that our initial attempts at parsing are based on the principles of minimal attachment and late closure and confirms our (quite sensible) bias to read sentences as subject-verb-object. (This bias is not shared by many languages; most other languages use different sentence structures such as subject-object-verb; see Bates, Devescovi, & Wulfeck, 2001).

SKIPPING UP THE GARDEN PATH

Badly worded headlines provide amusing examples of leading readers up the garden path. Consider the following examples.

Prostitutes Appeal to Pope
College Graduates Blind Senior Citizen
Complaints about NBA Refs Growing Ugly

Find some examples of garden-path sentences from newspapers or Internet sites. (There are, no doubt, Web sites explicitly devoted to these unfortunate headlines.) Analyze what you found by considering the following questions:

- How much effort did it take to "get" each interpretation of the headline/sentence?
- Which interpretation did you arrive at first?
- Was it easy to come up with the alternative?
- Was it difficult to figure out both interpretations?
- What parts of headlines/sentences (i.e., parts of speech) seem to be the most sensitive to misinterpretation?
- How did your general knowledge help you to disambiguate the headline/sentence?

The Importance of Semantics.   The difficulty we encounter when presented with ambiguous language stimuli like garden-path sentences makes a second aspect of sentence processing evident. Obviously, understanding the standard SVO syntactic structure that serves as the basis for so much of our communication in the English language is not enough for language understanding and production. If it was, you'd come up with sentences like "The hen polished the dictionary." As we said earlier, semantics refers to the manner in which we convey and understand the meaning of language. Most of the theorizing we've discussed thus far (in particular, Chomsky's approach) relegates semantics to a secondary role, while certainly not denying the importance of semantic factors in language.

One approach that highlights the importance of meaning is termed the **case-grammar approach** (Fillmore, 1968). This approach contends that sentences are parsed through the assignment of words to various **case roles,** which specify who (or what) is doing what to whom (or what) (tortured syntax indeed!). Consider the following example: "Jim shot the ball through the hoop." Rather than parsing the sentence into syntactic components like noun phrase and verb phrase, the case-grammar approach assumes that the sentence is understood by parsing it into the roles played by each word in the sentence. In the sample sentence above, Jim serves the case role of agent, the basketball serves the case role of patient, and the hoop serves the case role of goal. Understanding and producing sentences is an exercise in decomposing and composing the case-role assignments, rather than the syntactic-role assignments, for the words in the sentence.

Sentence Comprehension.   The importance of both syntax and semantics in sentence parsing and understanding is a given. Psycholinguistic researchers are interested in the specifics of the interplay between syntax and semantics. Does one have primary importance? Does one affect the other, or do semantic and syntactic analyses proceed independently of each other? Do these analyses occur in parallel or in serial?

According to what might be termed the **autonomous view,** the analyses of syntax and semantics proceed independently (i.e., autonomously) of each other, and the processing is serial. Sentence comprehension involves (in this precise order) computing the syntactic structure of the sentence followed by building a representation of the meaning being expressed in the sentence. The garden-path approach discussed above is an example of this type of approach. This view has the flavor of the information-processing approach, with its serial view of cognitive processes. An **interactionist view** of sentence comprehension proposes the same component processes but suggests that syntactic and semantic analyses occur in parallel (i.e., simultaneously). Furthermore, these processes depend on each other. This view has more of a connectionist flavor, in that it emphasizes parallel processing of different language modules. The autonomous and interactionist views highlight two separate but related issues: First, do syntactic and semantic processing proceed in parallel or in serial? Second, do syntactic and semantic processing proceed independently of each other, or do they interact?

Independent or Dependent Modules?   One source of evidence that syntax and semantics comprise distinct language modules is dissociations in performance between these two aspects of language. As you've seen in a number of places throughout the text, evidence that two processes may be based on fundamentally different mechanisms is provided by dissociations—instances in which one cognitive process is impacted by some variable while another process is not or when the process is affected in the opposite fashion. This logic has been used to argue for the independence of syntactic and semantic processing in speech. The most commonly cited dissociation is between two types of aphasia: Broca's aphasia and Wernicke's aphasia. **Broca's aphasia,** associated with frontal lobe brain damage, tends to involve a breakdown of structure; speech is telegraphic and incorrectly structured. However, use of content words (i.e., nouns and verbs) is less affected. So there seems to be a loss in syntactic ability but a preserved semantic ability. **Wernicke's aphasia,** which is associated with temporal lobe brain damage, tends to involve a breakdown of semantic aspects of language. Wernicke's aphasics speak in intact sentence structures but with a distorted choice of content words. So there seems to be a loss of semantic ability with preserved syntactic ability. This dissociation is consistent with the view that syntactic processing and semantic processing are based on separate, independent systems; if they were based on the same system, damage to one would mean damage to the other.

Serial or Parallel?   Earlier, we discussed the garden-path approach to sentence parsing, which assumes that we follow one syntactic interpretation of a sentence until that interpretation leads up the wrong path, in which case we regroup and reinterpret. The garden-path approach is consistent with the autonomous view; sentence parsing is ultimately guided by syntactic structure. Semantic (i.e., meaning-based) factors do not exert their effect until later stages of sentence comprehension. In other words, syntactic analysis is primary, and semantic analysis is, in some respects, secondary. If this is true, then syntactic analysis should proceed unaffected by meaning. However, if you think about it, the difficulty encountered in the processing of garden-path sentences could be viewed as either a syntactic or a semantic influence on parsing. After all, the juncture in the sentence that creates problems involves a change in meaning as well as a change in phrase structure. If there is an influence of semantic factors, then we might expect that the meaning of a sentence would influence whether or not the garden-path effect occurs.

A study addressing this general question was conducted by Pickering and Traxler (1998). They hypothesized that if semantic factors influence syntactic factors, then the difficulty induced by a garden-path sentence should be more severe when the initial interpretation makes sense than when it doesn't. In other words, silly sentences shouldn't be as likely to induce a garden-path effect. Consider these two sentences:

As the woman edited the magazine amused all the reporters.
As the woman sailed the magazine amused all the reporters.

Both of these are identical in terms of syntax, and both are garden-path sentences. According to the garden-path principles of late closure and minimal attachment, the phrase "the magazine" should be placed with the verb in each sentence, leading to difficulties in comprehension for both.

But there is a critical difference between the initial parts of these two sentences: one is plausible ("As the woman edited the magazine"), and one is not plausible ("As the woman sailed the magazine"). Does this semantic difference in these syntactically identical sentences affect comprehension of the sentence? Pickering and Traxler (1998) had subjects read garden-path sentences that were either plausible or implausible to investigate the possibility of semantic effects in comprehension. Their results demonstrated stronger garden-path effects for plausible sentences. The semantic plausibility of the sentence induced more of a "commitment" from readers; once a particular semantic interpretation was made, encountering a syntactic change that caused the interpretation to be wrong created more problems in comprehending the sentence. If the sentence was not semantically plausible, the correct syntactic decision was usually made, reducing the difficulty normally seen with garden-path sentences. Interestingly, implausible sentences did produce some garden-path effects, indicating the importance of syntactic factors.

The cognitive struggle in which we seem to engage when faced with the syntactic ambiguity of garden-path sentences can be compared to what happens when we're faced with lexical ambiguity (i.e., a word with two different meanings). You'll recall (from Chapter 9) that, somewhat surprisingly, all interpretations of a word are considered (however briefly) before context finally leads to the selection of the appropriate interpretation. The same general pattern seems to apply to garden-path sentences, at least to some degree; multiple interpretations are considered, and context biases one of them. This finding seems to support the interactionist view that syntactic and semantic analyses occur in parallel.

Working Memory and Parsing.   It should come as no surprise that the online processing of sentences is influenced by moment-to-moment demands on attention. Research demonstrates that the strength of garden-path effects depends on working memory capacity. Just and Carpenter (1992) compared subjects with high and low working memory capacity in their comprehension of garden-path sentences. As you read earlier, a garden-path sentence like "The evidence examined by the lawyer shocked the jury" is less likely to lead to interpretation difficulties because the verb "Examined" can't plausibly go along with "The evidence" (i.e., evidence is an inanimate object so it could not examine something). However, Just and Carpenter found that comprehension depended on capacity. Readers with high capacity were more likely than those with lower capacity to use the status of the noun "evidence" to disambiguate the remainder of the sentence. So, difficulties in interpreting garden-path sentences may arise from capacity limitations rather than from the serial processing of syntax and semantics. So the debate continues, providing fertile ground for further research.

Parsing: A Cross-Linguistic Comparison.   Almost all of the research discussed in this chapter is based on research with native English speakers, who speak and read in, what else . . .

English! As Bates, Devescovi, and Wulfeck (2001) note, this is an unfortunate state of affairs. To some extent, psycholinguistics involves the search for universal principles of language processing. Obviously, if psycholinguistic research is dominated by studies using English, the results are severely limited in their generalizability. This is especially true when one considers the vast differences that exist between the languages of the world with regard to what MacWhinney and Bates (1989) term the *cue validity of grammatical structures* in comprehending sentences. In other words, how do particular combinations of words tip off a comprehender to the meaning of a sentence? As we noted earlier, in English, word order is an extremely powerful cue. Consider these words: *cow chased horse.* Given English speakers rigid adherence to the subject-verb-object sentence structure, English speakers would almost universally interpret this word combination as meaning that the cow (the subject) chased (verb) the horse (object), even though the idea expressed seems a bit strange. But the validity of this particular word ordering as a cue is by no means universal.

In an exhaustive analysis of the cue validity of various languages, MacWhinney and Bates compared native speakers from over a dozen different language backgrounds in order to assess the hierarchy of cues used to comprehend sentences. More specifically, the researchers were interested in cross-linguistic differences in which sentence cues were used for actor assignment. In our cow example above, the cow is the actor (to English speakers, at least). What other cues can affect actor assignment, and how do these differ among languages? To assess this, MacWhinney and Bates report a series of studies that employed a "Who did it?" task (Bates, Devescovi, & Wulfeck, 2001) under different presentation conditions. Simple sentences—like "The cow chased the horse" or "The rock kissed the cow"—were used to find out how speakers of various languages would determine who did the chasing and the kissing.

Two conditions employed in these studies varied the syntactic relationship (whether the verb agreed with the first noun or the second noun) and the semantic relationship between the two nouns (e.g., animate-animate, inanimate-animate, animate-inanimate). The investigators were interested in determining which cues would win out in determining "who did what to whom." The results yielded some intriguing differences. As expected,

English speakers rigidly followed word order as a cue, asserting that the cow did the chasing and the rock did the kissing. However, for the latter sentence ("The rock kissed the cow"), animacy overruled word order for most other languages. (Rocks are inanimate objects; therefore they can't kiss. So the cow must have kissed the rock.) When word order was pitted against verb agreement, as in "The cows is chasing the horse," English speakers once again relied on word order rather than agreement, ascribing the action to the cow. Speakers of more richly inflected languages (languages that feature numerous permutations of a given word based on its number, gender, tense, or grammatical relations to other words) tended to favor agreement over word order. Since "horse" and "is" are both singular forms, they belong together. To sum up: the evidence on cross-linguistic differences in sentence comprehension supports the conclusion that speakers of a given language demonstrate processing biases that reflect the structure and the statistical biases present within their own language (Bates, Devescovi, & Wulfeck, 2001).

Developmental Factors.   Given the subtleties involved in comprehending the syntax and semantics of language, it's no small wonder that children are able to do it so quickly. The consensus is that children have basic knowledge of language's patterns and regularities in phonology, morphology, and semantics in place by age 3 (Jusczyk, 1997; Pinker, 1994c), but their understanding of syntax and the concomitant ability to successfully parse sentences seems to lag behind (e.g., Friederici, 1983). This difference is reflected by their fairly quick mastery of content words relative to function words. Content words carry most of the meaning of a sentence. These would include nouns (e.g., *banana, dog*), many verbs (e.g., *grow, laugh*), and adjectives (e.g., *pretty, fair*). Function words, as their name would imply, are used to describe relationships among the content words. These include pronouns (e.g., *it, she*), prepositions (e.g., *on, under*), and conjunctions (e.g., *and, while*), among others. Hahne, Eckstein, and Friederici (2004) propose that early in childhood, toddlers rely more on the semantic context provided by content words. At around age 8 or 9, reliance on contextual factors becomes less dominant, as children develop a better sense of syntactic rules and relations.

In an attempt to more clearly delineate developmental changes in the processing of syntactic and semantic relations as well as to map out their time course, Hahne et al. investigated event-related potentials while youngsters processed sentences. It turns out that, in adults, semantic and syntactic violations are associated with distinct neurological markers as indicated by event-related potentials. As you read earlier in the chapter, the N400 response is particularly sensitive to the semantics of language, and a particularly strong N400 occurs after the presentation of a semantically incongruous word ("The quarterback threw the vase"). In contrast to this N400 response to semantic violation, syntactic violations (i.e., "I is hungry") are associated with two distinct markers: a response termed *early left anterior negativity* (ELAN) and also a late positive response approximately 600 ms after stimulus presentation—a P600 wave. To get a sense of the developing sensitivity to syntactic and semantic factors in language, Hahne and colleagues tested children from ages 6 to 13, presenting them with correct, semantically incorrect, and syntactically incorrect sentences. Subjects were to judge the correctness of each sentence, and ERPs were recorded.

The behavioral data weren't surprising; detection of semantic violations was better for the older children. Few errors were committed, even by the seven-and eight-year-olds. The ERP data revealed a slightly delayed N400 response for the seven-and eight-year-old children, and an adult-like N400 response for 13-year-olds. So for younger children, the detection of semantic anomalies is somewhat delayed. Perhaps the most interesting finding was the complete lack of an ELAN response (a response to syntactic violation) in six-year-olds, indicating that syntactic processing is established relatively late in development. These findings fit with previous research indicating that syntactic processing lags behind semantic processing.

Language: Learned or Innate?

Chomsky's theory (at least many of the assumptions underlying it) remained the dominant force in psycholinguistic research for years. His assumptions that language is nonlearnable and depends on rules that are with us from birth have been considered practically sacrosanct. But a serious challenge to this view has been mounted by a recent approach that suggests that the structural aspects of language may be learnable. You'll recall that Chomsky argued that a simple associationistic account could not possibly explain the rapid development and astounding creativity of language. The notion that language is learned is highly improbable, due to what Chomsky termed "the poverty of the stimulus." How can children possibly learn language? Children hear grammatical and ungrammatical sentences that aren't labeled as "grammatical" and "ungrammatical"; what they hear is widely variable; and they don't get any sort of negative evidence—that is, what is not allowable, given the structure of the language. So basically, with almost no direction, children learn language and learn it rapidly. Given that the learning environment provides no help (i.e., is an impoverished stimulus), language cannot possibly be learned based solely on environmental input (although certainly environmental input is critical).

Well, it turns out that the stimulus for language learning may not be so impoverished after all. An up-and-coming approach has reintroduced the notion that language may indeed be learnable, based simply on the incoming data. The challenge to Chomsky's approach comes not from a return to a behavioristic approach but from the neural network approach to cognition. And the associations that may account for the learning and use of language are not the stimulus-response associations postulated by the behaviorists, but the associations of neural networks distributed throughout the human brain. The same neural networks that carry out perceiving, recognizing, and remembering may also be responsible for learning and implementing linguistic knowledge about sentence structure and word meaning. A special modular system need not be proposed to explain language learning and use (i.e., a nonmodular approach to language may suffice).

Recall the connectionist approach to cognition that we discussed in Chapter 1. According to this approach, knowledge is embodied in distributed networks of excitatory and inhibitory connections between neuronlike units in the brain. These networks "learn" (i.e., are modified) through experience. Network connections are built up, solidified, and modified as we experience the world day to day. According to the **constraint-based approach** to language (e.g., Chang, Dell, & Bock, 2006; Seidenberg, 1997), the gradual development and fine-tuning of neural networks during early linguistic experience play an important role in the rapid learning of language as well as in the cross-cultural consistency in the rate of language development.

Language is full of the probabilistic constraints that can be discovered by neural networks and exploited during the process of language learning. To get a better handle on the constraint-based approach, think back to the speech perception research that demonstrated infants' ability to compute word boundaries. With as little as two minutes of exposure to speech, infants could use the probability of syllable pairs occurring within and between experimenter-defined words to distinguish experimenter-defined words from similar words in which the syllables were rearranged. The same type of probabilistic constraints are present within sentences. Consider the following examples (from Seidenberg, 1997):

1. The plane left for the East Coast.
2. The plane left for the reporter was missing.
3. The note left for the reporter was missing.

What constraints are available for the processing of these sentences? It turns out there are several. First, the meaning of *plane* as a vehicle is much more likely than its other meanings. Also, the word *left* is used more often in the active form (as in sentence 1) than in the passive form (as in sentences 2 and 3). Also, the phrase "The plane left" imposes constraints on interpreting the relationships between the words; "plane" could not possibly be a modifier of "left," so "The plane left" cannot be a noun phrase. Another constraint is apparent in comparing sentences 2 and 3: sentence 3 is easier to comprehend, because it is much more plausible for a note to be left than it is for a plane to be left. In sentence 2, both senses of "The plane left" need to be considered, causing a temporary "hiccup" in comprehension. Constraints like these can be easily and rapidly learned by a neural network through repeated experience with linguistic strings (i.e., sentences). Combine this idea with the recent findings regarding infants' stunning abilities to do a probability analysis on a string of speech sounds in the space of two minutes, and you have the beginnings of a compelling argument for how language might be learned in the absence of any special grammar-learning module.

Not everyone is persuaded by the constraint-based approach. Pinker (1996) notes that while probabilistic constraints might allow infants to learn how syllables combine to form words, this does not generalize to their learning how words combine to form sentences. Words comprise a finite set of items, all of which can be deciphered and committed to memory. Sentences do not comprise a finite set of possibilities; they're an open-class (i.e., theoretically limitless) set and cannot all be committed to memory. Also, grammar doesn't just sequence words; it combines words hierarchically and relates them to a meaning. So learning how syllables are sequenced and learning how words are sequenced are different "computational" problems. What works for deciphering words won't work for comprehending and producing sentences on the fly.

It's also important to note that in many ways, the debate over whether language is learned or innate oversimplifies matters. There is no doubt that the acquisition of language involves both sorts of mechanisms. As Yang (2004) notes, a human baby can learn language, but her pet kitten cannot. Therefore, there must be some biological substrate for language learning that the kitty lacks. And it is just as clear that this biological substrate alone does not lead to the emergence of language; sounds, words, and grammar all vary among languages, so it's quite obvious that they must be learned on the basis of linguistic experience.

STOP *and* REVIEW!

1. Distinguish between the surface structure and the deep structure of language.
2. What are garden-path sentences?
3. Autonomous view is to interactionist view as
   a. syntax is to semantics.
   b. simultaneous is to sequential.
   c. serial is to parallel.
   d. case grammar is to syntax.
4. True or false? Children understand function words before they understand content words.
5. What is the basic idea behind the constraint-based view of language learning?

➤ Phrase structure is an important basis for understanding sentences, but it is incomplete. According to transformational grammar, sentences exist as both deep structures that represent meaning and surface structures that convey it. Sentences can have the same surface structure but different deep structures. Also, different surface structures may be associated with the same deep structure.

➤ Some approaches to sentence comprehension place primary emphasis on syntax. According to the garden-path approach, we parse sentences according to syntactic rules and test one interpretation at a time. Difficulty in the processing of garden-path sentences is consistent with this approach. Garden-path sentences are associated with longer reading times, longer fixations, and more regressive saccades.

➤ Some approaches to sentence comprehension stress the importance of semantics. One example of this is the case-grammar approach. According to this approach, sentences are parsed by assigning words to various case roles that reflect the roles of the concept within the given sentence. According to the autonomous view of sentence comprehension, syntactic and semantic processing are independent and operate serially, with syntactic processing occurring before a semantic analysis. According to the interactionist view, syntactic and semantic processing occur interactively and in parallel.

➤ Parsing is dependent on working memory, and the exact form of sentence parsing differs across languages. Developmental studies of syntax and semantics indicate that children acquire the ability to use content words before the ability to use function words; there is a corresponding difference in the development of syntactic understanding, relative to semantic understanding.

➤ A connectionist approach (i.e., the constraint-based model) proposes that language is learnable via the same cognitive and brain mechanisms used for other tasks. Probabilistic constraints within language can be exploited by neural networks during the language-learning process. The acquisition of language no doubt involves both innate and learned mechanisms.

Language Production

Whereas volumes of research have been produced on the topics of speech perception and how syntactic and semantic factors influence comprehension, comparatively little research has been done on the processes underlying speech production. What are the processes involved in producing syntactically correct and semantically appropriate chains of speech?

Can you imagine why there might be such a discrepancy in the amount of research on the production, as opposed to the perception, of language? The reason is, in large part, methodological. It's much easier to control what someone experiences than it is to control what someone talks about or says. What someone reads or listens to can be controlled by an experimenter in a laboratory, and their reaction to it can be straightforwardly assessed in terms of accuracy. However, what someone says is a spontaneous and generative product of what they're thinking, and it's difficult to control this spontaneity and generativity. Indeed, even if you could manage to control it, you would no longer be studying true language production.

Stages in Language Production

In spite of the methodological difficulties inherent in the investigation of speech production, researchers have begun to get a better handle on the processes involved. One useful framework for research on language production was proposed by Levelt and colleagues (Levelt, 1989; Levelt, Rolofs, & Meyer, 1999). This framework can be characterized as an information-processing approach in that it proposes four sequential steps in the production of language. The first step is *conceptualizing* what we want to say; the next step is *planning*, in which we formulate what is termed a *linguistic plan*—basically, organizing our thoughts in terms of language. The third step is *articulating* the linguistic plan. Finally, language production involves a process of *self-monitoring* in which we keep track of what we're saying and whether the message and tone are as intended. We should note here that this section will deal primarily with the *mechanics*, or basic processes, involved in the planning and production of speech.

Conceptualizing.   As you can imagine, some of the four processes proposed by Levelt and colleagues are easier to investigate than others. Not much research has been conducted on the conceptualization stage; this makes sense, for the reasons discussed above. There is no objective way to find out how ideas come together in anticipation of speech. Many believe that there is a sort of "mentalese"—a representational system distinct from language—from which linguistic expression proceeds, but there is little agreement on its form (Carroll, 1994). It seems obvious that this first stage of speaking exists, but it's hard to say much about it. Most research on language production has been done on the latter three stages.

Planning and Articulating.   Most of the research on language production has dealt with the processes by which we devise our linguistic plans and articulate them in speech. You might think that getting a handle on how people devise a linguistic plan would be nearly as difficult as figuring out how they conceptualize their thoughts. However, there is a rich source of data available that has served as the primary database for research and theory. This batadase—oops! . . . database—is slips of the tongue.

Slips of the Tongue. You may do it several times a day: you get tongue-tied, you put the right word in the wrong slot of the sentence—in other words, you commit what psycholinguists term **slips of the tongue.** Slips of the tongue provide a valuable window into the processes involved in language production. They're also a close cousin of the action slips we discussed in Chapter 4. In fact, slips of the tongue are a type of action slip that we did not discuss, leaving it for discussion in this chapter

Types of Slips. Systematic research into naturally occurring slips of the tongue has identified eight basic categories. Table 10.3 provides examples of each category, taken from the students in our cognitive psychology classes. A **shift** occurs when one speech segment disappears from its appropriate location and appears somewhere else: "He was dunk in prublic." (The phoneme /r/ disappears from *drunk* and appears in *public*.) An **exchange** occurs when two segments change places (both segments disappear from their appropriate location): "Do you want water in your lemon?" (The words *lemon* and *water* switch places.) An **anticipation** occurs when a later segment replaces an earlier segment but does not disappear from its appropriate location. "Twitch on the television." (The later phoneme /t/ replaces the earlier phoneme /s/.) The opposite of an anticipation is a **perseveration,** in which an earlier segment replaces a later segment but does not disappear from its appropriate location: "I haven't deleted the diles yet." (The early phoneme /d/ replaces the later phoneme /f/.) A **deletion** refers to leaving something out: "I have to wind the tape." (The morpheme *re* is deleted from *rewind*). An **addition** refers to inserting something: "The girl's story is *un*believable." (The morpheme *un* is added to *believable*). A **substitution** occurs when an intruder replaces an intended segment: "Lets play some TV." (The word *play* replaces the word *watch*.) Finally, a **blend** occurs when two words combine into one, apparently because they are both being considered for selection. For example, one of Bridget's students came out with the unique exclamation of "My *gooshness*" (probably after having seen her grade on one of Bridget's killer tests), the second "word" of which represents a blend of *goodness* and *gosh*.

Table 10.3 Categories of Speech Errors, with Examples

Type of Error	Example
Shift	He was dunk in prublic (drunk in public).
Exchange	Do you want water in your lemon (lemon in your water)?
Anticipation	Twitch on the television (switch on the television).
Perseveration	I haven't deleted the diles yet (deleted the files yet).
Addition	The girl's story is unbelievable (believable).
Deletion	Before I take the tape back I need to wind it (rewind it).
Substitution	Let's play some TV (watch some TV).
Blend	Oh, my gooshness (gosh/goodness).

In looking at the samples of each type of error given in Table 10.3, you might notice that they can occur at any linguistic level, be it a sound (phoneme), a morpheme (e.g., suffixes or prefixes), or a word. And if an utterance contains a slip of the tongue, it tends to be at only one linguistic level; you typically wouldn't switch two phonemes and switch two words within the same utterance.

In addition to noting these eight categories of error that occur with some regularity, Garrett (1975) and Fromkin (1973) note several additional consistencies in slips of the tongue. Elements within an utterance that interact

- tend to come from similar positions within a word (switching the initial segments of two words rather than switching the end of one word with the beginning of another)
- tend to be similar to one another (e.g., consonants switched with consonants)
- receive the same sort of stress (i.e., emphasis, or accent) they would have had if they had not interacted
- seem to be based on phonological, rather than semantic, similarity (e.g., saying "*Sesame Street* crackers" instead of "sesame seed crackers")

Slips of the tongue also seem to obey the rules of phonology: even when sounds are switched, the resulting errant "word" sounds like a word. For example, what slip would you expect from a combination of *slippery* and *slick?* If you said *slickery,* you're right; neither *slickpery* nor *slipkery* fit in with English morphology and would not be the type of error we'd make.

Theoretical Accounts.   A number of explanations for slips of the tongue have been proposed. One major dimension along which these accounts differ is whether the planning and articulation of speech involve serial (step-by-step) or parallel (simultaneous) processes and whether these processes interact with one another. Serial accounts of linguistic planning have been proposed by Fromkin (1973) and Garrett (1988, 1992); their general structure is presented in Figure 10.6. Basically, these models propose a number of substages within the broader stages of linguistic planning. Once we conceptualize what we want to say, we then determine the stress patterns and syntactic structure for our utterance. Then content words and free morphemes are added. (These are the words that convey the meaning of the sentence.) Next, bound morphemes (prefixes and suffixes) are added, followed by the addition of function words and overt articulation.

One important assumption of these models is that the linguistic planning stages are independent of one another. Consistent with this assumption, many slips seem to occur at only one level of planning. Consider this classic slip of the tongue reported by Fromkin (1973): "a weekend for maniacs." The intended phrase was "a maniac for weekends." There are several interesting things about this error. First, the stress pattern of the sentence remained the same, as if that had been determined separately. The content words "weekend" and "maniac" switched places, but the *s* morpheme was left stranded at the end of the sentence rather than moved with the word "maniac" this suggests that the suffix *s* was added separately from the content word "weekend." Also, and perhaps most interesting, the sound generated for the stranded morpheme *s* fits the new context. An *s* at the end of *weekends* is a /z/ sound, but the *s* at the end of *maniac* is a "hissing" /s/ sound.

Stage 1—conceptualization, determination of stress patterns, determination of syntactical structure

———— ———— ———— ———— ———— ————

Stage 2—content words and free morphemes added

              student   *prepare*   *test*

———— ———— ———— ———— ———— ————

Stage 3—bound morphemes added

             students prepar*ed*   test

———— ———— ———— ———— ———— ————

Stage 4—function words added

  The   students   prepared   *for*   *the*   test

Stage 5—overt articulation

Figure 10.6 Serial speech production accounts for the articulation of the idea of "students preparing for a test in the past."

When "weekend" and "maniac" switch places, the /s/ sound is adjusted to match its new context; this phenomenon is termed *accommodation*. Accommodation suggests that sounds are assembled after (and independently of) assembly of the words in the sentence.

Other accounts of linguistic planning propose parallel processing: processors for the production of speech exist at a number of distinct levels (as just proposed), but these processors are capable of operating simultaneously (e.g., Dell, 1986; Dell, Chang, & Griffin, 1999; MacKay, 1987). These models propose that words in the lexicon are represented at four different levels—in terms of their sound (phonology), morphology, syntactic roles, and meaning. Processing units at each of these levels work in parallel, and may excite or inhibit processing within the same level as well as at other levels.

The study of slips of the tongue has a long and distinguished history within the discipline of psychology. No less than Sigmund Freud, the founder of psychoanalysis himself, investigated such slips of the tongue; they even bear his name—the so-called *Freudian slip.* Freud's view of these errors was decidedly different from those just described. Freud's interpretation of these sorts of errors was not in terms of the cognitive processes that lead to the errors, but in terms of what Freud viewed as the *unconscious motivation* for these errors. For Freud, slips of the tongue were a window into a person's fears, anxieties, or wishes. The person who goes into Dairy Queen and orders ice cream topped with "Reese's penis" (instead of "Reese's Pieces"—true story!) has done more than made a word error. According to Freud, this slip *means* something; it reflects something about unconscious motivation (although for this particular example, we dare not go any further).

Is there any truth to Freud's claim? It seems unlikely that every slip of the tongue we make has a hidden meaning. But could unconscious thoughts play a role in slips of the tongue? You might imagine that addressing this question by noting naturally occurring

Research Theme: Consciousness

errors (as the studies discussed previously have primarily done) would yield a biased sample of errors and leave many questions unanswered. When someone commits a slip, it's anybody's guess as to why it occurred. However, if you can set up a situation in which slips are under experimental control, you have a more reliable way of assessing their causes.

Motley (1985) reports an intriguing series of studies assessing the Freudian account of slips of the tongue. Motley and Baars (1979) used a laboratory procedure that induced subjects to make slips (e.g., saying "fluit fries" instead of "fruit flies"). Motley and Baars had subjects read two-word phrases (like "fruit fly") silently; every so often, a buzzer sounded. On these occasions, subjects were to read the presented pair out loud; of course, these trials were the ones of interest. Just to make errors a little more likely, the researchers preceded these spoken trials with a series of phrases that "primed the pump," so to speak. For example, to make the error "fluit fries" more likely to occur, the immediately preceding trials would be similar (e.g., "flag fright").

So where does hidden motivation come in? To engage subjects in a given motivational frame, Motley and Baars varied the context in which the study was conducted. They preoccupied one group of subjects with shock anxiety; these subjects were hooked up to (bogus) electrodes and told that they would be receiving an occasional electric shock during the procedure (although they never did). Another group was preoccupied with what might be called (for want of a better phrase) sexual anxiety; they were tested by "an attractive and provocatively dressed woman" (p. 118). A control condition was tested using an identical procedure but with neither environmental manipulation. The word pairs presented to subjects, when rearranged, referred to either shock-related concerns (e.g., the pair *worst cottage* was presented so that the likely error was *cursed wattage)* or sex-related concerns (e.g., the pair *share boulders* was presented, with the likely error being *bare shoulders*—no, we're not kidding).

Let's take a look at the design of the Motley and Baars study. The study was a 3×2 factorial, with six main conditions. One independent variable was type of anxiety induced in subjects. This was an experimental-context variable with three levels (shock anxiety vs. sexual anxiety vs. no anxiety). The other independent variable was the type of word pair presented to subjects, a materials variable with two levels (sex related or shock related). The dependent variable was the number of slips.

The results were consistent with the Freudian view of slips of the tongue. As you can see in Figure 10.7, subjects who were anxious about possible shocks were more likely to make shock-related errors; subjects (all men, by the way) who were anxious about sexual material were more likely to make sex-related errors. It is important to note that the number of shock-related slips in the sexual-anxiety condition (and the number of sex-related slips in the shock-anxiety condition) were not different from the number of slips made in the no-anxiety condition. This indicates that "anxiety" in general did not lead to more slips. An increase in the number of slips (relative to the control condition) was the result of the specific type of anxiety that led to a specific type of slip. This humorous finding in no way discounts or qualifies what we've said about slips, the regularities they feature, or the possible underlying mechanisms. It simply adds another dimension to their explanation; in some cases, it seems that slips of the tongue can be made more likely by contextual variables, like what is currently occupying one's mind. But certainly, many

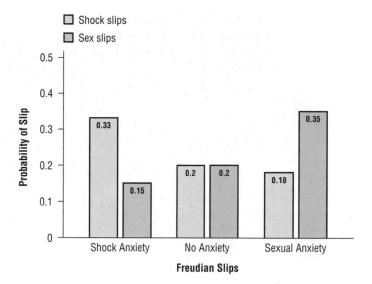

Figure 10.7 Results from Motley and Baars (1985).

From Motley, M. T. (1985). Slips of the tongue. *Scientific American, 253,* 116–127. Reprinted by permission.

(probably most) speech errors are more innocent, resulting from the misassemblage of linguistic units.

STOP *and* THINK!

FRIDIAN SLEUPS

Over the next few weeks, monitor your own and others' conversations for speech errors.

1. Take note of what type they are (following the classification scheme provided in Table 10.3, p. 423).
2. Note when they seem to occur.
3. Record whether any of them seem "motivated" in the Freudian sense.
4. Indicate the level (phoneme, morpheme, word) at which the slip occurred.
5. For the serial account of linguistic planning, indicate the stage at which the slip occurred.

Self-Monitoring. The final stage in Levelt and colleagues' (1989) conceptualization of speech production is self-monitoring, which refers to the processes whereby we keep track of what we're saying and change it online if necessary. It's unclear whether we actually edit what we say before we say it, but the fact that we edit what we have already said is not in doubt (Carroll, 1994). Often we engage in *self-repair*—we stop ourselves and correct what we've just said. Levelt (1983) noted that self-repairs have a consistent structure. First, we interrupt ourselves when we detect an error. Second, we issue what might be termed an *editing expression*, like "um," "oh, wait," or "sorry." Finally, we "repair" what we've just said by saying such things as "er . . . I mean."

STOP *and* **REVIEW!**

1. Name and briefly describe the four stages in language production.
2. Which of these is not a type of speech slip?
   a. an anticipation
   b. a perseveration
   c. a blend
   d. a delay
3. True or false? The Freudian view of motivated speech slips has received some empirical support.
4. Describe the process of self-monitoring.

➤ The four stages in language production are conceptualizing (determining what it is we want to say), planning (organizing our thoughts in terms of language), articulating (executing the linguistic plan), and self-monitoring (keeping track of content and tone).

➤ Slips of the tongue offer insight into the planning and articulation of speech. Slips of the tongue include shifts, exchanges, anticipations, perseverations, deletions, additions, substitutions, and blends. Slips can occur at any linguistic level—phoneme, morpheme, or word. Interacting speech elements tend to come from similar positions in words and receive the same sort of stress. Errors often seem to be based primarily on phonological similarity.

➤ A serial account of slips of the tongue proposes that after conceptualizing, we determine the syntactic structure for the utterance. Free morphemes are added, followed by bound morphemes and function words. Then appropriate phonological segments are assembled and articulated. Parallel processing accounts propose that words in the lexicon are represented at each linguistic level (phonology, morphology, syntactic, and semantic) and work in parallel, exciting or inhibiting processing within that level. Research indicates that slips of the tongue can be motivated.

➤ The final stage of speech production is self-monitoring. Often we engage in self-repair—we stop ourselves and correct what we've just said. Self-repairs have a consistent structure—first, we interrupt ourselves when we detect an error; second, we issue an editing expression; finally, we repair what we've just said.

Language in Nonhumans

One philosophical and empirical question that has fueled much debate is whether nonhuman species are capable of language (see Hillix, 2007, for a detailed history and review of the evidence). There is no question that they are capable of communication—the exchange of information through some type of signal. Even the lowly insect is capable of basic information exchange. Von Frisch (1967) demonstrated that honeybees produce a complex dance that signals to other members of the hive the location of nectar. Many other species engage in various sorts of communication. For example, vervet monkeys use a variety of calls to warn other vervets of specific predatory dangers, such as the presence of snakes or eagles. These calls elicit specific predator-appropriate avoidance behaviors (Demers, 1988).

So, nonhuman species can communicate, but is this communication considered language? Your intuition is probably that it isn't, and most researchers would agree. Let's consider these nonhuman communication systems in relation to the design features of a language that were discussed at the begining of this chapter. Semanticity is present to some extent. The dances of the honeybee and the warning cries of the vervet monkey might be considered "words" of a sort because they do mean something (e.g., "an eagle is approaching"). Also, animal language is not completely arbitrary. For example, the vervet warning sign for "an eagle is approaching" includes looking up, which does relate to the content of the message. Animal language systems are rigid and don't allow for change, so displacement (e.g., "an eagle will approach tomorrow") isn't possible. Nor do animal communication systems have the numerous symbols and rule systems that allow for endless novel combinations (productivity). The rigidity of animal language systems prevents prevarication—the deliberate misrepresentation of information (e.g., a wiseacre vervet issuing a snake warning when there is no danger)—as well as the ability to reflect on the communication system itself. Clearly, the built-in communication systems of honeybees, vervet monkeys, and the like fall well short of the design features that are at the heart of human language. Some research into the possibility of animal language has been directed at finding out whether nonhumans have the capability to learn and use systems of words and rules.

Are they using language?

Language Training Projects

Over the past 30 years, a substantial number of language training projects have been conducted with a range of nonhuman species in order to determine whether language is or is not a uniquely human faculty. These projects have investigated the representational and communicative abilities of common chimpanzees (e.g., Gardner & Gardner, 1975; Premack, 1970; Premack, 1983; Terrace, Petitto, Sanders, & Bever, 1979), pygmy (bonobo) chimpanzees (Savage-Rumbaugh, Rumbaugh, & Boysen, 1980), sea lions (Gisiner & Schusterman, 1992), bottle-nosed dolphins (Herman, Kuczaj, & Holder, 1993), and African gray parrots (Pepperberg, 1999a, b; 2006).

The criteria applied to assess whether other species exhibit language essentially boil down to the two components of language described earlier: words and rules. First, do apes, parrots, and other animals learn to associate labels with objects in the world? Second, can these animals take the symbols they've learned and spontaneously combine them in unique and novel ways using rules? You do this every time you open your mouth or sit down at the word processor to type something. Are nonhumans capable of this novel language generation? In a recent review of language training projects, Savage-Rumbaugh and Brakke (1996) provide a useful scheme for considering the successes of these training projects and the extent to which these successes might be labeled "language." The bottom-line conclusion that these authors reach is that however impressive the results of these training projects might be, they do not reveal that nonhumans use language (see Rivas, 2005, for an ape-signing review that reaches a similar conclusion).

Are they using language?

Still, their scheme provides a useful lens through which to examine exactly what language is, a lens that provides a complement to our discussion thus far.

Labeling: Is It Word Learning?

Let's take a look at whether nonhuman species are capable of mastering this first component of language: Can they learn to apply words to concepts? Almost all language training projects involve teaching the animal students labels for salient objects in their environment. For example, the Premacks (e.g., Premack & Premack, 1983) taught their chimpanzee, Sarah, to associate a set of plastic chips with objects in her environment. She was trained extensively on these "words" and was required to place the chips on a magnetized board in response to questions. Sarah was quite successful in learning and producing symbols in the appropriate context.

Similar (and quite astounding) successes have been reported by Pepperberg in her studies of African gray parrots, most notably her parrot Alex (Pepperberg, 1999a, b; 2006). In the training model, one trainer (trainer A) asks another (trainer B) to name an object (e.g., key). After trainer B does so successfully, trainer A asks Alex to do so. This procedure is repeated, with trainers A and B occasionally changing roles and with Alex being encouraged to participate. Another interesting aspect to the procedure is Alex's reward. Rather than getting some type of treat, Alex is simply given the thing that he named to grasp in his beak for a moment. The criterion for learning is 80% accuracy in naming an object or one of its properties. Using this method, Alex has learned dozens of symbols, including object words (e.g., *paper* and *rock*), color words, and numbers. And another contestant has recently been entered into the animal language fray—none other than man's best friend, Fido (or Rover, or . . . pick your favorite dog name). Kaminski, Call, and Fischer (2004) report the case of Rico, a border collie who learned to label over 200 small toys with different labels, with a high degree of accuracy.

These results are quite impressive, but do they demonstrate linguistic ability? Researchers (e.g., Markman & Abelev, 2004; Savage-Rumbaugh & Brakken, 1996) aren't convinced. Sarah, Alex, Rico, and others have succeeded in associating labels with objects, to be sure, but it's not clear whether the labels are truly *referential*. Think of how humans use words. If I tell you that I'm going to the library to get a book to read, the word *book* refers to the same (or very similar) concept in our respective heads. Note that I'm not holding up a book and saying "book." In the naming studies described above, the labels are not used in a referential manner. An object is simply held up, and the chimp, parrot, or border collie gives a label that they've associated with it. There's no evidence that the label *is* the thing.

Language as Learning to Do as You Are Told.

Savage-Rumbaugh and Brakke (1996) discuss a second possible manifestation of language that has been observed in language training studies: appropriate responses to commands issued in some sort of artificial language. These research projects help to study the second component of language—rules. Appropriate responses to requests or commands generated from the rules of a language would indicate a capacity for grammar. Interestingly, sea mammals have been the subject of some of these studies—namely, the sea lions Rockie and Gertie (e.g., Schusterman & Krieger, 1988) and the bottle-nosed dolphins Ake and Phoenix (e.g., Herman, Richards, & Wolz, 1984). These studies have investigated whether these animals can respond appropriately to symbolic relations such as "fetch the hoop to the frisbee" or "surfboard basket tailtouch." Although the ability to respond to these sorts of commands seems a bit more language-like than simply labeling objects, Savage-Rumbaugh and Brakke note that when compared to the language of children, these instances of communication fall short of language. The only reason the dolphins engaged in these interactions was to get a fish. Outside of this context, they would have no reason to engage in the communication. In stark contrast, a child uses language in a much more intentional and deliberate way. If a child plays a new game and enjoys it, they are able to refer to the game later in a request to play it again. No such capacity is evident in these sea mammals. Savage-Rumbaugh and Brakke do note that the animals may be capable of more, but given the limits of the testing situation, their abilities fall well short of linguistic expression.

Language as Engaging in Social Routines.   Language involves the use of words and rules in spontaneous interactions with others. By its very nature, language is social; it involves intentional and referential communication between at least two people. To assess the ability of nonhumans to apply the words and rules of a language in this context, a number of researchers have conducted what Savage-Rumbaugh and Brakke (1996) refer to as *cross-fostering studies* (e.g., Gardner & Gardner, 1975; Terrace et al., 1979). In these studies, selected signs from American Sign Language (ASL) were taught to chimpanzees within the context of daily interactions. Communication occurred throughout the day, and the experimenters treated the chimpanzees' gesturing as intentional even if it wasn't, just as adults do with young children. Eventually, the chimpanzees (most notably the star pupil Washoe) started to produce symbols, just as small children start to produce words.

So was Washoe learning language? In spite of the surface similarities between this training situation and a child learning language, there were some critical differences. To help the chimps learn the signs, the experimenters shaped their hands into the appropriate signs until the chimps "got it." Once the sign was learned, the chimps had to give it in order to gain access to certain desired activities (e.g., food or tickle games). Here, the signs served the same function as the labels learned by dolphins and sea lions: the signs are simply responses made to achieve a particular end. The animals aren't really communicating any type of idea or intention; their utterances seem limited to requests and are never used referentially (Rivas, 2006). So once again, we have evidence for successful labeling and manipulation of symbols but not for truly linguistic capabilities.

Kanzi and the Bonobos.   Although many, if not most, researchers would agree that the results discussed thus far fall well short of human language, some striking results have been found in investigations of the linguistic abilities of the pygmy chimpanzee, or bonobo. Kanzi is perhaps the most famous student in this breed, which has undergone extensive investigation by Savage-Rumbaugh and colleagues. Bonobos are more similar to humans (in terms of their social and sexual interactions) than are common chimpanzees (like Sarah and Washoe). Savage-Rumbaugh suspected this similarity might indicate a similarity in the development of communicative behavior.

The work of Savage-Rumbaugh and colleagues with Kanzi is noteworthy in a number of respects. First is the manner in which Kanzi learned; initially his learning was

Figure 10.8 Lexigraphic symbols used in the bonobo language studies of Savage-Rumbaugh and colleagues.
Courtesy of Language Research Center, Georgia State University.

spontaneous. Trainers were teaching Kanzi's mother, Matata, to use a system of symbols, termed *lexigrams* (see Figure 10.8). When Matata was separated from Kanzi for breeding purposes, the researchers were surprised to learn that he had picked up many of the lexigraphic signs. In subsequent investigations, the focus was squarely on Kanzi and his ability to learn and manipulate these lexigraphic symbols.

Kanzi's learning was fast and spontaneous. It wasn't necessary to explicitly train him in the lexigraphic language. He learned simply through constant interaction and interchange with caretakers about the events and routines of each day. As they spoke, the caretakers would point to whatever symbols happened to be relevant. In addition to speaking and referring to lexigraphic symbols, caretakers also used informal gestures and a smattering of ASL signs. Another noteworthy difference in the study of Kanzi was that the human communication system was combined with Kanzi's physical environment. Rather than raising Kanzi as a human child and attempting to engage him in humanlike conversation about objects and activities chosen by humans (as had been done with Sarah and Washoe), the communication system was allowed to evolve during Kanzi's everyday adventures in his 55-acre playground. Finally, the work with Kanzi was noteworthy in the sheer volume of data recorded by the researchers. Using automated, rigorous, and consistent data-recording methods, Savage-Rumbaugh and colleagues amassed a corpus of over 13,000 utterances generated by Kanzi over a four-month period.

A painstaking analysis of the utterances generated by Kanzi indicated that he was quite capable of generating novel combinations of symbols. And these combinations weren't just random strings of symbols and gestures. It was clear that Kanzi made a distinction between types of words (nouns and verbs, basically) and was able to place these types in the appropriate slots of an utterance. Even more impressive, the analysis also indicated that Kanzi made up his own grammatical rules and used them consistently, a sign of the productivity that characterizes human language. In sum, work with Kanzi has yielded the most impressive evidence to date of language-like abilities in nonhumans. First, Kanzi learned the language spontaneously, in the absence of formal instruction, just as it is with human children. Second, the symbols Kanzi used seemed truly referential in nature. Third, Kanzi combined the symbols in a novel and rule-governed manner. And importantly, these utterances were not initiated by external events in the immediate context.

What Makes Language Special?

Some, the prominent linguists Noam Chomsky and Steven Pinker among them, remain unconvinced by the demonstrations offered in the preceding studies. As impressive and surprising as these nonhumans' abilities may be, they are not using language. This nativistic view of language holds that nonhuman animals are simply not equipped neurologically to learn a complex system of language; language is based in specific brain structures that have evolved only in humans. But still, there is heated debate. Opponents of Chomsky's view (e.g., Greenfield & Savage-Rumbaugh, 1990), referring to it as "creationist," point out that given the (99%) genetic similarity between humans and other primates, it would be surprising if there *wasn't* some degree of similarity in nonhuman primates' linguistic abilities (but this is an oversimplification; see Pinker, 1994a, for a rejoinder to this genetic claim).

Assuming that human language is "special" and unique to humans begs a question: What is at the heart of its "specialness"? What makes language the truly astounding creative instrument that it is, and distinguishes it from the labeling and communicative behaviors of nonhuman animals? Hauser, Chomsky, and Fitch (2002) point to one particular characteristic, **recursion,** a decidedly difficult concept to define simply. Let's start with what some apparently believe to be a funny joke about recursion: *In order to understand recursion, one must first understand recursion."* In the context of language, recursion basically refers to embedding sentences within sentences; this can theoretically be done ad infinitum, (or ad nauseum, judging from some of our students' run-on sentences). Consider an example: "The student wrote the paper that the professor assigned, which was worth 25% of the semester grade, which was one of four grades that the student would receive at the end of the semester, which was his last semester at college." . . . You get the idea. According to Hauser et al., the universal grammar of human language that allows for recursion is *the* defining feature, and the only one that truly distinguishes it from animal communication systems.

By no stretch is Hauser et al.'s (2002) view shared by all researchers. Pinker and Jackendoff (2005) dispute the claim that recursion is the only distinguishing feature of human language. They argue that many nonrecursive aspects of language—its phonology, morphology, grammatical agreement, word learning—distinguish human language. And some tantalizing recent evidence suggests that recursion might not be unique to the human species. Gentner, Fenn, Margoliash, and Nusbaum (2006) reported evidence of recursive syntactic pattern learning by, of all things, starlings. So stay tuned; the animal language debate continues.

STOP *and* **REVIEW!**

1. True or false? Animal language fails to demonstrate any of the design features that characterize human language.
2. What does it mean that animal use of language labels is not referential?
3. The most compelling evidence for the use of language by nonhuman animals comes from studies of
   a. parrots.
   b. seals.
   c. bonobo chimps.
   d. dogs.
4. What do some linguists consider the defining characteristic of language?

➤ Animal communication does exhibit a few of the design features that characterize human language, but due to its lack of productivity, animal communication seems to fall well short of language. A number of projects have attempted to train language-like abilities in a variety of nonhuman species.

➤ Although animals are able to learn labels or symbols for a wide array of objects and concepts, it is doubtful whether these labels are truly referential—that is, that they truly represent the concepts. Animals also fail to show evidence of using grammar intentionally or deliberately; they do so only within a prescribed context, and do so to get a reward.

➤ The most impressive evidence of language-like abilities has been shown with Kanzi and other bonobo chimps. Trained with a cross-fostering technique that involved the spontaneous use of symbols in day-to-day interactions with his trainers, Kanzi generated a wide array of novel sign combinations that seemed to indicate a rudimentary use of grammar.

➤ Those who hold the nativistic view of language are skeptical that any animal is truly capable of demonstrating language, the key to which may be recursion—or the ability of language to embed sentences and phrases within other sentences and phrases, theoretically without limit.

GLOSSARY

addition: a speech error in which an inappropriate segment is inserted into an utterance (p. 423)

anticipation: a speech error in which a later segment replaces an earlier segment but does not disappear from its appropriate location (p. 423)

arbitrariness: the lack of an inherent relationship between the symbols of language and what they represent (p. 384)

auditory theory of speech perception: the idea that the basic mechanisms that accomplish auditory perception are the same ones we use to decode speech (p. 392)

autonomous view: the idea that the analyses of syntax and semantics proceed independently and in a serial manner (p. 415)

blend: a speech error in which two words combine into one, apparently because they are both being considered for selection (p. 423)

bound morphemes: morphemes that need to be used in conjunction with a free morpheme (i.e., prefixes and suffixes) (p. 396)

Broca's aphasia: a language disorder that tends to feature syntactic difficulties in language production (p. 415)

case-grammar approach: an approach to sentence comprehension emphasizing the assignment of words to various semantic case roles (p. 414)

case roles: specify who is doing what to whom (p. 414)

categorical perception: our tendency to perceive phonemes in a relatively broad (i.e., categorical) fashion (p. 391)

coarticulation: the overlap in the acoustic signal produced by consecutive phonemes; phonemes are articulated together to some extent (p. 390)

cohort model: a model of spoken word recognition proposing that words are recognized by activating the entire set of possible words based on the word's initial sound, with a subsequent narrowing of the candidate set as more of the word is perceived (p. 397)

constituents: the component phrases of a sentence (p. 410)

constraint-based approach: the idea that language is learned through gradual development and fine-tuning of neural networks during early linguistic experience, picking up on probabilistic constraints of language (p. 419)

deep structure: the idea being expressed by a given phrase structure (p. 411)

deletion: a speech error in which a segment is left out of an utterance (p. 423)

design features: the characteristics that communication systems share (p. 384)

direct-access view: the view that orthography provides the major route to word recognition (p. 406)

displacement: the ability that language allows us for communication about things not in the present moment (p. 385)

dual-route view: the idea that word recognition can proceed by either direct (visual label only) or indirect (visual label plus phonological representation) routes (p. 407)

exchange: a speech error in which two speech segments within an utterance change places (p. 423)

fixations: the brief pauses in eye movements during which the eye takes in information (p. 403)

free morphemes: morphemes that can stand alone (p. 396)

garden-path approach: a theory of sentence processing that assumes that readers follow a simple, word-by-word path through the sentence, testing one syntactic structure until it's proved wrong (p. 412)

gaze duration: the summed duration of fixations (p. 403)

gazes: consecutive fixations in the same location (p. 403)

grammar: the rules that govern how the symbols of a language may be combined. (p. 384)

indirect-access (or **phonological**) **view:** the view that word recognition goes through the phonological representation of the word prior to the word's identification (p. 406)

interactionist view: the idea that the analyses of syntax and semantics proceed in parallel and interact (p. 415)

language: a set of symbols and rules for the combination of these symbols that allow for communication and comprehension among individuals (p. 383)

linguistic competence: knowledge of language and its rules (p. 383)

linguistic performance: the manner in which language is actually used (p. 383)

mirror neurons: neurons that appear to react the same way when perceiving an act and when performing the act (p. 394)

modular view: the view that some cognitive processes (e.g., language) are accomplished by a set of structures and/or processes devoted exclusively to that process and to nothing else (p. 386)

mondegreens: misheard word boundaries (p. 401)

morpheme: the smallest unit of language that carries meaning (p. 396)

morphology: the aspect of language that deals with manipulating and changing phonemes to produce different words and word forms (p. 396)

motherese: the melodic and exaggerated manner in which adults speak to infants, which seems to aid in the development of their speech perception abilities (p. 394)

motor theory of speech perception: the idea that a common set of representations underlies speech perception and speech production and that implicit knowledge about how speech sounds are articulated aids in the perception of the sounds (p. 391)

nonmodular view: a view that cognitive processes occur via general purpose mechanisms that subserve many different processes (p. 386)

orthography: the physical structure of a written word (p. 406)

overregularization: the overapplication of a morphological rule, such as adding *-ed* to an irregular verb (p. 396)

parsing: the identification of the component elements of a sentence and their grammatical relation to one another (p. 412)

perceptual span: the amount of text that the eyes can cover effectively to the right of any given fixation (p. 405)

perseveration: a speech error in which an earlier segment replaces a later segment but does not disappear from its appropriate location (p. 423)

phone: the smallest unit of speech that is discriminable in terms of its acoustic properties (p. 389)

phoneme: the categories of speech sounds that are clearly different and that change the meaning of a spoken signal (p. 389)

phonemic restoration effect: the tendency for our perceptual system to "fill in" missing speech sounds (p. 396)

phonics approach: an approach to teaching reading that emphasizes the mapping of sounds to letters (p. 408)

phonology: the aspect of language that deals with the analysis of basic speech sounds (p. 388)

phonotactic knowledge: sensitivity to the rules that govern phoneme (i.e., sound) combinations in a given language (p. 398)

prevarication: the ability that language allows us for misrepresentation and deception (p. 385)

productivity: the fact that words and rules for their combination allow for an infinite array of new messages to be formed (p. 385)

recursion: the ability of language to embed sentences and phrases within other sentences and phrases, theoretically without limit (p. 434)

reflectiveness: the ability that language allows us for reflecting on language itself (p. 385)

regressive saccades: backward eye movements (p. 405)

saccades: the discrete movements that our eyes make from one point to another when we're reading, taking in a visual scene, or searching for an object (p. 403)

saccadic suppression: the fact that, during saccades, we take in little or no information (p. 403)

semanticity: the fact that symbols of language refer to meaningful aspects of the real world (p. 384)

semantics: the rules governing the effective transmission of meaning (p. 410)

shift: a speech error in which one speech segment disappears from its appropriate location and reappears somewhere else (p. 423)

slips of the tongue: speech errors (p. 423)

substitution: a speech error in which an intruder replaces an intended segment in an utterance (p. 423)

suprasegmental factors: the aspects of the speech signal—such as rate, stress, and intonation—over and above the actual phonemes (p. 390)

surface structure: the phrase structure used to express an idea (p. 411)

syntax: the set of rules that specify legal combinations of words within a given language (p. 410)

transformational grammar: Chomsky's view that language is based on a set of innate syntactic rules that allow for movement between ideas and the structures we use to communicate those ideas (p. 410)

universal grammar: Chomsky's view of language as a uniquely human ability to understand and produce an infinite number of sentences based on an implicit understanding of surface structure and deep structure (p. 410)

Wernicke's aphasia: a language disorder that tends to feature semantic difficulties in language production (p. 415)

whole-language approach: an approach to teaching reading that emphasizes the role of story content and context (and de-emphasizes the role of phonics) (p. 408)

whole-word approach: an approach to teaching reading that emphasizes the wholistic apprehension of complete words (p. 408)

11

Problem Solving

Have you ever been faced with a really tough problem, one that seems nearly insurmountable—perhaps the mound of tests and assignments facing you right now? What are the basic processes that people engage in as they attempt to arrive at solutions to problems? What obstacles tend to get in their way, and how might these obstacles be overcome?

What's happening when you get stuck in a mental rut? In these cases, it sometimes seems helpful to take a break and walk away from the problem. This seems to be exactly when the solution pops into your head. Does taking a break help problem solving, and if so, why?

How does one get to be an expert? Is it possible for anyone to become an expert at anything? If someone becomes an expert in a particular domain, does this have implications for their performance in other domains? Are there any drawbacks to expertise?

Some people just seem to have brilliant, creative minds. What exactly *is* creativity? What underlies creativity? Are people born with the ability to be creative? Can anyone be creative?

What Is a Problem?

Chances are, you've got a big problem facing you. More than likely, you're approaching the end of your semester, and you have to engage in quite a balancing act. You no doubt have papers to write, presentations to give, and/or exams to study for. Oh, and let's not forget about the 30 hours a week that you're working and the fact that you need to maintain a B average in order to keep your scholarship, or a C average to maintain your parents' support, or (fill in the appropriate constraint here). Grappling with this complex scenario involves the processes that a cognitive psychologist would term **problem solving.**

A **problem** consists of several basic components: an **initial state** (the situation at the beginning of the problem), a **goal state** (the solution to the problem), a set of *rules* (or constraints) that must be followed, and usually, a set of *obstacles* that must be overcome. In the present example, the initial state is you, in a panic, staring at a blank computer screen, trying to get a start on your first paper. The goal state is finished research papers and sterling performance (OK, B-level performance) on several finals, which will result in a happy trip home for semester break. The rules and obstacles are numerous. The research paper topics are difficult, and many of the sources you're found are not in the school's library. You have only two weeks to finish everything. You're working at Starbucks, and they just asked you to work extra hours because of heavy business lately . . . shall we go on? *Problem solving* seems a most apt term.

Well-Defined and Ill-Defined Problems

The problems we face every day, from the morning crossword puzzle to retrieving our keys from a locked car, can be classified along a continuum from well defined to ill defined. **Well-defined problems** are clear and structured; the initial state, goal state, and constraints are all understood, and once you reach a solution, it's easily assessed. Solving an **anagram** (unscrambling letters to form a word) is an extremely well-defined problem. The initial state of this problem is the set of scrambled letters; the goal state is a word; the constraints are to use only the letters provided. Once you arrive at a solution, it's clear whether you're right or wrong. In contrast to well-defined problems, an **ill-defined problem** is fuzzy and abstract. One of the term papers you have to write is a good example of an ill-defined problem. You're not quite sure where you're starting, where you need to get to, or what the constraints are. The topic is up to you, the length is up to you, and you're not 100% sure "what the professor wants." In addition, once you've come up with a solution, you're really not sure if it's a good one. You may think the paper is good, but you're not the one grading it. Needless to say, ill-defined problems tend to present more of a challenge to the solver.

Routine and Nonroutine Problems

Problems also vary in terms of how familiar we are with the procedures they involve. A **routine problem** is one that can be solved by applying well-practiced procedures. Consider the task of writing a psychology research paper. For a senior psychology major, this may be a fairly routine problem, consisting of individual tasks that have been performed many times: identifying a topic, searching the library, and organizing the paper. But a first-time psychology student, taking their first course in research methods, would likely find this problem decidedly nonroutine, having never identified a research topic, searched research literature, or organized a research paper. As you might expect, people tend to find more challenge in a **nonroutine problem.**

Consider the relation between how routine a problem is and whether the problem is well or ill defined. You might imagine that as the procedures involved in solving problems become more routine, people have an easier time giving the problem some definition. Let's turn back to psychology students. For the senior psychology major, four years of psychology classes have made the procedures involved in writing a research paper increasingly routine. As a result, the student has an easier time conceptualizing and proceeding with the assignment (i.e., the problem is more well defined). For our beginning student, all of the subtasks involved in writing a research paper are nonroutine. So, this student will have a more difficult time *defining the problem* (i.e., the problem is more ill defined).

Problem-Solving Research: Some Methodological Challenges

In many ways, problem solving is the culmination of all of the processes that make up our cognitive arsenal. Completing all of your end-of-semester assignments requires perception (to take in the problem information), pattern recognition (to recognize words in the paper guidelines and on the final exams), attention and working memory (to hold the information in conscious awareness when necessary) and language (to understand the exam items).

As a result of this complexity, problem solving often occurs over a much longer time interval than many of the cognitive processes previously discussed in the text (such as naming a word or remembering a string of digits). The time required to solve a problem presents a challenge to researchers. Often, subjects can be presented with only one problem within a reasonable time frame (which precludes the study of many everyday problems!). Therefore, assessing problem solving in terms of accuracy rate (as is the practice in many other domains of cognitive psychology) provides a rather gross estimate of problem-solving proficiency. Measuring solution times provides some useful information but doesn't shed much light on the nature of the processing that occurs during problem solving. Take the country dance problem presented in Figure 11.1; it may take someone a few moments to solve this problem, and the solution is either yes or no, with a brief justification. In reality, almost everyone solves this problem (the correct answer is no), and they solve it fairly quickly. But the fact that 95% of people solve a given problem in an average of 30 seconds tells us nothing about exactly how the problem was solved.

One Saturday night at a local country dance, 40 people, 20 men and 20 women showed up to dance. The dance was a "contra dance," in which men and women face each other in lines. From 8:00 to 10:00 P.M. there were 20 heterosexual couples (consisting of one man and one woman each; i.e., two women or two men cannot dance together) dancing on the floor. At 10:00 P.M., however, 2 women left, leaving 38 people to dance. Could the dance caller make arrangements so that the remaining people could all dance together at the same time in 19 heterosexual couples? The dance caller must remain a caller only and cannot take a partner. Answer yes or no, and give the reasoning behind your answer.

Figure 11.1 Can you solve this problem?

From Gick, M. L., & McGarry, S. J. (1992). Learning from mistakes. Inducing analagous solution failures to a source problem produces later successes in analogical transfer. *Journal of Experimental Psychology: Learning, Memory and Cognition, 18,* 623–639. Copyright 1992 by the American Psychological Association. Reprinted by permission.

Verbal Protocols.   In order to gain a window into the processes of problem solving, researchers have made extensive use of verbal protocols. **Verbal protocols** are reports generated by problem solvers as they "think out loud" during the solution process. You might also recall that in Chapter 7, we discussed a study by Lampinen, Meier, Arnal, and Leding (2005) in which verbal protocols were used to gain insight into which processes might underlie encoding and false remembering within a list-learning paradigm. Verbal protocols might be considered a close cousin of the introspective technique employed in the early days of psychology by the structuralists (discussed in Chapter 1). Recall that the structuralists attempted to gain insight into the components of conscious experience by asking people to introspect and report on a variety of perceptual experiences. Whereas structuralist introspections provided rather static descriptions of the contents of awareness for relatively short and discrete periods of time, verbal protocols attempt to give a more dynamic view of cognitive processing as it occurs over a longer span of time.

As is the case with introspective reports of any type, verbal protocols have a number of potentially serious limitations. First, not everyone has the verbal ability required to reflect accurately on what they're thinking. Second, there is no way to assess the accuracy of a verbal report; indeed, it may be that the most important processes cannot be verbalized at all. Finally, the mere act of thinking out loud may interfere with or change the very nature of the thought processes being described. In the years since introspection was reintroduced as a legitimate means of gathering data about thought processes, debate has raged over its validity. Some (e.g., Nisbett & Wilson, 1977) argue that the interpretational difficulties associated with verbal protocols render them essentially useless as a means of analyzing higher thought processes. Others (e.g., Ericsson & Simon, 1980, 1984) have demonstrated that in most cases, verbalizing cognitive processing has a minimal influence on performance. In spite of their potential problems, verbal protocols have proved valuable to problem-solving researchers, and no doubt their use will continue.

STOP *and* THINK!

THINKING OUT LOUD

Pick out some everyday problem (like choosing the courses you have to take next semester, or planning a birthday party), and spend about 15 minutes solving it. Here's the catch: Think out loud while you're doing it:

1. Collect your own verbal protocol (you might use a tape recorder to record your observations).
2. Observe the sorts of processes your mind seems to go through as you're "talking it out."
3. Reflect on your own protocol and how it demonstrates problem-solving principles.

The Varied Nature of Problems.   The complexity of problem solving presents another challenge to researchers. The term *problem* can apply to a breathtakingly diverse set of circumstances, from solving math problems to writing a term paper to figuring out an alternative route home during rush-hour traffic. Getting problem solving into the cognitive psychology laboratory can be a challenging task indeed. In most studies, researchers use fairly short, discrete, circumscribed sorts of problems—much like the brainteasers and puzzles you see in newspapers, magazines, and puzzle books. This makes the investigation of problem solving more tractable. It is assumed that the basic processes used for these sorts of problems are the same ones we employ when we face complex problems like planning a wedding.

Mayer (1992) provides some order to the diversity by distinguishing between five sorts of problems. **Transformation problems** present the solver with a goal state; the solver must find the proper strategies, or "moves," that will eventually transform the initial state into the goal state. **Arrangement problems** involve presentation of all the necessary elements to solve the problem; the solver must figure out how the elements are to be arranged. In **induction problems,** the solver is given a series of exemplars or instances and must figure out the pattern or rule that relates the instances. In **deduction problems,** premises or conditions are given, and the solver must determine whether a conclusion fits these premises. Actually, deduction and induction are forms of everyday reasoning and will be discussed in more depth in Chapter 12. Finally, **divergent problems** require the solver to generate as many solutions as possible to a given problem. It's important to note that many of the complex problems we face every day are actually sets of problems that may involve aspects of any or all of these five problem types. Now that you have read about each of these problem types, examine the problems presented in Figure 11.2. Try to determine the type of problem that each represents.

1. Tower of Hanoi Problem

    The rings must be rearranged so that the pyramid on the far left peg ends up on the far right peg. The following constraints must be observed:
    A larger ring can never be above a smaller one.
    Only one ring can be moved at a time

2. "KIGVIN"
    Rearrange the letters to form another word.

3. Think of as many uses for a brick as you can.

4. "All professors are caring people" and "All caring people are good";
    would you accept the conclusion that "All professors are good"?

5. Take a look at the following number sequence:
    8, 5, 4, 1, 7, 6, 10, 0
    What is the next number in the sequence?

Figure 11.2 Some sample problems from studies of problem solving. Can you identify each type?

1. Transformation 2. Arrangement 3. Divergent 4. Deduction 5. Induction

1. Name the main components of a problem.
2. True or false? A well-defined problem has a solution that is not easily assessed.
3. What are verbal protocols, and why are they employed in problem-solving research?
4. Identify and define the five types of problems.

➤ A problem consists of an initial state (the situation at the beginning of the problem), a goal state (the solution to the problem), a set of rules (or constraints) to follow, and a set of obstacles that must be overcome.

➤ Problems range from well defined (clear and structured, solution easily assessed) to ill defined (fuzzy and abstract, solution not easily assessed). Problems also vary along a continuum from routine (involving well-practiced procedures) to nonroutine (involving less familiar procedures).

➤ Revealing the nature of problem-solving processes presents a methodological challenge to researchers due to the time and complexity involved. Reaction time and accuracy are limited in the information they provide about problem solving. Therefore, problem-solving researchers often use verbal protocols—verbal reports generated by problem solvers during the solution process.

➤ Problem types include transformation (solver must transform the initial state into the goal), arrangement (solver must figure out how the presented problem elements are to be arranged), induction (solver must figure out the rule that relates the presented examples), deduction (premises given and solver must determine if a conclusion follows), and divergent (solver generates as many solutions to a given problem as possible).

Approaches to the Study of Problem Solving

The study of problem solving has a surprisingly rich and varied history. Believe it or not, some of the earliest work on problem solving was conducted with a veritable menagerie of animal subjects, including rats, cats, monkeys, and those titans of cognition, goldfish (Dewsbury, 2000). In many ways, the evolution of problem-solving research mirrors the evolution of cognitive psychology in general, as outlined in Chapter 1. The key players in the debate over the processes underlying problem solving have been behaviorists, Gestalt psychologists, and information-processing psychologists.

Behaviorism: Problem Solving as Associative Learning

One of the first systematic studies of problem solving was conducted by E. L. Thorndike in the late 1800s. Thorndike was interested in the basic processes involved in learning. His subjects were cats, which he placed in a predicament that cats most definitely do not

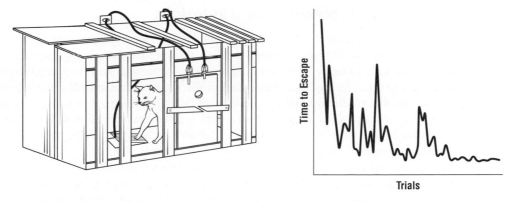

Figure 11.3 A rendition of Thorndike's puzzle box and idealized response data showing trial-and-error learning.

enjoy. He put cats in what he termed "puzzle boxes." Basically, these were homemade enclosures; this posed a problem for his feline subjects because cats hate being enclosed. Phrased in terms of the problem components, the initial state was being in an enclosed space; the goal state was to be outside of the enclosure. The constraint was basically the enclosure itself and the fact that its construction prevented escape. Thorndike was interested in whether the ability to solve this confinement problem would appear suddenly as an insight, or gradually through a process of trial and error.

Take a look at Figure 11.3, which shows the puzzle box along with the solution times for a sample cat, graphed over a series of trials. The cats basically learned through trial and error. When first placed in the box, the cats behaved more or less randomly—meowing, scratching, and pawing in a vain attempt to escape their predicament. But as you can see in the figure, over the course of many trials, they eventually figured out how to escape, finally learning the response well enough to quickly escape whenever placed in the situation.

Thorndike described this learning process with what he termed the **law of effect.** According to the law of effect, if a response leads to a satisfying outcome, the connection between the response and the situation in which it took place (in this case, the puzzle box) will be strengthened. If a response leads to a nonsatisfying outcome, this connection will be weakened. Over the course of many experiences in the box, consider what happens: Ineffective responses like crying and scratching will weaken and disappear, while more effective responses that get the cat closer to escape will increase. So eventually, the cat will engage only in those effective responses and quickly exit the box. Behaviorists believe that, contrary to what you might think intuitively, problem solving is essentially a "mindless" process whereby learned responses automatically play themselves out. As you might recall from Chapter 1, this stimulus-response account is preferred by behaviorists for all varieties of behavior, not just problem solving.

Gestalt Psychology: Problem Solving as Insight

Gestalt psychologists have a radically different (and decidedly more cognitive) view of problem solving. Recall from Chapter 1 the basic tenets of the Gestalt approach: the mind has an inherent tendency to organize incoming information, and these organizational processes are the defining feature of cognition. So, rather than a mindless playing out of associations that gradually build up over time, problem solving involves a restructuring or reorganization of problem elements that results in a sudden realization of the solution.

Consider the work of the pioneering Gestalt psychologist Wolfgang Kohler, who conducted extensive investigations of problem solving in apes (Kohler, 1925). In one task, an ape was put in a pen with some crates, and something desirable (like a banana) was suspended from the ceiling, just out of reach. The solution to this problem was to drag the crates over and use them as steps to reach the banana. What interested Kohler was the manner in which apes seemed to be solving this problem (and other ones like it). Contrary to the gradual trial-and-error process observed by Thorndike, Kohler noticed that apes sat for a while as if they were pondering the problem; then all of a sudden they would jump up, push the crates to the appropriate spot, stack them, and fetch their treat. What led to this sudden solution? For Gestalt psychologists, problem solving involves a process of restructuring whereby problem elements are suddenly reorganized and seen in a new way. The sudden and successful restructuring of problem elements is termed **insight,** and this is a major focus of the Gestalt approach.

Contrasting the Behaviorist and Gestalt Views.   The Gestalt approach character-izes problem solving as a process of apprehending relationships between problem ele-ments, and failures in problem solving as failures to correctly or completely encode these relationships. This view contrasts sharply with the behaviorist characterization of problem solving as the mindless execution of a well-learned response. A behaviorist would have explained the apes' behavior as a series of simple responses learned through association. Over the course of many experiences in acquiring food that was difficult to attain, the apes formed a dominant response of stacking and standing on objects in order to do so, much as Thorndike's cats learned appropriate escape responses after many trials of confinement.

Both the behaviorist and the Gestalt approaches to problem solving are compelling in some ways but deficient in others. The appeal of the behaviorist approach is its precision and simplicity. Many seemingly complex behaviors can be characterized as sets of simple responses that are based on a straightforward association mechanism. But as discussed in Chapter 1, the behaviorists are limited in what they can explain via a simple stimulus-response (S-R) association mechanism. This analysis seems to apply fairly well to the behav-ior of Thorndike's cats but fails to explain more novel and creative behavior. The Gestalt approach has the converse set of strengths and limitations. To its credit, it attempts to explain novel and creative behavior in terms of mental representations, but to its detriment, it is imprecise and vague. Gestalt psychologists have never provided really satisfactory (i.e., testable) definitions for concepts like "insight" and "restructuring of problem elements." The notion of insight was (and still is, to some researchers) problematic in that it's circularly defined. Insight is said to have occurred when a person suddenly arrives at a solution that had previously been difficult to reach. But when asked for an explanation of how the problem was solved, the explanation is . . . insight. You can't use insight as both the phenomenon to be explained *and* as the explanation.

Let's finish our evaluation of these two approaches by applying them to your end-of-semester problem. You have to fit writing research papers and studying for several final exams into the space of two weeks. It's hard to imagine your solution to this problem as the triggering of a series of associations that have been built up through experience. Behavior in this situation is much too complex and unpredictable to be adequately explained in such simple terms. But it's also hard to imagine that you're going to sit in your room and then all of a sudden, in a burst of insight, exclaim, "I know exactly how to successfully write these papers and ace these exams!" It seems that what's needed is a view that has the precision of behaviorism but that also allows for novel and creative solutions to problems. In the 1950s, the information-processing approach emerged as the dominant paradigm for explaining problem solving.

Cognitive Psychology: Problem Solving as Information Processing

You'll recall from Chapter 1 that one of the major factors in the emergence of cognitive psychology was the development of the computer, which served notice that intelligent behavior (of a sort) was not the exclusive province of human beings. Early cognitive psychologists (e.g., Newell, Shaw, & Simon, 1958) felt that computer programs might serve as useful tools for modeling human problem solving. Just as a computer solves problems by executing programs that use information stored in some type of database, humans solve problems by applying mental processes to representations in memory. So, if you design a computer program that can solve a reasoning problem, you've essentially proposed a possible theory for how humans do the same.

The General Problem Solver.   Newell and Simon (1972) originated the conceptualization of problem solving as a step-by-step progression from an initial state to a goal state. They did so within the framework of a computer program termed the **General Problem Solver (GPS)**, which they proposed as a general model of human problem solving—one that can be applied to any problem. Basically, the GPS approach to problem solving attempts to minimize the "distance" between an initial state and a goal state by breaking the problem down into a series of subgoals. This **subgoal analysis** is accomplished through the application of **operators,** which is basically a fancy word for problem-solving techniques. These techniques are applied (at a microlevel) to reduce the difference between the current state and the current subgoal state and (at a macrolevel) to reduce the difference between the initial state and the final goal state. Figure 11.4 lists a possible set of subgoals for your end-of-semester problem. Another important aspect of GPS is the notion of problem space. **Problem space** basically refers to the problem solver's mental representation of the initial state, the goal state, all possible intermediate

Subgoal 1
Study for cognitive psych exam (read the book, outline notes, meet with study group)

Subgoal 2
Study for physics exam (read the book, meet with prof to discuss unclear points, highlight important passages in reading)

Subgoal 3
Finalize paper topic for psychology (check with prof about topic, go to library, see if there are enough relevant resources)

Figure 11.4 A set of subgoals that one might attempt to reach for the end-of-semester problem (along with nested subgoals).

Table 11.1 A Sampling of the Stages Involved in Problem Solving

Wallas	Bransford & Stein	Polya
Preparation	Identify the problem.	Understand the problem.
Incubation	Define the problem correctly.	Devise a plan.
Illumination	Explore your options.	Carry out the plan.
Verification	Act on the chosen strategy.	
	Look back and evaluate.	

(subgoal) states, and the operators that can be applied to reach these subgoals. Hence, the problem-solving process is essentially an excursion through problem space.

Note the features that define GPS as an information-processing model. First, information in the external world (e.g., the problem information) is transformed into an internal (mental) representation. Then, in a sequential fashion, various mental operations are applied to this representation to transform it into other representations that are closer and closer to the goal state. This general information-processing framework has served as the model for modern problem-solving research. Given this, it should come as no surprise that problem solving is usually characterized as a steplike progression through a series of stages. Table 11.1 lists three such characterizations by different researchers (e.g., Bransford & Stein, 1993; Polya, 1957; Wallas, 1926). From these, a pretty standard picture emerges. Problem solving involves an initial phase in which the problem is defined and a representation formed. Then, the problem solver embarks on a process of generating and testing possible solutions.

STOP *and* **REVIEW!**

1. Which of these concepts would a behaviorist NOT make reference to, in explaining problem solving?
   a. responses
   b. behavior
   c. insight
   d. learning
2. True or false? Insight involves the restructuring of problem elements.
3. Describe the basic idea behind the General Problem Solver.

➤ Behaviorists viewed problem solving as a learning process that can be described in terms of the law of effect (if a response leads to a satisfying outcome, the connection between the response and the situation will be strengthened; if a response leads to a nonsatisfying outcome, this connection will be weakened). Problem solving is viewed as the formation of increasingly complex chains of stimulus-response connections.

➤ The Gestalt psychologists viewed problem solving as a process whereby the elements of a problem must be restructured. Often, problem restructuring results in a sudden insight regarding problem solution.

➤ The information-processing approach views problem solving as a stagelike progression from starting state to goal state. One of the first attempts to model this process was within the framework of a computer program termed *General Problem Solver*. GPS models problem solving as successive reductions in "distance" between an initial state and a goal state by breaking a problem into a series of subgoals (subgoal analysis).

Problem Representation

As stated above, problem solving involves a process of converting presented information into some type of internal mental representation. Within the framework of GPS, **problem representation** involves correctly specifying the problem space—in other words, correctly identifying the initial state as well as the operators that may be applied within the constraints of the problem. The process of problem representation may seem automatic or trivial in some respects, but it is a critical component of successful problem solving. And the ways in which problems can be represented are as varied as problems themselves. Let's look at a few examples. As you read each one, try to solve it, taking note of the particular manner in which you represent the problem.

1. Once there was a monk who lived in a monastery at the foot of a mountain. Every year, the monk made a pilgrimage to the top of the mountain to fast and pray. He would start out on the mountain path at 6 a.m., climbing and resting as the spirit struck him, but making sure that he reached the shrine at exactly 6 p.m. that evening. He then prayed and fasted all night. At exactly 6 a.m. the next day, he began to descend the mountain path, resting here and there along the way, but making sure that he reached his monastery by 6 p.m. of that day. Prove that there must be a spot along the path that the monk will pass at exactly the same time on the two days.

2. A man bought a white horse for $60 and then sold it for $70. Then he bought it back for $80 and sold it for $90. What was his net gain (or net loss) in the horse business?

Clearly, these two problems would lead the problem solver to form different problem representations. The problem about the monk (based on Duncker, 1945) leads the problem solver to form a visual representation of the monk ascending and descending the mountain. The horse-trading problem leads the problem solver to form an arithmetic representation, given that the solver must add and subtract the appropriate numbers to come up with a solution. Not only will these problems lead to different representations, but the ability to solve the problems depends critically on the exact nature of the representation. Take the monk problem: one possible representation is to form two separate visualizations—one of the monk ascending and another of him descending. A much more effective representation is to imagine these two excursions superimposed; it immediately becomes apparent that there must be a point of intersection. This point would be the critical spot in the path (see Figure 11.5).

Figure 11.5 The monk problem proves to be much more manageable when represented appropriately. Visualization makes it apparent that the ascent up the mountain and the descent down the mountain must intersect at some point.

The horse-trading problem was used in a study by Maier and Burke (1967), who found that less than 40% of subjects could successfully solve it. Did you? The answer is $20. The key to an easy solution, once again, is problem representation. Consider this similar problem:

> A man bought a white horse for $60 and then sold it for $70. Then he bought a black horse for $80 and sold it for $90. What was his net gain (or net loss) in the horse business?

This problem seems similar to problem 2 above. But it's not just similar; it's pretty much identical. When presented this way, as two separate transactions involving different horses instead of a continuous pair of transactions involving the same horse, everyone gets the solution. Clearly, the manner in which the problem solver mentally "sets up" the problem has powerful implications for whether it is solved.

Rigidity in Representation

The initial representation of a problem is critical to its eventual solution. Failure in representation might result from a number of factors: the problem elements may not have received sufficient attention; the problem elements may not have been understood; or previous experience with similar problems may have led to encoding the problem elements in a rigid manner. Let's consider the following induction problem previously presented in Figure 11.2.

Take a look at the following number sequence: 8, 5, 4, 1, 7, 6, 10, 0. Now, attempt to figure out the rule that generated the sequence. This challenging problem is not what it seems to be. In an attempt to identify some pattern in these differences, you no doubt attempted to calculate the difference between each consecutive pair of numbers in this way: "Let's see, 8 and 5 differ by 3, 5 and 4 differ by 1, 4 and 1 differ by 3. . . ." If you followed this line of reasoning, you could add and subtract all day and still not come up with the correct solution. The key to the problem lies in viewing the numbers as words rather than as numerical values. Does this hint help? The numbers in the sequence are arranged alphabetically. However, given that in your experience, most number sequences are arranged numerically, not alphabetically, you no doubt struggled quite a bit with this problem.

Mental Set. This tendency to rely on habits and procedures used in the past is termed **mental set.** A mental set can interfere with your ability to solve everyday problems. An anecdote from our life provides an (embarrassing for Bridget) example of mental set. We drove to a restaurant for dinner, and Bridget was delayed in exiting the car because she was looking for something in her purse. Greg, unaware of this, locked the door with the remote lock control. After finding what she needed, Bridget attempted to unlock the car with her automatic lock control, but with no success. So she sat there, unable to figure out how to get out of the car. After letting her wait long enough to maximize his own amusement, Greg pointed to the lock and motioned for her to lift it. Bridget had used the automatic locking control so regularly that it was the only option in her mind at that moment—reflecting her mental set.

Mental set tends to affect the representation phase of problem solving, as past experience leads to an inappropriate representation of the problem. For Bridget, her past experience with the car led her to represent the problem of unlocking the car in only one way (with the automatic lock control). In the number sequence problem, your tendency to view digits numerically instead of in terms of verbal labels most likely prevented you from solving the problem. Consider if the problem had been presented in this way: eight, five, four, one, seven, six, ten, zero. Chances are, the correct solution would have come to you more easily. People seem to make unnecessary assumptions or follow habits acquired through past experience that impede the problem-solving process.

Functional Fixedness.   Take a look at one of the classics of problem-solving research—Duncker's candle problem. This problem provides a nice example of a close cousin of mental set termed **functional fixedness.** Functional fixedness refers to people's tendency to view objects in a narrow, fixed sense—that is, in terms of the typical functions of the object. In his classic experiment, Duncker presented subjects with a number of objects, including the following critical materials: matches, tacks, boxes, and candles. The problem was to attach the candles to the wall and light them.

In order to influence the solvers' problem representations, Duncker presented the materials in one of three conditions (see Figure 11.6). In the functional fixedness condition, the boxes were each filled with one of the three critical materials: candles, matches, and tacks. In the first control condition, the boxes sat empty, alongside the other materials. In a second control condition, the boxes contained materials not critical to the solution, like buttons. The correct solution is to tack the boxes to the wall and use them as candleholders, placing a candle in each box, which can then be safely lit. The key to solving this problem is to view the boxes as boxes, not as boxes of matches, tacks, or candles. Note that this is an issue of problem representation. In the first control condition, all of the subjects successfully solved the problem. But in the functional fixedness and second control conditions (in which the boxes were narrowly perceived as containers for the objects they were holding), less than one-third of the subjects successfully solved the problem.

STOP *and* THINK!

MENTAL RUTS

Try and think of times when you were absolutely stuck on some type of problem.

1. Describe the circumstances.
2. Note how you were able to overcome whatever obstacle(s) blocked your way.
3. Classify your examples as (a) mental set or (b) functional fixedness.

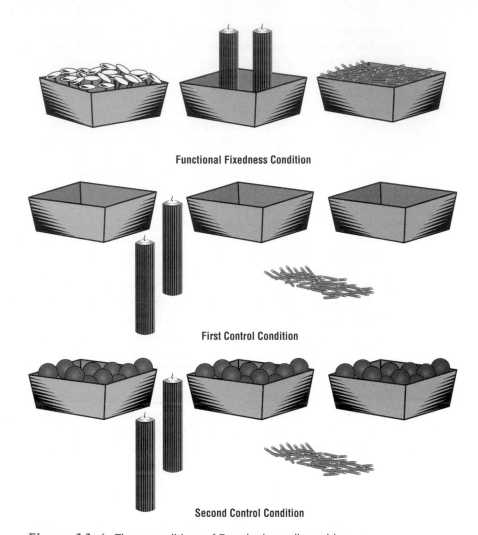

Figure 11.6 Three conditions of Duncker's candle problem.

Adapted from Duncker, K. (1945). On problem solving. *Psychological Monographs, 58,* 1–112. Copyright 1945 by the American Psychological Association.

Research Theme: Development

One developmental perspective on functional fixedness holds that older children are more likely than younger ones to demonstrate functional fixedness. That is, they're slower to realize that some object can be used in an atypical way to solve a problem. Why might be this be? Some analyses (e.g., German & Johnson, 2002; Matan & Carrey, 2001) suggest that by age 6 or so, children have come to learn the conventional functions of artifact category members. Recall from Chapter 5 that artifact categories are categories of human-made objects (i.e., artifacts) that are organized by convention rather than by inherent characteristics. Once the conventional function is learned, youngsters begin to have trouble seeing the objects' potential for unusual or novel uses. Consistent with this view, German and Defeyter (2000) found that older children were slower than younger children to solve a problem by using an artifact (e.g., a bucket) for an atypical purpose when the typical purpose had been primed by demonstrating it.

German and Barrett (2005) note that functional fixedness has typically been demonstrated in technologically sophisticated cultures that have seemingly endless numbers of "artifacts" designed to perform every function under the sun—can openers, bottle stoppers, lint rollers, fondue forks, olive trays, cat litter scoops, . . . this could go on for pages. It could be that having such a (as German and Barrett term it) "technologically promiscuous" culture leads us to view every artifact we encounter in terms of a narrowly prescribed function, making us more prone to functional fixedness (seriously, what else would you *want* to use a cat scoop for?). The complementary prediction would be that a "technologically sparse" culture might be more able to discern alternative uses for objects, given that culture's less proscribed technology. To test this idea, German and Barrett conducted a study of functional fixedness in a technologically sparse culture—the Shuar of Ecuador, a horticultural and hunting society with relatively few artifacts; the ones they do have are fairly simple and nonspecialized (e.g., axes, pots, fishhooks, and the like). Would this simpler approach to objects be associated with a lessened tendency to fixate on the function of an object?

Research Theme: Culture

The task presented by the researchers involved using provided props to solve a problem posed by a simple story; the *spoon task* is depicted in Figure 11.7. For this task, subjects (adolescent and young adults from Shuar villages) were required to construct a bridge for a story character who needed to cross a river. The objects they were given were a spoon (the target object, and the only one long enough to do the job), a cup filled with rice, a smaller plastic cup, an eraser, a lollipop stick, and a small clear ball. Subjects were presented with these materials in one of two conditions. In a baseline condition, all materials were presented separately and next to one another. In the functional fixedness condition, the spoon was in the cup of rice. This latter condition was considered the "prime" for functional fixedness. The solution was to bridge the river with the spoon. Two times were recorded: the time it took a subject to select the spoon, and the time it took a subject to use it to solve the problem successfully.

The results indicated that, just like their technologically promiscuous counterparts in more modernized cultures, the Shuar were susceptible to functional fixedness. In the

Figure 11.7 The two conditions of the "spoon task" used by German and Barrett (2005) to test functional fixedness in the Shuar of Ecuador.

From German, T. P. & Barrett, H. C. (2005). Functional fixedness in a technologically sparse culture. *Psychological Science, 16*(1), 1–5. Published by Blackwell, Inc. Reprinted with permission.

functional fixedness condition, it took subjects much longer to (a) select and (b) use the spoon as the solution (33 and 45 seconds, respectively), relative to the baseline condition (25 and 20 seconds, respectively). Priming the function of the spoon made it more difficult for subjects to use the spoon in an atypical manner. German and Barrett surmise that even in a technologically sparse culture, representations of concepts (e.g., spoons) in semantic memory must have design information—what the object is intended for—as a core property.

It's important to note that thinking of things in the same old way is not always a bad thing. As noted by Bransford and Stein (1993), most situations in life require that we think conventionally as opposed to nonconventionally. Conventional, everyday thinking (because it tends to rely on processes that have become automatic, as discussed in Chapter 4) tends to be quick and requires little conscious effort, allowing us to do other things at the same time. The best-case scenario for effective problem solving may be to balance conventional and nonconventional thinking, sticking with the basics unless the circumstances demand a more creative solution.

Stereotypes as a Threat to Problem Representation

"Here's a math word problem." Does this statement make the hair on the back of your neck stand up? Most of us have been plagued by word problems throughout our school years. In order to solve these problems, you must represent the problem in proper mathematical form. This, as we all know, seems an impossible task at times. Consider this comment from a fellow sufferer: "I have no idea how to set up a formula for this. I really don't know what to do with this one."

This person obviously is having difficulty with problem representation. What factors contribute to such difficulty? Limitations in mathematical knowledge and/or ability, you might be thinking. Perhaps the above comment makes more sense when you consider that the comment comes from a female problem solver. Aha, you may think, that's it—women aren't very good at math, right? Well, yes, according to a common cultural stereotype, though the real story is infinitely more complex than that. A woman's belief in this stereotype can interfere with her ability to devise a strategy to represent a mathematical problem properly and, consequently, her ability to solve it. Surprisingly (and troublingly), the comment above came from a woman with a strong mathematical background who participated in a study on the effects of stereotype threat on mathematical problem solving.

Quinn and Spencer (2001) were interested in why women who have strong math skills underperform in comparison to their male peers. They believed that the answer resides in the interaction between the cultural stereotype about women's math ability and the testing situation. This interaction creates **stereotype threat.** Stereotype threat occurs when a member of a negatively stereotyped group feels that the stereotype might be used to judge their behavior, thus resulting in a negative judgment that will propagate the stereotype. Take the woman who made the above comment, reflecting her difficulty or frustration when confronting a math problem. She may have felt that the difficulty she was having would be used by others to validate and perpetuate the stereotype that women aren't good at math. The anxiety created by this apprehension may have interfered with her ability to accurately represent the problem, and her performance suffered, not because as a woman she is inherently inferior in math, but because of a self-fulfilling prophecy driven by this stereotype.

Word problem: A sporting goods store sold 64 Frisbees in one week, some for $3.00 and the rest for $4.00 each. If receipts from Frisbee sales for the week totaled $204, what is the fewest number of $4.00 Frisbees that could have been sold?

Numeric/algebraic equivalent: $3(64 - x) + 4(x) = 204$

$x =$

(a) 24   (b) 12   (c) 8   (d) 4   (e) 2

Figure 11.8 Sample problem used by Quinn and Spencer (2001) in both word and numeric/algebraic form.

From Quinn, D. M., & Spencer, S. J. (2001). The interference of stereotype threat with women's generation of mathematical problem-solving strategies. *Journal of Social Issues, 57,* 55–71. Copyright 2001 by Blackwell, Inc. Reprinted by permission.

In order to test this idea, Quinn and Spencer (2001) had men and women solve either math word problems or numeric/algebraic equivalents of the word problems. A sample problem is presented in Figure 11.8. The mathematical knowledge necessary to answer these problems was equivalent in both conditions; however, the word problem condition required subjects to transform the problem into its proper mathematical representation. The results are presented in the top panel of Table 11.2. Men outperformed women on word problems only; on the more straightforward numeric/algebraic problems, men and women did not differ. Apparently, women had the mathematical ability to solve the problem but ran into interference in conditions that required an involved stage of problem representation. Quinn and Spencer assumed this interference was produced by stereotype threat.

In order to test this assumption, the authors manipulated the level of stereotype threat in the situation. Subjects in a low-stereotype-threat condition were told that the test had been shown previously to be gender fair, yielding equivalent performance

Research Theme: Individual Differences

Table 11.2 Results from Quinn and Spencer (2001)

Correct Solutions (%)		Problem Type	
		Word	Numeric
Gender	Female	8	38
	Male	20	40

Correct Solutions (%)		Stereotype Threat	
		High	Low
Gender	Female	26	39
	Male	45	34

Failures (%)		Stereotype Threat	
		High	Low
Gender	Female	14	4
	Male	2	9

From Quinn, D. M., & Spencer, S. J. (2001). The interference of stereotype threat with women's generation of mathematical problem-solving strategies. *Journal of Social Issues, 57,* 55–71. Copyright 2001 by Blackwell, Inc. Reprinted by permission.

between men and women. Subjects in the high-threat conditions were not given this information. The results are presented in the middle panel of Table 11.2. In the high-stereotype-threat condition, men outperformed women; in the low-stereotype-threat condition, there were no sex-related differences.

In order to determine if the deficits found were really due to difficulties in problem representation, subjects in the second experiment were recorded while solving the problems. (Remember the verbal protocol procedure we discussed earlier?) The number of problems in which subjects could not determine a strategy (i.e., proper problem representation) to solve the problem (i.e., a "failure rate") was assessed. The results are presented in the bottom panel of Table 11.2. In the high-stereotype-threat condition, women had higher failure rates than men. In the low-threat condition, these failure rates were equivalent. It appears that when stereotype threat is reduced, women perform equally as well as men, quite possibly because an obstacle to successful problem representation was removed. Some more recent and complementary evidence (Schmader & Johns, 2003) indicates that the effect of stereotype threat on problem solving may be rooted in working memory; the priming of a stereotype leads to extra resource-demanding processing that interferes with finding a solution.

Research Theme: Culture

You may be wondering whether stereotypes lead to advantages in performance in circumstances in which the stereotype is a positive one. For example, another cultural stereotype characterizes Asians as more accomplished math problem solvers than their Western counterparts; might this stereotype enhance Asians' performance on math tasks? Evidence would indicate that this indeed is the case. Asian-Americans who are primed by the math stereotype do better than those who are unprimed (Shih, Ambady, Richeson, Fujita, & Gray, 2002). And it's not just a difference in cultural sensitivity to stereotypes in general. Shih, Pittinsky, and Trahan (2006) tested Asian-American women on verbal tasks (a situation in which the stereotype is negative), and showed that priming a negative stereotype about verbal skills had detrimental effects on performance. So it would seem that the specific impact of stereotypes on cognition (adaptive or maladaptive) depends on the particular task as well as on the stereotypes.

STOP *and* **REVIEW!**

1. What processes are involved in problem representation?
2. Define (a) mental set and (b) functional fixedness.

➤ The GPS has led researchers to explore the various stages of the problem-solving process. Problem representation involves correctly identifying the initial state as well as the operators that may be applied within the constraints of the problem. The initial problem representation is critical to the eventual solution to a problem. Failure to represent a problem correctly is likely to hinder finding a solution.

➤ Rigidity in the representation phase can be seen in cases of mental set (the tendency to rely on habits and procedures used in the past) and functional fixedness (the tendency to view objects in terms of their typical functions). Problem representation can also be hindered by stereotype threat (which occurs when a member of a negatively stereotyped group feels that the stereotype will be used to judge their behavior).

Problem Solution

Once a problem has been successfully transformed from externally presented information into an internal representation, the next phase of the problem-solving process involves searching for, testing, and evaluating problem solutions. Within the context of Newell and Simon's (1972) information-processing approach, problem solution amounts to traveling through the problem space. Two general approaches to this excursion are through algorithms and through heuristics; each approach has different implications for exactly how the problem space is traversed.

Algorithms

An **algorithm** is basically a set of rules that can be applied systematically to solve certain types of problems. A mathematical formula is a good example of an algorithm. Suppose I were to tell you that the two shorter sides of a right triangle had lengths of 3 inches and 4 inches. You could easily apply a well-known algorithm (the Pythagorean theorem) to calculate the length of the hypotenuse (5 inches). Algorithms are very powerful problem-solving techniques; applied correctly, an algorithm will always lead to the correct solution, if one exists. But it's not a perfect world; algorithms are seldom if ever used to solve problems on a day-to-day basis.

For human problem solvers, algorithms are often unfeasible, for a couple of reasons. The Pythagorean theorem is easy enough to apply, but consider a more difficult problem. Suppose someone asked you to solve the word anagram *kigvin* (an arrangement problem previously presented in Figure 11.2). You could solve this problem algorithmically by systematically working through every possible letter combination, but you would have to consider hundreds of possibilities. Think of it in terms of problem space; obviously, hundreds of possible sequences comprise this extremely large problem space. The exhaustive nature of algorithms makes them overly tedious and quite impractical, at least for humans. On the other hand, computers are well suited to algorithmic problem solving because they are well suited for what algorithms require: speed, power, and reliable application. A second factor that limits the usefulness of algorithms is that there simply aren't any for most of the problems we face on a daily basis. Alas, life is not a right triangle. There is no algorithm for deciding on a college major or a career, for figuring out how to complete two papers and study for three finals over the space of two weeks, or for deciding how to be happy in life. These very complex and ill-defined problems demand a more flexible, dynamic approach.

Heuristics

Given the strengths (flexibility) and limitations (computing power) of the human problem solver, along with the fact that most problems are ill defined and have relatively large problem spaces, heuristic problem solving is much more effective. **Heuristics** are general strategies, or rules of thumb, that can be applied to various problems. Heuristics serve as "shortcuts" through problem space. Take another look at the anagram *kigvin*. Immediately, you reject certain possibilities because of your morphological knowledge of the English language. For example, no English words start with *gk* or *vg* or *ikn,* so these

Heuristics come in handy when playing games.

would not be explicitly considered. While the algorithmic approach entails the consideration of every possible solution, the strength of the heuristic approach is that the trip through problem space is faster; the solutions come more quickly. But unlike algorithms, heuristics do not guarantee a correct solution. (By the way, the solution is *viking*.)

Specific heuristics exist for specific problem domains. One of our favorite card games is euchre, the object of which is to win tricks by playing high, or trump, cards. When dealt a hand in euchre (or any card game, for that matter), you certainly can't consider every possible play of the cards in preparation for your bid (although it seems like some people do!). Instead, you do a quick heuristic evaluation of your hand. If you have at least two cards that are pretty certain to win a trick, then a bid is a good risk. In addition to the heuristics that apply to specific situations, there are a number of general-purpose heuristics that can be applied to a wide array of problems.

STOP *and* THINK!

YOUR OWN HEURISTICS

Consider the personal problem solving you do every day.

- Are there any everyday problems for which you use algorithms?
- What types of problems do these tend to be?

You no doubt use heuristics a great deal.

1. Generate a list of strategies, or shortcuts, you use to solve everyday problems.
2. List the heuristics you use in your favorite game or sport to make it more likely you'll succeed.

Means-End Analysis.   The General Problem Solver developed by Newell and Simon utilizes the heuristic known as means-end analysis. **Means-end analysis** involves breaking a problem into smaller subgoals in which accomplishing each subgoal moves the solver closer to the final goal—the problem's solution. As the term *means-end analysis* implies, the solver systematically attempts to devise means to get to each of the subgoal's ends. Means-end analysis can be an effective way to solve a transformation problem, which involves moving from the initial state to the goal state through a series of transformations. For example, your problem of writing some papers and studying for several final exams isn't going to be solved overnight. It's going to be manageable only if you break it up into a series of subgoals and systematically accomplish each. As you do, you will slowly but surely reach your goal.

STOP *and* THINK!

MAKING BIG PROBLEMS INTO LITTLE ONES

As you have read, one pretty effective problem-solving heuristic is means-end analysis, which essentially amounts to breaking a problem into smaller parts. Consider these everyday problems:

> finding a job
> finding an apartment
> planning a spring break trip
> raising a child
> planning a wedding
> deciding what to do on the weekend

For each of these problems,

1. Try to break the general goal into a series of subgoals.
2. See if you can break these subgoals into still smaller subgoals.

Analogies.   Before you read on, take a look at the mutilated checkerboard problem described in Figure 11.9 and try to come up with a solution. Did you solve it? Chances are, you didn't; this is a fairly difficult problem. Did the problem ring any bells? Remind you of anything else in the chapter? It turns out that this problem is analogous to the country dance problem discussed earlier and presented in Figure 11.1. As in that problem, the key to the solution lies in realizing that it is going to be impossible to pair off each of the black-and-white combinations of the checkerboard if two squares of the same color are removed, just as it is

---

You are given a checkerboard and 32 dominoes. Each domino covers adjacent squares on the board. Thus, 32 dominoes can cover all 64 squares of the checkerboard. Now suppose two squares are cut off at diagonally opposite corners of the board. If possible, show how you would place 31 dominoes on the board so that all 62 of the remaining squares are covered. If you think it is impossible, give a proof of why.

Figure 11.9 The mutilated checkerboard problem.

From Wickelgren, W. A. (1974). *How to solve problems.* New York: Freeman. Copyright 1974 by W. H. Freeman and Company. Reprinted by permission.

Suppose you are a doctor faced with a patient who has a malignant tumor in his stomach. It is impossible to operate on the tumor, but unless the tumor is destroyed, the patient will die. There is a kind of ray that can be used to destroy the tumor. If the rays reach the tumor all at once at a sufficiently high intensity, the tumor will be destroyed. Unfortunately, at this intensity, the healthy tissue that the rays pass through on the way to the tumor will also be destroyed. At lower intensities, the rays are harmless to healthy tissue, but they will not affect the tumor either. What type of procedure might be used to destroy the tumor with the rays and at the same time avoid destroying the healthy tissue?

Figure 11.10 The radiation problem.

From Duncker, K. (1945). On problem solving. *Psychological Monographs, 58,* 1–112.

impossible to form man-woman dance partnerings if there is not an equal number of men and women.

The connection between these problems is an example of an analogic relationship. **Analogies**—using problems that have already been solved as aids for representing and solving the problem currently being faced—is potentially one of the most powerful heuristics. Have you ever said, "Hey, this is just like the time when . . ."? If so, you've been thinking in terms of an analogy. The use of analogies in problem solving has been investigated extensively by problem-solving researchers (much more than any of the other heuristics), and the news isn't too good. Research indicates that problem solvers are unlikely to use analogies to aid in problem solving unless the problem solvers are practically "hit over the head" with the connections between problems. This is why you may not have realized the connection between the mutilated checkerboard and country dance problems. But, as you'll see, there are conditions that encourage the successful application of analogies.

Duncker (the problem-solving pioneer who developed the candle problem) developed what has become known as the radiation problem, presented in Figure 11.10. Can you solve it? The correct solution is to aim many radiation beams (at sufficiently weak intensity to avoid damage) at the tumor from different angles. Hence, the tumor receives the summed energy of the radiation (and is destroyed), while the surrounding tissue is unharmed. In a classic series of studies, Gick and Holyoak (1980, 1983) utilized the radiation problem developed by Duncker (1945) to investigate whether an analogous problem might help solvers succeed at finding a solution to it.

In their initial series of investigations on whether analogies might aid in problem solving, Gick and Holyoak (1980) presented subjects with one of several stories analogous to the radiation problem. For example, in the commander problem, a military commander is trying to capture the military headquarters of an opposing force. The headquarters are located on an island connected to the surrounding area by several bridges. A bridge can accommodate only a few tanks, which will not be enough for a successful attack. Therefore, the military commander conducts the attack by sending a few tanks across each bridge; this results in enough tanks arriving at the island for a successful attack. After looking over this initial story (the *source problem*) under the guise of a story-comprehension task, subjects were given the radiation problem (the *target problem*). Some subjects were given only the target problem; in this condition, 10% came up with the convergence solution. Some subjects were instructed to memorize the source problem and then try to solve the target problem. In this condition, 30% of subjects came up with the convergence solution. A comparison of these two conditions indicates that 20% of subjects spontaneously noticed the analogous relationship and used it.

In a follow-up series of investigations, Gick and Holyoak (1983) set out to determine the conditions under which analogical transfer would occur. They attempted to get

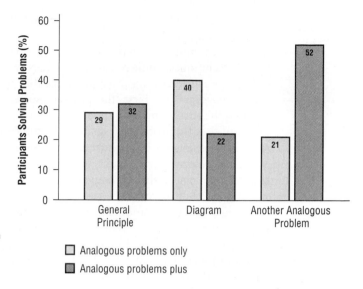

Figure 11.11 Results from Gick and Holyoak (1983).

From Gick, M. L., & Holyoak, K. J. (1983). Schema induction and analogical transfer. *Cognitive Psychology, 15,* 1–38. Copyright 1983, Elsevier Science (USA). Reprinted by permission.

solvers to notice and use analogies under three different conditions. In the analogy-plus-general-principle condition, subjects received an analogous problem plus an extra passage that basically stated the underlying principle (or, in Gick and Holyoak's terms, the underlying *schema*)—namely, that simultaneously applying small forces from different locations is as effective as applying one large force from the same location. In the analogy-plus-diagram condition, subjects received an analogous problem plus a diagram (multiple arrows converging on one location) that sketched out the underlying schema. Alternatively, in the analogy-plus-another-analogous-problem condition, the subjects received two analogous problems and were asked to find the relationship between them. Which of these three conditions (if any) do you think would be most likely to lead to the transfer of the analogy?

Figure 11.11 summarizes the results from experiments that tested these different conditions. Each pair of bars represents a comparison between one of the three conditions discussed above to an analogy-alone condition in which the subjects received just one analogous problem. As you can see, only one of the analogy hints was successful. Providing a diagram (analogy-plus-diagram condition) or a statement of the general principle underlying the problem (analogy-plus-general-principle condition) did not help subjects to spontaneously recognize and use the analogy. However, when subjects read and related two analogous stories (analogy-plus-another-analogous-problem condition), they were able to use the knowledge in the new problem. Gick and Holyoak explain that in this condition, solvers were able to map the connections between the two different problems. This mapping process is a defining feature of analogical reasoning and is a critical determinant of whether an analogous problem is going to be an aid. Gick and Holyoak term this mapping process *schema induction*. A schema is a mental representation of facts and procedures that apply to a specific object or situation. In this context, a schema is a mental representation of the underlying principles that multiple problems share. Once this schema is formed, the problem solver can make use of it in solving analogous problems.

Let's examine the steps that are necessary for analogies to succeed as problem-solving techniques. Some researchers (e.g., Novick & Holyoak, 1991) summarize the role of analogy by describing three processes that might be termed *noticing, mapping,* and *schema development*. First, the problem solver must *notice* that a relationship exists between the two problems in question. Next, the solver must be able to *map* the key elements of the two problems (e.g., that the tumor in the radiation problem can be represented as the military headquarters in the commander problem). Finally, the solver must arrive at a general *schema* underlying the problems that will allow for the solution of the target problem (i.e., the convergence schema).

A good deal of research (e.g., Holyoak & Koh, 1987; Ross, 1987) reveals that the first stage, where a relationship must be noticed, is a major culprit in failures of analogical problem solving. Why is this the case? It's basically a failure of memory; the problem currently being faced fails to trigger the memory of other problems that may be helpful. A hint to specifically use the related problem (which serves as a retrieval cue) leads the solver to use the previous problem. But in most everyday cases of problem solving, there's no one to provide hints about other analogous problems. So what factors promote the spontaneous recognition and retrieval of a related problem? One answer to this question relates to the types of features the two problem situations may or may not share.

Surface vs. Structural Features.   Our ability to notice, map, and develop schemata depends on the particular *type of similarity.* Researchers generally distinguish between the *surface features* and the *structural features* of problems (e.g., Gentner, 1989). **Surface features** are the specific elements of the problem. If two problems share surface similarity, this means that the parts of the problems look pretty similar. A fiasco that occurred while printing the first draft of this very chapter serves as a good example. One of our printers (the newer one) decided to start munching paper as it printed, and it shut down. As we flailed around, looking for the printer manual to get instructions on clearing a paper jam from the new printer, we realized (via analogy) that this printer probably would work like our old printer. Paper jams on our old printer get cleared by opening up the back of the printer. Sure enough, the same principle applied to the new printer. The two problems shared surface features, we noticed the relationship, and the problem was solved.

Structural features are the underlying relationships among the surface features of the two problems. If two problems are structurally similar, they may look quite different on the surface but have underlying similarities in terms of their relationships. Does this sound familiar? Remember the distinction we made in Chapter 10 between surface structure and deep structure? Two sentences could have different surface structures (i.e., look similar) but have the same deep structures (i.e., mean the same thing). For example, "The dog chased the cat" and "The cat was chased by the dog" have different structures but the same meaning (i.e., deep structures).

Think about the radiation and commander problems. These problems are completely different in terms of their surface features: military attack versus cancer. Yet in terms of structural features, they are pretty much the same. Both require the use of many smaller forces applied simultaneously from different directions. In spite of the fundamental (structural) similarity between the radiation and commander problems, their dissimilarity on the surface is likely to prevent your making a connection between the two. Simply put, in many circumstances, structural similarity is not enough to cue your memory regarding previous problems; the reminder must be more obvious.

Speaking of reminders, recall our earlier discussion of verbal protocols—think-out-loud reports that help researchers get a handle on the processes underlying problem solving. Might these serve another purpose? You might have the intuition, or even the personal experience, that "talking through" a problem helps you solve it. This has been found to be true in many circumstances of learning and problem solving (e.g., Chi, 1996). How about the case of analogy? Perhaps thinking through a problem out loud would lead one to stumble upon the connections that might unlock a problem solution. Lane and Schooler (2004) investigated the effects of verbalizing on the apprehension and retrieval of analogies by having subjects read 16 short scenarios. A few minutes later, they were asked to read eight more test scenarios and decide which of the original ones seemed like the best analogy. It turns out that each of these eight scenarios was indeed related to two of the original scenarios; each of these test scenarios had been designed to bear a superficial relation (surface similarity) with one of the encoded scenarios and a deeper relation (structural similarity) with another of the encoded scenarios. Half of the subjects "thought out loud" during this retrieval task, while the other half worked silently.

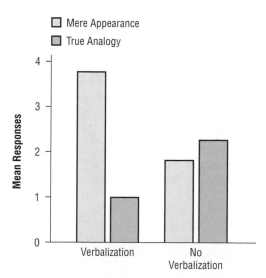

☐ Mere Appearance
☐ True Analogy

Figure 11.12 Results from Lane and Schooler's (2004) study of the effects of verbalization on analogy retrieval.

From Lane, S. M. & Schooler, J. W. (2004). Skimming the surface: Verbal overshadowing of analogical retrieval. *Psychological Science, 15*(11), 715–719. Published by Blackwell, Inc. Reprinted with permission.

In terms of design, this was a simple 2 × 2 factorial One independent variable was a materials variable—type of relation among the test scenarios and original scenarios (superficial and deep). A second independent variable was the instructional variable of whether or not subjects were told to verbalize during retrieval. Figure 11.12 presents the results from the four conditions yielded by this factorial. As you can see, verbalizing seemed to have converse effects on the discovery of different sorts of analogies. Verbalizing seemed to encourage subjects to see superficial analogies (surface similarity) at the expense of deeper analogies (structural similarity). Lane and Schooler explain these results by proposing that the requirement of verbalization leads one to focus on superficial similarities because these are easier to talk about. Basically, verbalization biases people toward verbalizable processes.

Even though a good deal of research indicates that people aren't too good at picking up on analogies unless the relationship is pretty obvious (Gick & Holyoak, 1980, 1983; Hayes & Simon, 1977), a study by Blanchette and Dunbar (2000) provides a hopeful assessment of analogy use. As you've read, people often fail to pick up on analogies unless there is surface similarity.

But the seeming ineffectiveness of structural similarity for analogy use is deceiving; some research suggests that it might be (at least in part) an artifact of the cognitive psychology laboratory. Several studies of real-world problem solving indicate that the analogies people use are based on structural features, not surface ones (e.g., Dunbar, 1995). In their study, Blanchette and Dunbar had subjects produce their own analogies to various target problems, and the characteristics of these generated analogies were evaluated. The results indicated that when analogies were produced by subjects, the analogies shared structural similarity, rather than surface similarity, with the target problem. This finding indicates that people in everyday circumstances may actually be more sensitive to structural similarity than had been suggested by earlier research.

STOP *and* **REVIEW!**

1. Which of the following is FALSE about algorithms?
   a. They involve a systematic application of rules.
   b. They involve the exhaustive application of rules.
   c. They guarantee a solution.
   d. They are most useful in everyday problem-solving situations.
2. True or false? Heuristics are preferable to algorithms.
3. What is an analogy? What steps are necessary for people to notice and use analogies?
4. When do people tend to successfully use analogies?

➤ Algorithms involve the systematic and exhaustive application of rules for specific types of problems. Algorithms guarantee a solution if correctly applied. For human problem solvers, algorithms are limited in their usefulness because their exhaustive nature makes their use tedious. Also, algorithms do not exist for most everyday problems.

➤ Heuristics are rules of thumb. They're generally preferable to algorithms because they tend to be more efficient. Heuristics include means-end analysis (breaking a problem into smaller subgoals and the use of analogies (the application of previous solution procedures to current problems).

➤ Research indicates that people often fail to spontaneously make the critical connections between analogous problems. The steps necessary to make the connection are *noticing* that a relationship exists, *mapping* the problem elements, and *schema development*, detecting a general principle underlying the problems. Many failures in analogical problem solving occur in the noticing stage.

➤ Making the connection between two analogous problems is more likely if the two problems share surface features (problem elements) than if they share only structural features (the underlying relationships). However, in everyday situations, people may actually be more sensitive to structural similarity than laboratory research would indicate.

Experts: Masters of Representation and Solution

A good deal of research in the area of problem solving has been devoted to the notion of **expertise,** which can be defined as exceptional knowledge and/or performance in some specific problem domain. For some time, it was commonly believed that the exceptional performance of an expert reflected some innate capacity or talent. Since the advent of cognitive psychology in the 1950s, however, this view has given way to what might be termed an *information-processing account* of expertise (Ericsson & Charness, 1994). Rather than viewing expert performance as the product of innate capacities, many researchers now view it as an outgrowth of learning and repetition over the course of years that produces an extensive body of knowledge and an extremely well-learned set of skills. One estimate is that expertise involves approximately 10 years of continuous exposure to a given domain, comprising thousands of hours of practice (Ericsson & Charness, 1994).

For the past 50 years, researchers have investigated differences in the cognitive processing of experts and novices. Table 11.3 provides a list of some of the areas in which researchers have investigated expert performance (based on Vicente & Wang, 1998). To some extent, experts might be considered *skilled memorizers* (Deakin & Allard, 1991); in fact, one popular framework for explaining expertise effects in problem solving is termed *skilled-memory theory* (Ericsson & Polson, 1988). According to this framework, there are a number of fundamental differences between experts and novices, all to the advantage of experts. First, the semantic networks that we talked about in Chapter 9 are much more richly elaborated in experts. Second, experts have quicker and more direct access to long-term memory. Third, information is more easily encoded into long-term memory by experts, and the speed of this encoding improves with practice. It is critical to note here that these memory skills seem to be specific to the domain in which they were acquired in the first place; there's no reason to believe that a waiter who's exceptionally good at remembering drink orders is going to be exceptionally good at remembering chessboard configurations (although some evidence indicates that there can be transfer of expertise; see Kimball & Holyoak, 2000, for a brief review).

Table 11.3 The Many Areas of Expertise Investigated by Problem-Solving Researchers

chess	gymnastics
computer programming	figure skating
medical diagnosis	basketball
bridge	ballet
Othello	algebra
baseball	musical notation
field hockey	maps
football	soap opera knowledge
serving tables	soccer

ANALYZING YOUR EXPERTISE

Table 11.3 lists over a dozen areas of expertise that have been investigated by cognitive researchers. Below are some of the advantages that experts have over novices:

richer semantic networks
faster retrieval from memory
faster encoding into memory

Consider some area of your "personal expertise"; it can be anything—a game you're good at, a skill you've developed at work, athletic performance.

1. Reflect on how your expertise demonstrates these characteristics.
2. Compare your performance in your domain with that of a novice.

Expert Advantages

The core of problem solving is memory—the long-term memory that allows for the storage of domain-related general knowledge and specific episodes and the working memory that allows for quick and efficient online processing of problem information. A groundbreaking investigation of expert memory was conducted by de Groot (1946/1978), who investigated memory in chess players of varying skill levels by presenting them with brief glimpses of meaningful board positions and then having them reconstruct the boards. Perhaps not surprisingly, recall differed as a function of expertise, with the best players recalling the boards almost perfectly.

Another classic study by Chase and Simon (1973) replicated de Groot's findings but included an encoding condition in which the chess pieces were randomly rearranged to find out whether the advantage enjoyed by experts was a general one (good working memory overall) or a specific one (exceptionally good working memory for chess game configurations the experts had seen before). Interestingly, while expert chess players remembered game configurations better than novices, they demonstrated no superiority in memory for random board configurations. Chase and Simon explained the superiority in the former condition by appealing to the notion of chunking in working memory (discussed in Chapter 4). According to this account, experts can instantly recognize game board configurations based on their extensive knowledge and experience base. As a result, they can easily and quickly chunk pieces, and these chunks become increasingly larger and more complex; each of the 7 ± 2 (the magical number) chunks in memory contains more information.

Later evidence has demonstrated that the superior memory exhibited by the experts in these studies is not an exclusive function of working memory, because it doesn't seem subject to many of the limits you read about in Chapter 4. For example, Charness (1976) found that expert memory for chess positions was not diminished by delay, even with an interfering task. Also, Gobet and Simon (1996) found that chess masters who quickly glimpsed several game boards were able to process more chunks than the typical view of working memory would allow. Ericsson and Kintsch (1995) propose the idea of **long-term working memory** to explain expert advantages in online processing. Basically, this theory states that experts can bypass the limits of working memory by using the information in working memory to directly access LTM; in essence, working memory serves as a retrieval cue for information in LTM.

Aside from the general advantages in the power and efficiency of memory within their domain area, expert problem solvers also use general strategies that differ from those of novices. For example, Chi, Feltovich, and Glaser (1981) found that experts tend to search problem space in a forward fashion, reasoning from givens toward the goal. Novices, on the other hand, tend to think about the goal and reason backward about the steps that will lead there. Also, experts are much better at picking up on structural features of problems, whereas novices are more likely to focus on surface features. Given what you've learned about analogy, you've probably inferred (correctly) that experts are more likely to recognize analogous problems or situations when faced with a new problem or situation (within their area of expertise).

Another perspective on expertise is proposed by Lemaire and Siegler (1995), who conceptualize differences between novices and experts in terms of strategy use. Their Adaptive Strategy Model proposes four "layers" of difference, the first being *strategy existence*. Although experts and novices may have some strategies in common, experts have many more at their disposal. A second layer is *strategy base rate*, which refers to the notion that experts in a given domain know which strategies tend to work generally, and are biased toward selecting those strategies. The third layer is *strategy choice*, which refers to experts' advantage in discerning which strategies should be chosen for a specific circumstance. Finally, *strategy execution* refers to the expert advantage over the novice in actually carrying out the strategy, in terms of speed and accuracy. The Adaptive Strategy Model has been quite successful as an account of problem solving across a wide variety of domains, from something as simple and well defined as children learning multiplication (Lemaire & Siegler, 1995) to something as complex and ill defined as platoon leadership in the Army (Schunn, McGregor, & Saner, 2005).

Expert Disadvantages: Costs of Expertise

Although experts enjoy tremendous advantages in processing (primarily within their own domains), there is what might be considered a "downside" to expertise. For example, in the Chase and Simon (1973) study, novices were actually a little better at recall of randomly arranged chess pieces. Also, some studies of medical expertise (e.g., Rikers, Schmidt, & Boshuizen, 2000; Schmidt & Boshuizen, 1993) have revealed that those at an intermediate level of knowledge (e.g., residents in a teaching hospital) actually remember more information about specific patient cases than do experts (e.g., experienced physicians); this has been termed the **intermediate effect**. Rikers et al. (2000) offer an "encapsulation hypothesis" to account for the intermediate effect, proposing that medical experts chunk case information into higher-level summarizing concepts, and then tend to recall these concepts rather than the specific case information. A study by Wimmers, Schmidt, Verkoeijen, and van de Wiel (2005) suggests that when experts are

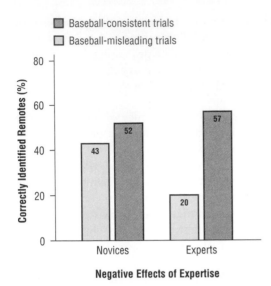

Negative Effects of Expertise

Figure 11.13 Results from Wiley's (1998) study of mental set.

From Wiley, J. (1998). Expertise as mental set: The effects of domain knowledge in creative problem solving. *Memory and Cognition, 26,* 716–730. Reprinted by permission of the Psychonomic Society, Inc.

required to more explicitly elaborate on the cases they are encoding, the expected expert advantage emerges. This suggests that experts tend to chunk information into higher-level organizing concepts that might gloss over detail. When asked to recall case information, they tend to recall these higher-level concepts at the expense of finer details (unless specifically asked to provide it).

An investigation by Wiley (1998) suggests that expertise itself may actually function as a type of mental set. In her experiment, Wiley wanted to find out whether expertise might prevent solvers from coming up with creative solutions to problems, due to their tendency to think of things in an automatic, expertise-driven fashion. She employed the Remote Associates Test (RAT), in which solvers look at three apparently unrelated words and generate one word that ties the triplet together. For example, if presented with *apple, family, house,* the remote associate is *tree* (apple *tree,* family *tree,* and *tree*house). The ability to make the connection between the three terms and come up with the remote associate is taken as a sign of creativity.

Wiley tested experts and novices in baseball, presenting them with RAT items. On all trials, the first word (e.g., *plate*) formed a baseball phrase (home plate). The remote associate (*home*) was further supported by the second word (e.g., *broken*—broken home). However, the third word presented was the critical one. On baseball-consistent trials, the third word presented (e.g., *rest*) was also consistent with the baseball interpretation of the remote associate (rest home). This was not the case on baseball-misleading trials; to the contrary, although a baseball-related word seemed likely given the first two words, the third word rendered the baseball-related term incorrect (e.g., *plate, broken, shot—glass*).

Can you see where this experiment is going? Wiley suspected that baseball experts would be likely to start thinking *baseball* as soon as they saw the word *plate,* the result being that they would be stumped if the final word didn't match the word they had generated. The results supported her hypothesis. As you can see in Figure 11.13, performance of the expert subjects was very poor if they were misled; their ability to make creative connections was stifled by their tendency to think in terms of their area of expertise.

 **STOP** *and* **REVIEW!**

1. Define expertise.
2. True or false? Expertise is a skill that extends beyond a given problem domain.
3. Explain the advantages experts have over novices.

➤ Expertise (exceptional knowledge and/or performance in some specific problem domain) is due to learning and repetition over years that produce an extensive body of knowledge and an extremely well-learned set of skills.

➤ According to skilled-memory theory, knowledge networks are more richly elaborated in experts. Experts have quicker and more direct access to long-term memory and more quickly and easily encode information into long-term memory. Expert memory skills are limited to the domain of expertise.

➤ Experts seem able to bypass the limits of working memory by using WM information to access LTM directly. Processing advantages of experts come at the expense of memory for detail. The intermediate effect indicates that people with intermediate knowledge are better at detail retention. The tendency to think within an area of expertise can serve as a mental set.

Insight and Creativity

At the end of the last section, you read about a study in which experts were actually a bit impeded in problem solving due to their expertise. You shouldn't take the results of this study as evidence that expertise generally inhibits creativity; quite the contrary, the extensive knowledge and processing proficiency possessed by experts is important in their ability to find creative solutions. In this section, we'll take a closer look at the notion of creativity—what exactly is it? What are the processes that lead to creative products? For that matter, what *are* creative products? Can creativity be measured? Enhanced? Exhibited by anybody?

Based on an extensive analysis of several cases in which great thinkers made significant breakthroughs, Wallas (1926) proposed that the processes leading up to a creative breakthrough can be described in terms of four stages. In the first stage of *preparation,* the solver gathers information and makes initial attempts at problem solution. This initial stage corresponds roughly to the problem-representation phase of processing discussed earlier. Often, these attempts are stymied, leading to a period of *incubation,* which might be described as productive inactivity. You may have had the experience that when you were trying to solve a problem, putting it aside for a time seemed to allow for a breakthrough. We'll examine the empirical evidence for this experience later. After the incubation period, the problem solver arrives at a critical insight—an important realization or understanding that leads to what Wallas termed *illumination*. Ever see a cartoon where a lightbulb appears over a character's head? A solution to a problem has occurred suddenly, probably with a tangible "Aha!" feeling for the solver. The final stage comprising creative thought is *verification*, in which the problem solver assesses whether the solution will actually work.

The Wallas framework provides a useful description of problem solving but is, by no means, an accepted theory. It was based on Wallas's introspections about the creative process and case studies on the introspections of creative individuals. Although too vague to really test, the theory has provided fodder for two of the more intriguing questions in problem-solving research. First, what is the nature of the ubiquitous experience we term *insight*? Do solutions to problems really appear out of nowhere? Second, if sudden breakthroughs in problem solving are a reality, can these be encouraged by a period of incubation?

Insight

One problem-solving phenomenon that has been a topic of extensive debate and investigation since the beginning of research on problem solving is the notion of insight. As we discussed earlier, *insight* involves the sudden realization of a problem's solution (or of a key idea necessary to the solution). The debate over the nature (or the very existence) of insight goes back to the Gestalt views of problem solving. Gestalt psychologists believe that the key to problem solution lies in a restructuring of the problem elements, which, if successful, leads to a sudden realization of the problem's solution. This sudden realization is insight. The notion of insight is controversial; many theorists believe that problem solving is an incremental process of getting closer and closer to a solution rather than a sudden realization. Another problem is that insight (until relatively recently) never has been clearly defined or experimentally demonstrated by Gestalt psychologists.

Even if insight is a reality, it would not apply to every problem. Many researchers (Gilhooly & Murphy, 2005) make a distinction between noninsight and insight problems (which can be seen as loosely analogous to the earlier distinction between ill-defined and well-defined problems). **Noninsight problems** are those that are likely solved through incremental, or "grind out the solution," processes. They require analytical, step-by-step processing—like the problems in logic, arithmetic, chess, and the like. The transformation problem called the Tower of Hanoi (previously presented in Figure 11.2) is an example of a noninsight problem—no simple breakthrough is going to give you the answer. **Insight problems** are those in which the solution appears suddenly. Figure 11.14 presents a couple of these so-called insight problems, along with a couple of noninsight problems.

Two of the key assumptions about insightful problem solving are (1) that it involves a mistaken assumption that, once removed, will clear the way to a successful solution of the problem, and (2) that the solver is hit with the solution suddenly, "out of the blue," and has what might be termed an "Aha!" experience. Let's take a look at some research that has addressed these fundamental assumptions.

Removal of a Mistaken Assumption?   The notion of insight was an integral part of much of the early work on problem solving, but as many researchers have noted (e.g., Weisberg & Alba, 1981), the concept is typically vaguely defined, and until the 1980s had

Examples of Insight Problems

Water lilies double in area every 24 hours. At the beginning of summer, there is one water lily on the lake. It takes 60 days for the lake to become completely covered with water lilies. On which day is the lake half-covered?

A prisoner was attempting to escape from a tower. He found in his cell a rope which was half long enough to permit him to reach the ground safely. He divided the rope in half, and tied the two parts together and escaped. How could he have done this?

Examples of Noninsight Problems

Three people play a game in which one person loses and two people win each round. The one who loses must double the amount of money that each of the players has at that time. The three players agree to play three games. At the end of the three games, each player has lost one game, and each person has $8. What was the original stake of each player?

Next week I am going to have lunch with my friend, visit the new art gallery, go to the social security office, and have my teeth checked at the dentist. My friend cannot meet me on Wednesday; the social security office is closed weekends; the dentist has office hours only on Tuesday, Friday, and Saturday; the art gallery is closed Tuesday, Thursday, and weekends. What day can I do everything I planned?

Figure 11.14 Some examples of insight and noninsight problems used in the study by Metcalfe and Weibe (1987).

From Metcalfe, J., & Weibe, D. (1987). Intuition in insight and noninsight problem solving. *Memory and Cognition, 15,* 238–246. Reprinted by permission of the Psychonomic Society, Inc.

not really been put to the empirical test. This may have been due in part to the intuitive appeal of the idea. But intuitive appeal and common sense are poor bases for knowledge. However, since the 1980s, insight has become one of the most hotly researched topics in problem solving. Many of these studies (e.g., Lung & Dominowski, 1985; MacGregor, Ormerod, & Chronicle, 2001;Weisberg & Alba, 1981) employed what is possibly the most thoroughly investigated insight problem, the *nine-dot problem*—in which subjects must connect all the dots with one continuous line. This problem (surprisingly difficult for most) and its solution are presented in Figure 11.15.

One focus of research has been the notion that the difficulty of insight problems is that they involve one key—but errant—perception or assumption that if removed, would lead to an easy solution. You'll recall that earlier in the chapter we discussed Duncker's candle problem and the assumption that the difficulty in solving it stems from

Figure 11.15 The nine-dot problem and solution.

From Weisberg, R. W., & Alba, J. W. (1981). An examination of the alleged role of "fixation" in the solution of several "insight" problems. *Journal of Experimental Psychology: General, 110,* 169–192. Copyright 1981 by the American Psychology Association. Reprinted by permission.

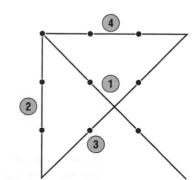

a would-be solver's failure to perceive the box of tacks in a different manner (i.e., as a candleholder). In the nine-dot problem, the mental set of staying within this boundary is the primary block that prevents successful solution. According to the notion of insight, removing this mental set should reveal an easy solution. A review of research on the nine-dot problem by Kershaw and Ohlsson (2004) takes issue with this research assumption. They contend that the difficulty with insight problems—the reason that they can't be solved with a simple hint about a faulty mental set—is that they're overdetermined. That is, they have multiple causes and sources of difficulty, rather than just one.

According to Kershaw and Ohlsson, three sources of difficulty are evident in the nine-dot problem (as well as in many other insight problems). *Perceptual factors* relate to the Gestalt organizational principles mentioned in Chapter 3—figure-ground, proximity, similarity, and the like. These affordances, or ways of initially seeing problems, can have a dramatic impact on our ability to successfully break through to a solution. *Process factors* relate to the information-processing demands of the problem, like the size of the problem space and the complexity of the solution. Finally, *knowledge factors* involve prior knowledge that a solver brings to bear on a problem. This is often where mental set can interfere, as a problem solver repeatedly tries ineffective approaches because of prior success with them in other contexts. Any combination of these factors (i.e., not just one of them) might come into play as people try to solve an insight problem and find themselves at an impasse.

The "Aha!" Experience.   Another defining feature of the insight experience is a sudden and tangible feeling of discovery, usually described as an "Aha!" experience. The issue of what someone is thinking as they think relates to metacognition. Metacognition refers to a person's knowledge of their own thought processes. In a series of clever experiments, Metcalfe (Metcalfe, 1986a; Metcalfe & Weibe, 1987) investigated the metacognition of problem solvers faced with different sorts of problems. Metcalfe and Weibe (1987) developed one of the more interesting dependent variables in cognitive psychology—*ratings of warmth* collected from problem solvers during their problem-solving attempts. You know the old "hot and cold" game when you're looking for something? If the hider tells you you're cold, you're nowhere near the hidden object; if you're hot, you're practically on top of it.

Metcalfe and Weibe adapted this game to problem solving by having subjects rate how warm they were with regard to the solution of a problem. Their reasoning was as follows: if insight involves sudden realization of the solution, solvers who are working on an insight problem should have no clue whether they're close to a solution or not, and their warmth ratings should reflect this. They should report little warmth throughout the problem-solving interval until a solution finally appears. With a noninsight problem, however, the metacognition should be different: subjects should realize that they're getting closer and closer to a solution, given the grind-it-out nature of a noninsight problem. To test their hypothesis, Metcalfe and Weibe (1987, experiment 2) presented subjects with noninsight problems and insight problems like the ones previously presented in Figure 11.14. They were allowed four minutes for each problem, and within that interval, they were to rate their warmth every 15 seconds by making a mark on a scale. In addition to rating warmth, solvers were asked to judge whether or not they would be able to solve each of the problems.

The results revealed some interesting differences in the metacognitive processes underlying the solution of insight and noninsight problems. Simply put, metacognition was not nearly as good for the insight problems. Let's take a look at the warmth ratings. These were incremental for the noninsight problems, increasing gradually throughout the solution interval. Subjects felt as if they were nearing a solution when they really were near a solution. For the insight problems, however, the warmth ratings didn't really increase at all throughout the solution interval until the problem was solved. So subjects really had no idea if and when they were approaching a solution. The other metacognitive judgment ("Will I be able to solve this problem?") paralleled the warmth ratings. For the noninsight problems, subjects were decent judges of whether they would be able to solve the problems. However, for the insight problems, subjects were relatively poor judges of solution probability. They demonstrated overconfidence, underestimating how difficult the problems were.

The results from both metacognitive judgments indicate a fundamental difference between insight and noninsight problems. Subjects' metacognitions about noninsight problems were more accurate and more predictive of actual performance. Metacognitions about insight problems tended to be unrelated to (or even negatively related to; see Metcalfe and Wiebe, 1987) the probability of eventual solution. Metcalfe and Wiebe (1987) suggest that the processes underlying the solution of insight and noninsight problems may be fundamentally different and that the pattern of warmth ratings observed during a solution can be used as an indicator of whether a problem involves insight, thereby avoiding the circularity problem in defining insight.

In a critique of the metacognitive studies of insight, Weisberg (1992) lodges a number of objections to these conclusions. He acknowledges the subjective "Aha!" experience produced by some problems but points out that this does not necessarily mean that the problems are solved suddenly, as the Gestalt position suggests. It may be that step-by-step processes are involved but that the solver is unaware of them.

Intuition as Insight.   The issue of whether insight problem solving involves special, unconscious processes—like a sudden restructuring of problem elements or removal of some mistaken  information—still stirs controversy in the field. Certainly, insight problems do seem unique phenomenologically—that is, in terms of the conscious experience that a problem solver has. Insight problem solving feels like an all-or-none process that occurs suddenly. But, as we just mentioned, an alternative conceptualization is that insight problem solving (like noninsight problem solving) is really more gradual, but the gradual progress is not open to conscious awareness.

This latter analysis of insight problem solving is supported by some fascinating research by Bowers, Regehr, Balthazard, and Parker (1990). These authors propose a two-stage model of insight (which they term *intuition*). In stage 1, the *guiding stage,* mnemonic networks relevant to the problem are activated, and this activation begins to spread. In essence, the problem solver is working on the problem unconsciously; the results of this unconscious processing may serve as a basis for a hunch or intuition regarding the solution. In stage 2 (the *integrative stage*), the buildup of activation reaches enough strength to break through into conscious awareness. This transition from stage 1 to stage 2 is insight.

Bowers and colleagues employed what they called *intuition tasks* (similar to an insight problem) to test this two-stage model of insight. One experiment used what the researchers termed the *dyads of triads* task, adapted from the Remote Associates Test you read about earlier. Subjects were faced with two triads of words (e.g., *notch-flight-spin* and *clear-role-force*). For one of the triads, the words had a common associate; for the other one, no common associate existed. (In this example, words in the first triad all relate to *top;* words in the second triad have no common associate.) Subjects were given 8 to 12 seconds to solve each triad; if they couldn't, they were asked to give a simple guess about which of the two triads was *coherent*—in other words, which triad was the one that could be related to one word. They also rated their confidence in this judgment.

Let's relate the procedure to the two-stage model of insight and see what predictions the model generates. According to this view, when faced with the three words in a triad, unconscious processes immediately begin working on a problem (the guiding stage). Although solvers cannot report on these processes, evidence for the solution is building up unconsciously through spreading activation, which can serve as the basis for a hunch, or intuition, about the answer. This hunch should allow subjects to succeed on the second task, picking which of the triads is coherent, even if they can't come up with the solution (i.e., even if they never reach the integrative stage).

The results provided support for the researchers' proposal. Subjects were able to guess which triad was coherent at a rate well above chance, even when they couldn't come up with the solution. This suggests that incremental processes outside conscious awareness are at work on a problem, providing evidence for hunches or intuitions that are not open to the conscious awareness necessary for accurate metacognitive judgments. This may explain why Metcalfe (1986a, b; Metcalfe & Weibe, 1987) found that warmth judgments were poor indicators of whether solvers were close to an answer; subjects were getting closer to the solution, but they were not consciously aware of it. An appropriate analogy might be to liken the process to that of a sunrise (Wittgenstein, 1969): "Our subjective experience is that the new day suddenly dawns, but the amount of light actually grows continuously over a fairly protracted period of time" (Siegler, 2000, p. 79). When solving problems, you may have the subjective experience that you arrived at the solution suddenly, when in reality you were (unconsciously) approaching that solution incrementally.

Does Incubation Lead to Insight?   One of the more controversial notions within the study of problem solving is **incubation,** or the idea that taking a break in problem solving leads to a quicker solution than does continuing effort. The idea is that the break allows for the elements of the problem to be reorganized or for unconscious processes to continue to work on the problem (perhaps as described above) and that this unconscious processing will not take place if conscious work on the problem continues. The anecdotal evidence for incubation is strong; everyday problem solvers, including scientists, artists, and writers, often observe that some critical realization or breakthrough occurs only after a period of frustration and setting the problem aside (Wallas, 1926). However, anecdotal evidence is viewed skeptically by scientists. As intuitive as it seems, this phenomenon has proved to be elusive quarry for problem-solving researchers, who, more often than not, have failed to find incubation effects (e.g., Dominowski & Jenrick, 1972; Olton, 1979; Olton & Johnson, 1976).

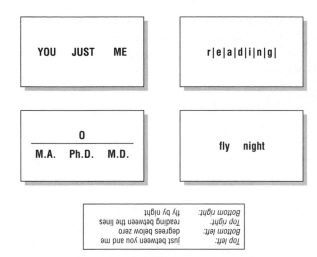

YOU   JUST   ME

r|e|a|d|i|n|g|

0
_____
M.A.   Ph.D.   M.D.

fly   night

Top left: just between you and me
Bottom left: degrees below zero
Top right: reading between the lines
Bottom right: fly by night

Figure 11.16 Sample rebus problems: Can you come up with the saying represented by each?

From Smith, S. M., & Blankenship, S. E. (1989). Incubation effects. *Bulletin of the Psychonomic Society, 27,* 311–314. Reprinted by permission of the Psychonomic Society, Inc.

Smith (1995) suggests that incubation effects do occur, but only under specific circumstances—namely, when a problem is doable and when the solver is blocked in some way from the solution. The incubation period allows the interfering information to be forgotten, clearing the way for a solution. This effect was nicely demonstrated in a study by Smith and Blankenship (1989). In this study, subjects attempted to solve rebus problems—basically, word puzzles in which pictures and words are used to indicate a common phrase. Some examples are given in Figure 11.16. In their experiment, Smith and Blankenship had subjects solve these puzzles; for some, they provided a pair of misleading cue words. For example, in the fourth rebus problem presented in the figure, *fly* and *night* were presented as misleading cues; they're misleading because they suggest two compound words that are not correct solutions (i.e., *flypaper* and *overnight*). Then the researchers retested unsolved rebuses either immediately or after varying periods of incubation. After attempting to solve the rebus again, subjects were asked to recall the cue word that went along with it originally. Consistent with Smith's (1995) analysis, longer break periods were associated with higher probabilities of solution. Memory for the misleading cues provides a possible explanation; memory for the misleading cues decreased as incubation time increased. Apparently, as the misleading cue was forgotten, the problem became more solvable.

Smith (1995) offers a contextual view of incubation, which is basically the encoding specificity principle in reverse. If you'll recall from Chapter 6, the *encoding specificity principle* states that retrieval will be effective to the degree that retrieval conditions match encoding conditions. The *contextual view* of incubation states that when problem solving is stymied, a solution will come more easily if there is a contextual change from the previous situation. Essentially, staying in the same situation continually reinstates the circumstances in which the failure to find a solution was first encountered, increasing the likelihood that the failure will continue. Changing the environment prevents this reinstatement, making success more likely. Smith provides some anecdotal support for this idea, noting that a number of famous cases of incubation followed by insight took place when the problem solver was in a completely different environment than usual.

One example of a decidedly different environment in which incubation might lead to a problem-solving breakthrough is . . . sleep! Categorically different from the waking state in many ways, you must agree. But as you know, the brain is far from inactive during sleep, and there is many an anecdote of thinkers having some type of creative breakthrough during sleep. For example, Kekule's discovery of the structure of the organic compound benzene seems to have resulted from a special process like sudden restructuring or insight that reportedly occurred after he had dreamed about snakes biting each other's tails. Recent empirical research seems to bear out the anecdotal suggestion that sleep aids in creative insights (see Wagner, Gais, Haider, Verleger, & Born, 2004).

Creativity

When someone has an insight, demonstrating the ability to hurdle over the problem-solving obstacles that block us mere mortals, what do we say about them? It's quite likely that we would comment on their **creativity**. Creative individuals are able to think "outside the box"—to come up with new ideas, view old problems from a fresh perspective, and connect seemingly disparate problem situations. Because creativity might seem like the pinnacle of thought in many ways, it might surprise you to learn that it hadn't received much attention in psychology until J. P. Guilford issued a wake-up call at the 1950 meeting of the American Psychological Association in his presidential address. Even relatively recently, some (e.g., Sternberg & Lubart, 1996) have decried the lack of research in the area, relative to its importance. But the last couple of decades or so have witnessed a considerable surge in research into the creative process, from a breathtakingly diverse range of perspectives. And according to Runco (2004), it's a good thing, because the understanding of creativity is of paramount importance today, as technological advances occur in the blink of an eye, and the world becomes increasingly complex.

What Is Creativity?   Experts on creativity generally agree that creative solutions have two components—novelty and appropriateness (Lubart, 1994; Sternberg, 2004). Creative solutions are novel, different from previous solutions, and usually unexpected. Yet surprise and originality alone do not make a problem solution creative. The solution must also satisfy the constraints of the problem at hand; it must fulfill a need and be sensible and useful. Let's think back to your end-of-semester problem. One "solution" to the problem might be to fake your death. That way, you wouldn't need to hand in the assignments or take the tests. Although it certainly fulfills the criterion of novelty, this solution is entirely inappropriate, failing to fit within the problem constraints. It would be considered aberrant rather than creative.

One of the most-cited frameworks for describing and investigating creativity was originally proposed by Rhodes (1961/1987), who suggested that creativity can be informed by a focus on several dimensions, which he labeled *person, process, press*, and *product*. Sternberg (2005) has a similar proposal, suggesting that there are discriminable *creativities*, rather than one general monolithic characteristic, that we can label *creativity*.

Person.   First, there is evidence that creativity, to some extent, is related to aspects of the *person*, or personality. Creative persons are thought to exhibit a number of personality characteristics, including broad interests, appreciation of complexity, tolerance of ambiguity, self-confidence, independence, and sensible risk taking (Barron & Harrington, 1981; Feist, 1999). In addition, creative individuals seem to have a high degree of intrinsic motivation for their fields (Amabile, 1990). Runco (2004) adds other important defining characteristics of creative people: flexibility and reactivity. The creative individual must be flexible and able to react effectively to changes in technology, circumstances, and opportunity.

Simonton (2000) also notes some developmental aspects of creativity, characterizing it as a constantly developing ability rather than a static attribute that some lucky folks are born with. According to Simonton's review (and perhaps counter to intuition), creativity is not always the product of a particularly *comfortable* environment. In fact, a person's potential to exhibit creativity seems dependent on having had a diverse set of life experiences, which then enhance an individual's ability to take fresh perspectives. Creative potential also depends on a person having faced sufficiently challenging life experiences, which helps develop the ability to persevere (Simonton, 1994). Such perseverance is important for creative problem solving, which, by definition, includes numerous obstacles. It's useful at this point to note the correlational nature of this personality data. It's not clear whether creativity is the *product* of or the *cause* of this type of personality. It could also be the case that some third variable leads to the emergence of someone with propensities toward creativity and these particular personality characteristics.

Process.   Creativity can also refer to a specific set of *processes*. Two contradictory ideas about cognitive processing in creativity have been proffered—one view asserts that creativity involves special processes and abilities, like the ability to quickly restructure problem information and to connect seemingly remote possibilities. Conversely, another view contends that creative thinking is the product of the garden-variety cognitive processing that we've discussed throughout the text, such as attention and memory. So which view is closer to the truth? The **creative cognition approach** (Smith, 2003; Smith, Ward, & Finke, 1994) argues that the answer is probably that creative thinking can be the result of *either* type of process, or of both.

What specific cognitive processes seem to be important? You've no doubt picked up on some of them in our foregoing survey of problem solving. Two that seem especially important are attention and memory. That might seem obvious, so let's get a little more specific. Attentional deployment seems to be important in creativity. More specifically, wide and diffuse attentional deployment seems to be associated with creative problem solving (Martindale & Greenough, 1973; Wallach, 1970). Memory in the form of general knowledge is also vital. Recall the discussion of expertise earlier in the chapter; experts have a larger knowledge base from which to work, enhancing their chances of producing a creative solution, relative to a novice in the area. However, as you read earlier, expertise can also inhibit problem solving in cases where expertise functions as a mental set, as in the Wiley (1998) study.

Sternberg and Davidson (1982; Davidson, 1995) cite three processes as important in reaching creative insights. *Selective encoding* involves distinguishing between relevant and irrelevant information in the domain of expertise. Creative individuals are better at distinguishing useful information from red herrings. *Selective combination* involves going beyond discovering and encoding the information to the combination of that information in new and productive ways. Finally, *selective comparison* involves relating new information to old information in novel ways. The processes involved in applying analogies from one problem to another could be considered processes of selective comparison.

Press.   Odd word choice—but Rhodes needed a "p" word, so it made the list. Press refers to the notion that creative behavior does not occur in a vacuum, that it's subject to various external pressures and contextual factors. Simonton (2000) makes a similar point. Creative acts are also products of interpersonal, disciplinary, and sociocultural environments. Research on creativity indicates a sensitivity to a number of interpersonal factors. For example, some evidence (e.g., Amabile, 1996) indicates that being evaluated by others can decrease creativity. The popular notion of **brainstorming** refers to the supposed creative benefit of generating ideas in groups. Unfortunately, research evidence fails to support a relationship between brainstorming and creativity. Still, the technique enjoys great popularity in corporate settings. Another social component of creativity is the disciplinary environment in which it takes place, in part because experts in a given area define what is deemed creative. Finally, creativity is partially dependent on the sociocultural milieu in which one's work is conducted. According to Simonton, cultural diversity enhances creativity; a civilization's creativity tends to thrive when it opens itself up to alien influences through immigration or foreign study.

Product.   The final approach to creativity in the Rhodes (1961/1987) scheme is *product,* which refers to the outcome yielded by the creative process, be it a painting, poem, design, or new technology. Quite often, this approach is applied to case analyses of famously creative individuals like Picasso, Freud, Einstein, or da Vinci. The analysis of creativity from this perspective is a challenge, as its evaluation requires some type of objective standard. One such standard is productivity; some of the most creative individuals exhibited incredibly productive periods. Analyses of these "bursts of creativity" no doubt lend some insights into the creative process (Simonton, 1984). However, productivity is a narrow window on the creative process—although productivity and creativity may be associated, *more* doesn't always mean *better.* Another problem with using famous cases to illuminate creative processes is that it's limited in generalizability and applicability. The factors that made Einstein a brilliant and creative thinker were no doubt fairly unique to his abilities and life experiences.

A Taxonomy of Creative Processes and Products.
Dietrich (2004) proposes a useful scheme that imposes some order on the disparate research into creativity. In addition, he sketches the brain systems that are implicated in each of creativity's various manifestations. Although his neuropsychological analysis is beyond the scope of our discussion here, his taxonomy does provide an interesting framework for thinking about creativity.

Dietrich's scheme is captured by the simple matrix pictured in Figure 11.17. As you can see, Dietrich characterizes creative insights as a product of two distinct dimensions: processing mode and knowledge domain. *Processing mode* refers to whether creative insight emerges as the result of a deliberate and effortful search, or whether it emerges spontaneously as an unexpected flash of insight. *Knowledge domain* refers to the nature of the creative insight, and whether it is characterized more by a cognitive or by an emotional breakthrough.

Dietrich makes a point of emphasizing that the two key dimensions are continual, rather than dichotomies. A given creative product won't necessarily fall neatly into one of the four bins pictured. According to Dietrich, examples of *deliberate-cognitive* creativity would include the deliberate piecing together of the DNA structure and the systematic approach to inventing seen in Thomas Edison's work. *Spontaneous-cognitive* creativity would include Kekule's discovery of the structure of benzene (mentioned briefly earlier

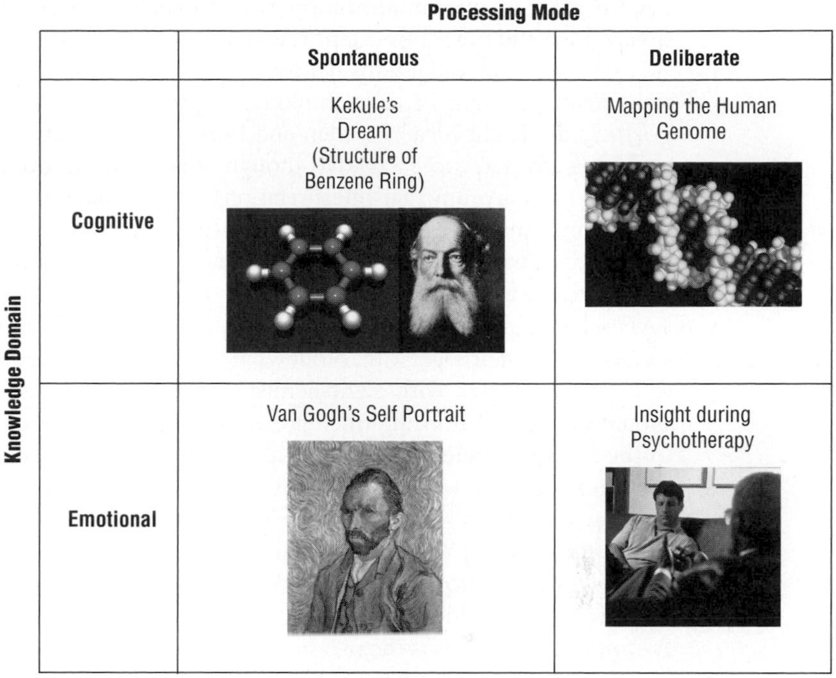

Processing Mode

		Spontaneous	Deliberate
Knowledge Domain	**Cognitive**	Kekule's Dream (Structure of Benzene Ring)	Mapping the Human Genome
	Emotional	Van Gogh's Self Portrait	Insight during Psychotherapy

Figure 11.17 Four types of creative processes/products proposed by Dietrich (2004).

From Dietrich, A. (2004). The cognitive neuroscience of creativity. *Psychonomic Bulletin & Review*, *11*(6), 1011–1026. Published by the Psychonomic Society. Adapted with permission.

in the chapter) and Newton's supposed realization of the principle of gravity upon seeing an apple fall to the ground. *Deliberate-emotional* creativity would be exemplified by the insight of a psychotherapy client who has just had an emotional breakthrough. Finally, *spontaneous-emotional* creativity would involve the intense emotional experiences that are often said to lead to artistic creation.

Creativity, Insight, and the Brain

You've seen throughout the text the important role of brain research in specifying the nature of various cognitive processes. Although creativity and insight might seem like difficult research nuts to crack, neuroscientists are beginning to get a handle on the brain processes that underlie creativity—seemingly the most mysterious of the cognitive processes.

Research Theme: Neuroscience

Hemisphericity and Creativity. As you've seen in a number of places throughout the text, one of the major questions addressed by cognitive neuroscientists is the relative role of each brain hemisphere in accomplishing various cognitive tasks. As we noted in Chapter 2, the distinction between the left and right hemispheres is quite often overgeneralized in the popular press, with the left hemisphere labeled as the constrained "logical" hemisphere and the right as the unfettered "creative" hemisphere. Although this is undoubtedly an oversimplification, recent evidence does suggest that the right hemisphere plays the more important role in creativity.

A series of investigations by Bowden and Beeman (1998) examines the role of the right hemisphere in creative thinking. Appropriately enough, their article is entitled "Getting the Right Idea." Bowden and Beeman begin with the assumption that insight problems involve more creative thought than noninsight problems, because insight problems require unusual interpretations and arrangements of problem elements. In other words, insight problems involve venturing into usually unexplored problem space.

Bowden and Beeman employed the Remote Associates Test (RAT). These researchers combined the logic of priming (which we discussed in many previous chapters) with the RAT to investigate the relative roles of the left and right hemispheres in making creative connections. Their logic was as follows: if the solution of an insight problem is associated to a greater degree with right-hemisphere activation, then solution-related concepts should show more priming when presented to the right hemisphere than when presented to the left hemisphere. In their study, subjects were presented with a word triad for 15 seconds during which subjects attempted to come up with the solution word. After they had generated the solution, or after time had run out, the screen was erased, and then a target word was presented for pronunciation. On half of the trials, this target word was the solution word for the Remote Associates Test. On the other half, the target word was a nonsolution word (a word that did not relate the three words together). Pronunciation time was the measure of interest.

Critical to note here is exactly where the target word was presented. Sometimes it was presented left of fixation (i.e., to the right hemisphere) and sometimes right of fixation (i.e., to the left hemisphere). The researchers reasoned that if the right hemisphere is more involved in creative problem solving, then pronunciation times should reveal more priming (i.e., faster pronunciation times for solution than nonsolution words) when presented to the right hemisphere. Why? Because the increased activation of the right hemisphere when solving (or attempting to solve) a problem should translate into an enhanced ability to say the solution word relative to saying the nonsolution word.

The results are shown in Figure 11.18a. What you see are priming scores. These scores were calculated by taking pronunciation times for nonsolution words (which boils down to basic word-naming RT) and subtracting the reaction times for solution words. Remember—these were the words on which subjects had actively been working, so no doubt this "active work" served to speed up identification. The figure plots this increase in reaction time.

First, take a look at the solved-problem condition—here you see a priming effect in the reading of solution words, regardless of which hemisphere they were presented to; however, there was significantly more priming for words presented to the *right hemisphere* than there was for words presented to the left hemisphere, indicating greater activation in the right hemisphere. Now look at the unsolved problems, which offer an even more compelling picture. In this condition, subjects looked at the three words, but were unable to generate the solution word. In this situation, a priming effect was found *only* for words presented to the right hemisphere (the small priming effect in the left hemisphere was not significantly greater than 0). This indicates that when a solution has not yet been consciously reached, the right hemisphere "knows what's coming," and is speeded

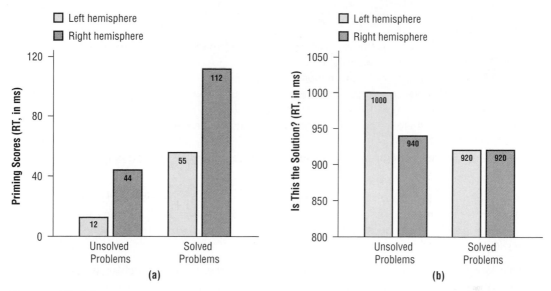

Figure 11.18   Results from Bowden and Beeman's (1998) study of hemispheric activation during insight problem solving.

From Bowden, E. M., & Beeman, M. J. (1998). Getting the right idea: Semantic activation in the right hemisphere may help solve insight problems. *Psychological Science, 9,* 435–440. Copyright 1998 by Blackwell, Inc. Reprinted by permission.

up in naming the solution word. The left hemisphere doesn't know what's coming, and is not speeded up.

In a follow-up study, Bowden and Beeman used exactly the same procedure but changed the required response. After presentation of the target word, subjects had to make a simple yes or no response—yes if the word was the solution word, or no if it wasn't. The results are presented in Figure 11.18b. Not surprisingly, there was no difference between the right and left hemispheres for solved problems. Given that the solution had already been figured out, saying yes or no was trivially easy for either hemisphere. More interesting is the unsolved problem data. In this situation, subjects were still engaged in solution processes. As you can see, the right hemisphere was much faster than the left hemisphere at classifying whether the presented word was the solution or not, indicating that only the right hemisphere was "aware" of the solution.

Subsequent research by Jung-Beeman, Bowden, and colleagues (e.g., Beeman & Bowden, 2000; Bowden & Jung-Beeman, 2003; Bowden, Jung-Beeman, Fleck, & Kounios, 2005) has clarified and extended this analysis of how creative problem solving occurs in the brain. For example, Bowden et al. (2005) found insightful problem solving to be associated with a couple of distinct neural signatures. First, brain-imaging results from fMRI scans revealed increased activity in a right-hemisphere area termed the *anterior superior temporal gyrus,* relative to activity during noninsight solutions. In addition, EEG recordings made during insight problem solving revealed a sudden burst of neural activity in this same region immediately preceding insight solutions.

STOP *and* **REVIEW!**

1. The illumination phase of problem solving is synonymous with
   a. insight.
   b. incubation.
   c. problem representation.
   d. creativity.
2. Describe the major difference between noninsight and insight problems.
3. What is incubation?
4. True or false? The left hemisphere seems particularly important in the solution of insight problems.

➤ Wallas proposes a four-stage model of problem solving. In the preparation stage, the solver gathers information. This is followed by a period of incubation (productive inactivity), which leads to illumination or insight (sudden realization of a problem's solution); the solution is checked in a verification phase.

➤ Noninsight problems are solved through incremental processes; insight problems are those in which the solution appears suddenly. Research has cast some doubt on the assumption that insight involves an "all-or-none" breakthrough, although metacognitive research verifies that people do have an "Aha!" experience as they arrive at the solution to an insight problem.

➤ It is not clear whether a period of incubation (taking a break from problem solving) enhances problem solving, but a problem's solution can be preceded by unconscious activation of problem-related concepts. One view of incubation states that a contextual change from the solution-blocking situation increases the likelihood of finding a solution.

➤ Creative problem solving is viewed as the product of a number of disparate influences, including aspects of the person, cognitive processing, and the particular context and pressures at play. Right-hemisphere activation seems to be particularly important in arriving at creative insights.

GLOSSARY

algorithm: a set of rules that can be applied systematically to solve certain types of problems (p. 457)

analogies: using problems that have already been solved as aids for representing and solving the problem currently being faced (p. 460)

arrangement problems: problems in which the solver must figure out how to put together the problem elements (p. 443)

brainstorming: the practice of generating ideas in a group setting, with no constraints on what can be suggested (p. 478)

creative cognition approach: the view that creative thinking involves both special and ordinary cognitive processing (p. 477)

creativity: the ability to come up with novel and appropriate solutions to problems (p. 476)

deduction problems: problems in which premises are given and the solver must determine whether a conclusion fits these premises (p. 443)

divergent problems: problems in which the solver must generate as many solutions as possible to a given problem (p. 443)

expertise: exceptional knowledge and/or performance in some specific problem domain (p. 465)

functional fixedness: people's tendency to view objects in a narrow, fixed sense—that is, in terms of the typical uses of the object (p. 451)

General Problem Solver (GPS): a general computer model of problem solving that works by minimizing the "distance" between an initial state and a goal state by breaking a problem into a series of subgoals (p. 447)

goal state: the solution to a problem (p. 440)

heuristics: general strategies, or "rules of thumb," that can be applied to various problems (p. 457)

ill-defined problem: a problem that is poorly structured; the initial state, goal state, and constraints are not well understood, and once you reach a solution, it's not easy to assess (p. 440)

incubation: the idea that taking a break in problem solving leads to a quicker solution than does continuing effort (p. 474)

induction problems: problems in which the solver is given a series of instances and must figure out the rule that relates the instances (p. 443)

initial state: the situation that exists at the beginning of a problem (p. 440)

insight: the sudden and successful restructuring of problem elements to reach a solution (p. 446)

insight problems: problems in which the solution appears suddenly (p. 470)

intermediate effect: the finding that those at an intermediate level of knowledge actually remember more information than do experts (p. 467)

law of effect: Thorndike's principle of associative learning that if a response leads to a satisfying outcome, the connection between the response and the situation in which it took place will be strengthened; if a response leads to a nonsatisfying outcome, that connection will be weakened (p. 445)

long-term working memory: the theory that experts bypass the limits of working memory by using the information in working memory to directly access long-term memory (p. 467)

means-end analysis: breaking a problem into smaller subgoals, where accomplishing each subgoal moves the solver closer to the solution (p. 459)

mental set: the tendency to rely on habits and procedures used in the past (p. 450)

noninsight problems: problems that are likely to be solved through incremental processes (p. 470)

nonroutine problem: a problem that requires the application of unfamiliar procedures in order to reach a solution (p. 441)

operators: problem-solving techniques (p. 447)

problem: a situation in which we're faced with an initial state, a goal state, a set of rules that must be followed, and a set of obstacles that must be overcome (p. 440)

problem representation: the process of correctly identifying the initial state as well as the operators that may be applied within the constraints of the problem (p. 449)

problem solving: the processes involved in moving from an initial state to a goal state, in the face of constraints that must be observed and obstacles that must be overcome (p. 440)

problem space: the problem solver's mental representation of the initial state, goal states, all intermediate (subgoal) states, and the operators that can be applied to reach these subgoals (p. 447)

routine problem: a problem that can be solved by applying well-practiced procedures (p. 440)

stereotype threat: a situation that occurs when a member of a negatively stereotyped group feels that their behavior might fit the stereotype, thus perpetuating it (p. 454)

structural features: the underlying relationships among the elements of a problem (p. 462)

subgoal analysis: breaking a problem into a series of subgoals (p. 447)

surface features: the specific elements of a problem (p. 462)

transformation problems: problems in which the solver must find the proper strategies, or "moves,"

that will eventually convert the initial state into the goal state (p. 443)

verbal protocols: reports generated by problem solvers as they "think out loud" during the solution process (p. 442)

well-defined problems: problems that are clear and structured and in which the initial state, goal state, and constraints are all understood (p. 440)

12

Reasoning, Judgment, and Decision Making

People sometimes make ill-advised choices, or adopt beliefs that don't seem very sound. In fact, they're outright illogical. What are some of the basic steps in logical reasoning, and what are some of the factors that trip people up?

Sometimes you make decisions quickly, based on an intuition or hunch. Other times you make decisions after a long and laborious process of weighing and considering alternatives. How do these modes of reasoning differ? Which one is better, or more likely to lead to a rational choice?

Why is it that people seem to inflate beyond reason the likelihood of certain bad things happening? For example, after the September 11 terrorist attacks in 2001, many people were afraid to fly. It seems that this dramatic rise in fear was unjustified. But why did it occur?

"I could have told you that would happen." You hear it all the time, and you've probably said it yourself. The counter to this mundane claim is, "Yeah, well, hindsight is 20/20." Do our hindsight judgments and views of events reflect what we really would have thought or said beforehand, in foresight?

Consider the following evaluations:

- If you don't manage your time effectively, then you aren't going to do well in your classes.
  My roommate is bombing all of his classes.
  He's not very good at time management.

- All my professors are cool.
  Cool people wouldn't get worked up about extending a paper deadline.
  So my professor shouldn't have a problem with giving the class an extra week.
- There's been a "pop" quiz every other Monday for two months.
  It's Sunday night, two weeks after the last quiz.
  I'd better get ready for a quiz tomorrow.
- Boy, that guy is sure a tall drink of water.
  He's at least 6' 6".
  He must be a basketball player.
- Should I buy that brand of new truck?
  The consumer magazines rave about it, but a friend of my brother's bought one, and
      it was a real lemon.
  I'd better not.

Complex Thinking:
Reasoning, Judgment, and Decision Making

Each of these seemingly simple evaluations is actually quite complex at its core. Each involves making certain assumptions and arriving at a conclusion. For some, there is incomplete or missing information; others entail an educated guess. In other words, each scenario involves the processes we'll be discussing next: **reasoning, judgment,** and **decision making.** It's appropriate that a book about the processes of cognition ends with a chapter on complex thought processes that put all of the component parts of cognition together. Think about it (hopefully, after reading this text, you've grown fond of that phrase): In each case, your attention is required to take in the information; pattern recognition helps you to identify the elements within each scenario; working memory allows you to consider the alternatives; long-term memory serves as the database from which you build your assumptions; and language allows you to express and process each of the assertions.

The chapter title—"Reasoning, Judgment, and Decision Making"—connotes that each of these elements depends on different processes and/or presents different challenges. The major difference among them seems to relate primarily to what each requires. Reasoning involves evaluation of a conclusion based solely on given information. Decision making and judgment require that you go beyond the information given. With judgment, you apply reasoning processes about given information, but you must use the given information to arrive at a conclusion (rather than simply evaluate a given conclusion). The pop quiz example involves judgment; you discern a pattern in particular events and form a conclusion (i.e., "Pop quizzes occur every two weeks"). Unlike in the first two examples, you must go beyond the information given.

Decision making involves an even further progression beyond the given information—to situations that involve uncertainty or risk. In decision making, you must evaluate given information, arrive at a judgment, and, based on this judgment, make a choice among several possible alternatives. This is "risky," because it involves a considerable amount of guesswork. Decision-making situations often provide limited information or require a degree of knowledge or computational skill that is well beyond the range of what humans can do. Take the car-buying scenario above; there's no possible way you can know every fact about every car, and there is no easy way to combine what information you have to arrive at the correct choice. Indeed, in this case, it's not even clear what the correct choice would be! So in cases of decision making, we stray well beyond the given information into uncertain territory.

The Focus on Errors

As you'll see, the emphasis in research on reasoning, judgment, and decision making has been on the mistakes people make. In fact, after reading about all of the ways in which these processes go wrong, you may think that people are idiots. Quite the contrary; errors may be seen as the price we pay for quick and efficient processing. So why the emphasis on error? One reason, noted by Nobel Prize–winning psychologist Daniel Kahneman (1991), is informativeness. The conditions under which our thinking fails us reveal important aspects of cognitive processing. You've seen a number of examples of this throughout the text; theories of memory have been richly informed by the phenomena of memory distortion (Chapter 7); the nature of automaticity is revealed by our susceptibility to action slips (Chapter 4). Along the same lines, the patterns of error that are evident in reasoning, judgment, and decision making inform us about how these processes typically operate.

The fact that so much research focuses on errors begs a question: How exactly do we know that a given chain of reasoning, judgment, or decision making is in error? What is the benchmark against which we compare people's thinking in order to evaluate whether the thinking was accurate or proper? This question relates to a distinction researchers make between two approaches to the study of reasoning, judgment, and decision making. One approach, termed a **normative approach,** describes how we *ought* to think in a given situation. As you'll see, we often fall short of this ideal, so researchers have developed what is termed a **descriptive approach.** This approach, as the label would imply, describes how we actually *do* think.

Let's consider an example that allows for a comparison of the approaches. Suppose a woman told you that she has 10 children—all boys. Suppose you were then asked to estimate the probability of her having a girl in her next pregnancy. What would be your answer? According to a normative analysis, your answer should be 50/50. But people often overestimate the probability of the next child being a girl. They look at the long run of boys, and because this seems so unusual and unlikely, they think that it is especially likely that the situation will "return to normal" (in other words, become half boys and half girls). One descriptive model of judgment claims that people use a principle termed *representativeness.* (We'll discuss this principle in more detail later; here, we'll keep it simple.) In this example, people will see 10 boys in a row as very nonrepresentative of what should happen in 10 pregnancies. For this sequence to be representative, there should be as many boys as girls; therefore, a girl being born next will be seen as especially likely. Although this judgment violates the principles of basic probability (which serve as the normative model here), people often make it. As you'll see, normative models of reasoning, judgment, and decision making are not always a reasonable standard against which to compare human thought. People aren't calculators and few are statisticians, so they usually don't have all of the information they need to follow a normative model.

Bounded Rationality.   You're going to see throughout this chapter that people violate normative models of reasoning, judgment, and decision making. Does this mean that human beings are irrational? As we'll see, there is no one simple answer to this question. Adherence to or deviance from rational thought and behavior depends on a variety of factors, not to mention exactly how we define *rational*. Baron (1999) contends that rationality is not necessarily the same as accuracy (getting the "right" answer), and that irrationality is not necessarily the same as error (getting the "wrong" answer). By Baron's analysis, rationality involves choosing the methods that help us attain our goals, whatever those may be. We can reason well but still have a decision work out badly; conversely, we can reason badly yet still luck into a good outcome.

The simple notion that there are limits to our powers of reason—that we show what is termed **bounded rationality**—isn't disputed. However, there are some profound differences of interpretation when it comes to how one should view bounded rationality. In many ways, these differing views represent a version of the glass as half empty/half full debate. As stated earlier, historically most of the research evidence on these processes has seen the glass as half empty. It's focused on errors and has used them as a vehicle to examine what's *wrong* with the human reasoner, judger, or decision maker, and how their conclusions, judgments, and decisions might differ from the "rational" standard. The more recent approach (championed by Gigerenzer and colleagues) has been to view the heuristics used by human thinkers as "simple heuristics that make us smart" (Gigerenzer & Todd, 1999). The approaches you're going to read about in the coming pages are not signs of stupid humans making mistake after mistake; rather, they are signs of extremely well-adapted humans making the best decisions possible given cognitive limitations and contextual demands.

It's interesting to note that this debate is symptomatic of a wider trend in psychological theory and research. For nearly a century, many would claim that psychology has accentuated the negative aspects of human mental processes and behavior. From clinical psychologists' focus on psychopathology to social psychologists' emphasis on the dark side of human behavior as evidenced by studies of social influence to cognitive psychologists' emphasis on errant cognitions such as memory distortion and reasoning errors, it's clear that human failings have fascinated psychologists. The current trend in the field is to investigate more positive aspects of human behavior—what humans do right. The entire field of *positive psychology* is a testament to this emerging trend (also, see Krueger & Funder, 2004, for an extensive discussion of this issue within the field of social psychology).

Dual-Process Views.   Currently, many researchers adopt what is typically termed a *dual-process view* of reasoning, judgment, and decision making (e.g., Evans, 2003; Sloman, 1996; Stanovich, 2004; Stanovich & West, 2000). According to this view, the human thinker operates in one of two modes, depending on the particular nature of the situation at hand. In many ways, this distinction is similar to the controlled-automatic distinction we discussed in Chapter 4. In what might be termed a *heuristic mode* (also called *System 1*), the processes used for thinking operate quickly and without much deliberation—that is, automatically. You may recall the notion of a problem-solving heuristic from Chapter 11 as a shortcut or strategy that helps make a problem more manageable and solvable; the idea is similar here. The heuristic mode of thinking is fast and efficient, just like the use of heuristics in problem solving, and like those heuristics, is based on previous experiences and beliefs. The heuristic mode of thinking actually doesn't sound much like "thinking" in the colloquial sense. The colloquial term that might apply to the heuristic mode of thinking is *intuition*, which, in contrast to its mystical connotations, has recently found firm empirical footing in the experimental psychology literature (Frantz, 2003; Hogarth, 2005; Lieberman, 2000).

The heuristic mode contrasts powerfully with what is termed an analytic mode of thought (also termed *System 2*). In this mode, reasoning, judging, and decision making processes are relatively slow, deliberate, and controlled. In addition, the analytic mode is more cognitively demanding than the heuristic mode; that is, it demands a good deal of working memory capacity. Because of this demand and the fact that we have limited working memory capacity, we often reason and make judgments and decisions in the heuristic mode, as you'll see throughout our discussion this chapter.

STOP *and* **REVIEW!**

1. Distinguish among reasoning, judgment, and decision making.
2. Normative is to descriptive as
   a. how we do think is to how we ought to think.
   b. how we ought to think is to how we do think.
   c. reasoning is to judgment.
   d. judgment is to reasoning.
3. What are the two processes in the dual-process view of reasoning?

➤ Reasoning involves evaluating conclusions based solely on given information. Judgment involves the application of reasoning processes to given information and the use of this information to arrive at a conclusion. Decision making involves evaluating given information, making a judgment, and choosing among several possible alternatives based on this analysis.

➤ Research on thinking emphasizes error because analyzing the types of mistakes people make and when they make them can be quite informative with regard to typical cognitive processing. Normative models of decision making provide descriptions of how we *ought to* think, given objective standards of rationality. Descriptive models of decision making provide descriptions of how we *do* think in actual situations.

➤ Researchers now conceptualize bounded rationality as part of an adaptive approach to reasoning, judgment, and decision making given limited capacity and contextual demands. Dual-process theories of reasoning, judgment, and decision making propose that reasoning, judgments, and decisions are made in an automatic, low-demand heuristic mode and/or a controlled, high-cognitive-demand analytic mode.

Reasoning

Deductive Reasoning

Determining if a specific conclusion is valid based on general principles or assertions (i.e., **premises**) is termed **deductive reasoning**. Think about the way psychology experiments are often conducted. Let's say you want to do a study about memory encoding and retrieval.

First, you would review the literature to examine the theories concerning the relationship between these two concepts. Then you would find the encoding specificity principle, which states that retrieval is best when the conditions at retrieval match those at encoding; this is your *general premise*. From this general premise, you would make a *specific prediction* (conclusion) about what should happen when you vary the mood of people at encoding and retrieval: people will retrieve more information if their mood during retrieval is the same as their mood at encoding. In this example, you would go from a general principle (encoding specificity) and make a specific conclusion (about mood) based on that principle.

Deductive reasoning is like solving a well-defined problem (discussed in Chapter 11) in that deductive-reasoning problems involve a large degree of constraint and the conclusion is easily assessed. It's also like a well-defined problem in that an algorithmic approach is appropriate for solution. Recall that algorithms are step-by-step, formulaic approaches to solving problems. As you'll see, algorithms exist for solving deductive-reasoning problems; if you have taken a course in logic, you've learned some of these techniques. Two forms of deductive reasoning have received a great deal of attention from cognitive researchers: syllogistic reasoning and conditional reasoning (see Evans, 2002, for a review).

Syllogistic Reasoning.   The first type of deductive reasoning is called **syllogistic reasoning.** Consider the following *syllogism* (no doubt a familiar sight if you've had a logic course):

> All students are bright.
> All bright people complete assigned work on time.
> Therefore, all students complete assigned work on time.

Syllogisms consist of two premises and a conclusion. The premises and conclusion may begin with a *universal quantifier* (*all*) or a *particular quantifier* (*some*). Also, the terms within a syllogism may be stated positively ("All A are B") or negatively ("All A are not B"). Syllogisms are either valid or invalid—that is, the conclusion either does or does not hold, given the premises. There is an important difference between the validity of an argument and the truth value of an argument. When we speak of an argument being *valid,* we're just saying that the conclusion does follow from the premises. However (and this is important), it says nothing about whether the premises themselves are true. The truth value of an argument depends on *both* validity of the argument form *and* the truth of the premises. Consider this argument:

> All professors are comedians.
> All comedians are funny.
> Therefore, all professors are funny.

This argument is valid in form; the conclusion does follow from the premises. However, the truth (or soundness) of the argument also depends on the truth of the premises. You could take issue with either premise; if either premise is false, then the argument is not true (i.e., it is not sound).

Confused? You're not alone. People are quite often bedeviled by these sorts of reasoning problems, and consequently they make predictable errors. Try your hand at these (from Sternberg & Ben-Zeev, 2001):

1. All A are B.
   All C are B.
   Therefore, all A are C.
2. No oranges are apples.
   No lemons are oranges.
   Therefore, no apples are lemons.

Are these conclusions valid, based on their respective premises? No, they aren't, although many believe they are (Wilkins, 1928). What underlies these reasoning errors?

Atmosphere Effects.   One classic description of syllogistic reasoning errors is termed the **atmosphere effect** (Woodworth & Sells, 1935). According to this explanation, the quantifiers used in the premises combine to form an "atmosphere" within which the validity of the conclusion is assessed. For example, the premises in syllogism 1 create a "positive universal atmosphere" (stated positively and using universal quantifiers). This produces an erroneous tendency to claim that the universal and positive conclusion ("All A are C") is valid. A similar account would explain why people mistakenly think the conclusion in syllogism 2 is valid. The premises in this syllogism produce a "negative universal atmosphere" (stated negatively and using negative quantifiers), which produces the tendency to agree that the universal and negative conclusion ("No apples are lemons") is valid. What if the quantifiers are mixed (*some* and *all*) or the positive and negative statements are mixed? Consider this example:

All A are B.
Some C are not B.
Therefore, some C are not A.

In this case, the syllogism seems to take on a "particular and negative atmosphere." Therefore, the particular and negative conclusion ("Some C are not A") is likely to be accepted (in this case, correctly, as this is a valid syllogism).

Belief Bias.   Consider our earlier distinction between validity and truth value. Often, our beliefs about truth interfere with our ability to assess argument validity. Rather than evaluating the validity of the argument form, people can be swayed by the believability of the premises. Consider the following example:

All intelligent beings are Simpsons fans.
All dolphins are intelligent beings.
Therefore, all dolphins are Simpsons fans.

You probably looked at this conclusion and thought, "Dolphins can't be Simpsons fans" and therefore concluded that it was invalid. However, this is a perfectly valid conclusion, given the premises. The validity of a conclusion in no way depends on how nonsensical the premises sound. The tendency to allow belief to interfere with the evaluation of conclusions in syllogistic arguments has been termed **belief bias.** Consider another example:

All smart people are reasonable.
All Democrats are smart people.
Therefore, all Democrats are reasonable.

If you are a Democrat you would probably be more likely to believe that this conclusion is valid, because it agrees with your prior beliefs. However, if you are a Republican you would probably believe the conclusion to be invalid, because it is contrary to your prior beliefs. Belief bias can have serious ramifications: we are prone to uncritically accept conclusions if we agree with them and to uncritically reject conclusions if we disagree with them. Belief bias is one of a number of phenomena that you'll read about in this chapter in which our knowledge and beliefs hinder, rather than facilitate, the processes of thought.

STOP *and* THINK!

I LOVE LOGIC

Read the following syllogisms and conclude which are valid and which are invalid. Answers are below.

1. Some politicians are dishonest people.
   All dishonest people are untrustworthy.
   Therefore, some politicians are untrustworthy.
2. All college students are curious.
   All curious people read books.
   Therefore, all college students read books.
3. No rock fans are priests.
   All priests are religious.
   Therefore, no rock fans are religious.
4. Some lawyers are ambulance chasers.
   Some ambulance chasers are unethical.
   Therefore, some lawyers are unethical.

Now answer these questions:

- For which syllogisms was this determination difficult?
- Which were easier?
- Why?

Find some willing friends and see how well they reason. Ask them the questions above or try out some questions from the text to see if your friends demonstrate the biases you've been reading about.

1. valid   2. valid   3. invalid   4. invalid

The finding of belief bias represents a paradigmatic contrast between the two modes of reasoning discussed earlier, heuristic and analytic. In fact, this is a circumstance in which the two modes of operation are both influencing performance, and are essentially in conflict (Evans, 2003). The quick, heuristic, intuitive mode of reasoning is influenced by the believability of the conclusion—does it seem reasonable or not, based on previous experience? Meanwhile, the slower analytic mode is trudging along, attempting to evaluate the validity of the conclusion given the premises. But because this mode takes more working memory capacity than the heuristic mode, it is often abandoned in cases in which working memory capacity is limited. In line with this analysis, working memory capacity is negatively correlated with susceptibility to the belief-bias effect (Stanovich & West, 1997) and with deductive reasoning in general (Copeland & Radvansky, 2004).

Also consistent with this analysis is the finding of age-related decrements in reasoning. You'll recall from our discussion in Chapter 6 that older adults fare less well on tasks that involve self-initiated cognitive processes. Another age-related change that occurs in the later phases of the life span is a loss in efficiency of working memory processes (see Reuter-Lorenz & Sylvester, 2005, for a review), especially for complex cognitive tasks like reasoning. Gilinsky and Judd (1994) found that older subjects were more susceptible to the belief-bias effect than were younger subjects, lending support to the notion that a heuristic mode of reasoning is adopted in situations in which working memory is limited.

Conditional Reasoning: Minding Your P's and Q's.   The second form of deductive reasoning is called **conditional reasoning** (or *if-then reasoning*) and involves evaluating whether a particular conclusion is valid given that certain conditions (premises) hold. For example, consider the following premises 1 and 2 and the conclusion (3):

1. If someone likes Winnie-the-Pooh, then they're a sensitive person.
2. Mary likes Winnie-the-Pooh.
3. Therefore, Mary is a sensitive person.

The *conditional statement* (1) provides the rule that is expressed in an *if-then* format: if P (some sort of antecedent condition), then Q (some sort of consequent condition).

So is statement 3 a valid conclusion, based on premises 1 and 2? Yes, given that sensitive people like Winnie-the-Pooh and given that Mary likes Winnie-the-Pooh, one can validly conclude that Mary is a sensitive person. Notice that the evaluation of a conclusion is in terms of validity, not truth. (See our earlier example about professors being funny!) It may not be true that people who like Winnie-the-Pooh are sensitive, but this is irrelevant to determining the validity of the conclusion. In conditional-reasoning tasks, like syllogistic-reasoning tasks, the goal is to determine only whether the conclusion can be derived logically from the premises.

Let's try another version of the reasoning problem. Once again, assess whether conclusion (3) is valid—that is, does it flow logically from premises 1 and 2?

1. If someone likes Winnie-the-Pooh, then they're a sensitive person.
2. Mary is a sensitive person.
3. Therefore, Mary likes Winnie-the-Pooh.

It seems, on the face of it, that the conclusion (3) is valid: Winnie-the-Pooh and sensitivity go together. But in reality, the conclusion is invalid. It could be that Mary is a sensitive person who couldn't care less about Winnie-the-Pooh. There are many reasons besides liking Winnie-the-Pooh that can indicate a person's sensitivity. People fall prey fairly easily to validating these sorts of erroneous conclusions. In actuality, conditional-reasoning conclusions can be evaluated quite easily if one applies a set of logical rules. Consider again the

Condition statement:

If a person likes Winnie-the-Pooh, then they're a sensitive person.
            (Antecedent)   *(Consequent)*

Four conditional-reasoning scenarios:

	Affirm	**Deny**
Antecedent	Mary likes Winnie-the-Pooh. Therefore, Mary is a sensitive person.	Mary does not like Winnie-the-Pooh. Therefore, Mary is not a sensitive person.
Consequent	Mary is a sensitive person. Therefore, Mary likes Winnie-the-Pooh.	Mary is not a sensitive person. Therefore, Mary does not like Winnie-the-Pooh.

Figure 12.1 Conditional-reasoning forms.

argument form of conditional-reasoning problems. Line 1 gives the if (antecedent)–then (consequent) contingency—that is, "If someone likes Winnie-the-Pooh, then they are a sensitive person." Line 2 either affirms or denies either the antecedent ("Mary does or does not like Winnie-the-Pooh") or the consequent ("Mary is or is not a sensitive person"). This creates four different argument forms, which are outlined in Figure 12.1.

Two of the forms have already been discussed. The first example is termed *affirming the antecedent*—"Mary likes Winnie-the-Pooh; therefore, Mary is a sensitive person." (In logic lingo, this argument form is termed *modus ponens*.) It is valid to conclude that Mary is a sensitive person, because the conditional statement gives us that rule: if a person likes Winnie-the-Pooh, then they're a sensitive person. It is stated that Mary likes Winnie-the-Pooh; therefore, she must be a sensitive person. The second example we discussed above was (can you guess?) *affirming the consequent*—"Mary is a sensitive person; therefore, Mary likes Winnie-the-Pooh." As you saw, this is invalid; it does not necessarily follow that Mary likes Winnie-the-Pooh given that she is a sensitive person. The conditional statement does not say anything about what sensitive people will like or will not like. It tells only what it means if a person likes Winnie-the-Pooh.

The other two argument forms involve denying each part of the conditional statement. *Denying the antecedent*—"Mary does not like Winnie-the-Pooh; therefore, Mary is not a sensitive person"—is invalid. If she does not like Winnie-the-Pooh, this does not necessarily mean that she is not a sensitive person. There are many other correlates of sensitivity; liking Winnie-the-Pooh is just one of them. Finally, *denying the consequent*—"Mary is not sensitive; therefore, Mary does not like Winnie-the-Pooh"—is valid. (Logicians call this *modus tollens*.) If Mary is not sensitive, it is valid to conclude that she does not like Winnie-the-Pooh. According to the conditional statement, liking Winnie-the-Pooh means the person is sensitive. Given that we know that Mary is not sensitive, she must not like Winnie-the-Pooh.

As you might imagine, people run into a fair amount of difficulty when judging the validity of conclusions derived from if-then statements. No one walks around with a card in their pocket describing the valid and invalid argument forms. So what types of errors are common in these sorts of reasoning tasks? One tendency people have is to interpret the initial conditional statement as *biconditional*—thinking that "If *p*, then *q*" also means

Conditional statement:

If a person likes Winnie-the-Pooh (antecedent), then they're a sensitive person (consequent).

Affirm: Mary likes Winnie-the-Pooh.

Conclusion is valid, affirming the antecedent.

Biconditional assumption:

If a someone is a sensitive person (antecedent), then *they like Winnie-the-Pooh* (consequent).

Affirm: Mary likes Winnie-the-Pooh.

Conclusion is invalid, affirming the consequent.

Figure 12.2 Affirming the antecedent leads to a valid conclusion. However, affirming the consequent leads to an invalid conclusion and a common fallacy.

"If q, then p" (Wyer & Srull, 1989). In the problem above, people would tend to think that "If someone likes Winnie-the-Pooh, then they're a sensitive person" also means "If someone is a sensitive person, then they like Winnie-the-Pooh." But conditional statements don't work that way. By assuming that the if-then statement is biconditional, we are essentially assuming that p can be an antecedent or a consequent. If we affirm p, this leads to a valid conclusion only if p is an antecedent. If we make the biconditional assumption and assume that p can also be the consequent, then affirming p leads to an invalid conclusion (see Figure 12.2).

STOP *and* THINK!

I LOVE LOGIC, THE SEQUEL

Try out the following conditional-reasoning problems:

1. If I do really well on my GREs, then I'll get into graduate school.
   I got into graduate school.
   Therefore, I did well on my GREs.
2. If someone likes *South Park*, then they have a crude sense of humor.
   Joan likes *South Park*.
   Therefore, Joan has a crude sense of humor
3. If someone watches *The Simpsons*, they must be intelligent.
   Becky does not watch *The Simpsons*.
   Therefore, Becky is not intelligent.
4. If the tickets for the rock concert are under $50, then I will go to the concert.
   I did not go to the concert.
   Therefore, the tickets for the concert were not under $50.

Now answer these questions:

- Does each conclusion follow from its premises?
- Which are difficult?
- Which are easier?
- Why?
- What is the form of the argument (e.g., affirming the consequent)?

1. affirming the consequent (invalid)   2. affirming the antecedent (valid)
3. denying the antecedent (invalid)   4. denying the consequent (valid)

If a card has a vowel on one side. then it must have an even number on the other side.

(a) Classic Version

If a person is under age 21, then they should be drinking a nonalcoholic beverage.

(b) Deontic Version

Figure 12.3 Two versions of the Wason Selection Task. Does one seem easier than the other?

From Wason, P. C., & Johnson-Laird, P. N. (1970). A conflict between selection and evaluating information in an inferential task. *British Journal of Psychology, 68,* 325–331. Copyright 1970, the British Journal of Psychology. Reprinted with kind permission of the British Psychological Society.

Wason's Selection Task. One of the most investigated conditional-reasoning tasks is the Wason Selection Task (WST). The classic version of this task is depicted in Figure 12.3a. The reasoner must decide which of the four cards needs to be turned over in order to determine whether the following if-then statement holds: if a card has a vowel on one side, then it must have an even number on the opposite side. Can you figure out which cards should be turned over? If you had a logic guide (as we mentioned earlier), you would realize that to test this conditional rule, you need to apply modus ponens and modus tollens. In other words, you would need to turn over the *E* card (affirming the antecedent "if vowel"), and the 7 card (denying the consequent "then even number"). However, people rarely choose this combination of cards; in fact, they choose these particular cards less than 10% of the time (Sternberg, 2001). The most common choices are to turn over the *E* and the 6 cards (nearly half choose 6, which amounts to the error of affirming the consequent) or only the *E* card. (About 33% choose this option.)

Why does this task pose such difficulty? One reason is the biconditional thinking discussed above: "If *p*, then *q*" is often misinterpreted to imply "If *q*, then *p*." As a result, the WST if-then statement is inappropriately interpreted as also meaning "If a card has an even number on one side, it must have a vowel on the other." Based on this invalid assumption, it seems that the 6 card must be turned over (applying the valid rule of affirming the antecedent). But the if-then statement is not biconditional. Turning over the 6 card demonstrates the error of affirming the consequent.

The selection tendencies revealed on the WST have been cited as evidence for a confirmatory bias in reasoning. **Confirmatory bias** refers to our tendency to seek out or notice evidence that is consistent with a particular hypothesis rather than evidence that would be inconsistent with the hypothesis. Once again, consider the selection task "If vowel, then even number." What would support, or help confirm, the validity of this rule? Answer: a vowel with an even number on the other side. What cards are most commonly turned over? Answer: even numbers and vowels. If you'd thought in terms of disconfirmation— what should not be the case, given the rule—you'd have realized that odd numbers never go with vowels. Thinking along these lines would more likely lead one to (correctly) turn over the *E* and 7 cards.

Deontic Versions of the WST. People don't perform poorly on all versions of the Wason Selection Task. Consider the deontic version in Figure 12.3b. In this case, the selection scenario is presented in a deontic context—that is, in terms of a social contract or a right (Griggs & Cox, 1982). The rule to be tested is "If a person is consuming alcohol, then the person must be at least 21 years old." Under these conditions, people are much more likely to turn over the correct cards—the age 17 card, and the beer card. A number of studies have demonstrated improved performance on the WST in such a context. Based on these findings, some (e.g., Cosmides, 1989) have gone as far as to suggest that **deontic reasoning** is a special form of thought that has evolved to allow people to reason about their own duties and social obligations—that is, the things they should or shouldn't do. However, this assertion is controversial. Some (e.g., Almor & Sloman, 1996; Kirby, 1994) have challenged it, showing that people can perform the selection task very well under conditions that do not involve some type of social contract.

Rules or Models?   Explanations for how we reason deductively generally fall into one of two camps. One view might be termed a "strict" or *rule-based account* of deductive reasoning (Rips, 1994). Basically, this view contends that people possess the representational equivalent of logic rules (basically, a mental version of the ones discussed earlier). These rules are then applied to the premises to determine if the conclusion is valid. A contrasting view is the *mental models view* of Johnson-Laird and colleagues (e.g., Bauer & Johnson-Laird, 1993; Johnson-Laird & Byrne, 2002). According to this approach, we first form a mental model based on the information in the premises and our own previous experience. Next, we search for a mental model in which the premises would be true but the stated conclusion would be false. If we find such a model, we deem the conclusion invalid; if we don't find such a model, we deem the conclusion valid. Currently, the jury is still out regarding whether a rule-based account or a mental models account provides a better explanation for deductive reasoning. It may well be that people rely on both sorts of processes (e.g., Oberauer, 2006; Smith, Langston, & Nisbett, 1992).

Inductive Reasoning

The flip side of the reasoning coin is **inductive reasoning.** Rather than working from general premises to arrive at a specific conclusion, we take the opposite tack, moving from specific pieces of data or information, and working toward a general conclusion. Think about theory development in psychology. Based on the results of specific empirical investigations, researchers will develop a general theory that explains each specific finding. Unlike deductive reasoning, where conclusions can be labeled *valid* or *invalid* with absolute certainty, inductive reasoning leads to uncertain conclusions that vary in their strength.

For an everyday example of inductive reasoning, consider the following:

Professor X gets upset when asked if she'll issue a paper extension.
Professor Y won't accept late papers.
Professor Z takes 20% off each day a paper is late.

You might (correctly) induce from these specific pieces of data that professors find late papers unacceptable. Note the differences between this type of inductive reasoning and deductive reasoning. If this were a deductive-reasoning situation, you would be given the general principle—"Professors find late papers unacceptable"—and would need to determine if the specific statements about Professors X, Y, and Z follow from that general principle. In the above inductive-reasoning example, you are inferring the general principle

("Professors find late papers unacceptable") based on specific pieces of information about Professors X, Y, and Z. Deductive reasoning moves from general to specific, while inductive reasoning moves from specific to general.

Bisanz, Bisanz, and Korpan (1994) describe some characteristics that seem to typify inductive reasoning. First, the product of inductive reasoning (the general principle) is not necessarily correct. Suppose you make the assumption that professors won't accept late papers or extend paper deadlines; you may miss an opportunity to get an extension. This characteristic of inductive reasoning provides a sharp contrast to deductive reasoning, in which the validity of a conclusion is inherent in the premises. Inductive arguments are evaluated in terms of their strength rather than in terms of their validity; in other words, how solid the conclusion is based on the evidence. Second, as Rips (1990) points out, with inductive reasoning, there is a need for constraint on the conclusions reached. If there were no constraints, you could come up with some pretty wild conclusions based on the evidence. For example, given the pieces of evidence from Professors X, Y, and Z, you could induce that people whose last names are letters of the alphabet don't like late papers. As you can see, constraint is needed in order to avoid unreasonable conclusions.

Confirmatory Bias Revisited.   Earlier we discussed Wason's Selection Task, which reveals people's tendency to seek out information consistent with a given hypothesis in deductive reasoning. The same effect can found for inductive reasoning. A classic study investigated the confirmatory bias within the context of social cognition—the information processing we perform about other people. Snyder and Swann (1978) had subjects simulate the role of an interviewer whose task it was to discover whether an interviewee was extroverted (outgoing) or introverted (shy). The subjects were given a suggested set of questions to ask the interviewee and were instructed to use the questions they thought would be the most diagnostic—in other words, the ones that would definitely determine whether the person was extroverted or not. Note how this situation involved inductive reasoning; the interviewers were to use the information derived from the answers to the questions to arrive at a general conclusion (i.e., that the person was extroverted). Rather than seeking out information that might have been incongruent with what they were thinking, the interviewers tended to ask questions that were congruent with their hypothesis. If they expected an extrovert, then they asked questions that would reveal extroversion (e.g., "What are some reasons you like parties?"). Any answer would serve only to bolster the interviewer's already-held idea. Interviewers tended not to ask questions that would be inconsistent with extroversion and reveal contrary evidence. Nickerson (1998) provides a wide-ranging review of confirmatory bias and its role in real-world reasoning and judgment.

Rules or Instances?   What mental structures and processes underlie inductive reasoning? Here there is a theoretical debate similar to the one found in deductive reasoning. Basically, researchers disagree over whether induction is based on formal, rule-driven processes or on more context-bound, experience-based heuristic processing. The rule-based view—termed the "strict" or *syntactic view* of inductive reasoning—states that inductive reasoning involves special processes and representations that operate in the abstract, outside of any real-life context. Conversely, the experience-based view, which Rips (1990) terms the *loose view,* contends that inductive reasoning is a little more "messy." According to this view, inductive reasoning involves updating the strengths of one's beliefs based on the recall of specific instances. In this view, inductive reasoning is strongly influenced by real-world context and does not involve special mental structures or built-in logic steps. Sloman (1996) proposes a likely scenario—that both types of processes, formal and loose, are involved in inductive reasoning.

The Omnipresence of Inductive Reasoning.   Inductive reasoning is pervasive; in some form, it underlies just about every other process we've talked about. The hallmark of cognition is going beyond the given information to form a new conclusion. Let's reassess two of the cognitive processes we discussed in previous chapters through the lens of inductive reasoning.

Inductive Reasoning in Categorization.   The processes of categorization and concept formation are, by their very nature, inductive. As you learned in Chapter 5, forming a concept or category involves making a connection between specific instances that seem similar in some manner; in other words, concept formation and categorization involve deriving a general principle (i.e., a category) from specific examples (i.e., the members of the category).

Inductive reasoning provides another window through which to view the phenomenon known as the *typicality effect* (which you read about in Chapter 9)—the finding that some members of a category are more readily identified as such. Rips (1974) extended these findings beyond simple judgments of category membership to inferences induced from knowledge about category members. Consider the following inductive arguments:

1. Robins are susceptible to disease A.
    Therefore, all birds are susceptible to disease A.
2. Turkeys are susceptible to disease B.
    Therefore, all birds are susceptible to disease B.

Subjects rated argument 1 as more likely to be true, because robins are seen as more typical birds than turkeys. The typicality effect seems to carry over to reasoning about unknown properties; inferences from typical category members are "safer bets."

Another interesting phenomenon observed in inductive reasoning about categories might be termed a *diversity effect* (Rips, 1974). Which of the following inductive arguments seems stronger?

1. Robins are susceptible to disease Y.
    Sparrows are susceptible to disease Y.
    Therefore, all birds are susceptible to disease Y.
2. Cardinals are susceptible to disease Z.
    Turkeys are susceptible to disease Z.
    Therefore, all birds are susceptible to disease Z.

In this case, people tend to rate the second argument as stronger because cardinals and turkeys represent a more diverse set of birds relative to robins and sparrows. Because of this diversity, the conclusion seems more warranted and more likely to be true.

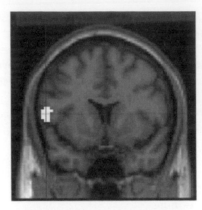

Deductive Reasoning
All animals with 32 teeth are cats.
No cats are dogs.
No dogs have 32 teeth.

Figure 12.4 Results from Goel and Dolan's (2004) study of the brain regions involved in deductive reasoning and inductive reasoning.

Goel, V. & Dolan, R. J. (2004). Differential involvement of left prefrontal cortex in inductive and deductive reasoning. *Cognition, 93*(3), B109–B121. Published by Elsevier. Reprinted with permission.

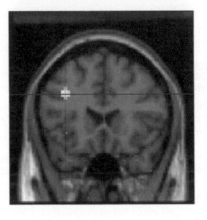

Inductive Reasoning
House cats have 32 teeth.
Lions have 32 teeth.
All felines have 32 teeth.

Inductive Reasoning in Problem Solving. Another set of cognitive processes that depends critically on inductive reasoning is problem solving—more specifically, solving problems by analogy. As you learned in Chapter 11, analogies are a potentially powerful but underused tool; people often fail to make the necessary connections between problem situations. Making these connections involves the processes of inductive reasoning. Recall that in using analogies, people must recognize that two situations share superficial and/or structural characteristics and must use the connection between the two to come to a general solution that can be transferred to similar problems. So, specific problem situations are used to generate a general problem-solution procedure.

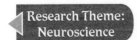

Research Theme: Neuroscience

Deduction and Induction: A Neural Dissociation? As you've read, deduction and induction involve fundamentally different processes. Deduction involves evaluating whether a conclusion is valid or invalid, based on logical relations among specific premises and a conclusion. Induction involves an estimate of an argument's plausibility. Given these differences, it is perhaps not surprising that some research has revealed that these forms of reasoning are associated with distinct loci of brain activity. Goel and Dolan (2004) gave subjects inductive- and deductive-reasoning tasks during an fMRI scan to localize the brain networks that underlie reasoning. Generally, their results replicated earlier ones (e.g., Gazzaniga, 1985, 1998), demonstrating widespread activation: Both induction and deduction were associated with bilateral (i.e., both hemispheres) activation of dorsal frontal, parietal, and occipital cortical areas, in addition to activation of left-hemisphere prefrontal areas.

But a deeper look at this left-hemisphere activation (see Figure 12.4) revealed deductive reasoning to be associated with greater activation in left inferior prefrontal areas, relative to inductive reasoning, which was associated with greater activation in left dorsolateral prefrontal areas. Goel and Dolan (2004) link this dissociation in processing to other cognitive functions. Given deductive reasoning's reliance on the particular form of an argument—a "syntax" of sorts—it makes sense that it's associated with increased activation in Broca's area, which, as you'll recall from Chapter 10, is involved in processing the syntactic aspects of speech. And, given inductive reasoning's reliance on accessing and evaluating world knowledge (i.e., semantic memory), it makes sense that inductive reasoning is associated with the brain regions activated during semantic memory retrieval.

STOP *and* **REVIEW!**

1. Define belief bias.
2. Which of these is a valid form of argument?
   a. affirming the antecedent
   b. affirming the consequent
   c. denying the antecedent
   d. denying the consequent
3. Describe the confirmatory bias in reasoning.
4. What is inductive reasoning?

➤ Deductive reasoning involves determining whether a conclusion is valid based on premises. Syllogistic reasoning involves deciding whether two premises necessitate a conclusion. The atmosphere effect occurs when quantifiers combine to form an atmosphere, resulting in inaccurate assessments of argument validity. Belief bias occurs when believability of premises and conclusions interferes with judgments of validity.

➤ Conditional reasoning involves evaluating whether a particular conclusion is valid given that certain conditions hold. A conditional statement fits the form *If P* (antecedent), *then Q* (consequent). Affirming the antecedent and denying the consequent are valid forms; denying the antecedent and affirming the consequent are invalid forms.

➤ People often wrongly assume that conditional statements are actually biconditional (*If p then q* also means *If q then p*). Confirmatory bias refers to our tendency to seek evidence that affirms our hypotheses, and is less likely to be shown in some applied contexts. The rule-based account of reasoning contends that people possess the mental representational equivalent of logic rules. The mental models view contends that we base reasoning on models we build based on premises and our own previous experience.

➤ Inductive reasoning involves using specific information to arrive at a general conclusion. Confirmatory bias leads to errors in inductive reasoning. Induction underlies a host of other cognitive processes, such as the use of analogy in problem solving, the formation of categories, and judgments about category members. Some evidence points to a neural dissociation between deduction and induction. Deductive reasoning is based in left-hemisphere areas associated with syntactic processing, while inductive reasoning is based in left hemisphere associated with semantic memory retrieval.

Judgment

As you've seen, inductive reasoning involves arriving at general conclusions based on specific pieces of what might be called "data." Judgment is an extension of inductive reasoning. Hastie and Dawes (2001) define *judgment* as "the human ability to infer, estimate, and predict the character of unknown events" (p. 48). Judgment is much more a process of making educated guesses, based on (sometimes quite severely) limited information along with our previous knowledge, expectations, and beliefs. We make these sorts of judgments all the time. For example, when a friend tells you that there's this really interesting person they'd like to fix you up with, you're very likely to gather some initial data and arrive at a judgment. Your impression will be different if you find out that this person is a sculptor rather than a business major. Right or wrong, this information is likely to lead you to strikingly different inferences (i.e., judgments) about this individual.

Much of the research on judgment has been conducted by social psychologists interested in how we perceive and think about other people. Indeed, much of the work in social cognition (the study of how we process information about other people) is concerned with the factors that underlie our judgments of others (such as our hypothetical sculptor or business student). Stereotypes—the set of beliefs that we hold about members of certain groups—are largely based on the processes of judgment.

Even though judgments can be overly broad or outright wrong, it seems necessary for us to make them. In almost every situation requiring a judgment, we usually don't have all of the information we need to arrive at an accurate conclusion. Even if we did, we do not possess the computational power required to successfully combine the information. So we make educated guesses. Does this sound familiar? It should, since it is similar to something you read about in Chapter 11—that is, our reliance on heuristics, or "rules of thumb," for solving certain types of problems. Heuristics serve as shortcuts across the problem space; with heuristics, one needn't consider every possible course of action to solve a problem. In the case of judgment, heuristics are rough assumptions we make that reduce the need for complete data and computational skill.

As you read through the following sections, keep in mind the contrasting views of heuristics posed earlier in the chapter. The dominant view has been to perceive heuristics as examples of suboptimal thinking tools that are employed by the overloaded thinker, leading to errors and biases in judgment. The alternative, proposed by Gigerenzer and colleagues, is that heuristics are "fast and frugal" approaches to thinking that have evolved as an effective solution to the everyday reasoning situations we face on a day-to-day basis. As we stated earlier, these views aren't as different as they might seem. Both acknowledge the usefulness of heuristics; they differ in the spin they put on what such heuristic thinking indicates.

Basing Judgments on Memory: The Availability Heuristic

Scan the names in Table 12.1 and then come back to the reading. There were a total of 21 names. Try to estimate the number of first names that began with *J*, began with *C*, and began with *B*. Do you have your estimates? You may have guessed that there were more names that began with *J* than with the other letters. If you did, you fell victim to what is termed the *availability heuristic*. The **availability heuristic** indicates that we base our estimates of likelihood, or probability, on the ease with which we can think of examples. In this case, the names that begin with *J* are relatively well known, while those names that begin with *C* or *B* are not. Therefore, *J* names seem more numerous because it is easier to remember famous rather than nonfamous names.

Consider why you would need such a heuristic in this situation. Given the characteristics of human attention and memory, it's simply not possible to memorize 21 names with a brief glimpse. Therefore, you rely on a fairly sensible strategy: when asked about the names, you try and think of as many names as you can and see what letter these names begin with. In other words, you turn to the information that is available in memory. The problem, as you saw in detail in Chapter 7, is that memory is not always the most reliable database. When the availability heuristic is applied, systematic biases in memory can lead to systematic biases in judgment. Just because something seems like a common occurrence doesn't mean that it is. So availability in memory is not always the best basis for judgment; it is affected by a host of factors that can distort our judgment.

Biased Encoding.   The availability heuristic is based on the ease of retrieval from memory. But something may be easier to get out of memory because it is overrepresented in memory. Why might this occur? Consider the exercise you just did. Because the names that start with *J* are more familiar than the other names, you were much more likely to have encoded them successfully. So your memory retrieval is biased because the information you've stored is biased.

Another study, conducted by Lichtenstein, Slovic, Fischhoff, Layman, and Comb (1978) on the cheery subject of causes of death, provides another example. Before we talk

Table 12.1 Availability and Frequency Estimation

Jimmy Stewart	John Kerry	J. K. Rowling
Bob Smitson	Carl Pavano	Chris Baines
Jack Kerouac	Beth Feynman	Jackie Robinson
Charlie Horton	Bobbi Castel	Cory Lidle
Cecil Patterson	Barbara Edison	Claude Shelet
Bill Arnold	Jennifer Aniston	Bruce Thomas
Charlene Tilton	Joan Crawford	Bess Severson

Table 12.2 Availability and Judgment

A. Tornadoes	A. Motor vehicle accidents
B. Extreme cold	B. Stroke
A. Homicide	A. Food poisoning
B. Stomach cancer	B. Smallpox vaccination
A. All cancers	A. Floods
B. Heart disease	B. Asthma

From Lichtenstein, S. (1978). Judged frequency of lethal events. *Journal of Experimental Psychology: Human Learning and Memory, 4,* 551–578. Copyright 1978 by the American Psychological Association. Reprinted by permission.

about the study, try it yourself. Look at the causes-of-death pairs listed in Table 12.2. For each pair, decide which of the two causes results in more deaths. If you're like the subjects in this study, you overestimated the frequency of some causes of death and underestimated others. For example, at the time this study was conducted, there were more deaths from stomach cancer than from homicide, more from asthma than from flood, more from stroke than from motor vehicle accidents, and more from extreme cold than from tornadoes. But the subjects in the study tended to make the opposite estimates, overestimating the number of deaths caused by homicides, floods, auto accidents, and tornadoes and underestimating the number of deaths caused by stomach cancer, asthma, stroke, and extreme cold. When faced with this estimation task, the only possible way to do it is to sample memory for examples. In this case, however, you're likely to come up with a biased sample, because the first member of each cause-of-death pair (e.g., floods) is "front-page news." The very nature of such events is dramatic, and therefore deaths from such causes are more likely to be reported on the evening news and in magazines and newspapers. The second member of each pair (e.g., asthma) is undramatic. (When was the last time your newspaper reported someone dying of asthma?) The bias in reporting of these types of death leads to a biased knowledge base.

Your authors' personal experience in teaching in different geographic locales provides an example of the effects of a biased knowledge base. (Keep in mind that this example is anecdotal and subject to our own processes of memory distortion!) We began our teaching careers in Indiana, where tornadoes are probably the most serious weather hazard; in other words, they're front-page news. Hoosiers hear a great deal about tornadoes and encode lots of information about the damage they wreak. We now teach in Minnesota, where the extreme cold is front-page news. Minnesotans are exposed to conditions of extreme cold for several months every year and thus are likely to encode information about this hazard. In line with the experiential differences between our two populations of students, when we've asked students to compare tornadoes and extreme cold as causes of death, Indiana students were clearly biased toward saying "tornadoes." But since our move to Minnesota, we've heard more people claim "extreme cold" as the more common cause of death. Once again, the information that is encoded in memory exerts an influence on our judgments; differences or biases in encoding lead to differences or biases in judgment.

Which is the cause of more deaths?

The media no doubt serve as one source of encoding-based availability biases. Vivid news reports of certain types of events lead us to overestimate those events' frequency and likelihood. For example, as Hastie and Dawes (2001) point out, when a former psychiatric patient commits a crime, the fact that they were formerly in treatment is often mentioned in the news report. But how often do we hear the negative case—"Harold Smith, who has never received psychiatric treatment, was arrested for murder today"? So being a former psychiatric patient and committing a crime are vividly connected. These biases in reporting can lead to biases in people's knowledge database. Many researchers would contend that the media's vivid reporting is at the root of many public anxieties, such as the safety of drinking water, the likelihood of school shootings, and the chances of a plane crash. This is not to say that these issues are of no concern, but that there is little doubt that vivid and intense reports may increase their prominence in memory in disproportion to their actual danger.

Does vivid media coverage lead people to worry too much about certain events?

Biased Retrieval.   So the availability heuristic leads us astray when our memory contains a biased sample of information. Availability can also lead us astray if the sampling process itself is biased. Try the following demonstration, based on Tversky and Kahneman (1973), and estimate whether there are more of number 1 or number 2:

1. six-letter words that have the letter *n* as the fifth letter
2. words that fit the pattern __ __ __ *ing*

Participants in Tversky and Kahneman's study estimated that words of type 2 were much more likely than words of type 1. Can you see why this is a rather silly answer and why the answer must be type 1? The set of words defined by type 1 includes every single word that fits type 2—that is, words that fit type 2 are six letters long with the fifth letter being *n!* Therefore, there have to be more words that fit category 1. But making this judgment requires a person to sample memory, and people generate a biased sample because it's easier to think of words that end in *-ing* than it is to think of words that have *n* as the fifth letter. Note that the problem here is not one of encoding; the information stored in memory really does have more words with *n* as the fifth letter than words that fit the pattern __ __ __ *ing*. The problem here is one of retrieval; being asked to think of examples of words that end in *-ing* serves as a more precise, hence easier-to-use, retrieval cue.

Another instance of a retrieval-based bias in the use of the availability heuristic relates to recency. One of the most tried-and-true principles of memory research (going all the way back to Ebbinghaus's ubiquitous forgetting curve, discussed in Chapter 1) is that more recent events are easier to retrieve than more remote events. This is true for both immediate (working) memory and long-term memory. Therefore, the availability heuristic can lead us to overestimate the frequency of events because of their recency. Consider again the news reports of tragedies such as the hijackings on September 11, 2001. In addition to being selectively encoded into memory (as described above), these events also impact our judgment more when they've occurred recently and their aftermath is fresh in our minds. Therefore, people probably felt that the likelihood of being a victim of a terrorist attack was greater immediately after the World Trade Center disaster than it was prior to the attacks. In reality, the probability may be less, because of the heightened security that resulted from that disaster.

Another availability-related result of the September 11 terrorist attacks was a drastically reduced willingness to fly, due to what some term **dread risk** (Slovic, 1987). Dread risk refers to our tendency to avoid situations in which many people may be killed at the same time while simultaneously being relatively impervious to risky situations in which deaths are more spread out. But avoiding dread risk results in a cruel irony, as noted by Myers (2001); the fear that swept the country after the 9/11 attacks of getting onto a plane no doubt caused people to drive rather than fly (Greg actually decided to drive rather than fly to see his family in Cincinnati in October 2001), leading to an elevated number of traffic fatalities. This speculation was confirmed by a later analysis of traffic accident data by Gigerenzer (2004). In the three months of 2001 remaining after the 9/11 attacks, the number of fatal traffic accidents was greatly elevated, relative to baseline rates from other years during the same period. So, indeed, the September 11 attacks may have led to a second toll of lives due to the impact of raw emotions on people's judgments and subsequent decisions.

STOP *and* **THINK!**

ASSESSING AVAILABILITY

Consider the following question: Do you think there are more words in the English language that start with the letter *k* or that have *k* as the third letter? Now answer these questions:

- How did you arrive at your answer?
- Which of the judgment heuristics came into play?
- How might your judgment have been biased?

Find two friends to be "research subjects." Vary the conditions under which you give them this problem. For one of your "research subjects," have them answer quickly. Tell the other to take as much time as needed to think about it. These two different conditions correspond to the dual modes of reasoning discussed earlier.

- What would you expect under these two conditions?
- Why?

Illusory Correlations.   Everyone has heard claims or stories like the following:

I know a couple who had just given up trying to get pregnant, started to look into adoption, and then bam! They got pregnant!

Because of the vividness of some examples like the above, people see relationships where none likely exist. To know if starting adoption proceedings really is associated with an increase in the chances of getting pregnant, one needs to know four different pieces of information: (1) how frequently people who can't conceive start adoption and get pregnant, (2) how frequently people who can't conceive start adoption and do not get pregnant, (3) how frequently people who can conceive start adoption and get pregnant, and (4) how frequently people who can conceive start adoption and do not get pregnant (see Table 12.3). All four pieces of data allow for an assessment of whether the circumstance (i.e., getting pregnant after starting adoption proceedings) occurs an inordinate number of times. Of course, people can't readily bring to mind all four pieces of information; they tend to rely on only the first piece, which essentially boils down to noticing coincidences. When one notices primarily (or only) coincidences, two events will seem to be linked even when they're not. This perception is termed **illusory correlation.**

One well-known example of an illusory correlation is the "*Sports Illustrated* jinx," which goes something like this: if an athlete appears on the cover of this well-known sports magazine, then they are doomed to suffer some calamity soon after—a season-ending injury, an awful performance slump, or personal problems. Of course, the correlation between appearing on the cover of *Sports Illustrated* and having some calamity occur is nonexistent; but people notice when such an appearance is followed by some bad event, and they don't notice other combinations of events, such as someone appearing on the cover and continuing to excel. This is also an example of the statistical principle termed *regression to the mean.* Sometimes an athlete performs below their average, sometimes above their average, but most of the time their performance hovers right around their average. (That's why it's called the average!) After performing far above or below their average, performance will tend to *regress toward the average.* Athletes appear on the cover of *Sports Illustrated* only when they perform well above average. So of course, their performance will tend to move back (i.e., regress) toward their mean level of performance.

It's important to note that (as with all of the judgment heuristics) the availability heuristic can be quite useful. If, based on thinking of examples from memory, you come

---

Table 12.3 Influence of Coincidental Events

Our tendency to notice distinctive coincidences causes us to be overly influenced by coincidental evidence.

	Get Pregnant	Don't Get Pregnant
Start adoption proceedings	Distinctive coincidence	Nonevent
Don't start adoption proceedings	Nonevent	Nonevent

to the conclusion that your professor is going to be a trifle annoyed (or worse) when you hand in a late paper, this is most likely an accurate judgment. Use of the availability heuristic tends to get us into trouble only when there are especially memorable examples that seem to carry the weight of a thousand.

A Recognition Heuristic.   This underscores the point that Gigerenzer and colleagues make with regard to bounded rationality. Reasoning is adaptive; we simply cannot consider all of the data, nor do we have access to it. In fact, sometimes a *lack of data* can be informative! Such is the case with another memory-based judgment tool termed the *recognition heuristic* (e.g., Goldstein & Gigerenzer, 2002). The **recognition heuristic** is often used when we're faced with two alternatives—one that's recognizable and one that's not. Under these conditions, we tend to infer that the recognizable alternative has the higher value on whatever criterion is of interest. Let's look at a concrete example from a study by Gigerenzer and Hoffrege (1995). In one study, they asked Americans and Germans to pick which city had the higher population: San Diego or San Antonio. Nearly two-thirds of Americans correctly picked San Diego; obviously, fewer Germans would answer correctly, right? Guess again; *all* of the Germans correctly surmised that San Diego was the more populous city. According to the researchers, the Germans used their having heard of San Diego to infer that it must be more noteworthy in terms of the criterion characteristic, in this case, population.

Basing Judgments on Similarity: The Representativeness Heuristic

We've all made judgments based on similarity. For example, we see an unusually tall person, say, 6' 8", and we make an assumption that anybody so tall must play basketball. But think about it. Most people, even tall people, don't play basketball. So why do we make such judgments? When trying to place a person in a particular category (e.g., basketball player), we have a tendency to base our judgment on the similarity between the person and the stereotype we hold about that category. If you met Greg, you'd soon realize that he's a big fan of the Cincinnati Bengals professional football team. Given that, you might brand him a sports fan, and assume that he also likes the Cincinnati Reds (you'd be correct). Judgments like this rely on what is termed the **representativeness heuristic:** we assess the degree to which the object represents (is similar to) our basic idea (or stereotype) of that object.

Ignoring Base Rates.   Let's consider a classic demonstration of this heuristic from a study by Kahneman and Tversky (1973, p. 241). Subjects were given the following instructions:

> A panel of psychologists have interviewed and administered personality tests to 30 engineers and 70 lawyers, all successful in their fields. On the basis of this information, thumbnail descriptions for each of these individuals have been written. For each description, please indicate the probability that the person described is an engineer, from 1 to 100.

Subjects were then given the following description:

> Jack is a 45-year-old man. He is married and has 4 children. He is generally conservative, careful, and ambitious. He shows no interest in political and social issues and spends most of his time on his many hobbies, which include home carpentry, sailing, and mathematical puzzles.

Subjects were required to rate the probability that Jack was an engineer. Probabilities would dictate that an engineer would be pulled from the 100 names about 30% of the time, because 30% is the proportion of engineers in this sample. This type of statistical information is termed *base rate*—the rate of occurrence of a particular category in the population or sample (i.e., how often a certain event tends to occur). Consider this example: The base rate of professional football players in the general population is quite low. The base rate of males in the general population is relatively high. If you select somebody out of the population at random, you're very unlikely to pick a professional football player. However, you're about 50% likely to pick a male. Now consider the engineer-lawyer problem above. Given that there are 30 engineers in the sample, the probability that a randomly drawn name is an engineer is 30/100, or 30%. Indeed, when subjects were asked to estimate the probabilities without the personality description, that is the guess they made. But the description, which just happened to fit their stereotype of an engineer, overruled this base-rate information, leading subjects to overestimate the probability (50%) that Jack was an engineer.

Use of the representativeness heuristic, and the concomitant tendency to ignore base rates, may relate to the use of the controversial practice known as racial profiling. Racial profiling involves the assumption that a certain type of criminal (i.e., a drug dealer) fits a certain profile; in many cases, the profile includes race as a prominent component. For example, in racial profiling, the "typical" or "average" drug dealer is often assumed to be young, black, and male. As is the case with the biased use of the representativeness heuristic (discussed above), use of the heuristic in this situation leads to judgment errors. Operating on the basis of this profile, police will be especially prone to detain and question individuals that fit, or represent, this profile. Just as we expect that 10 pregnancies should result in a mixture of boys and girls, so do we tend to expect criminals to fit a particular racial profile. Just as in the engineer-lawyer example, this expectation leads to biases in judgment and in subsequent behavior.

Table 12.4 presents data from a study on traffic patterns conducted by Harris (1999). In this study, more than 5,000 cars were observed on a state highway over the course of about two

Racial profiling: A misapplication of the representativeness heuristic?

Table 12.4 Profiling as an Instance of the Representativeness Heuristic

---

Harris's (1999) observational study revealed that although African-Americans comprise a small minority of drivers who are committing traffic violations, they comprise the majority of drivers who are actually pulled over.

	Caucasian	African-American	Other Minorities
(a) Drivers observed	4,314 (76%)	973 (17%)	241 (4%)
Offenders observed	4,000 (74%)	938 (18%)	232 (4%)

	Caucasian	African-American	Other Minorities
(b) Drivers searched (out of 823)	162 (19.7%)	600 (73%)	61 (7.3%)

From Harris, D. A. (1999). *Driving while black: Racial profiling on our nation's highways.* ACLU Report. Washington, DC: ACLU. Reprinted by permission of the author and the American Civil Liberties Union.

days, and the race of the driver was noted (this was possible in 97% of the cases). Also recorded was the number of drivers who were actually violating traffic laws at the time they were observed. Table 12.4a presents the number of drivers overall, as well as the number of violators, as a function of racial group. Note that the percentage of violators per racial group is a rough estimate of the base rate of individuals who could potentially be pulled over; as you can see, 74% are white and 18% are African-American. Now look at Table 12.4b, which presents the number of motorists stopped in an 18-month period along the same stretch of highway. Over this time span, 823 motorists were stopped and searched. Just going by the base rate, you would expect that 609 (74%) of these motorists would be white. However, the traffic stops show that 600 (73%) of the motorists were African-American. So although the base rate suggests that whites would be much more likely violators of traffic laws (and hence eligible to be stopped), actual behavior deviated strikingly from this baseline. The representativeness heuristic is strongly implicated as the culprit.

The Conjunction Fallacy. Base rates aren't the only type of information people ignore when they make probability judgments. In their classic investigation of judgment heuristics, Tversky and Kahneman (1983, p. 299) presented the following problem to subjects:

> Linda is 31 years old; she's single, outspoken, and very bright. She majored in philosophy. As a student, she was deeply consumed with issues of discrimination and social justice, and also participated in anti-nuclear demonstrations.

Based on this information about Linda, subjects were asked to decide whether it was more likely that she was (1) a bank teller or (2) a bank teller who was active in the feminist movement. Which do you think? If you said 2, you agreed with the vast majority of Tversky and Kahneman's subjects. If you think about it, there's no possible way that 2 could be more likely than 1, because 1 includes 2! If you think about the universe of bank tellers, you can imagine that some subset of them would consider themselves feminist bank tellers; so the chances of Linda being a feminist bank teller have to be smaller than (or at the very least the same as) the probability of her being a bank teller. Figure 12.5 makes this apparent.

Figure 12.5 Is it more likely that Linda is a bank teller or that she is a bank teller and a feminist?

Another way to look at it is that being a bank teller and a feminist is the conjunction of two events. The probability of a conjunction between two independent events is the probability of one multiplied by the probability of the other. Since probabilities are almost always less than 1, conjunctions almost always have to be less likely than either event considered alone. For example, if the probability of event 1 is 0.5 and the probability of event 2 is 0.5, the probability of the conjunction of event 1 and event 2 is 0.25 (less than the 0.5 probability of either event in isolation). Failure to use this knowledge in the Linda problem is termed the **conjunction fallacy**. The conjunction fallacy is another compelling demonstration of the power of stereotypes. Because Linda fits the stereotype (i.e., is representative) of a liberal individual, we assume that she has to be a feminist, and we use this information as the basis for our judgment.

Criticisms of Kahneman and Tversky.   Not everyone buys the conjunction fallacy and Kahneman and Tversky's interpretation of it. In fact, there are a number of general criticisms of the approach to judgment taken in these studies. One of these has already been discussed—what many see as the "half-empty" view of judgment that is implicit in the approach, which compares judgment to an ideal or rational standard. Another objection to the research program of Kahneman and Tversky relates to their methodology. Many researchers have claimed that the scenarios presented to subjects in these judgment tasks were a bit odd in their structure, and that there was often more than one *rational construal,* or reasonable way of viewing the problem. So what appears to be an "irrational" judgment when compared with an ideal or normative standard might be perfectly rational when considered within the context of the subject's construal of the problem. Actually, these complaints have been lodged against each of the research paradigms discussed throughout this chapter, but we'll discuss the objection in the context of the conjunction fallacy, because this is the task that has perhaps been most roundly criticized (Stanovich, 1999). In fact, Margolis (1987) goes as far as to say that "many critics have insisted that in fact it is Kahneman and Tversky, not their subjects, who have failed to grasp the logic of the problem" (p. 158).

Follow-up analysis of and research on the conjunction fallacy seems to indicate that the critics have a point. As Stanovich (1999) notes, people may not be likely to apply a probability analysis to the conjunction fallacy. Rather, the question has some subtle linguistic cues and implications that are likely to lead to certain inferences on the part of the subject. The subject's answer may be the result of these linguistic influences rather than a failure to understand probabilities. Hilton (1995) points out that when subjects read the possibility "Linda is a bank teller" and also read the possibility "Linda is a bank teller and active in the feminist movement," they take "Linda is a bank teller" as implying that "Linda is a bank teller and not active in the feminist movement." Given that both options include "Linda is a bank teller" and that the second option includes additional information about the feminist movement, it is reasonable to infer that the first option also includes information about the feminist movement (albeit implicitly). If this is the interpretation, then the choice commonly made by subjects seems rational rather than irrational. This task-construal analysis of the conjunction "fallacy" (as well as of other judgment tasks) implies that what looks like irrationality and rash judgment is actually adaptive decision making that makes the most of our limited capacity, given the demands of the situation.

Misperception of Event Clusters. When a given event has two different ways of working out, such as a coin flip, people tend to misconstrue what a random sequence should look like. That is, they tend to underestimate the number of streaks, or clusters of like events, that would occur in a truly random sequence. For example, look at the following two coin-flip sequences (where H is heads, and T is tails) and judge which is more likely:

H T H T T H T H H T H T
H H H H H H T T T T T T

If you think that the first sequence is a more likely outcome, you're incorrect—but not alone (Tversky & Kahneman, 1974). Each sequence has an equally low probability of occurring—namely $(1/2)^{12}$. But because the first sequence represents how we picture the outcome of 12 coin flips, it's perceived as more likely. Runs of like events (six heads, then six tails) are perceived as extremely unlikely.

The Hot Hand. The tendency to misperceive event clusters as indicating nonrandomness may underlie what sports fans term a "hot hand." This pet phrase of sports announcers refers to situations in which it seems a player can do no wrong; for example, in basketball, a player has made six straight shots. While in the midst of these streaks, players are often said to be "in the zone" or "white hot." A study by Gilovich, Vallone, and Tversky (1983) suggests that the player's shots are nothing more than a random sequence dictated by the player's overall shooting percentage. These researchers were interested in whether there was any truth to the claim that players get "hot," and they investigated this by looking at the official shooting statistics of the 1983 Philadelphia 76ers (the only team to keep shot-by-shot records). If a hot-hand phenomenon exists, then the probability of making any particular shot should be higher, given that some number of immediately previous shots have been made. In other words, the probability of making any given shot should be higher if the player is hot, and this "heat"

Is there such a thing as a "hot hand"?

should carry over to subsequent shots. The study indicated that there was no relationship between making a basket and having made any number of previous baskets. A shooter is just as likely to make a shot after having missed the previous three baskets as they are if they'd made each previous shot. There was no support for the idea of a hot hand. So although clusters of events seem unlikely, they do arise, even within completely random sequences.

The existence of the hot-hand fallacy has held up to a good deal of scrutiny; it really does seem to be a misperception (Adams, 1992; Kass & Raftery, 1995), in spite of the strident objections of basketball coaches everywhere. But Burns (2004) has a most interesting take on the hot-hand belief, one that fits well with the adaptive view of heuristic thinking discussed at the outset of the chapter. According to his analysis, it may be adaptive to believe in the hot hand. If behavior is altered by this belief, and the alterations in behavior enhance the chances of success, then the belief is beneficial even though it's fallacious. Burns's (2004) analysis proceeds as follows: Every time a basketball team has the ball, they face the decision of who should take the next shot. There are a number of cues they might use to choose which player. One is a player's shooting percentage. It makes sense to get the ball to the player who hits their shots at a higher rate than other players. It's also true that those with higher shooting percentages are going to have more streaks, because they make more shots. Therefore, streaks provide information. So regardless of whether the hot hand is a misperception, it is a useful heuristic to use in order to arrive at quick judgments.

The Gambler's Fallacy.   The representativeness heuristic, and its relation to the misperception of event clusters, also underlies what Tversky Kahneman and (1971) term the **gambler's fallacy**. This refers to the belief that after a run of bad luck (or a run of a certain type of outcome), a change is "due" to occur. Because a run of events seems so unlikely, sometimes people believe that a return to normalcy is likely to occur. This misperception leads to people's prolonged stays at the blackjack table; if a you are on losing streak, you may feel that a winning streak has to be right around the corner. But in this situation, future events (i.e., better card hands) have nothing to do with whether you've won or lost previously. Nonetheless, people often overestimate the probability of winning after a losing streak and continue to play.

Basing Judgments on Initial Estimates: The Anchoring-and-Adjustment Heuristic

In many cases of judgment, people start with an idea, or standard, in mind. Say you were guessing how much money the average college student makes from working part time over the course of the school year. As we've seen, there's no way you can possibly know or calculate this value, so you do the next best thing: you use a rule of thumb to help educate your guess. If you are a working college student, you might recall that you earn $8.10 per hour and work 15 hours a week at your job. Based on this knowledge, you may estimate that the average working college student makes around $100 to $150 a week. Although the information from your own work experience is helpful to start the estimation

The gambler's fallacy: My luck *has* to turn soon.

process, it may exert too much influence, essentially "anchoring" your judgment. That is, our initial estimate or first impression tends to make us overly biased toward it. The heuristic involved in these judgments is termed **anchoring and adjustment.** We often make an initial estimate, based on previous knowledge or on presented information, and then make adjustments to that initial anchor to arrive at a final judgment. But just as an anchor holds a ship in place, your initial estimate can hold your guess in place, and you can fail to make sufficient adjustments.

Chapman and Bornstein (1996) investigated anchoring and adjustment in the context of personal-injury awards. In their study, subjects read a (simulated) one-page discussion of a personal-injury suit involving a woman who developed ovarian cancer after taking birth-control pills. The only manipulation in the study (experiment 1) was the amount of money requested by the plaintiff for compensation—$100, $20,000, $5 million, and $1 billion. After reading the case with one of the four anchoring values, subjects made a number of judgments, including compensatory damages and the likelihood that the defendant caused the plaintiff's injuries.

The results are described aptly by the title of the article: "The More You Ask For, the More You Get." The amount of compensatory damages awarded to the fictional plaintiff mirrored the anchor; the higher the anchor, the more money was awarded. Perhaps even more surprising was what the researchers termed a *cross-modality anchoring effect:* higher monetary anchors were not only associated with greater awards, but were also associated with higher ratings of defendant blame. Although the procedure was quite different from an actual jury trial in important ways, there still seem to be important ramifications of the anchoring-and-adjustment heuristic in this setting.

STOP *and* THINK!

I HAVE NO IDEA . . .

Consider the following questions and decide whether the proposed estimate is greater than or less than the number designated. Come up with a quick answer, making your guess as precise as you can.

1. number of electoral votes belonging to Ohio for a presidential election—less than or more than 6?
   Your guess _____
2. number of times *Hello Dolly* was performed on Broadway—less than or more than 5,000?
   Your guess _____
3. number of men who have served as pope—less than or more than 100?
   Your guess _____
4. total area of the state of Utah, in square miles—less than or more than 100,000 square miles?
   Your guess _____
5. distance from Neptune to the sun—less than or more than 5 billion miles?
   Your guess _____

Compare your answers to the actual answers at end of this paragraph.

- How far off were you?
- Did the "anchor" presented in the question affect your answer?
- Did it make your guess too high or too low?
- What is your explanation for this?

1. 12   2. 2,844   3. 300   4. 36,420   5. 2.8 billion

The Spotlight Effect.   Gilovich and colleagues (Gilovich, Krueger, & Medvec, 2002; Gilovich, Medvec, & Savitsky, 2000) cite anchoring and adjustment as the underlying cause of what they term the *spotlight effect*. The **spotlight effect** refers to our tendency to believe that others notice our actions and appearance more than they actually do—in other words, we believe that the "social spotlight" shines more brightly on us than it actually does. In three of their studies, these researchers had subjects don a T-shirt that was embarrassing (Barry Manilow or Vanilla Ice) and then enter a room where other people were assembled and stay for a few minutes. Afterward, the subjects were asked to estimate how many of the people assembled in the room had noticed their T-shirt. The results clearly demonstrated the spotlight effect: subjects guessed that about twice as many people noticed their T-shirt as actually did. The result was even stronger in a later study, in which subjects were asked to wear a nonembarrassing (perhaps even cool) T-shirt of their choice (with Martin Luther King, Jr., Bob Marley, or Jerry Seinfeld); the result was the same: subjects thought everyone had noticed their T-shirt, but few did.

So how is this an example of anchoring and adjustment? The researchers suspected that subjects would be overly aware of and self-conscious about their T-shirt and that this intense self-awareness would serve as an anchor, leading to overestimates of how many other people noticed it. They tested this idea in a disarmingly simple manner. After subjects estimated the number of people who had noticed their T-shirts, the experimenters asked subjects if they had considered any other number. The researchers' logic was simple: If subjects' guesses were based on the very high anchor of their own self-consciousness, then their initial estimate likely would be even higher than their final estimate. The results from these two experiments supported this anchoring-and-adjustment interpretation.

Biased Evaluation of Our Judgments

We've seen that people employ some pretty reasonable-sounding judgment heuristics in situations in which information, computational power, or both are lacking. We've also seen that people tend to overrely on heuristics, which sometimes leads to biased judgments. Sometimes we're not so good at estimating how much we know or when we knew it. We now turn to a couple of biases of this sort.

Hindsight Bias. "I could have told you that was going to happen." Who hasn't heard (or offered) this little gem of wisdom? People always seem to be sure after something has

occurred that they knew things would work out just that way. This tendency is termed **hindsight bias** (and sometimes, quite descriptively, the *I-knew-it-all-along effect*).

A good example of an everyday situation that may be powerfully influenced by the hindsight bias is civil litigation. Civil suits involve disputes in which a plaintiff claims that they are the victim of some type of harm caused by the defendant. The purpose of the suit is to determine whether the plaintiff is entitled to some type of monetary compensation. When a jury or judge has to make a determination about liability, they are required to judge whether the defendant could have foreseen what was going to happen and acted accordingly. But, as described above, people often fall victim to a hindsight bias. Therefore, they're likely to believe that "they knew it all along"— that they could have foreseen the events that led to the plaintiff's injury and therefore the defendant should have seen it coming, too.

A study by Hastie, Schkade, and Payne (1999) provides a dramatic demonstration of the hindsight bias in the context of a civil case with a plaintiff seeking punitive damages. The scenario they used was based on an actual case of a California train derailment and a resulting

Inappropriately self-conscious?

Was this accident foreseeable?

toxic herbicide spill. The case was presented in two slightly different ways. In the fore-sight condition, subjects were told that there was a potentially dangerous situation devel-oping along mountainous railroad tracks in California and that the National Transportation Safety Board (NTSB) had deemed the situation unsafe and ordered the railroad to stop operations. Expert testimony supporting the NTSB finding was also pre-sented. Subjects were told that the railroad had appealed the NTSB order and were to evaluate whether the appeal should be upheld. In other words, subjects had to demon-strate foresight, judging how likely it would be that an accident would occur.

In the hindsight condition, subjects were given basically the same information, with one important addition: there had already been a train derailment with an associated toxic spill. Instead of ruling on an appeal of an NTSB order, subjects were instructed to decide whether punitive damages against the railroad were in order. These subjects were susceptible to hindsight bias; they knew that an accident had occurred and were basically asked whether the railroad should have seen it coming. The procedure required that all subjects give an overall probability of an accident. The question in the foresight condition was: "Estimate the probability that a serious accident will happen." The question in the hindsight condition was: "*Ignoring what you now know,* what probability *would you have*

Table 12.5 "They Should Have Seen It Coming"

Judgments on Elements of Liability	Foresight Condition	Hindsight Condition
Defendant was (would be) reckless.	2.89	5.12
Risk was (is) foreseeable.	3.40	5.52
Defendant is (would be) liable for accident.	3.50	6.08
Defendant disregarded (is disregarding) grave risk.	3.36	5.59
Defendant was (is being) malicious.	1.80	2.12

Note: 1 = definitely "no"; 10 = definitely "yes."
From Hastie, R., Schkade, D. A., & Payne, J. W. (1999). Juror judgments in civil cases: Hindsight effects on judgments of liability for punitive damages. *Law and Human Behavior, 23,* 445–470. Reprinted by permission of Kluwer Academic/Plenum Publishers.

estimated for a serious accident happening?" (emphasis added). In addition to this overall judgment, subjects in both conditions were asked to judge various elements of liability.

The results demonstrated a striking hindsight bias. The average probability estimate for the occurrence of an accident was 0.34 in foresight and 0.59 in hindsight; indeed, hindsight subjects were fairly certain that they could have predicted the accident. Judgment on the elements of liability are presented in Table 12.5. Hindsight subjects rated the railroad company more harshly for each of these elements (except maliciousness, which was not statistically significant but was in the predicted direction). Notice that the exact same rating questions were presented to the foresight and hindsight subjects. All questions related generally to the core issue of whether the company should have foreseen the accident. The hindsight subjects were overwhelmingly more likely to say yes, based on knowledge they had gained after the fact.

Hastie, Schkade, and Payne (1999) contend that this type of hindsight bias is nearly inevitable when people are asked to reason about the causes and precursors to everyday events; this is pretty much what happens when juries or judges in civil trials consider punitive damages. To ameliorate the effects of hindsight bias, the authors offer a number of suggestions, including taking the question of punitive damages out of the hands of jurors and placing it in the hands of experts who might be less likely to fall victim to hindsight bias, given their extensive knowledge in the particular area.

Miscalibration of Confidence.   The fact that we overestimate the extent to which we knew something was going to happen demonstrates an insensitivity to what we knew and when we knew it. This general lack of sensitivity is also revealed by the finding that we have a general tendency to be overconfident (or, in some circumstances, underconfident) about what we know. In other words, we are not very good at calibrating our confidence. If confidence were perfectly calibrated to what we know, then our confidence would match our knowledge. If we were 50% sure about some set of facts, then we would get 50% of them correct. If we were 100% sure about another set of facts, then we would get all of them correct.

Many studies have investigated confidence calibration and revealed it to be "off" in a fairly systematic manner. For example, Fischhoff, Slovic, and Lichtenstein (1977) had people answer general knowledge questions (e.g., "Is absinthe a type of liqueur or a type of precious stone?") and also rate their confidence that they had given a correct answer. If subjects were completely guessing, their confidence rating should have been 50%. Also, if confidence was well calibrated, then the average confidence value should have matched the average percentage correct. The researchers found that subjects tended to be overconfident; for questions about which they were 100% confident, they managed to get only 75% or so correct. This **miscalibration of confidence** seems to be most serious in cases when we're extremely confident; it seems that people who are "absolutely sure" are the ones most likely to be wrong. It's important to note that although overconfidence is common, it is not always the rule. In cases in which answers are rather easy to arrive at, we are actually a little underconfident. For instance, having taken a test that was fairly easy, you may be a little cautious in your estimation of how you did, perhaps to avoid "getting your hopes up." In this type of situation, people are a little too cautious in their estimates. (By the way, absinthe is a liqueur.)

CONFIDENCE CALIBRATION

Your task here is to set a 90% confidence interval for each answer. In other words, your answer will be a range within which you're 90% sure the answer falls. Try to set your ranges so that they're not too narrow (overconfident) or too wide (underconfident).

I am 90% confident the answer falls between:

1. Estimated number of tigers (all types) in the wild as of 2007   _____ and _____
2. Year in which the first professional baseball team was established   _____ and _____
3. Highest recorded temperature in Oslo, Norway   _____ and _____
4. Length of the Amazon River   _____ and _____
5. Average salary in 2007 for an NBA player   _____ and _____
6. Population of Dublin as of 2006 census   _____ and _____
7. Estimated number of civilian casualties in World War I   _____ and _____
8. Year in which Genghis Khan was born   _____ and _____
9. Approximation gestation period of a giant panda   _____ and _____
10. Number of nations that belong to the UN   _____ and _____

If your confidence is well calibrated to your accuracy, you should be correct on 90% or more of your intervals (answers on the bottom of this page).

- Did you show good calibration of confidence?
- Was your range too narrow (overconfident)?
- Too wide (underconfident)?
- What is your explanation?

1. 6000   2. 1869   3. 95 degrees Fahrenheit; 35 Celsius   4. 4195 mi/6712 km   5. $5.2 million   6. 505,000   7. 10 million   8. 1162   9. 145 days   10. 192 nations

Plous (1993) notes the potentially grave consequences of overconfidence, citing a study by Bedau and Radelet (1987) on wrongful convictions for capital crimes. This study revealed 350 documented instances of innocent defendants being wrongfully convicted. Plous points out that this is an example of overconfidence. The standard of proof in a criminal trial is a volume of evidence that would suggest that a defendant is "guilty beyond a reasonable doubt." Obviously, the convictions of these innocent individuals were instances of overconfident juries that failed to find reasonable doubt when there was some to be found.

STOP *and* **REVIEW!**

1. What are heuristics, and why are they used?
2. Define the availability heuristic.
3. When people make judgments based on representativeness, they're basing their judgments on
   a. recency in memory.
   b. similarity.
   c. their first impressions.
   d. what they thought they knew before.
4. Describe the spotlight effect and what heuristic seems to be implicated.
5. True or false? Research fails to support the old saying that "Hindsight is 20/20."

➤ The processes of judgment involve arriving at some conclusion about unknown events. Because of limits in capacity and information, we rely on heuristics, "shortcuts" that allow us to make quick judgments.

➤ The availability heuristic is the tendency to make judgments based on how easily an example can be brought to mind. Biases in the encoding and retrieval of events can lead to biased application of the availability heuristic. An illusory correlation is made when the vividness of an example causes someone to see a relationship between events when none exists. The recognition heuristic is the tendency to choose a familiar alternative over an unfamiliar one when asked to pick which is greater on some dimension.

➤ The representativeness heuristic involves making judgments based on the similarity between an event or person and our stereotype of it/them. This heuristic can lead to a tendency to ignore basic principles of probability which results in the conjunction fallacy (the belief that two events are more likely than just one of the events). The conjunction fallacy (and other thinking biases) might sometimes be attributable not to irrationality but to alternative construals that subjects might have of the problems.

➤ People tend to misperceive event clusters as nonrandom, leading to a fallacious belief in a "hot hand" and the gambler's fallacy. The anchoring-and-adjustment heuristic occurs when a person makes an initial estimate and then fails to make sufficient adjustments to arrive at their final estimate. Anchoring and adjustment seem to underlie the spotlight effect, our tendency to believe that others notice our actions and appearance more than they actually do.

➤ Judgments about our own judgments are also suspect. The hindsight bias refers to our tendency, after an event has happened, to inflate the degree to which we knew that something was going to happen. Miscalibration of confidence refers to the fact that the confidence we have in our judgments is not always a good indicator of our judgments' accuracy.

Decision Making

Despite the errors that occur when we make judgments, these judgments form an important part of the database for the process of decision making. For example, consider the following conversation:

> *Person A:* If there's a good chance that Tom will be at the party, then I think we should go. What do you think the chances are he'll go?
> *Person B:* Oh, I'm pretty sure he'll be there.
> *Person A:* OK, then let's go.

In this situation, the decision (going to the party) is based on the judgment of another event happening (whether Tom will be there). But decision making goes beyond this judgment to include a choice between alternatives: Do you go to the party or stay home? The fact that decision making involves choice introduces another element to the thinking mix—that of risk, or uncertainty. When you choose among a number of alternatives, there is always a chance that your choice will be the wrong one.

The consequences in the above decision-making scenario are not dire. If Tom isn't at the party, you still might have a good time. But what if the decision were a bigger one? For example, suppose you had to decide on a contractor for an important building renovation and the contingent event was whether or not a particular company would come in on budget. The consequences of a faulty judgment in this situation could be serious. According to the *threshold approach to choice* (Clemen, 1991), if a decision (e.g., choosing a given contractor or not) depends on the likelihood of another event happening (e.g., coming in on budget), then the attractiveness of the option should increase as the probability of the other event increases. Once that probability reaches a minimal level of certainty, the alternative will be chosen. Given what you just learned about the relationship between confidence and judgment, you might anticipate that overconfidence will be at play in this situation: the minimal level of certainty may be reached too easily.

 **Research Theme: Culture**

Is the minimal level of certainty likely to vary with culture? Would you be more concerned about overconfidence if the decision maker was American or Chinese? If you are like the subjects in a study by Yates, Lee, and Shinotsuka (1996), you're probably thinking that the American would be more likely to fall victim to overconfidence. But you, like the study subjects, are wrong. People from the Chinese culture show a greater overconfidence in their judgments than do Americans. What accounts for this difference?

Before addressing this question, the researchers wanted to be sure that the finding was reliable and practical. The difference in overconfidence had been demonstrated within the limited context of answering general knowledge questions like "For which is the gestation period longer, (a) humans or (b) chimpanzees?" Using this type of question can assess whether overconfidence is present, but it cannot assess the ramifications. In decision-making situations, there are ramifications of our judgments. Therefore, Yates, Lee, Shinotsuka, Patalano, and Sieck (1998) wanted to investigate whether overconfidence generalizes to the type of judgments needed to make practical decisions. In addition, these researchers wanted to determine if the greater overconfidence exhibited by Chinese subjects would be found in a decision-making situation.

Subjects from the United States and Taiwan were asked to take the role of a physician in a situation in which two new diseases that shared similar symptoms were discovered. They were instructed to examine a series of patient profiles, make a decision as to which disease the patient had, and rate their confidence in that judgment. They then received feedback concerning the accuracy of that diagnosis. The assumption was that over time, subjects would learn which configuration of symptoms was diagnostic for each disease and that this would affect their decision. Feedback was given in order to help subjects calibrate their confidence.

The results indicated that all subjects showed overconfidence; they were more confident in the accuracy of their decisions than was warranted by the actual measure of accuracy. This overconfidence effect was greater than that normally found with general knowledge questions. Furthermore, Chinese subjects showed more overconfidence than American subjects, indicating that this cross-cultural difference in overconfidence in judgment generalizes to decision-making situations.

The authors suggest that cultural differences in approaches to cognitive tasks may be responsible for this difference. It is common in Chinese culture to emphasize the importance of memorization in the acquisition of knowledge. Given the prevalent belief that memory is veridical (i.e., that it must be true) rather than reconstructive (i.e., that it is subject to reconstructive processes, as you read about in Chapter 7), cultures that rely on a memory strategy (in this case, memorization) would be more likely to show overconfidence. The authors conclude that "in situations where decisions are made using the logic underlying common Western ways of construing decision problems, ignoring the cultures of decision makers is risky" (p. 115).

Expected Utility: A Normative Approach

The study of simple choice and decision making has a long history. Economists have always been interested in the factors involved in choice and what type of model describes rational choice behavior. One of the most well-established theories of decision making is **expected utility theory.** Basically, this theory states that when faced with some type of uncertain choice, we make our decisions based on two factors—the expected utility of the outcomes and their respective probability. Utility refers to whatever end a person would like to achieve, be it happiness, money, or something else. Baron (1999) suggests that *good* might be a better word to use; utility refers to the amount of good that comes out of a decision (Broome, 1991). So basically, we weigh the good that might come out of each alternative against the costs of that alternative. We also assess the probability of each alternative occurring. Whichever alternative provides the best combination of "good" and "likelihood of occurring" will be the one we choose. Consider these choices:

Flip a coin; if it turns up heads, you get $40.
Roll the dice; if it comes up 4, you get $50.

Most people would probably choose the first option because it seems like a better combination of good and probability. You stand to get $10 less than if you choose the second option, but the probability of winning in the first option is much greater. This greater probability offsets the slight difference in monetary value.

Violations of Expected Utility. Expected utility theory provides a normative description of decision making—that is, it lays out the ways human beings would choose among alternatives if humans were perfectly rational decision makers. Given that expected utility theory provides a view of the ideal decision maker, it serves as a useful baseline against which actual decision making can be compared. So what should the ideal decision maker do and not do? Let's take a look at one of the normative predictions made by expected utility theory. According to the principle, our choices should show *invariance;* that is, a decision maker's choices should not depend on the way a choice is presented. (In other words, a preference should be invariant across different sorts of situations.) If I prefer choice A over choice B in situation 1, then I should prefer choice A over choice B in situation 14 (as long as A and B are identical in the two situations).

As you'll see, it's quite easy to get people to violate the assumption of invariance. People often do switch their preferences of one outcome over another, based only on how these outcomes are presented, thereby demonstrating *irrationality.* Consider the **preference reversals** shown in a classic series of studies by Lichtenstein and Slovic (1971, 1973). Their general procedure involved having subjects look at two different gambles and decide (1) which gamble they would like to play and (2) how much the gamble was worth. Try this for yourself. Look at the choices in Figure 12.6. First, imagine which gamble you would choose; then for each pair, imagine that you "own" the gamble and are trying to sell it—how much will you charge? You would think that a rational person would be consistent. If they preferred one gamble over the other, they would also say it was worth more and set a higher price for it. (Is this what you did?) Lichtenstein and Slovic expected otherwise; they thought that the choice of which gamble to play would be influenced by the probability of winning, whereas the choice of the selling price for the gamble would depend on the potential dollar amount to be won. Think about why this preference reversal is irrational. If subjects think that one gamble should go for a higher price than the other gamble, why didn't they choose it? And this result is not limited to questionnaires about theoretical choices given within a laboratory setting. Lichtenstein and Slovic (1973) found exactly the same results when they conducted the study in a Las Vegas casino (in which the sample included a number of card dealers!).

The preference reversal phenomenon is only one of a number of phenomena that demonstrate the inadequacy of expected utility as a descriptive model of decision making. The expected utility model fails to provide a good description of how we make choices in many circumstances because it assumes too much; humans rarely, if ever, have all of the information necessary to make a decision. Even if we did, we would lack the ability to combine and weigh the information accurately. Also, expected utility proposes that we base our decisions on expected consequences, but there is no real way to foresee consequences with any certainty. Expected utility is still one of the most common yardsticks by which the rationality of human decision making is measured, but

1. 80% chance to win $4.00
    20% chance to lose $.50
	4. 10% chance to win $40.00
	    90% chance to lose $1.00

2. 95% chance to win $3.00
    5% chance to lose $2.00
	5. 50% chance to win $6.50
	    50% chance to lose $1.00

3. 99% chance to win $4.00
    1% chance to lose $1.00
	6. 33% chance to win $16.00
	    67% chance to lose $2.00

Figure 12.6 Sample choices in preference reversal experiments.

From Lichtenstein, S., & Slovic, P. (1971). Reversals of preference between bids and choices in gambling choices. *Journal of Experimental Psychology, 89,* 46–55. Copyright 1971 by the American Psychological Association. Reprinted by permission.

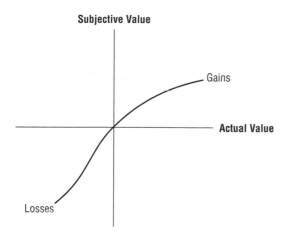

Figure 12.7 Hypothetical value function proposed in prospect theory.

From Kahneman, D., & Tversky, A. (1984). Choices, values, and frames. *American Psychologist, 39,* 341–350. Copyright 1984 by the American Psychologial Association. Reprinted by permission.

psychologists have attempted to develop descriptive models of how we actually do make decisions in order to accommodate "irrationality."

Prospect Theory: A Descriptive Approach

One popular alternative to expected utility theory is Kahneman and Tversky's (1979) prospect theory. **Prospect theory** is a descriptive model of decision making that attempts to describe how we make decisions and why our decisions violate the expected utility model. According to prospect theory, decisions are not valued based on the absolute value of the end result, as proposed by expected utility; instead, we value decisions based on the amount of gain or loss from what we have right now. Another important feature of the model is that it proposes that gains and losses are on different scales of value. Figure 12.7 plots the value that we place on gains and losses. Gains are to the right of center, and losses are to the left. Note that the value we attach to gains increases more slowly as a function of the size of the gain than does the (negative) value we place on losses as a function of the size of the loss. Basically, we feel losses more acutely than we feel gains; the psychological pain associated with losing $50 is greater than the psychological pleasure of gaining $50. Prospect theory predicts that people will be especially averse to loss and will show differences in preference depending on how alternatives are presented, or framed.

Framing.   Prospect theory predicts that our preferences will change whenever our reference point (i.e., what we have right now) changes. This means that decisions can be influenced by how information is presented. If information is presented in terms of a positive "gain frame" (emphasizing the certainty of what we have right now), we will be more likely to avoid risk (i.e., risk averse) and pick the surer bet. However, if the same information is presented in a negative "loss frame" (emphasizing what we might lose if we make a particular decision), we will be more likely to take a risk (i.e., risk prone) to avoid this loss. **Framing** is the term used to describe the effects on our decisions of how a scenario is presented.

Consider the results of a classic study by Tversky and Kahneman (1981, p. 453). Subjects were presented with this scenario and two choices:

Imagine that the U.S. is preparing for the outbreak of an unusual Asian disease, which is expected to kill 600 people. Two alternative programs for combating the disease have been proposed. Assume that the exact scientific estimate of the consequences of the program is as follows:

If program A is adopted, 200 people will be saved.

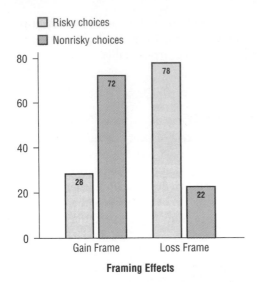

Figure 12.8 Results from Tversky and Kahneman (1981).

From Tversky, A., & Kahneman, D. (1981). The framing of decisions and the psychology of choice. *Science, 211*, 453–458. Copyright 1981 by the American Psychological Association. Reprinted by permission.

If program B is adopted, there is a $^1/_3$ probability that 600 people will be saved, and a $^2/_3$ probability that no one will be saved.

Other subjects were presented with exactly the same problem but different choices:

If program C is adopted, 400 people will die.

If program D is adopted, there is a $^1/_3$ probability that nobody will die, and a $^2/_3$ probability that 600 people will die.

If you look closely, you'll note something a little peculiar: the choice between A and B is exactly the same as the choice between C and D, but they're worded differently. The first choice is presented in terms of what is to be gained, while the second is presented in terms of what is to be lost. Figure 12.8 shows the number of people who picked the nonrisky (options A and C) and risky (options B and D) alternatives as a function of how the alternatives were presented. As you can see, when the alternatives were presented in a gain frame, people were *risk averse*—unwilling to take a risk and preferring the "sure" alternative. But when the exact same choices were reworded and presented in a loss frame, people were *risk prone*—much more willing to take a risk to avoid loss.

You may wonder what this has to do with anything. Does this framing of alternatives have real-life implications? The answer is yes. Studies of medical decision making (McNeil, Pauker, Sox, & Tversky, 1986), decisions about health-related behaviors (Rothman & Salovey, 1997), and decisions about the continuation of romantic relationships (Boon & Griffin, 1996) have all shown influences of framing. So the effects of framing are seen in real-world contexts and seem to be wide ranging.

> **Research Theme:
> Neuroscience**

Risky Decision Making in the Brain. A spate of recent research has investigated the brain areas thought to be involved in decision making (e.g., Gonzalez, Dana, Koshino, & Just, 2005; Sanfey, Loewenstein, McClure, & Cohen, 2006; Trepel, Fox, & Poldrack, 2005). An fMRI study by Gonzalez, Dana, Koshino, and Just (2005) was designed to reveal a possible interaction between the frame in which a problem is presented and the amount of effort expended in arriving at a decision. Brain activity was monitored as subjects made decisions within standard framing scenarios that resembled the "Asian disease problem." The behavioral results replicated the standard finding nicely. In a gain frame, a sure thing was preferred to a risk while in a loss frame, the risk was preferred to the sure thing.

The brain-imaging results proved intriguing and indicated differences in cognitive effort between the two conditions. Overall, much of the brain activity occurred in frontal and parietal regions, indicating the involvement of working memory and, to some extent, mental imagery. But especially intriguing were the differences in relative amounts of brain activity between framing conditions. When things were framed in terms of gains, brain-imaging results indicated that the brain was considerably less active when faced with the certain alternative, relative to when it was faced with the risky alternative. The converse relationship was shown when choices were framed in terms of losses. In this case, the brain was considerably less active when faced with the risky alternative, relative to when it was faced with the certain alternative. These findings present an intriguing parallel to the oft-replicated behavioral result, and suggest that another consideration in decision making is the desire to minimize cognitive effort.

Psychological Accounting.   The research on framing indicates that we make different choices depending on how the alternatives are worded or framed. Kahneman and Tversky (1981, p. 457) demonstrate a similar effect in people's consideration of the outcomes of their decisions. According to the *psychological accounting principle,* people will make different decisions depending on how the outcome is felt or perceived. Consider the following scenarios:

1. Imagine that you have decided to see a play for which admission is $10 a ticket. As you enter the theater, you discover that you have lost a $10 bill. Would you still pay $10 for a ticket to the play?
2. Imagine that you have decided to see a play for which admission is $10 a ticket. As you enter the theater, you discover that you have lost the ticket. The seat was not marked, and the ticket cannot be recovered. Would you pay $10 for a ticket to the play?

In these scenarios, what is being manipulated is not the cost or benefit; it's the way that subjects are likely to think about the extra $10 that needs to be spent. Kahneman and Tversky (1981) term this a *difference in psychological accounting.* In both scenarios, an extra 10 bucks needs to be shelled out. In which scenario does this seem more painful? In Kahneman and Tversky's study, subjects were less willing to purchase a ticket in scenario 2. Why should this be? In that scenario, $10 has already been invested for the play, so spending another $10 seems an unattractive alternative. In scenario 1, we simply have lost $10, money that could have been spent for anything. So it seems that we are less averse to losing money from our general "psychological account" than we are from our "play account," which has already been tapped for the $10 play ticket. But this distinction is a little silly. In both scenarios, we're out $20, and we get to see a play; so there should be no difference in our willingness to spend 10 more dollars.

Sunk Costs.   Another interesting variation on the notion of psychological accounting relates to what has been termed the **sunk-cost effect.** This effect was demonstrated by Arkes and Blumer (1985). In one experiment, subjects were to imagine that they had purchased tickets for two different ski trips: one ticket (for a ski trip to Wisconsin) cost $50, while the other ticket (for a ski trip to Michigan) cost $100. The scenario made it clear that the trip to Wisconsin was preferable because it would be more enjoyable. Then a complication arose: the two trips were on the same weekend, and the tickets were nonrefundable. Which trip would you choose to go on? Most subjects chose the Michigan trip even though the Wisconsin trip was touted as being more enjoyable.

Why? Because, according to their "psychological accounting," not going to Michigan would waste more money. Keep in mind, however, that the costs were already "sunk." Subjects were out $150 no matter what. But because more money was invested in the Michigan trip, subjects felt that they had to follow through on this particular investment. When people have invested more time, effort, or money into a given situation, they feel more compelled to go ahead with it, sometimes "throwing good money after bad."

STOP *and* THINK!

TV DINNERS

Read the following problem and make the choice yourself; then enlist a friend or two and see how they choose (from Arkes & Blumer, 1985):

On your way home you buy a TV dinner on sale for $3 at a local grocery store. A few hours later, you decide it is time for dinner, so you get ready to put the TV dinner in the oven. Then you get an idea. You call up a friend to ask if he would like to come over for a quick TV dinner and then watch a good movie. Your friend says, "Sure." So you go out to buy a second TV dinner. However, all of the on-sale TV dinners are gone. You therefore have to spend $5 (the regular price) for a TV dinner identical to the one you just bought for $3. You go home and put both dinners in the oven. When the two dinners are fully cooked, you get a call. Your friend is ill and cannot come. You are not hungry enough to eat both dinners. You cannot freeze one. You must eat one and discard the other. Which one do you eat?

Notice that there is no difference between the TV dinners in terms of their quality or the type of food; the only difference is that you spent more money on one of them.

- Did this make a difference in your decision?
- Did it make a difference to your friends?
- How do you explain this?

Affect and Decision Making.   The framing and psychological accounting effects just discussed underscore the role that affect and subjective feelings can play in decision making. Positive and negative outcomes *feel* different to us, with predictable implications for the decisions we make. In other words, *affect* is an important determinant of decision making, and can have a sizable impact on your psychological accounting processes.

Hsee and Rottenstreich (2004) make this point by highlighting an important dimension of choice that interacts with affect, which they term *scope*; it basically refers to the sweep of a decision or action—how much impact will it have? Consider a concrete example of the joint influence of affect and scope provided by Hsee and Rottenstreich. Suppose you gave $10 to help save one endangered panda—feels pretty good, doesn't it? Now, how much would you give to save four endangered pandas? Of course, the answer to this question depends on whether the subjective value you derive from saving pandas

"Awwwww!" How might emotion impact decision making?

is somehow multiplicative. Would you feel four times as good? Probably not, but this scenario raises the question of the joint effect of subjective value and scope on decision making.

The authors propose a dual-process view of the relative impact of scope and subjective value on decision making. Their dual-process approach does map nicely onto the dual-process view of thought discussed earlier in the chapter. Hsee and Rottenstreich label their version of the dual processes a *deliberate mode* (which would map onto the conscious, System 2 reasoning discussed earlier) and an *affective mode* (which would map onto the unconscious, System 1 reasoning discussed earlier). When we're in a deliberate decision-making mode, we value things by calculation (e.g., four is better than two); when we're in an affective decision-making mode, we value things by feeling. Figure 12.9 depicts the relationship between these two valuation modes. The x-axis of this graph represents scope, while the y-axis represents the subjective value of a stimulus. Here's what the function tells us: In the deliberate decision-making mode (represented by the dotted line), as scope increases subjective value increases correspondingly. By contrast, in the affective decision-making mode (represented by the solid line), scope doesn't matter nearly as much. We're affected only by the presence or absence of a stimulus.

Take the panda question we asked above. According to Hsee and Rottenstreich (2004), how we feel about helping one or four pandas depends on what decision-making mode we're in. If we're in a deliberative decision-making mode, helping four pandas is going to seem much better than helping just one, and we're likely to value these different options accordingly. However, if we're in an affective decision-making mode, all that matters is we're helping pandas. The difference between helping one and helping four isn't very salient. But you will notice that in the affective decision-making mode, saving one panda is valued much more highly than it is in the deliberative mode.

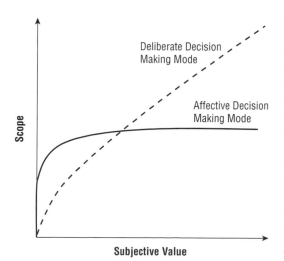

Figure 12.9 A comparison of affective and deliberate decision-making.

Hsee, C. K. & Rottenstreich, Y. (2004). Music, pandas, and muggers: On the affective psychology of value. *Journal of Experimental Psychology: General, 133*(1), 23–30. Published by the American Psychological Association. Reprinted with permission.

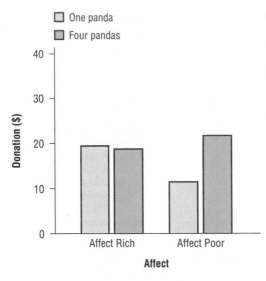

Figure 12.10 Results from Hsee and Rottenstreich (2004) study of affect and decision making.

Hsee, C. K. & Rottenstreich, Y. (2004). Music, pandas, and muggers: On the affective psychology of value. *Journal of Experimental Psychology: General, 133*(1), 23–30. Published by the American Psychological Association. Reprinted with permission.

So where is this going? Well, this model has some interesting predictions about how we'll value outcomes and make decisions, based on which decision-making mode is "primed." In one of their experiments, Hsee and Rottenstreich (2004) asked subjects to imagine that a zoology team had discovered some endangered pandas in a remote Asian region. They were going to save these pandas and were soliciting donations. The researchers manipulated two independent variables. The first was the instruction variable of scope; subjects were told that one panda would be saved or that four pandas would be saved. The other independent variable was the experimental-context variable of presentation mode, which was either affect low or affect rich. In the affect-low condition, subjects were shown a map of where the pandas had been found, with each panda represented by a black dot. In the affect-rich condition, instead of black dots, cute little pictures of pandas like 529 were used.

The results are depicted in Figure 12.10 and support Hsee and Rottenstreich's analysis. When the situation was affect rich and subjects had viewed pictures of one cute little panda or four cute little pandas, their offered donations were comparably large. When the situation was affect poor and subjects had viewed lifeless black dots, they were influenced by the number of pandas being saved, and donated considerably more in the case of four pandas, relative to the case of only one. These findings add another layer to the analysis of value originally proposed by Tversky and Kahneman in prospect theory. The subjective value of our choices is determined in part by our own affective mode at the time we make a choice.

STOP *and* REVIEW!

1. On what do we base our choices, according to expected utility theory?
2. True or false? According to prospect theory, gains carry more psychological weight than losses.
3. Describe the sunk-cost effect.

➤ Decision making involves choosing among alternatives that have different costs, benefits, and consequences. Expected utility theory, a normative approach to decision making, contends that choices are based on the attractiveness of consequences and the probability of the consequence. The outcome with the best combination is chosen. Choices should not vary with how choices are presented. Preference reversals indicate that they do.

➤ Prospect theory, a descriptive model, assumes that people make decisions based on what they have right now and interpret gains and losses on different scales, losses being more psychologically powerful. This theory predicts the framing effect, whereby people are risk averse when faced with certain gains, and risk prone when faced with certain losses.

➤ According to the psychological accounting principle, people make different decisions depending on how they feel about each outcome. The sunk-cost effect states that people overuse the resources already invested in a particular course of action as a decision criterion. Some research shows that affect plays an important role in the decisions we make. If affect is primed, a different set of decision processes is engaged, relative to when affect is not primed.

GLOSSARY

anchoring and adjustment: making an initial estimate based on knowledge or on presented information and making adjustments to that initial anchor to arrive at a final judgment (p. 515)

atmosphere effect: quantifiers used in syllogistic reasoning premises combine to form an "atmosphere" within which the validity of the conclusion is assessed (p. 491)

availability heuristic: the basing of our estimates of likelihood, or probability, on the ease with which we can think of examples (p. 503)

belief bias: the tendency to allow belief to interfere with the evaluation of conclusions in syllogistic reasoning (p. 491)

bounded rationality: the notion that there are limits to our powers of reasoning, judgment, and decision making (p. 488)

conditional reasoning: a deductive-reasoning task that involves evaluating whether a particular conclusion is valid given that certain conditions hold (p. 493)

confirmatory bias: our tendency to seek out or notice evidence that is consistent with a particular hypothesis rather than evidence that would be inconsistent with the hypothesis (p. 496)

conjunction fallacy: judging the joint probability of two events as more likely than just one event, due to the representativeness heuristic (p. 512)

decision making: a process that involves evaluating given information, making a judgment, and, based on these, making a choice among several possible alternatives (p. 486)

deductive reasoning: determining if a specific conclusion is valid based on general premises (p. 489)

deontic reasoning: reasoning about one's own duties and social obligations (p. 497)

descriptive approach: an approach to reasoning, judgment, and decision making that describes how we actually think (p. 487)

dread risk: our tendency to avoid situations in which many people may be killed at the same time while simultaneously being relatively impervious to risky situations in which deaths are more spread out (p. 507)

expected utility theory: the theory that states that when faced with uncertainty in choice, we make our decisions based on two factors—the expected utility of the outcomes and the respective probability of those outcomes (p. 523)

framing: the effect that how scenarios are presented affects our choice of behavior (p. 525)

gambler's fallacy: the belief that after a run of one certain type of outcome, a change is "due" to occur (p. 514)

hindsight bias: the tendency to believe after a chance event has occurred that we could have predicted that outcome (p. 517)

illusory correlation: when two events are vividly experienced together (i.e., a coincidence) and seem to be linked even when they're not (p. 508)

inductive reasoning: reasoning in which we move from specific pieces of data or information toward a general conclusion (p. 497)

judgment: the application of reasoning processes about given information and the use of this information to arrive at a conclusion (p. 486)

miscalibration of confidence: the tendency to be overconfident (or underconfident) in our judgments and decisions (p. 520)

normative approach: an approach to reasoning, judgment, and decision making that describes how we ought to think in a given situation (p. 487)

preference reversals: switching our preferences of one outcome over another based only on how these outcomes are presented (p. 524)

premises: the general principles or assertions that form the basis for deductive reasoning (p. 489)

prospect theory: the idea that decisions are based on the amount of gain or loss from what we have right now (p. 525)

reasoning: the evaluation of a conclusion based solely on given information (p. 486)

recognition heuristic: the tendency to choose a familiar alternative over an unfamiliar one when asked to pick which is greater on some dimension (p. 509)

representativeness heuristic: basing estimates of likelihood on the degree to which an object represents (is similar to) our basic idea (or stereotype) of that object (p. 509)

spotlight effect: the tendency to believe that others notice our actions and appearance more than they actually do (p. 516)

sunk-cost effect: the tendency to continue investing in a given situation (even in the face of loss) after we have spent a good deal of time, effort, or money (p. 527)

syllogistic reasoning: determining whether a conclusion is valid given the truth of quantified (i.e., *all, some,* or *none*) premises (p. 490)

References

Adams, R. M. (1992). The "hot hand" revisited: Successful basketball shooting as a function of intershot interval. *Perceptual & Motor Skills, 74,* 934.

Addis, D. R., Alana, T., & Schacter, D. L. (2007). Remembering the past and imagining the future: Common and distinct neural substrates during event construction and elaboration. *Neuropsychologia, 45,* 1363–1377.

Addis, D. R., Moscovitch, M., Crawley, A. P., & McAndrews, M. P. (2004). Recollective qualities modulate hippocampal activation during autobiographical memory retrieval. *Hippocampus, 14,* 752–762.

Allen, G. A., Mahler, W. A., & Estes, W. K. (1969). Effects of recall tests on long-term retention of paired associates. *Journal of Verbal Learning and Verbal Behavior, 8,* 463–470.

Allopenna, P. D., Magnuson, J. S., & Tanenhaus, M. K. (1998). Tracking the time course of spoken word recognition using eye movements: Evidence for continuous mapping models. *Journal of Memory and Language, 38,* 419–439.

Almor, A., & Sloman, S. A. (1996). Is deontic reasoning special? *Psychological Review, 103,* 174–180.

Amabile, T. M. (1990). Within you, without you: The social psychology of creativity, and beyond. In M. A. Runco & R. S. Albert (Eds.), *Theories of Creativity.* Newbury Park, CA: Sage.

Amabile, T. M. (1996). *Creativity in context.* Boulder, CO: Westview Press.

Anderson, J. R. (1974). Retrieval of propositional information from long-term memory. *Cognitive Psychology, 6,* 451–474.

Anderson, J. R. (1976). *Language, memory, and thought.* Hillsdale, NJ: Erlbaum.

Anderson, J. R. (1978). Arguments concerning representations for mental imagery. *Psychological Review, 86,* 395–406.

Anderson, J. R. (1982). Acquisition of cognitive skill. *Psychological Review, 89,* 369–406.

Anderson, J. R., & Bower, G. H. (1973). Human associative memory. Washington, DC: Winston.

Anderson, J. R., & Reder, L. M. (1999). The fan effect: New results and new theories. *Journal of Experimental Psychology: General, 128,* 186–197.

Anderson, M. C., & Bell, T. (2001). Forgetting our facts: The role of inhibitory processes in the loss of propositional knowledge. *Journal of Experimental Psychology: General, 130,* 544–570.

Anderson, M. C., Bjork, R. A., & Bjork, E. L. (1994). Remembering can cause forgetting: Retrieval dynamics in long-term memory. *Journal of Experimental Psychology: Learning, Memory, & Cognition, 20,* 1063–1087.

Anderson, S. J., & Conway, M. A. (1993). Investigating the structure of autobiographical memories. *Journal of Experimental Psychology: Learning, Memory, and Cognition, 19,* 1178–1191.

Andersson, J., & Roennberg, J. (1996). Collaboration and memory: Effects of dyadic retrieval on different memory tasks. *Applied Cognitive Psychology, 10,* 171–181.

Arbib, M. A. (2003). The evolving mirror system: A neural basis for language readiness. In M. H. Christiansen & S. Kirby (Eds.), *Language evolution. Studies in the evolution of language* (pp. 182–200). New York: Oxford University Press.

Arias, C., Curet, C. A., Moyano, H. F., Joekes, S. (1993). Echolocation: A study of auditory functioning in blind and sighted subjects. *Journal of Visual Impairment and Blindness, 87,* 73–77.

Arkes, H. R., & Blumer, C. (1985). The psychology of sunk cost. *Organizational Behavior and Human Decision Processes, 35,* 124–140.

Atchley, R., & Kwasny, K. M. (2003). Using event-related potentials to examine hemispheric differences in semantic processing. *Brain and Cognition, 53,* 133–138.

Atkinson, R. C., & Shiffrin, R. M. (1968). Human memory: A proposed system and its control processes. In W. K. Spence & J. T. Spence (Eds.), *The psychology of learning and motivation,* Vol. 2: *Advances in learning and theory* (pp. 89–195). New York: Academic Press.

Atran, S. (1990). *Cognitive foundations of natural history.* New York: Cambridge University Press.

Atran, S. (1998). Folbiology and the anthropology of science. Cognitive universals and cultural particulars. *Behavioral and Brain Sciences, 21,* 547–609.

Awh, E., Jonides, J., Smith, E. E., Schumacher, E. H., Koeppe, R. A., & Katz, S. (1996). Dissociation of storage and rehearsal in verbal working memory: Evidence from positron emission tomography. *Psychological Science, 7,* 25–31.

Bachevalier, J., & Mishkin, M. (1984). An early and a late developing system for learning and retention in infant monkeys. *Behavioral Neuroscience, 98,* 70–77.

Baddeley, A. D. (1966). Short-term memory for word sequences as a function of acoustic, semantic, and formal similarity. *Quarterly Journal of Experimental Psychology, 18,* 362–365.

Baddeley, A. D. (1986). *Working memory*. Oxford: Oxford University Press.

Baddeley, A. D. (1993). Working memory or working attention? In A. Baddeley & L. Weiskrantz (Eds.), *Attention: Selection, awareness, and control: A tribute to Donald Broadbent* (pp. 152–170). Glouchestershire, UK: Clarendon Press.

Baddeley, A. (2000a). The episodic buffer: A new component of working memory? *Trends in Cognitive Sciences, 4,* 417–423.

Baddeley, A. D. (2000b). Short-term working memory. In E. Tulving & F. I. M. Craik (Eds.), *The Oxford handbook of memory* (pp. 77–92). New York: Oxford University Press.

Baddeley, A. (2003). Working memory: Looking back and looking forward. *Nature Reviews Neuroscience, 4,* 829–839.

Baddeley, A. D., Lewis, V., & Vallar, G. (1984). Exploring the articulatory loop. *Quarterly Journal of Experimental Psychology, 36,* 233–252.

Baddeley, T. N., & Buchanan, M. (1975). Word length and the structure of short-term memory. *Journal of Verbal Learning and Verbal Behavior, 14,* 575–589.

Badets, A., Blandin, Y., Bouquet, C. A., & Shea, C. H. (2006). The intention superiority effect in motor skill learning. *Journal of Experimental Psychology: Learning, Memory, and Cognition, 32,* 491–505.

Bahrick, H. P. (1979). Maintenance of knowledge: Questions about memory we forgot to ask. *Journal of Experimental Psychology: General, 108,* 296–308.

Bahrick, H. P. (1984). Semantic memory content in permastore: Fifty years of memory for Spanish learned in school. *Journal of Experimental Psychology: General, 113,* 1–29.

Bahrick, H. P. (2000). Long-term maintenance of knowledge. In E. Tulving and F. I. M. Craik (Eds.), *The Oxford handbook of memory* (pp. 347–362). New York: Academic Press.

Bahrick, H. P. (2005). The long-term neglect of long-term memory: Reasons and remedies. In A. F. Healy (Ed.), *Experimental cognitive psychology and its applications. Decade of behavior* (pp. 89–100). Washington, DC: American Psychological Association.

Bahrick, H. P., & Hall, L. K. (1991). Lifetime maintenance of high school mathematics content. *Journal of Experimental Psychology: General, 120,* 20–33.

Bahrick, H. P., Hall, L. K., & Berger, S. A. (1996). Accuracy and distortion in memory for high school grades. *Psychological Science, 7,* 265–271.

Balch, W. R., Bowman, K., & Mohler, L. A. (1992). Music-dependent memory in immediate and delayed word recall. *Memory and Cognition, 20,* 21–28.

Balota, D. A., Pollatsek, A., & Rayner, K. (1985). The interaction of contextual constraints and parafoveal visual information in reading. *Cognitive Psychology, 17,* 364–390.

Banaji, M. R., & Crowder, R. G. (1989). The bankruptcy of everyday memory. *American Psychologist, 44,* 1185–1193.

Bar, M., & Aminoff, E. (2003). Cortical analysis of visual context. *Neuron, 38,* 347–358.

Bar, M., & Biederman, I. (1998). Subliminal visual priming. *Psychological Science, 9,* 464–469.

Baron, J. (1999). *Thinking and deciding* (3rd ed.). New York: Cambridge University Press.

Baron-Cohen, S., Burt, L., Smith-Laittan, F., & Harrison, J. (1996). Synaesthesia: Prevalence and familiarity. *Perception, 25,* 1073–1080.

Barron, F., & Harrington, D. M. (1981). Creativity, intelligence, and personality. *Annual Review of Psychology, 32,* 439–476.

Barsalou, L. W. (1983). Ad hoc categories. *Memory and Cognition, 11,* 211–227.

Barsalou, L. W. (1988). The content and organization of autobiographical memories. In U. Neisser & E. Winograd (Eds.), *Remembering reconsidered: Ecological and traditional approaches to the study of cognition* (pp. 193–243). New York: Cambridge University Press.

Bass, E., & Davis, L. (1988). *The courage to heal: A guide for women survivors of childhood sexual abuse*. New York: Harper and Row.

Bates, E., Devescovi, A., & Wulfeck, B. (2001). Psycholinguistics: A cross-language perspective. *Annual Review of Psychology, 52,* 369–396.

Battig, W., & Montague, P. (1969). Category norms of verbal items in 56 categories: A replication and extension of the Connecticut category norms. *Journal of Experimental Psychology, 80,* 1–46.

Bauer, M. I., & Johnson-Laird, P. N. (1993). How diagrams can improve reasoning. *Psychological Science, 4,* 372–378.

Bauer, P. J. (2004). Getting explicit memory off the ground: Steps toward construction of a neuro-developmental account of changes in the first two years of life. *Developmental Review, 24,* 347–373.

Beck, D. M., & Palmer, S. E. (2002). Top-down influences on perceptual grouping. *Journal of Experimental Psychology: Human Perception and Performance, 28,* 1071–1084.

Bedau, H. A., & Radelet, M. L. (1987). Miscarriages of justice in potentially capital cases. *Stanford Law Review, 40,* 21–179.

Beede, K. E., & Kass, S. J. (2006). Engrossed in conversation: The impact of cell phones on simulated driving performance. *Accident Analysis & Prevention, 38,* 415–421.

Beeman, M. J., & Bowden, E. M. (2000). The right hemisphere maintains solution-related activation for yet-to-be-solved problems. *Memory & Cognition, 28,* 1231–1241.

Behrman, B. W., & Davey, S. L. (2001). Eyewitness identification in actual criminal cases: An archival analysis. *Law and Human Behavior, 25,* 475–491.

Behrmann, M. (2000). The mind's eye mapped onto the brain's matter. *Current Directions in Psychological Science, 9,* 50–54.

Bellezza, F. S. (1982). Updating memory using mnemonic devices. *Cognitive Psychology, 14,* 301–327.

Beluggi, U., Klima, E. S., & Siple, P. (1974). Remembering in signs. *Cognition, 3,* 83–125.

Berlin, B. (1992). *Ethnobiological classification.* Princeton, NJ: Princeton University Press.

Berntsen, D. (1996). Involuntary biographical memories. *Applied Cognitive Psychology, 10,* 435–454.

Berntsen, D. (1998). Voluntary and involuntary access to autobiographical memory. *Applied Cognitive Psychology, 6,* 113–141.

Berntsen, D., & Hall, N. M. (2004). The episodic nature of involuntary autobiographical memories. *Memory & Cognition, 32,* 789–803.

Berrios, G. E. (1995). Deja vu in France during the 19th century: A conceptual history. *Comprehensive Psychiatry, 36,* 123–129.

Bertelson, P. (1999). Ventriloquism: A case of crossmodal perceptual grouping. In G. Aschersleben, T. Bachmann, & J. Müsseler (Eds.), *Cognitive contributions to the perception of spatial and temporal events. Advances in psychology, 129,* (pp. 347–362). Amsterdam, Netherlands: North-Holland/Elsevier Science Publishers.

Besner, D., & Stolz, J. A. (1999). Unconsciously controlled processing: The Stroop effect reconsidered. *Psychonomic Bulletin and Review, 6,* 449–455.

Besner, D., Stolz, J. A., & Boutilier, C. (1997). The Stroop effect and the myth of automaticity. *Psychonomic Bulletin and Review, 4,* 221–225.

Besson, M., Faita, F., Peretz, I., Bonnel, A.-M., & Requin, J. (1998). Singing in the brain: Independence of lyrics and tunes. *Psychological Science, 9,* 494–498.

Best, C. T., & Avery, R. A. (1999). Left-hemisphere advantage for click consonants is determined by linguistic significance and experience. *Psychological Science, 10,* 65–70.

Best, C. T., Hoffman, H., & Glanville, B. B. (1982). Development of infant-ear asymmetries for speech and music. *Perception and Psychophysics, 31,* 75–85.

Biederman, I. (1987). Recognition-by-components: A theory of human image understanding. *Psychological Review, 94,* 115–147.

Biederman, I., & Cooper, E. E. (1991). Priming contour-deleted images: Evidence for intermediate representations in visual object recognition. *Cognitive Psychology, 23,* 393–419.

Biederman, I., & Gerhardstein, P. C. (1993). Recognizing depth-rotated objects: Evidence and conditions for three-dimensional viewpoint invariance. *Journal of Experimental Psychology: Learning, Memory, and Cognition, 19,* 1162–1182.

Biederman, I., Mezzanotte, R. J., & Rabinowitz, J. C. (1982). Scene perception: Detecting and judging objects undergoing relational violations. *Cognitive Psychology, 14,* 143–177.

Bisanz, T., Bisanz, M., & Korpan, J. (1994). Inductive reasoning. In R. J. Sternberg (Ed.), *Thinking and problem solving* (pp. 179–213). New York: Academic Press.

Bisiach, E., & Luzzatti, C. (1978). Unilateral neglect of representational space. *Cortex, 14,* 129–133.

Bjork, R. A., & Whitten, W. B. (1974). Recency-sensitive retrieval processes in long-term free recall. *Cognitive Psychology, 6,* 173–189.

Blanchard, I., Pollatsek, A., & Rayner, K. (1989). The acquisition of parafoveal word information in reading. *Perception and Psychophysics, 46,* 85–94.

Blanchette, I., & Dunbar, K. (2000). How analogies are generated: The roles of structural and superficial similarity. *Memory and Cognition, 28,* 108–124.

Blaney, P. H. (1986). Affect and memory: A review. *Psychological Bulletin, 99,* 229–246.

Block, N. (1995). On a confusion about a question of consciousness. *Behavioral and Brain Sciences, 18,* 227–287.

Bohannon, J. N., & Symons, V. L. (1992). Flashbulb memories: Confidence, consistency, and quality. In E. Winograd & U. Neisser (Eds.), *Affect and accuracy in recall: Studies of "flashbulb" memories* (pp. 65–91). New York: Cambridge University Press.

Boon, S. D., & Griffin, D. W. (1996). The construction of risk in relationships: The role of framing in decisions about intimate relationships. *Personal Relationships, 3,* 293–306.

Bothwell, R. K., Brigham, J. C., & Malpass, R. S. (1989). Cross-racial identification. *Personality and Social Psychology Bulletin, 15,* 19–25.

Bowden, E. M., & Beeman, M. J. (1998). Getting the right idea: Semantic activation in the right hemisphere may help solve insight problems. *Psychological Science, 9,* 435–440.

Bowden, E. M., & Jung-Beeman, M. (2003). Aha! Insight experience correlates with solution activation in the right hemisphere. *Psychonomic Bulletin & Review, 10,* 730–737.

Bowden, E. M., Jung-Beeman, M., Fleck, J., & Kounios, J. (2005). New approaches to demystifying insight. *Trends in Cognitive Sciences, 9,* 322–328.

Bowen, R. W., Pola, J., & Matin, L. (1974). Visual persistence: Effects of flash luminance, duration, and energy. *Vision Research, 14,* 295–303.

Bower, G. H., Black, J. B., & Turner, T. J. (1979). Scripts in memory for text. *Cognitive Psychology, 11,* 177–120.

Bower, G. H., Clark, M. C., Lesgold, A. M., & Winzenz, D. (1969). Hierarchical schemes in recall of categorized word lists. *Journal of Verbal Learning and Verbal Behavior, 8,* 323–343.

Bowers, K. S., Regehr, G., Balthazard, C., & Parker, K. (1990). Intuition in the context of discovery. *Cognitive Psychology, 22,* 72–110.

Bowers, G. H., & Schacter, D. S. (1993). Priming of novel information in amnesic patients. In P. Graf & M. Masson (Eds.), *Implicit memory: New directions in cognition, development and neuropsychology* (pp. 303–326). Hillsdale, NJ: Erlbaum.

Boyce, S. J., & Pollatsek, A. (1992). Identification of objects in scenes: The role of scene background in object naming. *Journal of Experimental Psychology: Learning, Memory, and Cognition, 18,* 531–543.

Brandimonte, M. A., & Gerbino, W. (1993). Mental image reversal and verbal recoding: When ducks become rabbits. *Memory and Cognition, 21,* 23–33.

Bransford, J. D., & Stein, B. S. (1993). *The IDEAL problem solver* (2nd ed.). New York: Freeman.

Brédart, S., Brennen, T., Delchambre, M., McNeill, A., & Burton, A. M. (2005). Naming very familiar people: When retrieving names is faster than retrieving semantic biographical information. *British Journal of Psychology, 96,* 205–214.

Bregman, A. S. (1990). *Auditory scene analysis: The perceptual organization of sound.* Cambridge, MA: MIT Press.

Brewer, N., & Wells, G. L. (2006). The confidence-accuracy relationship in eyewitness identification: Effects of lineup instructions, foil similarity, and target-absent base rates. *Journal of Experimental Psychology: Applied, 12,* 11–30.

Brewer, W. (1986). What is autobiographical memory? In D. C. Rubin (Ed.), *Autobiographical memory* (pp. 25–49). Cambridge, UK: Cambridge University Press.

Brewer, W. F. (1988). Memory for randomly sampled autobiographical events. In U. Neisser & E. Winograd (Eds.), *Remembering reconsidered: Ecological and traditional approaches to the study of memory* (Emory Symposia in Cognition, vol. 2, pp. 21–90). Cambridge, UK: Cambridge University Press.

Brewin, C. R., Christodoulides, J., & Hutchinson, G. (1996). Intrusive thoughts and intrusive memories in a nonclinical sample. *Cognition and Emotion, 10,* 107–112.

Briem, V., & Hedman, L. R. (1995). Behavioural effects of mobile telephone use during simulated driving. *Ergonomics, 38,* 2536–2562.

Briere, J., & Conte, J. (1993). Self-reported amnesia for abuse in adults molested as children. *Journal of Traumatic Stress, 6,* 21–31.

Brigham, J. C. (1990). Target person distinctiveness and attractiveness as moderator variables in the confidence-accuracy relationship in eyewitness identification. *Basic and Applied Social Psychology, 11,* 101–115.

Broadbent, D. A. (1958). *Perception and communication.* London: Pergamon Press.

Brooks, L. R. (1967). Spatial and verbal components of the act of recall. *Canadian Journal of Psychology, 22,* 349–366.

Brooks, L. R. (1978). Nonanalytic concept formation and memory for instances. In E. Rosch & B. B. Lloyd (Eds.), *Cognition and categorization* (pp. 169–211). Hillsdale, NJ: Erlbaum.

Brooks, L. R. (1987). Decentralized control of categorization: The role of prior processing episodes. In U. Neisser (Ed.), *Concepts and conceptual development: The ecological and intellectual factors in categorization* (pp. 141–174). Cambridge, UK: Cambridge University Press.

Broome, J. (1991). Utilitarian metaphysics? In J. Elster & J. E. Roemer (Eds.), *Interpersonal comparisons of well being* (pp. 70–97). New York: Cambridge University Press.

Bross, M., & Borenstein, M. (1982). Temporal auditory acuity in blind and sighted subjects: A signal detection analysis. *Perceptual and Motor Skills, 55,* 963–966.

Brown, A. S. (1991). A review of the tip-of-the-tongue experience. *Psychological Bulletin, 109,* 204–223.

Brown, A. S. (2003). A review of the déjà vu experience. *Psychological Bulletin, 129,* 394–413.

Brown, A. S. (2004). The déjà vu illusion. *Current Directions in Psychological Science, 13,* 256–259.

Brown, A. S., & Murphy, D. R. (1989). Cryptomnesia: Delineating inadvertent plagiarism. *Journal of Experimental Psychology: Learning, Memory, and Cognition, 15,* 432–442.

Brown, E., Deffenbacher, K., & Sturgill, W. (1977). Memory for faces and the circumstances of encounter. *Journal of Applied Psychology, 62,* 311–318.

Brown, R., & Kulik, J. (1977). Flashbulb memories. *Cognition, 5,* 73–99.

Brown, R., & McNeill, D. (1966). The "tip of the tongue" phenomenon. *Journal of Verbal Learning and Verbal Behavior, 5,* 325–337.

Bruce, D. (1989). Functional explanations of memory. In L. W. Poon, D. C. Rubin, & B. C. Wilson (Eds.), *Everyday cognition in adulthood and later life* (pp. 44–58). New York: Cambridge University Press.

Bruce, V., & Young, A. W. (1986). Understanding face recognition. *British Journal of Psychology, 77,* 305–327.

Bruck, M., & Ceci, S. J. (1997). The suggestibility of young children. *Current Directions in Psychological Science, 6,* 75–79.

Bruck, M., & Ceci, S. J. (1999). Children's suggestibility. *Annual Review of Psychology, 50,* 419–439.

Bruck, M., & Ceci, S. (2004). Forensic developmental psychology. *Current Directions in Psychological Science, 13,* 229–232.

Bruck, M., Ceci, S. J., & Francoeur, E. (2000). Children's use of anatomically detailed dolls to report genital touching in a medical examination: Developmental and gender comparisons. *Journal of Experimental Psychology: Applied, 6,* 74–83.

Bruck, M., Ceci, S. J., Francoeur, E., & Renick, A. (1995). Anatomically detailed dolls do not facilitate preschoolers' reports of a pediatric examination involving genital touching. *Journal of Experimental Psychology: Applied, 1,* 95–109.

Bruner, J. (1990). *Acts of meaning.* Cambridge, MA: Harvard University Press.

Bruner, J. (1996). *The culture of education.* Cambridge, MA: Harvard University Press.

Brysbaert, M., & Vitu, F. (1998). Word skipping: Implications for theories of eye movement control in reading. In G. Underwood (Ed.), *Eye guidance in reading and scene perception* (pp. 125–147). Amsterdam: Elsevier Science.

Bunting, M. F., Conway, A. R. A., & Heitz, R. P. (2004). Individual differences in the fan effect and working memory capacity. *Journal of Memory and Language, 51,* 604–622.

Burke, D. M., MacKay, D. G., Worthley, J. S., & Wade, E. (1991). On the tip of the tongue: What causes word finding failures in young and older adults? *Journal of Memory and Language, 30,* 542–579.

Burke, D. M., & Shafto, M. A. (2004). Aging and language production. *Current Directions in Psychological Science, 13,* 21–24.

Burns, B. D. (2004). Heuristics as beliefs and as behaviors: The adaptiveness of the "hot hand." *Cognitive Psychology, 48,* 295–331.

Burton, M. A., & Bruce, V. (1992). I recognize your face, but I can't remember your name: A simple explanation? *British Journal of Psychology, 83,* 45–60.

Calvert, G. A., Bullmore, E. T., & Brammer, R. (1997). Activation of auditory cortex during silent lipreading. *Science, 276,* 593–596.

Campbell, R., & Dodd, B. (1980). Hearing by eye. *Quarterly Journal of Experimental Psychology, 32,* 85–99.

Caramazza, A., & Brones., I. (1980). Semantic classification by bilinguals. *Canadian Journal of Psychology, 34,* 77–81.

Carmichael, L., Hogan, H. P., & Walters, A. A. (1932). An experimental psychology of the effect of language on the reproduction of visually perceived form. *Journal of Experimental Psychology, 15,* 73–86.

Carreiras, M., Gernsbacher, M. A., & Villa, V. (1995). The advantage of first mention in Spanish. *Psychonomic Bulletin and Review, 2,* 124–129.

Carrier, M., & Pashler, H. (1992). The influence of retrieval on retention. *Memory and Cognition, 20,* 633–642.

Carroll, D. W. (1994). *Psychology of language* (2nd ed.). Pacific Grove, CA: Brooks/Cole.

Carver, R. P. (1971). Pupil dilation and its relationship to information processing during reading and listening. *Journal of Applied Psychology, 55,* 126–134.

Castles, A., & Coltheart, M. (2004). Is there a causal link from phonological awareness to success in learning to read? *Cognition, 91,* 77–111.

Cave, K. R., & Bichot, N. P. (1999). Visuospatial attention: Beyond a spotlight model. *Psychonomic Bulletin & Review, 6,* 204–223.

Ceci, S. J., & Bruck, M. (1993). Suggestibility of the child witness: A historical review and synthesis. *Psychological Bulletin, 113,* 403–439.

Chang, F., Dell, G. S., & Bock, K. (2006). Becoming syntactic. *Psychological Review, 113,* 234–272.

Chang, T. M. (1986). Semantic memory: Facts and models. *Psychological Bulletin, 99,* 199–220.

Channon, S. E., & Baker, J. E. (1996). Depression and problem-solving performance on a fault-diagnosis task. *Applied Cognitive Psychology, 10,* 327–336.

Chapman, G. B., & Bornstein, B. H. (1996). The more you ask for, the more you get: Anchoring in personal injury verdicts. *Applied Cognitive Psychology, 10,* 519–540.

Charness, N. (1976). Memory for chess positions: Resistance to interference. *Journal of Experimental Psychology:*

Human Learning and Memory, 2, 641–653.

Chase, K., & Ericsson, W. G. (1982). Exceptional memory. *American Scientist, 70,* 607–615.

Chase, W. G., & Simon, H. A. (1973). Perception in chess. *Cognitive Psychology, 4,* 55–81.

Cheesman, J., & Merikle, P. M. (1984). Priming with and without awareness. *Perception & Psychophysics, 36,* 387–395.

Cherry, E. C. (1953). Some experiments on the recognition of speech, with one and with two ears. *Journal of the Acoustical Society of America, 25,* 975–979.

Chi, M. T. H. (1996). Constructing self-explanations and scaffolded explanations in tutoring. *Applied Cognitive Psychology, 10,* 33–49.

Chi, M. T. H., Feltovich, P. J., & Glaser, R. (1981). Categorization and representation of physics problems by experts and novices. *Cognitive Science, 5,* 121–152.

Chomsky, N. (1957). *Syntactic structures.* The Hague: Mouton.

Chomsky, N. (1959). A review of Skinner's *Verbal behavior. Language, 35,* 26–58.

Chomsky, N. (1986). *Knowledge of language: Its nature, origin, and use.* New York: Praeger.

Christiansen, S.-A. (1989). Flashbulb memories: Special, but not so special. *Memory and Cognition, 17,* 435–443.

Christiansen, S.-A. (1992). Emotional stress and eyewitness memory: A critical review. *Psychological Bulletin, 112,* 284–309.

Chu, S., & Downes, J. J. (2000). Long live Proust: The odour-cued autobiographical memory bump. *Cognition, 75,* B41–B50.

Claparede, E. (1951). Recognition and "me-ness." In D. Rapaport (Ed.), *Organization and pathology of thought* (pp. 58–75). New York: Columbia University Press. (Reprinted from *Archives de Psychologie,* 1911, *11,* 79–90.)

Clark, H. H., & Haviland, S. E. (1977). Comprehension and the given-new contract. In R. O. Freedle (Ed.), *Discourse production and comprehension*. Norwood: Ablex.

Cohen, G., & Faulkner, D. (1986). Memory for proper names: Age differences in retrieval. *British Journal of Psychology, 4,* 187–197.

Cole, J. (1995). *Pride and a daily marathon*. Cambridge, MA: MIT Press.

Cole, N. S. (1997). *The ETS gender study: How females and males perform in educational settings*. Princeton, NJ: Educational Testing Services.

Colegate, R. L., Hoffman, J. E., & Eriksen, C. W. (1973). Selective encoding from multielement visual displays. *Perception & Psychophysics, 14,* 217–224.

Collins, A. M., & Loftus, E. F. (1975). A spreading-activation theory of semantic processing. *Psychological Review, 82,* 407–428.

Collins, A. M., & Quillian, M. R. (1969). Retrieval time from semantic memory. *Journal of Verbal Learning and Verbal Behavior, 8,* 240–247.

Collins, A. M., & Quillian, M. R. (1970). Does category size affect reaction time? *Journal of Verbal Learning and Verbal Behavior, 9,* 432–438.

Coltheart, M., Rastle, K., Perry, C., Langdon, R., & Ziegler, J. (2001). DRC: A dual route cascaded model of visual word recognition and reading aloud. *Psychological Review, 108,* 204–256.

Coltheart, V. (1993). Effects of phonological similarity and concurrent irrelevant articulation on short-term memory recall of repeated and novel lists. *Memory and Cognition, 21,* 539–545.

Conrad, C. (1972). Cognitive economy in semantic memory. *Journal of Experimental Psychology, 92,* 149–154.

Conrad, R. (1964). Acoustic confusions in immediate memory. *British Journal of Psychology, 55,* 75–84.

Conrad, R., & Hull, A. J. (1968). Input modality and the serial position

curve in short-term memory. *Psychonomic Science, 10,* 135–136.

Conway, A. R. A., Cowan, N., & Bunting, M. F. (2001). The cocktail party phenomenon revisited: The importance of WM capacity. *Psychonomic Bulletin & Review, 8,* 331–335.

Conway, M. A. (1990). *Autobiographical memory: An introduction*. Buckingham, UK: Open University Press.

Conway, M. A. (1991). In defense of everyday memory. *American Psychologist, 46,* 19–26.

Conway, M. A. (1997). Introduction: Models and data. In M. A. Conway (Ed.), *Cognitive models of memory*. Cambridge, MA: MIT Press.

Conway, M. A., & Bekerian, D. A. (1987). Organization in autobiographical memory. *Memory and Cognition, 15,* 119–132.

Conway, M. A., Cohen, G., & Stanhope, N. (1991). On the very long-term retention of knowledge acquired through formal education: Twelve years of cognitive psychology. *Journal of Experimental Psychology: General, 120,* 395–409.

Conway, M. A., & Pleydell-Pearce, C. W. 2001. The construction of autobiographical memories in the self memory system. *Psychological Review, 107,* 261–288.

Conway, M. A., Pleydell-Pearce, C. W., & Whitecross, S. E. (2001). The neuroanatomy of autobiographical memory: A slow cortical potential study of autobiographical memory retrieval. *Journal of Memory and Language, 45,* 493–524.

Conway, M. A., Turk, D. J., Miller, S. L., Logan, J., Nebes, R. D., Meltzer, C., & Becker, J. T. (1999). A positron emission tomography (PET) study of autobiographical memory retrieval. *Memory, 7,* 679–702.

Cooper, L. A. (1975). Mental rotation of random two-dimensional shapes. *Cognitive Psychology, 7,* 20–43.

Cooper, L. A., & Lang, R. (1996). Imagery and visual-spatial representations. In E. L. Bjork & R. A. Bjork

(Eds.), *Memory* (pp. 129–164). New York: Academic Press.

Cooper, L. A., & Schacter, D. L. (1992). Priming and recognition of transformed three-dimensional objects: Effects of size and reflection. *Journal of Experimental Psychology: Learning, Memory, and Cognition, 18,* 43–57.

Cooper, L. A., & Shepard, R. N. (1975). Mental rotation in the identification of left and right hands. *Journal of Experimental Psychology: Human Perception and Performance, 1,* 48–56.

Cornoldi, D., & de Beni, R. (1991). Memory for discourse: Loci mnemonics and the oral presentation effect. *Applied Cognitive Psychology, 5,* 511–518.

Correa-Chávez, M., Rogoff, B., & Arauz, R. M. (2005). Cultural patterns in attending to two events at once. *Child Development, 76,* 664–678.

Corteen, R. S., & Wood, B. (1972). Autonomic responses to shock-associated words in an unattended channel. *Journal of Experimental Psychology, 94,* 308–313.

Cosmides, L. (1989). The logic of social exchange: Has natural selection shaped how humans reason? Studies with the Wason selection task. *Cognition, 31,* 187–276.

Courtois, C. A. (1997). Delayed memories of child sexual abuse: Critique of the controversy and clinical guidelines. In M. Conway (Ed.), *Recovered memories and false memories* (pp. 206–229). Oxford: Oxford University Press.

Cowan, N. (1988). Evolving conceptions of memory storage, selective attention, and their mutual constraints within the human information-processing system. *Psychological Bulletin, 104,* 163–191.

Cowan, N. (1995). *Attention and memory: An integrated framework*. New York: Oxford University Press.

Cowan, N. (2001). The magical number 4 in short-term memory:

A reconsideration of mental storage capacity. *Behavioral and Brain Sciences, 24,* 87–185.

Cox, S. D., & Wollen, K. A. (1981). Bizarreness and recall. *Bulletin of the Psychonomic Society, 18,* 244–245.

Craig, J. C., & Rollman, G. B. (1999). Somesthesis. *Annual Review of Psychology, 50,* 305–331.

Craik, F. I. M. (1986). A functional account of age differences in memory. In F. Klix & H. Hagendorf (Eds.), *Human memory and cognitive capabilities: Mechanisms and performances* (pp. 409–422). Amsterdam: Elsevier-North-Holland.

Craik, F. I. M., & Lockhart, R. S. (1972). Levels of processing: A framework for memory research. *Journal of Verbal Learning and Verbal Behavior, 11,* 671–684.

Craik, F. I. M., & McDowd, J. M. (1987). Age differences in recall and recognition. *Journal of Experimental Psychology: Learning, Memory, and Cognition, 13,* 474–479.

Craik, F. I. M., & Tulving, E. (1975). Depth of processing and the retention of words in episodic memory. *Journal of Experimental Psychology: General, 104,* 268–294.

Craik, F. I. M., & Watkins, M. J. (1973). The role of rehearsal in short-term memory. *Journal of Verbal Learning and Verbal Behavior, 12,* 599–607.

Crowder, R. G. (1976). *Principles of learning and memory.* Hillsdale, NJ: Erlbaum.

Crowder, R. G. (1993). Short-term memory: Where do we stand? *Memory and Cognition, 21,* 142–145.

Crowder, R. G., & Morton, J. (1969). Precategorical acoustic storage (PAS). *Perception & Psychophysics, 6,* 365–373.

Cutler, A., & Butterfield, S. (1992). Rhythmic cues to speech segmentation: Evidence from juncture misperception. *Journal of Memory and Language, 31,* 218–236.

Cutler, A., & Carter, D. M. (1987). The predominance of strong initial syllables in the English vocabulary.

Computer Speech and Language, 2, 133–142.

Cutler, B. L., & Penrod, S. D. (1989). Moderators of the confidence-accuracy relationship in face recognition: The roles of information-processing and base rates. *Applied Cognitive Psychology, 3,* 95–107.

Cutler, B. L., & Penrod, S. D. (1995). *Mistaken identification: Eyewitnesses, psychology, and the law.* New York: Cambridge University Press.

Cutler, B. L., Penrod, S. D., & Martens, T. K. (1987). Improving the reliability of eyewitness identifications: Putting context into context. *Journal of Applied Psychology, 72,* 629–637.

Daneman, M., & Merikle, P. M. (1996). Working memory and language comprehension: A meta-analysis. *Psychonomic Bulletin and Review, 3,* 422–433.

Darwin, C. J., Turvey, M. T., & Crowder, R. G. (1973). An auditory analogue of the Sperling partial-report procedure. *Cognitive Psychology, 3,* 255–267.

Davenport, J. L., & Potter, M. C. (2004). Scene consistency in object and background perception. *Psychological Science, 15,* 559–564.

Davidson, J. E. (1995). The suddenness of insight. In R. J. Sternberg & J. E. Davidson (Eds.), *The nature of insight* (pp. 125–155). Cambridge, MA: MIT Press.

Davis, P. J. (1999). Gender differences in autobiographical memory for emotional experiences. *Journal of Personality and Social Psychology, 76,* 498–510.

Deakin, J. M., & Allard, F. (1991). Skilled memory in expert figure skaters. *Memory and Cognition, 19,* 79–86.

De Beni, R. (1988). The aid given by the "Loci" memory technique in the memorization of passages. In M. M. Gruneberg, P. E. Morris, & R. N. Sykes (Eds.), *Practical aspects of memory: Current research and issues* (Vol. 2, pp. 421–425). Chichester: Wiley & Sons.

Deese, J. (1959). On the prediction of occurrence of particular verbal intrusions in immediate recall. *Journal of Experimental Psychology, 58,* 17–22.

Deffenbacher, K. A. (1980). Eyewitness accuracy and confidence: Can we infer anything about their relationship? *Law and Human Behavior, 4,* 243–260.

Deffenbacher, K. A. (1994). Effects of arousal on everyday memory. *Human Performance, 7,* 141–161.

Deffenbacher, K. A., Bornstein, B. H., Penrod, S., & McGorty, E. K. (2004). A meta-analytic review of the effects of high stress on eyewitness memory. *Law and Human Behavior, 28,* 687–706.

de Groot, A. D. (1978). *Thought and choice in chess.* The Hague, Netherlands: Mouton. (Original work published 1946).

Dell, G. S. (1986). A spreading-activation theory of retrieval in sentence production. *Psychological Review, 93,* 283–321.

Della Sala, S., Gray, C., Baddeley, A., Allamano, N., & Wilson, L. (1999). Pattern span: A tool for unwelding visuo-spatial memory. *Neuropsychologia, 37,* 1189–1199.

Demers, R. A. (1988). Linguistics and animal communication. In F. J. Newmeyer (Ed.), *Language: Psychological and biological aspects* (pp. 314–345). Cambridge, UK: Cambridge University Press.

Denes, P. B., & Pinson, E. N. (1993). *The Speech Chain.* Murray Hill, NJ: Bell Telephone.

Desor, J. A., & Beauchamp, G. K. (1974). The human capacity to transmit olfactory information. *Perception & Psychophysics, 16,* 551–556.

D'Esposito, M., Detre, J. A., Aguirre, G. K., Stallcup, M., Alsop, D. C., Tippett, L. J., & Farah, M. (1997). A functional MRI study of mental image generation. *Neuropsychologia, 35,* 725–730.

Dewsbury, D. A. (2000). Comparative cognition in the 1930's. *Psychonomic Bulletin and Review, 7,* 267–283.

Diamond, A., & Doar, B. (1989). The performance of human infants on a measure of frontal cortex function, the delayed response task. *Developmental Psychobiology, 22,* 271–294.

Diamond, R., & Carey, S. (1986). Why faces are and are not special: An effect of expertise. *Journal of Experimental Psychology: General, 115,* 107–117.

Diehl, R. L., Lotto, A. J., & Holt, L. L. (2004). Speech perception. *Annual Review of Psychology, 55,* 149–179.

Dietrich, A. (2004). The cognitive neuroscience of creativity. *Psychonomic Bulletin & Review, 11,* 1011–1026.

Di Lollo, V. (1980). Temporal integration in visual memory. *Journal of Experimental Psychology: General, 109,* 75–97.

Dodson, C. S., & Hege, A. C. G. (2005). Speeded retrieval abolishes the false-memory suppression effect: Evidence for the distinctiveness heuristic. *Psychonomic Bulletin & Review, 12,* 726–731.

Dodson, C. S., & Schacter, D. L. (2001a). "If I had said it, I would have remembered it": Reducing false memories with a distinctiveness heuristic. *Psychonomic Bulletin and Review, 8,* 155–161.

Dodson, C. S., & Schacter, D. L. (2001b). Memory distortion. In B. Rapp (Ed.), *The handbook of cognitive neuropsychology: What deficits reveal about the human mind* (pp. 445–463). New York: Psychology Press.

Dominowski, R. L., & Jenrick, R. (1972). Effects of hints and interpolated activity on solution of an insight problem. *Psychonomic Science, 26,* 335–338.

Dornburg, C. C., & McDaniel, M. A. (2006). The cognitive interview enhances long-term free recall of older adults. *Psychology and Aging, 21,* 196–200.

Dror, I. E., & Kosslyn, S. M. (1994). Mental imagery and aging. *Psychology and Aging, 9,* 90–102.

Druckman, D., & Bjork, R. A. (1991). *In the mind's eye: Enhancing human performance.* Washington, DC: National Academy Press.

Dunbar, K. (1995). How scientists really reason: Scientific reasoning in real-world laboratories. In R. J. Sternberg & J. E. Davidson (Eds.), *The nature of insight* (pp. 369–395). Cambridge, MA: MIT Press.

Duncker, K. (1945). On problem solving. *Psychological Monographs, 58,* 1–112.

Dunning, D., & Perretta, S. (2002). Automaticity and eyewitness accuracy: A 10- to 12-second rule for distinguishing accurate from inaccurate positive identifications. *Journal of Applied Psychology, 87,* 951–962.

Eals, M., & Silverman, I. (1994). The hunter-gatherer theory of spatial sex differences: Proximate factors mediating the female advantage in recall of object arrays. *Ethology and Sociobiology, 15,* 95–105.

Easterbrook, J. A. (1959). The effect of emotion on cue utilization and the organization of behavior. *Psychological Review, 66,* 183–201.

Edelman, S., & Bülthoff, H. H. (1992). Orientation dependence in the recognition of familiar and novel views of three-dimensional objects. *Vision Research, 32,* 2385–2400.

Eich, E. (1980). The cue-dependent nature of state-dependent retrieval. *Memory and Cognition, 8,* 157–173.

Eich, E. (1984). Memory for unattended events: Remembering with and without awareness. *Memory and Cognition, 12,* 105–111.

Eich, E., & Metcalfe, J. (1989). Mood-dependent memory for internal vs. external events. *Journal of Experimental Psychology: Learning, Memory, and Cognition, 15,* 443–455.

Eichenbaum, H., & Fortin, N. (2003). Episodic memory and the hippocampus: It's about time. *Current Directions in Psychological Science, 12,* 53–57.

Einstein, G. O., & McDaniel, M. A. (1990). Normal aging and prospective memory. *Journal of Experimental Psychology: Learning, Memory, and Cognition, 16,* 717–726.

Einstein, G. O., McDaniel, M. A., Richardson, S. L., Guynn, M. J., & Cunfer, B. (1995). Aging and prospective memory: Examining the influences of self-initiated retrieval processes. *Journal of Experimental Psychology: Learning, Memory, and Cognition, 21,* 996–1007.

Ellis, A. W. (1984). *Reading, writing, and dyslexia: A cognitive analysis.* London: Erlbaum.

Engelkamp, J., & Zimmer, H. D. (1985). Motor programs and their relation to semantic memory. *German Journal of Psychology, 9,* 239–254.

Engle, R. (2002). Working memory capacity as executive attention. *Current Directions in Psychological Science, 11,* 19–23.

Engle, R. W., & Kane, M. J. (2004). Executive attention, working memory capacity, and a two-factor theory of cognitive control. In B. H. Ross, (Ed.), *The psychology of learning and motivation: Advances in research and theory* (Vol. 44, pp. 145–199). New York: Elsevier Science.

Erickson, R. P. (1982). Studies on the perception of taste: Do primaries exist? *Physiology and Behavior, 28,* 57–62.

Erickson, R. P., Priolo, C. V., Warwick, Z. S., & Schiffman, S. S. (1990). Synthesis of tastes other than the "primaries": Implications for neural coding theories and the concept of suppression. *Chemical Senses, 15,* 495–504.

Ericsson, K. A. (1985). Memory skill. *Canadian Journal of Psychology, 39,* 188–231.

Ericsson, K. A., & Charness, N. (1994). Expert performance: Its structure and acquisition. *American Psychologist, 49,* 725–747.

Ericsson, K. A., Chase, W. G., & Faloon, S. (1980). Acquisition of a memory skill. *Science, 208,* 1181–1182.

Ericsson, K. A., & Kintsch, W. (1995). Long-term working memory. *Psychological Review, 102,* 211–245.

Ericsson, K. A., & Polson, P. G. (1988). An experimental analysis of the mechanisms of a memory skill. *Journal of Experimental Psychology: Learning, Memory, & Cognition, 14,* 305–316.

Ericsson, K. A., & Simon, H. E. (1980). Verbal reports as data. *Psychological Review, 87,* 215–251.

Ericsson, K. A., & Simon, H. E. (1984). *Protocol analysis.* Cambridge, MA: MIT Press.

Eriksen, C. W., & Yeh, Y. (1985). Allocation of attention in the visual field. *Journal of Experimental Psychology: Human Perception and Performance, 11,* 583–597.

Erikson, E. H. (1950). Growth and crises of the healthy personality. *Symposium on the Healthy Personality.* 91–146.

Evans, J., Williams, J. M., O'Loughlin, S., & Howells, K. (1992). Autobiographical memory and problem-solving strategies of parasuicide patients. *Psychological Medicine, 22,* 399–405.

Evans, J. B. T. (2002). Logic and human reasoning: An assessment of the deduction paradigm. *Psychological Bulletin, 128,* 978–996.

Evans, J. B. T. (2003). In two minds: Dual-process accounts of reasoning. *Trends in Cognitive Sciences, 7,* 454–459.

Evans, M. A., Shedden, J. M., Hevenor, S. J., & Hahn, M. C. (2000). The effect of variability of unattended information on global and local processing: Evidence for lateralization at early stages of processing. *Neuropsychologia, 38,* 225–239.

Fabiani, D., Stadler, R., & Wessels, F. (2000). True but not false memories produce a sensory signature in human lateralized brain potentials. *Journal of Cognitive Neuroscience, 12,* 941–949.

Falk, D. (2004). Prelinguistic evolution in early hominids: Whence motherese? *Behavioral and Brain Sciences, 27,* 491–541.

Farah, M. J. (1991). Patterns of co-occurrence among the associative agnosias: Implications for visual object representation. *Cognitive Neuropsychology, 8,* 1–19.

Feist, G. J. (1999). The influence of personality on artistic and scientific creativity. In R. J. Sternberg (Ed.), *Handbook of creativity* (pp. 273–296). New York: Cambridge University Press.

Fernald, A. (1985). Four-month-old infants prefer to listen to motherese. *Infant Behavior and Development, 8,* 181–195.

Fernald, A., & Simon, T. (1984). Expanded intonation contours in mothers' speech to newborns. *Developmental Psychology, 20,* 104–113.

Fillmore, C. J. (1968). The case for case. In E. Bach & R. T. Harms (Eds.), *Universals of linguistic form* (pp. 101–190). New York: Holt, Rinehart, & Winston.

Fink, G. R., Markowitsch, H. J., & Reinkemeier, M. (1996). Cerebral representation of one's own past: Neural networks involved in autobiographical memory. *Journal of Neuroscience, 16,* 4275–4282.

Finke, R. A., & Pinker, S. (1982). Spontaneous imagery scanning in mental extrapolation. *Journal of Experimental Psychology: Learning, Memory, and Cognition, 8,* 142–147.

Finke, R. A., & Pinker, S. (1983). Directional scanning of remembered visual patterns. *Journal of Experimental Psychology: Learning, Memory, and Cognition, 9,* 398–410.

Finke, R. A., & Shepard, R. N. (1986). Visual functions of mental imagery. In L. Kaufman, J. P. Thomas, & K. Boff (Eds.), *Handbook of perception and human performance,* Vol. 2: *Cognitive processes and performance* (pp. 1–55). New York: Wiley.

Fischhoff, B., Slovic, P., & Lichtenstein, S. (1977). Knowing with certainty: The appropriateness of extreme confidence. *Journal of Experimental Psychology: Human Perception and Performance, 4,* 552–564.

Fisher, R. P., & Geiselman, R. E. (1992). *Memory-enhancing techniques for investigative interviewing: The cognitive interview.* Springfield, IL: Thomas.

Fivush, R. (1991). Gender and emotion in mother/child conversations about the past. *Journal of Narrative and Life History, 1,* 325–341.

Fivush, R., Gray, J. T., & Fromhoff, F. A. (1987). Two-year-olds talk about the past. *Cognitive Development, 2,* 393–409.

Foss, D. J. (1969). Decision processes during sentence comprehension: Effects of lexical item difficulty and position upon decision times. *Journal of Verbal Learning and Verbal Behavior, 8,* 457–462.

Foss, D. J. (1970). Some effects of ambiguity upon sentence comprehension. *Journal of Verbal Learning and Verbal Behavior, 9,* 699–706.

Fowler, C. A., Galantucci, B., & Saltzman, E. (2003). Motor theories of perception. In M. Arbib (Ed.), *The handbook of brain theory and neural networks* (pp. 705–707). Cambridge, MA: MIT Press.

Frantz, R. (2003). Herbert Simon. Artificial intelligence as a framework for understanding intuition. *Journal of Economic Psychology, 24,* 265–277.

Frazier, L., & Rayner, K. (1982). Making and correcting errors during sentence comprehension: Eye movements in the analysis of structurally ambiguous sentences. *Cognitive Psychology, 14,* 178–210.

Friederici, A. D. (1983). Children's sensitivity to function words during sentence comprehension. *Linguistics, 21,* 717–739.

Fromkin, V. A. (1973). *Speech errors as linguistic evidence.* The Hague: Mouton.

Gardiner, J. M. (1988). Functional aspects of recollective experience. *Memory and Cognition, 16,* 309–313.

Gardiner, J. M., & Parkin, A. J. (1990). Attention and recollective experience in recognition memory. *Memory and Cognition, 18,* 579–583.

Gardiner, J. M., & Richardson-Klavehn, A. (2000). Remembering and knowing. In E. Tulving & F. I. M. Craik (Eds.), *The Oxford handbook of memory* (pp. 229–244). New York: Oxford University Press.

Gardner, B. T., & Gardner, R. A. (1975). Evidence for sentence constituents in the early utterances of child and chimpanzee. *Journal of Experimental Psychology: General, 104*, 244–267.

Gardner, H. (1983). *Frames of mind: A theory of multiple intelligence.* New York: Basic Books.

Gardner, H. (1985). *The mind's new science: A history of the cognitive revolution.* New York: Basic Books.

Garrett, M. F. (1975). The analysis of sentence production. In G. Bower (Ed.), *The psychology of learning and motivation: Advances in research and theory* (Vol. 9). New York: Academic Press.

Garrett, M. F. (1988). Processes in language production. In F. J. Newmeyer (Ed.), *Language: Psychological and biological aspects* (pp. 69–96). Cambridge: Cambridge University Press.

Garrett, M. F. (1992). Disorders of lexical selection. *Cognition, 42*, 143–180.

Garry, M., Manning, C. G., Loftus, E. F., & Sherman, S. J. (1996). Imagination inflation: Imagining a childhood event inflates confidence that it occurred. *Psychonomic Bulletin and Review, 3*, 208–214.

Garry, M., & Wade, K. A. (2005). Actually, a picture is worth less than 45 words: Narratives produce more false memories than photographs do. *Psychonomic Bulletin & Review, 12*, 359–366.

Gaskell, M. G., & Marslen-Wilson, W. D. (2001). Lexical ambiguity resolution and spoken word recognition: Bridging the gap. *Journal of Memory and Language, 44*, 325–349.

Gauthier, I., Curran, T., Curby, K. M., & Collins, D. (2003). Perceptual interference supports a non-modular account of face processing. *Nature Neuroscience, 6*, 428–432.

Gauthier, I., Skudlarski, P., Gore, J. C., & Anderson, A. W. (2000). Expertise for cars and birds recruits brain areas involved in face recognition. *Nature Neuroscience, 3*, 191–197.

Gazzaniga, M. S. (1985). *The social brain.* New York: Basic Books.

Gazzaniga, M. S. (1998). *The mind's past.* Berkeley, CA: University of California Press.

Gazzaniga, M. S., Ivry, R. B., & Mangun, G. R. (1998). *Cognitive neuroscience: The biology of the mind.* New York: Norton.

Gazzaniga, M. S., & Smylie, C. S. (1984). Dissociation of language and cognition. *Brain, 107*, 145–153.

Gelman, S. A. (2003). *The essential child: Origins of essentialism in everyday thought.* New York: Oxford University Press.

Gelman, S. A. (2004). Psychological essentialism in children. *Trends in Cognitive Sciences, 8*, 404–409.

Gelman, S. A., & Wellman, H. M. (1991). Insides and essences: Early understandings of the nonobvious. *Cognition, 38*, 213–244.

Gentner, D. (1989). The mechanisms of analogical learning. In S. Vosniadou & A. Ortony (Eds.), *Similarity and analogical reasoning* (pp. 199–241). New York: Cambridge University Press.

Geraerts, E., Arnold, M. M., Lindsay, D. S., Merckelbach, H., Jelicic, M., & Hauer, B. (2006). Forgetting of prior remembering in persons reporting recovered memories of childhood sexual abuse. *Psychological Science, 17*, 1002–1008.

German, T. P., & Barrett, H. C. (2005). Functional fixedness in a technologically sparse culture. *Psychological Science, 16*, 1–5.

German, T. P., & Johnson, S. C. (2002). Function and the origins of the design stance. *Journal of Cognition and Development, 3*, 279–300.

Gernsbacher, M. A. (1989). Mechanisms that improve referential access. *Cognition, 32*, 99–156.

Gernsbacher. M. A. (1991). *Language comprehension as structure building.* Hillsdale, NJ: Erlbaum.

Gernsbacher, M. A. (1997). Two decades of structure building. *Discourse Processes, 23*, 365–204.

Gernsbacher, M. A., & Hargreaves. (1988). Accessing sentence participants: The advantage of first mention. *Journal of Memory and Language, 27*, 699–717.

Gibbs, R. W. (2006). *Embodiment and cognitive science.* New York: Cambridge University Press.

Gibson, J. J. (1966). The problem of temporal order in sensation and perception. *Journal of Psychology, 62*, 141–149.

Gibson, J. J. (1987). *The perception of the visual world.* New York: Houghton-Mifflin.

Gick, M. L., & Holyoak, K. J. (1980). Analogical problem solving. *Cognitive Psychology, 12*, 306–335.

Gick, M. L., & Holyoak, K. J. (1983). Schema induction and analogical transfer. *Cognitive Psychology, 15*, 1–38.

Gigerenzer, G. (2004). Dread risk, September 11, and fatal traffic accidents. *Psychological Science, 15*, 286–287.

Gigerenzer, G., & Hoffrage, U. (1995). How to improve Bayesian reasoning without instruction. Frequency formats. *Psychological Review, 102*, 684–704.

Gigerenzer, G., & Todd, P. M. (1999). *Simple heuristics that make us smart. Evolution and cognition.* New York: Oxford University Press.

Gilhooly, K. J., & Murphy, P. (2005). Differentiating insight from non-insight problems. *Thinking & Reasoning, 11*, 279–302.

Gilinsky, A. S., & Judd, B. B. (1994). Working memory and bias in reasoning across the life span. *Psychology and Aging, 9*, 356–371.

Gillund, G., & Shiffrin, R. M. (1984). A retrieval model for both recognition and recall. *Psychological Review, 91*, 1–67.

Gilovich, T., Kruger, J., & Medvec, V. H. (2002). The spotlight effect revisited: Overestimating the manifest variability of our actions and appearance. *Journal of Experimental Social Psychology, 38,* 93–99.

Gilovich, T., Medvec, V., & Savitsky, K. (2000). The spotlight effect in social judgment: An egocentric bias in the estimates of the salience of one's own actions and appearance. *Journal of Personality and Social Psychology, 75,* 332–346.

Gilovich, T., Vallone, R., & Tversky, A. (1983). The hot hand in basketball: On the misperception of random sequences. *Cognitive Psychology, 17,* 295–314.

Gisiner, R., & Schusterman, R. J. (1992). Sequence, syntax, and semantics: Responses of a language-trained sea lion (Zalophus Californianus) to novel sign combinations. *Journal of Comparative Psychology, 106,* 78–91.

Gleaves, D. H., Smith, S. M., Butler, L. D., & Spiegel, D. (2004). False and recovered memories in the laboratory and clinic: A review of experimental and clinical evidence. *Clinical Psychology: Science and Practice, 11,* 3–28.

Glenberg, A. M. (1974). Influences of retrieval processes on the spacing effect in free recall. *Journal of Experimental Psychology: Human Learning and Memory, 3,* 282–294.

Glenn, C. G. (1978). The role of episodic structure and of story length in children's recall of simple stories. *Journal of Verbal Learning and Verbal Behavior, 17,* 229–247.

Gobet, F., & Simon, H. A. (1996). Recall of rapidly presented random chess positions is a function of skill. *Psychonomic Bulletin and Review, 3,* 159–163.

Godden, D. R., & Baddeley, A. D. (1975). Context-dependent memory in two natural environments: On land and underwater. *British Journal of Psychology, 66,* 325–331.

Goel, V., & Dolan, R. J. (2004). Differential involvement of left prefrontal cortex in inductive and deductive reasoning. *Cognition, 93,* B109–B121.

Goel, V., Gold, B., Kapur, S., & Houle, S. (1998). Neuroanatomical correlates of human reasoning. *Journal of Cognitive Neuroscience, 10,* 293–302.

Goff, L. M., & Roediger, H. L. (1998). Imagination inflation for action events: Repeated imaginings lead to illusory recollections. *Memory and Cognition, 26,* 20–33.

Goldinger, S. D., Luce, P. A., & Pisoni, D. B. (1989). Priming lexical neighbors of spoken words: Effects of competition and inhibition. *Journal of Memory and Language, 28,* 501–518.

Goldstein, D. G., & Gigerenzer, G. (2002). Models of ecological rationality: The recognition heuristic. *Psychological Review, 109,* 75–90.

Goldstone, R. L., & Kersten, A. (2003). Concepts and categorization. In A. F. Healy & R. W. Proctor (Eds.), *Handbook of psychology: Experimental psychology* (Vol. 4, pp. 599–621). Hoboken, NJ: John Wiley & Sons, Inc.

Gonzalez, C., Dana, J., Koshino, H., & Just, M. (2005). The framing effect and risky decisions: Examining cognitive functions with fMRI. *Journal of Economic Psychology, 26,* 1–20.

Goodman, G. S., Quas, J. A., Batterman-Faunce, J. M., Riddlesberger, M. M., & Kuhn, J. (1994). Predictors of accurate and inaccurate memories of traumatic events experienced in childhood. *Consciousness and Cognition, 3,* 269–294.

Gopnik, A., & Sobel, D. M. (2000). Detecting blickets: How young children use information about novel causal powers in categorization and induction. *Child Development, 71,* 1205–1222.

Goschke, T., & Kuhl, J. (1993). Representation of intentions: Persisting activation in memory.

Journal of Experimental Psychology: Learning, Memory, and Cognition, 19, 1211–1226.

Graham, S. A., Kilbreath, C. S., & Welder, A. N. (2004). Thirteen-month-olds rely on shared labels and shape similarity for inductive inferences. *Child Development, 75,* 409–427.

Grainger, J., & Whitney, C. (2004). Does the huamn mnid raed wrods as a wlohe? *Trends in Cognitive Sciences, 8,* 58–59.

Grant, H. M., Bredahl, L. C., Clay, J., Ferrie, J., Groves, J. E., McDorman, T. A., & Dark, V. J. (1998). Context-dependent memory for meaningful material: Information for students. *Applied Cognitive Psychology, 12,* 617–623.

Gratton, G., Corballis, P. M., & Jain, S. (1997). Hemispheric organization of visual memories. *Journal of Cognitive Neuroscience, 9,* 92–104.

Greene, R. L. (1992). *Human memory: Paradigms and paradoxes.* Hillsdale, NJ: Erlbaum.

Greenfield, P. M., & Savage-Rumbaugh, E. S. (1990). Grammatical combination in *Pan paniscus:* Processes of learning and invention in the evolution and development of language. In S. T. Parker & K. R. Gibson (Eds.), *"Language" and intelligence in monkeys and apes: Comparative developmental perspectives* (pp. 540–578). Cambridge: Cambridge University Press.

Greenwald, A. G., Spangenberg, E. R., Pratkanis, A. R., & Eskenazi, J. (1991). Double-blind tests of subliminal self-help audiotapes. *Psychological Science, 2,* 119–122.

Grice, H. P. (1975). Logic and conversation. In P. Cole & J. L. Morgan (Eds.), *Syntax and semantics: Vol. 3: Speech acts* (pp. 41–58). New York: Seminar Press.

Griggs, R. A., & Cox, G. R. (1982). The elusive thematic-materials effect in Wason's selection task. *British Journal of Psychology, 73,* 407–420.

Groninger, L. D. (1971). Mnemonic imagery and forgetting. *Psychonomic Science, 23,* 161–163.

Gruneberg, M. M., Smith, R. L., & Winfrow, P. (1973). An investigation into response blockaging. *Acta Psychologica, 37,* 187–196.

Haber, R. N. (1983). The impending demise of the icon: A critique of the concept of iconic storage in visual information processing. *Behavioral and Brain Sciences, 6,* 1–54.

Habermas, T., & Bluck, S. (2000). Getting a life: The emergence of the life story in adolescence. *Psychological Bulletin, 126,* 748–769.

Habib, R., Nyberg, L., & Tulving, E. (2003). Hemispheric asymmetries of memory: The HERA model revisited. *Trends in Cognitive Sciences, 7,* 241–245.

Hahne, A., Eckstein, K., & Friederici, A. D. (2004). Brain signatures of syntactic and semantic processes during children's language development. *Journal of Cognitive Neuroscience, 16,* 1302–1318.

Halpern, D. F. (2000). *Sex differences in cognitive abilities* (3rd ed.). Mahwah, NJ: Erlbaum.

Hampton, J. A. (1993). Conjunctions of visually-based categories: Overextension and compensation. *Journal of Experimental Psychology: Learning, Memory, and Cognition, 22,* 378–396.

Han, J. J., Leichtman, M. D., & Yang, Q. (1998). Autobiographical memory in Korean, Chinese, and American children. *Developmental Psychology, 34,* 701–713.

Hanley, J. R., & Cowell, E. S. (1988). The effects of different types of retrieval cues on the recall of names of famous faces. *Memory and Cognition, 16,* 545–555.

Hanson, V. L. (1982). Short-term recall by deaf signers of American Sign Language: Implications of encoding strategy for order recall. *Journal of Experimental Psychology: Learning, Memory, and Cognition, 8,* 572–583.

Harley, T. A. (1995). *The psychology of language: From data to theory.* East Sussex, UK: Taylor & Francis.

Harris, D. A. (1999). Driving while black: Racial profiling on our nation's highways. Washington, DC: American Civil Liberties Union.

Harris, J. E. (1980). Memory aids people use: Two interview studies. *Memory and Cognition, 8,* 31–38.

Harrison, J. E., & Baron-Cohen, S. (1997). Synaesthesia: A review of psychological theories. In J. E. Harris & S. Baron-Cohen (Eds.), *Synaesthesia: Classic and contemporary readings.* (pp. 109–122). Oxford: Blackwell.

Hartley, A. A. (1992). Attention. In F. I. M. Craik & T. A. Salthouse (Eds.), *The handbook of aging and cognition* (pp. 3–49). Hillsdale, NJ: Erlbaum.

Harvey, A. G. (2005). Unwanted intrusive thoughts in insomnia. In D. A. Clark (Ed.), *Intrusive thoughts in clinical disorders: Theory, research, and treatment* (pp. 86–118). New York: Guilford Press.

Hashtroudi, S., Johnson, M. K., & Chrosniak, L. D. (1989). Aging and source monitoring. *Psychology and Aging, 4,* 106–112.

Haskell, T. R., MacDonald, M. C., & Seidenberg, M. S. (2003). Language learning and innateness: Some implications of compounds research. *Cognitive Psychology, 47,* 119–163.

Hastie, R., & Dawes, R. M. (2001). *Rational choice in an uncertain world: The psychology of judgment and decision making.* London: Sage.

Hastie, R., Schkade, D. A., & Payne, J. W. (1999). Juror judgments in civil cases: Hindsight effects on judgments of liability for punitive damages. *Law and Human Behavior, 23,* 445–470.

Hauser, M. D., Chomsky, N., & Fitch, W. T. (2002). The faculty of language: What is it, who has it, and how did it evolve? *Science, 298,* 1569–1579.

Hayes, J. R., & Simon, H. A. (1977). Psychological differences among problem isomorphs. In N. J.

Castellan, D. B. Pisoni, & J. R. Potts (Eds.), *Cognitive theory.* Hillsdale, NJ: Erlbaum.

Hayward, W. G. (2003). After the viewpoint debate: Where next in object recognition? *Trends in Cognitive Sciences, 7,* 425–427.

Hayward, W. G., & Tarr, M. J. (1997). Testing conditions for viewpoint invariance in object recognition. *Journal of Experimental Psychology: Human Perception and Performance, 23,* 1511–1521.

Hebb, D. O. (1949). *The organization of behavior: A neuropsychological theory.* London: Wiley.

Henry, J. D., MacLeod, M. S., Phillips, L. H., & Crawford, J. R. (2004). A meta-analytic review of prospective memory and aging. *Psychology and Aging, 19,* 27–39.

Herlitz, A., Nilsson, L. G., & Backman, L. (1997). Gender differences in episodic memory. *Memory & Cognition, 25,* 801–811.

Herman, J. L., & Schatzow, E. (1987). Recovery and verification of memories of childhood sexual trauma. *Psychoanalytic Psychology, 4,* 1–14.

Herman, J. S. (1992). *Trauma and recovery.* New York: Basic Books.

Herman, L. M., Kuczaj, S. A., & Holder, M. D. (1993). Response to anomalous gestural sequences by a language-trained dolphin: Evidence for processing of semantic relations and syntactic information. *Journal of Experimental Psychology: General, 122,* 184–194.

Herman, L. M., Richards, D. G., & Wolz, J. P. (1984). Comprehension of sentences by bottlenosed dolphins. *Cognition, 16,* 129–219.

Herz, R. S., & Cupchik, G. C. (1992). An experimental characterization of odor-evoked memories in humans. *Chemical Senses, 17,* 519–528.

Hicks, M., & Marsh, J. (1999). Attempts to reduce the incidence of false recall with source monitoring. *Journal of Experimental Psychology: Learning, Memory, and Cognition, 25,* 1195–1209.

Hillix, W. A. (2007). The past, present, and possible futures of animal language research. In D. A. Washburn (Ed.), *Primate perspectives on behavior and cognition* (pp. 223–234). Washington, DC: American Psychological Association.

Hilton, D. J. (1995). The social context of reasoning: Conversational inference and rational judgment. *Psychological Bulletin, 118,* 248–271.

Hintzman, D. L. (1986). "Schema abstraction" in a multiple-trace memory model. *Psychological Review, 93,* 411–428.

Hintzman, D. L., Block, R. A., & Summers, J. J. (1973). Modality tags and memory for repetitions: Locus of the spacing effect. *Journal of Verbal Learning and Verbal Behavior, 12,* 229–238.

Hitch, G. J., & Baddeley, A. D. (1976).Verbal reasoning and working memory. *Quarterly Journal of Experimental Psychology, 28,* 603–621.

Hockett, C. F. (1960). The origin of speech. *Scientific American, 203,* 89–96.

Hogan, R. M., & Kintsch, W. (1971). Differential effects of study and test trials on long-term recognition and recall. *Journal of Verbal Learning and Verbal Behavior, 10,* 562–567.

Hogarth, R. M. (2005). Deciding analytically or trusting your intuition? The advantages and disadvantages of analytic and intuitive thought. In T. Betsch & S. Haberstroh (Eds.), *The routines of decision making* (pp. 67–82). Mahwah, NJ: Lawrence Erlbaum Associates Publishers.

Holbrook, M. E., & Schindler, R. M. (1989). Some exploratory findings on the development of musical tastes. *Journal of Consumer Research, 16,* 119–124.

Hollingworth, A. (1998). Does consistent scene context facilitate object perception? *Journal of Experimental Psychology: General, 127,* 398–415.

Hollins, M., Faldowski, R., Rao, S., & Young, F. (1993). Perceptual dimensions of tactile surface texture: A multidimensional scaling analysis. *Perception & Psychophysics, 54,* 697–705.

Holyoak, K. J., & Koh, K. (1987). Surface and structural similarity in analogical transfer. *Memory and Cognition, 15,* 332–340.

Horwitz, B., Rumsey, J. M., & Donohue, B. C. (1998). Functional connectivity of the angular gyrus in normal reading and dyslexia. *Proceedings of the National Academy of Sciences, USA, 95,* 8939–8944.

Hötting, K., & Röder, B. (2004). Hearing cheats touch, but less in congenitally blind than in sighted individuals. *Psychological Science, 15,* 60–64.

Howe, M. L., & Courage, M. L. (1993). On resolving the enigma of childhood amnesia. *Psychological Bulletin, 113,* 305–326.

Howe, M. L., & Courage, M. L. (1997). The emergence and early development of autobiographical memory. *Psychological Review, 104,* 499–523.

Howe, M. L., Courage, M. L., & Edison, S. C. (2003). When autobiographical memory begins. *Developmental Review, 23,* 471–494.

Howe, M. L., Courage, M. L., & Peterson, C. (1994). How can I remember when "I" wasn't there: Long-term retention of traumatic experience and the emergence of the cognitive self. *Consciousness and Cognition, 3,* 327–355.

Hsee, C. K., & Rottenstreich, Y. (2004). Music, pandas, and muggers: On the affective psychology of value. *Journal of Experimental Psychology: General, 133,* 23–30.

Hulme, C., Roodenrys, S., Brown, G., & Mercer, R. (1995). The role of long-term memory mechanisms in memory span. *British Journal of Psychology, 86,* 527–536.

Hunt, R. R., & Einstein, G. O. (1981). Relational and item-specific information in memory. *Journal of Verbal Learning and Verbal Behavior, 20,* 497–514.

Hyde, T. S., & Jenkins, J. J. (1969). Differential effects of incidental tasks on the organization of recall of a list of highly associated words. *Journal of Experimental Psychology, 82,* 472–481.

Hyman, I. E., Husband, T. H., & Billings, F. J. (1995). False memories of childhood experiences. *Applied Cognitive Psychology, 9,* 181–197.

Hyman, I. E., & Pentland, J. (1996). The role of imagination in the creation of false childhood memories. *Journal of Memory and Language, 35,* 101–117.

Hyman, I. E., & Rubin, D. C. (1990). Memorabeatlia: A naturalistic study of long-term memory. *Memory and Cognition, 18,* 205–214.

Intons-Peterson, M., & Fournier, J. (1986). External and internal memory aids: When and how do we use them? *Journal of Experimental Psychology: General, 115,* 267–280.

Irwin, D. E. (1992). Memory for position and identity across eye movements. *Journal of Experimental Psychology: Learning, Memory, and Cognition, 18,* 307–317.

Iverson, P. (1995). Auditory stream segregation by musical timbre: Effects of static and dynamic acoustic attributes. *Journal of Experimental Psychology: Human Perception and Performance, 21,* 751–763.

Jacobs, W. J., & Nadel, L. (1998). Neurobiology of reconstructed memory. *Psychology, Public Policy, & Law, 4,* 1110–1134.

Jacoby, L. L. (1983). Remembering the data: Analyzing interactive processes in reading. *Journal of Verbal Learning and Verbal Behavior, 22,* 485–508.

Jacoby, L. L., & Dallas, M. (1981). On the relationship between autobiographical memory and perceptual learning. *Journal of Experimental Psychology: General, 110,* 306–340.

Jacoby, L. L. (1991). A process dissociation framework: Separating automatic from intentional uses of memory. *Journal of Memory and Language, 30,* 513–541.

Jaffe, J., & Feldstein, S. (1970). *Rhythms of dialogue.* New York: Academic Press.

James, W. (1890). *The principles of psychology.* New York: Holt.

Jenkins, J. J. (1979). Four points to remember: A tetrahedral model of memory experiments. In L. S. Cermak & F. I. M. Craik (Eds.), *Levels of processing in human memory* (pp. 429–446). Hillsdale, NJ: Erlbaum.

Jennings, J. M., & Jacoby, L. L. (1993). Automatic versus intentional uses of memory: Aging, attention, and control. *Psychology and Aging, 8,* 283–293.

Johnson, M. K. (1988). Reality monitoring: An experimental phenomenological approach. *Journal of Experimental Psychology: General, 117,* 390–394.

Johnson, M. K., Foley, M. A., Suengas, A. G., & Raye, C. L. (1988). Phenomenal characteristics of memories for perceived and imagined autobiographical events. *Journal of Experimental Psychology: General, 117,* 371–376.

Johnson, M. K., Nolde, S. F., & Leonardis, D. M. (1996). Emotional focus and source monitoring. *Journal of Memory and Language, 35,* 135–156.

Johnson, R., Jr. (1984). P300: a model of the variables controlling its amplitude. *Annals of the New York Academy of Sciences, 425,* 223–229.

Johnson-Laird, P. N., & Byrne, R. M. (2002). Conditionals: A theory of meaning, pragmatics, and inference. *Psychological Review, 109,* 646–678.

Johnston, W. A., & Heinz, S. P. (1978). Flexibility and capacity demands of attention. *Journal of Experimental Psychology: General, 107,* 420–435.

Jones, G. V., & Langford, S. (1987). Phonological blocking in the tip of the tongue state. *Cognition, 26,* 115–122.

Jonides, J., Lacey, S. C., & Nee, D. E. (2005). Processes of working memory in mind and brain. *Current Directions in Psychological Science, 14,* 2–5.

Jonides, J., & Smith, E. E. (1997). The architecture of working memory. In M. D. Rugg (Ed.), *Cognitive neuroscience. Studies in cognition* (pp. 243–276). Cambridge, MA: MIT Press.

Joslyn, S., Loftus, E., McNoughton, A., & Powers, J. (2001). Memory for memory. *Memory & Cognition, 29,* 789–797.

Jusczyk, P. W. (1997). *The discovery of spoken language.* Cambridge, MA: MIT Press.

Just, M. A., & Carpenter, P. A. (1987). *The psychology of reading and language comprehension.* Boston: Allyn and Bacon.

Just, M. A., & Carpenter, P. A. (1992). A capacity theory of comprehension: Individual differences in working memory. *Psychological Review, 99,* 122–149.

Just, M. A., Carpenter, P. A., & Masson, M. E. J. (1982). *What eye fixations tell us about speed reading and skimming* (Technical report). Pittsburgh: Carnegie-Mellon University.

Kahneman, D. A. (1973). *Attention and effort.* Englewood Cliffs, NJ: Prentice-Hall.

Kahneman, D. (1991). Judgment and decision making: A personal view. *Psychological Science, 2,* 142–145.

Kahneman, D., & Tversky, A. (1984). Choices, values, and frames. *American Psychologist, 39,* 341–350.

Kako, E. (1999). Elements of syntax in the systems of three language-trained animals. *Animal Learning and Behavior, 27,* 1–14.

Kaminski, J., Call, J., & Fischer, J. (2004). Word learning in a domestic dog: Evidence for "fast mapping." *Science, 304,* 1682–1683.

Kane, M. J., & Engle, R. W. (2000). WM capacity, proactive interference, and divided attention: Limits on long-term memory retrieval. *Journal of Experimental Psychology: Learning, Memory, and Cognition, 26,* 336–358.

Kane, M. J., Poole, B. J., Tuholski, S. W., Engle, R. W. (2006). Working memory capacity and the top-down control of visual search: Exploring the boundaries of "executive attention." *Journal of Experimental Psychology: Learning, Memory, and Cognition, 32,* 749–777.

Kanwisher, N. (2006). What's in a face? *Science, 311,* 617–618.

Kanwisher, N., McDermott, J., & Chun, M. M. (1997). The fusiform face area: A module in human extrastriate cortex specialized for face perception. *Journal of Neuroscience, 17,* 4302–4311.

Kapur, S., Craik, F. I. M., Tulving, E., Wilson, A. A., Houle, S., & Brown, G. M. (1994). Neuroanatomical correlates of encoding in episodic memory: Levels of processing effects. *Proceedings of the National Academy of Sciences USA, 91,* 2008–2111.

Kass, R. E., & Raftery, A. E. (1995). Bayes factors. *Journal of the American Statistical Association, 90,* 773–795.

Keenan, J. P., Freund, S., Hamilton, R. H., Ganis, G., & Pascual-Leone, A. (2000). Hand-response differences in a self-face recognition task. *Neuropsychologia, 38,* 1047–1053.

Keenan, J. P., McCutcheon, B., Freund, S., Gallup, G. G., Sanders, G., & Pascual-Leone, A. (1999). Left-hand advantage in a self-face recognition task. *Neuropsychologia, 37,* 1421–1425.

Keenan, J. P., Wheeler, M. A., Gallup, G. G., & Pascual-Leone, J. (2000). Self-recognition and the right prefrontal cortex. *Trends in Cognitive Sciences, 4,* 338–344.

Kellogg, R. T. (1994). *The psychology of writing.* New York: Oxford University Press.

Kelley, C. M., & Lindsey, D. S. (1996). Conscious and unconscious forms of memory. In E. L. Bjork & R. A. Bjork (Eds.), *Memory* (pp. 31–63). New York: Academic Press.

Kemp, S. (1988). Dating recent and historical events. *Applied Cognitive Psychology, 16,* 181–188.

Keppel, G., & Underwood, B. J. (1962). Proactive inhibition in short-term retention of single items. *Journal of Verbal Learning and Verbal Behavior, 1,* 153–161.

Kershaw, T. C., & Ohlsson, S. (2004). Multiple causes of difficulty in insight: The case of the nine-dot problem. *Journal of Experimental*

Psychology: Learning, Memory, and Cognition, 30, 3–13.

Key, A. P. F., Dove, G. O., & Maguire, M. J. (2005). Linking brainwaves to the brain: An ERP primer. *Developmental Neuropsychology, 27*, 183–215.

Key, B. W. (1973). *Subliminal seduction*. Englewood Cliffs, NJ: Prentice Hall.

Kihlstrom, J. F. (2004). An unbalanced balancing act: Blocked, recovered, and false memories in the laboratory and clinic. *Clinical Psychology: Science and Practice, 11*, 34–41.

Kihlstrom, J. K. (1998). Exhumed memory. In S. J. Lynn & K. M. McConkey (Eds.), *Truth in memory* (pp. 3–31). New York: Guilford Press.

Kimball, D. R., & Holyoak, K. J. (2000). Transfer and expertise. In E. Tulving & F. I. M. Craik (Eds.), *The Oxford handbook of memory*. New York: Oxford University Press.

Kimble, G. A. (1985). *Psychology and learning*. Washington, DC: American Psychological Association.

King, A. (1991). Improving lecture comprehension: Effects of a metacognitive strategy. *Applied Cognitive Psychology, 5*, 331–346.

Kintsch, W. (1974). The representation of meaning in memory. Hillsdale, NJ: Erlbaum.

Kintsch, W. (1988). The role of knowledge in discourse comprehension. A construction-integration model. *Psychological Review, 95*, 163–182.

Kintsch, W. (1998). *Comprehension: A paradigm for cognition*. Cambridge: Cambridge University Press.

Kintsch, W., Healy, A., Hegarty, M., Pennington, B., & Salthouse, T. (1999). Models of working memory: Eight questions and some general answers. In A. Miyake & P. Shah (Eds.), *Models of working memory*. London: Cambridge University Press.

Kintsch, W., & Keenan, J. (1973). Reading rate and retention as a function of the number of propositions in the base structure of sentences. *Cognitive Psychology, 5*, 257–274.

Kintsch, W., & van Dijk, T. A. (1978). Toward a model of text comprehension and production. *Psychological Review, 85*, 363–394.

Kirby, K. N. (1994). Probabilities and utilities of fictional outcomes in Wason's four-card selection task. *Cognition, 51*, 1–28.

Kirsner, K., Smith, M. C., Lockhart, R. S., King, M. L., & Jain, M. (1984). The bilingual Lexicon: Language-specific units in an integrated. *Journal of Verbal Learning and verbal Behavior, 23*, 519–539.

Klatzky, R. L., & Lederman, S. J. (1995). Identifying objects from a haptic glance. *Perception & Psychophysics, 57*, 1111–1123.

Klatzky, R. L., Lederman, S. J., & Metzger, V. A. (1985). Identifying objects by touch: An "expert system." *Perception & Psychophysics, 37*, 299–302.

Klatzky, R. L., Lederman, S. J., & Reed, C. (1987). There's more to touch than meets the eye: The salience of object attributes with and without vision. *Journal of Experimental Psychology: General, 116*, 356–369.

Klein, G. S. (1964). Semantic power measured through the interference of words with color-naming. *American Journal of Psychology, 77*, 576–588.

Kleunder, K. R., Diehl, R. L., & Killeen, P. R. (1987). Japanese quail can learn phonetic categories. *Science, 237*, 1195–1197.

Knoch, D., Gianotti, L. R., Mohr, C., & Brugger, P. (2005). Synesthesia: When colors count. *Cognitive Brain Research, 25*, 372–374.

Kohler, W. (1925). *The mentality of apes*. New York: Harcourt, Brace, and Jovanovich.

Kohnken, G., Milne, R., Memon, A., & Bull, R. (1999). The cognitive interview: A meta-analysis. *Psychology, Crime, and Law, 5*, 3–27.

Kolb, B., & Whishaw, I. Q. (1996). *Human neuropsychology*. New York: W. H. Freeman and Company.

Komatsu, L. K. (1992). Recent views of conceptual structure. *Psychological Bulletin, 112*, 500–526.

Koriat, A. (1991). How do we know what we know? Exploring a process model of feeling of knowing. Paper presented at the international conference on memory. Lancaster, England.

Koriat, A., & Lieblich, I. (1974). What does a person in a TOT state know that a person in a don't know state doesn't know? *Memory & Cognition, 2*, 647–655.

Kosslyn, S. M. (1975). Information representation in visual images. *Cognitive Psychology, 7*, 341–370.

Kosslyn, S. M. (1981). The medium and the message in mental imagery: A theory. *Psychological Review, 88*, 46–66.

Kosslyn, S. M. (1994). *Image and brain: The resolution of the imagery debate*. Cambridge, MA: MIT Press.

Kosslyn, S. M. (2005). Mental images and the brain. *Cognitive Neuropsychology, 22*, 333–347.

Kosslyn, S. M., Ball, T. M., & Reiser, B. J. (1978). Visual images preserve metric spatial information: Evidence from studies of image scanning. *Journal of Experimental Psychology: Human Perception and Performance, 4*, 47–60.

Kosslyn, S. M., Chabris, C. F., Marsolek, C. J., & Koenig, O. (1992). Categorical vs. coordinate spatial relations: Computational analyses and computer simulations. *Journal of Experimental Psychology: Human Perception and Performance, 18*, 562–577.

Kosslyn, S. M., Murphy, G. L., Bernesderfer, M. E., & Feinstein, K. J. (1977). Category and continuum in mental comparisons. *Journal of Experimental Psychology: General, 106*, 341–375.

Kosslyn, S. M., Reiser, B. J., Farah, M. J., & Fliegel, S. L. (1983). Generating visual images: Units and relations. *Journal of Experimental Psychology: General, 112*, 278–303.

Kozar, B., Vaughn, R. E., Lord, R. H., & Whitfield, K. E. (1995). Basketball free-throw performance: Practice implications. *Journal of Sport Behavior, 18*, 123–129.

Kramer, A. F., & Larish, J. L. (1996). Aging and dual-task performance. In W. A. Rogers, A. D. Fisk, & N. Walker (Eds.), *Aging and skilled performance: Advances in theory and applications* (pp. 83–112). Hillsdale, NJ: Erlbaum.

Kramer, T. H., Buckhout, R., & Eugenio, P. (1989). Weapon focus, arousal, and eyewitness memory: Attention must be paid. *Applied Cognitive Psychology, 14,* 167–184.

Krueger, J. I., & Funder, D. C. (2004). Towards a balanced social psychology: Causes, consequences, and cures for the problem-seeking approach to social behavior and cognition. *Behavioral and Brain Sciences, 27,* 313–327.

Krueger, L. E. (1992). The word-superiority effect and phonological recoding. *Memory and Cognition, 20,* 685–694.

Kuhl, P. K., Williams, K. A., Lacerda, F., Stevens, K. N., & Lindblom, B. (1992). Linguistic experience alters phonetic perception in infants by 6 months of age. *Science, 255,* 606–608.

Kutas, N., & Hillyard, S. A. (1970). Reading senseless sentences: Brain potentials reflect semantic incongruity. *Science, 207,* 203–205.

Kutas, N., & Hillyard, S. A. (1980). Reading between the lines: Event-related brain potentials during natural sentence processing. *Brain and Language, 11,* 354–373.

Lachman, R., Lachman, J. R., & Butterfield, E. C. (1979). *Cognitive psychology and information processing: An introduction.* Hillsdale, NJ: Erlbaum.

Lakoff, G. (1972). *Women, fire, and dangerous things.* Chicago: University of Chicago Press.

Lakoff, R. (1975). *Language and woman's place.* New York: Harper & Row.

Lampinen, J. M., Meier, C. R., Arnal, J. D., & Leding, J. K. (2005). Compelling untruths: Content borrowing and vivid false memories. *Journal of Experimental Psychology: Learning, Memory, and Cognition, 31,* 954–963.

Lamy, D., & Tsal, Y. (2000). Object features, object locations, and object files: Which does selective attention activate and when? *Journal of Experimental Psychology: Human Perception and Performance, 26,* 1387–1400.

Lane, S. M., & Schooler, J. W. (2004). Skimming the surface: Verbal overshadowing of analogical retrieval. *Psychological Science, 15,* 715–719.

Larsen, S. F. (1996). Memorable books: Recall of reading and its personal context. In R. J. Kreuz & M. S. MacNealy (Eds.), *Empirical approaches to literature and aesthetics* (pp. 583–599). Norwood, NH: Ablex.

Lawless, H. T. (1997). Olfactory psychophysics. In G. K. Beauchamp & L. Bartoshuk (Eds.), *Tasting and smelling* (pp. 125–174). New York: Academic Press.

Lawless, H. T., & Engen, T. (1977). Associations to odors: Interference, mnemonics, and verbal labeling. *Journal of Experimental Psychology: Human Learning and Memory, 3,* 52–57.

Leahey, T. H. (1992). *A history of psychology: Main currents in psychological thought* (3rd ed.). Englewood Cliffs, NJ: Prentice-Hall.

Lederman, S. J., & Klatzky, R. L. (1990). Haptic classification of common objects: Knowledge-driven exploration. *Cognitive Psychology, 22,* 421–459.

Lemaire, P., & Siegler, R. S. (1995). Four aspects of strategic change: Contributions to children's learning of multiplication. *Journal of Experimental Psychology: General, 124,* 83–97.

Lesch, M. F., & Hancock, P. A. (2004). Driving performance during concurrent cell-phone use: Are drivers aware of their performance decrements? *Accident Analysis and Prevention, 36,* 471–480.

Levelt, W. J. M. (1983). Monitoring and self-report in speech. *Cognition, 14,* 41–104.

Levelt, W. J. M. (1989). *Speaking: From intention to articulation.* Cambridge, MA: MIT Press.

Levelt, W. J. M., Roelefs, A., & Meyer, A. S. (1999). A theory of lexical access in speech production. *Behavioral and Brain Sciences, 22,* 1–75.

Lewald, J. (2002). Opposing effects of head position on sound localization in blind and sighted subjects. *European Journal of Neuroscience, 15,* 1219–1224.

Liberman, A. M., Cooper, F. S., Shankweiler, D. P., & Studdert-Kennedy, M. (1967). Perception of the speech code. *Psychological Review, 74,* 431–461.

Liberman, A. M., Harris, K. S., Hoffman, H. S., & Griffith, B. C. (1957). The discrimination of speech sounds within and across phoneme boundaries. *Journal of Experimental Psychology, 54,* 358–368.

Liberman, A. M., & Whalen, D. H. (2000). On the relation of speech to language. *Trends in Cognitive Sciences, 4,* 187–196.

Lichtenstein, S. (1978). Judged frequency of lethal events. *Journal of Experimental Psychology: Human Learning and Memory, 4,* 551–578.

Lichtenstein, S., & Slovic, P. (1971). Reversals of preference between bids and choices in gambling choices. *Journal of Experimental Psychology, 89,* 46–55.

Lichtenstein, S., & Slovic, P. (1973). Response-induced reversals of preference in gambling: An extended replication in Las Vegas. *Journal of Experimental Psychology, 101,* 16–20.

Lieberman, M. D. (2000). Intuition: A social cognitive neuroscience approach. *Psychological Bulletin, 126,* 109–137.

Lien, M., Ruthruff, E., & Johnston, J. C. (2006). Attentional limitations in doing two tasks at once: The search for exceptions. *Current Directions in Psychological Science, 15,* 89–93.

Lindsay, D. S. (1990). Misleading suggestions can impair witness' ability to remember event details. *Journal of Experimental Psychology: Learning, Memory, and Cognition, 16,* 1077–1083.

Lindsay, D. S. (1998). Depolarizing views on recovered memory experiences. In S. J. Lynn & K. M. McConkey (Eds.), *Truth in memory* (pp. 481–494). New York: Guilford Press.

Lindsay, D. S., Hagen, L., Read, J. D., Wade, K. A., & Garry, M. (2004). True photographs and false memories. *Psychological Science, 15,* 149–154.

Lindsay, D. S., Ross, D. F., Smith, S. M., & Flanagan, S. (1999). Does race influence measures of lineup fairness? *Applied Cognitive Psychology, 13,* S109–S119.

Lindsay, R. C., & Wells, G. L. (1985). Improving eyewitness identifications from lineups: Simultaneous vs. sequential lineup presentation. *Journal of Applied Psychology, 70,* 556–564.

Linton, M. (1975). Transformations of memory in everyday life. In U. Neisser (Ed.), *Memory observed: Remembering in natural contexts* (pp. 77–92). San Francisco: Freeman.

Livesay, K., & Burgess, C. (1998). Mediated priming in high-dimensional semantic space: No effect of direct semantic relationships or co-occurrence. *Brain and Cognition, 37,* 102–105.

Loftus, E. F. (1975). Leading questions and the eyewitness report. *Cognitive Psychology, 7,* 560–572.

Loftus, E. F. (1976). Unconscious transference in eyewitness identification. *Law and Psychology Review, 2,* 93–98.

Loftus, E. F. (1979). *Eyewitness testimony.* Cambridge, MA: Harvard University Press.

Loftus, E. F. (1991). The glitter of everyday memory . . . and the gold. *American Psychologist, 46,* 16–18.

Loftus, E. F. (2005). A 30-year investigation of the malleability of memory. *Learning and Memory, 12,* 361–366.

Loftus, E. F., & Davis, D. (2006). Recovered memories. *Annual Review of Clinical Psychology, 2,* 469–498.

Loftus, E. F., Feldman, J., & Dashiell, R. (1995). The reality of illusory memories. In D. L. Schacter (Ed.), *Memory distortions: How minds, brains, and societies reconstruct the past* (pp. 47–68). Cambridge, MA: Harvard University Press.

Loftus, E. F., & Ketcham, K. (1991). *Witness for the defense: The accused, the eyewitness, and the expert who puts memory on trial.* New York: St. Martin's Press.

Loftus, E. F., Miller, D. G., & Burns, H. J. (1978). Semantic integration of verbal information into a visual memory. *Journal of Experimental Psychology: Human Learning and Memory, 4,* 19–31.

Loftus, E. F., & Pickrell, J. E. (1995). The formation of false memories. *Psychiatric Annals, 25,* 720–725.

Logan, G. D. (1988). Toward an instance-based theory of automatization. *Psychological Review, 95,* 492–527.

Logan, G. D. (1997). The automaticity of academic life: Unconscious applications of an implicit theory. In R. S. Wyer (Ed.), *The automaticity of everyday life, advances in social cognition.* Vol. 10, pp. 157–179. Mahweh, NJ: Erlbaum.

Logothetis, N. K., Pauls, J., & Poggio, T. (1995). Shape representation in the inferior temporal cortex of monkeys. *Current Biology, 7,* 645–651.

Loring-Meier, S., & Halpern, D. F. (1999). Sex differences in visuospatial working memory: Components of cognitive processing. *Psychonomic Bulletin and Review, 6,* 464–471.

Lovelace, E. (1987). Attributes that come to mind in the TOT state. *Bulletin of the Psychonomic Society, 25,* 370–372.

Lubart, T. I. (1994). Creativity. In R. J. Sternberg (Ed.), *Thinking and problem solving* (pp. 290–323). New York: Academic Press.

Luchins, A. M. (1942). Mechanization in problem solving—the effect of Einstellung. *Psychological Monographs, 54,* 95.

Lung, C., & Dominowski, R. L. (1985). Effects of strategy instructions and practice on nine-dot problem solving. *Journal of Experimental Psychology: Learning, Memory, and Cognition, 11,* 804–811.

Luo, C. R., Johnson, R. A., & Gallo, D. A. (1998). Automatic activation of phonological information in reading: Evidence from the semantic relatedness decision task. *Memory and Cognition, 26,* 833–843.

MacDonald, S., Uesiliana, K., & Hayne, H. (2000). Cross-cultural and gender differences in childhood amnesia. *Memory, 8,* 365–376.

MacGregor, J. N., Ormerod, T. C., & Chronicle, E. P. (2001). Information processing and insight: A process model of performance on the nine-dot and related problems. *Journal of Experimental Psychology: Learning, Memory, and Cognition, 27,* 176–201.

Mack, A., & Rock, I. (1998). *Inattentional blindness.* Cambridge, MA: MIT Press.

MacKay, D. G. (1987). *The organization of perception and action: A theory for language and other cognitive skills.* New York: Springer-Verlag.

MacWhinney, B., & Bates, E. (1989). *The cross-linguistic study of sentence processing.* New York: Cambridge University Press.

Madigan, S. (1974). Representational storage in picture memory. *Bulletin of the Psychonomic Society, 4,* 567–568.

Maier, N. R., & Burke, R. J. (1967). Influence of timing of hints on their effectiveness in problem solving. *Psychological Reports, 20,* 3–8.

Maki, R. H. (1998). Predicting performance on text: Delayed vs. immediate predictors and tests. *Memory and Cognition, 26,* 959–964.

Malt, B. C. (1989). An on-line investigation of prototype and exemplar strategies in classification. *Journal of Experimental Psychology: Learning, Memory, and Cognition, 15,* 539–555.

Malt, B. C. (1995). Category coherence in cross-cultural perspective. *Cognitive Psychology, 29,* 85–148.

Malt, B. C., & Smith, E. E. (1984). Correlated properties in natural categories. *Journal of Verbal Learning and Verbal Behavior, 23,* 250–269.

Mandler, J. A. (1987). On the psychological reality of story structure. *Discourse Processes, 10,* 1–29.

Marcel, A. J. (1983). Conscious and unconscious perception: Experiments on visual masking and word recognition. *Cognitive Psychology, 15,* 197–237.

Margolis, H. (1987). *Patterns, thinking, and cognition.* Chicago: University of Chicago Press.

Marian, V., & Neisser, U. (2000). Language-dependent recall of autobiographical memories. *Journal of Experimental Psychology: General, 129,* 361–368.

Marks, L. E. (1987). On cross-modal similarity: Auditory-visual interactions in speeded discrimination. *Journal of Experimental Psychology: Human Perception and Performance, 13,* 383–394.

Marr, D., & Nishihara, H. K. (1982). Representation and recognition of the spatial organization of three-dimensional shapes. *Proceedings of the Royal Society of London, Series B: Biological Sciences* (pp. 269–294). Cambridge, MA: MIT Press.

Marsh, R. L., Landau, J. D., & Hicks, J. L. (1997). Contributions of inadequate source monitoring to unconscious plagiarism during idea generation. *Journal of Experimental Psychology: Learning, Memory, and Cognition, 23,* 886–897.

Marslen-Wilson, W. D., & Welsh, A. (1978). Processing interactions and lexical access during word recognition in continuous speech. *Cognitive Psychology, 10,* 29–63.

Martindale, C. (1991). *Cognitive psychology: A neural-network approach.* Pacific Grove, CA: Brooks/Cole.

Martindale, C., & Greenough, J. (1973). The differential effect of increased arousal on creative and intellectual performance. *Journal of Genetic Psychology, 123,* 329–335.

Martino, G., & Marks, L. E. (2001). Synaesthesia: Strong and weak.

Current Directions in Psychological Science, 10, 61–65.

Massaro, D. W. (1972). Preperceptual images, processing time, and perceptual units in auditory perception. *Psychological Review, 79,* 124–145.

Massaro, D. W. (1975). *Experimental psychology and information processing.* Chicago: Rand-McNally.

Massaro, D. W. (1994). Psychological aspects of speech perception: Implications for research and theory. In M. A. Gernsbacher (Ed.), *Handbook of psycholinguistics* (pp. 219–263). New York: Academic Press.

Massaro, D. W., & Loftus, G. R. (1996). Sensory and perceptual storage: Data and theory. In E. L. Bjork & R. A. Bjork (Eds.), *Memory* (pp. 67–99). New York: Academic Press.

Matan, A., & Carey, S. (2001). Developmental changes within the core of artifact concepts. *Cognition, 78,* 1–26.

Matin, E. (1974). Saccadic suppression: A review and an analysis. *Psychological Bulletin, 81,* 899–917.

Mattingly, I. G., & Liberman, A. M. (1987). Specialized perceiving systems for speech and other biologically significant sounds. In G. M. Edelman, W. E. Gall, & W. M. Cowan (Eds.), *Auditory function: Neurological bases of hearing* (pp. 775–793). New York: Wiley.

Mattys, S. L., White, L., & Melhorn, J. F. (2005). Integration of multiple speech segmentation cues: A hierarchical framework. *Journal of Experimental Psychology: General, 134,* 477–500.

Mayer, R. (1992). *Thinking, problem solving, cognition* (2nd ed.). New York: Freeman.

Mazzoni, G. A. L., Loftus, E. F., & Kirsch, I. (2001). Changing beliefs about implausible autobiographical events: A little plausibility goes a long way. *Journal of Experimental Psychology: Applied, 7,* 51–59.

McBride-Chang, C., & Kail, R. V. (2002). Cross-cultural similarities in the predictors of reading acquisition. *Child Development, 73,* 1392–1407.

McBurney, D. M. (1974). Are there primary tastes for man? *Chemical Senses and Flavor, 1,* 17–28.

McBurney, D. M. (1986). Taste, smell, and flavor terminology: Taking the confusion out of fusion. In H. L. Meiselman & R. S. Rivlin (Eds.), *Clinical measurement of taste and smell* (pp. 117–125). New York: Macmillan.

McClaughlin, G. H. (1969). Reading at "impossible" speeds. *Journal of Reading, 12,* 449–454.

McClelland, J. L., & Elman, J. L. (1986). The TRACE model of speech perception. *Cognitive Psychology, 18,* 1–86.

McClelland, J. L., & Rumelhart, D. (1981). An interactive activation model of context effects in letter perception, I: An account of basic findings. *Psychological Review, 88,* 375–407.

McClelland, J. L., Thomas, A. G., McCandliss, B. D., & Fiez, J. A. (1999). Understanding failures of learning: Hebbian learning, competition for representational space, and some preliminary experimental data. In J. A. Reggia, E. Ruppin, & D. Glanzman (Eds.), *Progress in brain research* (Vol. 121). Amsterdam: Elsevier.

McCloskey, M., & Zaragoza, M. (1985). Misleading postevent information and memory for events: Arguments and evidence against memory impairment hypothesis. *Journal of Experimental Psychology: General, 114,* 1–16.

McCloskey, M., Wible, C. J., & Cohen, N. J. (1988). Is there a special flash-bulb-memory mechanism? *Journal of Experimental Psychology: General, 117,* 171–181.

McConkie, G. W., & Rayner, K. (1976). What guides a reader's eye movements? *Vision Research, 16,* 829–837.

McDaniel, M. A., & Einstein, G. O. (1986). Bizarre imagery as an effective memory aid: The importance of distinctiveness. *Journal of Experimental Psychology: Learning, Memory, & Cognition, 12,* 54–65.

McDaniel, M. A., & Einstein, G. O. (2005). Material-appropriate difficulty: A framework for determining when difficulty is desirable for improving learning In A. F. Healy (Ed.), *Experimental cognitive psychology and its applications. Decade of behavior* (pp. 73–85). Washington, DC: American Psychological Association.

McDaniel, M. A., Pressley, M., & Dunay, P. K. (1987). Long-term retention of vocabulary after keyword and context learning. *Journal of Educational Psychology, 79,* 87–89.

McDowd, J. M., & Craik, F. I. (1988). Effects of aging and task difficulty on divided attention performance. *Journal of Experimental Psychology: Human Perception and Performance, 14,* 267–280.

McDonald, J. L., & MacWhinney, B. (1995). The time course of anaphor resolution: Effects of implicit verb causality and gender. *Journal of Memory and Language, 34,* 543–566.

McGurk, J., & MacDonald, H. (1978). Visual influences on speech perception. *Perception & Psychophysics, 24,* 253–257.

McKoon, G. (1977). Organization of information in text memory. *Journal of Verbal Learning and Verbal Behavior, 16,* 247–260.

McKoon, G., & Ratcliff, R. (1992). Inferences during reading. *Psychological Review, 99,* 440–466.

McMackin, J., & Slovic, P. (2000). When does explicit justification impair decision making? *Applied Cognitive Psychology, 14,* 527–541.

McNally, R. J. (2003). Recovering memories of trauma: A view from the laboratory. *Current Directions in Psychological Science, 12,* 32–35.

McNamara, H. J., Long, J. B., & Wike, E. L. (1956). Learning without response under two conditions of external cues. *Journal of Comparative and Physiological Psychology, 49,* 477–480.

McNamara, T. P. (1992). Theories of priming I: Associative distance and lag. *Journal of Experimental*

Psychology: Learning, Memory, and Cognition, 18, 1173–1190.

McNamara, T. P. (1994). Knowledge representation. In R. L. Sternberg (Ed.), *Thinking and problem solving* (pp. 81–117). New York: Academic Press.

McNamara, T. P., & Altarriba, J. (1988). Depth of spreading activation revisited: Semantic mediated priming occurs in lexical decisions. *Journal of Memory and Language, 27,* 545–559.

McNeil, B. J., Pauker, S. G., Sox, H. C., & Tversky, A. (1986). On the elicitation of preferences for alternative therapies. In K. R. Hammond & H. R. Arkes (Eds.), *Judgment and decision making.* New York: Cambridge University Press.

McQuiston-Surrett, D., Malpass, R. S., & Tredoux, C. G. (2006). Sequential vs. simultaneous lineups: A review of methods, data, and theory. *Psychology, Public Policy, and Law, 12,* 137–169.

Medin, D. L., & Atran, S. (2004). The native mind: Biological categorization and reasoning in development and across cultures. *Psychological Review, 111,* 960–983.

Medin, D. L., & Coley, J. D. (1998). Concepts and categorization. In J. Hochberg (Ed.), *Perception and cognition at century's end* (pp. 403–439). San Diego, CA: Academic Press.

Medin, D. L., & Heit, E. (1999). Categorization. In D. Rumelhart & B. Martin (Eds.), *Handbook of cognition and perception* (pp. 99–143). New York: Academic Press.

Medin, D. L., Lynch, E. B., & Solomon K. O. (2000). Are there kinds of concepts? *Annual Review of Psychology, 52,* 121–147.

Medin, D. L., & Ortony, A. (1989). Psychological essentialism. In S. Vosniadou & A. Ortony (Eds.), *Similarity and analogical reasoning* (pp. 179–196). New York: Cambridge University Press.

Medin, D. L., & Rips, L. J. (2005). Concepts and categories: Memory, meaning, and metaphysics. In K.

Holyoak & R. G. Morrison (Eds.), *The Cambridge handbook of thinking and reasoning* (pp. 37–72). New York: Cambridge University Press.

Melton, A. W. (1963). Implications of short-term memory for a general theory of memory. *Journal of Verbal Learning and Verbal Behavior, 2,* 1–21.

Melton, A. W. (1970). The situation with respect to the spacing of repetitions and memory. *Journal of Verbal Learning and Verbal Behavior, 9,* 596–606.

Merckelbach, H., Smeets, T., Geraerts, E., Jelicic, M., Bouwen, A., & Smeets, E. (2006). I haven't thought about this for years! Dating recent recalls of vivid memories. *Applied Cognitive Psychology, 20,* 33–42.

Merikle, P. M. (1988). Subliminal auditory messages: An evaluation. *Psychology and Marketing, 5,* 355–372.

Mervis, C. B., & Rosch, E. (1981). Categorization of natural objects. *Annual Review of Psychology, 32,* 89–115.

Metcalfe, J. (1986a). Feeling of knowing in memory and problem solving. *Journal of Experimental Psychology: Learning, Memory, and Cognition, 12,* 288–294.

Metcalfe, J. (1986b). Premonitions of insight predict impending error. *Journal of Experimental Psychology: Learning, Memory, and Cognition, 12,* 623–634.

Metcalfe, J., & Weibe, D. (1987). Intuition in insight and noninsight problem solving. *Memory and Cognition, 15,* 238–246.

Metzger, R. L., Boschee, P. F., Haugen, T., & Schnobrich, B. L. (1979). The classroom as learning context: Changing rooms affects performance. *Journal of Educational Psychology, 71,* 440–442.

Miles, C., & Hardman, L. (1998). State-dependent memory produced by aerobic exercise. *Ergonomics, 41,* 20–28.

Miller, G. A. (1956). The magical number seven, plus or minus two: Some limits on our capacity for processing information. *Psychological Review, 63,* 81–97.

Miller, G. A. (1990). The place of language in a scientific psychology. *Psychological Science, 1,* 7–14.

Mills, C. B., Boteler, E. H., & Oliver, G. K. (1999). Digit synesthesia: A case study using a Stroop-type test. *Cognitive Neuropsychology, 16,* 181–191.

Moè, A., & De Beni, R. (2005). Stressing the efficacy of the loci method: Oral presentation and the subject-generation of the loci pathway with expository passages. *Applied Cognitive Psychology, 19,* 95–106.

Monti, L. A., Gabrieli, J. D. E., Wilson, R. S., Beckett, L. A., Grinnell, E., Lange, K. L., & Reminger, S. L. (1997). Sources of priming in text rereading: Intact implicit memory for new associations in older adults and in patients with Alzheimer's disease. *Psychology and Aging, 12,* 536–547.

Moore, C. M., & Egeth, H. (1997). Perception without attention: Evidence of grouping under conditions of inattention. *Journal of Experimental Psychology: Human Perception and Performance, 23,* 339–352.

Moore, T. E. (1996). Scientific consensus and expert testimony: Lessons from the Judas Priest trial. *Skeptical Inquirer, 20.*

Moors, A., & De Houwer, J. (2006). Automaticity: A theoretical and conceptual analysis. *Psychological Bulletin, 132,* 297–326.

Moray, N. (1959). Attention in dichotic listening: Affective cues and the influence of instructions. *Quarterly Journal of Experimental Psychology, 11,* 56–60.

Morris, C. D., Bransford, J. D., & Franks, J. J. (1977). Levels of processing versus transfer-appropriate processing. *Journal of Verbal Learning and Verbal Behavior, 16,* 519–533.

Morrot, G., Brochet, F., & Dubourdieu, D. (2001). The color of odors. *Brain and Language, 79,* 309–320.

Morton, J. (1969). Interaction of information in word recognition. *Psychological Review, 76,* 165–178.

Most, S. B., Scholl, B. J., Clifford, E. R., & Simons, D. J. (2005). What you see is what you set: Sustained inattentional blindness and the capture of awareness. *Psychological Review, 112,* 217–242.

Motley, M. T. (1985). Slips of the tongue. *Scientific American, 253,* 116–127.

Motley, M. T., & Baars, B. J. (1979). Effects of cognitive set upon laboratory-induced verbal (Freudian) slips. *Journal of Speech and Hearing Research, 22,* 421–432.

Mousty, P., & Bertelson, P. (1992). Finger movements in braille reading: The effect of local ambiguity. *Cognition, 43,* 67–84.

Mueller-Johnson, K., & Ceci, S. J. (2004). Memory and suggestibility in older adults: Live event participation and repeated interview. *Applied Cognitive Psychology, 18,* 1109–1127.

Murray, D. J. (1968). Articulation and acoustic confusability in short-term memory. *Journal of Experimental Psychology, 78,* 679–684.

Murray, J. E., Young, E., & Rhodes, G. (2000). Revisiting the perception of upside-down faces. *Psychological Science, 11,* 492–496.

Murray, W. S., & Kennedy, A. (1988). Spatial coding in the processing of anaphor by good and poor readers: Evidence from eye movement analyses. *Quarterly Journal of Experimental Psychology: Human Experimental Psychology, 40(4-A),* 693–718.

Myers, D. G. (2001, December). Do we fear the right things? *American Psychological Society Observer, 14,* 3.

Nadel, L., & Jacobs, W. J. (1998). Traumatic memory is special. *Current Directions in Psychological Science, 7,* 154–157.

Nadel, L., & Zola-Morgan, S. (1984). Infantile amnesia: A neurobiological perspective. In M. Moscovitch (Ed.), *Infant memory* (pp. 145–172). New York: Plenum Press.

Nairne, J. S. (1983). Associative processing during rote rehearsal. *Journal of Experimental Psychology: Learning, Memory, and Cognition, 9,* 3–20.

Nairne, J. S. (1992). The loss of positional certainty in long-term memory. *Psychological Science, 3,* 199–202.

Nairne, J. S. (1996). Short-term/working memory. In E. L. Bjork & R. A. Bjork (Eds.), *Memory: Handbook of perception and cognition.* New York: Academic Press.

Nairne, J. S. (2002a). The myth of the encoding-retrieval match. *Memory, 10,* 389–395.

Nairne, J. S. (2002b). Remembering over the short-term: The case against the standard model. *Annual Review of Psychology, 53,* 53–81.

Nairne, J. S., & Walters, V. L. (1983). Silent mouthing produces modality- and suffix-like effects. *Journal of Verbal Learning and Verbal Behavior, 22,* 475–483.

Nathan, D., & Snedeker, M. (1995). *Satan's silence: Ritual abuse and the making of a modern American witch hunt.* New York: Basic Books.

Navon, D. (1977). Forest before trees: The precedence of global features in visual perception. *Cognitive Psychology, 9,* 353–383.

Navon, D., & Gopher, D. (1979). On the economy of the human information processing system. *Psychological Review, 86,* 214–255.

Navon, D., & Miller, J. F. (2002). Queuing or sharing? A critical evaluation of the single-bottleneck notion. *Cognitive Psychology, 44,* 193–251.

Neath, I. (2000). Is "working memory" still a useful concept? *Contemporary Psychology, 45,* 410–412.

Neath, I., Surprenant, A. M., & Crowder, R. G. (1993). The context-dependent stimulus suffix effect. *Journal of Experimental Psychology: Learning, Memory, and Cognition, 19,* 698–703.

Needham, D. R., & Begg, I. M. (1991). Problem-oriented training promotes spontaneous analogical transfer: Memory-oriented training promotes memory for training. *Memory and Cognition, 19,* 543–557.

Neely, J. H. (1977). Semantic priming and retrieval from lexical memory: Roles of inhibitionless spreading activation and limited-capacity attention. *Journal of Experimental Psychology: General, 106,* 226–254.

Neisser, U. (1967). *Cognitive psychology.* New York: Appleton-Century-Crofts.

Neisser, U. (1978). Memory: What are the important questions? In M. M. Gruneberg, P. E. Morris, & R. N. Sykes (Eds.), *Practical aspects of memory.* New York: Academic Press.

Neisser, U. (1988). What is ordinary memory the memory of? In U. Neisser (Ed.), *Remembering reconsidered: Ecological and traditional approaches to the study of memory* (pp. 356–373). San Francisco: Freeman.

Neisser, U., & Harsch, N. (1992). Phantom flashbulbs: False recollections of hearing the news about Challenger. In E. Winograd & U. Neisser (Eds.), *Affect and accuracy in recall: Studies of "flashbulb" memories* (pp. 9–31). New York: Cambridge University Press.

Nelson, E. L., & Simpson, P. (1994). First glimpse: An initial investigation of subjects who have rejected their recovered visualizations as false memories. *Issues in Child Abuse Accusations, 6,* 123–133.

Nelson, K. (1993). The psychological and social origins of autobiographical memory. *Psychological Science, 4,* 7–14.

Nelson, K., & Fivush, R. (2004). The emergence of autobiographical memory: A social-cultural developmental theory. *Psychological Review, 111,* 486–511.

Nelson, T. O. (1984). A comparison of current measures of the accuracy of the feeling-of-knowing predictions. *Psychological Bulletin, 95,* 109–133.

Newell, A., Shaw, J. C., & Simon, H. A. (1958). Elements of a theory of human problem solving. *Psychological Review, 65,* 151–166.

Newell, A., & Simon, H. (1972). *Human problem solving.* Englewood Cliffs, NJ: Prentice Hall.

Nickerson, R. S. (1998). Confirmation bias: A ubiquitous phenomenon in many guises. *Review of General Psychology, 2,* 175–220.

Nisbett, R. E., & Masuda, T. (2003). Culture and point of view. *Proceedings of the National Academy of Sciences, 100,* 11163–11170.

Nisbett, R. E., & Wilson, T. D. (1977). Telling more than we can know: Verbal reports on mental processes. *Psychological Review, 84,* 231–259.

Norman, D. A. (1981). Categorization of action slips. *Psychological Review, 88,* 1–15.

Norman, D. A. (1988). *The psychology of everyday things.* New York: Basic Books.

Norman, D. A., & Bobrow, D. G. (1975). On data-limited and resource-limited processes. *Cognitive Psychology, 7,* 44–64.

Norman, D. A., & Bobrow, D. G. (1979). On the role of active memory processes in perception and cognition. In C. N. Cofer (Ed.), *The structure of human memory* (pp. 114–132). San Francisco: Freeman.

Norman, K. A., & Schacter, D. L. (1996). Implicit memory, explicit memory and false recollection. A cognitive neuroscience perspective. In L. M. Reder (Ed.), *Implicit memory and metacognition* (pp. 229–259). Hillsdale, NJ: Erlbaum.

Norris, D. (1994). Shortlist: A connectionist model of continuous speech recognition. *Cognition, 52,* 189–234.

Nosofsky, R. (1984). Choice, similarity, and the context theory of classification. *Journal of Experimental Psychology: Learning, Memory, and Cognition, 10,* 104–114.

Novick, L. R., & Holyoak, K. E. (1991). Mathematical problem solving by analogy. *Journal of Experimental Psychology: Learning, Memory, and Cognition, 17,* 398–415.

Nyberg, L., Cabeza, R., & Tulving, E. (1996). PET studies of encoding and retrieval: The HERA model. *Psychonomic Bulletin and Review, 3,* 135–148.

Oberauer, K. (2006). Reasoning with conditionals: A test of formal models of four theories. *Cognitive Psychology, 53,* 238–283.

Okado, Y., & Stark, C. E. L. (2005). Neural activity during encoding predicts false memories created by misinformation. *Learning & Memory, 12,* 3–11.

Olton, R. M. (1979). Experimental studies of incubation: Searching for the elusive. *Journal of Creative Behavior, 13,* 9–22.

Olton, R. M., & Johnson, D. M. (1976). Mechanisms of incubation in creative problem solving. *American Journal of Psychology, 89,* 617–630.

Ostergaard, A. L. (1999). Priming effects in amnesia: Now you see them, now you don't. *Journal of the International Neurological Society, 5,* 175–190.

Ostergaard, A. L., & Jernigan, T. L. (1993). Are word priming and explicit memory mediated by different brain structures? In P. Graf & M. E. J. Masson (Eds.), *Implicit memory: New directions in cognition, development, and neuropsychology* (pp. 327–349). Hillsdale, NJ: Erlbaum.

Paivio, A. (1971). *Imagery and verbal processes.* New York: Holt, Rinehart, & Winston.

Paivio, A., & Csapo, K. (1969). Concrete image and verbal memory codes. *Journal of Experimental Psychology, 80,* 279–285.

Paller, K. A. (2004). Electrical signals of memory and of the awareness of remembering. *Current Directions in Psychological Science, 13,* 49–55.

Paller, K. A., Hutson, C. A., Miller, B. B., & Boehm, S. G. (2003). Neural manifestations of memory with and without awareness. *Neuron, 38,* 507–516.

Palmer, S. E. (1975). The effects of contextual scenes on the identification of objects. *Memory and Cognition, 3,* 519–526.

Palmer, S. E. (1999). Perceptual grouping: It's later than you think. *Current Directions in Psychological Science, 11,* 101–106.

Palmer, S. E. (2003). Visual perception of objects. In A. F. Healy & R. F. Proctor (Eds.), *Handbook of psychology: Experimental psychology* (Vol. 4, pp. 179–211). Hoboken, NJ: John Wiley & Sons, Inc.

Palmer, S., Rosch, E., & Chase, P. (1981). Canonical perspective and the perception of objects. In J. Long & A. Baddeley (Eds.), *Attention & performance IX* (pp. 135–151) Hillsdale, NJ: Erlbaum.

Park, D. C., Hertzog, C., Kidder, D. P., & Morrell, R. W. (1997). Effect of age on event-based and time-based prospective memory. *Psychology and Aging, 12,* 314–327.

Park, D. C., Smith, A. D., & Cavanaugh, J. C. (1990). Metamemories of memory researchers. *Memory and Cognition, 18,* 321–327.

Parsons, L. M. (1987). Imagined spatial transformations of one's body. *Journal of Experimental Psychology: General, 116,* 172–191.

Pashler, H. (1992). Attentional limitations in doing two tasks at the same time. *Current Directions in Psychological Science, 1,* 44–48.

Pashler, H. (1994). Dual-task interference in simple tasks: Data and theory. *Psychological Bulletin, 16,* 220–244.

Pashler, H., & Carrier, M. (1996). Structures, processes, and the flow of information. In E. L. Bjork & R. A. Bjork (Eds.), *Handbook of perception and cognition: Memory* (pp. 3–29). New York: Academic Press.

Patterson, K., & Besner, D. (1984). Is the right hemisphere literate? *Cognitive Neuropsychology, 1,* 315–341.

Pavani, F., Spence, C., & Driver, J. (2000). Visual capture of touch: Out-of-body experiences with rubber gloves. *Psychological Science, 11,* 353–359.

Payne, J. D., Jackson, E. D., Ryan, L., Hoscheidt, S., Jacobs, W. J., & Nadel, L. (2006). The impact of stress on neutral and emotional aspects of episodic memory. *Memory, 14,* 1–16.

Payne, J. D., Nadel, L., Britton, W. B., & Jacobs, W. J. (2004). The biopsychology of trauma and memory. In D. Reisberg & P. Hertel (Eds.), *Memory and emotion. Series in affective science* (pp. 76–128). New York: Oxford University Press.

Pepperberg, I. M. (1999a). *The Alex studies: Cognitive and communicative abilities of grey parrots.* Cambridge, MA: Harvard University Press.

Pepperberg, I. M. (1999b). Cognitive and communicative abilities of grey parrots. *Current Directions in Psychological Science, 11,* 83–87.

Pepperberg, I. M. (2006). Cognitive and communicative abilities of grey parrots. *Applied Animal Behaviour Science, 100,* 77–86.

Peretz, I., Radeau, M., & Arguin, M. (2004). Two-way interactions between music and language: Evidence from priming recognition of tune and lyrics in familiar songs. *Memory & Cognition, 32,* 142–152.

Perfect, T. J., & Harris, L. J. (2003). Adult age differences in unconscious transference: Source confusion or identity blending? *Memory & Cognition, 31*(4), 570–580.

Petersen, S. E., Fox, P. T., Posner, M. I., Mintun, M., & Raichle, M. E. (1988). Positron emission tomography studies of the cortical anatomy of single-word processing. *Nature, 331,* 585–589.

Peterson, C., & Bell, M. (1996). Children's memory for traumatic injury. *Child Development, 67,* 3045–3070.

Peterson, L., & Peterson, M. J. (1959). Short-term retention of individual verbal items. *Journal of Experimental Psychology, 58,* 193–198.

Pezdek, K. (2003). Event memory and autobiographical memory for the events of September 11, 2001. *Applied Cognitive Psychology, 17,* 1033–1045.

Piaget, J. (1929). *The child's conception of the world.* New York: Harcourt-Brace.

Pickering, M. J., & Traxler, M. J. (1998). Plausibility and recovery from garden paths: An eye-movement study. *Journal of Experimental Psychology: Learning, Memory, and Cognition, 24,* 940–961.

Pillemer, D. B. (1984). Flashbulb memories of the assassination attempt on President Reagan. *Cognition, 16,* 63–80.

Pillemer, D. B. (1998). *Momentous events, vivid memories.* Cambridge, MA: Harvard University Press.

Pillemer, D. B., & White, S. H. (1989). Childhood events recalled by children and adults. In H. W. Reese (Ed.), *Advances in child development and behavior* (Vol. 21, pp. 297–340). San Diego, CA: Academic Press.

Pinker, S. (1990). Language acquisition. In L. R. Gleitman (Ed.), *Language: An invitation to cognitive science,* (Vol. 1, pp. 199–241). Cambridge, MA: MIT Press.

Pinker, S. (1991). Rules of language. *Science, 253,* 530–535.

Pinker, S. (1994a). How could a child use verb syntax to learn verb semantics? *Lingua, 92,* 377–410.

Pinker, S. (1994b). *How the mind works.* New York: Norton.

Pinker, S. (1994c). *The language instinct.* New York: William Morrow & Co.

Pinker, S. (1999). *Words and rules.* New York: Basic Books.

Pinker, S., Choate, P. A., & Finke, R. A. (1984). Mental extrapolations in patterns constructed from memory. *Memory and Cognition, 12,* 207–218.

Plous, S. (1993). *The psychology of judgment and decision-making.* New York: McGraw-Hill.

Polusny, M. A., & Follette, V. M. (1996). Remembering childhood sexual abuse: A national survey of psychologists' clinical practices, beliefs, and personal experiences. *Professional Psychology Research and Practice, 27,* 41–52.

Poole, D. A., Lindsay, D. S., Memon, A., & Bull, R. (1995). Psychotherapy and the recovery of memories of childhood sexual abuse. *Journal of Consulting and Clinical Psychology, 63,* 426–437.

Posner, M. I. (1980). Orienting of attention. *Quarterly Journal of Experimental Psychology, 32,* 3–25.

Posner, M. I., Goldsmith, R., & Welton, K. E. (1967). Perceived distance and the classification of distorted patterns. *Journal of Experimental Psychology, 73,* 28–38.

Posner, M. I., & Snyder, C. R. R. (1975). Facilitation and inhibition in the processing of signals. In P. M. A. Rabbitt & S. Dornic (Eds.), *Attention and performance V* (pp. 669–682). New York: Academic Press.

Povinelli, D. J., Landry, A. M., Theall, L. A., Clark, B. R., & Castille, C. M. (1999). Development of young children's understanding that the recent past is causally bound to the present. *Developmental Psychology, 35,* 1426–1439.

Premack, D. (1970). A functional analysis of language. *Journal of the Experimental Analysis of Behavior, 14,* 107–125.

Premack, D., & Premack, A. J. (1983). The mind of an ape. New York: Norton.

Principe, G. F., Kanaya, T., Ceci, S. J., & Singh, M. (2006). Believing is seeing: How rumors can engender false memories in preschoolers. *Psychological Science, 17,* 243–248.

Proctor, R. W., & Fangini, C. A. (1978). Effects of distractor-stimulus modality in the Brown-Peterson distractor task. *Journal of Experimental Psychology: Human Learning and Memory, 4,* 676–684.

Proffitt, D. R. (2006). Embodied perception and the economy of action. *Perspectives on Psychological Science, 1,* 110–122.

Proffitt, D. R., Bhalla, M., Gossweiler, R., & Midgett, J. (1995). Perceiving geographical slant. *Psychonomic Bulletin & Review, 2,* 409–428.

Pugh, K. R., Mencl, W. E., Shaywitz, B. A., Shaywitz, S. E., Fulbright, R. K., Constable, R. T., Skudlarski, P., Marchione, K. E., Jenner, A. R., Fletcher, J. M., Liberman, A. M., Shankweiler, D. P., Katz, L., Lacadie, C., Gore, J. C. (2000). The angular gyrus in developmental dyslexia: Task-specific differences in functional connectivity within posterior cortex. *Psychological Science, 11,* 51–56.

Pylyshyn, Z. W. (1973). What the mind's eye tells the mind's brain: A critique of mental imagery. *Psychological Bulletin, 80,* 1–24.

Pylyshyn, Z. W. (1981). The imagery debate: Analogue media vs. tacit knowledge. *Psychological Review, 88,* 16–45.

Pylyshyn, Z. W. (2002). Mental imagery: In search of a theory. *Behavioral and Brain Sciences, 25,* 157–238.

Pylyshyn, Z. (2003). Return of the mental image: Are there really pictures in the brain? *Trends in Cognitive Sciences, 7,* 113–118.

Pylyshyn, Z. (2004). The illusion of explanation: The experience of volition, mental effort, and mental imagery. *Behavioral and Brain Sciences, 27,* 672–673.

Pynoos, R. S., & Nader, K. (1989). Children's memory and proximity to violence. *Journal of the American Academy of Child and Adolescent Psychiatry, 28,* 236–241.

Quinn, D. M., & Spencer, S. J. (2001). The interference of stereotype threat with women's generation of mathematical problem-solving strategies. *Journal of Social Issues, 57,* 55–71.

Radford, B. (1999). The ten-percent myth. *Skeptical Inquirer, 23.*

Rajaram, S. (1993). Remembering and knowing: Two means of access to the personal past. *Memory and Cognition, 21,* 89–102.

Rappold, V. A., & Hashtroudi, S. (1991). Does organization improve priming? *Journal of Experimental Psychology: Learning, Memory, and Cognition, 17,* 103–114.

Rastle, K. G., & Burke, D. M. (1996). Priming the tip of the tongue: Effects of prior processing on word retrieval in young and older adults. *Journal of Memory and Language, 35,* 585–605.

Rauschecker, J. P., & Tian, B. (2000). Mechanisms and streams for processing of "what" and "where" in auditory cortex. *Proceedings of the National Academy of Sciences, 97,* 11800–11806.

Rawson, K. A., Dunlosky, J., & Thiede, K. W. (2000). The re-reading effect: Metacomprehension accuracy improves across reading trials. *Memory and Cognition, 28,* 1004–1010.

Rayner, K. (1998). Eye movements in reading and information processing: Twenty years of research. *Psychological Bulletin, 124,* 374–422.

Rayner, K., Foorman, B. R., Perfetti, C. A., Pesetsky, D., & Seidenberg, M. S. (2001). How psychological science informs the teaching of reading. *Psychological Science in the Public Interest, 2,* 31–74.

Rayner, K., Foorman, B. R., Perfetti, C. A., Pesetsky, D., & Seidenberg, M. S. (2002). How should reading be taught? *Scientific American, 287,* 85–91.

Rayner, K., & Morris, R. K. (1992). Eye movement control in reading: Evidence against semantic preprocessing. *Journal of Experimental Psychology: Human Perception and Performance, 18,* 164–172.

Rayner, K., & Pollatsek, A. (1983). Is visual information integrated across saccades? *Perception & Psychophysics, 34,* 39–48.

Rayner, K., & Pollatsek, A. (1989). *The psychology of reading.* Englewood Cliffs, NJ: Prentice Hall.

Rayner, K., & Well, A. D. (1996). Effects of contextual constraint on eye movements in reading: A further examination. *Psychological Bulletin and Review, 3,* 504–509.

Rayner, K., White, S. J., Johnson, R. L., & Liversedge, S. P. (2006). Raeding wrods with jumbled lettres: There is a cost. *Psychological Science, 17,* 192–193.

Reason, J. T. (1984). Lapses of attention in everyday life. In R. Parasuraman & D. R. Davies (Eds.), *Varieties of attention* (pp. 515–549). New York: Academic Press.

Reason, J. T., & Lucas, D. (1984). Using cognitive diaries to investigate naturally occurring memory blocks. In J. E. Harris & P. E. Morris (Eds.), *Everyday memory, actions, and absentmindedness* (pp. 53–69). New York: Academic Press.

Reed, C. L., Klatzky, R. L., & Halgren, E. (2005). What vs. where in touch: An fMRI study. *NeuroImage, 25,* 718–726.

Reed, C. L., Stone, V., Bozova, S., & Tanaka, J. (2003). The body inversion effect. *Psychological Science, 14,* 302–308.

Reed, C. L., Stone, V. E., Grubb, J. D., & McGoldrick, J. E. (2006). Turning configural processing upside down: Part- and whole body postures. *Journal of Experimental Psychology: Human Perception & Performance, 32,* 73–87.

Reed, G. (1974). *The psychology of anomalous experience.* Boston: Houghton-Mifflin.

Reese, E., & Fivush, R. (1993). Parental styles of talking about the past. *Developmental Psychology, 29,* 506–516.

Reicher, G. (1969). Perceptual recognition as a function of meaningfulness of stimulus material. *Journal of Experimental Psychology, 81,* 275–280.

Reisberg, D., Pearson, D. G., & Kosslyn, S. M. (2003). Intuitions and introspections about imagery: The role of imagery experience in shaping an investigator's theoretical views. *Applied Cognitive Psychology, 17,* 147–160.

Rensink, R. A. (2002). Change detection. *Annual Review of Psychology. 53,* 245–277.

Repp, B. H. (1984). Closure duration and release burst amplitude cues to stop consonant manner and place of articulation. *Language and Speech, 27,* 245–254.

Reuter-Lorenz, P. A., & Sylvester, C. C. (2005). The cognitive neuroscience of working memory and aging. In R. Cabeza, L. Nyberg, & D. Park (Eds.), *Cognitive neuroscience of aging: Linking cognitive and cerebral aging* (pp. 186–217). New York: Oxford University Press.

Rhodes, M. (1961/1987). An analysis of creativity. In S. G. Isaksen (Ed.), *Frontiers of creativity research: Beyond the basics* (pp. 216–222). Buffalo, NY: Bearly.

Riby, L. M., Perfect, T. J., & Stollery, B. T. (2004). The effects of age and task domain on dual task performance: A meta-analysis. *European Journal of Cognitive Psychology, 16,* 868–891.

Richman, C. L., Mitchell, D. B., & Reznick, J. S. (1979). Mental travel: Some reservations. *Journal of Experimental Psychology: Human Perception and Performance, 5,* 13–18.

Rikers, R. M., Schmidt, H. G., & Boshuizen, H. P. (2000). Knowledge encapsulation and the intermediate effect. *Contemporary Educational Psychology, 25,* 150–166.

Rips, L. J. (1974). Inductive judgments about natural categories. *Journal of Verbal Learning and Verbal Behavior, 14,* 665–681.

Rips, L. J. (1989). Similarity, typicality, and categorization. In S. Vosniadu & A. Ortony (Eds.), *Similarity and analogical reasoning* (pp. 21–59). Cambridge, UK: Cambridge University Press.

Rips, L. J. (1990). Reasoning. *Annual Review of Psychology, 41,* 321–353.

Rips, L. J. (1994). Deduction and its cognitive basis. In R. J. Sternberg (Ed.), *Thinking and problem solving* (pp. 149–178). New York: Academic Press.

Rips, L. J., Shoben, E. J., & Smith, E. E. (1973). Semantic distance and the verification of semantic relations. *Journal of Verbal Learning and Verbal Behavior, 12,* 1–20.

Risset, J. C. (1991). Speech and music combined: An overview. In J. Sundberg, I. Nord, & R. Carlson (Eds.), *Music, language, speech, and brain* (pp. 368–379). New York: Cambridge University Press.

Rivas, E. (2005). Recent use of signs by chimpanzees (Pan troglodytes) in interactions with humans. *Journal of Comparative Psychology, 119,* 404–417.

Roalf, D., Lowery, N., & Turetsky, B. I. (2006). Behavioral and physiological findings of gender differences in global-local visual processing. *Brain and Cognition, 60,* 32–42.

Robertson, D. A., Gernsbacher, M. A., Guidotti, S. J., Robertson, R. R., Irwin, W., Mock, B. J., & Campana, M. E. (2000). Functional neuroanatomy of the cognitive process of mapping during discourse comprehension. *Psychological Science, 11,* 255–260.

Rochat, P. (1999). Direct perception and representation in infancy. In E. Winograd, R. Fivush, & W. Hirst (Eds.), *Ecological approaches to cognition: Essays in honor of Ulric Neisser* (pp. 3–30). Mahwah, NJ: Erlbaum.

Rock, I. (1984). *Perception.* New York: Scientific American Books.

Roediger, H. L. (1990). Implicit memory: Retention without remembering. *American Psychologist, 45,* 1043–1056.

Roediger, H. L., & Bergman, E. T. (1998). The controversy over recovered memories. *Psychology, Public Policy, and Law, 4,* 1091–1109.

Roediger, H. L., & Gallo, D. A. (2004). Associative memory illusions. In R. F. Pohl (Ed.), *Cognitive illusions: A handbook on fallacies and biases in thinking, judgment and memory.* New York: Oxford University Press.

Roediger, H. L., & Guynn, M. J. (1996). Retrieval processes. In E. L. Bjork & R. A. Bjork (Eds.), *Handbook of perception and cognition: Memory* (pp. 197–236). New York: Academic Press.

Roediger, H. L., & Karpicke, J. D. (2006). Test-enhanced learning: Taking memory tests improves long-term retention. *Psychological Science, 17,* 249–255.

Roediger, H. L., & McDermott, K. B. (1995). Creating false memories: Remembering words not presented in lists. *Journal of Experimental Psychology: Learning, Memory, and Cognition, 21,* 803–814.

Roediger, H. L., Meade, M. L., & Bergman, E. T. (2001). Social contagion of memory. *Psychonomic Bulletin and Review, 8*, 365–371.

Roediger, R. (2004, March). What happened to behaviorism? *American Psychological Society Observer, 17* (3), Presidential Column.

Rogers, T. B., Kuiper, N. A., & Kirker, W. S. (1977). Self reference and the encoding of personal information. *Journal of Personality and Social Psychology, 35*, 677–688.

Rogoff, B., Paradise, R., Mejia Arauz, R., Correa-Chavez, M., & Angelillo, C. (2003). Firsthand learning through intent participation. *Annual Review of Psychology, 54*, 175–203.

Rosch, E. (1973). Natural categories. *Cognitive Psychology, 4*, 328–350.

Rosch, E. (1975a). Cognitive reference points. *Cognitive Psychology, 7*, 532–547.

Rosch, E. (1975b). Cognitive representations of semantic categories. *Journal of Experimental Psychology: General, 104*, 192–233.

Rosch, E. (1976). Basic objects in natural categories. *Cognitive Psychology, 8*, 382–439.

Rosch, E. (1978). Principles of categorization. In E. Rosch & B. B. Lloyd (Eds.), *Cognition and categorization* (pp. 27–48). Hillsdale, NJ: Erlbaum.

Rosch, E., & Mervis, C. B. (1975). Family resemblances: Studies in the internal structure of categories. *Cognitive Psychology, 7*, 573–605.

Rosenbluth, R., Grossman, E. S., & Kaitz, R. (2000). Performance of early-blind and sighted children on olfactory tasks. *Perception, 29*, 101–110.

Ross, B. H. (1987). This is like that: The use of earlier examples and the separation of similarity effects. *Journal of Experimental Psychology: Learning, Memory, and Cognition, 13*, 629–639.

Ross, B. H., & Spalding, T. L. (1994). Concepts and categories. In R. J. Sternberg (Ed.), *Handbook of perception and cognition,* Vol. 2: *Thinking and problem solving* (pp. 119–148). San Diego, CA: Academic Press.

Ross, D. R., Ceci, S. J., Dunning, D., & Toglia, M. P. (1994). Unconscious transference and mistaken identity: When a witness misidentifies a familiar but innocent person. *Journal of Applied Psychology, 79*, 918–930.

Roth, E. M., & Shoben, E. J. (1983). The effect of context on the structure of categories. *Cognitive Psychology, 15*, 346–378.

Rothman, A. J., & Salovey, P. (1997). Shaping perceptions to motivate healthy behavior: The role of message framing. *Psychological Bulletin, 121*, 3–19.

Rozin, P. (1982). "Taste-smell confusions" and the duality of the olfactory sense. *Perception and Psychophysics, 31*, 397–401.

Rubin, D. C., Groth, E., & Goldsmith, D. J. (1984). Olfactory cuing of autobiographical memory. *American Journal of Psychology, 97*, 493–507.

Rubin, D. C., Rahhal, T. A., & Poon, L. W. (1998). Things learned in early adulthood are remembered best. *Memory and Cognition, 26*, 3–19.

Rubin, D. C., Wetzler, S. E., & Nebes, R. D. (1986). Autobiographical memory across the lifespan. In D. C. Rubin (Ed.), *Autobiographical memory* (pp. 202–221). Cambridge, UK: Cambridge University Press.

Rumelhart, D. E. (1975). Notes on a schema for stories. In D. G. Bobrow & A. M. Collins (Eds.), *Representation and understanding* (pp. 211–236). New York: Academic Press.

Runco, M. A. (1991). *Divergent thinking.* Norwood, NJ: Ablex.

Runco, M. A. (2004). Creativity. *Annual Review of Psychology, 55*, 657–687.

Sachs, J. (1967). Recognition memory for syntactic and semantic aspects of connected discourse. *Perception and Psychophysics, 2*, 437–442.

Sacks, H., Schegloff, E. A., & Jefferson, G. (1974). A simplest systematics for the organization of turn-taking in conversation. *Language, 50*, 696–735.

Saffran, J. R., Aslin, R. N., & Newport, E. C. (1996). Statistical learning in 8-month old infants. *Science, 274*, 1926–1928.

Salaman, E. (1970). *A collection of moments: A study of involuntary memories.* London: Longman.

Saldana, H. M., & Rosenblum, L. D. (1993). Visual influences on auditory pluck and bow judgments. *Perception & Psychophysics, 54*, 406–416.

Sanfey, A. G., Loewenstein, G., McClure, S. M., & Cohen, J. D. (2006). Neuroeconomics: Crosscurrents in research on decision-making. *Trends in Cognitive Sciences, 10*, 108–116.

Saufley, W. H., Otaka, S. R., & Bravaresco, J. L. (1986). Context effects: Classroom tests and context independence. *Memory and Cognition, 13*, 522–528.

Savage-Rumbaugh, E. S., & Brakke, K. E. (1996). Animal language: Methodological and interpretive issues. In M. Bekoff & D. Jamieson (Eds.), *Readings in animal cognition.* Cambridge, MA: MIT Press.

Savage-Rumbaugh, E. S., Rumbaugh, D. M., & Boysen, S. (1980). Do apes use language? *American Scientist, 68*, 49–61.

Schab, L. (1990). Odors and the remembrance of things past. *Journal of Experimental Psychology: Learning, Memory, and Cognition, 16*, 648–655.

Schacter, D. L. (1989). *Memory.* In M. I. Posner (Ed.), *Foundations of cognitive science.* Cambridge, MA: MIT Press.

Schacter, D. L. (1996). *Searching for memory: The brain, the mind, and the past.* New York: Basic Books.

Schacter, D. L. (2001). *The seven sins of memory: How the mind forgets and remembers.* New York: Houghton-Mifflin.

Schacter, D. L., Cooper, L. A., & Delaney, S. M. (1990). Implicit memory for unfamiliar objects depends on access to structural descriptions. *Journal of Experimental Psychology: General,* 5–24.

Schacter, D. L., Cooper, L. A., Delaney, S. M., & Tharan, M. (1991). Implicit memory for possible and impossible objects: Constraints on the construction of structural descriptions. *Journal of Experimental Psychology: Learning, Memory, and Cognition, 17,* 3–19.

Schacter, D. L., & Moscovitch, M. (1984). Infants, amnesia, and dissociable memory systems. In M. Moscovitch (Ed.), *Infant memory* (pp. 173–216). New York: Plenum Press.

Schacter, D. L., Norman, K. A., & Koutsaal, W. (1997). The recovered memories debate: A cognitive neuroscience perspective. In M. A. Conway (Ed.), *Recovered memories and false memories* (pp. 63–99). Oxford: Oxford University Press.

Schank, R. C., & Abelson, R. B. (1977). *Scripts, plans, goals, and understanding: An inquiry into human knowledge structures.* Hillsdale, NJ: Erlbaum.

Schank, R. C., & Cleary, C. (1994). Making machines creative. In S. M. Smith, T. B. Ward, & R. A. Finke (Eds.), *The creative cognition approach* (pp. 229–247). Cambridge, MA: MIT Press.

Schegloff, E. A. (1972). Sequencing in conversational openings. In J. J. Gumpetz & D. Hymes (Eds.), *Directions in sociolinguistic: The ethnography of communication* (pp. 346–380). New York: Holt, Rinehart, & Winston.

Schiano, D. J., & Watkins, M. J. (1981). Speech-like coding of pictures in short-term memory. *Memory and Cognition, 9,* 110–114.

Schmidt, H. P., & Boshuizen, H. G. (1993). On the origin of intermediate effects in clinical case recall. *Memory and Cognition, 21,* 338–351.

Schmidt, S. R. (1991). Can we have a distinctive theory of memory? *Memory and Cognition, 19,* 523–542.

Schmidt, S. R. (2004). Autobiographical memories for the September 11th attacks: Reconstructive errors and emotional impairment of memory. *Memory & Cognition, 32,* 443–454.

Schmolck, H., Buffalo, L. R., & Squire, L. R. (2000). Memory distortions develop over time: Recollections of the O. J. Simpson trial verdict after

15 and 32 months. *Psychological Science, 11,* 39–45.

Schneider, W., & Shiffrin, R. M. (1977). Controlled and automatic human information processing I: Detection, search, and attention. *Psychological Review, 84,* 1–66.

Schooler, J. W. (1994). Seeking the core: The issues and evidence surrounding recovered accounts of sexual trauma. *Consciousness and Cognition, 3,* 452–469.

Schooler, J. W., Bendiksen, M. A., & Ambadar, Z. (1997). Taking the middle line: Can we accommodate both fabricated and recovered memories of sexual abuse? In M. Conway (Ed.), *Recovered memories and false memories* (pp. 251–292). Oxford: Oxford University Press.

Schooler, J. W., & Eich, E. (2000). Memory for emotional events. In E. Tulving & F. I. M. Craik (Eds.), *The Oxford handbook of memory.* New York: Oxford University Press.

Schunn, C. D., McGregor, M. U., & Saner, L. D. (2005). Expertise in ill-defined problem-solving domains as effective strategy use. *Memory & Cognition, 33,* 1377–1387.

Schusterman, R. J., & Krieger, K. (1988). Artificial language comprehension and size transposition by a California sea lion (Zalophis Californianus). *Journal of Comparative Psychology, 100,* 348–355.

Schwartz, B. L. (1999). Sparkling at the end of the tongue: The etiology of tip-of-the-tongue phenomenology. *Psychonomic Bulletin & Review, 6,* 379–393.

Schwartz, B. L. (2001). The relation of tip-of-the-tongue states and retrieval time. *Memory & Cognition, 29,* 117–126.

Schwartz, B. L. (2002). The phenomenology of naturally-occurring tip-of-the-tongue states: A diary study. In S. Shohov (Ed.), *Advances in psychology research* (Vol. 8, pp. 73–84). Hauppauge, NY: Nova Science Publishers.

Schwartz, B. L., & Frazier, L. D. (2005). Tip-of-the-tongue states and aging:

Contrasting psycholinguistic and metacognitive perspectives. *Journal of General Psychology, 132,* 377–391.

Schweickert, R., McDaniel, M. A., & Riegler, G. (1993). Effects of generation on immediate memory span and delayed unexpected free recall. *Quarterly Journal of Experimental Psychology: Human Experimental Psychology, 47,* 781–804.

Scoboria, A., Mazzoni, G., Kirsch, I., & Milling, L. S. (2002). Immediate and persisting effects of misleading questions and hypnosis on memory reports. *Journal of Experimental Psychology: Applied, 8,* 26–32.

Seabrook, R., Brown, G., & Solity, J. E. (2005). Distributed and massed practice: From laboratory to classroom. *Applied Cognitive Psychology, 19,* 107–122.

Searlemann, A., & Herrmann, D. (1994). *Memory from a broader perspective.* New York: McGraw-Hill.

Sehulster, J. R. (1996). In my era: Evidence for the perception of a special period of the past. *Memory, 4,* 145–158.

Seidenberg, M. S. (1997). Language acquisition and use: Learning and applying probabilistic constraints. *Science, 275,* 1599–1603.

Sekuler, R., & Blake, R. (1994). *Perception* (3rd ed.). New York: McGraw-Hill.

Selfridge, O. (1959). Pandemonium: A paradigm for learning. In D. V. Blake and A. M. Uttley (Eds.), *Proceedings of the symposium on mechanisation of thought processes* (pp. 511–529). London: H. M. Stationary Office.

Serafine, M. L., Crowder, R. J., & Repp, B. H. (1984). Integration of melody and text in memory for songs. *Cognition, 16,* 285–303.

Sergent, J., & Signoret, J. L. (1992). Varieties of functional deficits in prosopagnosia. *Cerebral Cortex, 2,* 375–388.

Shapiro, P. N., & Penrod, S. (1986). Meta-analysis of facial identification studies. *Psychological Bulletin, 100,* 139–156.

Shepard, R. N., & Metzler, J. (1971). Mental rotation of three-dimensional objects. *Science, 171,* 201–203.

Shiffrin, R. M., & Nosofsky, R. M. (1994). Seven plus or minus two: A commentary on capacity limitations. *Psychological Review, 101,* 357–361.

Shih, M., Ambady, N., Richeson, J. A., Fujita, K., & Gray, H. M. (2002). Stereotype performance boosts: The impact of self-relevance and the manner of stereotype activation. *Journal of Personality and Social Psychology, 83,* 638–647.

Shih, M., Pittinsky, T. L., & Trahan, A. (2006). Domain-specific effects of stereotypes on performance. *Self and Identity, 5,* 1–14.

Shipherd, J. C., & Beck, J. G. (2005). The role of thought suppression in posttraumatic stress disorder. *Behavior Therapy, 36,* 277–287.

Shors, T. J. (2006). Stressful experience and learning across the lifespan. *Annual Review of Psychology, 57,* 55–85.

Shriberg, L. K., Levin, J. R., McCormick, C. B., & Pressley, M. (1982). Learning about "famous" people via the keyword method. *Journal of Educational Psychology, 74,* 238–247.

Siegler, R. S. (2000). Unconscious insights. *Current Directions in Psychological Science, 9,* 79–83.

Simons, D. J., & Chabris, C. F. (1999). Gorillas in our midst: Sustained inattentional blindness for dynamic events. *Perception, 28,* 1059–1074.

Simons, D. J., & Levin, D. T. (1997). Change blindness. *Trends in Cognitive Sciences, 1,* 261–267.

Simonton, D. K. (1994). *Greatness: Who makes history and why.* New York, NY: Guilford Press.

Simonton, D. K. (2000). Creativity: Cognitive, personal, social, and developmental aspects. *American Psychologist, 55,* 151–158.

Singer, M. (1980). The role of case-filling inferences in the coherence of brief passages. *Discourse Processes, 3,* 185–201.

Singer, M. (1990). *Psychology of language.* Hillsdale, NJ: Erlbaum.

Sloboda, J. (1986). *The musical mind: The cognitive psychology of music.* London: Oxford University Press.

Sloman, S. A. (1996). The empirical case for two systems of reasoning. *Psychological Bulletin, 119,* 3–22.

Slotnick, S. D., & Schacter, D. L. (2004). A sensory signature that distinguishes true from false memories. *Nature Neuroscience, 7,* 664–672.

Slovic, P. (1987). Perception of risk. *Science, 236,* 280–285.

Smári, J. (2001). Fifteen years of suppression of white bears and other thoughts: What are the lessons for obsessive-compulsive disorder research and treatment? *Scandinavian Journal of Behaviour Therapy, 30,* 147–160.

Smith, E. E., Langston, C., & Nisbett, R. E. (1992). The case for rules in reasoning. *Cognitive Science, 16,* 1–40.

Smith, E. E., Shoben, E. J., & Rips, L. J. (1974). Structure and process in semantic memory: A featural model for semantic decisions. *Psychological Review, 81,* 214–241.

Smith, E. R., & Branscombe, N. R. (1988). Category accessibility as implicit memory. *Journal of Experimental Social Psychology, 24,* 490–504.

Smith, M. A. (1983). Hypnotic memory enhancement: Does it work? *Psychological Bulletin, 94,* 387–407.

Smith, R. S., Doty, R. L., Burlingame, G. K., & McKeown, D. A. (1993). Smell and taste function in the visually impaired. *Perception & Psychophysics, 54,* 649–655.

Smith, S. M. (1979). Remembering in and out of context. *Journal of Experimental Psychology: Human Learning and Memory, 5,* 460–471.

Smith, S. M. (1988). Environmental context-dependent memory. In G. M. Davies & D. M. Thomson (Eds.), *Memory in context: Context in memory.* New York: Wiley.

Smith, S. M. (1995). Getting into and out of mental ruts: A theory of fixation, incubation, and insight. In R. J. Sternberg & J. E. Davidson (Eds.), *The nature of insight.* Cambridge, MA: MIT Press.

Smith, S. M. (2003). The constraining effects of initial ideas. In P. B. Paulus & B. A. Nijstad (Eds.), *Group creativity: Innovation through collaboration* (pp. 15–31). New York: Oxford University Press.

Smith, S. M., & Blankenship, S. E. (1991). Incubation effects. *Bulletin of the Psychonomic Society, 27,* 311–314.

Smith, S. M., Ward, T. B., & Finke, R. A. (1994). *The creative cognition approach.* Cambridge, MA: MIT Press.

Snyder, M., & Swann, W. B. (1978). Hypothesis-testing in social interaction. *Journal of Personality and Social Psychology, 36,* 1202–1212.

Solomon, K. O., Medin, D. L., & Lynch, E. B. (1999). Concepts do more than categorize. *Trends in Cognitive Science, 3,* 99–105.

Soto, D., & Blanco, M. J. (2004). Spatial attention and object-based attention: A comparison within a single task. *Vision Research, 44,* 69–81.

Sousa, P., Atran, S., & Medin, D. L. (2002). Essentialism and folk biology: Evidence from Brazil. *Journal of Cognition and Culture, 2,* 195–223.

Sperling, G. (1960). The information available in brief visual presentation. *Psychological Monographs, 74,* 1–29.

Squire, L. A. (1987). *Memory and brain.* New York: Oxford University Press.

Squire, L. A., & Zola-Morgan, S. (1988). Memory: Brain systems and behavior. *Trends in Neuroscience, 11,* 170–175.

Squire, L. R. (1993). The organization of declarative and nondeclarative memory. In T. Ono (Ed.), *Brain mechanisms of perception and memory: From neurons to behavior.* New York: Oxford University Press.

Squire, L. R. (2004). Memory systems of the brain: A brief history and current perspective. *Neurobiology of Learning and Memory, 82,* 171–177.

Squire, L. R., Knowlton, B., & Musen, G. (1993). The structure and organization of memory. *Annual Review of Psychology, 44,* 453–495.

Stanovich, K. E. (1999). *Who is rational? Studies of individual differences in reasoning.* Mahweh, NJ: Erlbaum.

Stanovich, K. E. (2004). Balance in psychological research: The dual process perspective: Comment. *Behavioral and Brain Sciences, 27,* 357–358.

Stanovich, K. E., & West, R. F. (1997). Reasoning independently of prior belief and individual differences in actively open-minded thinking. *Journal of Educational Psychology, 89,* 342–357.

Stanovich, K. E., & West, R. F. (2000). Individual differences in reasoning: Implications for the rationality debate? *Behavioral and Brain Sciences, 23,* 645–726.

Steblay, N., Dysart, J., Fulero, S., & Lindsay, R. C. L. (2001). Eyewitness accuracy rates in sequential and simultaneous lineup presentations: A meta-analytic comparison. *Law and Human Behavior, 25,* 459–473.

Sternberg, R. J. (2006). The nature of creativity. *Creativity Research Journal, 18,* 87–98.

Sternberg, R. J., & Ben-Zeev, T. (2001). *Complex cognition.* New York: Oxford University Press.

Sternberg, R. J., & Davidson, J. E. (1983). Insight in the gifted. *Educational Psychologist, 18,* 51–57.

Sternberg, R. J., & Davidson, J. E. (1995). *The nature of insight.* Cambridge, MA: MIT Press.

Sternberg, R. J., & Lubart, T. I. (1996). Investing in creativity. *American Psychologist, 51,* 677–688.

Stevens, J. C., Foulke, E., & Patterson, M. Q. (1996). Tactile acuity, aging, and braille reading in long-term blindness. *Journal of Experimental Psychology: Applied, 2,* 91–106.

Stevens, S. S., & Newman, E. B. (1934). The localization of pure tone.

Proceedings of the National Academy of Sciences, 20, 593–596.

Stolz, J. A., & Besner, D. (1999). On the myth of automatic semantic activation in reading. *Current Directions in Psychological Science, 8,* 61–65.

Strayer, D. L., & Drews, F. A. (2004). Profiles in driver distraction: Effects of cell phone conversations on younger and older drivers. *Human Factors, 46,* 640–649.

Strayer, D. L., Drews, F. A., & Johnston, W. A. (2003). Cell phone-induced failures of visual attention during simulated driving. *Journal of Experimental Psychology: Applied, 9* (1), 23–32.

Strayer, D. L., & Johnston, W. A. (2001). Driven to distraction: Dual-task studies of simulated driving and conversing on a cellular telephone. *Psychological Science, 12,* 462–466.

Stroop, J. R. (1935). Studies of interference in serial verbal reactions. *Journal of Experimental Psychology, 35,* 643–662.

Sulin, R. A., & Dooling, D. J. (1974). Intrusion of a thematic idea in retention of prose. *Journal of Experimental Psychology, 103,* 255–262.

Sutton, S., Tueting, P., & Zubin, J. (1967). Information delivery and the sensory evoked potential. *Science, 155*(3768), 1436–1439.

Symons, C. S., & Johnson, B. T. (1997). The self-reference in memory: A meta-analysis. *Psychological Bulletin, 121,* 371–394.

Talarico, J. M., & Rubin, D. C. (2003). Confidence, not consistency, characterizes flashbulb memories. *Psychological Science, 14,* 455–461.

Tanaka, J. (2006). The entry point of face recognition. *Journal of Experimental Psychology: General, 130,* 534–543.

Tanaka, J. W., & Farah, M. J. (1993). Parts and wholes in face recognition. *Quarterly Journal of Experimental Psychology, 46A,* 225–245.

Tarr, M. J. (2000). Pattern recognition. In A. Kazdin (Ed.), *Encyclopedia of psychology.* Washington, DC:

American Psychological Association.

Tarr, M. J., & Bülthoff, H. H. (1995). Is human object recognition better described by geon-structural-descriptions or by multiple-views? *Journal of Experimental Psychology: Human Perception and Performance, 21,* 1494–1505.

Tarr, M. J., & Cheng, Y. D. (2003). Learning to see faces and objects. *Trends in Cognitive Science, 7,* 23–30.

Tarr, M. J., & Pinker, S. (1989). Mental rotation and orientation-dependence in shape recognition. *Cognitive Psychology, 21,* 233–282.

Tarr, M. J., & Vuong, Q. C. (2002). Visual object recognition. In H. Pashler & S. Yantis (Eds.), *Steven's handbook of experimental psychology* (3rd ed.). Vol. 1: *Sensation and perception* (pp. 287–314). Hoboken, NJ: John Wiley & Sons, Inc.

Telford, C. W. (1931). The refractory phase of voluntary and associative responses. *Journal of Experimental Psychology, 14,* 1–36.

Terr, L. C. (1979). Children of Chowchilla: A study of psychic trauma. *Psychoanalytic Study of the Child, 34,* 547–623.

Terrace, H. S., Petitto, L. A., Sanders, R. J., & Bever, T. G. (1979). Can an ape create a sentence? *Science, 206,* 891–902.

Thomas, A. K., & Sommers, M. S. (2005). Attention to item-specific processing eliminates age effects in false memories. *Journal of Memory and Language, 52* (1), 71–86.

Thomas, E. L. (1962). Eye movements in speed reading. In R. G. Stauffer (Ed.), *Speed reading: Practices and procedures* (vol. 10). Newark: University of Delaware, Reading Study Center.

Thompson, P. (1980). Margaret Thatcher: A new illusion. *Perception, 9,* 483–484.

Thompson, W. C., Clarke-Stewart, K., & LePore, S. J. (1997). What did the janitor do? Suggestive interviewing and the accuracy of children's accounts. *Law and Human Behavior, 21,* 405–426.

Thomson, D. M., & Tulving, E. (1970). Associative encoding and retrieval. *Journal of Experimental Psychology, 86,* 255–262.

Thomson, R., Murachver, T., & Green, J. (2001). Where is the gender in gendered language? *Psychological Science, 12,* 171–175.

Thorndyke, P. W. (1977). Cognitive structures in comprehension and memory of narrative discourse. *Cognitive Psychology, 9,* 77–110.

Tinker, M. A. (1939). Illumination standards for effective and comfortable reading. *Journal of Consulting Psychology, 3,* 11–19.

Tinker, M. A. (1958). Recent studies of eye movements in reading. *Psychological Bulletin, 55,* 215–231.

Tolman, E. C. (1948). Cognitive maps in rats and men. *Psychological Review, 55,* 189–208.

Tolman, E. C., & Honzik, C. H. (1930). Introduction and removal of reward, and maze performance in rats. *University of California Publications in Psychology, 4,* 257–275.

Treffner, P. J., & Barrett, R. (2004). Hands-free mobile phone speech while driving degrades coordination and control. *Transportation Research Part F: Traffic Psychology and Behavior, 7,* 229–246.

Treisman, A. (1960). Contextual cues in selective listening. *Quarterly Journal of Experimental Psychology, 12,* 242–248.

Treisman, A., & Gormican, S. (1988). Feature analysis in early vision: Evidence from search asymmetries. *Psychological Review, 95,* 15–48.

Trepel, C., Fox, C. R., & Poldrack, R. A. (2005). Prospect theory on the brain? Toward a cognitive neuroscience of decision under risk. *Cognitive Brain Research, 23,* 34–50.

Tronsky, L. N. (2005). Strategy use, the development of automaticity, and working memory involvement in complex multiplication. *Memory & Cognition, 33,* 927–940.

Trout, J. D. (2001). The biological basis of speech: What to infer from talking to the animals. *Psychological Review, 108,* 523–549.

Trout, J. D. (2003). Biological specializations for speech: What can the animals tell us? *Current Directions in Psychological Science, 12,* 155–159.

Tulving, E. (1962). Subjective organization in free recall of "unrelated" words. *Psychological Review, 69,* 344–354.

Tulving, E. (1972). Episodic and semantic memory. In E. Tulving & W. Donaldson (Eds.), *Organization of memory.* New York: Academic Press.

Tulving, E. (1983). *Elements of episodic memory.* New York: Oxford University Press.

Tulving, E. (1991). Memory research is not a zero-sum game. *American Psychologist, 46,* 41–42.

Tulving, E. (2002). Episodic memory: From mind to brain. *Annual Review of Psychology, 53,* 1–25.

Tulving, E., Kapur, S., Craik, F. I. M., Moscovitch, M., & Houle, S. (1994). Hemispheric encoding/retrieval asymmetry in episodic memory: Positron emission tomography findings. *Proceedings of the National Academy of Sciences USA, 91,* 2016–2020.

Tulving, E., & Pearlstone, Z. (1966). Availability vs. accessibility of information in memory for words. *Journal of Verbal Learning and Verbal Behavior, 5,* 381–391.

Tulving, E., & Schacter, D. L. (1990). Priming and human memory systems. *Science, 247,* 301–306.

Tulving, E., & Thomson, D. M. (1973). Encoding specificity and retrieval processes in episodic memory. *Psychological Review, 80,* 359–380.

Tversky, A., & Kahneman, D. (1971). Belief in the law of small numbers. *Psychological Bulletin, 76,* 105–110.

Tversky, A., & Kahneman, D. (1973). Availability: A heuristic for judging frequency and probability. *Cognitive Psychology, 5,* 207–232.

Tversky, A., & Kahneman, D. (1974). Judgment under uncertainty: Heuristics and biases. *Science, 185,* 1124–1131.

Tversky, A., & Kahneman, D. (1981). The framing of decisions and the psychology of choice. *Science, 211,* 453–458.

Tversky, A., & Kahneman, D. (1983). Extensional vs. intuitive reasoning. The conjunction fallacy in probability judgment. *Psychological Review, 90,* 293–315.

Ullman, M., Corkin, S., Coppola, M., Hickok, G., Growdon, J. H., Koroshetz, W. J., & Pinker, S. (1997). A neural dissociation within language: Evidence that the mental dictionary is part of declarative memory, and that grammatical rules are processed by the procedural system. *Journal of Cognitive Neuroscience, 9,* 266–276.

Usher, J. A., & Neisser, U. (1993). Childhood amnesia and the beginnings of memory for four early life events. *Journal of Experimental Psychology: General, 122,* 155–165.

Uttal, W. R. (2003). *The new phrenology: The limits of localizing cognitive processes in the brain.* Cambridge, MA: MIT Press.

van der Kolk, B. A. (1994). The body keeps score: Memory and the evolving psychobiology of post-traumatic stress. *Harvard Review of Psychiatry, 1,* 253–265.

van Dijk, T. A., & Kintsch, W. (1983). *Strategies of discourse comprehension.* New York: Academic Press.

Van Orden, G. C. (1987). A ROWS is a ROSE: Spelling, sound, and reading. *Memory and Cognition, 15,* 181–198.

Vecera, S. P., Vogel, E. K., & Woodman, G. F. (2002). Lower ground: A new cue for figure-ground assignment. *Journal of Experimental Psychology: General, 131,* 194–205.

Vicente, K. J., & Wang, J. H. (1998). An ecological theory of expertise effects in memory recall. *Psychological Review, 105,* 33–57.

Vokey, J. R., & Read, J. D. (1988). Subliminal messages: Between the devil and the media. *American Psychologist, 39,* 1231–1239.

von Eckardt, B., & Potter, M. C. (1985). Clauses and the semantic representations of words. *Memory and Cognition, 13*, 371–376.

von Frisch, K. (1967). *The dance language and orientation of bees.* Cambridge, MA: Belknap Press.

von Restorff, H. (1933). Uber die Wirkung von Bereichsbildungen im Spurenfeld. *Psychologische Forschung, 18*, 299–342.

von Wright, J. M. (1972). On the problem of selection in iconic memory. *Scandinavian Journal of Psychology, 13*, 159–171.

Voss, J. F., Vesonder, G., & Spilich, T. (1980). Text generation and recall by high-knowledge and low-knowledge individuals. *Journal of Verbal Learning and Verbal Behavior, 19*, 651–667.

Voss, J. L., & Paller, K. A. (2006). Fluent conceptual processing and explicit memory for faces are electrophysiologically distinct. *Journal of Neuroscience, 26*, 926–933.

Vroomen, J., van Zon, M., & de Gelder, B. (1996). Cues to speech segmentation. Evidence from juncture misperceptions and word spotting. *Memory and Cognition, 24*, 744–755.

Wagenaar, W. A. (1986). My memory: A study of autobiographical memory over six years. *Cognitive Psychology, 18*, 225–252.

Wagner, U., Gais, S., Haider, H., Verleger, R., & Born, J. (2004). Sleep inspires insight. *Nature, 427*, 352–355.

Wakefield, H., & Underwager, R. C. (1994). *Return of the furies: An investigation into recovered memory therapy.* Chicago: Open Court.

Walker and Yekovich (1987). Activation and use of script-based antecedents in anaphoric reference. *Journal of Memory and Language, 26*, 673–691.

Wallace, W. P. (1965). Review of the historical, empirical, and theoretical status of the von Restorff phenomenon. *Psychological Bulletin, 63*, 410–424.

Wallach, M. A. (1970). Creativity. In P. Mussen (Ed.), *Carmichael's handbook of child psychology* (pp. 1211–1272). New York: Wiley.

Wallas, G. (1926). *The art of thought.* London: J. Cape.

Warren, P., & Marslen-Wilson, W. M. (1988). Cues to lexical choice: Discriminating place and voice. *Perception & Psychophysics, 43*, 21–30.

Warren, R. M. (1970). Perceptual restoration of missing speech sounds. *Science, 167*, 392–393.

Warrington, E. K., & Weiskrantz, L. (1970). Amnesic syndrome: Consolidation or retrieval? *Nature, 228*, 628–630.

Wason, P. C., & Johnson-Laird, P. N. (1970). A conflict between selection and evaluating information in an inferential task. *British Journal of Psychology, 68*, 325–335.

Watkins, M. J. (1990). Mediationism and the obfuscation of memory. *American Psychologist, 45*, 328–335.

Waugh, N. C., & Norman, D. A. (1965). Primary memory. *Psychological Review, 72*, 89–104.

Weber, N., Brewer, N., Wells, G. L., Semmler, C., & Keast, A. (2004). Eyewitness identification accuracy and response latency: The unruly 10–12-second rule. *Journal of Experimental Psychology: Applied, 10*, 139–147.

Wegner, D. M. (1994). Ironic processes of mental control. *Psychological Review, 101*, 34–52.

Wegner, D. M. (2003). The mind's best trick: How we experience conscious will. *Trends in Cognitive Sciences, 7*, 65–69.

Wegner, D. M., Ansfield, M., & Pilloff, D. (1998). The putt and the pendulum: Ironic effects of the mental control of action. *Psychological Science, 9*, 196–199.

Wegner, D. M., & Sparrow, B. (2004). Authorship processing. In M. Gazzaniga (Ed.), *The cognitive neurosciences* (3rd ed., pp. 1201–1209). Cambridge, MA: MIT Press.

Wegner, D. M., Sparrow, B., & Winerman, L. (2004). Vicarious agency: Experiencing control over the movements of others. *Journal of Personality and Social Psychology, 86*, 838–848.

Weisberg, R. W. (1992). Metacognition and insight during problem solving: Comment on Metcalfe. *Journal of Experimental Psychology: Learning, Memory, and Cognition, 18*, 426–431.

Weisberg, R. W. (1995). Prolegomena to theories of insight in problem solving. A taxonomy of problems. In R. J. Sternberg & J. E. Davidson (Eds.), *The nature of insight.* Cambridge, MA: MIT Press.

Weisberg, R. W., & Alba, J. W. (1981). An examination of the alleged role of "fixation" in the solution of several "insight" problems. *Journal of Experimental Psychology: General, 110*, 169–192.

Weiskrantz, L. (1986). *Blindsight: A case study and implications.* Oxford, UK: Oxford University Press.

Weldon, M. S. (2000). Remembering as a social process. In D. L. Medin (Ed.), *The psychology of learning and motivation* (Vol. 40, pp. 67–120). New York: Academic Press.

Wells, G. L. (1993). What do we know about eyewitness identification? *American Psychologist, 48*, 553–571.

Wells, G. L., & Bradfield, A. L. (1998). "Good, you identified the suspect": Feedback to witnesses distorts their reports of the witnessing experience. *Journal of Applied Psychology, 83*, 360–376.

Wells, G. L., Ferguson, T. J., & Lindsay, R. C. L. (1981). The tractability of eyewitness confidence and its implications for triers of fact. *Journal of Applied Psychology, 66*, 688–696.

Wells, G. L., Leippe, M. R., & Ostrom, T. M. (1979). Guidelines for empirically assessing the fairness of a lineup. *Law and Human Behavior, 3*, 285–293.

Wells, G. L., Malpass, R. S., Lindsay, R. C. L., Fisher, R. P., Turtle, J. W., & Fulero, S. M. (2000). From the lab to the police station: A successful application of eyewitness research. *American Psychologist, 55*, 581–598.

Wells, G. L., & Murray, D. M. (1984). Eyewitness confidence. In G. L. Wells & E. F. Loftus (Eds.), *Eyewitness testimony: Psychological perspectives*. New York: Cambridge University Press.

Wells, G. L., Olson, E. A., Charman, S. D. (2002). The confidence of eyewitnesses in their identifications from lineups. *Current Directions in Psychological Science, 11,* 151–154.

Wells, G. L., Rydell, S. M., & Seelau, E. P. (1993). On the selection of distractors for eyewitness lineups. *Journal of Applied Psychology, 78,* 835–844.

Wells, G. L., Small, M., Penrod, S. J., Malpass, R. S., Fulero, S. M., & Brimacombe, C. A. E. (1998). Eyewitness identification procedures: Recommendations for lineups and photospreads. *Law and Human Behavior, 22,* 603–647.

Wenger, S. K., Thompson, C. P., & Bartling, C. A. (1980). Recall facilitates subsequent retention. *Journal of Experimental Psychology: Human Learning and Memory, 1,* 210–221.

Wenzlaff, R. M., & Luxton, D. D. (2003). The role of thought suppression in depressive rumination. *Cognitive Therapy and Research, 27,* 293–308.

Wenzlaff, R. M., & Wegner, D. M. (2003). Thought suppression. *Annual Review of Psychology, 51,* 59–91.

Werker, J. F., & Yeung, H. H. (2005). Infant speech perception bootstraps word learning. *Trends in Cognitive Sciences, 9,* 519–527.

Wickens, C. D. (1984). Engineering psychology and human performance: Columbus, OH: Merrill.

Wickens, D. D., Dalezman, R. E., & Eggemeier, F. T. (1976). Multiple encoding of word attributes in memory. *Memory and Cognition, 4,* 307–310.

Wickelgren, W. A. (1974). How to solve problems. New York: Freeman.

Wiley, J. (1998). Expertise as mental set: The effects of domain knowledge in creative problem solving. *Memory and Cognition, 26,* 716–730.

Wilkins, M. C. (1928). The effect of changed material on ability to do formal syllogistic reasoning. *Archives of Psychology, 16*(102).

Williams, J. M. G. (1996). Depression and the specificity of autobiographical memory. In D. C. Rubin (Ed.), *Autobiographical memory: Studies in autobiographical memory*. New York: Cambridge University Press.

Williams, J. M. G., Ellis, N. C., Tyers, C., Healy, H., Rose, J., & MacLeod, C. (1996). The specificity of autobiographical memory and imageability about the future. *Memory and Cognition, 24,* 116–125.

Williams, J. M., & Scott, J. (1988). Autobiographical memory in depression. *Psychiatric Medicine, 18,* 689–695.

Williams, L. M. (1994). Recall of childhood trauma: A prospective study of women's memories of childhood abuse. *Journal of Consulting and Clinical Psychology, 62,* 1182–1186.

Wilson, M. (2002). Six views of embodied cognition. *Psychological Bulletin and Review, 9,* 625–636.

Wilson, M., & Emmorey, K. (1997). A visuospatial "phonological loop" in working memory: Evidence from American Sign Language. *Memory and Cognition, 25,* 313–320.

Wilson, M., & Emmorey, K. (1998). A "word-length effect" for sign-language: Further evidence for the role of language in structuring working memory. *Memory and Cognition, 26,* 584–590.

Wimmers, P. F., Schmidt, H. G., Verkoeijen, P. P., & van de Wiel, M. W. (2005). Inducing expertise effects in clinical case recall. *Medical Education, 39,* 949–957.

Wittgenstein, L. (1969). *On certainty*. New York: Harper & Row.

Wood, N. L., Stadler, M. A., & Cowan, N. (1997). Is there implicit memory without attention? A re-examination of task demands in Eich's (1984) procedure. *Memory and Cognition, 25,* 772–779.

Woodworth, R. S., & Sells, S. B. (1935). An atmosphere effect in syllogistic reasoning. *Journal of Experimental Psychology, 18,* 451–460.

Wyer, T. K., & Srull, R. S. (1989). *Memory and cognition in its social context*. Hillsdale, NJ: Erlbaum.

Yang, C. D. (2004). Universal grammar, statistics or both? *Trends in Cognitive Sciences, 8,* 451–456.

Yarmey, D. A. (1973). I recognize your face, but I can't remember your name: Further evidence on the tip-of-the-tongue phenomenon. *Memory and Cognition, 1,* 287–290.

Yates, F. A. (1968). *The art of memory*. Chicago: University of Chicago Press.

Yates, J. F., Lee, J., & Shinotsuka, H. (1996). Beliefs about overconfidence, including its cross-national variation. *Organizational Behavior and Human Decision Processes, 65,* 138–147.

Yates, J. F., Lee, J., Shinotsuka, H., Patalano, A. L., & Sieck, W. R. (1998). Cross-cultural variations in probability judgment accuracy: Beyond general knowledge overconfidence? *Organizational Behavior and Human Decision Processes, 74,* 89–117.

Yin, R. K. (1969). Looking at upside-down faces. *Journal of Experimental Psychology, 81,* 141–145.

Young, A. W., Ellis, A. W., & Flude, B. M. (1988). Accessing stored information about people. *Psychological Research, 50,* 111–115.

Yuille, J. C., & Paivio, A. (1969). Abstractness and recall of connected discourse. *Journal of Experimental Psychology, 82,* 467–471.

Zaragoza, M. S., McCloskey, M., & Jamis, M. (1987). Misleading postevent information and recall of the original event. Further evidence against the memory impairment hypothesis. *Journal of Experimental Psychology: Learning, Memory, and Cognition, 13,* 36–44.

Zattore, R. J., Evans, A. C., Meyer, E., & Gjedde, A. (1992). Lateralization of phonetic and pitch discrimination in speech processing. *Science, 256,* 846–849.

Zimmerman, D. H., & West, C. (1975). Sex roles, interruptions, and silences in conversation. In B. Thorne & N. Henley (Eds.), *Language and sex: Differences and dominance* (pp. 105–129). Rowley, MA: Newbury House.

Photo Credits

Name Index

565

Subject Index

Note: Italicized page numbers refer to the definition of the term in the chapter glossary.

absentmindedness, 132–134, 248, *287*
abuse, sexual, 280, 282–286
access consciousness, 95, 96–100, *116*
accessibility of memories, 225, *245*.
    See also retrieval
accidental features, 350
accommodation, 425
accuracy of response, 42–43, *70*, 345
action potentials, 58, 63, *70*
action slips, 132–134, *158*
Adaptive Strategy Model, 467
additions (speech error), 423, *435*
ad hoc categories, 188, *203*
adolescents, reminiscence bump in,
    297, 304–307, *330*
affective decision-making mode, 529
affirming the antecedent, 494
affirming the consequent, 494
aging
    cognitive function and, 127
    deductive reasoning and, 493
    elderly eyewitnesses, 263
    free recall and, 342–343
    self-initiated retrieval and, 223–224
"Aha!" experience, 470, 472–473
algorithms, 130, 457
alternating attentional style, 128–129
American Psychological Association
    (APA), 286
American Sign Language (ASL),
    149–150, 432
amnesia
    childhood, 297, 298–304, *330*
    definition of, *245*
    implicit and explicit memory and,
        210, 239, 242
amygdala, 60, 61, 281
analogies, in problem solving, 459–464
analog representation, 373–379.
    See also visual imagery
anchoring-and-adjustment heuristic,
    514–517
anchoring category members, 194.
    See also prototype approach to
    categorization

animals, 428–435
    face recognition in, 184
    honeybee communication, 429
    language training projects, 430–434
    primates, *See* primates, nonhuman
    recursion and, 434–435, *437*
    speech perception by, 393
antecedents, 494
anterior superior temporal gyrus, 481
anthropology, 5
anticipation (speech error), 423, *435*
APA (American Psychological
    Association), 286
aphasia, 415, *436*
arbitrariness, in language symbols,
    384–385, *435*
arrangement problems, 443
articulation
    in language production, 422–423
    of phonemes, 390–391
    slips of the tongue, 424
articulatory loop, 148–151, *158*
articulatory suppression task,
    150, *158*
artifacts (artifact categories),
    188, *203*
artificial intelligence, 5
ASL (American Sign Language),
    149–150, 432
association, laws of, 6, *33*
association areas, 60
associative activation error, 133
associative chains, 359
atmosphere effects, 491
attention, 106–115
    auditory, 110–115
    definition of, 2, 120, *158*
    divided, 121–129, *159*
    executive, 154–155, *159*
    multimode theory of, 120–121, *159*
    object-based, 106, *117*
    role in long-term memory, 211
    spatial, 106, *118*
    visual, 106–110
attentional capture, 107, *116*

attentional efficiency, 130
attentional set, 110, *116*
attenuation theory, 114–115, *116*
audition. *See* hearing
auditory theory of speech perception,
    392–394, *435–436*
authorship processing, 96–99, *116*
autobiographical fact, 293, *330*
autobiographical memory, 289–330
    brain processes in, 316–317
    childhood amnesia, 297, 298–304,
        330
    definition of, *330*
    encoding specificity in, 309–311
    flashbulb memory, 321–326, *330*
    forgetting in, 307–308
    functions of, 328–329
    involuntary, 317–318
    memory *vs.* fact, 293–295, *330*
    methods of investigation, 295–296
    mood dependence on, 326–327, *330*
    reminiscence bump, 297, 304–307,
        330
    retention function, 297–298
    retrieval cues for, 311–313
    role of language in, 301–303
    self-memory system, 313–317, *330*
automaticity, 129–136
    accounts of, 130–132
    characteristics of, 130
    costs of, 132–136
    definition of, *159*
autonomous view of syntax and
    semantics, 415, *436*
availability heuristic, 503–509
    biased encoding in, 503–505
    biased retrieval in, 506–507
    illusory correlations, 508–509
    recognition heuristic, 509
availability of memories, 225, *245*

babies. *See* children; infants
backmasking, 104
basal ganglia, 61
base rates, 510–511